"To see this country happy...
is so much the wish of my soul.
Nothing on this side of Elysium can be
placed in competition with it."

– George Washington

Table of Contents

Part One

Chapter Three continued…

Chapter Four continued…

Chapter Four continued…

(Updated April 15, 2022)

Come senators, congressmen
Please heed the call
Don't stand in the doorway
Don't block up the hall
For he that gets hurt
Will be he who has stalled
There's a battle outside and it is ragin'
It'll soon shake your windows and rattle your walls
For the times they are a-changin'

– Bob Dylan

Chapter One

The Butterfly Effect

Once upon a time, a young boy got a horse as a present for his 12th birthday. It was a coveted gift and his entire village cheered and said, "Isn't this wonderful!" "We'll see," replied the wise Zen master who lived in the village.

Two years later, the boy was violently thrown off of his horse, shattering his leg and causing great dismay throughout the town. The villagers all cried, "How unfortunate this is for the boy!" "We'll see," replied the wise Zen master.

Shortly after the boy's fall, a brutal war broke out near the village, but the boy could not fight because of his broken leg. Relieved that the boy would remain safe, the whole village said, "This is so fortunate for the boy!"

"We'll see," replied the Zen master – fully aware that, for better or worse, even the best intentions have unintended consequences. Understanding that events rarely occur in isolation and that seemingly random actions are often closely interconnected…and somewhere close by a butterfly flapped its wings.

The Butterfly Effect is the idea that small changes in the early state of a system can cause significant and unpredictable changes to its future state.

For example, the flutter of a butterfly's wings in Africa could possibly alter the atmosphere *just enough* to change a hurricane's path from across the Gulf of Mexico to up the East Coast.

Although the butterfly does not cause the hurricane, it's a small part of a larger sequence of events that causes a major change in the ultimate outcome.

Most often The Butterfly Effect is associated with chaos theory, a field of study in mathematics. However, this profound concept extends far beyond mathematical equations or weather patterns.

The power of this phenomenon is what Americans so desperately need to embrace to solve our national challenges and change the way our dysfunctional political system operates once and for all.

Just as the butterfly and the hurricane are elaborately connected, our domestic and foreign policies are linked in intricate ways. If we don't pay close attention, a policy decision that we make today can have significant consequences down the road – in ways we may never have considered.

Passing a three-strikes law today can cause significant over-incarceration tomorrow. Increasing domestic ethanol quotas today can cause a massive worldwide food shortage tomorrow. Redlining neighborhoods today can cause a substantial wealth gap tomorrow.

Overthrowing a *Glass-Steagall Act* today can contribute to a devastating subprime financial crisis tomorrow. Arming the Afghan mujahideen without appropriate oversight today can fortify terrorism tomorrow.

As fabulous as America is – and it really is an extraordinary country – it's no wonder we're not operating at maximum capacity. Instead of recognizing the wisdom of The Butterfly Effect and approaching our policies comprehensively, our politicians act like they exist in total isolation from one another.

Their actions (and inactions) suggest that they think our long-term economic health is separate and apart from our unstable entitlement programs, ridiculously convoluted tax code, schizophrenic immigration policy, non-evolving energy practices, suffocating debt, and severe inequality of both income and opportunity.

They evidently think that our ability to preserve supremacy within the international power structure is separate and apart from the way we educate our children, the way we treat the planet, the cost and quality of our health care, our level of investment in research and development, and the condition of our infrastructure.

Worse, politicians from both major parties seem to think we don't even notice this is going on. They constantly underestimate the American people. They act as if we aren't smart, capable adults – like we can't comprehend the magnitude of our problems or handle the hard choices we must make to solve them. This is not only false...it's downright insulting.

Regardless of our political affiliation – if we still have any at all – We the American people know it is impossible to safeguard our long-term economic health without a sensible plan to stabilize our entitlement programs; an uncomplicated tax code; a smart immigration policy; an evolving, self-reliant energy policy; manageable debt; and fair and equitable opportunities for every American.

We the People know it is impossible to retain our status as a superpower without properly educated children; a healthy planet; affordable, high-quality health care; a strong commitment to innovative research and development; and modern, cutting-edge infrastructure.

We the People fully recognize that it's impossible to sustain freedom and liberty without sacrifice and that, thanks to decades of political incompetence and irresponsibility, the time has finally come to buckle down and get serious about protecting our future.

Americans know an ugly truth is better than a pretty lie. No inspiring political speeches or hopeful campaign promises can disguise the harsh reality anymore: The future of America is in jeopardy. We know that an ugly truth is better than a pretty lie because when we know and accept the truth, we can finally do something about it.

The time has come for serious people to come up with serious solutions. From immigration to entitlements to our fiscal crisis – to the racial health, education and wealth gaps to criminal justice reform – we have to make very difficult decisions and come together as a nation to fix this.

Einstein once said, "The significant problems we face cannot be solved at the same level of thinking we were at when we created them." Therefore, we have to move beyond the ineffectual thinking of our past.

For politicians to view our challenges compartmentally – as opposed to comprehensively – is a lazy, irresponsible approach and does nothing more than waste precious time, as we are now so painfully aware.

Because there are so many problems to solve, the only plausible answer is to be boldly strategic in our attack. We can no longer expect half-measures and incremental ideas to work in systems that have collapsed. Instead, we need to embrace a full and fundamental restructuring.

As we begin to make revolutionary changes, it is essential that we always make today's decisions with tomorrow seared in our minds. Our best bet is to always keep our eyes firmly on the horizon and visualize the future we want for our *shining city upon the hill,* not only in the 21st century, but far beyond.

The Butterfly Effect can work either for us or against us. Decisions can be altruistic and intelligent and therefore have a positive impact on our future. Or they can be self-serving and illogical and therefore lead this nation into chaos.

Lately it's been the latter, but that trend is about to end. This book will prove that even the slightest disruption can transform our severely broken political system. Better yet, a large one can transform the world.

§§§

Not to make this all about me, but a little about me. If a butterfly in Africa had flapped its wings a second earlier, I might be in the United States Congress.

After completing graduate school, I officially launched a congressional campaign in the great state of Texas. By nature, I'm an optimistic person. For years, when people insisted our political system was hopelessly unchangeable, I would fight them until the bitter end.

And I knew for a fact I was just the person to save it. I actually thought that when Americans got a taste of me, they would follow me like the second coming of Lincoln, Roosevelt and Reagan, or, in the case of Texans, Sam Houston, Davy Crockett and Robert Earl Keen.

From the beginning, with the energy of the innocent, I was undaunted, enthusiastically speaking at fire departments, pie suppers, political forums, and every kind of fair, festival and fiesta imaginable. This was not difficult given that East Texas can find any reason for events that involve funnel cake.

I was on the Kiwanis, Rotary and Lions Club circuit, went to church five times every Sunday, and ate six times a day. I even entered a homemade float in five Christmas parades where amazingly supportive family members marched down brightly lit streets, throwing candy canes with my picture plastered to them. Believe me, dignity goes on hiatus during a political campaign. These were the honeymoon days – before reality dawned.

To ensure full disclosure, I ran on the Republican ticket in the 2004 election, but I'm most certainly not one. Before all of you Democrats get too excited, I'm not a member of your gang either.

I have news for both sides: Just like most Americans, I am impossible to compartmentalize.

Like most Americans, I am rational and balanced. Like most Americans, I recognize the absurdity of stale platforms that rely on three or four bullet points to solve every problem. Like most Americans, I don't choose the answer before I even hear the question. Like most Americans, I realize many challenges are a product of their time and, therefore, no solution is everlasting.

Although Jim Turner – the Democratic incumbent for the Texas 2nd congressional district and my original opponent in the election – seemed to be an upstanding family man, it was obvious (to me anyway) that things were oppressively stagnant and new blood was overdue.

It broke my heart to see the vulnerable condition of East Texas, my beloved home and a microcosm of rural America.

Town squares were in danger of becoming ghost towns as industry dwindled, and the educational and health care systems were taking the full brunt of a state legislature that continually made disastrous decisions on behalf of the people they were elected to protect (this has been happening ever since, by the way).

This may sound like political b.s., but my main motivation was an overwhelming desire to be a voice for the people who never seem to be heard. Aren't I just wonderful?

Because I had lived outside the *pine curtain* for several years, I had absolutely no idea how I would be received upon my return. I anticipated many thinking I was too young, too blonde or just flat too Union. After all, I had lived in Massachusetts, for goodness' sake! For many East Texans, living even a short time in the state that spawned the Kennedy clan would contaminate me for life. Twenty-five years in Texas could not possibly vaccinate me from their Yankee, liberal ways!

Despite the initial uncertainty, the positive reception I received from most everyone meant the world to me and is something I will never forget. Republicans in the 2nd district were thrilled to have me, mainly because there hadn't been a serious Republican candidate in years. They were so excited they sometimes forgot to ask what I actually stood for which, after reading these books, I'm certain you will recognize as borrowed time for my campaign.

Although my age and hair color did not necessarily deter people – though I must confess, I did have my hairdresser put in lowlights for a few months – the Harvard thing did rub some people the wrong way. This controversy was brought to my attention by a group of ladies having lunch at high noon at a busy restaurant on the Jasper square.

Oh! Have I mentioned that I was born and raised in Jasper, Texas? Yes, *that* Jasper, the town with the unfortunate legacy of three White supremacists dragging James Byrd, a Black man, behind their truck and to his death in 1998. Much more on this later.

Back to lunch. I had returned to my hometown in full anticipation of a ticker-tape parade or, at a minimum, a "Jasper: Home of Emily Mathews" welcome sign. After all, people, I was running for Congress! Can you believe what I've made of myself?

What I got instead was, "You went to Harvard," one particularly austere lady stated with dismay in the middle of the very crowded parlor (and not in her inside voice). "That just turns me off. Why couldn't you stay home and go to school around here?" To which I quickly replied, "Did someone tell you Harvard? They meant Stephen F. Austin

State, the 'Harvard of the South'." It never came up again, so I guess she spread it around.

What I also got in lieu of a much-deserved parade were several meetings with super angry people who said the most racist things I had ever heard – a shocking wakeup call in a campaign full of many (note: I attended plenty of other Republican meetings where this was not the case. I'm certainly not painting the entire group with the same brush). Although I've witnessed outrageous racism in my lifetime, I was stunned by how little had changed with these particular people.

This is probably a good spot to describe the general scene I encountered at these "First Tuesday of the Month Meeting of the (insert county name) Republicans" meetings, though I doubt I'm a talented enough writer to accurately capture the true essence of them. These gatherings should really be in one of those *100 Things You Must Do Before You Die* books.

You must first understand that for dyed-in-the-wool Republicans in East Texas – and I know and <u>LOVE</u> many, especially those in my family! – these meetings are second in importance only to church services.

It's serious business and the agenda rarely wavers from its order: anti-abortion petition, anti-gay marriage petition, anti-prayer in school ban petition and last, but certainly the most fun, Democrat-bashing (which, because it's encouraged at any point during the meeting, doesn't really have a set place on the program).

The focal point of the room – generally located in a courthouse basement, bank community room or, of course, a church – is the table that holds the food which: 1) is flanked by the United States flag on the left and the Texas flag on the right; 2) is draped with a plastic red, white and blue tablecloth decorated with stars and stripes; and 3) holds the pimento cheese sandwiches, the potato salad, and the sugar cookies that have been covered with red, white and blue sprinkles. Even before the prayer or the pledge, the participants of the meeting go through that table like Grant through Richmond.

Sometimes these meetings get really entertaining, mainly because they become contentious in some way. Once there was almost a fistfight when one local treasurer suggested that the monthly meeting be moved from the Mexican restaurant to the fish place since, being a buffet, a tip would no longer be required.

Another fun night was an election bake sale, a popular event highlighted by an auction of each candidate's "homemade" baked goods. Thank goodness for my precious grandmother who armed me with three pecan pies and a pound cake that killed.

This night, one of the candidates for sheriff accused his opponent of killing his dog with a shotgun and another announced that the incumbent's son was the biggest drug dealer in the entire county. Both revelations caused the entire crowd to erupt in – depending on their take on the situation – fierce applause, feigned disbelief, or obvious delight that they were finally going to see some action.

Although this was infinitely more entertaining than Grandpa Joe reading the entire Declaration of Independence – which we had endured the previous week – there were two additional components of the meeting that upped the ante: 1) There was a full bar set up in the back (an interesting but, as far as I was concerned, very welcomed development given that this was a dry county), and 2) Several of those attending were carrying a variety of weapons, which included an exposed machete strapped to one of the candidate's legs.

To be fair, this particular individual was questioned about the machete when he arrived, but he assured everyone that, although it had been dark for nearly two hours, he had come straight to the meeting from clearing brush. Everyone seemed content with that answer until his eighth Johnnie Walker on the rocks happened to coincide with that nasty little accusation about the dog.

So, hopefully you have a visual of the scene unfolding at one of those meetings with the angry people saying racist things. As I outlined my brilliant plans for infrastructure and national security, a KKK fossil < I'm not just arbitrarily accusing him of this; I was good friends with his daughter growing up and he actually was in the KKK > stood up and made the most disgusting, bigoted comments imaginable.

As one who doesn't sugarcoat hideous behavior for fear of enabling it, I originally had the entire statement written here. But in the end, I couldn't stomach the thought of seeing it in print.

After his moment of glory and amid the appreciative high-fives of his fellow wannabe Klansmen, he heroically sauntered to the plastic tablecloth-covered food table and filled his plastic plate with plastic tasting green bean casserole (okay, that last one was harsh).

Somewhat recovered from the meeting of the plantation brotherhood, I bravely forged onward.

At the time, the Texas 2nd district was composed of 19 counties. You may remember this as the district of Congressman Charlie Wilson who, in one of the largest CIA covert operations in history, armed half of Afghanistan to help defeat the Soviets in the 1980s.

He was also a player. If you have read or seen *Charlie Wilson's War* and therefore know the dirt, Charlie's onetime girlfriend and *Playboy* cover girl is my fourth cousin, but that's another story.

The fact that "Good-Time Charlie" had been the congressman for this district was a source of immense comfort to me. Although I was nervous about some of the skeletons in my closet, nothing I had done compared with driving drunk and leaving the scene of an accident I caused or snorting cocaine with strippers in a hot tub in Vegas (or I guess I should say, nothing that I can remember or there is photographic evidence of). Heck, if these constituents forgave Charlie for all of that while he was actually *in* Congress, they may at least consider giving me a pass on Harvard and other such indiscretions.

I never got the chance to find out. Little did we know that the 2nd district was about to be obliterated by the worst and most dangerous Texas Legislature in history. After securing a majority in the state legislature in 2002, and in an effort to unseat all of the state's "Anglo Democrats," the Texas Republicans launched a ferocious redistricting campaign to redraw the U.S. Congressional districts in their party's favor.

Every ten years, the U.S. Census Bureau conducts a census and uses the data to assign each state the number of seats it will have in the U.S. House of Representatives for the next ten years. Individual states then draw legislative boundaries for congressional districts and state legislative districts. This process is conducted by the state legislature in some states, while a few states use independent commissions. In Texas, the state legislature is responsible for drawing U.S. Congressional districts.

Despite the fact that congressional redistricting in Texas had occurred once every ten years for over a century, the Texas Republicans were now hell-bent on redrawing lines that had been approved by the legislature just two years earlier.

In its purest form, redistricting gives states the ability to appropriately respond to population shifts and to ensure that no geographic area is underrepresented.

Unfortunately, opportunist politicians have kidnapped the system and have made the despicable habit of drawing districts for competitive advantage standard operating procedure. Sophisticated voter profiling and a significant advancement in mapping technology allow legislators to essentially pick and choose the voters that will ensure their party's victory.

The prevailing system in most states is railroaded by partisan collusion and protects the interest of political parties to the detriment of the American citizen. Redistricting (to revise legislative districts) is certainly legal, but gerrymandering (to divide an area into election districts to give one political party an electoral majority while concentrating the voting strength of the opposition in as few districts as possible) is absolutely not.

Gerrymandering is one of the most blatant abuses of power in government and is a perfect example of partisan politics at its very worst. Its tentacles poison far more than just an election or two; gerrymandering is the breeding ground for the deep ideological split between Republicans and Democrats in Washington.

It's a rare occurrence when an unconstrained, freethinking candidate actually makes it through this mess, because these fabricated districts are drawn specifically to capture the crazed party faithful, especially in primaries... and the crazed party faithful demand likeminded candidates. Therefore, the possibility of a moderate candidate is largely eliminated, and the vast majority of this country is silenced.

The Texas redistricting battle was horrifying to watch. The stories that spewed from my great state warmed my heart with pride: legislative sessions erupted into fistfights, multiple lawsuits tied-up every level of the court system, and Republicans atrociously abused their power while Democrats shamelessly fled to other states to avoid a final vote.

In a dazzling display of failed leadership, Governor Rick Perry called three special legislative sessions – each at an astronomical cost to the state – to help his fellow Republicans manipulate the new map (don't even get me started on this guy).

To make the situation far more deadly, this ridiculousness happened while Texas was in absolute peril. At the beginning of the legislative session, Texas had a $10 billion budget deficit, a legislative typo delayed $800 million in school funding, and 60 schools were suing Texas over a $26 billion school finance disaster. Seems to me these people shouldn't have so much time on their hands.

In the end, the Texas delegation in the United States House of Representatives shifted from 17 to 15 in favor of the Democrats to 21 to 11 in favor of the Republicans.

One of the many lawsuits that challenged the Texas Legislature's redistricting plan was eventually heard by the U.S. Supreme Court and, despite overruling one of the districts as racial gerrymandering, the conservative-leaning court upheld the statewide redistricting as Constitutional…a decision that is perplexing given that the Republican's new map was as convoluted as an inkblot in the Rorschach test.

The majority of the members of the 2003 Texas Legislature should be seriously ashamed and owe every Texan an apology for their dereliction of duty.

I guess I shouldn't be surprised. This is, after all, the state that unanimously passed a motion to commemorate the "heroic actions" of the Boston Strangler, a motion that a jokester member of the state legislature introduced to prove that his colleagues continually passed legislation without even reading it.

Eight weeks before the 2004 primary election, after campaigning for months in the 2nd district, I suddenly found myself in the newly scrambled 1st district with only three of my original 19 counties going with me.

If you think this ticked me off, think how Jim Turner must have felt. Jim had been the congressman for these 19 counties for eight years and with one stroke of the pen, his constituents were scattered among three newly drawn districts. Since gerrymandering virtually ensured his defeat, Jim decided not to run for re-election.

Democrat Max Sandlin, who had represented the 1st district for four terms, did decide to run, though the Texas Republicans had ultimately sealed his fate as well. Now that the votes were completely stacked in his favor, whoever won the Republican primary would be the next congressman for the newly drawn 1st congressional district.

Forced into a new district with only two months to go, I went from a non-contested primary to a race with multiple opponents, including a judge, a lawyer, a doctor and a sitting state legislator named Wayne Christian (whose last name is incredibly ironic). All were, typically, ultra-conservative White men.

Although redistricting killed any chance I had to win, this part of the campaign was a complete blast. Freed by the absolute certainty of defeat, I could say anything I damned well pleased, and being in Congress was becoming less and less appealing anyway.

The day of the election dawned and, predictably, I got clobbered. Louie Gohmert (yes, you read that right) won the primary and went on to win the general election against Max Sandlin. < then went on to try to destroy our democracy, but we'll get into that later >

I honestly didn't care who won as long as it wasn't Wayne Christian. Now listen, lots can happen in almost two decades, and God can absolutely work miracles in people's hearts. But at the time, I found Wayne to be the stereotypical self-serving politician straight out of central casting, whose only mission is to manipulate the political arena for his own personal agenda.

The two of us went round-after-round during the campaign, which I enjoyed immensely and remains a highlight of the experience. Word on the street is that, even after all these years, Wayne's face gets as red as a cherry tomato when he hears my name. Needless to say, he doesn't like me very much which I take as a compliment.

Wayne was a member of the aforementioned Texas Legislature and led the fight (surprise, surprise) to redraw the districts. He made it no secret that he and then House Majority Leader Tom DeLay drew the new Texas 1st district just for him, although these days he isn't quite as vocal about it given his buddy DeLay's criminal conviction for money-laundering (or after what DeLay should have actually gone to prison for, his *Dancing With the Stars* appearance).

Two of Wayne's favorite sayings – and believe me, we heard them ten thousand times during the campaign – were something to the effect of "the only thing our kids need to succeed is a Christian mommy and daddy who live in the same house" and always a crowd favorite, "God made Adam and Eve not Adam and Steve."

Interestingly enough, Wayne never outlined his ten-point plan on how to miraculously give every child a Christian mommy and daddy who live in the same house. Maybe he has a clone factory somewhere.

In any event. I'm still suspicious that Wayne is the creator of the bumper sticker, usually stuck opposite a Peeing Calvin decal, "If you can't feed 'em don't breed 'em." But I digress.

Chapter Two

Let's Get This Party Started

"I ask for, not at once no government,
but *at once* a better government.
Let every man make known what kind
of government would command his respect,
and that will be one step toward obtaining it."

– Henry David Thoreau –

We Now *Know*

Donald Trump has done this country a huge favor. We owe him a debt of gratitude because, in just four years – love him or hate him – he has exposed every single weakness within our government and uncovered the deep fault lines that have destabilized this nation for decades.

Before him, it was like this slow *drip, drip, drip*. We could feel in our hearts that things were off, but had a hard time identifying exactly what those things were. Most of us assumed a day of reckoning was coming eventually, and it most certainly was. Donald Trump just accelerated the process.

Pre-Trump, so many actions, events, and potential policy outcomes were purely theoretical. Across America, we settled in at dinner tables with our families or sat across from co-workers at lunch and argued (with little evidence other than our, obviously brilliant, gut feelings) about the size our government should be and the role it should play, or if trade wars really do pay off, or if a $29.7 trillion debt was really *that* big of a deal, or if significant tax cuts for rich people and Wall Street really do, in fact, stoke the entire economy.

We debated the current status of our checks and balances and whether the executive branch had too much power. We discussed what would happen if we failed to see the warning signs of an international pandemic and, if a pandemic did indeed reach our shores, the role our institutions and basic science should play.

We innocently asked ourselves – in the naïve manner of people who are certain something like this could never happen to them – what it must be like to live in a country where the president called the press "the enemy of the people" and democratically-held elections "rigged" and "stolen." Or one where the president likened the United States intelligence agencies to Nazi Germany while, ironically, actual Nazi wannabes stormed the national Capitol.

We probably would have asked ourselves, if we could have even imagined it, what would happen if our president sold out our intelligence agencies in front of the entire world by siding with Russian President Vladimir Putin in Helsinki or if he shared highly classified information with the Russian foreign minister and Russian ambassador in the Oval Office.

Or, what would happen if our commander-in-chief verbally attacked combat veterans and Gold Star families or said that our military generals and top Pentagon brass just want to "do nothing but fight wars" so "all of those wonderful companies that make the bombs and make the planes and make everything else stay happy" – essentially accusing them of putting our armed forces into combat for nothing more than money.

We asked one another if it really was America's duty to open our doors to a certain number of refugees, then talked about how proud we were to live in a country where, even when we inevitably had to turn people away, it was always done with their dignity and respect in mind.

We waxed poetic about America's role in the world. What, for example, would happen if we legitimized Kim Jong-un by meeting with him face-to-face, or to what extent our outrage should be if a *Washington Post* contributing columnist was murdered in cold blood by the Saudis in their Consulate in Turkey.

Or what it would be like if the United States undermined NATO, or if we withdrew from major international agreements like the *Joint Comprehensive Plan of Action* (a.k.a. the Iranian nuclear deal), the *Intermediate-Range Nuclear Forces Treaty*, the *Open Skies Treaty*, the *Paris Climate Accord*, the T*rans-Pacific Partnership*, and several organizations within the United Nations system including the UN Human Rights Council, the UN Educational Scientific and Cultural Organization, and the UN Relief and Works Agency.

We questioned – but only hypothetically because we thought it too unthinkable to even contemplate – what would happen if we suddenly abandoned the Syrian Democratic Forces (SDF), our loyal allies who served beside us in our fight against the Islamic State, or if we abruptly retreated from the entire world, including from our most trusted allies (the entire world, that is, except for authoritarian leaders like Vladimir Putin, Rodrigo Duterte, and Recep Tayyip Erdoğan).

Pre-Trump, we regarded these topics as largely theoretical because, for the most part, we had never witnessed the real-life implications of them. But now, we have first-hand knowledge of the value and/or consequences of these scenarios because we have actually lived through them – and have the battle scars to prove it.

We now *know*.

At the same time, the Covid-19 pandemic also exposed many things. I mean, like huge, major things. The entire episode can be summed up in the warning Buffett gave us years ago (Warren, not

Jimmy): "It's only when the tide goes out that you learn who's been swimming naked."

We learned that our Strategic National Stockpile – our national repository of things like antibiotics, vaccines and other critical medical supplies – had been neglected for years. We discovered that our economy was not nearly as fortified as we would like to believe and that our government was tragically unprepared for an international crisis. We had front row seats, yet again, to the unimaginative "solutions" of the United States Congress.

We were also cruelly reminded of the massive health, economic and educational disparities that exist for people of color. Taken together, like a perfect storm, the depravity of Donald Trump, the devastation of Covid, and the documented murder of George Floyd brightly illuminated the grave injustices many Black Americans have been shackled to for centuries.

Demons that, in truth, are more dangerous than ever because – as opposed to crosses openly burning on lawns – they are now intricately woven into the fabric of our nation, perpetuating division, desolation, and damaging cycles and patterns that are difficult to identify and harder still to solve.

But here again we owe Donald Trump a debt of gratitude. By giving – through his racist and inflammatory words and deeds – formally closeted bigots permission to be loud, proud and at times homicidal, he helped expose blatant racism in a way that now, finally, cannot be ignored.

This is a gift. It is always better to know exactly who the enemy is, because then you know exactly who and what you are fighting against. As Sun Tzu said in *The Art of War*, "If you know the enemy and know yourself, you need not fear the result of a hundred battles."

Don't get me wrong, the revolting images from the Charlottesville domestic terrorist attack in August 2017 – where, among other things, racists chanted Nazi slogans, made monkey sounds, and, in the grand finale, a car bulldozed into a crowd of counter-protesters, killing one and leaving nineteen others injured – and the ones from the insurrection assault on our Capitol are nauseating, but at least most of these despicable racists ditched the white hoods and showed us their faces.

Uncovering their wickedness is the beginning of the end for them because, eventually, goodness conquers evil every time.

Some of the things mentioned here are *subjective* and, therefore, leave room for opinion. For example, topics like the size our government should be and the role it should play, or whether we should or shouldn't have withdrawn from major international agreements.

On the other hand, many of the things mentioned here are *objective*. We actually have the data necessary to assess things like Donald Trump's trade wars and tax cuts. We actually have provable outcomes and can clearly track the relationship between cause and effect.

We now *know*.

Obliterating the *Game of Politics*

So now that we *know*, what can we *do*? A time will eventually come when Americans will demand better governance and true transformation will begin. I say that time is now.

The grim reality is that there is a lot about the contemporary American way of life that is unsustainable. I hate to be a buzz kill, but our Social Security and Medicare models are unsustainable; our criminal justice, health care and educational systems are unsustainable; our dependence on debt, social media, emissions and antidepressants is unsustainable; our cavernous inequality gaps are unsustainable and so on and so forth. Essentially, we are running on a treadmill that often carries us backward.

Perhaps more than anything else, our political system is unsustainable. Our current political environment reminds me of those tricky Chinese finger traps we played with as kids – the bamboo contraption where you stick one of your fingers in each end. After fighting it the entire recess, you finally realized that the harder you pulled, the tighter it became.

Although there are die-hards who love to jump into the mud of dirty political debates and duke it out, the rest of us usually get disgusted with the entire mess and just *tune out*. It's as if politics has become a reality television show from which we are disengaged; like we're watching an unavoidable train wreck from the side of the tracks.

§§§

It is abundantly clear that finding actual solutions to our problems is not the goal of most of our politicians, and it hasn't been for a really long time. Instead, it's all about *the game*.

The insidious game of politics is being played by two ineffectual teams with nothing more in their arsenal than high-dollar lobbying, unconstitutional executive orders, self-serving earmarks, and despicable little tricks like gerrymandering and voter suppression.

The game of politics is the reason that Russia was able to exploit our deep internal division and interfere in our sacred elections; why our total public debt is $29.7 trillion, our federal budget deficit reached $3.13 trillion, and the reason we even know the term *fiscal cliff;* and why the U.S. debt rating was downgraded for the first time in history – over a decade ago – because of "the gulf between the political parties."

It is why, a full year after Joe Biden took the oath of office, only 41 percent of his nominees for Senate-confirmed jobs had been approved, leaving us with very important positions like ambassadors not being filled < worse, in order to even get many of those 41 percent approved, Democrats had to kiss-up to Republicans in ridiculous ways. Republican Senator Tom Cotton refused to move forward with the confirmation process of five U.S. attorney nominees until Democratic Senator Dick Durbin publicly apologized to him for interrupting him eight months before. I'm sorry…*what?* I swear, these people act like they are five >.

The game of politics is why too many parentless children are still stranded at our border and why over 37 million Americans are trapped in poverty. It is why our checks and balances are completely out of whack and why lobbyists almost exclusively write our public policy. It's the reason our early response to Covid-19 was a disaster, why our infrastructure is falling down, and why our allies are confused and concerned.

The game of politics is why atrocities like "enhanced interrogation techniques" (i.e., torture) and Guantánamo called into question our national core values and threatened our global image; why Iran and China are resentful and resurgent; and why Vladimir Putin and Kim Jong-un are essentially shooting us the bird.

It cannot be denied: The *game of politics* has brought this country to the brink, to the point where we literally have no choice but to make serious, significant changes.

I'm pretty sure most of us believe this to be true, but we always get stumped by the million-dollar question: How in the world do we do it?

I am convinced there is only one answer to this question. To truly disrupt the game of politics, we have to fundamentally change the way it is played. And realistically, there is only one way to fundamentally change the way it is played: Add more players to the game.

It is absolutely imperative we get this done because nothing will truly change as long as there are only two teams playing the game. That's just Social Psych 101.

Realistic Conflict Theory says that hostilities and resentments – along with feelings of prejudgment and discrimination – emerge when groups compete over a perceived scarcity of resources (in this case, political power). These emotions are amplified when the groups feel there can only be one winner and one loser. Sound familiar?

It would be terrific if our current political meltdown was caused solely by the election of Donald Trump or Hillary Clinton's emails or because of some procedural issue or because the right person hasn't yet fallen out of the sky to save us. Maybe then it would be relatively easy to fix. But this background noise is not what holds us back.

This is:

The reason true change eludes us is that we always attempt it within the constraints of an irreparably broken political system. The focus is always on tweaking elements of the system instead of eliminating the entire archaic, two-party system itself.

That is just not going to work. We are far beyond a small tweak here and there. Incremental change takes too long and we cannot vote our way out of this mess with our current two-party choices, or within the toxic environment that has evolved around them.

Think about it: If we just stick with the two major parties, overthrowing Congress at the voting booth is not only a fantasy, it wouldn't work anyway. Let's say we actually replaced every single member of Congress. At this point, their replacements would be other Republicans and Democrats.

Clearly, there aren't 535 Abraham Lincolns running around in either party. But, even if both major parties had super deep benches filled with Lincolns, they would still be forced to operate within the failed two-party setup – and we're all well aware that the destructive consequences of this dynamic get uglier and uglier by the day.

It is painfully obvious that our fractured political system is not going to miraculously heal itself and, due in large part to our poisonous political environment, most of our current leaders (who may otherwise be very solid, decent people) are not going to suddenly mutate into brilliant problem-solvers.

It just isn't going to happen. And every second we buy into that fairytale, we lose valuable time. This may sound depressing, but it's actually liberating! To lose the delusion and accept the truth sets us free.

Okay, so maybe we've been asleep at the wheel for a while, but this country has tremendous resilience. Americans don't reject national reflection – we embrace it. We don't allow momentary lapses in judgment to derail us – we gain wisdom that makes us even stronger.

§§§

The *Great American Reset* is finally here! We can absolutely change our direction, and we will. Regardless of our individual beliefs, it is critical we join together for positive progress. *We have been underestimated long enough.*

Together we will overcome the tremendous challenges we face and, channeling our very best angels, unleash the greatest version of both ourselves and our country.

What in the heck have we been waiting for? Americans are the most dynamic and innovative people in the world. We are courageous, convicted and confident and we possess a unique sense of assertiveness and adaptability.

We have all of the necessary ingredients – unlimited talent and intelligence, unparalleled freedom of opportunity, and vast economic resources – to cultivate the strength and goodness of America that we all know exists but that, thanks to partisan politics, has been compromised.

We simply need to incorporate the final component: a way to harness unrelenting will.

Challenging authority is our right, our responsibility, our legacy. Since the two-party political dynamic in America has completely broken down, we will simply step in and fix this madness ourselves.

The most beautiful thing about living in America is that we have the freedom and power to create a better future for ourselves without waiting for some piece of elusive legislation to pass. We don't need anyone's permission to define our destiny. Is this not the greatest country on the planet?!?

The exciting news is that once we take matters into our own hands, our future will be brighter than ever! The American spirit is unmatched, and we can achieve absolutely anything we put our minds to. It's a good thing too, because the time has finally come to tackle the most important effort we will ever take as fellow citizens: *Saving our country*.

We better get busy because, I hate to break it to you, there's no one else to do it. No one is sequestered in a secret room somewhere trying to figure this mess out. We seem to have this crazy notion that somebody – anybody! – is working on groundbreaking, nonpartisan solutions for us, but they are not. It's you and me, my fellow Americans! That's it.

On my first day of graduate school the dean made a joke: "Your first six weeks at Harvard, you will look around in awe at the people around you and think, 'how in the world did *I* get here'? The remainder of the time, you will look in disbelief at those around you and think, 'how in the world did *you* get here'?"

Don't get me wrong, I met the most brilliant people there, but it was at times reminiscent of Dorothy's immense surprise as she pulled down the curtain to reveal the all too human Wizard.

I like most of singer/songwriter John Mayer's songs, and plus he's pretty hot. But his song *Waiting on the World to Change* drives me nuts. "One day our generation is gonna rule the population, so we keep on waiting, waiting on the world to change" seems to insinuate that younger generations have little choice but to sit around with our thumbs up our… well, otherwise occupied…until the old regime is finished screwing everything up.

Do tell, who exactly is going to change the world if we all just sit around and wait? What age should we all hit before we jump in and help fix this?

I absolutely share John's frustration – "now we see everything that's going wrong with the world and those who lead it, we just feel like we don't have the means to rise above and beat it" – but we better get busy and find the means because our lame excuses are no longer an alternative.

In the absence of our involvement, we relinquish our future to people we half-heartedly elect and then are shocked when they fail to come through for us. No more!

Every single American needs to take their share of responsibility for the future of this country. It's important to have strong leaders and decision makers, but it's far more critical to have active, responsible citizens.

§§§

The time has come for each of us to honestly question our commitment to the future of this nation. Will our legacy be something we are proud of, or will we forever be known as the former superpower that recklessly relinquished our prominence because we lacked the will to protect it?

Deep down, do we really want to make the necessary changes or are we satisfied with accepting our political circus as some sort of perverse entertainment? We certainly have that privilege as a free nation but, if that is our position, we better brace ourselves for its severe consequences.

Our superpower as Americans is that we have the freedom and power to change the things we don't like. That we take that right for granted is a colossal understatement.

It feels like we all anticipate someone more qualified or smarter or less busy than ourselves to do something about all of this. Everyone is certainly eager to convey their disapproval and complain about the problems, but often the person that criticizes blames *someone else* or advocates that *someone else* take action.

It's true that identifying the challenges is a crucial component of the process, but to stop there is like hitting faulty brakes at the edge of a cliff. Imagine the difference if we reject finger pointing and the blame game, and go a step further: look inward, feel a compulsion to act, and introduce potential solutions into the political conversation.

I could not be prouder to be an American. Americans are optimistic not only for our own future, but also for our capacity to create a brighter tomorrow on a global scale. We are aware of our imperfections and have a deep desire to correct our indiscretions but remain completely faithful to the belief that the United States is the best place to be.

But the absolute greatest privilege of being an American is the freedom we have to continually assess our government, our leaders, and our political and moral direction.

Without that privilege, America would be lost. With it, anything is possible.

1787 National Committee

What makes a great leader? Given our current crop, it's easy to forget the genuine characteristics.

In late 1776, General George Washington and his army were seriously screwed. The American Revolution had taken a dreadful toll on what was, from the beginning, a ragtag army.

When Washington first took control earlier that year, it wasn't even an army at all. As Washington described it, he had more like the "raw materials" for an army with no name, no uniforms, no flag, no discipline, no military experience and only 10,000 pounds of gunpowder. Made up of crude and tattered shelters, the filthy encampments were ravaged by dysentery, typhus and typhoid fever. The conditions were about as nasty as nasty can get.

Nevertheless, Washington took command with "the look and bearing of a man accustomed to respect and to being obeyed. He was not austere. There was no hint of arrogance. 'Amiable' and 'modest' were words frequently used to describe him, and there was a softness in his eyes that people remembered."

According to Nathanael Greene, a major general of the Continental Army, when Washington arrived "joy was visible on every countenance, and it seemed as if the spirit of conquest breathed through the whole army." But things went downhill, fast. Just months into his command, the Continental Army had suffered several agonizing losses and men were deserting by the hundreds. Those who stayed were sick, starving, exhausted and dispirited.

Many of Washington's troops and two of his closest confidants – Joseph Reed, his most trusted friend, and General Charles Lee, his second-in-command – had lost faith in him entirely. The effort of the rebels was all but lost.

Then came the defining moment that proved we were destined to be a nation: The Battle of Trenton and Washington's night crossing of the Delaware.

On December 26, 1776, with his options running out and with just 2,400 men, General George Washington commanded his depleted troops across the Delaware River north of Trenton, New Jersey in severely treacherous conditions.

Once across, he led the Continental Army against Hessian soldiers and captured almost their entire force. This essential American victory reignited the spirit of the rebels in the colonies and proved that victory was possible.

Many factors contributed to America's independence, but none were more profound than Washington's conviction, perseverance and leadership.

Through times of immense despair and loneliness – "The reflection upon my situation and that of this army produces many an uneasy hour when all around me are wrapped in sleep. Few people know the predicament we are in." – Washington never lost faith.

He also never forgot what was at stake: "The fate of unborn millions will now depend, under God, on the courage and conduct of this army."

True leaders inspire others to fight harder, reach higher, dream wider and feel deeper. Leaders bravely and without hesitation confront the concerns and challenges of those they lead and take them where they sometimes don't want to go, but to where they need to be.

True leaders don't watch polls. True leaders don't consider November elections. True leaders don't surrender to party pressure or punt to political advisors. True leaders don't backtrack when things get tough.

In 1787, delegates from twelve states met for four sweltering months to write a document they entitled The Constitution of the United States of America.

The debate at the Constitutional Convention was extensive and often heated given the vast differences in the philosophies and motivations of the attendees, coupled with the significance of the issues being decided (proportional representation, how to elect the president, and the fate of slavery, just to name a few).

In the end, regardless of how contentious the debate, 55 men listened, compromised and periodically changed their minds, and they eventually created one of the most powerful documents in world history.

Its first seven words say it all: We the People of the United States. The U.S. Constitution is a grant of power *by* the people to elected officers and representatives that work *for* the people. There should be no confusion on this point because the intention of the document is undeniable.

Nevertheless, somewhere down the line, the people of this country were relegated to the sidelines and the intention of our forefathers has been thoroughly desecrated. The central theme throughout all of the founding documents, and the point that is made the most explicit, is that the ultimate power resides with the people.

The brilliant architects of the Constitution gave each of us an enormous responsibility when they established America as a republic, and they made it very clear that our duty extends far beyond stepping up to a ballot box.

To refresh your memory, a *republic* is a government having a chief of state where supreme power resides in a body of citizens entitled to vote. That's us! See how much control we are given in this setup?!? It's fascinating how easily we forget how much power we actually have.

As Benjamin Franklin left the Constitutional Convention, a woman asked him, "Well, Doctor, what have we got, a republic or a monarchy?" He responded, "A republic, if you can keep it."

'Ol Benjy was so wise. Democratic republics aren't sustained by placing power in the hands of the people alone. Whether ours succeeds or fails will be determined by our commitment to active and informed participation.

Well, that plus our adamant refusal to let two unproductive and ineffective political parties hijack our country.

In his farewell address to the nation, President George Washington praised our system's ability to represent individual differences. But, even way back then, he identified political parties as a specific threat to our union: "One of the expedients of party to acquire influence within particular districts is to misrepresent the opinions and aims of other districts. You cannot shield yourselves too much against the jealousies and heartburnings which spring from these misrepresentations."

He further warned that parties “serve to organize faction, to give it an artificial and extraordinary force; to put, in the place of the delegated will of the nation, the will of a party.”

Washington went on to say that, if these factions are tolerated, “cunning, ambitious and unprincipled men will be enabled to subvert the power of the people and to usurp for themselves the reins of government.” George’s prediction proved 1000% correct. This is exactly what has happened.

§§§

Although at times it feels like things have completely unraveled in our country, it’s actually a huge relief to finally be in this exact place – because now we can finally start turning this thing around.

1787 is a new American political party. Our mission has three parts:

Part One of the 1787 Mission

To find smart and sustainable solutions – with common sense and little drama – so we can create the America we all know is possible.

To best tackle this, I view our challenges as two paths that can be navigated <u>at the same time</u>, equally successfully. The *Path of Policies* is a straightforward path that we will take to address our most pressing policy issues. The *Path of Politics* is a more twisted one! This is the path we will take to end the glaring corruption in our political system.

Part Two of the 1787 Mission

Obliterate the *game of politics* so we can actually get these smart and sustainable solutions across the finish line – and actually *do something*!

Part Three of the 1787 Mission

Have a great time doing all of it!! Aren't you tired of everyone being mean and cranky because of politics? We need to chill out and start having fun again, America!

When an organization "nominates qualified candidates for president and various congressional offices in numerous states" as 1787 will, the U.S. Federal Election Commission (FEC) automatically classifies it as a national party committee. But that is where the "political party" distinction ends.

1787 is a new and improved brand of leadership that will never, as George Washington warned, "serve to organize faction, to give it an artificial and extraordinary force; to put, in the place of the delegated will of the nation, the will of a party."

In fact, with 1787 it's virtually impossible for the will of the party to overshadow the will of the people because 1787 members are in complete control of its direction. Think of 1787 like a democracy within the U.S. democracy, where every outcome is a *majority rule* of the members.

You can also think of 1787 as a modern-day Constitutional Convention, where committed citizens engage in respectful, nonpartisan conversation not to change the U.S. Constitution in any way, but to enhance and strengthen the extraordinary freedoms that our country was founded on.

At the annual 1787 convention – which features productive conversation, enlightening policy presentations, intelligent debate and super fun parties galore – 1787 members will vote on each policy issue to define the prevailing policy direction and platform. Also, members will nominate candidates for president of the United States, vice president of the United States, and congressional candidates.

Those members unable to attend the convention in person can submit their votes, analysis, presentations and comments virtually, or via email, text or the 1787 website. The rules and procedures are detailed on the 1787 website.

There are over 140 policy issues addressed on the website and within the three volumes of this book. Our goal is to provide unfiltered, unbiased information that is exhaustively researched. This way, we can actually have the knowledge necessary to make an intelligent decision rather than make up our minds based on 280 characters!! :)

Armed with knowledge, we bad ass Americans will be fully equipped to solve our problems and save our country! Doesn't this sound like a total blast? We can actually solve our problems, America! And it's not even that hard!

Will we all agree on everything? Of course not, but that's the point. Every policy deserves its own evaluation outside the context of misguided labels and political maneuvering …and the more qualified, diverse and experienced input, the better the outcome will be.

Walt Whitman said it best, "I hear America singing, the varied carols I hear." It is our variety of opinions and experiences that will stimulate colorful debate on our nation's most pressing issues. Only then can we expect sustainable solutions.

There will always be a certain amount of disagreement, but I think we'll be shocked by how straightforward the answers actually are when we drown out the noise of special interest groups, ideological labels, and the paralyzing backlash of a hard-core base. In many cases, it literally comes down to just doing the math.

This has never been tried before. Sure, there are existing political movements and so-called third parties, but the political movements are usually born out of frustration and anger and the third parties are generally based on a singular issue (Green Party) or just a severe extension of one of the two major parties (Libertarian Party).

This is one of the main reasons third parties have never really caught on. Previous efforts haven't worked because the outsiders were practically identical to one of the major party candidates. At that point, why take the chance? It's the *better the devil you know than the devil you don't* syndrome. The revolutionary course I am describing will only work if the motivation behind it transcends single issues, individual egos, and just one election cycle.

I assure you this one does. 1787 is motivated by one thing and one thing only: To cultivate the greatest version of the United States of America.

§§§

The destructive, archaic two-party structure has run its course. It's time to level the playing field in American politics by shattering this debilitating dynamic once and for all.

If you think I sound naïve, I ask you: Why not? Why can't a country of smart, innovative and empowered people unite to demand a larger voice in defining our future? We have nothing to lose and everything to gain because the alternative is just not working.

It's understandable that we "ordinary" Americans feel as powerless as David as we face the Goliath of special interest groups and national party affiliation, but there is enormous strength in even relatively small numbers.

Consider the extraordinary power of special interest groups. They have enormous influence in Washington and exert unparalleled control over our leaders. The American Israel Public Affairs Committee (AIPAC) is one of the most influential lobbying groups in Washington but has just over 100,000 members.

The National Education Association (NEA), one of the top influences in the Democratic party, has only three million members but their efforts consistently obstruct a ton of educational proposals.

There are reportedly just five million members of the National Rifle Association (NRA) – even in complete internal disarray, the undisputed master of the Republican Party – but they have historically blocked just about everything regarding gun control.

Hey, "ordinary" Americans, don't forget that there are over 255 million adults in the United States. AIPAC's members are only 0.04 percent of the entire adult population. The NEA members are only 1 percent and the NRA's members are only 2 percent.

I'm not completely delusional. I fully recognize the uphill battle we face. For one, our current political system is designed to be an impenetrable fortress, purposefully constructed to protect the two-party system in every way. The Electoral College, ballot access and debate rules, and endless other hurdles combine to make the playing field extraordinarily inequitable for new players.

There is also no question that those currently in charge will do everything in their power to try to stop us because this idea threatens their very existence. It's in their best interest to keep us alienated from one another because when we actually join forces, their Machiavellian gig will be up.

Many people think money rules Washington, but the power created by financial contributions is nothing in the face of an alliance that can take their power away. Our success is their worst nightmare because, when we prove that we are a force to be reckoned with, we will literally change the way this country is run.

All that said, I also know – with zero doubt – that there is a pathway to victory if we stand together. There will *always* be people who fight to protect the status quo, but that's really not even an option anymore. Clearly things can't stay as they are, and we won't change things if we are not daring, bold and brave.

Times are changing and changing fast. A new political party will eventually win. I guarantee you that, fellow Americans. Even before another party wins and regardless of how long winning takes, viable choice in and of itself will elevate the conversation and up *everyone's* game. Competition will instantly force Republicans and Democrats into seriousness.

To The Establishment I say: Bring it on! Take your best shot and try with all of your might to stop us, but it won't work this time. Your glory days are over.

§§§

I know there will be plenty of skepticism, so let's just jump right into it. Hmmm…okay, here's a good one. Some would argue that, even after actually winning, there are still major challenges for new players. Without strong congressional allies, for example, the existing parties can make it virtually impossible for newbies to build legislative consensus.

Those who believe this think way too small. For one, the argument makes little sense because gridlock can't possibly get any worse than it is right now. Nevertheless, the argument is not completely flawed.

Obviously, presidents and congressmen need congressional support to get things done. But this argument assumes that a third party or independent candidate has actually made it to the White House and/or Congress. When this finally happens, this concern becomes irrelevant because the rules of the game will have been completely turned upside down. At that point, none of the old rules apply.

When this finally happens, the American people will have essentially revolted against the two-party system. Any member of Congress who ignores such a clear message won't be around long anyway, not to mention the existing members of Congress who are probably as sick of this foolishness as we are.

In all seriousness, I imagine that, deep down, at least some members of the two major parties would love to break this little party up themselves. There are 535 members of Congress. How many do you actually see on TV or read about in the newspaper? My guess is less than 20 and that's only if you watch cable news. For the most part, those most visible are those most partisan.

However, I imagine that there are at least a few members of Congress who would welcome a disruption in the perpetual political tug of war. I imagine that, given the chance, there are a few who would actually love to do their actual *job* – regardless of the initial next to their name.

Here's another question asked by skeptics: How can a third party possibly win the presidency as long as we have the Electoral College? This is a really great question.

Many of us probably agree that the Electoral College needs to go. Under our current system of voting, some votes in the United States matter way more than others and that's just not the American way. I'll put it this way: Mathematically, a candidate could win the presidency by winning as little as 23 percent of the popular vote, which is illogical.

America is a representative democracy and, as such, all votes for the U.S. president should count equally. A few say that the Electoral College shouldn't be messed with because this process was the fervent wish of the Founding Fathers. However, this is a total mis-characterization of their intent.

In truth, the Electoral College was born out of a compromise that James Madison struck at the Constitutional Convention in 1787, when one group wanted Congress to elect the president and another group wanted to have direct elections. < Thank God they didn't land on having Congress *always* elect the president! Can you imagine? >

Twenty-three decades later, it makes zero sense that the U.S. president, who is supposed to represent every single American, was ultimately chosen in 2020 by essentially the people who live in Georgia, Florida, Arizona, Nevada, North Carolina, Wisconsin, Michigan, and Pennsylvania.

A constitutional amendment is the cleanest way to abolish the Electoral College but is by far the most difficult to achieve. Under Article V of the U.S. Constitution, there are two ways to pass an amendment: 1) receive two-thirds approval from both the House and Senate, plus ratification by three-fourths of the state legislatures (which, currently, is 38 states), or 2) if two-thirds of the state legislatures call for a Constitutional Convention.

Because neither of these will likely happen anytime soon, we should go with Plan B and replace statewide *winner-take-all* laws with the *National Popular Vote Interstate Compact* (NPVIC), which would basically accomplish the same goal.

States with *winner-take-all* laws – which is every state except Maine and Nebraska – require the state to cast its electoral votes for the candidate with the most popular votes in the state. The NPVIC is an agreement directly between the states that commits each state to cast its electoral votes for the presidential candidate who wins the national popular vote. As of the 2020 election, fifteen states plus Washington, D.C. had signed on to this pact, representing a total of 196 electoral votes.

< Incidentally, another thing we need to do is clarify the somewhat murky *Electoral Count Act of 1887*, the legislation that currently regulates the Electoral College selection process. It is critical that we do this as quickly as possible to guarantee that Congress understands its role in the process of counting electoral votes. The asinine things some members of Congress were saying before and on January 6, 2021 about their (and the vice president's) outsized authority were downright embarrassing in their ignorance.

The United States Constitution is clear: States are the arbiters of their own elections for presidential electors. Congress and/or the vice president of the United States have ZERO authority to second-guess, change, or just decide not to count the slate of electors submitted to them by each state, or to hold up the electoral vote count to "investigate" alleged election fraud or election "irregularities."

Congress and/or the vice president have ZERO authority to reject slates from states when no competing slates of electors exist. The only time Congress can object to Electoral College votes is if the appointment of the electors was not "lawfully certified," or the votes were not "regularly given." This is an extremely high – almost impossible to clear – bar because, in the end, majorities in both chambers must agree with the objection. As a result, objections to the electoral count vote are purely political theatre, like it was on January 6, 2021. >

Passing a constitutional amendment to abolish the Electoral College and the *National Popular Vote Interstate Compact* are both great possibilities for the future but, as I said earlier, neither will likely happen anytime soon. So, because we are a new party, our best bet is to focus on an interesting workaround the Founding Fathers provided for us.

Meet the good 'ol 12th Amendment. The guys at the Constitutional Convention came up with Article II Section 1 which addresses the Electoral College. Then, in 1803, Congress passed an amendment to Article II, which led to the 12th Amendment.

The 12th Amendment provides a way for 1787 to block both major parties from receiving 270 electoral votes, which is what a candidate must have to become president. If no presidential candidate gets to 270, the election moves to Congress where the House of Representatives chooses one of the top three electoral vote-getters to be president. This is the amendment the Republicans were trying to trigger with their completely baseless, shot-in-the-dark objections on January 6, 2021.

Here's how it works. Let's say that, in 2024, the three top electoral vote getters are the Republican candidate, the Democratic candidate, and the 1787 candidate. For this 12th Amendment strategy to work, 1787 has to win just one state with enough electoral votes to deny the Republicans and Democrats 270 – and we absolutely can. I personally believe that at least 17 states will be in play in 2024, and we plan to win a heck of a lot more than just one of those.

In the House of Representatives, each state delegation gets one vote and 26 of the states must vote for the same candidate. That's your new president.

In the meantime, the vice president is chosen by the Senate. But the Senate chooses only from the top two electoral vote getters, unlike the House who chooses from the top three. This means that, in 2024, the vice president will be either the Republican or Democratic candidate. Basically, whichever party has the majority in the Senate will vote for their party's vice-presidential candidate. That's your new vice president.

The political make-up of the House of Representatives goes back and forth – and we have a midterm election between now and 2024 – but based on history, there is a reasonable chance that neither the Republican nor the Democratic candidate will win the 26 states necessary to become president. The kicker is that, if neither party's candidate wins 26 states, the vice president remains the acting president.

So, let's say the Democratic candidate wins the vice presidency. At that point, members of the Republican party would have to decide if they would rather have the 1787 presidential candidate be president or keep the Democratic vice president as acting president.

Given the way Republicans and Democrats feel about each other these days, I bet anything that the Republicans' decision would be to vote for the 1787 candidate over the Democrat.

See?!? There is more than one way to skin this cat!

1787's Honor Code

† 1787 fiercely defends the constitutional rights of every American. We respect every race, color, religion, and creed that combine to make America truly exceptional. We deeply believe in the First Amendment and that all men and women are created equal.

† 1787 rejects political vitriol and hateful rhetoric in any form. 1787 strives to bring Americans together and has no patience for those who try to rip us apart. We commit to a high level of civility and a positive public conversation.

† 1787 believes in evidence-based facts. The initial 1787 Policy Recommendations are meant only to begin the conversation and have a blueprint to work from. We want *every* American to work hard to prove these wrong because that is the best way to find the best solutions.

† 1787 has a deep level of faith in the United States intelligence communities, the U.S. military, and the U.S. judiciary. We believe these institutions exist to protect and defend us from harm, and we greatly appreciate their dedication.

† 1787 honors and respects our friends and allies around the world. We believe that, for the United States to prosper and thrive, we must fully engage in the global community and not only regain but solidify our role as a world leader.

† 1787 highly respects and steadfastly defends the "mainstream" news media. We believe that the Fourth Estate contributes significantly to the health of our democracy and without high-level journalism, its very survival would be at risk.

1787's Position on Civil & Human Rights

- † 1787 believes deeply in civil rights and personal liberty.

- † Every adult citizen of the United States should have the freedom to make personal choices for his or her life and be responsible for those decisions. This belief does not mean that the leadership or any other member of 1787 necessarily approves or disapproves of other people's choices.

- † 1787 will fight to end discrimination in all forms – including discrimination based on race, sex, ethnicity or national origin, language, religion, sexual orientation, gender identity, age, or disability.

- † 1787 believes that government should not restrict personal relationships. Sexual orientation, preference, gender, or gender identity should not be a factor in issues such as marriage and equal federal rights, child custody, adoption, immigration or military service laws.

- † 1787 supports the freedom to participate in – or abstain from – any religious activities that do not violate the rights of others. We adamantly oppose any government interaction that either promotes or attacks any specific religion.

The Gang Who Can't Shoot Straight

Obviously, I'm far from the first person to have this opinion about new political parties. In fact, every single presidential election year, our country has endured the inevitable but largely pointless debate over the fantasy of a competitive third party. The final verdict has always been the same: Third parties have no chance of winning, which makes them nothing more than "spoilers" – an assessment that has been accurate since the 1912 presidential race between Theodore Roosevelt and William Howard Taft.

The spoiler argument certainly held true in 1992, when Ross Perot sent Bill Clinton to the White House and George H.W. Bush home, and in 2016, when the number of votes that third-party candidates received in key battleground states was larger than Donald Trump's margin of victory.

But now – suddenly – the "third party" debate has become pointless for an entirely different reason: It is obsolete.

Earlier, I said that it's time to shatter the destructive, archaic two-party dynamic. Because of the way elections inherently work, only a competitive third party or independent candidate can ultimately make that happen. But this once herculean task is a heck of a lot easier now, because the death of the two-party system has already been initiated, not from the landing blow of a third party at the ballot box, but because the two major parties have finally blown *themselves* apart.

It started in the Republican Party way before Donald Trump. The man who once said that he "probably identifies more as Democrat" did not hijack the Republican Party; rather he was the most predictable next phase of a decades-long natural progression.

The slow but sure downfall of the Republican Party started years ago, the minute the self-described fiscally responsible party abandoned its own rules regarding traditional conservative policy, which included their spending money like drunken sailors.

Sluggish wages, shuttered factories, Wall Street bailouts, and incredibly reckless foreign wars and the massive deficits that funded them soon collided with a largely Christian Caucasian hard-core base that was feeling increasingly hostile, defensive and aggrieved.

From the point of view of these constituents, they and their families worked for generations in jobs that helped build the very backbone of America. They believed they had, for generations, lived by a strict moral code – with God, country, and family at the center of everything.

But suddenly, based on my personal research and conversations with them, many felt America no longer looked like the country they once knew.

They started to feel marginalized, both culturally and politically. They felt like elites were mocking them, cheered on by their highbrow friends in the biased mainstream media. They started to believe their livelihoods were being threatened by minorities, immigrants and globalization. They sensed they were getting shafted big-time by the swamp, deep state, and rapidly changing demographics.

< Note: An analysis of the first 377 people arrested and/or charged in the January 6th attack on the Capitol, conducted by the Chicago Project on Security and Threats, revealed that 95 percent were White, 85 percent were male, and that "counties with the most significant declines in the non-Hispanic White population were the most likely to produce insurrectionists who now face charges. The counties that had the greatest decline in White population had an 18 percent chance of sending an insurrectionist to D.C., while the counties that saw the least decline in the White population had only a 3 percent chance." >

Eight years of having to endure a "Socialist" in the White House – a Black one at that! – not only exasperated their pain and perceived alienation…it threatened their entire way of life. To them, the radical left's depraved public policy and depleted values threatened Christianity itself. Taken together, all of this eventually destroyed their trust in government leaders and institutions, which they had always been highly suspicious of in the first place.

To prevent a full-scale revolt, the Republican Party inadvertently escalated its own downfall by making the decision to play only to this slice of its base through identity politics and making practically everything about abortion, gay people and guns…which I suppose is somewhat logical when, according to the Public Religion Research

Institute (PRRI) – a nonprofit, nonpartisan organization that conducts independent research – around three-quarters (73 percent) of your party belongs to a White Christian religious group.

But even severely narrowing things down to abortion, gay people and guns wasn't enough for the ever-hardening base. Enough is enough, they thought. Clearly, the only way to conquer the deep state, shifting demographics, and an increasingly connected world is to shut all of it down completely, a pivot that crushed five of the remaining pillars of the Grand Old Party of yesteryear – faith in civic institutions, international leadership, moral rectitude, responsible immigration, and global trade.

So, the stage was already set that fateful day when Mr. MAGA himself descended down that escalator. The shift from thoughtful conservatism to nihilistic populism was complete.

Listen, it's music to my ears if this is the party Republicans decide they want. It only makes them easier to defeat because this strategy is unsustainable for one reason: America is rapidly becoming more urban and diverse and, although they try <u>really</u> hard, there is absolutely nothing they can do about it.

…and they just cannot deal. The reality is that the Republican Party's current approach is far too narrow to survive long-term in a country where there are Black people, Hispanic people, gay people, young people and women.

Add to *that*, many of the Republican high-profile "stars" seem to be embracing authoritarianism and autocracy more by the day (we'll circle back to this later) and come off increasingly callous, petty and mean. Add to *that*, the Republican Party has abandoned even the slightest attempt to introduce new ideas and solid public policy. I mean, we certainly know what they are *against,* but what is the party even *for* anymore? Does anyone know?

Even when Republicans controlled all three branches of government at the beginning of the Trump presidency, the three distinct factions within the party – conservatives, moderates and Trump Republicans – could not agree on anything beyond a tax cut. Essentially, they produced zero productive policy achievements, not even ones for evil immigration or "repeal and replace!"

This vision vacuum didn't start in 2016; it has existed for decades. Democrats have won the popular vote in seven out of the last eight presidential elections, which is a pretty glaring clue that most Americans aren't really buying whatever it is you are selling. If it weren't for aggressive gerrymandering, the Republican Party would *already* be out of business.

Absent a huge dose of serious soul-searching, the death of the Republican Party is coming. Maybe not today or tomorrow – or, even in 2022 or 2024 – but it *is* going to happen sooner rather than later, just based on demographics alone.

According to the Pew Research Center, a nonpartisan fact tank, in 2018 the most common age for Hispanic Americans was 11; the most common age for Black Americans was 27; and the most common age for Asian Americans was 29. The most common age for White Americans was 58. Uh oh.

TargetSmart – a Democratic political data and data services firm that analyzed 2020 voter data on over 98 percent of American voters – found that "nationally, total turnout increased by 12 percent relative to 2016. Turnout among AAPI [Asian American and Pacific Islander] voters surged by 43 percent and Latino turnout increased by almost a third of all votes cast." Further, "non-college educated Whites dropped from 53.8 percent of the electorate in 2016 to 49.2 percent in 2020."

The Public Religion Research Institute (PRRI) found that White Christians now account for only 43 percent of all adults living in the United States. In 1976, that number was 81 percent. Plus, the number of people living in rural America, whose votes the Republican Party relies heavily on, is declining.

It's true that Donald Trump did marginally better than expected with communities of color in the 2020 election – which completely baffles me – but it's not nearly enough. Even with a slight bump in support, Donald Trump only won 12 percent of the Black vote and 32 percent of the Hispanic/Latino vote. He only won the vote of 42 percent of women and 36 percent of voters 18-29 years old.

This all creates a self-fulfilling prophecy for the GOP: Their largely Christian Caucasian hard-core base is quickly becoming outnumbered;

which only makes them angrier, more resentful, and more insular; which forces the party to say and do silly and senseless things; which alienates the party from even more Americans and makes the numbers against them grow even more.

Rest assured, the leaders of the Republican Party have seen all of this evidence too, which makes doubling down on their current path an even more bizarre choice.

Instead of building a larger coalition by designing and promoting policies that American voters might actually embrace – or calling Joe Biden out on a pretty liberal agenda (more on this in a minute) – Republicans spend their time and energy passing state-level draconian election laws (that allow them to try to rig elections) and anti-protest legislation (which includes things like granting immunity to drivers who crash into protesters on public streets) – all the while perpetuating ridiculous culture wars that delight their diehard supporters but make the rest of America nauseous.

< I mean, seriously guys. For example, according to Gallup, only 3.1 percent of Americans identify as bisexual, 1.4 percent as gay, 0.7 percent as lesbian and 0.6 percent as transgender. Is *this* really the hill you want to die on, Republicans? Fighting against – and, like a bunch of nosy Gladys Kravitz-es, interfering in the lives of – Americans who, by the way, have exactly the same constitutional right to live an authentic life as you do? *This* is the kind of thing you are busy worrying about? Give me a break. I actually have a theory on this, and it involves the concept of *methinks thou doth protest too much*, but I digress. >

This approach is going to backfire on them big-time, as we clearly saw in the Georgia 2020 Senate runoff election, when two Republicans who should have easily won were both defeated by Democrats.

Plus, many in the party seem determined to keep the Republican base-whisperer Donald Trump as its standard-bearer, which I find strange since he is the first president since Herbert Hoover to lose the White House, the Senate, and the House of Representatives for his party in just four years. Meaning, he is the epitome of what he projects others to be: a loser.

Although it took a while, cracks within the party are starting to show. In mid-May 2021, over 150 prominent Republicans – including former Cabinet officials, governors and party leaders, Members of Congress, and high-level staff – threatened to leave the GOP and start a new party if the Republican Party does not make serious changes, fast.

My guess is that the Republican National Committee is so detached from reality at this point that they won't take this threat seriously, but they should. This is bad news for them because they really don't have the people to lose. Gallup, a global analytics firm, released a poll in early April 2021 that found:

> "An average of 49 percent of U.S. adults identified with the Democratic Party or said they are independents who lean toward the Democratic Party. That compares with 40 percent who identified as Republicans or Republican leaners. The nine-percentage-point Democratic advantage is the largest Gallup has measured since the fourth quarter of 2012. In recent years, Democratic advantages have typically been between four and six percentage points."

Worse, at a time when sane and sensible Republicans are leaving or threatening to leave the party, their de facto leader Trump has welcomed in – with open arms – complete wackos. ...people like self-described "proud Islamophobe" Laura Loomer, who beat out five opponents to win the 2020 Republican congressional primary in Florida's 21st District.

Loomer – who gained the support of the Republican Party of Florida and was joined on the campaign trail by Donald Trump's daughter-in-law, Lara Trump – is a real gem.

For example, when she heard that over 2,000 migrants had died crossing the Mediterranean in 2017, she tweeted, "Good. Here's to 2,000 more," alongside a clapping emoji. Or when she said, in addition to many, many horrific racist comments, "Islam is a cancer on society. Islam is a cancer on humanity, and Muslims should not be allowed to seek positions of political office in this country. It should be illegal."

Umm, can you even be a member of Congress if you have never read the U.S. Constitution?

Although her extremist views got her banned from almost every social media platform, Donald Trump remained super supportive of her: "Great going Laura. You have a great chance against a Pelosi puppet!"

Thank God Loomer lost the 2020 general election, but other lunatics unfortunately won. And Donald was so supportive! "Lauren Boebert for Congress – we have to get her in, she's incredible, she's a fighter who knows how to win. She's taken our country by storm – she's taken *me* by storm."

This is a woman who openly expressed support for QAnon – the far-right loony-toon conspiracy theory cult that believes America is run by a cabal of blood-drinking cannibals, Satan worshippers, and child sex traffickers – and even called Q a "patriot." Even though she has since dialed her Q worship back a little, at least publicly, she was once very clear: "Everything that I've heard of Q, I hope that this is real because it only means that America is getting stronger and better, and people are returning to conservative values."

(there is much more on election "fraud," the January 6th insurrection, and the dangers of QAnon in the next chapter)

In the days *before* the January 6th attack on the U.S. Capitol, Boebert tweeted, "Remember these next 48 hours. These are some of the most important days in American history." The day *of* the attack, she tweeted, "Today is 1776," before sending out the exact locations of multiple Democratic lawmakers that some in the crowd were literally hunting down. In the days *after* the attack, she got into a standoff with Capitol police for refusing to go through the newly installed metal detectors at the entrance of the House chamber because she was carrying a gun (which is prohibited by law).

Donald also celebrated kooks like Representative Marjorie Taylor Greene (R-GA), another early supporter of QAnon. The admiration was mutual: Donald Trump is the best person to stop "this global cabal of Satan-worshiping pedophiles," Greene proudly declared!

Among other truly idiotic things, Greene was adamant that the Sandy Hook and Parkland school shootings were faked by anti-gun activists; that wildfires in California were started by Jewish space lasers; and that "George Soros is the piece of crap that turned in – he's a Jew – he turned in his own people over to the Nazis," which is just a flat out lie. She also called the January 6th insurrection at the U.S. Capitol a "1776 moment" and showed support for the execution of several of her congressional colleagues.

During the 2020 election, the fact that the FBI called QAnon out by name (warning of "conspiracy theory-driven domestic extremists") didn't slow Donald Trump and his cronies down one bit. Instead, Donald went all in, calling Greene a "future Republican Star" who is "strong on everything and never gives up – a real WINNER!"

Supporting cuckoo birds was not the only way Donald promoted QAnon during his time in the Oval Office. He retweeted pro-QAnon accounts hundreds of times and his two older sons referenced the whacked-out theories on their own social media accounts. Donald's deputy communications director and two of his personal lawyers all repeatedly shared QAnon posts and memes.

The Trump administration's first national security adviser Michael T. Flynn – a former military general who was fired 24 days into the administration for lying to the FBI, then was convicted for it, then was given a presidential pardon – is now literally selling QAnon T-shirts. He also joined Digital Soldiers, a group that expresses support of QAnon and other crazy conspiracy theories. There is actually a video of him online taking QAnon's "digital soldier" oath (you just have to Google this…it will skeeve you out).

When pressed publicly about QAnon, Donald not only refused to denounce the movement but said, "I heard these are people that love our country...I understand they like me very much. Which I appreciate."

Lest you think Laura Loomer, Lauren Boebert and Marjorie Taylor Greene are unfortunate one-off candidates, you should know that 81 primary congressional candidates in the 2020 election endorsed or supported QAnon theories, and 24 of those (22 Republicans, two independents) actually won a spot on the general election ballot.

Looking to the 2022 midterms, Trump sycophant Rep. Matt Gaetz (R-FL) made a declaration that should send chills down the backs of every rational Republican: "We are going to take power after this next election. And when we do, it's not going to be the days of Paul Ryan and Trey Gowdy. It's gonna be the days of Jim Jordan and Marjorie Taylor Greene and Gosar and myself." < Just FYI, Paul Gosar from Arizona recently posted a video that illustrated him killing a Democratic member of Congress. >

Donald Trump is working hard to help make this dream a reality, fervently searching for the most loyal, but often radical, MAGA candidates: "Saving America starts by saving the G.O.P. from RINOs [Republicans in name only], sellouts and known losers!"

It appears that the ex-president's main mission is to brutally punish anyone that he perceives did not sufficiently support him during the 2020 election drama. If a Republican candidate happens to believe that the 2020 election was not stolen or rejects the craziest of conspiracy theories or slighted him (in his sole opinion) in any way, he wants them to go *down*. Bigly.

Although most congressional Republicans don't believe conspiracy theory trash – Senator Mitch McConnell even said that the "looney lies and conspiracy theories" that Greene endorses is a "cancer" on the Republican Party – don't believe the 2020 election was stolen and, in private conversations, readily admit they cannot stand Donald Trump, there has been an alarming lack of pushback across most of their ranks, as there was throughout almost all of his presidency, regardless of his behavior.

In fact, 199 Republican members of the House of Representatives effectively came to Greene's defense when the House leadership sought to remove her from the Education and Budget Committees for promoting violence against fellow House members. For example, in one of her campaign ads, Greene is holding a gun beside photos of Democratic Representatives Alexandria Ocasio-Cortez, Ilhan Omar and Rashida Tlaib, with the caption, "Squad's worst nightmare."

Only 11 Republicans voted to remove her from the committees which, based on the hostile threats toward her colleagues, is the very least of what should have happened.

This is not just a Washington problem. Unfortunately for sane Republicans, crazies are now entrenched in every level of the party.

In early January 2021, after the Capitol insurrection, the chairman of the Nye County, Nevada Republicans, Chris Zimmerman, released a conspiracy-laced manifesto that said in part: "Let me be clear: Trump will be president for another four years. Biden will not be president…Indeed, we will have a new administration made up of a new vice president and cabinet, as the current ones have all made their treason complete."

Zimmerman also said that "the president, following the capitol incident, left DC on a 'Doomsday' aircraft (used for communications in the event of a nuclear war) with his family and was in Abilene, TX. This aircraft was confirmed by both flight trackers and eyes on the ground." Additionally, he said the emergency broadcast system would be used to facilitate "messages from the president to the public" and "high-profile arrests" would be made.

Zimmerman also wrote that a defense contractor "used satellites to change the votes from our election in the USA from Italy. These Dominion voting machines were actively sending data to Germany, Serbia, China, Iran and now Rome. This corruption is MUCH bigger that any of us expected but none of us would have believed it until now… It's 1776 all over again!"

Meanwhile, the Oregon Republican Party passed a resolution that declared "the violence at the Capitol was a 'false flag' operation designed to discredit President Trump, his supporters, and all conservative Republicans." They further said that the 10 House Republicans that voted for Donald Trump's impeachment "conspired to surrender our nation to Leftist forces seeking to establish a dictatorship."

In Wyoming, the state Republican Party passed a formal resolution condemning Representative Liz Cheney for criticizing, and being disloyal to, Donald Trump (this was before House Republicans booted her from her leadership position for the same egregious crime), and the Arizona Republican Party did the same to Cindy McCain, former U.S. Senator Jeff Flake, and Governor Doug Ducey. The state parties in Louisiana, North Carolina and South Carolina followed suit, as did county-level GOP officials in Illinois, Kentucky, Nebraska, Michigan and Washington.

Don't underestimate what a huge problem this is for the Republican Party. Even the always reliably conservative *Wall Street Journal* editorial page said, "If bowing before all things Trump is the litmus test for being a loyal Republican, the party should get used to continued losses in the suburbs."

Primary elections are the main reason this is such a disaster for the party. Most people who vote in primaries tend to be the crazed party faithful, and the crazed party faithful demand likeminded candidates.

Primaries have always been a balancing act for both parties, but never before have so many Americans been completely detached from reality. This phenomenon all but guarantees the Republican primaries will be jammed with total crackpots, and they very possibly may win. But unfortunately for Republicans, besides the occasional Marjorie Taylor Greenes, crackpots <u>are</u> <u>not</u> going to win general elections.

Already, there are ominous signs for the Republicans. The National Republican Congressional Committee has resorted to threatening its members to get them to make automatic monthly donations: "We need to know we haven't lost you to the Radical Left. If you UNCHECK this box, we will have to tell Trump you're a DEFECTOR & sided with the Dems. CHECK this box and we can win back the House and get Trump to run." Good grief. What is this, 1940s New York City?

As bad as things are for the Republican Party, the disconnect in the Democratic Party may be even worse. In fact, when it comes to public policy, the Democratic moderate and liberal wings may as well be on opposite planets. They cannot even agree on what economic system America should have.

Will Rogers once joked, "I am not a member of any organized political party – I am a Democrat." This is how I've always viewed the Democratic Party. It's essentially everyone in America who wants to identify with a political party but can't stomach being a Republican. That's why it's often described as a "big tent" party.

This is not a criticism. There are many positive attributes that come with being inclusive, with tolerance, empathy and compassion being at the top of my personal list. But being a "big tent" party is also what will ultimately be the Democratic Party's undoing. The widely disparate views within the party worked just fine for decades – mainly because the far left-wing was relatively small and contained – but that dynamic has changed significantly.

Even though Joe Biden won the 2020 Democratic presidential primary – a feat only achieved because establishment lions (namely South Carolina congressman Jim Clyburn) stepped in when far left-wingers Bernie Sanders and Elizabeth Warren moved to frontrunner status – progressives had been on a roll electorally and had already been extremely successful in heavily influencing the Democratic Party's platform.

In a relatively short time, "The Squad" – and its three highest-profile members, Representatives Alexandria Ocasio-Cortez (D-NY), Rashida Tlaib (D-MI) and Ilhan Omar (D-MN) – had already managed to push the Democratic House leadership to the left.

Ocasio-Cortez, a member of the Democratic Socialists of America, even nominated self-described democratic socialist Bernie Sanders to be president at the 2020 Democratic National Convention, even though Biden had the nomination sewn up, and she is working with other progressives to challenge moderate Democratic candidates in the 2022 midterms (since 2016, the far-left has already been successful in unseating five establishment Democrats).

Senator Bernie Sanders is now the chairman of the powerful Budget Committee, which has enormous influence over tax and spending thanks to a budget mechanism called reconciliation, which allows legislation to pass with a simple majority. Senator Sanders and others have made it clear that they intend to push the limits of this power.

By design, congressional Democrats of all stripes stuck together like glue in the first few months of Joe Biden's presidency, which was fairly easy because passing the coronavirus relief package was low hanging fruit.

But trouble is a-brew'n. One must look no further than the Democrat's inter-party feud over *Build Back Better*, voting rights, and the U.S. providing weapons to Israel to strike the Palestinians to see that the ideological split in the party is becoming wider and deeper by the day – and will eventually become a bridge too far for all sides.

I'm not saying that the super liberal slice of the Democratic party is large enough to overtake the entire thing. However, I do believe there are *just enough* of them to become "spoilers" within their own party.

Even though President Biden is proving to be far more progressive than many on the far left originally thought – for example, his *American Rescue Plan* and his proposed *American Jobs Plan* and *American Families Plan* have a combined price tag of over $6 trillion (more on this in Chapter Four) – it's still not sufficiently left for "The Squad" and the like. In response to the $2.3 trillion *American Jobs Plan,* Ocasio-Cortez tweeted, "This is not nearly enough."

The cracks are showing more and more every day. Although Joe Biden won the top of the ticket in 2020, Democrats down ballot fell well short of expectations. It was actually pretty bad. Democrats even lost New Hampshire's legislature.

Today, the Republican Party controls 30 state legislatures to the Democratic Party's 18, meaning Republicans control 61 percent of them. Republicans have "state control" – this is when the same party holds both legislative chambers <u>and</u> the governorship – of 23 states. Democrats have state control of just 15.

Several states and cities are faltering under Democratic leadership, badly. Analysis by WalletHub, a personal finance website, finds that Red States have a much lower tax burden than Blue States and that taxpayers in Red States get a much better Return on Investment (ROI) than those in Blue States (the state's color is determined by how the state voted in the 2020 election).

Both the state of New York and New York City have been horribly mismanaged and are terribly expensive places to live. Meanwhile, even in the midst of the Covid-19 crisis, then Democratic Mayor Bill de Blasio and Democratic Governor Andrew Cuomo squabbled with one another like spoiled children – until Cuomo was forced to resign due to multiple scandals.

The state of New York has the highest Overall Tax Burden of any state, but ranks 19th in Overall Government Services, 37th in Health, 41st in Economy, and 44th in Taxpayer's Return on Investment.

California has the 10th highest Overall Tax Burden but ranks 37th in Overall Government Services, 36th in Safety, 45th in Economy, and

49th in Taxpayer's Return on Investment. California has the third-highest cost of living (behind Hawaii and Washington, D.C.).

As a result, people and businesses are fleeing New York and California. California's population decreased last year for the first time on record. This is serious business because – remember – the number of people in a state translates into how many congressional seats (i.e., political power) that state has.

Centrist Democrats have already shown they are ready to push back against the far-left wing, hard. By refusing to change Senate rules to weaken the filibuster, Democratic Senators Joe Manchin (West Virginia) and Kyrsten Sinema (Arizona) have essentially put a halt to President Biden's agenda mere months before the 2022 midterm elections.

The outrage from the far left-wing of the party has been fierce. Rep. Cori Bush (D-MO) called Manchin's position "anti-Black, anti-child, anti-woman and anti-immigrant."

Even before this move, the Democratic establishment pounced after the party's poor performance in 2020, squarely laying the blame on the far left for their aggressive and vocal support of things like *Medicare for All*, the *Green New Deal*, and *Defunding the Police*. < I want to go on record as saying the phrase *defunding the police* is without a doubt the most ridiculous and counterproductive marketing approach in history. >

Listen, it's music to my ears if the far left keeps pushing these ideas. It only makes it easier to defeat them because this path – together with bloated budgets and astronomical spending – is unsustainable for one reason: Regardless of how many people such as Bernie Sanders or Alexandria Ocasio-Cortez periodically emerge, the reality is that America's economic system is capitalism. Period.

This is a fact that isn't going to change and for this we should be exceedingly grateful. As the old saying goes, capitalism is the worst kind of economy until you try all the rest.

It is my belief that those on the far-left have gotten their hopes up – and that the modern-day conception of "socialism" in the United States has gotten twisted – because 1) the true definition of socialism has been completely watered down and 2) a couple of interesting public polls.

A Harris Poll conducted in February 2019 revealed that 49.6 percent of Millennials and Gen Z-ers agreed with the statement: "I prefer living in a socialist country;" 73.2 percent agreed with the statement: "Government should provide universal health care" and 67.1 percent agreed with the statement: "Government should provide tuition-free college." A Gallup poll released in May 2019 found that "43 percent of Americans say socialism would be a good thing for the country."

Let's be absolutely clear: These polls are measuring what I like to call *sunny-side-up socialism*, not what true socialism actually is. A perfect example of this perversion of socialism is when Bernie Sanders points to Denmark as an example of his brand of socialism … which is strange because Denmark is not a socialist country.

Even the 25th Prime Minister of Denmark Lars Løkke Rasmussen rejected Bernie's definition when he remarked, "I know that some people in the U.S. associate the Nordic model with some sort of socialism. Therefore, I would like to make one thing clear. Denmark is far from a socialist planned economy. Denmark is a market economy. The Nordic model is an expanded welfare state which provides a high level of security to its citizens, but it is also a successful market economy with much freedom to pursue your dreams and live your life as you wish."

Aha! There it is. These polls are not measuring what Americans think of socialism à la Joseph Stalin or Chairman Mao Zedong. Rather, the term has come to mean something entirely different to many Americans. When "socialism" is mentioned in America today, it is more about the view/approach one takes to the welfare state, not whether or not the government should have complete control over our lives.

To me, the American view/approach to the welfare state is a spectrum: On the far end of one side there is zero help for citizens. Sink or swim, everyone is pretty much on their own. On the far end of the other side everything is provided to citizens for basically free.

Where the United States should land on that spectrum is an entirely different conversation – and we'll get into my recommendations for this in the second book – but the term "socialism" should not be a part of the conversation regardless of who is having it.

The fact is that Merriam-Webster defines socialism this way: "Any of various economic and political theories advocating collective or governmental ownership and administration of the means of production and distribution of goods; a system of society or group living in which there is no private property; a system or condition of society in which the means of production are owned and controlled by the state."

...and that is just not going to happen in the United States of America. Period. Believe me, the polls I referenced earlier would look far different if the question asked was: "Do you agree with this statement: I want the United States government to take all of my private property from me, tax me at a rate of 90 percent, and then be completely in charge of running every single thing about my life."

If that were the alternative, I imagine most of us would just work to improve the system we've already got! :)

At the beginning of this section, I said that the two major parties have finally blown *themselves* apart. It's true. For years, the significant divisions within the parties have acted much like water that freezes inside a rock and eventually breaks it apart. In truth, what all of this proves is there have actually been multiple parties for years, even though they have cleverly disguised themselves as two.

This is yet another reason we must have more players in the game. The ideological fractures and growing divisions within the existing parties will only make our overall national gridlock much worse. It's already really bad, but as the only two major parties get more internally jammed up, we are guaranteed that absolutely nothing gets solved. Ever.

The Democratic and Republican Parties have had 194 and 168 years, respectively, to get this right, yet things have progressively gotten worse. We cannot afford to waste any more time traveling the path of least resistance – and voting for the lesser of the *who in the heck cares* – simply because the two major parties, however wounded, believe they have the perpetual right to keep the playing field all to themselves.

They don't.

Why I Wrote These Books & Tips on How to Read Them

This book turned out to be really, really (really) long. In fact, it was so long that I had to ultimately break it into three (obviously, I had a lot to get off my chest). Because of the length, I thought an explanation of how this is all arranged may be helpful. While I believe every word written here is solid gold – and I cannot imagine you not cancelling all of your weekend plans to read it in one sitting – I also recognize that you may actually have a life.

When I initially started to work on the concept of 1787, I had this Pollyanna dream that we could all sit around a table – or in a beautiful rolling field, dressed in groovy dresses and daisy chains in our hair – and thoughtfully come up with solutions for our national challenges.

Looking back – and knowing what I know now – I'm pretty sure I was just trying to dodge the grind that is unavoidable when trying to make something like this work. I still hope my original dream will be the way 1787 ultimately works, but I also understand that someone had to provide, at a minimum, a place to begin the conversation…or we would all just be sitting around staring at an empty white board in a field somewhere. :)

Because 1787 is brand new and third parties are viewed by many with a healthy (and understandable) skepticism, I also knew that simply filing paperwork and announcing that we plan to change the world wasn't going to cut it. There is no way anyone could be expected to take this effort seriously unless I clearly laid out what my vision for 1787 is all about.

That said, this is the only time I will weigh in on policy in this manner. Earlier, I explained that 1787 members are in complete control of its direction, kind of like a democracy within the U.S. democracy where every outcome is a *majority rule* of the members. Because this is the very beginning of 1787, everything within these three books is exclusively my take on things. But beginning with our first convention, my vote on policy issues will be counted just like every other member's. Hopefully, I will continue to be the Chairman of the organization, but that too is up to the 1787 members.

The only thing that cannot be changed by any means, as set forth in the Bylaws, is that 1787 and its members must always remain faithful to 1787's original *Honor Code* and position on *Civil & Human Rights*.

This all leads to one of my biggest concerns. Since I've covered such a wide variety of topics in these books, my fear is that it will seem like I think I know everything about everything. I assure you that is not the case. In no way do I pretend to be an expert on any of these topics. My recommendations are only intended to provide a starting point for the difficult conversations that we so badly need to have in this country. Nothing more, nothing less.

The goal is to gather as many good ideas as possible, then create solutions that allow for a certain amount of flexibility so we can appropriately respond to changes in the national condition or when we all, together, discover a better way – a perpetual work in progress. Hopefully, seeing all of these topics together in one place will make it easier for every American to work hard to prove these initial ideas wrong, or at least offer recommendations they think may be better. That is the *very best* way to find the *very best* solutions!

Please believe, I honestly don't care where the answers come from or what ideology they align with. I just want the very best ones.

So, here's how this is all laid out. This first book explains 1787's worldview, at least to this point, and has policy issues sprinkled throughout, used mainly as examples. It's written in a way (hopefully) where you can check out the topics in the *Table of Contents*, then skip around to those that most interest you. The second book deals with social justice issues and is arranged the same way as this one.

The third book (a.k.a. *The Policy Guide*) includes every policy issue imaginable – including the ones addressed in books one and two – as well as 1787's initial policy recommendations for them. You can find detailed information on each of the recommendations, as well as the justification for its inclusion, at www.1787forAmerica.org.

You're awesome for taking the time to explore this! I really appreciate it because I deeply believe there is nothing more extraordinary than when empowered people come together for positive change. Robert Kennedy once said, "Each time a man stands up for an ideal, or acts to improve the lot of others, or strikes out against injustice, he sends forth a tiny ripple of hope, and crossing each other from a million different centers of energy and daring those ripples build a current which can sweep down the mightiest walls of oppression and resistance."

To build a current powerful enough to achieve the magnitude of transformation this country needs, we must be completely united in our efforts. I hope this provides a place for us to begin.

Chapter Three

The Truth Will Set Us Free

A Note to Donald Trump Supporters

First and most importantly, I want you to know that I respect you. Admittedly, I don't share your support for Donald Trump and several of his allies in the United States Congress, but not for one second would I ever judge you for your choices or think badly of you in any way. Please always remember, although I may not be a fan of *his*, that has nothing to do with how I view *you*. That's just not the way I think or behave.

My view toward this does not extend to the wingnuts (that is, the violent and destructive ones) who participated in the attack on the U.S. Capitol on January 6th but, again, I know that those bad apples don't represent *you* and are certainly not reflective of who *you* are.

There are no ulterior motives on this end. The only dog I have in this hunt is my love for America, and I know you love America too. The way I personally feel about one person – or even an entire group of people, like those who violently stormed the Capitol – will never distract me from doing what I believe is best for this country, whatever side of politics it comes from.

I say all of that to say this: There are things in these books that you may take issue with, maybe passionately so. This is not me trying to pick on your guy; he's just inextricably linked to most of these issues. He *was* our last president, after all.

To every extent possible, I have tried to validate everything I say here with actual facts and evidence – and you'll be glad to know my sources are not just from *The New York Times* and *The Washington Post*! – so I hope you will take a minute to go to the sources and fact check me when something doesn't go down well.

All I ask is that you keep an open mind. If anything is going to truly change in our country – both policy-wise and between one another – we have to erase our minds of the disheartening political darkness of the past, not to change who we are or who we support politically, but just to get things back level again.

So, I stand before you much like Agent K in the movie *Men in Black*, who used a neuralyzer to wipe people's memories clean.

*** Bright Flash of Light! ***

Good riddance frustration, disappointment and despair. Farewell derision, finger pointing and the blame game. Hasta la vista fractured interests, partisan posturing and inconsistent policy. A new day has finally come.

If you have decided to continue reading, I really, really appreciate your willingness to hear me out. Thank you.

Some Perspective on Our Political Division

It feels like everyone and everything is severely split in our country right now. According to the media, social media, public polls, and even what we see with our own eyes, it appears Americans are more divided than ever before. There has even been talk of another "civil war," a thought that transformed from being "just talk" into violent action at the U.S. Capitol on January 6, 2021.

But! I don't believe the division is as bad as it seems. Okay, I get it. I'm fully aware that politics, particularly during the Trump presidency, has divided families, devastated marriages, and destroyed lifelong friendships.

I'm fully aware that some people have acted like complete jerks and shameless bullies on social media, and that some have rioted and caused massive mayhem and destruction. Even a 9x6 piece of cloth used to cover one's face now creates a huge political uproar.

I'm also aware that political division has caused the mental health of Americans to suffer, has made our country a target of international online influence operations, and that, if something doesn't change pretty quickly, puts our very democracy at risk (we'll get to all of these in a few minutes). Actually, the potential destruction caused by political division is the very reason I even thought of starting 1787.

Political tribalism (where people feel protective of their chosen group) has quickly turned into political sectarianism (where one group hates the other group even more than they love their own). This is a huge problem and there are ideas in these books that aim to solve it.

But that said, it's important we maintain a practical perspective on our current situation. If we don't, political division will eventually become a self-fulfilling prophecy that we cannot escape.

Not to be overly dramatic, but I believe that maintaining proper perspective is perhaps the only thing that can keep half of this country from saying "screw it" and just giving up on the other half.

Let's start here: Regardless of our personal views on political and social issues – and despite our race, religion or social class – we all want pretty standard things for our lives.

All of us simply want to live a happy, productive life. We want to earn a respectable living and be able to enjoy the social security that we have contributed to. We want to properly educate our children and know that they will always breathe clean air and have satisfactory health care.

We want to be with our friends and family who unconditionally love us and want the very best for us. We want to feel safe with those we have come to fear abroad as well as with those who live among us.

At the end of the day, when you tune out all of the noise, the tapestry that binds all Americans is tightly woven with the common threads of freedom, optimism and hope.

The truth is that what forges a bond between us is far more powerful than what separates us. The constitution of this country – established with a firm foundation by the Constitution – is unyielding. The hallmarks of the American experience are a commonality of decency that permeates throughout this country and an unrelenting faith that we will find our way.

And we will. Personally, I find it amazing we coexist as peacefully as we do. This may seem like an odd thing to say in the wake of nationwide protests, riots, and an actual insurrection, but stick with me for a minute.

This country of over 330 million people represents a fabulous array of races, cultures and religions. We are far (far!) more diverse than anywhere on the entire planet.

The official U.S. census doesn't collect information on religion affiliation, but the U.S. Census Bureau does have data on "self-described religious identification." In the latest data available, 41 religious groups were reported.

There were five racial categories to choose from in the latest census, although there are likely way more than that represented in America. The Census Bureau codes 1,333 individual languages and language groups in the United States, a number so large they have to collapse them into a more manageable 42.

330 million people…41 religious groups…5 races…1,333 different languages. That is A LOT of people and A LOT of diversity.

Still, with that many people and that many differences, there are relatively few conflicts. Sure, there are instances of road rage here and there, or the occasional late-night bar brawl but, on the whole, we all live among one another in relative harmony. I find that extraordinary!

< Again, I'm not downplaying the issues of police brutality, mass shootings, or anti-democratic mob riots in the least. And I realize that crime is on the rise. We obviously have major problems to solve in all of these areas and I address them all in these books, exhaustively. >

Certainly, every violent crime is tragic, but the percentage of our violent crimes (murder and nonnegligent manslaughter, rape, robbery and aggravated assault) to our population is 0.36 percent. Think about that: 0.36 percent. That's just incredible to me.

Even during the highly emotional protests against racial injustice in 2020 – or what the U.S. Department of Justice called "demonstrations" – only around 300 people across 29 states and Washington, D.C. faced federal criminal charges. That may seem high until you consider that there were over 10,600 demonstrations across America.

Listen, I don't like conflict, so I hate that families, marriages and friendships are suffering because of politics and that people are getting bullied on social media. I hate that even a relatively small number of people get stung by violence. Even 0.36 percent is still 0.36 percent. Without a doubt, there are heartbreaking stories associated with everyone involved in that number.

But I can tell you this with absolute certainty: The angry posts and violent scenes that have recently dominated media and social media are not a true reflection of America on the whole.

When we are all our best selves, none of those ugly words and images show who we really are. Not even close. In the best version of ourselves, Americans donate money, time, food and free services to those affected by government shutdowns and international pandemics.

When we are our best selves, Americans risk their own lives to save their neighbors in Louisiana after a devastating hurricane. Americans are people who, in an emergency – without a moment's hesitation and with no assessment of skin color – reach our hands into dirty, murky water in hurricane-battered Houston to lift up another human being in need and carry the oldest and youngest on our backs to safety.

When we are our best selves, Americans lend blankets and generators to those who have no water or power during an ice storm.

During the storm and its aftermath, Americans invite complete strangers into their homes and even pay for their hotel rooms. In our best selves, Americans are like Houston's own "Mattress Mack," who, during hurricanes and ice storms, opens his furniture store to thousands of stranded people, offering them food and a warm, safe place to rest.

In our essence, this is who we are. We're Americans, dammit! And we're wonderful people!

So then, why do we feel like one half of America hates the other half? Why do we feel so attacked? Why do we feel so misunderstood? Why do we feel so hopeless?

There is just one answer, my fellow Americans: Because we are being manipulated by outside forces. Big time! This is not just a gut feeling. I can, and will, prove this in the following pages.

Here's how we will attack this complicated topic: First, to successfully construct a new paradigm, we need to deconstruct the old one and learn from the lessons it teaches. We'll also talk about some of the ways manipulative people try to gaslight others (gaslighting means manipulating others by psychological means, sometimes to the point they question their own sanity) and why truth even matters in the first place.

Next, we'll talk about how, logistically, this even happens, and then about the real-world affects it has on all of us when it does.

The thought of being manipulated is disturbing, but the great news is that now that we have identified the problem, we can fix it. There are several ways we can begin to fight back immediately. The dragons that have exploited us can absolutely be slayed.

And we must slay them. Right now. As a nation – <u>one</u> nation – we have to put a stop to this, because we cannot allow ourselves to be played any more than we already have been. We <u>cannot</u> let outside forces turn us into something we are <u>not</u>.

Deconstructing a Haunted House of Lies

Truth Matters

"The truth is still the truth, even if no one believes it.
A lie is still a lie, even if everyone believes it."

– Unknown –

Truth has taken a serious beating lately. So much so that it feels like we are living in an episode of *The Twilight Zone*, where up is down, down is up, the sky is yellow, fire is blue – and a lot of people have lost the ability to even know the difference.

There has always been an element of dishonesty in politics, but we have gone way beyond little white lies told on the campaign trail. Many of the lies our leaders tell now don't just target their opponents track record or enhance their own, they target reality itself.

To make matters far worse, there seem to be many more people willing to relinquish the power of their paint-by-number belief systems to master manipulators who happily color in the blanks for them.

As a result, truth is now whatever each person or group of people want it to be. Truth has become a personal choice instead of a touchstone.

Whereas, in the good 'ol days, when most of us let facts and reality determine our truth, there are now those who work it exactly backward – deciding first what they want the truth to be, then seeking out whatever post, tweet, conspiracy theory, or cable news host confirms it.

This confirmation bias is not hard to find – regardless of how outlandish it may be – because in our daily lives, we absorb a dizzying kaleidoscope of data that bombards us from all directions.

Overwhelmed by this information onslaught, it's no wonder most people gravitate toward the sources they are most comfortable with on social media, newspapers, radio, and television – which, through repetition and a total lack of dissent, ultimately combine to create an echo chamber that only amplifies and reenforces the original belief.

Operating in this manner may take less mental energy and its familiarity and consistency may provide temporary comfort, but it only serves to perpetuate our distrust of one another and deepen our political divide. Preaching to the choir takes minimal effort and requires minimal leadership. It's not courageous, it's redundant.

Proverbs 12:19 reminds us that "truthful lips endure forever, but a lying tongue lasts only a moment." Guys, we have to make absolutely certain this phenomenon of deception has just been an unfortunate moment in our history and that the moment has now passed.

As a civil society, we have to get back to a place where we can, at a minimum, agree on a basic set of facts. Whatever we decide to do about that set of facts is an entirely different issue, but we have to at least start from a place of truth.

This was way easier in the good 'ol days when families would sit together each night and watch Walter Cronkite, David Brinkley and Edward R. Murrow speak the truth, not as they individually viewed it, but as the way it actually was. People across America all heard the same facts.

I'm not naïve enough to believe we will ever get back to that exact place, but there are many ways we can recapture its essence.

To successfully construct a new paradigm, we need to first deconstruct the old one and learn from the lessons it teaches.

Visualize the United States of America as a house. For decades, when viewed from the outside, our house looked amazing! It was bright and cheerful, and carefully maintained. In fact, our house looked so perfect from the outside that very few guessed it was in danger of rotting from within.

The construction of our house, like all houses, started with the foundation. In many ways, the foundation is everything because without a strong foundation, the stability of the entire house is at risk.

Unfortunately, the foundation of our house – which was originally created to be rock-solid by brilliant men in 1787 – is now in danger of deteriorating into dust, thanks to the severe erosion caused by partisan politics.

Extreme partisanship has made our politics spiteful, angry and mean. It has created a venomous atmosphere where whatever side you happen to be on is "good," and everyone and everything else is "evil."

The two major parties are always bristled for a fight, retreating to their respective corners with their fangs out, zealously lying-in wait to retaliate against the most recent infraction against their gang. This only amplifies extreme party loyalty and perpetuates the *us v. them* mentality that leads to the furthering flourishing of turf warfare. It's just gross.

It is on this weakened foundation that the walls of our house now stand. When the walls of our house were originally constructed, they were built with the durable – and once thought indestructible – planks of life, liberty and the pursuit of happiness. They were built from a blueprint that envisioned the strongest, most resilient republic ever conceived.

Imagine the walls of our house represent each American individually. They embody the walls that each of us – at once emotional, societal and political – have built for ourselves and around ourselves.

Take, for example, the life experiences of many hard-core Trump supporters. If you are not one of them, imagine the walls they have likely built around *their* own hearts.

I said this earlier, but it bears repeating. From the point of view of these Americans, they and their families worked for generations in jobs that helped build the very backbone of America. They believed they had, for generations, lived by a strict moral code – with God, country, and family at the center of everything.

But suddenly, many felt America no longer looked like the country they once knew. They started to feel marginalized, both culturally and politically. They felt like elites were mocking them, cheered on by their highbrow friends in the biased mainstream media. They started to believe their livelihoods were being threatened by minorities, immigrants and globalization. They sensed they were getting shafted big-time by the swamp, deep state, and rapidly changing demographics.

Worse, to them, the radical left's depraved public policy and depleted values threatened Christianity itself. Taken together, all of this eventually destroyed their trust in government leaders and institutions, which they had always been highly suspicious of in the first place.

As the foundation of our house crumbled and the walls around the hearts of some White Americans solidified, the ghosts of our past remained active and destructive for Black Americans. Our house was more haunted than ever before.

Still today, the scars branded as far back as slavery remain painfully evident for many of these Americans. Generations of pervasive disparity has taken an egregious toll on members of this community, a population uniquely susceptible to the inequitable cycles of preceding generations.

The struggle shows up every single day and in every single system. The issues facing vulnerable communities are linked in complex ways… inadequate education, uneven health care, low or no employment, episodic poverty, dangerous and segregated housing, addiction, predatory lending, and an extremely unfair criminal justice system, just to name a few.

With a damaged foundation and unstable walls on all sides, our haunted house had been reduced to kindling – just barely able to hold its own weight.

Into this perfect storm walked Donald Trump…holding a match.

The Gaslighting of America: Four Examples

Example One:

The Total Distortion of Economic Accomplishments

The misinformation spread about Donald Trump's economic performance drives me bananas. Most politicians – and don't kid yourself, Donald Trump IS most certainly a politician – stretch the truth to a certain degree, but this guy takes it to an artform.

Obviously, political dishonesty did not start with Donald Trump. In politics, deceit is called "spin," which makes it seem more harmless than it really is. In reality, spin is not harmless. It's propaganda. Spin is not excusable just because it's come to be expected in American politics. It's just another lie.

The false narrative about Donald Trump's economic record drives me nuts for two reasons: 1) It's just flat wrong for people with power and a platform – whether it be the White House briefing room or a cable news channel – to bald-face lie to the American public and not be held accountable for it, and 2) We have to start operating from a place of truth. Please, America. Let's please at least agree on that.

To hear Donald Trump and Fox News tell it, during the Trump administration the U.S. economy was stronger than ever before. Best! Economy! Ever!

In their fairytale, Donald Trump, the genius financial mastermind, inherited a wrecked economy in recession. Even though Satan himself, President Barack Obama, had run the economy into the ground, Donald John Trump miraculously turned it around! Bigly!

This is just not true. I'm sorry, Republicans, but it's just not. Although the United States was in the Great Recession when Obama began his presidency, we pulled out of it by June 2009, five months after he took the oath of office.

On the other hand, the U.S. plowed right into a recession in February 2020, three years *after* Donald Trump took office. This recession – the worst since the Great Depression – ended 128 months of economic expansion, the longest run in U.S. history.

The truth is this: The economy that Donald Trump inherited had been on a slow but steady mend for years, and that upward trajectory simply continued during the early years of his administration.

< I'm leaving 2020 out of this discussion because, thanks to the pandemic – which is another indictment of Donald Trump but a separate conversation – the entire year is an outlier. This is really nice of me because, as you can imagine, including 2020 would make things look far worse for DJT. >

None of this is my opinion. Everything I say here is backed-up by facts released by the United States government. A government, by the way, that Donald Trump just ran for four years.

I'm certain he will claim that what I'm saying is *Fake News*! But if he does, he'll just be admitting that he is a terrible executive because, if these numbers that came straight from the United States government are inaccurate, that happened on *his* watch. He loses either way.

The U.S. Gross Domestic Product (GDP) is the total value of all the finished goods and services produced in the United States within a specific timeframe. The U.S. Bureau of Economic Analysis (BEA) – the federal agency that provides official macroeconomic and industry statistics – reports that America's GDP grew from $14.45 trillion in 2009, the year President Obama took office, to $21.43 trillion in 2019.

GDP is an interesting number to look at, but the GDP growth rate (i.e., the Percent Change from the Preceding Period in Real Gross Domestic Product) is maybe a better indicator of the nation's overall economic health because it measures how fast the economy is growing.

During the Trump presidency, the annual GDP growth rate was 2.3 percent, 3 percent, and 2.2 percent. < the growth rate in 2020 was -3.5 percent but, again, I'm leaving 2020 out >

By this measure, looking year over year, economic growth in Donald Trump's first three years (an average of 2.5 percent) looked a lot like it did during President Obama's last three years (an average of 2.4 percent).

To put Donald's economic performance into better perspective, let's look at additional presidencies. The annual growth rate during…

- † John F. Kennedy's shortened presidency reached 6.1 percent and 4.4 percent.
- † Lyndon B. Johnson's presidency reached 5.8 percent, 6.5 percent, 6.6 percent, and 4.9 percent.
- † Richard Nixon's presidency reached 3.1 percent, 3.3 percent, 5.3 percent, and 5.6 percent.
- † Gerald Ford's short presidency reached 5.4 percent.
- † Jimmy Carter's presidency reached 4.6 percent, 5.5 percent, and 3.2 percent.
- † During the Reagan administration, the annual growth rate broke 3 percent in six of the eight years of his presidency. Four of those years broke 4 percent and one year even reached 7.2 percent.
- † Two years of President George H.W. Bush's presidency broke 3 percent.
- † President Clinton's administration broke 3 percent in six of his eight years as president. Five of those years actually broke 4 percent.
- † Two years of President George W. Bush's presidency broke 3 percent.

The annual growth rate of GDP is worth noting, but breaking it down by quarters is sometimes more telling. Donald often brags about the last quarter of 2017 (3.9 percent) and the first quarter of 2018 (3.8 percent), the only quarters in the Trump presidency that broke 3 percent.

However, in President Obama's second term, the growth rate broke 3 percent in six quarters (3.6 percent, 3.2 percent, 3.2 percent, 5.5

percent, 5 percent, and 3.8 percent). You'll notice that the growth rate even exceeded 5 percent twice.

In President Obama's first term, the growth rate broke 3 percent five times (4.5 percent, 3.7 percent, 3 percent, 4.7 percent, 3.2 percent). You'll notice that the growth rate even exceeded 4 percent twice.

Okay, I have never used the word "percent" so much in my life, but I just wanted to show you that Donald Trump's GDP numbers don't even come close to being The! Best! Ever! And it's important to remember that his relatively slow growth happened in spite of very costly tax cuts and a $1.3 trillion spending bill, both of which should have stimulated the economy. (more on this in Chapter Four)

Next up, the stock market. Throughout his presidency, Donald loved to hype the hot stock market. Best! Stock Market! Ever!

I hate to break it to him, but stock market returns during his presidency rank 8th when compared to other presidents. Yes, 8th. Behind, in order, Bill Clinton, Barack Obama, Dwight Eisenhower, Ronald Reagan, Harry Truman, George H.W. Bush, and Lyndon Johnson.

During the 2020 presidential election, Donald loved to say things like "if Biden is elected, the market will crash" and that a Biden presidency would be the "biggest single headwind (to the stock market) is if he got in" and, in a tweet, "If you want your 401k's and stocks, which are getting closer to an all-time high (NASDAQ is already there), to disintegrate and disappear, vote for the Radical Left Do Nothing Democrats and Corrupt Joe Biden."

However, from the day of the 2020 election through early May 2021, the Dow increased roughly 26 percent, compared to the 14 percent for the same period after Donald Trump was elected president. In fact, from the day President Biden took office to early May 2021, the stock market performed better than every single president since the 1960s.

In the end, in 2021, the S&P 500 gained 26.9 percent, the Dow Jones Industrial Average gained 18.7 percent and the Nasdaq Composite gained 21.4 percent. Not bad.

Ironically, the stock market usually does much better under Democratic presidents. I know this is counterintuitive given what both parties supposedly represent, but it's true.

According to *Forbes* magazine, "From 1952 through June 2020, annualized real stock market returns under Democrats have been 10.6 percent compared with 4.8 percent for Republicans."

Next up, jobs. Until Covid-19 hit, Donald Trump loved to talk about how many jobs he was creating. The! Best! Jobs! Ever!

In 2017, his first year in office, America added 2.109 million jobs. In 2018, Donald's best year in regard to job creation, America added 2.314 million jobs and, in 2019, 2.096 million jobs were added.

However, the job growth in the last three years of President Obama's second term were higher than in Donald Trump's BEST year – 3.004 million (2014), 2.72 million (2015), and 2.345 million (2016).

In the end, around 1.6 million <u>more</u> jobs were created in the last three years of President Obama's presidency than in Donald Trump's first three.

Much has been said about the low unemployment rate during Donald Trump's tenure, which led to higher wages. It's true that by October 2019, the unemployment rate had fallen to its lowest level in fifty years. However, the unemployment rate was already 4.7 percent when he became president and had been on a steady decline since 2011.

A quick word about Donald Trump's claims of working "miracles" in the manufacturing sector. This too is false. The manufacturing sector was in a technical recession – which is triggered when output falls for at least six months – for the entirety of 2019. That year, U.S. factory production decreased 1.3 percent, making it the worst year for manufacturing since 2015.

The PMI, or the Purchasing Managers' Index – the most common way to measure the health of manufacturing – plummeted. In December 2019, another popular gauge of the manufacturing sector's health – a survey of purchasing managers from the Institute for Supply Management – fell to its lowest level since the Great Recession. (more on this later in this chapter)

EXAMPLE TWO:

THE ELECTION FRAUD LIE

There is no question that Donald Trump is an exceptional liar, but he has knocked his election "fraud" lie out of the park. This lie should go directly into the Lying Hall of Fame. Best. Executed. Lie. Ever!

Donald Trump's election "fraud" lie was clearly executed by a man who has had seventy years of experience in the art of deceiving others. It was Machiavelli who said that "one who deceives will always find those who allow themselves to be deceived."

But it was Voltaire who made the absolutely terrifying but brilliant observation: "Those who can make you believe absurdities can make you commit atrocities." We have to pay attention to what's going on here, America.

A masterful liar starts early, sometimes years before the big lie is even told. Donald did this when, even before his 2016 presidential campaign began, he started calling the MSM (that stands for "mainstream media," for all you non-Trumpers) "fake news" and "enemy of the people." He repeated this over and over and over and over – incessantly – which is another mind trick used by skillful liars.

As a result, if I happen to mention to a hardcore Trump supporter that *The Washington Post* reports that Donald Trump made 30,573 false or misleading claims during his presidency – which they do, often accompanied by video evidence of him actually telling the falsehood – s/he will likely dismiss it out of hand because *The Washington Post* is obviously The Devil. It's absolute genius.

Donald also started early with talk of the "deep state." Although he never officially defined what this means, I gather from context that it's the horribly corrupt members of the evil status quo who operate in the shadows of our big bad government.

So, by the time he needed to tell the big lie – meaning, when he wanted to save face after he lost the 2020 presidential election – many of his supporters had lost all trust in the people who work in any level of government, as well as the agencies and institutions they work for. Again, genius.

But here is the God's honest truth about widespread election fraud: It is, in fact, a straight-up lie. Widespread voter fraud in the United States <u>does</u> <u>not</u> <u>exist.</u>

This is not just my opinion, it's a fact. There is overwhelming evidence to prove widespread election fraud untrue, and this proof doesn't just come from the evil MSM. It comes directly from election experts and officials from both parties, transcripts from multiple courts of law and state legislatures, and from the mouths of judges themselves – many of whom were appointed by Donald J. Trump.

Honestly, we shouldn't even need all this proof because widespread election fraud can be discredited by common sense alone.

For one, the United States of America doesn't have one voting system, we have fifty. Plus, doesn't it strike you as odd that the "fraud" only affected Donald Trump, not other Republicans down ballot? And that the only states accused of massive fraud are the battleground states that Donald Trump thought he was going to win but lost? Would he really have us believe that the states he won are the only ones that miraculously have no fraud. Come on now, people.

You may ask me, if *The Washington Post* is to be believed, Donald Trump told tens of thousands of other lies. So why, Emily, are you dedicating an entire section to this one?

Answer: Because this lie is wildly un-American and incredibly damaging. It's a dagger through the very heart of democracy itself. Out of everything anyone in American politics has ever lied about, this is by far the most potentially devastating. It has to stop.

Even though we shouldn't need proof, I've got plenty. The Trump campaign and his cronies took their allegations to court in multiple states. Well over 60 cases have been dismissed. Just two actions – literally two – were even remotely successful. One gave voters a little less time to fix errors on mail-in ballots and the other allowed election observers to stand a little closer to the vote counting process.

Judges on all levels of the court system rejected this nonsense, including 38 appointed by Republicans.

Soon after Donald Trump's first 2020 election fraud accusation, 59 of America's leading computer scientists and election security experts called Donald Trump's claims of voter fraud "unsubstantiated" and "technically incoherent."

These people are not part of some conspiracy or members of some kind of deep state. They are experts from both political parties.

In part, their joint letter said, "Anyone asserting that a U.S. election was 'rigged' is making an extraordinary claim, one that must be supported by persuasive and verifiable evidence." Without evidence, they say, the claims are "simply speculation."

In conclusion, they wrote, "To our collective knowledge, no credible evidence has been put forth that supports a conclusion that the 2020 election outcome in any state has been altered through technical compromise."

That was just the beginning of the pushback against these false claims. After Donald Trump tweeted that voting machines made by Dominion Voting Systems "deleted 2.7 million Trump votes nationwide," the Election Infrastructure Government Coordinating Council (GCC) Executive Committee – which includes top officials from the Cybersecurity and Infrastructure Security Agency, the U.S. Election Assistance Commission, the National Association of Secretaries of State, National Association of State Election Directors, and members of the Election Infrastructure Sector Coordinating Council – released a statement:

"The November 3rd election was the most secure in American history… All of the states with close results in the 2020 presidential race have paper records of each vote, allowing the ability to go back and count each ballot if necessary. This is an added benefit for security and resilience. This process allows for the identification and correction of any mistakes or errors. There is no evidence that any voting system deleted or lost votes, changed votes, or was in any way compromised."

< Quick Commercial Break: Dominion Voting Systems is suing Fox News for defamation – to the tune of $1.6 billion – claiming the

network spread disinformation about the company in the wake of the 2020 election. In the complaint, Dominion's attorneys said: "The truth matters. Lies have consequences. Fox sold a false story of election fraud in order to serve its own commercial purposes, severely injuring Dominion in the process. If this case does not rise to the level of defamation by a broadcaster, then nothing does."

In December 2021, Delaware Superior Court Judge Eric Davis rejected Fox News' request to dismiss the lawsuit, which allows Dominion to now request documents from Fox, as well as interview the network's high command.

Dominion is also suing Trump attorney Rudy Giuliani for defamation, claiming over $1.3 billion in damages. Dominion CEO John Poulos explained it this way: "Rudy Giuliani actively propagated disinformation to purposefully mislead voters. Because Giuliani and others incessantly repeated the false claims about my company on a range of media platforms, some of our own family and friends are among the Americans who were duped."

Dominion legal counsel Thomas Clare added: "These lies have had an incalculable amount of damage on Dominion and our country. We will hold him [Giuliani], and the many that have abetted him, accountable for their profiteering lies."

Mr. Clare later followed-up: "The best way to vindicate the truth is in the courts where there's cross-examination where we have the opportunity to take discovery, where there are rules, where evidence is required to be submitted. And that is the process that we are very much looking forward to in order to vindicate the company and to get the truth out there."

Dominion is also suing former Trump attorney Sidney Powell and the My Pillow guy for defamation, for $1.3 billion each.

On March 22, 2021, Sidney Powell – who once called the "stealing" of the 2020 election "the greatest crime of the century if not the life of the world" – petitioned a federal court to drop the case against her and get this: In the filing to dismiss, her attorneys actually argued that "reasonable people would not accept [such statements she made against Dominion] as fact but view them only as claims that await testing by the courts through the adversary process." Essentially, her defense is that surely no one is stupid enough to believe a word she says.

Incidentally, Ms. Powell has also been ordered by Michigan U.S. District Judge Linda V. Parker to pay a hefty fine for "a historic and profound abuse of the judicial process." Judge Parker went on to say that the fine was an "appropriate sanction" that was "needed to deter Plaintiffs' counsel and others from engaging in similar misconduct in the future."

Michigan Attorney General Dana Nessel agreed wholeheartedly with the ruling: "The awarding of fees further holds accountable the attorneys who worked to distort our democracy in favor of lining their own pockets. These attorneys demonstrated a flagrant disregard for the law and attempted to use the courts to further a false and destructive narrative."

Smartmatic USA Corporation, another election technology company, is also suing Fox Corporation and three of its hosts – Lou Dobbs, Maria Bartiromo and Jeanine Pirro – for defaming the company. Rudy Giuliani and Sidney Powell are also being sued. Smartmatic is seeking $2.7 billion in damages.

The company argues that Rudy and Sidney "created a story about Smartmatic" and that "Fox joined the conspiracy to defame and disparage Smartmatic and its election technology and software. The story turned neighbor against neighbor. The story led a mob to attack the U.S. Capitol."

The basics of the case are similar to the Dominion case but, while Dominion's technology was used in 24 states in the 2020 election, Smartmatic only provided election services for Los Angeles County.

In a statement, Smartmatic chief executive Antonio Mugica said, "Fox is responsible for this disinformation campaign, which has damaged democracy worldwide and irreparably harmed Smartmatic and other stakeholders who contribute to modern elections." The company has identified "100 false statements and implications."

His statement continued, "Mr. Giuliani and Ms. Powell needed a platform to use to spread their story. They found a willing partner in Fox News."

Incidentally, U.S. District Judge Linda V. Parker of Michigan has ordered sanctions against nine lawyers affiliated with Donald Trump's legal team, including Sidney Powell. In her ruling, Judge Parker called the actions of these attorneys "a historic and profound abuse of the judicial process."

She continued, "This case was never about fraud. It was about undermining the People's faith in our democracy and debasing the judicial process to do so."

It is "one thing," she wrote, "to take on the charge of vindicating rights associated with an allegedly fraudulent election," but quite another to deceive "a federal court and the American people into believing that rights were infringed. This is what happened here." Commercial Break Over! >

After the Election Infrastructure Government Coordinating Council (GCC) statement, Christopher Krebs, then the head of the Cybersecurity and Infrastructure Security Agency (CISA) – a division of the Department of Homeland Security that helps states secure the voting process – went on to call the claims of election fraud "nonsense" and "farcical."

In an interview with *60 Minutes*, Krebs reiterated that 95 percent of the ballots cast had paper records backing them up. Plus, in states where there were hand recounts, the results were virtually the same as when the machine counted them.

Although Donald Trump had already fired Krebs for saying the 2020 election was the safest in history, after the *60 Minutes* interview Trump attorney Joseph diGenova said Krebs should be "drawn and quartered, taken out at dawn and shot."

Krebs is now suing the Trump campaign, Joseph diGenova, and the conservative news channel *Newsmax* for defamation. According to the lawsuit, Donald Trump accused him of, among other things, treason, and diGenova's comments "led to an avalanche of despicably offensive and frighteningly threatening statements" against Krebs… to the point that one of Krebs' five young children said, "Daddy's going to get executed?"

On November 29, 2020, Donald Trump, in quite possibly the longest run-on sentence in history, said on Fox News that "(the election) is total fraud. And how the FBI and Department of Justice – I don't know – maybe they're involved, but how people are getting away with this stuff – it's unbelievable. … You would think, if you're in the FBI or Department of Justice, this is – this is the biggest thing you could be looking at. Where are they? I have not seen anything. … It's an embarrassment to our country."

But two days later, none other than the Trump administration's Attorney General William Barr – who long before had proven to be a Donald Trump sycophant – reiterated that, although the Justice Department had followed-up on complaints of voter fraud, his department had not seen "fraud on a scale that could have affected a different outcome in the election."

Specifically, Barr said, "There's been one assertion that would be systemic fraud and that would be the claim that machines were programmed essentially to skew the election results. And the Department of Homeland Security (DHS) and Department of Justice (DOJ) have looked into that, and so far, we haven't seen anything to substantiate that." It sounds like to me that a competent lawyer finally got through to him.

Seven months after the election, the Justice Department released a treasure trove of emails to the House Oversight Committee. The emails detail how Donald Trump, his chief of staff Mark Meadows, and a few other minions relentlessly pressured the United States Justice Department to help overturn the legal election results. Mark Meadows went as far as asking then-acting Attorney General Jeffery Rosen to investigate already discredited conspiracy theories like the one claiming that someone in Italy somehow remotely changed the election results in America.

Mr. Rosen joined former Attorney General Bill Barr, former acting Solicitor General Jeffrey Wall, and White House counsel Pat Cipollone in refusing to indulge Donald Trump's deranged obsession on any level.

When it was clear that Mr. Rosen was not going to break the law for him, Donald Trump decided he would replace Rosen with Jeffrey Clark, one of his faithful worker bees – an idea that was squelched only when multiple senior Justice Department officials threatened to resign en masse. After Rosen forwarded Mark Meadows' email about the Italian nonsense to his acting deputy Richard Donoghue, Donoghue replied, "Pure insanity."

In October 2021, the Senate Judiciary Committee issued a report called *Subverting Justice: How the Former President and His Allies Pressured the Department of Justice (DOJ) to Overturn the 2020 Election.* The key findings of the initial report include the following:

† President Trump repeatedly asked DOJ leadership to endorse his false claims that the election was stolen and to assist his efforts to overturn the election results.

† White House Chief of Staff Mark Meadows asked Acting Attorney General Rosen to initiate election fraud investigations on multiple occasions, violating longstanding restrictions on White House-DOJ communications about specific law-enforcement matters.

† After personally meeting with Trump, Jeffrey Bossert Clark pushed Rosen and Donoghue to assist Trump's election subversion scheme – and told Rosen he would decline Trump's potential offer to install him as Acting Attorney General if Rosen agreed to aid that scheme.

† Trump allies with links to the "Stop the Steal" movement and the January 6 insurrection participated in the pressure campaign against DOJ.

† Trump forced the resignation of U.S. Attorney Byung Jin ("BJay") Pak, whom he believed was not doing enough to address false claims of election fraud in Georgia. Trump then went outside the line of succession when naming an Acting U.S. Attorney, bypassing First Assistant U.S. Attorney Kurt Erskine and instead appointing Bobby Christine because he

believed Christine would "do something" about his election fraud claims.

† By pursuing false claims of election fraud before votes were certified, DOJ deviated from longstanding practice meant to avoid inserting DOJ itself as an issue in the election.

Donald Trump's voter fraud claims fared even worse in American courts. Although *anyone* can say *anything* (even if they eventually get sued) on cable television, social media or at a press conference, the standard of proof is a little different in a court of law, to say the least. Attorneys are bound by a strict code of professional responsibility, which includes *duty of candor* to the courts and the *duty to avoid frivolous claims*.

Which means they cannot just make stuff up, and they certainly cannot lie to a judge. Which means that most all of them bolted from Team Trump almost immediately. Two large law firms withdrew as the Trump campaign's counsel only days after filing lawsuits. This led to several new lawyers joining the team, but they also resigned within days.

This left, as Trump's lawyers, only the self-described "elite, strike force team" – which included Rudy Giuliani, Jenna Ellis and, for a little while, the aforementioned kook Sidney Powell – whose collective conduct even former Republican governor of New Jersey and Trump ally Chris Christie called "a national embarrassment." Chris wasn't finished:

> "This is outrageous conduct by any lawyer. They allege fraud outside the courtroom but when they go inside the courtroom, they don't plead fraud and they don't argue fraud.
>
> We cannot continue to act as if something happened here that didn't happen. You have an obligation to present the evidence. The evidence has not been presented. And you must conclude – as Tucker Carlson even concluded the other night – that if you're unwilling to come forward and present the evidence, it must mean the evidence doesn't exist.

I think you've heard lots of Republicans starting to say this. I said it on election night. And I hope more say it going forward, because the country is what has to matter the most. As much as I'm a strong Republican – I love my party – it's the country that has to come first."

When Christie brought up Fox News host Tucker Carlson, he was referring to when Carlson called Sidney Powell out on his show: "She never demonstrated that a single actual vote was moved illegitimately by software from one candidate to another. Not one."

As we all know, in a court of law you actually need a little something called evidence. Unfortunately for Donald Trump and his attorneys, they had none. Zero. Nada. This led to some pretty humiliating moments for them.

One of the worst came two days after the election in Philadelphia. The Trump campaign filed an emergency petition to stop the vote count, claiming Republican observers had been unfairly banned from the room where votes were being counted.

Under intense questioning by Judge Paul S. Diamond, a U.S. District Judge appointed by President George W. Bush, Trump campaign attorney Jerome Marcus admitted that Republicans did, in fact, have a "nonzero number of people in the room," which is a ridiculous way to say there were, in fact, Republicans allowed in the room.

Seemingly annoyed and still unsatisfied with the answer, Judge Diamond then said: "I am asking you as a member of the bar of this court, are people representing Donald J. Trump for President, representing the plaintiff, in that room?" To which Marcus had to answer, "Yes." Judge Diamond then responded, "I'm sorry, then what's your problem?"

Elsewhere in Pennsylvania, in a joint stipulation of facts in Bucks County, the Trump legal team conceded that the "petitioners do not allege, and there is no evidence, that any of the challenged ballots were cast by, or on behalf of, a deceased person." They also conceded there was no "fraud," "misconduct," or "impropriety" in connection with the ballots they were challenging.

Because the question was answered before the case even started, the Honorable Robert O. Baldi stopped the farce, saying: "The parties specifically stipulated in their comprehensive stipulation of facts that there exists no evidence of any fraud, misconduct, or any impropriety with respect to the challenged ballots. There is nothing in the record and nothing alleged that would lead to the conclusion that any of the challenged ballots were submitted by someone not qualified or entitled to vote in this election."

Judge James C. Crumlish III rejected a Trump campaign petition that aimed to invalidate nearly 8,349 mail-in ballots because the voter failed to enter certain information, such as their address.

During a hearing, Judge Crumlish asked Trump attorney Linda Kerns: "Would you agree with me that you are not proceeding based on allegations of fraud or misconduct; is that correct?" She answered, "I am not proceeding on those allegations," which led Judge Crumlish to rule that the Trump campaign was "not contending that there has been fraud, that there is evidence of fraud or that the ballots in question were not filled out by the elector in whose name the ballot was issued."

Not one to be left out of the fun, Rudy Giuliani was in Pennsylvania when he stood outside the now infamous Four Seasons Total Landscaping Company and said, "This is a gross miscarriage of the process that would assure that these ballots are not fraudulent. It's a fraud, an absolute fraud." < I am determined not to make any jokes in this section because of its seriousness, but it is extremely difficult with all of the ammunition Rudy has given us, including his *Borat* performance and hair dye meltdown. The jokes are just writing themselves in my brain, but I'll try to be a patriot and behave. >

Then – I'm not making this up – he went right into a federal courtroom just days later and at first alleged "widespread, nationwide voter fraud" and that local election officials were part of a "little mafia," but eventually admitted to Republican U.S. District Judge Matthew W. Brann that "this is not a fraud case."

In yet another Pennsylvania courtroom, after repeatedly asking direct questions and not getting back direct answers, Judge Richard P. Haaz finally pointedly asked Trump attorney Jonathan Goldstein if he was accusing electors or the Board of the County of fraud.

Goldstein responded: "Your Honor, accusing people of fraud is a pretty big step. And it is rare that I call somebody a liar, and I am not calling the Board of the [Democratic National Committee] or anybody else involved in this a liar. Everybody is coming to this with good faith. The DNC is coming with good faith. We're all just trying to get an election done. We think these were a mistake, but we think they are a fatal mistake, and these ballots ought not be counted."

Judge Haaz then asked: "I am asking you a specific question, and I am looking for a specific answer. Are you claiming that there is any fraud in connection with these 592 disputed ballots?" Goldstein responded, "To my knowledge at present, no."

The judge again, "Are you claiming that there is any undue or improper influence upon the elector with respect to these 592 ballots?" Goldstein again responded, "To my knowledge at present, no."

But Pennsylvania judges weren't through. The aforementioned U.S. District Judge Brann, a Republican and former member of the conservative Federalist Society, rejected a petition by the Trump campaign to block the certification of the state's vote because certain counties allowed voters to correct errors on their ballots.

Judge Brann's decision was 37-pages of scorched earth. Among other harsh words, Judge Brann said that the Trump campaign's assertions "strained legal arguments without merit and speculative accusations."

He went on to say that "in the United States of America, this cannot justify the disenfranchisement of a single voter, let alone all the voters of its sixth most populated state."

But Judge Brann saved the best for last: "This claim, like Frankenstein's Monster, has been haphazardly stitched together."

Judge Stephanos Bibas of the U.S. Court of Appeals for the 3rd Circuit, who was appointed by Donald Trump, wrote this for the unanimous majority after a complete rejection of an emergency injunction to overturn Pennsylvania's vote certification: "Free, fair elections are the lifeblood of our democracy. Charges of unfairness are serious. But calling an election unfair does not make it so. Charges require specific allegations and then proof. We have neither here.

Voters, not lawyers, choose the President. Ballots, not briefs, decide elections."

At the end of November, the Pennsylvania Supreme Court unanimously dismissed a petition by the Trump campaign to invalidate over 2.5 million mail-in ballots. The decision said, in part, "The want of due diligence demonstrated in this matter is unmistakable," and admonished the campaign for a "complete failure to act with due diligence in commencing their factual constitutional challenge."

Of the case, Justice David N. Wecht said the Republicans "failed to allege that even a single mail-in ballot was fraudulently cast or counted…It is not our role to lend legitimacy to such transparent and untimely efforts to subvert the will of Pennsylvania voters. Courts should not decide elections when the will of the voters is clear."

The ruling was dismissed with prejudice, meaning the Trump campaign can never file another petition on the same claim.

The final nail in the Pennsylvania coffin was hammered when the United States Supreme Court denied a requested injunction in a one-sentence order, with no explanation and no noted dissenting votes.

< I'll spare you the details of the second instance in which the U.S. Supreme Court rejected a lawsuit around this foolishness, this time when Texans, led by Representative Louis Gohmert (my former opponent, you may remember) decided they were going to sue other states over how they ran their elections. Hello, 10th amendment? I'll spare you partly because it's humiliating to me as a Texan, but mainly because it's just so stupid. You can always count on Texas! #texasproud >

But even a U.S. Supreme Court verdict didn't stop Donald Trump, who called the Republican speaker of the Pennsylvania House of Representatives, Bryan Cutler, at least twice to see how Pennsylvania Republicans were going to stop this madness – to which Mr. Cutler made clear they had no power or intention to do so.

One last thing before we leave Pennsylvania. After the 2020 election, a letter carrier named Richard Hopkins told federal investigators that he heard his supervisors at the Erie post office discussing a plan to backdate mail-in ballots – a claim that Republicans naturally jumped on.

Even though the Erie postmaster immediately said the allegations were "100% false," Senator Lindsey Graham (R-SC) used Hopkins' statement as an example in a letter to the Justice Department demanding an investigation into the Pennsylvania election results. Donald Trump called Hopkins a "brave patriot" on Twitter.

Unfortunately for Lindsey and Donald, Hopkins recanted his claim rather quickly when he was questioned by the Postal Service's Office of Inspector General. The Inspector General's final report said that Hopkins "revised his initial claims, eventually stating that he had not heard a conversation about ballots at all – rather he saw the Postmaster and Supervisor having a discussion and assumed it was about fraudulent ballot backdating."

Further, he "acknowledged that he had no evidence of any backdated presidential ballots and could not recall any specific words said by the postmaster or supervisor."

The final report reached the conclusion that "both the interview of the Erie County Election Supervisor and the physical examination of ballots produced no evidence of any backdated presidential election ballots at the Erie, PA Post Office."

In Nevada, Trump ally and former Nevada lawmaker Sharron Angle petitioned the court to block vote certification in Clark County, where Las Vegas is located and by far the most populous county in the state. She essentially wanted to throw out the results of the entire election.

After hearing the case, Judge Gloria Sturman wasn't having it: "How do you get to that's sufficient to throw out an entire election?"

Unsurprisingly, Judge Sturman denied the petition, calling the petition "a really extreme request" and saying that not only was there no evidence to support the charge of voter fraud, but that "as a matter of public policy, this is just a bad idea."

In another Nevada courtroom, District Judge James T. Russell dismissed all voter fraud claims made by the Trump campaign with prejudice, writing that the campaign "did not prove under any standard of proof that illegal votes were cast and counted, or legal votes were not counted at all, due to voter fraud, nor in an amount equal to or greater than" Joe Biden's margin of victory.

The judge also dismissed witness declarations that had been put into evidence by the Trump campaign, describing them as "self-serving statements of little or no evidentiary value."

In Wisconsin, United States District Court Judge Pamela Pepper wrote this in her opinion to dismiss a bid to overturn the election results: "Federal judges do not appoint the president in this country. One wonders why the plaintiffs came to federal court and asked a federal judge to do so."

The Wisconsin Supreme Court declined to hear the Trump campaign's case to challenge the election results in their state, saying it first had to be heard by lower courts.

Conservative member Justice Brian Hagedorn wrote in the opinion, "We do well as a judicial body to abide by time-tested judicial norms, even – and maybe especially – in high-profile cases. Following the law governing challenges to election results is no threat to the rule of law."

Justice Hagedorn continued, "It can be easy to blithely move on to the next case with a petition so obviously lacking, but this is sobering. The relief being sought by the petitioners is the most dramatic invocation of judicial power I have ever seen. Judicial acquiescence to such entreaties built on so flimsy a foundation would do indelible damage to every future election. This is a dangerous path we are being asked to tread."

Next, the Trump campaign filed a federal lawsuit in the state, asking that the lawsuit be "remanded" back to the state legislature, a request U.S. District Judge Brett H. Ludwig – who was appointed by Donald J. Trump himself – called "bizarre" and "very odd."

Judge Ludwig wrote, "This court has allowed the plaintiff the chance to make his case, and he has lost on the merits," then he threw the case right out. But not before he added this:

"This is an extraordinary case. A sitting president who did not prevail in his bid for re-election has asked for federal court help in setting aside the popular vote based on disputed election administration issues he plainly could have raised before the vote occurred."

Judge Ludwig continued, "In his reply brief, plaintiff 'asks that the Rule of Law be followed.' It has been."

Things weren't going much better in Georgia, where another Trump ally brought a suit claiming that his company had uncovered evidence of inconsistencies in electronic voting machines.

The judge, who was appointed by Donald Trump, finally got around to the million-dollar question: "I understand that's your argument, but what's your evidence?" Then he too threw the case right out.

Another Trump campaign attempt centered around a charge that 53 ballots were possibly backdated. Problem was, when the two people who could supposedly speak to this were called to testify, they both said they had no idea if the ballots were received after the deadline.

Superior Court Judge James Bass dismissed the case right then with one sentence: "I'm denying the request and dismissing the petition." Later, in his written opinion, Judge Bass was more circumspect: "The Court finds that there is no evidence that the ballots referenced in the petition were received after 7:00 p.m. on election day, thereby making those ballots invalid. Additionally, there is no evidence that the Chatham County Board of Elections or the Chatham County Board of Registrars has failed to comply with the law."

At the same time, there were tons of other shenanigans going on in Georgia. Georgia Secretary of State Brad Raffensperger, a Republican who voted for Donald Trump, revealed he was being pressured by other Republicans, including Senator Lindsey Graham, to unethically intervene in the electoral process, and that he and his wife were receiving death threats (his wife, sexually explicit ones) – to the point that he had to enlist a security detail.

One text sent to Raffensperger said, "You better not botch this recount. Your life depends on it." In response, Raffensperger simply said, "Numbers don't lie."

Finally, sufficiently fed-up and understandably furious, Gabriel Sterling, a top Georgia election official, held a press conference and said, "Someone's going to get hurt, someone's going to get shot, someone's going to get killed. It's not right."

Sterling used as an example "a 20-something tech in Gwinnett County" who had received "death threats and a noose put out saying he should be hung for treason because he was transferring a report on batches from an EMS to a county computer so he could read it."

He continued, "His family is getting harassed now. There's a noose out there with his name on it. And it's not right. I've got police protection outside my house. Fine. You know, I took a higher-profile job. I get it, the secretary ran for office; his wife knew that, too. This kid took a job. He just took a job, and it's just wrong."

In the midst of the chaos, Donald Trump called Georgia's governor, Republican Brian Kemp and pressured him to call a special session of the legislature to override the state's election result and send an entirely new slate of electors to the Electoral College. < I literally cannot believe I am writing this about an America election. Honduras, maybe. Philippines, sure. But the United States of America? No way. >

Thankfully, after the ballots had been counted three separate times, Governor Kemp certified his states election results, saying: "As governor, I have a solemn responsibility to follow the law, and that is what I will continue to do. We must all work together to ensure citizens have confidence in future elections in our state."

But wait! If poor Governor Kemp thought that formally certifying the results was going to get Georgia out of Donald's crosshairs, he was dead wrong. Weeks later – three days before the Electoral College was constitutionally required to meet, to be exact – Donald made his infamous (recorded) call to Secretary of State Raffensperger, saying, "So look. All I want to do is this. I just want to find 11,780 votes, which is one more than we have. Because we won the state."

A few minutes later, Donald Trump said again, "So what are we going to do here, folks? I only need 11,000 votes. Fellas, I need 11,000 votes. Give me a break."

In October 2021, the Brookings Institution – a research group – released a report called *Fulton County, Georgia's Trump Investigation: An Analysis of the Reported Facts and Applicable Law*. The report said in part:

> "President Trump lost the 2020 election in Georgia by a margin of nearly 12,000 votes, and that outcome was confirmed and certified by the duly designated election

> officials in the state, with Republican Secretary of State Raffensperger and Republican Governor Kemp at the top of the process. Those officials formally certified the result 17 days after the election following a hand recount of all ballots cast, which altered the original count by only a few hundred votes. That result was recertified by Raffensperger on December 7.
>
> Notwithstanding the absence of any facts suggesting irregularity or any reason to question the result thus certified, the Georgia electoral process and vote count was subjected to sustained assault by the ex-president and his supporters."

The report sets forth several civil and criminal charges that could be pursued because of Donald Trump's conduct, including:

> "Solicitation of conduct by officials that would amount to election fraud; intentional interference with an election official's performance of election-related duties; and conspiracy, meaning an agreement among multiple people, to engage in electoral fraud.
>
> Other possible statutory violations include an array of general prohibitions not limited to conduct impacting on elections, but rather focused on more broadly applicable duties encompassing election misconduct of the kind here alleged, such as false statements in connections with official matters, attempts to influence government officials in improper ways, solicitation of action violative of public officer oaths, and several other provisions. Finally, it is possible, as mentioned in a public statement by the Fulton County District Attorney, that consideration might be given to action under the Georgia *Racketeer Influenced and Corrupt Organizations* (RICO) *Act,* since violation of a number of the statutes referenced above constitute predicate acts that are the essential building blocks in developing a prosecution under that statute."

Eight months after the election – after three audits of the election results, including a hand recount – Georgia Superior Court Judge Brian

Amero dismissed seven of the nine claims in one of the last remaining lawsuits (this one involved claims of fraudulent mail-in ballots in Fulton County). The other two counts were not dismissed because they sought records from Georgia's open records law. This came as a blow to the plaintiffs, who had planned to inspect the ballots *with high-powered microscopes* like they did in Arizona (more on this in a minute).

Meanwhile, in Arizona, Trump campaign attorney Kory Langhofer finally acknowledged, after trying super hard to bob and weave, that the campaign's case he was bringing was "not a fraud case." He continued, "We are not alleging fraud in this lawsuit. We are not alleging anyone is stealing the election. It is not a stealing-the-election case."

Langhofer also shut down the idea that a limited number of glitches in voting machines happened as a result of intentional fraud, saying they were "good-faith errors in operating machines."

After extreme pressure from the Trump campaign to disregard the popular vote and declare Trump the winner of Arizona's electoral votes, Rusty Bowers, the Republican speaker of the Arizona House of Representatives, finally had to make a definitive statement:

"As a conservative Republican, I don't like the results of the presidential election. I voted for President Trump and worked hard to reelect him. But I cannot and will not entertain a suggestion that we violate current law to change the outcome of a certified election."

The Republican-led Board of Supervisors in Maricopa County, Arizona – the second largest voting jurisdiction in the United States – voted unanimously to certify the county's election results, with the board chairman saying definitively there was no evidence of fraud or misconduct "and that is with a big zero."

But believe it or not, it didn't end there. Six months after the 2020 election, the Maricopa County Board of Supervisors was still dealing with the 2020 election. In late April 2021, Arizona Republicans hired a private company named Cyber Ninjas (seriously?) to start a hand recount of the almost 2.1 million ballots cast in Maricopa County.

This included the Cyber Ninjas using UV lights and microscopes to investigate whether the ballots were made of bamboo...which, of course, would prove that the ballots had been illegally smuggled into Arizona from Asia. (This story is 100% true, I promise. I could not possibly make this s#@# up. It would actually be really funny if it wasn't completely undermining our democracy).

Weeks into the bogus recount, the four Republicans and one Democrat on the Board of Supervisors finally had enough. Calling the recount "a sham process," "circus," and "a grift disguised as an audit" in a letter to Arizona state Senate President Karen Fann, the Board called for the "spectacle that is harming all of us" to end because "our state has become a laughingstock. Worse, this 'audit' is encouraging our citizens to distrust elections, which weakens our democratic republic."

They continued, "It is time to make a choice to defend the Constitution and the Republic. We stand united together to defend the Constitution and the Republic in our opposition to the Big Lie. We ask everyone to join us in standing for the truth."

In January 2022, the Maricopa County Elections Department released a report called *Correcting the Record: Maricopa County's In-Depth Analysis of the Senate Inquiry*. The report, in part, said:

> "The November 2020 General Election was administered with integrity and the results were accurate and reliable. This has been proven through statutorily required accuracy tests, court cases, hand counts performed by the political parties, and post-election audits.
>
> After an in-depth analysis and review of the reports and presentations issued by the Senate's contractors, we determined that nearly every finding included faulty analysis, inaccurate claims, misleading conclusions, and a lack of understanding of federal and state election laws.
>
> Our review of the claims made by Cyber Ninjas, CyFIR, EchoMail, and the Senate's Audit Liaisons, found: 1) 22 were misleading. The claims lead the reader to assume a conclusion that is not supported by the evidence, 2) 41 were inaccurate. The claims include flawed or misstated analysis, and 13 were false. The claims are demonstrably false and can be proven false using materials provided to the Senate."

The same day this report was released, a superior court judge declared Cyber Ninjas in contempt of court for not releasing their records to *The Arizona Republic* newspaper, which requested them under the *Freedom of Information Act*. The judge imposed a $50,000-a-day fine for every day the records were not produced. Within the week, attorneys for the Cyber Ninjas reported the firm insolvent.

Things in Michigan were downright painful to watch at times, and not just because armed, Trump-supporting, American-flag-waving protestors surrounded the home of Michigan's Secretary of State Jocelyn Benson when she was decorating for Christmas with her 4-year-old son.

One of the protesters, Genevieve Peters, said, "We are over here in the fricking dead of night, man. We are letting her know that we're not taking this bullshit election, we are not standing down, we are not giving up you are not going to take this election from a man that has earned it completely 100% by a freaking landslide. Let me tell you: This ain't over."

Early on, a Republican poll watcher reported that *someone* told her that *someone* had backdated mail-in ballots so they would be counted. While introducing this allegation in court, the Trump attorney kept insisting this testimony was not hearsay (i.e., information that someone received from another person that can't be substantiated).

After going round and round about testimony that is the very definition of hearsay, Judge Cynthia D. Stephens was incredulous. She not only declared the testimony hearsay, but she said it was "inadmissible hearsay within hearsay."

In another Michigan courtroom, Judge Timothy M. Kenny rejected the Trump campaign's effort to delay the certification of votes in Detroit, saying that allegations of misconduct were "not credible." "It would be an unprecedented exercise of judicial activism for this court to stop the certification process," not to mention it would "undermine faith in the electoral system."

Judge Kenny also said in his ruling that one of the Republican affidavits in particular was "rife with speculation and guess-work about sinister motives."

In Wayne County, Michigan's largest, Donald Trump personally called a member of the board of canvassers who, after the call, tried to take back her vote to certify Joe Biden's victory (which is not possible). Donald then invited Michigan's Senate Majority Leader Mike Shirkey and House Speaker Lee Chatfield, both Republicans, to the White House for a chat.

One can only imagine the conversation that went on in that meeting but, nevertheless, afterward the Michigan legislators issued a joint statement saying:

> "We have not yet been made aware of any information that would change the outcome of the election in Michigan and as legislative leaders, we will follow the law and follow the normal process regarding Michigan's electors, just as we have said throughout this election.
>
> Michigan's certification process should be a deliberate process free from threats and intimidation. Allegations of fraudulent behavior should be taken seriously, thoroughly investigated, and if proven, prosecuted to the full extent of the law. And the candidates who win the most votes win elections and Michigan's electoral votes. These are simple truths that should provide confidence in our elections."

Michigan's secretary of state concurred: "We have not seen any evidence of fraud or foul play in the actual administration of the election. What we have seen is that it was smooth, transparent, secure and accurate."

In the end – eight months after the election – a Republican-led Michigan state Senate Oversight Committee released a report putting voter fraud claims to rest for good.

The report said, in part: "This Committee found no evidence of widespread or systematic fraud in Michigan's prosecution of the 2020 election" and that citizens of Michigan should watch out for "those who have pushed demonstrably false theories for their own personal gain."

Committee Chairman, Republican Senator Edward McBroom, started his personal letter that accompanied the report this way:

"When I agreed to begin investigating the election, rumors and uncertainty were rampant. Allegations of markers bleeding through ballots, voter intimidation, dead voters, mystery ballot dumps, foreign interference, and ballot harvesting were just a few of the issues during the first days following the November 2020 election. Emotions and confusion were running wild across the country. Fears and hopes were had by every person, including myself."

Then came this extraordinary statement:

"'All politicians lie' is the popular axiom. Unfortunately, lies and deceit are not exclusive to politicians. Throughout our investigation, members have been actively following and engaged with various persons and reports. We have collectively spent innumerable hours watching and listening and reading. Some of these people and reports are true. Unfortunately, many of them are not, either because of a misunderstanding or an outright deception. As is often the case, the truth is not as attractive or as immediately desirable as the lies and the lies contain elements of truth."

He then concluded with:

"At this point, I feel confident to assert the results of the Michigan election are accurately represented by the certified and audited results. While the Committee was unable to exhaust every possibility, we were able to delve thoroughly into enough to reasonably reach this conclusion. The strongest conclusion comes in regard to Antrim County < note: this involved false claims about voting machines. > All compelling theories that sprang forth from the rumors surrounding Antrim County are diminished so significantly as for it to be a complete waste of time to consider them further."

That's not to say there was *zero* fraud in the 2020 election. An *Associated Press* review of "every potential case of voter fraud in the six battleground states disputed by former President Donald Trump has found fewer than 475 – a number that would have made no difference in the 2020 presidential election." This represents just 0.15 percent of Joe Biden's victory margin in these battleground states (and remember, not all these disputed ballots were cast for Biden).

< Note: The *Associated Press* review, a process that took months and encompassed more than 300 local election offices, is one the most comprehensive examinations of suspected voter fraud in last year's presidential election. It relies on information collected at the local level, where officials must reconcile their ballots and account for discrepancies, and includes a handful of separate cases cited by secretaries of state and state attorneys general. >

The AP's investigation also confirmed that there was "no collusion intended to rig the voting. Virtually every case was based on an individual acting alone to cast additional ballots."

For instance, officials in Wisconsin charged one woman with voter fraud when she allegedly tried to use her dead partner's name to vote. Michigan charged two people with fraud when they forged their daughters' names to get ballots. One man was charged in Pennsylvania for using his dead mother's name to vote for, you guessed it, Donald Trump. Wow, that's one hell of a conspiracy.

My favorite case of voter fraud is Donald Kirk Hartle of Las Vegas. Several days after the 2020 election, Donald told a news crew that someone stole his dead wife's ballot!!! Oh No! He just couldn't imagine who would take "advantage of his grief." "That is pretty sickening to me, to be honest with you," he lamented. Well, unfortunately for Donald Kirk Hartle, Nevada's attorney general's office investigated the matter, and discovered that the thief was no other than Donald Kirk Hartle himself! He has now been charged with two felonies.

And all of this is just what happened in the 2020 election. You may remember that Donald Trump also claimed election fraud in the 2016 presidential election.

Even though he won the 2016 election, Donald Trump didn't like that he lost the popular vote by 2.8 million votes so, of course, it had to be fraud – which is a tricky thing to claim when you actually won the Electoral College and, therefore, the presidency.

On November 27, 2016, Donald Trump tweeted, "In addition to winning the Electoral College in a landslide, I won the popular vote if you deduct the millions of people who voted illegally."

To back-up this claim, the Trump White House incorrectly cited a Pew Center report on voter fraud. In response, the author of the Pew Center report, David Becker, tweeted, "As I've noted before, voting integrity was better in this election than ever before. Zero evidence of fraud."

Several months earlier, when the Trump campaign first cited Becker's report to support their allegations of voter fraud, Becker tweeted: "As primary author of the report the Trump camp cited today, I can confirm that report made no findings re: voter fraud. We found millions of out-of-date registration records due to people moving or dying but found no evidence that voter fraud resulted."

Ironically, even as Donald Trump was claiming – with zero proof – that between 3 million and 5 million ballots were illegally cast in the 2016 election, his own lawyers were adamantly claiming in a Michigan courtroom that "all available evidence suggests that the 2016 general election was not tainted by fraud or mistake," as they fought to block a recount effort by Green Party candidate Jill Stein.

Likewise, in a court filing in Pennsylvania, legal representatives for Donald Trump and his campaign said, "There is no evidence – or even any allegation – that any tampering with Pennsylvania's voting systems actually occurred."

In this case, the Trump attorneys went even further: "The absence of any evidence of tampering is no surprise. Before the election, Secretary of State Pedro Cortés assured Pennsylvanian voters that Pennsylvania's voting systems are 'secure,' and criticized contrary suggestions as 'not only wrong and uninformed, but also dangerous.'"

My favorite example of this whole issue being complete b.s. is the fate of Donald Trump's own Presidential Commission on Election Integrity, which was convened after the 2016 election, met just twice, and never issued a report on their findings.

Maine's secretary of state who was initially appointed to the Commission, Democrat Matt Dunlap, told author David Daley, "It was a dishonest effort from the very beginning. It was never really meant to uncover anything. It was meant to backfill an unprovable thesis that there's voter fraud – then to issue a fake report justifying laws or executive orders that change the fundamental nature of how we run elections. I think that might have been the real danger that we averted."

It wasn't just Democrats who became disenchanted with the Commission. The effort got off to a rough start when Kris Kobach – Kansas' former secretary of state and the vice chairman of the Commission (stay tuned for more about this genius) – demanded that state election officials give the Commission tons of voter data, to include Social Security numbers, party registration and voting history.

Needless to say, that request did not go over well, and most all of the election officials seemingly felt the way Mississippi Secretary of State Delbert Hosemann, a Republican, did about the request: "They can go jump in the Gulf of Mexico."

In the end, a court order forced the Trump administration to turn over documents from the Commission to Matt Dunlap, who promptly posted them on a website.

An analysis of the documents by the *Associated Press* led them to say, "The now-disbanded voting integrity commission launched by the Trump administration uncovered no evidence to support claims of widespread voter fraud."

One of the big accusations in 2016 was that there were thousands upon thousands of non-citizens voting. This is a total distortion of the truth.

On January 27, 2019, Donald Trump tweeted: "58,000 non-citizens voted in Texas, with 95,000 non-citizens registered to vote. These numbers are just the tip of the iceberg. All over the country, especially in California, voter fraud is rampant. Must be stopped. Strong voter ID!" – a premise that Texas Attorney General Ken Paxton was more than happy to help promote.

The truth – which neither Donald Trump nor Ken Paxton bothered to later clarify – is that, yes, the Texas Department of Public Safety did indeed flag 95,000 names of potential non-citizens who were possibly registered to vote. But THEN, the state of Texas and individual counties began clearing names from that list as the citizenship status of people on the list were confirmed.

The *Texas Tribune* reported that, very quickly, "the number of registered voters flagged by the state began to plummet...Soon after, the citizenship review effort buckled, revealing itself as a ham-handed exercise that threatened to jeopardize the votes of thousands of legitimate voters across the state. The secretary of state's office eventually walked back its initial findings after embarrassing errors in the data revealed that tens of thousands of the voters the state flagged were citizens."

Things in Florida went about the same way. In 2012, there were reports that up to 200,000 registered voters in Florida may not have been U.S. citizens. After a thorough investigation by then Governor Rick Scott, a Republican, the actual number turned out to be 207.

Six years later, the same Rick Scott, now running for the U.S. Senate, claimed that the votes from Broward County – a county in Florida that generally votes Democratic – were tainted.

Once again, this was proven false. On May 21, 2020, the Florida Department of Law Enforcement released a report that found "no evidence of fraudulent intent" and "no evidence of fraudulent intent to use the altered forms by the Florida Democratic Party after more than a year-long investigation into alleged vote-by-mail fraud."

Another Donald Trump favorite in 2016 was his claim that "thousands" of people were "brought in on buses" to New Hampshire from neighboring Massachusetts to "illegally" vote.

After a months-long investigation by the New Hampshire Secretary of State and the state's Department of Justice, this was proven completely false.

The Boston Globe reported that "the two state agencies found that among the approximately 743,000 voters who cast ballots in the 2016 general election, just four appeared to have voted illegally, mostly out of confusion about where they were supposed to vote. For example, some said they were told to go to an incorrect location, others thought they were allowed to vote any place where they own property."

The article continues, "Of the 6,000 who registered to vote on Election Day and signed an affidavit swearing to be a state resident, just 66 in 15 communities did not ultimately have their identities verified. While the state could not confirm exactly why they couldn't contact those people, Associate Attorney General Anne Edwards cautioned: 'No one should reach any conclusion that an unlawful vote was cast, because we have not been able to identify these voters.'"

It's now time to circle back to good 'ol Kris Kobach from Kansas, our genius from Donald Trump's Presidential Commission on Election Integrity. This is a guy who couldn't actually win his campaign for governor or the U.S. Senate, even with the advantage of trying to cheat.

Former secretary of state Kobach was super proud of the fact that changes he made in the state's voter identification laws – some of the strictest in American history – probably, in his estimation, would remove as many as 20,000 people from the voter rolls.

Problem is that, even after an extensive investigation by Kobach himself, he could only find 127 ineligible individuals who actually voted (or tried) to vote. In the end, Kobach obtained nine convictions and, as *NBC News* reports, "most were older individuals who had misunderstood their voting rights – and just one was a noncitizen." That's some impressive law enforcement there, buddy!

§§§

At the risk of overkill, here's even more evidence that widespread voter fraud is a complete farce:

In 2020, the Texas attorney general's office almost doubled the number of hours its staff spent on tracking down election fraud than they did in 2018. Even after 22,000 hours spent investigating, Attorney General Ken Paxton's office uncovered only 16 minor cases of voter fraud. All 16 cases involved people putting false addresses on their voter forms.

The Houston Chronicle reports that "in its 15 years in existence, the (election integrity) unit has prosecuted a few dozen cases in which offenders received jail time, none of them involving widespread fraud."

Joseph Fishkin, a professor of election law at the University of Texas, puts it this way: "This is not the only voter fraud effort to pour in a lot of resources and end up with a relatively small number of cases found. Finding very few defendants, even if they can charge some with multiple offenses, is consistent with the possibility that there just isn't that much fraud to prosecute."

§

According to the Brennan Center for Justice at New York University School of Law, "Allegations of widespread voter fraud often prove greatly exaggerated. It is easy to grab headlines with a lurid claim ("Tens of thousands may be voting illegally!"), but the follow-up – when any exists – is not usually deemed newsworthy.

On closer examination, many of the claims of voter fraud amount to a great deal of smoke without much fire. The allegations simply do not pan out. These inflated claims are not harmless. Crying 'wolf' when the allegations are unsubstantiated distracts attention from real problems that need real solutions. If we can move beyond the fixation on voter fraud, we will be able to focus on the real changes our elections need, from universal registration all the way down to sufficient parking at the poll site.

Moreover, these claims of voter fraud are frequently used to justify policies that do not solve the alleged wrongs, but that could well disenfranchise legitimate voters. Overly restrictive identification requirements for voters at the polls – which address a sort of voter fraud more rare than death by lightning – is only the most prominent example."

§

A study from Columbia University reveals that:

"Voter fraud is extremely rare. At the federal level, records show that only 24 people were convicted of or pleaded guilty to illegal voting between 2002 and 2005, an average of eight people a year.

The available state-level evidence of voter fraud, culled from interviews, reviews of newspaper coverage and court proceedings, while not definitive, is also negligible. The lack of evidence of voter fraud is not because of a failure to codify it. It is not as if the states have failed to detail the ways voters could corrupt elections. There are hundreds of examples drawn from state election codes and constitutions that illustrate the precision with which the states have criminalized voter and election fraud.

If we use the same standards for judging voter fraud crime rates as we do for other crimes, we must conclude that the lack of evidence of arrests, indictments or convictions for any of the practices defined as voter fraud means very little fraud is being committed. Most voter fraud allegations turn out to be something other than fraud. A review of news stories over a recent two-year period found that reports of voter fraud were most often limited to local races and individual acts and fell into three categories: unsubstantiated or false claims by the loser of a close race, mischief and administrative or voter error.

There is a long history in America of elites using voter fraud allegations to restrict and shape the electorate. In the late nineteenth century when newly freed Black Americans were swept into electoral politics, and where Blacks were the majority of the electorate, it was the Democrats who were threatened by a loss of power, and it was the Democratic party that erected new rules said to be necessary to respond to alleged fraud by Black voters.

Today, the success of voter registration drives among minorities and low-income people in recent years threatens to expand the base of the Democratic party and tip the balance of power away from the Republicans. Consequently, the use of baseless voter fraud allegations for partisan advantage has become the exclusive domain of Republican party activists.

The historically disenfranchised are often the target of voter fraud allegations. Fraud allegations today typically point the finger at those belonging to the same categories of voters accused of fraud in the past – the marginalized and formerly disenfranchised, urban dwellers, immigrants, blacks, and lower status voters. These populations are mostly found among those still struggling for full inclusion in American life."

§

From Rutgers University-Camden:

"Are fraudulent voters undermining U.S. elections? The simple answer is no. Rather, the threat comes from the myth of voter fraud used to justify rules that restrict full and equal voting rights.

Twenty-four (24) journalism students at twelve universities reviewed some 2,000 public records and identified just six cases of voter impersonation between 2000 and 2012.

Under Republican President George W. Bush, the U.S. Justice Department searched for voter fraud. But in the first three years of the program, just 26 people were convicted or pled guilty to illegal registration or voting. Out of 197,056,035 votes cast in the two federal elections held during that period, the rate of voter fraud was a minuscule 0.00000132 percent.

No state considering or passing restrictive voter identification laws has documented an actual problem with voter fraud. In litigation over the new voter identification laws in Wisconsin, Indiana, Georgia and Pennsylvania, election officials testified they have never seen cases of voter impersonation at the polls. Indiana and Pennsylvania stipulated in court that they had experienced zero instances of voter fraud.

When federal authorities challenged voter identification laws in South Carolina and Texas, neither state provided any evidence of voter impersonation or any other type of fraud that could be deterred by requiring voters to present photo identification at the polls."

§

A *News21* – a national investigative reporting project funded by the Carnegie Corporation of New York and the John S. and James L. Knight Foundation – analysis of 2,068 alleged election-fraud cases since 2000 shows:

"That while fraud has occurred, the rate is infinitesimal, and in-person voter impersonation on Election Day, which prompted 37 state legislatures to enact or consider tough voter ID laws, is virtually non-existent.

In an exhaustive public records search, *News21* reporters sent thousands of requests to elections officers in all 50 states, asking for every case of fraudulent activity including registration fraud, absentee ballot fraud, vote buying, false election counts, campaign fraud, casting an ineligible vote, voting twice, voter impersonation fraud and intimidation.

Analysis of the resulting comprehensive *News21* election fraud database turned up 10 cases of voter impersonation. With 146 million registered voters in the United States during that time, those 10 cases represent one out of about every 15 million prospective voters."

Four Years Later...

"This year, *News21* reviewed cases in Arizona, Ohio, Georgia, Texas and Kansas, where politicians have expressed concern about voter fraud and found hundreds of allegations but few prosecutions between 2012 and 2016. Attorneys general in those states successfully prosecuted 38 cases, though other cases may have been litigated at the county level. At least one-third of those cases involved nonvoters, such as elections officials or volunteers. None of the cases prosecuted was for voter impersonation."

§

I could go on and on with this. The evidence that widespread voter fraud does not exist in the United States of America is endless, but we need to move on. There is no widespread voter fraud in the United States. It's just simply not true. Case closed.

EXAMPLE THREE

THE PERFECT SCAPEGOAT, ANTIFA

– the 1787 Recommendations for
Domestic Terrorism are in *The Policy Guide* –

Masterful liars need a boogeyman to deflect attention away from their deceit. This mind trick typically comes with a huge dose of projection: *I'm not lying, YOU ARE! I'm not a horrible person doing horrible things, YOU ARE! Some of my supporters aren't racist, violent lunatics, YOURS ARE!!*

Enter antifa. The protests for racial justice that took place after the murder of George Floyd were largely peaceful. However, when violence and destruction did take place sporadically across America, many right-wingers – including the sitting U.S. attorney general, the U.S. president, multiple members of Congress, and conservative cable channels – were quick to blame the antifascism activist movement antifa, and that narrative spread like wildfire across social media.

It didn't help that White supremacist groups were actually posing as antifa groups to stir the already boiling pot. For example, a White nationalist group named Identity Evropa started multiple Twitter accounts claiming to be national antifa organizations. These fake accounts repeatedly incited violence in the name of the Black Lives Matter movement.

Twitter finally shut down the accounts, but the damage was done. According to Zignal Labs – a media intelligence software service company – within two days of Identity Evropa's bogus accounts releasing tweets intended to stoke violence, antifa had already been mentioned nearly 300,000 times. The day after that, antifa was mentioned almost 1.5 million times. That's an increase of 1,200,000 million. In one day.

True to form, before the U.S. Capitol insurrection even ended on January 6th, right-wingers were back at it, saying (surprise, surprise) that antifa was the real monster wreaking havoc and – as Representative Matt Gaetz (R-FL) put it later that day, on the House floor no less – "masquerading as Trump supporters."

< Note: I fully address the events of January 6th, the days leading up to it, and its aftermath at the end of this chapter. But, for now, you should know that I firmly believe – and the evidence is very clear – that the attack on the U.S. Capitol was seditious and the perpetrators of the insurrection were Donald Trump supporters. >

During the riot, Representative Paul Gosar (R-AZ) said, "This has all the hallmarks of antifa provocation," and Representative Mo Brooks (R-AL) chimed in later that night, "There is some indication that fascist antifa elements were involved, that they embedded themselves in the Trump protests." The My Pillow wacko claimed that "there were probably some undercover antifa people that dressed as Trump people."

Conservative radio talk show host Todd Herman, who happened to be the guest host on Rush Limbaugh's radio show that day, referenced a tweet from yet another conservative radio guy Michael D. Brown that said: "Antifa or BLM or other insurgents could be doing it disguised as Trump supporters. Come on, man, have you never heard of psyops?" Yes, I have Mr. Brown…have YOU?

Then, Herman said to Limbaugh's millions and millions of listeners: "It's probably not Trump supporters who would do that. Antifa, BLM, that's what they do. Right?"

But here is the God's honest truth about antifa being behind or even remotely involved with the attack on the United States Capitol: It is just not true. Period. End of story.

… although you certainly wouldn't know it by looking at your Twitter feed. According to Zignal Labs, the blatantly false antifa narrative appeared 8,700 times throughout social media, cable television and Internet news outlets between 4pm and 5pm on January 6th alone. One tweet that said, "Remember, Antifa openly planned to dress as

Trump supporters and cause chaos today," also a lie, received 41,100 likes and shares.

On January 6th and 7th, the "MAGA didn't storm the Capitol, antifa did" lie was mentioned 411,099 times on social media, cable news, and online "news" websites. It was by far the most widely spread falsehood regarding the Capitol riot.

The afternoon of the 6th, the conservative news outlet *The Washington Times* published a story saying that XRVision, a facial recognition company, had identified antifa members at the Capitol. However, XRVision issued a statement that said the company's software did <u>not</u> identify antifa members but <u>did</u> identify members of neo-Nazi organizations and at least one QAnon supporter.

The XRVision statement said, in part: "Our attorney is in contact with *The Washington Times* and has instructed them to 'Cease and Desist' from any claims regarding sourcing of XRVision analytics, to retract the current claims, and publish an apology."

Even though *The Washington Times* removed the story less than 24-hours after it was posted, the damage was already done. Before it was taken down, Matt Gaetz and conservative television host Laura Ingraham, among many others, publicized the article, which eventually received 360,000 likes and shares on Facebook alone.

This right-wing gaslighting worked like a charm. In fact, a January 2021 poll conducted by the American Enterprise Institute – a nonpartisan, nonprofit organization – revealed that half of the Republicans they polled said that it was "mostly or completely accurate" to say that antifa "was mostly responsible for the violence that happened in the riots at the U.S. Capitol."

Within two days of the pro-Trump Capitol attack, the FBI made it clear that there was zero evidence to suggest antifa had anything to do with the death and destruction at the Capitol. Two months later, FBI Director Christopher Wray reiterated that fact when he testified before the Senate Judiciary Committee: "We have not, to date, seen any evidence of anarchist violent extremists or people subscribing to antifa in connection with the 6th."

When asked again if it were possible that antifa members were impersonating Trump supporters that day, Director Wray again said,

"We have not seen evidence of that at this stage. We have not seen any evidence of that."

Where did this obsession with antifa come from? Well, at least in part from Donald Trump, naturally. Among many other comments on the topic, in May 2020 Donald Trump tweeted: "The United States of America will be designating ANTIFA as a Terrorist Organization."

Four months later, he followed-up with this tweet: "And I look at (antifa) as a bunch of well funded ANARCHISTS & THUGS who are protected because the Comey/Mueller inspired FBI is simply unable, or unwilling, to find their funding source, and allows them to get away with "murder". LAW & ORDER!" < Note: I know this grammar is way off, but I wrote it exactly the way he did – which is not easy to do for someone with OCD and, well, pride. >

Donald didn't stop there. In fact, his antifa spin went next level. He even publicly accused an elderly peaceful protester – who was shoved down to the ground by police in Buffalo, New York, fracturing his skull – of being part of antifa, which was an absolutely ludicrous claim.

Not to be outdone, in the spring and summer of 2020, then Attorney General Bill Barr was trying everything he could possibly think of to blame antifa for the looting and riots that were periodically breaking out across America.

At one point, Barr even said, "I've talked to every police chief in every city where there has been major violence and they all have identified antifa as the ramrod for the violence. They are flying around the country. We know people who are flying around the country."

He also said, "There is clearly some high degree of organization involved at some of these events and coordinated tactics that we are seeing. Some of it relates to antifa, some of it relates to groups that act very much like antifa."

But as hard as Barr tried, the facts – including those from his own Justice Department – just couldn't back him up.

By early June 2020, 51 people faced federal charges related to the riots/protests. Of those already charged, 20 alleged crimes involved arson; 16 involved the illegal possession of a firearm, and 8 involved inciting a riot, civil disorder, and/or looting.

At that time, federal court records from the U.S. Justice Department showed zero links between any serious federal crimes that had occurred and anti-fascist groups. Hear this again: Zero.

According to the Department of Justice, by the end of September 2020, after Barr had established a "task force" to counter "anti-government extremists," over "300 individuals in 29 states and Washington, D.C., had been charged for crimes committed adjacent to or under the guise of peaceful demonstrations since the end of May."

Even though a few of the defendants self-identified as having far-left and/or anti-government views – and others who self-identified as having far-right views – there is zero evidence that any of them had ties to antifa.

In fact, the only reference to any extremist group in federal court documents during that time involved three men associated with a far-right extremist group called Boogaloo, who were charged with plotting violence in connection to a Las Vegas protest.

The Boogaloo Boys are a Hawaiian-shirt wearing anti-government, anti-law enforcement extremist movement. They are convinced that the government is determined to take their guns away and believe a second civil war is coming soon.

An intelligence bulletin that was distributed to police departments across the nation, issued by the FBI, the Department of Homeland Security and the National Counterterrorism Center, warned:

> Domestic terrorists "including militia extremists and groups who advocate a belief in the superiority of the White race have sought to bring about a second civil war, often referred to as a 'Boogaloo' by intentionally instigating violence at First Amendment-protected activities. Racially charged events, coupled with the accompanying widespread media attention, and the rapid dissemination of violent online rhetoric by extremists are likely to remain contributing factors to potentially ideologically motivated violence."

As for those police chiefs and other officials around the country who Barr claimed blamed antifa for being the "ramrod for the violence?" When asked directly about antifa, Josh Rubenstein, the public information director for the Los Angeles Police Department, said, "We saw no organized effort of antifa here in Los Angeles."

Medaria Arradondo, the Minneapolis chief of police, said: "As I sit here today, I have not received any sort of official information identifying any of the groups." The Sturgis, South Dakota Police Chief Geody VanDewater, said: "As far as we know (the protesters) were just local citizens from Rapid City and not affiliated with antifa."

Dermot Shea, New York City's police commissioner, said that most of the people arrested at the riots/protests were actually people who lived in New York and were simply taking advantage of the chaos to commit crimes. He made clear they were not driven by political ideology. John Miller, a New York City police official, confirmed this, saying the crimes were committed by just plain 'ol "regular criminal groups."

In Austin, a group that burglarized a Target store was initially identified as being affiliated with the anti-fascist activist movement, but people who are *actually* affiliated with the movement adamantly denied the group's affiliation, as did at least one of the defendant's attorneys.

You may have noticed that the Trump administration never got around to designating antifa a terrorist organization – mainly because antifa is not an actual organization at all.

Although there are organized, localized groups, antifa is not some sort of colossal, looming presence that has designated leadership and a hierarchical structure. In fact, the lack of structure is something they take pride in. Antifa is more what some people call an "affinity group."

FBI Director Christopher Wray underscored this distinction when he told members of the U.S. Congress, under oath, that while antifa is certainly the "real thing" and that the FBI had led "any number of properly predicated investigations into what we would describe as violent anarchist extremists," what people refer to as antifa "is not a group or an organization. It's a movement or an ideology."

Wray continued, "Trying to put a lot of these things into nice, neat, clean buckets is a bit of a challenge, because one of the things that we see more and more in the counterterrorism spaces is people who assemble together in some kind of mishmash…a bunch of different ideologies. Almost like a salad bar of ideologies, a little bit of this, a little bit of that, and what they're really about is the violence."

Indeed, the main thing that antifascism activists generally have in common is their distaste for anything racist, alt-right or, of course, fascist, and they generally show up when there are big gatherings of White nationalists. Antifascism activists send out "calls for action" and then like-minded people just show up.

Just as a review, the term *fascism* was created by Benito Mussolini, the Prime Minister of Italy from 1922 until 1943 and the man who established the first one-party fascist state in the world. Fascism is a form of authoritarian ultranationalism, with the hallmarks of dictatorial leadership and the aggressive silencing of any and all kinds of opposition.

At its core, antifascism is literally an opposition to fascism, which is a "political ideology and mass movement that dominated many parts of central, southern, and eastern Europe between 1919 and 1945 and that also had adherents in western Europe, the United States, South Africa, Japan, Latin America, and the Middle East."

So, just by reading a little more about what antifascism actually is, you can probably guess that the last thing anti-government, anti-capitalists want to be is tied to an organized political party. But that's exactly what Donald Trump, Bill Barr and cronies like Rudy Giuliani and conservative media outlets tried desperately to get people to believe.

They worked hard to conflate antifa with the Democratic party, which – although many people associated with antifa can be described as "far-left" – is 100% untrue. At one point Donald even said, "In my book, it's virtually part of (the Democratic) campaign, antifa."

Trump & Co. also worked hard to conflate antifa and the Black Lives Matter movement in an obvious attempt to position antifa as a "Black" organization…the perfect dog whistle for their tribe…and also 100% untrue.

Portland, Oregon offers a good example of these distinctions. Out of every American city that experienced protests/riots for racial justice and police reform in 2020, Portland endured perhaps the most vandalism, violence, and destruction.

As usual, Trump & Co. tried hard to blame antifa – and antifa alone – for the mayhem in Portland (and they all, of course, kept driving home the subtle theme that antifa is a "Black" organization led by Democrats).

Donald constantly tweeted things like: "The FBI and Law Enforcement must focus their energy on ANTIFA and the Radical Left, those who have spent the summer trying to burn down poorly run Democrat Cities throughout the USA!" and "These are Biden fools. ANTIFA RADICALS. Get them FBI, and get them now!" Rudy remarked that "antifa sprang into action and in a flash hijacked the protests into vicious, brutal riots."

Never mind that, after the 2020 protests had settled down, a spokesman for the U.S. Attorney's office in Portland told *Reuters* that his office had "not alleged defendant affiliation with any specific groups or ideologies in cases stemming from recent Portland protests… our cases focus purely on the criminal conduct alleged."

In truth, a lot of the violence in Portland was perpetrated by White *anarchists*. Even though many antifascists share certain principles with anarchists, the ideologies are not the same. For one, anarchists essentially believe there should be no central government. Although many antifascists are highly suspicious of government institutions, most don't go nearly that far.

The Washington Post reports that "from the assessments of the White mayor, Ted Wheeler, and the Black police chief, Chuck Lovell, this smaller faction (of self-described anarchists) comprises mostly White, middle-class students and others, who have made places such as churches, public libraries, small Black-owned businesses and a Boys & Girls Club the confounding targets of their vandalism."

For example, on May 25, 2021, the one-year anniversary of George Floyd's death, a peaceful crowd gathered in Portland to walk from Revolution Hall to the Burnside Bridge. Meanwhile, a crowd that included anarchists gathered downtown. According to the Portland Police Department, the downtown crowd – which included people wearing helmets and carrying gas masks – "pushed a dumpster against the Justice Center" and "lit a fire in the dumpster…while people chanted to burn the building down." Five people were arrested. All five were White.

Please know, I don't bring any of this up to defend antifa, or to suggest that groups and individuals associated with antifa are never violent or destructive. They most certainly can be.

On August 29, 2020, a self-identified antifa supporter shot and killed Aaron Danielson, a pro-Trump protester in Portland (the shooter was later killed by federal agents). Almost one year later, far-right groups and far-left groups – including antifascist demonstrators – violently clashed in Portland (and there were plenty of violent flare-ups in between).

Just hours after Joe Biden was sworn in as president, far-left demonstrators – including some who identified themselves as aligned with antifa – vandalized the Oregon Democratic Party headquarters in Portland, as well as the Immigration and Customs Enforcement office, several businesses, and a federal courthouse in Seattle.

I only bring this entire topic up to illustrate how absolutely imperative it is that we get our basic facts straight. These challenges are difficult enough to solve without having to plow through thorns of deceit.

There is this thing called the *Theory of Constraints*. Essentially, the *Theory of Constraints* says that we should identity the factors (i.e., constraints) that keep us from achieving a certain goal, then systematically remove or improve those constraints until they are no longer limiting our end result.

As we work to remove or improve constraints, it's important to keep in mind that if we identify the wrong constraint and work on *it* instead of the *actual* constraint, we will likely make the entire problem worse.

Let's say Jack owns a car dealership. Jack sells a lot of cars, but – it's really weird – he never has enough money to pay his bills at the end of the month. He must not be selling enough cars, he thinks!

So, Jack orders twice the number of cars from his wholesale car suppliers than he usually does and announces a contest among his salespeople to motivate them to sell every one of them. Jack's salespeople do great! They sell every car on the lot.

However, in the weeks following the contest, Jack had far less money in the bank than he did in the months before.

What Jack failed to realize is that he had identified the wrong constraint. The problem was never that Jack was selling too few cars. The problem was that Jack owed his wholesale car suppliers money for the cars he bought from them weeks before he actually sold the cars on his own lot. In other words, the terms of his Accounts Payable and Accounts Receivable were not aligned correctly, and *that* was the constraint.

Since Jack's constraint was a cash flow issue, it was made far worse when he ordered even more cars from his suppliers, because now he owed them *even more* money upfront.

To alleviate Jack's real constraint, the best move would be to contact his car suppliers and other creditors and match their payment terms to a time closer to when he actually sold the cars. This would allow him time to collect money from the cars he sells, then pay his bills, then pocket the difference (i.e., the profit).

You may be wondering why in the heck we took that little detour, but the *Theory of Constraints* concept is really instructive for most policy issues. It's especially important in this discussion, because we're not talking about cars, we're talking about life and death.

We cannot allow anyone to highjack the domestic terrorism conversation or allow them to misidentify antifa as our constraint. If we do, the insurrection on January 6th will be just the beginning of our troubles.

This is not the first time a constraint has been misidentified to protect far-right extremist groups. For years, the federal government and other law enforcement agencies did not give the rising threat of these groups the attention it demanded, keeping the focus instead on Islamic extremists.

For example, in a 2017 interview, then White House Deputy Assistant to President Trump Sebastian Gorka, said there "has never been a serious attack or a serious plot (in the United States) that was unconnected from ISIS or al-Qaeda."

When, in response, someone cited the Oklahoma City bombing – where Timothy McVeigh killed 168 people at the Alfred P. Murrah Federal Building in 1995, a horrific crime that remains the deadliest act of domestic terrorism in American history – Gorka responded, "It's this constant 'Oh, it's the White man. It's the White supremacists. That's the problem.' No, it isn't." (Gorka has long-standing ties to the alt-right, by the way)

His wife Katharine then chimed in and said that the United States should just close "radical mosques" and bar *Al Jazeera* from broadcasting in the United States to solve the problem of domestic terrorism.

In truth, analysis sponsored by the Triangle Center on Terrorism and Homeland Security at Duke University reveals that:

> "Muslim-American extremists caused no fatalities in 2020. The total number of fatalities in the United States from Muslim-American violent extremism since 9/11 remained at 141. Over this same period, there have been more than 309,000 murders in the United States. In other words, the number of fatalities caused by acts of violent extremism by Muslim-Americans in 19 years is about the same as the number of murders that take place every three days in the United States. In 2020 alone, 179 Americans were killed in mass killings according to the federal definition of mass killing as incidents involving three or more fatalities."
>
> The report continued, "Islamic extremism played almost no role in the considerable unrest that the United States experienced in 2020: protests for racial justice; protests against public health measures, including a plot to kidnap the governor of Michigan; protests leading up to and following the elections in November; and a vehicle suicide bombing in Nashville in December, whose motivation remains unknown."

The brutal truth is that neither Islamic extremists nor antifa are causing widespread violence and mayhem in America. Far-right extremists and White nationalist groups are.

Antifa is the perfect scapegoat for these groups and their champions, because the entire storyline feeds directly into the narrative that already plays loudly in their heads: antifa people, who are "probably Black," are crazies from the radical left who defend the wicked Black Lives Matter zealots. They are scary terrorists who are devoted to the Democratic Party and fight for their Socialist agenda, and are funded by people like the evil George Soros, blah blah blah…

But it's just not true. According to a database administered by the Center for Strategic and International Studies, from 1994 to August 2020 – when that self-identified antifa supporter shot and killed a pro-Trump protester in Portland – far right and White supremacist groups were found to be responsible for at least 329 murders. In that same timeframe, antifa and other anti-fascists groups were not found to be responsible for any. Not one. <u>Zero</u>.

The United States Institute of Peace – a federal institution, founded by Congress, tasked with promoting conflict resolution and prevention worldwide – has seen this trend for years now:

> "The last few years have seen a dramatic increase in the threat presented by the far right. There has been a 250 percent increase in far-right terrorist incidents since 2014. In Western countries, far-right extremism now accounts for 46 percent of attacks and 82 percent of deaths from terrorist attacks.
>
> The rise in far-right terrorism is part of a broader rise in political violence (including violent demonstrations and riots) in the West. This rise in political violence doesn't happen in a vacuum but is rather symptomatic of wider trends. Increasing political polarization and indications of the increased acceptability of political violence across the political spectrum in the United States present a foreboding picture of the future.
>
> Unless these trends are addressed, and efforts to remedy the social and political cleavages that have fueled their rise, they could lay the foundations for a further increase in political violence around the globe, particularly if coupled with the continued politicization and mainstreaming of far-right extremist views."

Analysis by *The Washington Post* of data compiled by the Center for Strategic and International Studies – a bipartisan, nonprofit policy research organization – revealed that:

> "Domestic terrorism incidents have soared to new highs in the United States, driven chiefly by White-supremacist, anti-Muslim and anti-government extremists on the far right. The surge reflects a growing threat from homegrown terrorism not seen in a quarter-century, with right-wing extremist attacks and plots greatly eclipsing those from the far left…Since 2015, right-wing extremists have been involved in 267 plots or attacks and 91 fatalities, the data shows. At the same time, attacks and plots ascribed to far-left views accounted for 66 incidents leading to 19 deaths."

Throughout the years, many people tried to raise the alarm on far-right extremist groups, but their efforts were at best ignored and at worst sabotaged. In 2009, Daryl Johnson, then a senior analyst for domestic terrorism at the U.S. Department of Homeland Security, wrote a private intelligence report specifically for members of law enforcement.

However, conservative media outlets leaked Johnson's report, causing a huge uproar because Johnson dared to use the term "right-wing extremism." The report also warned that American military veterans could be prime targets for domestic extremist recruitment.

Republicans went berserk, demanding an apology on behalf of veterans and calling for Johnson to be fired. Within a year, Johnson's entire department was dismantled and work on domestic terrorism threats came to a screeching halt.

Toward the end of the Obama administration, however, the Department of Homeland Security awarded grants to groups that countered violent extremism – like those that helped people who wanted to leave neo-Nazi and White supremacist groups – and that tried to prevent Americans from embracing these groups in the first place. In the first weeks of the Trump administration those grants were cancelled.

As a result of years of turning a blind eye, White supremacy – as terrorism scholar John Horgan, a Distinguished University Professor of

Psychology at Georgia State University puts it – "is far more dispersed and deeply ingrained ideology in Western society." Over the long-term "it will be far harder to defeat than jihadism."

This threat is made far worse by the fact that – as Daryl Johnson warned in 2009 and the FBI's *Counterterrorism Policy Directive and Policy Guide* finally confirmed – "domestic terrorism investigations focused on militia extremists, White supremacist extremists, and sovereign citizen extremists often have identified active links to law enforcement officers."

In fact, at least 81 active-duty U.S. military and U.S. veterans face charges as a result of the Capitol riot. These include people like former FBI official and Navy intelligence officer Thomas Caldwell, who gave military-style advice and organized training sessions for the Proud Boys, Oath Keepers and Three Percenters. (more on these groups in a minute…)

He also started a "death list" of his enemies, saying he would get rid of them by "killing them, shooting them, and mutilating their corpses to use them as shields."

And people like Larry Brock Jr. a guy who, after the election, told his Facebook audience that the United States was "now under occupation by a hostile governing force." He went on to say that he saw "no distinction between a group of Americans seizing power and governing with complete disregard to the Constitution and an invading force of Chinese communists accomplishing the same objective." He vowed to protect America "against all enemies foreign and domestic."

Reveal from The Center for Investigative Reporting found, in an investigation that led to over 50 internal departmental investigations, that "hundreds of active-duty and retired law enforcement officers from across the United States are members of Confederate, anti-Islam, misogynistic or anti-government militia groups on Facebook…Almost 150 of the officers they found are involved with violent anti-government groups such as the Oath Keepers and Three Percenters."

As reported jointly by *Buzz Feed* and Injustice Watch, The Plain View Project – launched by Philadelphia lawyer Emily Baker-White – "examined the accounts of about 2,900 officers from eight departments across the country and an additional 600 retired officers from those same departments. She compiled posts that represented troubling conduct in a database that is replete with racist imagery and memes, and in some cases long, vitriolic exchanges involving multiple officers."

"The project sought to compile posts, comments, and other public activity that could undermine public trust in the police and reinforce the views of critics, especially in minority communities, that the police are not there to protect them. Of the pages of officers whom the Plain View researchers could positively identify, about 1 in 5 of the current officers, and 2 in 5 of the retired officers, made public posts or comments that met that threshold – typically by displaying bias, applauding violence, scoffing at due process, or using dehumanizing language. The officers mocked Mexicans, women, and Black people, celebrated the Confederate flag, and showed a man wearing a kaffiyeh scarf in the crosshairs of a gun."

The good news is that after years of being behind the eight ball, many in the federal government finally caught up with reality, thank God.

In 2017, the Department of Homeland Security and the FBI admitted far-right extremists, particularly White supremacists, are indeed a huge problem, in a bulletin titled *White Supremacists Extremism Poses Persistent Threat of Lethal Violence*.

That was a start but, in March 2020, Department of Justice Inspector General Michael Horowitz issued a report that said the FBI had "not taken sufficient action" in regard to 'homegrown violent extremists.' Nearly 40 percent of counterterrorism assessments went unaddressed for 18 months after deficiencies were known to the FBI."

The report continued, "Since September 11, 2001, homegrown violent extremists (HVEs) have carried out over 20 attacks in the United States, some of which occurred after the FBI closed a counterterrorism investigation or assessment on the individual." Between 2009 and 2017 "at least six attacks committed in the United States were by individuals who the FBI had previously assessed or investigated."

I am happy to report that the FBI took this criticism to heart and started to make serious headway. In September 2020, FBI Director Wray told the U.S. Congress: "Within the domestic terrorism bucket, the category as a whole, racially motivated violent extremism is, I think, the biggest bucket within that larger group. And within the racially motivated violent extremist bucket, people subscribing to some kind of White supremacist-type ideology is certainly the biggest chunk of that."

Wray continued, "Of the domestic terrorism threats, we last year elevated racially motivated extremism to be a national threat priority commensurate with homegrown violent extremists." He said he put the threat on the same level as "jihadist-inspired people here."

The following month, the FBI charged six people affiliated with two White supremacist, neo-Nazi groups – named Atomwaffen Division and The Base – for a thwarted plot to kidnap Michigan Governor Gretchen Whitmer. Federal prosecutors also charged 13 people for plotting to start a civil war with the purpose of overthrowing the United States government.

Also in September 2020, then acting deputy secretary of the Department of Homeland Security Ken Cuccinelli told Congress, "When White supremacists act as terrorists, more people per incident are killed," and then acting director of the Department of Homeland Security Chad Wolf told members of the Senate Homeland Security and Government Affairs Committee that White supremacists presented "the most persistent and lethal threat when we talk about domestic violent extremists."

That same month, *The Wall Street Journal* reported that: "White supremacists were responsible for the most ideologically inspired extremist homicides in recent years, overtaking salafist and jihadist killings in the U.S., according to the Center for the Study of Hate and Extremism at California State University, San Bernardino. In 2019, White supremacists were responsible for 29 homicides, up from 17 in 2018, according to the center."

This all reached critical mass on January 6, 2021, when many of these groups converged to assault the United States Capitol. They showed up ready for battle, and several had the intention of killing and/or kidnapping the vice president and other members of Congress. (more on this later)

The Proud Boys were there. In fact, at least two dozen of them across multiple states have been charged with federal crimes from that day. This far-right nationalist group is dedicated to "reinstating a spirit of Western chauvinism" in America. Before the Capitol riot, one of its leaders, Joe Biggs, wrote: "Every law makers who breaks their own stupid F---ing laws should be dragged out of office and hung."

Proud Boy Dominic Pezzola, appropriately known as "Spaz," was one of the first to breach the Capitol. But his boys weren't far behind! Assistant U.S. Attorney Erik Kenerson explained, "The defendants' actions show planning, determination, and coordination," then charged Spaz and his buddy William Pepe with conspiracy.

The Three Percenters were there. This right-wing paramilitary-style outfit named themselves for the 3 percent of the American population that fought the British Army in the Revolution.

In the weeks before January 6th, the founder of the group, Stewart Rhodes, assured people that The Three Percenters would provide security in Washington, with "some of our most skilled special warfare veterans standing by armed, just outside D.C."

As the big day drew closer, the group encouraged people to join "President Trump's fight to defeat the enemies foreign and domestic who are attempting a coup."

"Prepare yourselves for whatever may come. Prepare your mind, body, and spirit for battle, and above all else, prepare to STAND!"

The Oath Keepers certainly wouldn't have missed the fun (although, I wonder if they still think it's fun after being charged with *seditious conspiracy*...more on this later). This far-right militia-style group, made up of largely former law enforcement and military veterans, "believes that the federal government has been co-opted by a shadowy conspiracy that is trying to strip American citizens of their rights," according to the FBI.

My fellow Americans, we <u>cannot</u>, under any circumstance, allow <u>anyone</u> to distract us with false narratives that take the heat off alt-right and White nationalist groups who, quite frankly, are getting scarier by the minute.

On January 27, 2021, three weeks after the Capitol assault, the Department of Homeland Security (DHS) issued a warning about the growing threat of "ideologically-motivated violent extremists": "Violent riots have continued in recent days and we remain concerned that individuals frustrated with the exercise of governmental authority and the presidential transition, as well as other perceived grievances and ideological causes fueled by false narratives, could continue to mobilize a broad range of ideologically-motivated actors to incite or commit violence."

A report released by the Office of the Director of National Intelligence in March 2021 says that "[Domestic Violent Extremist] attackers often radicalize independently by consuming violent extremist material online and mobilize without direction from a violent extremist organization, making detection and disruption difficult."

The report underscores that White supremacists have "the most persistent and concerning transnational connections because individuals with similar ideological beliefs exist outside of the United States." It revealed that some White supremacists had already "traveled abroad to network with like-minded individuals," and warns that these groups may get "escalating support from persons in the United States or abroad."

In May 2021, a joint analysis by the FBI and Department of Homeland Security (DHS) said that:

> "The FBI and DHS assessed *Racially or Ethnically Motivated Violent Extremists* (RMVEs), primarily those advocating for the superiority of the White race, likely would continue to be the most lethal *Domestic Violent Extremists* (DVE) threat to the Homeland.
>
> Our agencies had high confidence in this assessment based on the demonstrated capability of RMVEs in 2019 to select weapons and targets to conduct attacks, and the effectiveness of online RMVE messaging calling for increased violence. The year 2019 represented the most lethal year for DVE attacks since 1995, with five separate DVE attacks resulting in 32 deaths, 24 of which occurred during attacks conducted by RMVEs advocating for the superiority of the White race."

EXAMPLE FOUR:

TINFOIL HATS TO RED HATS: THE CONSPIRACY THEORY TRAP

One morning in Houston, David Lopez-Zuniga had just left his house for his job as an air-conditioner repairman, with the lunch his wife prepared on the seat next to him. As usual, his day was getting started before sunrise, so the lights of an SUV following way too closely behind him were glaring.

Suddenly, the SUV hit Mr. Lopez-Zuniga's small truck on the passenger side, forcing him off the highway. Mark Aguirre, the driver of the SUV – a former Houston police captain turned private investigator – pointed a gun at Mr. Lopez-Zuniga and ordered him to get on the ground.

Class, welcome to Conspiracy Theory 101. In the past, conspiracy theories lived largely on the fringes of society, believed only by kooks and the tinfoil hat crew, who steadfastly insisted the earth is flat and that Area 51 exists, as do extraterrestrials and UFOs. For the most part, conspiracy theories were isolated and pretty harmless.

Conspiracy theorists seemed to ratchet things up after 9/11, when many claimed that the U.S. federal government was involved in the attack, and that the World Trade Center was destroyed not by international terrorists, but "controlled demolition."

Then came the theories that the fatal mass shooting at Sandy Hook Elementary School in Newtown, Connecticut never happened, nor did the high school shooting in Parkland, Florida. Oh! And one of my favorites, that forest fires in California were caused by Jewish space lasers.

Unfortunately, conspiracy theories have not only come roaring into the mainstream from the fringes, but they have also now made their way into the White House and U.S. Capitol.

Back to our story, where we last left Mr. Lopez-Zuniga on the ground with a gun pointed at his head. Mark Aguirre, the man who had his gun pointed at a completely baffled Mr. Lopez-Zuniga, was convinced he would find in the truck 750,000 mail-in ballots from the 2020 presidential election, signed by Hispanic children with untraceable fingerprints. (This story is 100% true, I promise. I'll say it again, I could not possibly make this s#@# up. It would actually be really funny if it wasn't completely undermining our democracy).

What was actually in Mr. Lopez-Zuniga's truck and on his property, both of which he allowed the police to search, was air conditioning equipment. Which makes sense since Mr. Lopez-Zuniga is, after all, *an air-conditioner repairman.*

So here's what happened. The Liberty Center for God and Country – a nonprofit organization started by a man named Steven F. Hotze, a well-known donor to the Texas Republican party – paid almost $300,000 to 20 private investigators for a six-week undercover investigation into what they were certain was illegal ballot retrievals in Houston. < like I've said before, you can always count on Texas! #texasproud >

To give you some context on what we're dealing with here, in 2015 Mr. Hotze started a campaign against the legalization of same-sex marriage, specifically because it would lead to schools teaching children as early as kindergarten to "practice sodomy."

Meanwhile, at the Aurora Medical Center in Grafton, Wisconsin, a pharmacist mired in conspiracy theories intentionally sabotaged 570 doses of the Covid-19 vaccine because he was convinced the vaccine could actually change people's DNA.

In a divorce petition, the wife of the pharmacist claimed that he told her that "if she didn't understand by now that he is right and that the world is crashing down around us, she is in serious denial. He continued to say that the government is planning cyberattacks and plans to shut down the power grid." The couple has two daughters.

In an earlier chapter, I mentioned QAnon, the preposterous conspiracy theory group that believes Donald Trump is saving America from a cabal of Satan worshipers and child sex traffickers. Yes, that was a member of QAnon, known as the Q Shaman, inside the Senate chamber on January 6th, shirtless and otherwise dressed in some sort of fur getup.

In August 2021, a California father and QAnon follower killed his 2-year-old son and 10-month-old daughter because he believed they had "serpent DNA" and were "going to grow into monsters." Killing them, he said, "was the only course of action that would save the world."

In early December 2016, Edgar Maddison Welch left his home in Salisbury, North Carolina and headed to Washington, D.C. He had heard Alex Jones – the host of the far-right *Info-Wars*, who started the "Sandy Hook Elementary massacre didn't happen" conspiracy theory – say that Hillary Clinton was sexually abusing children as part of satanic rituals in the basement of a pizza restaurant there, and he was horrified.

The Alex Jones' rant he heard went something like this: "When I think about all the children Hillary Clinton has personally murdered and chopped up and raped . . . yeah, you heard me right. Hillary Clinton has personally murdered children."

When Mr. Welch arrived at Comet Ping Pong, the scene of the "crime," with an AR-15 semiautomatic rifle, a .38 handgun and a folding knife, he went through the restaurant room by room, looking for children to rescue. He never got to the basement because the restaurant doesn't even have one.

This episode has come to be known as Pizzagate. The first Facebook post associated with Pizzagate appeared on October 29, 2016, around the time that federal agents confiscated former congressman Anthony Weiner's laptop to investigate his communications with a 15-year-old girl. Anthony Weiner is married to Huma Abedin, a close friend and staffer of Hillary Clinton (Huma and Anthony have since separated).

The original Pizzagate message was posted by a user named Carmen Katz: "My NYPD source said its much more vile and serious than classified material on Weiner's device. The email DETAIL the trips made by Weiner, Bill and Hillary on their pedophile billionaire friend's plane, the Lolita Express. Yup, Hillary has a well documented predilection for underage girls. . . . We're talking an international child enslavement and sex ring."

From there, the lie sprinted its way through social media, eventually getting the attention of a Twitter user named @DavidGoldbergNY, who retweeted Katz's post twice, adding: "I have been hearing the same thing from my NYPD buddies too. Next couple days will be interesting!" One of those tweets was retweeted 6,369 times.

Rolling Stone magazine reports that, "according to a sample of tweets with Pizzagate or related hashtags provided by Filippo Menczer, a professor of informatics at Indiana University, Pizzagate was shared roughly 1.4 million times by more than a quarter of a million accounts in its first five weeks of life – from @DavidGoldbergNY's tweet to the day Welch showed up at Comet Ping Pong."

"At least 14 Russia-linked accounts had tweeted about Pizzagate" and "at least 66 Trump campaign figures followed one or more of the most prolific Pizzagate tweeters." The clip of Alex Jones claiming Hillary Clinton raped and murdered children had already been viewed on YouTube more than 427,000 times.

For our next example, we head to the steps of the United States Supreme Court, where a group of doctors in white medical coats spread misinformation about the pandemic. "America's Frontline Doctors," as they called themselves, spewed falsehoods about, among other things, coronavirus vaccines, treatments and masks.

After Donald Trump promoted the video on social media and Donald Trump Jr. declared it a "must watch," views of the video went through the roof.

Social media platforms finally removed the video, but the damage was already done – yet again. By that time, versions of the video had been seen millions of times across social media platforms. One version was viewed on Facebook over 16 million times alone.

Donald Trump was perplexed by the removal of the video. "For some reason the Internet wanted to take them down and took them off. I think they are very respected doctors. There was a woman who was spectacular in her statements about it, that she's had tremendous success with it and they took her voice off. I don't know why they took her off. Maybe they had a good reason, maybe they didn't."

Let's take a closer look into this woman who was "spectacular in her statements." Stella Immanuel is a registered physician in Texas, where she operates a medical clinic located in a strip mall. She was born in Cameroon and received her medical degree in Nigeria.

To say this lady is a wackadoodle is an insult to wackadoodles. *The Daily Beast* reported that "she has often claimed that gynecological problems like cysts and endometriosis are in fact caused by people having sex in their dreams with demons and witches."

The article continues, "She alleges alien DNA is currently used in medical treatments, and that scientists are cooking up a vaccine to prevent people from being religious. And, she has said that the government is run in part not by humans but by 'reptilians' and other aliens." Well, that part may actually be true. :)

But wait! There's more. *The Daily Beast* again: "In sermons posted on YouTube and articles on her website, Immanuel claims that medical issues like endometriosis, cysts, infertility, and impotence are caused by sex with 'spirit husbands' and 'spirit wives' – a phenomenon Immanuel describes essentially as witches and demons having sex with people in a dreamworld…They are responsible for serious gynecological problems. We call them all kinds of names – endometriosis, we call them molar pregnancies, we call them fibroids, we call them cysts, but most of them are evil deposits from the spirit husband. They are responsible for miscarriages, impotence – men that can't get it up." I gotta tell ya, that's some church.

Those are all interesting examples, but for the best illustration of just how crazy and convoluted this has all gotten, meet Adam Rahuba. He is a food-delivery driver and DJ who lives on his friend's sofa.

Adam is a self-described democratic socialist and Bernie Sanders supporter who has taken homegrown trolling to an entirely new level – targeting conservative extremists, commentators, and media outlets.

Most of Adam's hoaxes incorporate something having to do with MAGA supporters, and use antifa as bait. For example, he once created a meme that showed photos of the crowd at a Trump rally that said, "Know any MAGA parents? Child Services will investigate any anonymous claim even without proof. Child Service agents tend to be liberal" – insinuating that people on the far-left were going to unlawfully take the children of Trump supporters away from their families.

Founder and former editor in chief of the far-right *Big League Politics* website, Patrick Howley, retweeted the post to his 42,000 Twitter followers, adding, "Self-identified ANTIFA operatives are filing false reports on Trump-supporting parents. Lots of sources say this is happening – don't let them say this was a joke." Which, of course, was exactly what it was.

For a July 4th ruse, Adam announced that antifa was having a flag burning "to peacefully protest for abolishing police nationwide." The event was to take place at the Gettysburg Cemetery in Gettysburg, PA.

Conservative media outlet *Breitbart News* reported on the story: "Should members of the 'antifa' movement carry out their plan to desecrate the graves of soldiers who fell at Gettysburg, they will join the Taliban, ISIS, and Turkish Islamists who have launched a campaign to destroy historic sites and desecrate graves of their enemies."

The Fox News website reported "possible disruptive or even violent actions by the militant left-wing group antifa at Gettysburg National Park."

Before Adam announced the antifa-organized July 4th flag-burning event, he published an Internet phone number to make it even more fun. *The Washington Post* published several of the recorded messages he received:

"Y'all going to get to real … surprised in Gettysburg. I cannot wait to participate, you n------loving f---s."

"I hope someone shoots every one of you motherf-----s. I pray to God in heaven for someone to shoot everyone involved in that event."

Sixteen local and federal law enforcement groups were activated to help monitor the event. They all gathered at a local middle school that had been turned into a command center. There were 100 Pennsylvania state troopers, mounted officers, and a helicopter.

Hundreds of armed counter protesters, including militiamen and White supremacist groups, showed up to stop the flag-burning madness. When the antifa crazies never showed up – because, of course, there never really were antifa crazies coming to this fake event – the counter protesters felt victorious, with many believing their very presence at the event frightened the antifa flag burners away.

According to Adam, he does this just to screw with people for his own amusement, calling his hijinks "performance art."

He told *The Washington Post*, "I've found myself very annoyed with the rise of right-wing populism. So, I thought I'd do my own thing to push back against them. The message here was that any idiot on the Internet can get a bunch of people to show up at a Union cemetery with a bunch of Confederate flags and Nazi tattoos on their necks that just make them look foolish."

This is quickly becoming a trend among the Gen Z set. For example, billboards claiming "Birds Aren't Real" have started to pop up in several major American cities. Birds Aren't Real followers have a strong presence on social media, plenty of merchandise for sale, and have even protested outside the Twitter headquarters, demanding that the company change its logo (which, of course, is a bird).

On the surface, the Birds Aren't Real people – and its leader, twenty-three-year-old Peter McIndoe – seemingly believe that regular 'ol birds are actually drones the U.S. government uses to spy on the American people. However, behind the scenes, the movement freely admits that it is nothing more than a parody, created to shine a light on the absurdity of modern-day misinformation and conspiracy theories.

Claire Chronis, a twenty-two-year-old Birds Aren't Real organizer from Pittsburgh, puts it this way: "It's a way to combat troubles in the world that you don't really have other ways of combating. My favorite way to describe the organization is fighting lunacy with lunacy."

Control Mind Control

This is all interesting, but how do lies and conspiracy theories become someone's truth? And, more importantly, what can we do about it? There are many ways this trash spreads, but I'll offer you my top three: social media, media, and straight up sabotage.

Social Media

– the 1787 Recommendations for
Social Media are in *The Policy Guide* –

"If you've built a chaos factory,
you can't dodge responsibility for the chaos.
Taking responsibility means having
the courage to think things through."

– Tim Cook, Chief Executive of Apple –

For almost two decades, as our politics fractured and misinformation flourished, multiple social media networks were emerging to provide a lightning-fast pathway for even the most asinine propaganda to spread.

Social media has enabled widespread deceit to infect the bloodstream of American society, poisoning our politics and enabling pathological collective delusions that are shared by millions of people on obscure platforms like Parler, Gab, 8kun and Telegram – as well as mainstream networks like Facebook, Twitter and all the rest.

This super-spreader superhighway changed everything. We already talked about the false antifa narrative that shot through social media on January 6th, which showed that social media is unrelenting even on our darkest days. This was also proven in the agonizing weeks in 2020 when Americans, in the midst of the Covid-19 crisis and subsequent economic turmoil, were enraged and broken-hearted over the killing of George Floyd by a police officer in Minneapolis.

Instead of bringing the country together in the midst of chaos and grief, social media firms enabled what is the equivalent of bomb-throwing. Instead of promoting productive discourse, they allowed hundreds of false, inflammatory posts to metastasize.

Some posts said George Floyd wasn't even dead at all. Others claimed that Derek Chauvin, the Minnesota police officer charged in Mr. Floyd's death, was actually an actor paid by the "deep state" and that George Soros, the billionaire investor and Democratic donor, was funding the protests.

This poor guy. I don't know where the conspiracy crazies got hold of his name, but for years George Soros has been one of their favorite villains. Sid Miller, the agriculture commissioner of the great state of Texas, seemed to speak for all of them when he said, "I have no doubt in my mind that George Soros is funding these so-called 'spontaneous' protests. Soros is pure evil and is hell-bent on destroying our country!"

During the week after Mr. Floyd's death, George Soros was mentioned in 34,000 tweets. On YouTube, over 90 videos in five languages were posted detailing various Soros conspiracy theories. He was mentioned in 72,000 posts on Facebook. Together, the ten most active Facebook posts about George Soros were shared over 110,000 times.

To see exactly how these lies spread, let's take a look at what happened with the 26-minute video called Plandemic.

Plandemic is a video that promotes misinformation about the coronavirus, falsely blaming a shady ring of scientific and political elites for manufacturing the virus to increase their power and bank accounts. The goal of the film, in the filmmaker's words, is to "expose the scientific and political elite who run the scam that is our global health system" (think big pharma, Bill Gates, the World Health Organization – and, naturally, poor George Soros).

In a grave tone, the Plandemic narrator says, "Now, as the fate of nations hang in the balance, Dr. Mikovits is naming names of those behind the plague of corruption that places all human life in danger."

Dr. Mikovits is Judy Mikovits, who the filmmaker calls "one of the most accomplished scientists of her generation." In reality, Judy Mikovits is a long-discredited virologist who claims that the aforementioned shadowy elite cabal is trying to bury her brilliant scientific theories.

In the video, Mikovits says that face masks actually "activate" the virus and that Covid-19 vaccines will surely kill millions of people – never mind that none had even been introduced at that time the video was filmed.

She also accuses Dr. Anthony Fauci – the head of the National Institute of Allergy and Infectious Diseases and another favorite villain of the crazies – of killing millions of people during the HIV/AIDS crisis.

Mikovits claims that it was *she* who was instrumental in discovering HIV but was put in jail for her scientific research by…wait for it…the aforementioned shadowy cabal of elites. In reality, she was put in jail for stealing proprietary information from a laboratory that had fired her.

Among many (many) others, *Science* magazine "fact-checked the video. None of these claims are true." The article then walks through every discredited claim – exhaustively, point by point – to prove it.

When Plandemic was first posted on May 4, 2020, it stayed on the fringes of the Internet for a few hours, circulating through conspiracy theory and anti-vaccine forums. However, pretty quickly, it crossed over into the mainstream.

The New York Times analyzed how exactly Plandemic blasted its way across the Internet. Here's what they found: In less than a day after the video's creator Mikki Willis uploaded the video, a QAnon Facebook group posted the video for its almost 25,000 members. From there, 1,660 people shared the video to their own pages.

At around the same time, Dr. Christiane Northup, an obstetrician-gynecologist who was once a "medical expert" on Oprah, shared the video with her nearly 500,000 followers. From there, over 1,000 people shared the video.

Incidentally, to this day, Northup denies the reality of the pandemic, saying "it doesn't make sense." Jonathan Jarry – a biological scientist at McGill University, a research university in Montreal, Quebec, Canada – said after watching her nightly ten-minute videos, "In this parallel universe, there are Indigo children, time travelers from the future, and geomancers performing acupuncture on Mother Earth by moving rocks around. Rarely have I witnessed such a smorgasbord of gobbledygook from someone who once had an active medical license."

By that evening, Plandemic hit the Reopen Alabama Facebook page. Reopen Alabama is a group that was, in the early days of the pandemic, advocating for shelter-in-place orders to be lifted. At the time, the group had 36,000 members and was linked with other Reopen America groups around the country. From there it spread like wildfire.

Soon, the video hit the Facebook page of Nick Catone, a professional mixed martial arts fighter and vocal anti-vaccine activist. Over 2,000 of his almost 70,000 followers "liked" the video.

The following day, Melissa Ackison, a candidate who ran in the Republican primary for Ohio's 26th District Senate seat (she lost), posted the video on her Facebook page for her 20,000 followers. Now the video was in the political mainstream, making its way to Republican groups around the Web.

By May 7th, YouTube, Vimeo and Facebook had removed Plandemic for violating their misinformation policies but, once again, the damage was done. In a little more than a week after Mr. Willis posted the video, it had been viewed over 8 million times across social media networks.

The story of how Plandemic stormed the Internet shows just how fast misinformation can spread – and just how difficult it is to get the toothpaste back in the tube – but nothing illustrates this better than what was discovered after Donald Trump got kicked off the social networks. This is actually pretty hard to believe, but it's true.

After Donald Trump and several of his closest allies were booted from Twitter two days after the January 6th Capitol riots, Zignal Labs found that online misinformation about election fraud fell – get this! – 73 percent. SEVENTY-THREE PERCENT.

"Election fraud" mentions plummeted from 2.5 million to 688,000 across social media platforms. The hashtag #FightforTrump fell 95 percent, and #HoldTheLine and the phrase "March for Trump" dropped over 95 percent.

During the week of November 16, 2020, every single one of the twenty most-engaged Facebook posts that included the word "election" came from Donald Trump. Every single one of them were also slapped with a false or misleading warning by independent fact checkers.

Over a four-week period beginning in mid-October 2020, Avaaz – a nonprofit organization that promotes global activism – analyzed 95,546 Facebook posts that included "voter fraud" in some way. Collectively, these posts were liked, shared or commented on almost 60 million times.

Their analysis revealed that only 33 of the 95,546 posts were responsible for over 13 million of the 60 million interactions. That's just extraordinary.

After analyzing over 55,000 online media stories, 5 million tweets, and 75,000 posts on public Facebook pages, the Berkman Klein Center for Internet & Society at Harvard University found that "Fox News and Donald Trump's own campaign were far more influential in spreading false beliefs than Russian trolls or Facebook clickbait artists."

In another analysis, the Election Integrity Partnership found that "posts from just 20 users were the source (original tweet) for approximately 20 percent of all of the retweets in their dataset. This means that a small number of accounts was responsible for a large portion of the spread of misleading election-related information."

...and the Donald Trump disinformation train didn't stop at elections. A study by Cornell University found "that media mentions of Donald Trump within the context of Covid-19 misinformation made up by far the largest share of the 'infodemic' of misinformation. Trump mentions comprised 37.9 percent of the overall misinformation conversation, well ahead of any other topics."

The researchers concluded that former president Donald Trump "was likely the largest driver of the Covid-19 misinformation infodemic. Only 16.4 percent of the misinformation conversation was 'fact checking' in nature, suggesting that the majority of Covid misinformation is conveyed by the media without question or correction."

These results are even more telling given that many conservatives are convinced that social media networks are drowning in political bias – against *them*.

That's just false. Right-wing users drive far more engagement than left-wingers, a fact that a Facebook executive acknowledged in an interview with *Politico* weeks before the 2020 election. The reason the political right has higher interactions rates is simple, the Facebook executive said. Their content is better at hitting visceral trigger points.

"Right-wing populism is always more engaging," the executive said, because the content triggers "an incredibly strong, primitive emotion" by engaging on such topics as "nation, protection, the other, anger, fear."

The *Politico* article continues, "In the final stretch of the 2020 campaign, the Facebook posts with the most engagement in the United States most days – measured by likes, comments, shares and reactions – were from conservative voices outside the mainstream media: Dan Bongino, Ben Shapiro, David Harris, Jr., Franklin Graham and 'Blue Lives Matter,'" according to the Facebook-owned tool Crowdtangle. "Trump's personal page also regularly made the top of the list, in effect allowing him to become a publisher in his own right and navigate around the traditional media."

The level of this impact is greatly enhanced by people like Guo Wengui, the Chinese real estate developer whose yacht Steve Bannon was on when Bannon was arrested for fraud.

A report from Graphika, a social media intelligence firm, called *Ants in a Web* reveals that "Wengui is at the center of a vast network of interrelated media entities which have disseminated online disinformation and promoted real-world harassment campaigns. Graphika has identified thousands of mostly-authentic social media accounts associated with this network which are active across platforms including Facebook, Instagram, YouTube, Twitter, Gab, Telegram, Parler, and Discord."

Although the network primarily focuses on the Chinese Communist Party (CCP) and anti-CCP dissidents, it also "acts as a prolific producer and amplifier of mis- and disinformation, including claims of voter fraud in the U.S., false information about Covid-19, and QAnon narratives."

The report says that "in the second half of 2020, content from the Guo media network was increasingly prevalent in the American right-wing social media environment. Activity within the Guo network spiked in the run-up to the November 2020 U.S. presidential election."

There are real-life consequences to this reality. Research conducted by the University of Virginia McIntire School of Commerce found that "the more time someone spends on Facebook, the more polarized their online news consumption becomes."

"What's more, Facebook usage is five times more polarizing for conservatives than for liberals. This evidence suggests Facebook indeed serves as an echo chamber, especially for its conservative users."

"Facebook and Reddit shape the news consumption of their conservative users in dramatically different ways. In months when a typical conservative visited Facebook more than usual, they read news that was about 30 percent more conservative than the online news they usually read. In contrast, during months when a typical conservative used Reddit more than usual, they read news that was far less conservative – about 50 percent more moderate than what they typically read."

§§§

Remember the good 'ol days, when the Internet was just a simple, innocent place to go for useful information like movie times and weather?

Just a simple place where you could track down your old high school boyfriend or girlfriend, to specifically see if their life had indeed gone on without you and to make sure their significant other was not as pretty or fun as you are?

How times have changed in such a short period of time. Over the last few years we have, unfortunately, seen the Internet's dark side.

We have seen foreign countries maliciously attack our sacred elections; intimate photos of women posted without their consent for revenge, or just a cheap thrill; fake social media accounts created to harass and embarrass ex-boyfriends and girlfriends; terrorist propaganda accounts enabled and empowered; and Americans accused of murder and other horrible crimes, with zero evidence – openly defamed, maligned and slandered with little recourse.

We have seen social media firms shamelessly sell us out by not only failing to protect our personal information, but actively pimp it out; we have seen truth and productive discourse replaced by disinformation and hate.

Like a slow-moving car crash, we have seen the Internet morph from an innocent, cuddly Calico kitten into an irresponsible, out-of-control Bengal tiger – weaponized for the destruction of almost everything we hold dear, from our personal privacy to our hallowed democracy.

The Cyberspace Solarium Commission, a bipartisan commission ordered by the U.S. Congress, put it this way: "The digital connectivity that has brought economic growth, technological dominance, and an improved quality of life to nearly every American has also created a strategic dilemma. The more digital connections people make and data they exchange, the more opportunities adversaries have to destroy private lives, disrupt critical infrastructure, and damage our economic and democratic institutions."

We have to get a handle on this, and fast. There are tons of issues that need to be addressed involving the Internet – everything from cybersecurity to online influence operations to cyber bullying (the recommendations for all of these are covered in these books) – but the behavior and responsibility of social networks is at the top of the list.

What's the big deal, one may ask, because Facebook and Twitter accounts are free anyway, right? Not even close.

Many services in the digital economy appear to be free, but you actually pay for them not with money, but with your personal data. In fact, your personal information is a currency far more valuable to social media companies than if you paid them a large monthly fee.

You and I are the product being sold here. Our likes and dislikes, our penchants and preferences, our vulnerabilities and insecurities. What we eat, when we sleep, why we vote, where we shop. Who we worship, who our friends are, who our enemies are…all sold to the highest bidder.

Social media companies not only have access to a mind-boggling pool of our personal data, but they also possess an unprecedented "social graph" that allows them to not only know the desires and habits of each of their members, but also how each of their members connects and interacts with their *other* members. This goldmine is invaluable to advertisers.

Until recently, these companies showed little regard for their actions, even though they knew exactly how they were manipulating their users and negatively affecting society. Their irresponsible behavior did not stop with enabling Russian bots and fake antifa accounts, or even the spread of disinformation, conspiracy theories and hate speech. They also punted on basic human decency.

For example, in 2018, Facebook employees created a slide presentation as part of an internal effort to understand how Facebook shapes user behavior, and how the company could possibly alleviate potential harmful effects.

One of the slides said: "Our algorithms exploit the human brain's attraction to divisiveness. If left unchecked, Facebook would feed users more and more divisive content in an effort to gain user attention and increase time on the platform."

Facebook founder and chief executive Mark Zuckerberg, along with other senior members of his team, seemingly buried the results of the research.

What's even more disturbing is that, according to *The Wall Street Journal*, "the concern was that some proposed changes would have disproportionately affected conservative users and publishers, at a time when the company faced accusations from the right of political bias."

In other words, the leaders of Facebook threw us all under the bus because of political pressure. I guess the Facebook executive conveniently left that out of his interview with *Politico*.

The Wall Street Journal also reported that "a 2016 presentation that names as author a Facebook researcher and sociologist, Monica Lee, found extremist content thriving in more than one-third of large German political groups on the platform."

"Swamped with racist, conspiracy-minded and pro-Russian content, the groups were disproportionately influenced by a subset of hyperactive users, the presentation notes. Most of them were private or secret. The high number of extremist groups was concerning, the presentation says."

"Worse was Facebook's realization that its algorithms were responsible for their growth. The 2016 presentation states that '64 percent of all extremist group joins are due to our recommendation tools' and that most of the activity came from the platform's Groups You Should Join and Discover algorithms: Our recommendation systems grow the problem.'"

Please reread that paragraph. Facebook has known for years that their own algorithms promote and even encourage extremism. That is truly beyond the pale.

In July 2020, Facebook released the results of a long-awaited audit of its civil rights policies. It wasn't good.

"With each success the auditors became more hopeful that Facebook would develop a more coherent and positive plan of action that demonstrated, in word and deed, the company's commitment to civil rights. Unfortunately, in our view Facebook's approach to civil rights remains too reactive and piecemeal."

Perhaps most exasperating to the auditors is Mark Zuckerberg's stance on political speech. Using the example of Donald Trump's May 2020 Facebook post that warned protesters "when the looting starts, the shooting starts," they said:

"After the company publicly left up the looting and shooting post, more than five political and merchandise ads have run on Facebook sending the same dangerous message that 'looters' and 'antifa terrorists' can or should be shot by armed citizens. The auditors do not believe that Facebook is sufficiently attuned to the depth of concern on the issue of polarization and the way that the algorithms used by Facebook inadvertently fuel extreme and polarizing content."

"When powerful politicians do not have to abide by the same rules that everyone else does, a hierarchy of speech is created that privileges certain voices over less powerful voices."

To be fair, social media firms were far more disciplined right before, during and after the 2020 election. According to *The Economist*, Facebook removed ten times the number of hate speech posts than they had two years ago. They also deactivate 17 million fake accounts every single day, double the number from three years ago.

Facebook also reinforced its security teams, conducted practice drills to plan for every possible election outcome, blocked new political ads for certain time periods, limited the number of people and/or groups with which a message can be shared, and strengthened transparency rules for advertisers.

Honestly, I'm grateful they are trying to do better but, because of their size and scale of impact on communication, media, and civil society on the whole, it's clear we cannot rely on their self-policing alone. The stakes are just way too high.

For one, cleaning this mess up flies directly in the face of their entire profit model, which is obviously a disincentive. Social media algorithms are designed to attract as much of the user's attention as possible, then push the user to interact with others. The algorithms don't distinguish between "good" and "bad" content, they just understand that they need to push the content that gets the most comments, clicks and shares.

Recent experience proves that this is a disaster waiting to happen. We now know that primitive emotion and extreme behavior generate more attention and interest than cats playing Pat-a-Cake, meaning these companies make more money on the extremes – which is exactly the reason Facebook executives buried their own research.

Thankfully, there is a silver lining to this. Because of the way social network business models work, social media companies *need us more than we need them*. They need as many of us as possible to participate, because their survival depends on "network effects" –

meaning, the more people they have using their services, the more valuable their services are.

This fact alone gives all of us social media users tremendous power. And we need to wield it. The good news is that it is absolutely possible to strike an appropriate balance between guardrails and innovation.

As we search for the best solutions to this challenge, we have to be extremely mindful of protecting self-expression and free speech. If we are not careful, those pesky unintended consequences could come and bite us really quickly. #TheButterflyEffect

In fact, let's talk about free speech for a minute, using an example that we have all just lived through.

After four years of political and societal chaos, the rubber finally met the road on January 6, 2021. After the pro-Trump mob assaulted the U.S. Capitol, Corporate America decided it had finally had enough – and they brought down the thunder.

Airbnb, AT&T, Dow, Google, Marriott International, Morgan Stanley, and the U.S. Chamber of Commerce announced their political action committees (PACs) would no longer contribute to the 147 Republican members of Congress who objected to certifying the election results.

American Airlines, Bank of America, Best Buy, Blue Cross Blue Shield, Boston Scientific, BP, Charles Schwab, Citigroup, Coca-Cola, Comcast, Commerce Bancshares, ConocoPhillips, CVS Health, Delta, ExxonMobil, Facebook, FedEx, Ford, General Motors, Goldman Sachs, Hilton, JPMorgan, Microsoft, UPS, Walmart, the Walt Disney Company, and Wells Fargo announced they were either reviewing their contribution strategy or stopping contributions altogether.

This is a huge blow because Corporate America PACs gave $91 million to members of the House of Representatives and $27 million to members of the Senate in the last election cycle alone.

Hallmark specifically asked Senator Josh Hawley (R-MO) and Senator Roger Marshall (R-KS) for their campaign contributions back, saying in a statement, "Hallmark believes the peaceful transition of power is part of the bedrock of our democratic system, and we abhor violence of any kind. The recent actions of Senators Josh Hawley and

Roger Marshall do not reflect our company's values." Additionally, Simon & Schuster canceled Josh Hawley's upcoming book contract.

As a reminder, Senator Hawley was the first person to announce his intention to object to the certification of the Electoral College vote count, and Senator Marshall supported the objections to the electoral votes for Arizona and Pennsylvania.

But that was nothing compared to the wrath Donald Trump incurred. Stripe, the online payment platform; Shopify, the e-commerce platform; and Snapchat, YouTube, Twitch, and Reddit banned him from their platforms – as, famously, did Twitter.

Facebook and Microsoft announced temporary suspensions for the Donald, saying they would reassess things after his presidential term ended.

Deutsche Bank and Signature Bank (his two largest lenders), the Professional Golfers' Association and the City of New York all announced they would no longer do business with him. Lehigh University and Wagner College both rescinded his honorary degrees.

Amazon Web Services announced it would no longer host pro-Trump social network Parler for violating its terms of service. Buck Sexton, a conservative talk radio host, was incensed, tweeting: "Every time I try to open my Parler app and can't because of big tech censorship, I'm reminded that the most powerful enemies of free speech got where they are by pretending to be its greatest advocates."

What Buck conveniently left out of his tweet is that Parler, a private company, was removed by Amazon, another private company. Ironically, he also forgot he was saying all of this "big tech censorship" business on Twitter, to a national audience.

Josh Hawley also didn't see the irony when he wrote a column titled "It's Time to Stand Up Against the Muzzling of America," which made the cover of the *New York Post*, along with a picture of a man with duct tape over his mouth. *The New York Post* has hundreds of thousands of readers. This hardly qualifies as "muzzling" him.

The irony was also lost on the members of the House of Representatives who, wearing masks bedazzled with the word "Censored," stood at a microphone on the House floor, where their complaints about being censored were broadcast across the entire nation.

The whining didn't stop there. Josh Hawley described his book cancellation as "Orwellian" and as "a direct assault on the First Amendment." He continued, "This is the Left looking to cancel everyone they don't approve of."

Jonathan Turley, a professor at the George Washington University Law School, called these acts "McCarthyism" and "censorship," and likened them to "blacklists." Representative Devin Nunes (R-CA) called these types of moves an "oppressive attack on our fundamental freedoms."

When Twitter permanently shut down Donald Trump's account, Senator Steve Daines (R-MT) tweeted, "Big Tech censoring [Donald Trump] & the free speech of American citizens is on par with communist countries like China and North Korea."

Of his father's Twitter banishment, Donald Trump Jr. said – once again, ironically, on Twitter to a national audience – "Free speech no longer exists in America."

Guys, or should I say crybabies, give me a freak'n break. You can't have it both ways, Republicans. It was <u>your</u> ideology that established these rules in the first place.

For decades, the Republican Party has worked hard to ensure that Corporate America – and Corporate America alone – has the right to decide how to run their companies.

In 1968, Supreme Court Justice Thurgood Marshall, the liberal lion, wrote the majority opinion that the owner of a private shopping mall could not exclude protestors from using the mall's passageways. This, Justice Marshall declared, would violate the protester's First Amendment rights.

This ruling stood until President Nixon appointed four conservative justices and the position of the Supreme Court was reversed. Now, private corporations were under no obligation to grant access to their property: "The Court today holds that the First Amendment poses no bar to a shopping center owner's prohibiting speech within his shopping center."

The First Amendment says: "Congress shall make no law respecting an establishment of religion or prohibiting the free exercise thereof; or abridging the freedom of speech, or of the press; or the right of the people peaceably to assemble, and to petition the Government for a redress of grievances."

These words protect American citizens against censorship imposed by the United States government, not *Amazon*. I seem to remember that conservatives were all for this distinction when businesses didn't want to make wedding cakes for gay couples, or when Hobby Lobby didn't want to provide birth control to its employees.

Look, here's the deal with free speech: every member of Congress, every president, and every American citizen has the right to say whatever they want to say, whenever they want to say it. BUT *everyone else* has the right to react to what is said in any way *they* choose. See, the funny thing about free speech is that it cuts both ways.

This topic always reminds me of the country band the Dixie Chicks, who have since changed their name to just The Chicks. In 2003, right before the U.S. invasion of Iraq, one of the members of the Dixie Chicks, Natalie Maines, told a London audience that the band was against the war and "ashamed" that President George W. Bush was from Texas.

This comment led to an enormous backlash from their fans, corporate boycotts, and their music being dropped from thousands of radio stations across America. Seventeen years later, Natalie said that she thinks her band was "one of the first to feel that 'cancel culture.'"

I love The Chicks and personally think the punishment didn't fit the crime in this case, but the fact remains that, as I just said, everyone has a right to say whatever they want but everyone else has the right to their personal reaction to it. If her fans were offended enough by her comments to stop buying her albums, then they had every right to be.

Someone yelling "Free Speech" after saying something controversial doesn't immunize them from the repercussions that may come with what they said. We're not on the freak'n playground playing Cooties.

In my view, this extends to hate speech. Go ahead and put on your fur and horns getup and storm the United States Capitol, along with your buddies who said they "were looking for Nancy to shoot her in the friggin' brain" – but you will all get arrested and face federal charges for your actions.

Go ahead, Marjorie Taylor Greene, and spew deranged, racist conspiracy theories and post photos of yourself pointing an AK-47 at other members of Congress – but you will lose your congressional committee assignments and (I know there is a long way to go, but I have faith in Georgia so I'm making a bold prediction) you will lose your congressional seat (please, we are begging you Georgia!).

Go ahead and incite your cult to riot and trash the United States Capitol. But you will get impeached, you will get kicked off your social media platforms, and you will be blacklisted by Corporate America. That's just the way the ball bounces buckaroo.

§§§

So, what do we do about all of this? There are recommendations in *The Policy Guide*, but I'll give you some of the biggies here. In my mind, the federal government and the social networks both have some heavy lifting to do.

To start, the federal government should do three things. First, Congress should pass – and properly enforce – data privacy legislation similar to the *General Data Protection Regulation* in Europe. The legislation must include *Purpose Limitation*, the requirement that data collected for one purpose cannot be used for another.

It's critical that we have a unified, national strategy regarding data protection as opposed to a patchwork approach across the states. Although some states are trying to put regulations in place, it is a difficult task given that the Internet spans all fifty states.

I completely understand the hesitation to regulate, but we really don't have much of a choice. The penalties we currently have in place don't seem to bother these guys in the least.

In 2012, the Federal Trade Commission (FTC) charged Facebook with eight separate privacy-related violations. According to a statement by the FTC, "To settle that case, Facebook agreed to an order that, among other things: 1) prohibited Facebook from making misrepresentations about the privacy or security of consumers' information, 2) prohibited Facebook from misrepresenting the extent to which it shares personal data, and 3) required Facebook to implement a reasonable privacy program."

Facebook basically ignored these penalties for seven years. Finally, in 2019, the FTC imposed a $5 billion civil penalty against Facebook, "the largest ever imposed on a company anywhere for violating consumers' privacy."

"Facebook flouted (the 2012) order in multiple ways, and the $5 billion settlement holds them accountable for putting profits over their privacy promises." I have seen little evidence that this is true so far, but I guess we'll see.

Two, Congress should pass a version of the *Honest Ads Act*, which requires public disclosures of all political and social issue advertising in social media, consistent with print, radio, and television standards.

Third, Congress should repeal Section 230 of the *Communications Decency Act*. This is harsh but absolutely necessary.

Section 230 says: "No provider or user of an interactive computer service shall be treated as the publisher or speaker of any information provided by another information content provider." This essentially says that social networks bear no responsibility for what their users say on their platforms.

First of all, the idea that these social media enterprises are simply platforms in service of their users and not publishers is ridiculous. Not only is Facebook a publisher, with 2.4 billion users and content that is published in 150 languages, Facebook is the largest publisher – of anything – in the entire world.

Section 230 has enabled social media firms to build hundreds of billions of dollars-worth of value largely unencumbered. It has shielded these companies from liability for content created by their users and allowed them to manage the content on their platforms – however defamatory – as they see fit.

Ironically, Congress' motivation to include this provision was to give these companies cover to remove or restrict posts they deem "obscene, lewd, lascivious, filthy, excessively violent, harassing or otherwise objectionable, whether or not such material is constitutionally protected."

It would have worked out great if, given this air-tight, blanket protection, these companies would have just done the right thing and enacted policies, processes and procedures that protect Americans and American democracy. If they had just done this, repealing Section 230 wouldn't even be necessary.

But they didn't and they don't deserve a mulligan. True, they did better during the 2020 election, but most of them did so kicking and screaming. I'm not sure how far we can trust that.

Repealing 230 will completely change the game. I'm not a litigious person, but legal threats work. The defamation lawsuits brought by Dominion Voting Systems and Smartmatic regarding voter fraud allegations have sent chills through conservative media. Fox Business canceled Lou Dobbs Tonight, its highest rated show, and Fox News started to fact-check its own anchors on-air. *Newsmax* even chastised the My Pillow lunatic.

These billion-dollar lawsuits come on the heels of a multi-million-dollar settlement with the family of a murdered Democratic National Committee (DNC) staffer, who Fox hosts falsely accused of leaking DNC emails. Such a prick move on their part...do these people have no shame?

Of course, once Section 230 is history, it would then be up to the social media companies to decide how to best protect themselves. And there are definitely ways they can. In fact, many of them have already started to at least try.

For example, on May 6, 2020, Facebook announced the first members of its new Oversight Board. Facebook created the Oversight Board, which is kind of like their version of the Supreme Court, to hold the company accountable for decisions regarding online speech. From the beginning, I was skeptical of this idea since Facebook chose the 20-member board and pays them from a $130 million trust.

However, although it's not a perfect solution, in my opinion the Oversight Board passed its first big test. In early May 2021, the Board announced its decision on whether or not Facebook's ban on Donald

Trump should be upheld. Their decision was that, because Donald Trump broke the social network's rules, the ban should be upheld for the next six months.

But, within that timeframe, the Board mandated that Facebook had to either make the ban permanent or establish a date when he could return to the platform. Calling the ban a "vague, standardless penalty," the Board made clear that the penalties Facebook impose in the future must be transparent and no longer arbitrary.

Moving forward, I believe the Facebook Oversight Board needs a much broader scope. For example, the committee currently oversees only material that has been taken *off* the platform. It would be helpful if this was extended to cover controversial material that has been reported to Facebook, but that is still visible on the platform.

Another solid move was that social networks, as we all well know, got way more serious about placing fact-check labels on certain posts, as well as linking others to accurate information.

This is certainly an idea worth exploring, but the effectiveness of these labels is unclear. One research study conducted jointly by the University of Regina, Harvard, Yale, and the Massachusetts Institute of Technology (MIT) found that:

> "Warnings may be rendered ineffective by politically motivated reasoning, whereby people are biased against believing information that challenges their political ideology. Indeed, such warnings might actually backfire and increase belief.
>
> Beyond the potential for warnings to backfire, there is an additional (potentially more serious) concern regarding misinformation warnings which the researchers refer to as the Implied Truth Effect. When attempting to fight misinformation using warnings, it is necessary for some third party to examine every new piece of information and either verify or dispute it. Given that it is much easier to produce misinformation than it is to assess its accuracy, it is almost certain that only a fraction of all misinformation will be successfully tagged with warnings.

Thus, the implication of the absence of a warning is ambiguous: does the lack of a warning simply mean that the headline in question has not yet been checked, or does it imply that the headline has been verified (which should lead to an increase in perceived accuracy)?

To the extent that people draw the latter inference, tagging some false news headlines will have the unintended side-effect of causing untagged headlines to be viewed as more accurate. Such an Implied Truth Effect, combined with the near impossibility of fact-checking all (or even most) headlines, could pose an important challenge for attempts to combat misinformation using warnings."

Another study conducted jointly by Dartmouth College and the University of Michigan was a little more optimistic but still found that:

"Both 'Disputed' and 'Rated False' tags modestly reduce belief in false news. Notably, the researchers found larger accuracy effects for the 'Disputed' tags than the study above. However, their results demonstrate that 'Rated False' tags, which specifically tell users when claims made in headlines are untrue, are more effective at reducing belief in misinformation than the 'Disputed' tags previously used by Facebook.

Encouragingly, we find no consistent evidence that the effects of these tags varies by the political congeniality of the headlines or that exposure to the tags increases the perceived accuracy of unlabeled false headlines (though our study lacks the precision necessary to detect the small 'implied truth' effect that the study above identifies).

By contrast, though general warnings about false news also appear to decrease belief in false headlines, the effect of a general warning is small compared to either type of tag. Moreover, general warnings also reduce belief in real news and do not enhance the effects of the 'Rated False' and 'Disputed' tags, suggesting that they are a less effective approach.

The results provide support for prior studies finding a negative effect of general warnings on belief in misinformation, but the finding that these warnings also reduce the perceived accuracy of true headlines suggest that they pose a potential hazard. False news may already increase distrust in legitimate information; unintended spillover effects from general warnings or related proposals to fight false information by increasing media literacy could exacerbate this problem.

The researchers' 'Disputed' and 'Rated False' tags, which more effectively reduce the perceived accuracy of false headlines without causing these spillover effects, may be a safer way to reduce belief in misinformation."

Finally, it would be smart for social networks to make their data available for audits by independent researchers. I don't think this should be mandatory by any means but, if Facebook were my client, I would encourage them to agree to this – to just improve their public image if nothing else. After all, almost two-thirds of Americans think social media causes harm.

The Media

It's hard to overstate my respect and gratitude for the Fourth Estate. To me, a free press is everything. I deeply believe the news media significantly contributes to the health of our democracy and, without high-level journalism, democracy's very survival would be at risk.

Take investigative journalism, which has been on fire lately. Holding individuals and corporations accountable is invaluable to our society, and journalists have been knocking it out of the park.

There was *Vice News'* reporting on White supremacist groups during and after the Charlottesville domestic terrorist attack; *ProPublica*'s investigation of child separation at the border, which included audio tapes of hysterical children detained by U.S. Customs and Border Protection, along with their explosive "Secret IRS Files" investigation (which we'll talk more about later).

There was *Buzz Feed*'s heartbreaking coverage of China's internment of Uyghurs; a deep dive into the Pandora Papers by *The Washington Post*, which uncovered a massive offshore financial system used to hide money and shield corrupt and criminal behavior; and incredible reporting by *The New York Times* on how the United States tried to hide an airstrike in Syria that killed dozens of civilians and Donald Trump's finances which, far from a "witch hunt," helps us evaluate how vulnerable any president or others in power are to bribery and/or blackmail (although Donald Trump seemed to think the demand for the release of his tax returns was nothing more than a personal attack, it was more about protecting the United States from foreign corruption and exploitation.)

That said, there is something that has really been bothering me over the past few years. I hate to say it, but there are other elements of the media – including print media (traditional journalism and opinion journalism) and broadcast media (talk radio, network television and cable news) – that have gotten a little sideways.

I mentioned earlier that some Americans, particularly those who lean right, believe that the "mainstream media" is just a propaganda machine for the Democrats – which is ironic because Democrats and others who still have faith in the "mainstream media" feel exactly the same way about the Republicans and their beloved Fox News.

One of my favorite things to do is switch back and forth between MSNBC and Fox News when big news stories break. Based on this unscientific experiment, I can personally attest to the fact that, depending on the cable news channel they watch, Americans are living on two completely different planets.

On cable news especially, it's pretty clear that certain channels align with either "Team Red" or "Team Blue." This loyalty is reenforced by what they choose to cover and how they cover it, the words of their hosts and anchors, and the guests they book.

...hmmm...the guests they book. Okay, let's put a pin in cable news for a minute and circle back to it after we address another issue happening with newspapers.

Because of my deep respect for journalists of all stripes, this is really hard for me to say, but: The lines have gotten way too blurry. What exactly do I mean by this? Let's start with this question: Why do Fox News viewers generally trust only Fox and nothing else?

Meet Mary. Mary is a life-long Republican, but she doesn't really have time to worry too much about politics. She works twelve hour shifts as a nurse, plus has three kids under ten.

In 2020, Mary was getting hit from all sides. Covid-19 was making her life hell at the hospital, and her friends and family, almost all Trump supporters, were in a constant frenzy over the upcoming election.

Because of all the craziness going on in the world, Mary decided she needed to pay a little more attention to the news. Out of an old habit, she tuned in to Fox.

She couldn't believe how bad things in America had gotten! Even though the election wasn't for another two months, Fox somehow already knew that the mail-in ballots were going to be fraudulent, and Joe Biden's son was some sort of spy for the Ukraine and China, and they had his laptop to prove it! Oh my!

But wait. Fox was also saying that the "China Virus" wasn't as bad as Democrats were claiming – it was really just like the flu – and that Democrats were hyping it up just to win the election – things she, as a nurse, knew not to be true.

After a few weeks, the false narratives about Covid started to make her question *all* of Fox's coverage, so she decided to change over to MSNBC for a while.

The Covid messaging on MSNBC was a lot better, she decided, but the negative Trump coverage was a little much. She thought: Does he not do *anything* that warrants a positive story? I heard something on the radio about some good things happening between Israel and countries in the Middle East, she thought. Why haven't I heard more about that here?

As someone who had already decided to vote for Donald Trump, this made her very uncomfortable. She switched back to Fox. MSNBC really is biased against Republicans, Mary tells her husband, and Trump…they really, really hate him. It's pretty clear MSNBC is "Team Blue," she said.

Mary also told him what she had witnessed on Joe Biden's inauguration day, when she was in a patient's room and MSNBC was on. Host Joy Reid gushed about the festivities: "They gave us fashion. They gave us celebrity. They gave us hope," her face glowing. Later, Rachel Maddow told her audience that she had used an entire box of Kleenex that day.

Right after the presidential race was officially called, Mary glanced up just in time to see CNN's Van Jones crying with relief and happiness over Joe Biden's win.

She had also heard something about *The New York Times*, under enormous pressure from its staff, taking down an article written by Republican Senator Tom Cotton – I mean, despite what you think of him, he is still a sitting United States Senator – and refusing to even publish an article written by one of the paper's very few conservative opinion columnists Bret Stephens. Yep, Mary said, just like I thought.

Roy Peter Clark – a senior scholar and vice president of the Poynter Institute for Media Studies, a nonprofit journalism school that owns the *Tampa Bay Times* and operates PolitiFact – wrote an article in response to the January 6th attack on the U.S. Capitol. Actually, he wrote an article about *another* article written in *The Washington Post* about the attack on the Capitol.

Of course, I quickly went to the referenced article and found the writing to be – as almost all *Washington Post* writing is – masterful. I also found most of the writing in the front-page piece perfectly appropriate: "With poles bearing blue Trump flags, the mob bashed through Capitol doors and windows, forcing their way past police officers unprepared for the onslaught. Lawmakers were evacuated shortly before an armed standoff at the House doors. The woman who was shot by a police officer was rushed to an ambulance, police said, and later died. Canisters of tear gas were fired across the rotunda's white marble floor, and on the steps outside the building, rioters flew Confederate flags."

No problem here, the journalists were simply reporting exactly what we all saw with our own eyes – nothing more, nothing less.

However, in other parts of the article, words used to describe the Capitol attack included "attempted coup," "saboteurs," and the phrase "much of it incited by the president's incendiary language."

Of *The Washington Post* article, Mr. Clark said, "I am astonished by the way the lead was written, and by an epiphany: Language that pushes the boundaries of traditional neutrality can be used in a responsible news report."

I could not disagree more with this statement. In all honesty, his words really scare me. It is absolutely imperative that news coverage be neutral, with the goal of nothing beyond presenting raw, vetted facts. The reader must then be trusted to make an independent, informed decision based on facts and facts alone. Please believe me when I say this is not a thread we should pull on.

The words/phrases "attempted coup," "saboteurs," and "much of it incited by the president's incendiary language" do not belong in a *Washington Post* front-page news story, at least not on the very day of the event when emotions are high, information is still being gathered, and investigations hadn't even started. They belong in its opinions and editorials section. Period.

< I have long believed that newspapers should make a better distinction between the news section and the opinion section on their websites. *The New York Times* has made a solid stab at this by

replacing the term "Op-Ed" with "Guest Essay" and clearly labeling it as such. >

In his article, Mr. Clark also references another author, Samuel Hayakawa, who wrote *Language in Thought and Action.*

In this seminal book, Hayakawa argues that reporters should avoid "loaded" language and always understand that it is not their job to declare something *good* or *bad.* Hayakawa warns that straightforward reporting is the only remedy for malicious propaganda which, around the time of his writing, had been widely disseminated by the Nazis.

He is so right. The only thing more dangerous than brazen lies told by a destructive leader is overcompensation – somehow convincing oneself that the actions of this person are so terrible that it gives everyone else permission to abandon their own moral principles.

Unfortunately, this very thing happened a lot throughout Donald Trump's presidency. Many journalists fell right into his trap, chasing every distraction he threw down and giving him the oxygen he so desperately craved.

Often, the media's calculation seemed to be that, since Donald Trump was such a danger to this country, they had the responsibility to fight back with anything and everything they had – even if it meant sacrificing a few basic journalism rules here and there. Hey, desperate times call for desperate measures, right?

<u>Wrong</u>. That's nothing more than misguided justification. Two wrongs <u>do</u> <u>not</u> make a right.

Listen, I get it. Journalists have one of the hardest jobs in the world, especially during a time when a sitting U.S. president was actively telling his followers to mentally and physically attack them.

Journalists are only human, after all, and each and every one has a deep love for his or her country. It would be ridiculous to believe that human beings can switch off their opinions and their world views every time their hands hit a keyboard or the camera lights come on.

This is the reason I could never be a journalist, as much as I would love to be. I would find it incredibly frustrating to not freely give my opinion whenever I wanted. And forget anyone trying to edit me! :) But that's why I'm not a journalist.

It's instructive to remember that Donald Trump's presidency came at a time when media was already going through an extremely difficult transition. The Internet has given anyone and everyone access to a public platform, which has cut deeply into traditional newsrooms.

Plus, let's face it, most straightforward new stories don't sell nearly as well as salacious ones. That's just a fact. Buy any reporter a shot or two of tequila and I bet anything most would admit that, while incredibly frustrating and utterly exhausting, the presidency of Donald J. Trump was on balance a huge windfall for them.

My fear is that these new realities create additional motivations for journalists. A decade ago, I would never know what my favorite newspaper reporter looked like. Even now, *The Economist* doesn't even include the name of the person who writes each article.

But today, I see news reporters and journalists everywhere, especially on cable news (and am I crazy or does it seem like many of them also have brand new gym memberships and stylists?!?). I buy and read their books which, more often than not, definitively reveal if they are Team Red or Team Blue.

Other Americans see this too. Republicans, for example, see that Chuck Todd – the host of *Meet the Press*, the longest-running television show in history and, until recently, one of the most trusted – also hosts a daily show on MSNBC...MSNBC which, in their minds, is solidly Team Blue. This, in turns, makes them distrustful of him and erodes his credibility as the host of *Meet the Press*.

This all feeds right into their already strong belief that the mainstream media is just a propaganda machine for the Democrats. And that, my friends, is why Fox News viewers generally trust only Fox and nothing else.

This is a problem. It's actually a major problem because Fox News and other conservative media outlets are themselves a major problem. In fact, with the exception of Donald Trump, I blame Fox News and other conservative media outlets more than anything else for the escalation of our national political division over the past five years.

One has to look no further than their reaction to the attack on the U.S. Capitol to know this is true. We've already covered the right-wing lies and misinformation about antifa, but that is just the tip of the iceberg. (Note: I fully address the events of January 6th, the days leading up to it, and its aftermath at the end of this chapter).

It comes as no surprise that the alt right media (à la *Newsmax* and *One America News*) stirred the pot before and after the Capitol riot. But Fox and its s#@+ stirrers – including but not limited to Sean Hannity, Tucker Carlson, Laura Ingraham, Maria Bartiromo, Lou Dobbs and Mark Levin – have some serious soul searching to do. What good are high ratings when you sell your country out? What exactly *is* the price for your soul?

What upsets me the most is the way these people just blatantly manipulate and mislead their audiences, who obviously trust them and rely on them for THE TRUTH. I honestly don't know how they sleep at night.

A perfect example is their duplicitous behavior on January 6th, when Fox hosts sent concerned text messages to Donald Trump's chief of staff Mark Meadows, then went on television and told their audience something completely different.

…and this didn't stop on January 6th. To this day, Fox hosts significantly downplay the events of that day, telling their viewers that it really wasn't that bad, or was caused by antifa, or, worse, that it was a "false flag" operation conceived and carried out by the United States government.

They say things like "many riots in American history < including the 2020 Black Lives Matter protests > were far worse than this" (Laura Ingraham), or "(the rioters) don't look like terrorists. They look like tourists" (Tucker Carlson).

On January 6th, as the violence at the Capitol escalated, Laura Ingraham texted to Trump's chief of staff: "Mark, the president needs to tell people in the Capitol to go home. This is hurting all of us. He is destroying his legacy."

However, hours later, she went on her show and told her viewers that true Trump supporters had virtually nothing to do with the mayhem: "From a chaotic Washington tonight, earlier today the Capitol was under siege by people who can only be described as antithetical to the MAGA movement," and perpetuated the "this is all antifa" b.s.

Sean Hannity also texted Mark Meadows: "Can he make a statement? Ask people to leave the Capitol." However, on his show later that evening, he tried hard to distract his audience with shiny objects: "Our election, frankly, was a train wreck." Then quickly followed up with an impressive pivot: "So how were officials not prepared? We got to answer that question. How did they allow the Capitol building to be breached in what seemed like less than a few minutes?"

But, as usual, the absolute worst offender was Tucker Carlson. To the three million people who buy into Tucker Swanson McNear Carlson's idiocy: I gotta tell ya, I am dumbfounded by the fact that anyone listens to a word this douche says. As long as I live, I will never understand this.

I could give so many examples but here are three particularly egregious ones. The first is his obvious love for anything authoritarian and autocratic. Recently, Tucker went to Hungary to interview Hungarian Prime Minister Viktor Orbán.

"If you care about Western civilization and democracy and families," Tucker said gravely to his viewers, "and the ferocious assault on all three of those things by the leaders of our global institutions, you should know what is happening here right now."

According to Tucker, Hungary is a "small country with a lot of lessons for the rest of us." Orbán, he gushed, "thinks families are more important than banks." "He believes countries need borders. For saying these things out loud, Orban has been vilified."

Well, that's not *exactly* what Orbán said. What he actually said were things like this: "We must defend Hungary as it is now. We must state that we do not want to be diverse. We do not want our own color, traditions and national culture to be mixed with those of others."

Okay, Tucker Swanson McNear Carlson, this nonsense needs to stop right now. Let's be honest about what is *really* going on here.

If you ever want to study a perfect example of how a traditional liberal democracy can backslide, look no further than Hungary and Viktor Orbán. < Note: the word "liberal" is not used here as it is often used to describe someone's political positions in U.S. politics. A *liberal democracy* refers to a representative democracy that protects individual liberty through established rule of law. On the other hand, an *illiberal democracy* places no (or very few) limits on the power of elected representatives. Orbán himself describes Hungary as an illiberal democracy. >

It's important to make crystal clear that Orbán is an authoritarian leader (one who favors strict obedience to authority over personal freedom) who champions autocracy (a government led by one person who has absolute power). For years, he has methodically shifted Hungary away from the traditions of liberal democracy by embracing far-right, nativist politics – effectively shutting down immigration; at once bribing and threatening the media; stacking the judiciary with close allies; and sabotaging free and fair elections through aggressive gerrymandering.

Naturally, Orbán wraps his populism in national sovereignty and antisemitic "Christian" identity while, at the same time, wages fierce culture wars against everything from multiculturalism to LGBTQ rights. He has worked to make the educational system in Hungary more "patriotic" – as defined by him – and spies on journalists and dissidents.

The scariest tool Orbán and his Fidesz party has used to centralize power for themselves is to place Hungary's three branches of government – the executive, legislative and judicial – firmly under Fidesz's control. Orbán calls this a "system of national co-operation," probably because it's less alarming than saying what it really is – a fully illiberal regime.

Freedom House – a U.S. government-funded nonprofit organization that conducts research and advocacy on democracy, political freedom, and human rights – put it this way:

> "Prime Minister Viktor Orbán's government in Hungary has dropped any pretense of respecting democratic institutions. After centralizing power, tilting the electoral playing field, taking over much of the media, and harassing critical civil society organizations since 2010, Orbán moved during 2019 to consolidate control over new areas of public life, including education and the arts.

> The 2020 adoption of an emergency law that allows the government to rule by decree indefinitely has further exposed the undemocratic character of Orbán's regime. Hungary's decline has been the most precipitous ever tracked in Nations in Transit; it was one of the three democratic frontrunners as of 2005, but in 2020 it became the first country to descend by two regime categories and leave the group of democracies entirely."

In 2018, Varieties of Democracy (V-Dem) also removed Hungary's status as a democracy (V-Dem measures democracy by assessing five high-level principles of democracy: electoral, liberal, participatory, deliberative, and egalitarian).

If you are wondering why Tucker slings this Hungarian propaganda to his three million viewers, V-Dem warns us of the terrifying truth:

> "V-Party's Illiberalism Index shows that the Republican party in the U.S. has retreated from upholding democratic norms in recent years. Its rhetoric is closer to authoritarian parties, such as the Justice and Development Party (AKP) in Turkey and Fidesz in Hungary. Conversely, the Democratic party has retained a commitment to longstanding democratic standards.
>
> The Republican party has not changed left-right placement but moved strongly in an illiberal direction. In this sense it is now more similar to autocratic ruling parties such as the Turkish AKP, and Fidesz in Hungary than to typical center-right governing parties in democracies such as the Conservatives in the UK or the Christian Democratic Union (CDU) in Germany.
>
> The data shows that the Republican Party in 2018 was far more illiberal than almost all other governing parties in democracies. Only very few governing parties in democracies in this millennium (15 percent) were considered more illiberal than the Republican Party in the U.S. Conversely, the Democratic Party was rated slightly less illiberal than the

typical party in democracies. The Republican party scores much higher than almost all parties in democracies on almost all of these indicators."

The second example of why I will never understand the reason anyone listens to Tucker Carlson is how he speaks about our military heroes.

First let me say, I have long been baffled by the way some conservatives allow people to talk about our military these days. What happened to conservatives being champions of our Armed Forces? What happened to conservatives being champions of law and order?

It was bad enough when many Republicans complicitly sat by and allowed a sitting United States president to call our military generals "dopes and babies," "suckers," and "losers." Now, it appears many are going to sit by and allow a man – who has probably never been in an Army Navy Surplus store much less contemplated wearing a military uniform – to trash the Chairman of our Joint Chiefs of Staff.

"He's not just a pig, he's stupid," Carlson said of four-star General Mark Milley – a combat veteran who has valiantly served the United States of America in five wars – when General Milley dared say that he studies a wide range of books and philosophies in order to "have some situational understanding about the country for which we are here to defend." …you know, when one of our four-star Generals dared to admit that he actually *studies* and *learns* things.

Well, needless to say, the cable television host who was once kicked off *Dancing With the Stars* in the first round was not impressed: "Hard to believe that man wears a uniform. He's just that unimpressive," Carlson said of this American military hero who has three degrees – from Princeton, Columbia and the Naval War College – plus these: two Defense Distinguished Service Medals, four Army Distinguished Service Medals, three Defense Superior Service Medals, three Legions of Merit, and four Bronze Stars.

This is despicable. What has happened here? At what point did this all go so horribly wrong?

But, circling back to our original topic of January 6th, the third – and by far most damaging – thing Tucker Swanson McNear Carlson has done is produce and air a "documentary" called *Patriot Purge*, which claims that January 6th was a "false flag" operation carried out by the U.S. government to target Trump supporters. The film's trailer bills it as "the true story behind 1/6" and "the War on Terror 2.0 and the plot against the people."

In Tucker's own words, "January 6 is being used as a pretext to strip millions of Americans – disfavored Americans – of their core constitutional rights." Then he said this: "The helicopters have left Afghanistan, and now they've landed here at home." Then this: "Our conclusion? The U.S. government has in fact launched a new war on terror. But it's not against al-Qaida, it's against American citizens." Oh, for the love of #@^%.

As a result of Carlson's propaganda, two longtime Fox News conservative contributors, Jonah Goldberg and Stephen Hayes, quit in protest, calling the film "totally outrageous" and saying that it "will lead to violence." Chris Wallace, the longtime Fox News anchor, resigned from the network after 18 years. Although he didn't specify the film as a specific reason for his exit, we do know that he raised significant concerns with the Fox News brass.

The very thought that an American – any American – would knowingly push these blatant lies is horrifying. But for a network who claims to traffic in "news" to allow it is reprehensible.

James Murdoch, the younger son of Fox Corp owner Rupert, said it best: "The damage is profound. The sacking of the Capitol is proof positive that what we thought was dangerous is indeed very much so. Those outlets that propagate lies to their audience have unleashed insidious and uncontrollable forces that will be with us for years." (James left his position as chief executive officer of 21st Century Fox in 2019)

And it goes on and on. A few weeks after the election, and before his death, Rush Limbaugh told his audience of over 15 million people listening on roughly 600 radio stations across the nation: "I actually think that we're trending toward secession. I am not advocating it, have not advocated it, never have advocated it, and probably wouldn't," but liberals use "force and intimidation and bullying tactics to get people who disagree with them to shut up."

A few weeks after that, Rush said that Joe Biden "didn't win this thing fair and square, and we are not going to be docile like we've been in the past and go away and wait till the next election." He continued, "Seventy-four-plus million Americans are not going to shut up, and you tell them that their views don't matter? You do not know what you're creating. You do not know the enemy you are manufacturing."

"It is time to fight," radio host Glenn Beck told his 10.5 million listeners two days before the attack. "It is time to rip and claw and rake. It is time to go to war, as the left went to war four years ago." Mark Levin told his equally large radio audience that stealing elections "is becoming the norm for the Democrat Party" and that they needed to "crush them, crush them. We need to kick their ass."

Broadcasting from Cincinnati two days before the attack, Bill Cunningham told his listeners that he would "never surrender and collapse and act as if it's OK when hundreds of thousands have voted illegally," while a day before the attack Dan Bongino told his audience that Democrats "rigged the rules to make sure that any potential outcome would go their way."

Still not convinced? Then just listen to what Peter Pomerantsev has to say. Peter was born in the Soviet Union then moved to London then moved back to Russia, where he became involved in Russian television production (he is now a professor at Johns Hopkins University).

In his production job in Russia, he saw first-hand how state propaganda is spread. Speaking to *The Washington Post* about Fox News and how the channel reminds him of Russia, he said, "It's the same game. It's the same rhetorical tactics, the same intellectual tactics, the same psychological tactics." Uh oh.

In an article that he himself wrote, Peter uses Sean Hannity as an example of Russian-style propaganda, which he calls the "dirtiest art form":

> "The typical Hannity monologue rises in a series of rhetorical questions until it topples over the edge of sense. On March 27, 2017, for example, a two-minute-long series of questions attacked rival network CBS's objectivity by asking whether its presenters ever questioned their criticism of George

W. Bush, whether they spiked stories which made Obama look bad, whether they had investigated Obama's ties to a former terrorist, his commitment to American-hating 'Black liberation theology' or recorded Obama's economic failings (here Hannity showed a list of stats on the screen, too briefly to read fully).

Had CBS, Hannity went on, listed all the laws Hillary Clinton violated when she used a private email server as Secretary of State? Exposed every one of her lies about the death of U.S. diplomats in Benghazi? Explored how media colluded with the Clinton campaign? Questioned how much time they had given to the 'conspiracy theory' that Trump's campaign colluded with Russia?

The effect of such a long list, where some of the charges are serious, others spurious, many debatable, and none explored, is to leave the mind exhausted and confused. The semantic patterns reinforce Hannity's main message: That we live in a world where there is no epistemological certainty anymore. For anyone familiar with Russian media this radical relativism is something very familiar."

One of the best examples of these mind games is the way conservative media weaponizes language to enflame its viewers (we already talked a little about this in the antifa section). This not only deepens the division in this country, but it also prevents us from having constructive conversations about really important issues.

I know it may feel like I'm picking on conservative media but, even though both sides do this to a certain degree, right-wingers are the only ones that have turned this tactic into a true artform. It would actually be impressive if it wasn't seriously damaging our country.

That they do this – on purpose – is not my opinion, it's a fact. I haven't cracked some secret code or anything…many conservatives openly admit that this is their strategy. For example, conservative writer and activist Christopher Rufo laid out (on Twitter, in detail) his and his buddies' plan for metastasizing the concept of critical race theory.

< Note: Encyclopedia Britannica defines critical race theory (CRT) as "an intellectual movement and loosely organized framework of legal analysis based on the premise that race is not a natural, biologically grounded feature of physically distinct subgroups of human beings but a socially constructed (culturally invented) category that is used to oppress and exploit people of color. Critical race theorists hold that the law and legal institutions in the United States are inherently racist insofar as they function to create and maintain social, economic, and political inequalities between Whites and non-Whites, especially African Americans." >

Here is Christopher Rufo's tweet:

> "We have successfully frozen their brand – 'critical race theory'– into the public conversation and are steadily driving up negative perceptions. We will eventually turn it toxic, as we put all of the various cultural insanities under that brand category.
>
> The goal is to have the public read something crazy in the newspaper and immediately think 'critical race theory.' We have decodified the term and will recodify it to annex the entire range of cultural constructions that are unpopular with Americans."

Really think about what he is publicly admitting in that tweet. He is essentially explaining to all of us that his grand plan is to weaponize the phrase "critical race theory" to the point that it becomes an all-encompassing catch phrase for *anything* having to do with race and culture that *he* doesn't like. This effectively makes the concept of CRT a giant blank screen that *anyone* can project *anything* they want onto, regardless of how untrue, inflammatory, or damaging it may be.

I've got to hand it to these guys, they have absolutely no problem saying the quiet part out loud.

To be clear: This is not me defending critical race theory (although I will give you my take on it in a few minutes). In fact, my argument here has nothing to do with the virtues or inadequacies of critical race theory at all. My point is that we cannot let a few rhetorical snipers at Fox News and other conservative media outlets – together with Republican lawmakers – highjack then pervert our national conversation about race, which is quite possibly the most important dialogue the current residents of this nation will ever have.

We are finally getting somewhere on this topic, America – which is probably why the snipers are freaking out. If we allow a few antagonists to disrupt our progress, we will forfeit the best chance we have had in decades to develop a sensible, productive path forward.

We have to act fast because this is happening in real time. Already – as a result of these guys using CRT as a grenade in their fabricated culture war – practically every racial complexity in this country, however innocuous, has been pulled into the vortex of the CRT tornado, creating a distorted narrative that is quickly spinning out of control.

So far, at least five Republican-led state legislatures have banned the teaching of "critical race theory" – as defined by them – in public schools, and many others are trying hard to do the same. In Tennessee, the legislature forbids teachers from suggesting that the rule of law is "a series of power relationships and struggles among racial or other groups."

In Idaho, the law cites critical race theory specifically, as does the law in Texas, which also explicitly mentions the *1619 Project*, a journalistic endeavor that was published in *The New York Times* in August 2019. According to the introduction to the initial article, the *1619 Project* "aims to reframe the country's history by placing the consequences of slavery and the contributions of Black Americans at the very center of our national narrative."

The Texas law also prohibits teaching that "slavery and racism are anything other than deviations from, betrayals of, or failures to live up to, the authentic founding principles of the United States."

The Florida Board of Education approved an amendment put forward by Governor Ron DeSantis that forbids any teaching that aims to "suppress or distort significant historical events, such as the Holocaust, slavery, the Civil War and Reconstruction, the civil rights movement and the contributions of women, African American and Hispanic people to our country."

…again, as defined by *them*:

> "Examples of theories that distort historical events and are inconsistent with State Board approved standards include the denial or minimization of the Holocaust, and the teaching of critical race theory, meaning the theory that racism is not merely the product of prejudice, but that racism is embedded in American society and its legal systems in order to uphold the supremacy of White persons.
>
> Instruction may not utilize material from the *1619 Project* and may not define American history as something other than the creation of a new nation based largely on universal principles stated in the Declaration of Independence. Instruction must include the U.S. Constitution, the Bill of Rights, and subsequent amendments."

With this as the backdrop, enter cable news. Sean Hannity kicked things off on Fox News: "Now, let's look at this critical race theory debate in the country. Now, this anti-American belief structure that is rooted in Marxism, it claims that White people are collectively all guilty of racism from birth just because they're White. Democrats want to teach this to every student in every school in America. They want them to learn this radical ideology from an early age."

Naturally, not to be outdone, Tucker Carlson, hot off of pushing his White nationalist conspiracy theory about "replacement" politics (i.e., the idea that Democrats are plotting to replace the (White) American electorate with "more obedient voters from the third world") told his audience, "In schools they are teaching this. Race hate."

He wasn't finished: "The question is, and this is the question that we should be meditating on day in and day out, is how do we get out of this vortex, this cycle, before it's too late? How do we save this country before we become Rwanda?"

Well, that escalated quickly. As a reminder, the genocide in Rwanda took the lives of hundreds of thousands of people who were part of the country's minority ethnic group.

This genius believes that critical race theory is "civilization-ending poison," and we will never know how rampant these teachings are across our schools until "we finally get cameras in the classroom…to oversee the people teaching your children, forming their minds."

Never one to be left out of the fun, Michael Savage over at *Newsmax* had this to say: "Now they're beating up White children in schoolrooms…Attacks on White people is exactly what was done to the Jews in Germany in the '30s. Don't fall for this garbage. This is the road to the death camps." Ahhh… playing the Nazi card. Of course. But really? "Death camps?" That's really where Michael Savage sees this going?

Senator Ted Cruz offered this: "Critical race theory is bigoted, it is a lie and it is every bit as racist as the Klansman in white sheets…critical race theory says America is fundamentally racist and irredeemably racist. Critical race theory seeks to turn us against each other."

Conservative writer Damon Linker wrote that those who oppose teaching CRT in schools "do not want their children taught in state-run and state-funded schools that the country was founded on an ideology of White supremacy in which every White child and family today is invariably complicit regardless of their personal views of their Black fellow citizens," then went on to twist himself into a pretzel trying to somehow link CRT to the Soviet Union.

One member of Utah's state school board suggested that phrases like *systemic racism*, *social justice*, *restorative justice, White Privilege*, *conscious/unconscious bias,* and even the word *diversity* are just "euphamisms" (ironically, she misspelled the word) for critical race theory.

Congressman Glenn Grothman (R-WI) – who, along with five other Republican congressmen, has introduced legislation to ban the teaching of critical race theory in Washington, D.C. public schools and charter schools – had this to say: "Students are being taught that they are defined by the color of their skin, not the content of their character. This neo-racist ideology should have no place in our public education system, especially in our nation's capital."

Others claim that the *Black Lives Matter* movement was organized solely on critical race theory and that every single violent act that took place during the protests against police brutality and racism in 2020 were fueled 100% by CRT.

Can you see what they are doing? This is Christopher Rufo's tweet playing out right before our very eyes. Let's illustrate this by using an example from your new favorite author…me!! The entirety of Part Two of this book series focuses on social justice issues (and, no, Utah school board lady who can't spell, I'm not using the term "social justice" as a euphemism for critical race theory). At one point in Part Two I say:

> Beginning in the 1930s, as part of President Franklin D. Roosevelt's *New Deal*, the Federal Housing Administration (FHA) created loan programs that lowered down payment requirements and extended the term of home loans from 5 to 30 years – all in an effort to make home ownership accessible to more Americans.
>
> To help banks determine who should get home loans, the government-run Home Owners' Loan Corporation established a system for appraising neighborhoods, now commonly referred to as "redlining." Essentially, the United States government created color-coded maps, assigning green for "good" neighborhoods and red for "bad" neighborhoods (literally drawing red lines around what they considered "bad" neighborhoods, hence the name).
>
> Black neighborhoods, pretty much across the board, were given both the color red and the worst grade (D), which classified them as "hazardous" places to underwrite mortgages because "colored infiltration is a definite adverse influence on neighborhood desirability." Naturally, without the ability for homeowners to obtain conventional financing, these neighborhoods significantly declined as businesses left, segregation and discrimination deepened, and predatory lending and slumlords thrived.
>
> In large cities, Black Americans were now confined almost exclusively to the "inner city" – where housing developments

were often the only housing option – and soon freeways bypassed them altogether. Although smaller in scale, Black Americans in rural areas fared no better as they were now relegated to the "wrong" side of town, or tracks as it were.

The very (very) few Black people who did obtain financing saw their property values plummet as White Americans refused to buy in what was now firmly considered "Black" neighborhoods.

I go on to say:

Redlining was devastating for Black Americans. Between 1934 and 1962, the federal government backed $120 billion of home loans. Over 98 percent of the loans went to White people.

This is a mind-blowing number, but this nefarious practice cut far deeper than Black people not getting to own a house ninety years ago. In truth, it was one of the very first bricks that built the impermeable wall that has prevented Black Americans from having the chance to fully participate in American capitalism.

You can clearly see this in the astonishing racial wealth gap that exists in this country today. The latest *Survey of Consumer Finances* released by the Federal Reserve revealed that the wealth of typical White households is eight times the wealth of typical Black households.

The median wealth (the number squarely in the middle of all the numbers) of White households is $188,200, compared to $24,100 for Black households. The mean wealth (the average) of White households is $983,400, compared to $142,500 for Black households.

And then I say this:

Redlining is a perfect example of how the staggering inequity that exists in this country – in everything from wealth

> to incomes to education to criminal justice – did not just miraculously happen.
>
> The uncomfortable, harsh truth is that the disparities that infect practically every one of our systems and institutions is a direct result of decades of irresponsible and, at times, downright racist public policy decisions.
>
> < Note: I'm pretty sure this is the spirit of what people mean when they use the term "systemic racism." I'm not a huge fan of this term because it fails to convey the multidimensional challenges of racism in this country. Inanimate entities – like systems – *reveal* racist cycles and *uncover* the consequences of racism, they don't *cause* it. Systems in and of themselves aren't the problem; the human-driven decisions made within those systems are. >
>
> As we search for solutions, we all need to understand that chronic inequality is not something that those trapped in its relentless grip can work – or even at times educate – themselves out of without a hand...and it is highly insulting to act like they can, or even should. In truth, the only way to close these persistent gaps is to enact policies that actively work to counteract the original ones.

This is not an example of critical race theory. Rather, it's simple, straight up cause and effect. If anyone in this country is naïve enough to believe that there are zero instances of Black people getting screwed by public policy over the years, they are out of their mind. From the jump, many decisions – made both intentionally and unintentionally – initiated and perpetuated pervasive, deep-rooted division and inequality. They just did. This is not my opinion. It's a well-documented fact.

Numbers don't lie. All we have to do is read the astonishingly unequal statistics scattered throughout these three books to know that these inequalities not only exist, but they are not healing on their own. (You can find 1787's solutions to this challenge in Chapter Four of this book and the entirety of Part Two of this book series.)

Please notice, did I insinuate, at any time, that "White people are collectively all guilty of racism from birth just because they're White"

(Sean Hannity)? Did I ever insinuate that "America is fundamentally racist and irredeemably racist" (Senator Ted Cruz)? Did I ever insinuate that "every White child and family today is invariably complicit" (Damon Linker)? Nope. Never. And I honestly don't feel that way.

But here is the problem: I guarantee you that the snipers will try their very best to bend my words to fit their "critical race theory" narrative. Many in their audiences, if they even take the time to read them, will pre-judge my words and approach them with phrases like "race hate," "death camps," "civilization-ending poison," and "anti-American belief structure that is rooted in Marxism" firmly burned into their brains. This is the trap that the snipers have set.

And consider this: The concept of critical race theory has been around for over four decades...which begs the question: Why now? Why, all of the sudden, is critical race theory being mentioned on Fox News a lot?

< *The Washington Post* reports that "the term 'critical race theory' was mentioned just 132 times on Fox News shows in 2020. In the first six months of 2021, CRT has been mentioned 1,860 times, according to a tally using the media monitoring service Critical Mention. After being mentioned just 51 times in February, it was mentioned 139 times in March and 314 times in April. It really blew up in May, when it was mentioned 589 times on the network's shows. In June, the topic was mentioned 737 times on Fox." On one Tuesday in June, "it was mentioned 48 times on shows across the network's lineup." >

Why now? Easy answer: At a time when randomly screaming Build That Wall, Stop the Steal, Lock Her Up, antifa, and China virus has become boring, the snipers need a new divisive, manipulative topic to fuel their culture war. Basically, they need a new boogeyman.

These are not harmless games being played. Unfortunately, the early evidence suggests that the snipers are getting exactly the results they wanted. Across America, school boards and concerned citizens are angrily and divisively debating critical race theory, along with other issues involving race and inclusivity that have gotten sucked into the CRT vortex, often with meetings erupting into shouting matches and even physical violence.

NBC News reported a story about an incident in Southlake, Texas, a predominately White suburb of Dallas, Texas that has stellar schools, an average household income of $230,000, and an average home price of $650,000. Two-thirds of the Southlake votes in the 2020 election were cast for Donald Trump.

In 2018, a video of "several White high school students laughing as they filmed themselves shouting the N-word at a party" went viral (because one of the geniuses in attendance posted it on Snapchat).

Sadly, this behavior came as no surprise to a nurse and mother of five Black woman named Robin Cornish. After all, "this was the city where, on the day after Rosa Parks died in 2005, elementary school children told her four oldest kids 'now you have to sit in the back of the bus.' It's where a sixth-grade boy once joked with her son: 'How do you get a Black out of a tree? You cut the rope.'"

"It's where, weeks after her husband (former offensive lineman for the Dallas Cowboys, Frank) died suddenly in 2008, a White boy on the football team told her son, 'Your mom is only voting for Obama because your dad is dead and she's going to need welfare.'"

What happened next was entirely predictable. When the video was first discovered, the school district facilitated listening sessions and – after two more instances, one being another racially charged video and the other involving spray-paint and racists slurs – established a diversity council to create a plan for greater inclusivity.

The diversity council's *Cultural Competence Action Plan* – a plan one member of the council described as "just a basic plan of human decency, empathy, kindness, inclusion and understanding about other cultures" – was released almost two years after the original video went viral. The plan required "diversity and inclusion training for all students as part of the K-12 curriculum, while amending the student code of conduct to specifically prohibit acts of discrimination, referred to in the document as 'microaggressions.'"

Well, as you can imagine, triggered White parents went nuts, with some "denouncing the diversity plan as 'Marxist' and 'leftist indoctrination' designed to 'fix a problem that doesn't exist.' The opponents said they, too, wanted all students to feel safe, but they argued that the district's plan would instead create 'diversity police' and amounted to 'reverse racism' against White children."

One father, who is White, said he was all for exposing kids to different cultures but believed this plan would "teach students 'how to be a victim' and force them to adopt 'a liberal ideology.'"

And, naturally, "several parents said the plan would infringe on their Christian values by teaching children about issues affecting gay and transgender classmates." Others "warned that the board had awoken Southlake's 'silent majority'" – which is always hilarious to hear from certain Trump Republicans because, regrettably, there is nothing silent about them.

Remember when Christopher Rufo came right out and told us that he and his buddies were going to "steadily drive up negative perceptions" and "annex the entire range of cultural constructions that are unpopular with Americans" until they "eventually turn it toxic?"

My fellow Americans, episodes like the one that happened at Southlake are heartbreaking. And completely unnecessary. Let's please, please, please not let them do this to us! We are better than this.

§§§

The hot button issue at the core of the critical race theory debate revolves around *how* racial and cultural issues are presented to students in our public schools. I'm sure you are *dying* to know my thoughts on this, so here is my take…

Although the state laws passed recently by conservative legislatures vary in language, most all of them have some sort of provision that resembles Tennessee's, where teachers are prohibited from teaching anything that may cause students to "feel discomfort, guilt, anguish or another form of psychological distress solely because of the individual's race or sex" or anything that can lead to "division between, or resentment of, a race, sex, religion, creed, nonviolent political affiliation, social class or class of people."

First of all, I find this hysterically hypocritical of Republicans – aren't they the very ones who say liberal schools are churning out a bunch of "snowflakes?" But beyond that, what does the language in the Tennessee bill even mean?

It is highly possible that the Holocaust may evoke very specific feelings of "anguish or another form of psychological distress" for Jewish students, but does that mean it shouldn't be taught in public schools? Should slavery not be taught simply because White students may "feel discomfort" by the fact that White people once did really, really horrible things to Black people?

The Holocaust and slavery are not revisionist history. They happened. Period. And there is absolutely no way that slavery – and the extremely difficult decades that followed for Black Americans – have no effect on some of our current day challenges. Republicans can pass all of the legislation they want, but they cannot change this fact.

It's also important to remember that, as W.E.B. DuBois' put it, changing "history into propaganda" cuts both ways. Just like Republicans don't want narratives like the *1619 Project* taught in schools, Democrats (and other people, like me) don't want the Trump administration's *1776 Report* – which is committed to the "restoration of American education," whatever that means – taught in schools.

On a personal level, as Republicans fight to keep certain racial themes *out* of schools, I am just as concerned about the racial propaganda that is already *in* schools – falsehoods like the *Lost Cause* ridiculousness, a narrative that tries to rewrite history and say that the Civil War had nothing to do with the enslavement of Black people at all; rather it was about the moral and just goals of gaining economic prosperity, "state's rights," and preserving the "Southern way of life." It's almost impossible to believe, but the *Lost Cause* is still included in some textbooks in the South.

< To those who try to defend the *Lost Cause* nonsense, you can just save it. There is zero doubt that the main reason the South fought the Civil War was to preserve slave labor. One has to look no further than Confederate Vice President Alexander Hamilton Stephen's *Cornerstone Speech*, given in 1861, for confirmation of this: "Our new government is founded upon the great truth that the Negro is not equal to the White

man; that slavery subordination to the superior race is his natural and normal condition." >

Is the truth about why the *Civil War* was fought disturbing? Of course it is! It's appalling. But it is, in fact, the truth! Just because we acknowledge that White people did something bad in the past in no way suggests that every White person alive today is racist and that every White person alive today should feel guilty about every transgression perpetrated by their ancestors. And guess what? No one is trying to "take away" Christmas either. Calm down, White people.

I'm also concerned that certain proven historical events are, for whatever reason, *still* being left *out* of public schools. I'm not talking about sweeping, maybe controversial racial narratives; I'm talking about proven historical events.

The fact that this remains a problem became clear to me when I recently watched the coverage of the 100-year anniversary of the Tulsa Massacre. Imagine my surprise to learn there *even was* a Tulsa Massacre and something known as "Black Wall Street" since – despite having gone to three private universities and having read a ton about social justice issues – I had never heard one single thing about either of them.

Regardless of where we individually come down on critical race theory, surely we can all agree that we can't just jump from slavery right to the *Civil Rights Act*, skipping over the painful but documented historical facts in between.

So, where do we go from here? Before anything else, it is imperative that we get religious and political agendas out of our public schools. Like, yesterday. I write about the religion side of this equation extensively in Part Two of this book series, but the political side of the equation is just as important.

Teachers are incredibly influential in children's lives. As such, just as kids should not know what faith their public-school teacher subscribes to, they should also not know what political party their teacher is associated with or, God forbid, who they voted for. A public-school teacher has no more business hanging a *Black Lives Matter* banner in his/her classroom than wearing a MAGA hat while at school.

Does that mean that *Black Lives Matter* and MAGA – or discussions about how things like redlining affected, and still affects, the Black community, or if reparations are a good or bad idea – should *never* be discussed in public schools, or used as student-chosen topics for research papers or projects? Of course not.

Kids aren't stupid. They live in the real world just like the rest of us and should be given a safe space to express themselves on their journey to becoming well-rounded, knowledgeable, and discerning citizens. After all, isn't that what school is for?

Over the past few months, as the critical race theory debate went from being simmering hot embers to fully enflamed, I have often thought back to the day I went to the *National Museum of African American History and Culture* in Washington, D.C. (a part of the Smithsonian Institution) with seven White, Black, and Hispanic 17 and 18-year-old girls.

This museum is stunning in every way. It is aesthetically beautiful, but that pales in comparison to the power of its message. The exhibits are no frills and just present the facts in a very straightforward, non-manipulative way. Early in our visit, I noticed that, although our group had stayed together in other museums, each of us had broken off from the others and chose to absorb this museum independent of one another.

Afterward, we went to lunch and shared our thoughts about the experience. The highly intelligent and elegant way these girls analyzed and expressed what they had learned about the past and how they feel it relates to the present and future was incredible. Their analysis and insight was as impressive as it was inspiring.

Our kids don't need us to explain the complicated and at times hypocritical nature of our Founding Fathers and other historical figures like President Abraham Lincoln; they can read the actual words of these men and evaluate their actions for themselves. Our kids don't need our running commentary on how the horrors of slavery relate, or don't relate, to the racial inequities that exist today; they can absorb the stories and interpret modern-day statistics with their own brains. Our kids don't need us to supply them with, as Justice Thurgood Marshall put it, a "sensitive understanding of the Constitution's inherent defects and its promising evolution." They can study the Constitution and decide for themselves how they feel about those things.

It is not a teacher's job to tell our kids what to think. The job of a teacher is to challenge students to think creatively and to use higher order thinking and critical analytical skills.

Likewise, it is not the place of the school board to tell our kids what to think. The job of the school board is to ensure that students have a curriculum that offers a combination of theoretical and practical learning opportunities to promote integrated knowledge, enhance communication skills, and encourage self-management and personal development. At the end of the day, we need to make sure our kids have the skills they need to go beyond the acquisition of knowledge to problem solving and application.

If we focus on successfully providing *these* tools for our kids – and present them proven historical facts in an untainted, honest and straightforward way – they will each possess the ability to deconstruct, interpret, and critique the unbiased information they are give – and be fully capable of connecting the dots all on their own.

§§§

We took miles and miles of detours in this section but, remember, it started as *The Media* section. So, a final word to my heroes, the reporters and journalists out there: There are many worthwhile paths you can travel in your career, from being a traditional news reporter to being an opinion writer or cable commentator.

But it's important you choose one over the other because the lines get too blurry otherwise. You have to choose because we obviously need you, badly.

Online Influence Operations

The Russia "Hoax"

"(Political partisanship) opens the door to foreign influence and corruption, which finds a facilitated access to the government itself through the channels of party passions. Thus, the policy and the will of one country are subjected to the policy and will of another."

– President George Washington, *Farewell Address* (1796) –

Our vulnerability to online manipulation doesn't stop at our border. America's foreign adversaries have been persistent in their sabotage efforts – proving that our political division is not just a domestic challenge but a national security issue as well.

Russian President Vladimir Putin, for example, didn't cause our national division but, as any good KGB agent would, he masterfully leveraged it and, ultimately, deepened it.

Election interference is part of Putin's asymmetric-warfare strategy (asymmetric-warfare is essentially a conflict between two countries that have significantly uneven military capabilities, like the United States versus Russia).

These hybrid warfare tactics are designed to significantly raise the risk and cost of retaliation and to keep potential adversaries guessing. This creates a kind of gray zone between war and peace, where things don't necessarily escalate into overt military conflict, but where adversaries know the threat exists nonetheless. (more on this in Chapter Four)

It's incredibly important we understand exactly how Russia interfered in our 2016 and 2020 elections so we can make absolutely certain we never let this happen again.

Regrettably, our quest to find the truth about Russia's 2016 interference was railroaded by partisan politics. Even though Russia's transgressions are undeniable, a disturbingly large part of America still thinks the whole thing was a "hoax" because Donald Trump and his parrots still insist that it was.

Somehow – most likely because his campaign was included in the Special Counsel investigation – the fact that Russia interfered in the 2016 election got all tangled up with whether or not Russia interfered *to help Donald Trump win.*

As a result, in what I can only guess is an attempt to defend his legitimacy, Donald Trump never challenged Putin and, in the end, enabled him to do even more damage (like the damage Putin caused by initiating the largest, most comprehensive cyber hack in American history, which we will also cover in Chapter Four).

To be clear: Acknowledging that Russia interfered in our 2016 presidential election in no way undermines Donald Trump's victory. He won, fair and square. Russia screwing with our elections and what candidate they were or were not trying to help are completely separate issues.

Personally, I could not care less who Russia's interference helped or didn't help. That is entirely beside the point. The only point is that Russia attacked us and should have been held accountable for it, immediately. It was critical in that moment for the president of the United States to acknowledge the very serious threat of a foreign power interfering in American democracy.

That didn't happen, to say the least. At a news conference during the 2018 Russia–United States summit in Helsinki, Finland – with Donald Trump and Vladimir Putin standing right beside one another – an American reporter asked Donald Trump if he believed his own intelligence agencies in regard to the 2016 election interference or did he believe Putin. Donald Trump replied, "President Putin says it's not Russia. I don't see any reason why it would be." Say whaaaaaatttt?????

This is bad. Even though the U.S. Congress passed Russian sanctions in response to the election interference and the Mueller investigation ensnared quite a few Russians, these actions at best make a one-day story on limited international media outlets.

Standing on a podium in another country with the head Russian, siding with him over our own U.S. intelligence agencies? That's a multi-day headline and a huge long-term blow to our national security apparatus.

The mere appearance that Russia got away with this puts the United States at significant risk. After all, what kind of message did that spectacle send to China, Iran, North Korea, and other potential cyber attackers? This matters because, believe me, they are all just watching and waiting for their chance.

Look, I'm not naïve. I understand the United States also does this kind of stuff. That's just the nature of the ongoing cyberconflict we are now confronted with. < read more about this in the Cybersecurity section >

But that certainly doesn't mean we should just sit back and let other nation states attack us with no consequence. I mean, whose side are you on, Donald?

All of this only empowered Putin, which was evident in the 2020 election. Two months before the big day, FBI Director Christopher Wray said at a House of Representatives Homeland Security Committee hearing that "the intelligence community consensus is that Russia continues to try to influence our elections."

Wray continued, "We certainly have seen very active efforts by the Russians to influence our elections in 2020." He went on to describe Russia's behavior as a "steady drumbeat of misinformation."

On August 7, 2020, Director of the National Counterintelligence and Security Center (NCSC) William Evanina warned that: "Ahead of the 2020 U.S. elections, foreign states will continue to use covert and overt influence measures in their attempts to sway U.S. voters' preferences and perspectives, shift U.S. policies, increase discord in the United States, and undermine the American people's confidence in our democratic process."

Specifically, he said that the NCSC "assesses that Russia is using a range of measures to primarily denigrate Biden and what it sees as an anti-Russia 'establishment.'"

He continued, "This is consistent with Moscow's public criticism of Biden when he was Vice President for his role in the Obama

Administration's policies on Ukraine and its support for the anti-Putin opposition inside Russia. For example, pro-Russia Ukrainian parliamentarian Andrii Derkach is spreading claims about corruption – including through publicizing leaked phone calls – to undermine former Vice President Biden's candidacy and the Democratic Party. Some Kremlin-linked actors are also seeking to boost President Trump's candidacy on social media and Russian television."

A month later, the U.S. Treasury Department actually sanctioned Andrii Derkach for running an "influence campaign" against Joe Biden. In their announcement, they labeled Derkach as "an active Russian agent for over a decade" who has maintained "close connections with the Russian Intelligence Services."

The announcement also revealed that Derkach "has directly or indirectly engaged in, sponsored, concealed, or otherwise been complicit in foreign interference in an attempt to undermine the upcoming 2020 U.S. presidential election. Today's designation of Derkach is focused on exposing Russian malign influence campaigns and protecting our upcoming elections from foreign interference. This action is a clear signal to Moscow and its proxies that this activity will not be tolerated."

Then Treasury Secretary Steven Mnuchin was quoted in the statement confirming that "Andrii Derkach and other Russian agents employ manipulation and deceit to attempt to influence elections in the United States and elsewhere around the world. The United States will continue to use all the tools at its disposal to counter these Russian disinformation campaigns and uphold the integrity of our election system."

Incidentally, Rudy Giuliani, Donald Trump's cracker jack personal attorney, met at least three times with Derkach in the months leading to the sanctions, and amplified Derkach's propaganda on his own podcast and other media outlets.

Now that the dust has settled, we now know – thanks to the United States intelligence community – that Russia did interfere in 2020 but on a much smaller scale. Among other things, Russia tried to undermine Joe Biden's candidacy by spreading unsubstantiated allegations about him and his son. < Note: Iran also tried to influence the election but, contrary to the Trump Administration's claims, China did not. >

Nevertheless, Director of National Intelligence Avril Haines made clear that "foreign malign influence is an enduring challenge facing our country. These efforts by U.S. adversaries seek to exacerbate divisions and undermine confidence in our democratic institutions."

Actually, Putin probably didn't feel he needed to be as involved this time, because enough Americans were essentially doing his job for him by spreading disinformation and being hateful all on their own. Plus, the Russians were too busy pulling off a massive cyber hack that started in the Spring of 2020. < read more about this in Chapter Four >

Make no mistake though, thanks to the lack of blowback they received for the 2016 and 2020 attacks, you can bet your bottom dollar the Russians will be back, gunning for our future elections.

As former Director of National Intelligence Dan Coats said after the 2016 election, "Russia perceives its past efforts as successful" and views future elections "as a potential target for Russian influence operations."

So, let's review what we know so there will be zero doubt that online influence operations are not a hoax:

There is zero doubt that Vladimir Putin significantly intervened in the 2016 and 2020 U.S. presidential elections, threatening our democratic institutions and one of our most sacred constitutional rights.

There is zero doubt that Vladimir Putin purposefully and meticulously perpetrated these malicious acts with the intention of harming our democracy and polarizing the American public by sowing seeds of discord among us.

On January 6, 2017, the U.S. intelligence agencies released a report called *Assessing Russian Activities and Intentions in Recent U.S. Elections*. The report included analytic assessments drafted by the Central Intelligence Agency (CIA), the Federal Bureau of Investigation (FBI) and the National Security Agency (NSA) regarding "the motivation and scope of Moscow's intentions regarding U.S. elections and Moscow's use of cyber tools and media campaigns to influence U.S. public opinion." Here are their key judgements:

- † Russian efforts to influence the 2016 U.S. presidential election represent the most recent expression of Moscow's longstanding desire to undermine the U.S.-led liberal democratic order, but these activities demonstrated a significant escalation in directness, level of activity, and scope of effort compared to previous operations.

- † Russian President Vladimir Putin ordered an influence campaign in 2016 aimed at the U.S. presidential election. Russia's goals were to undermine public faith in the U.S. democratic process, denigrate Secretary Clinton, and harm her electability and potential presidency. Putin and the Russian Government developed a clear preference for President-elect Trump.

- † Putin and the Russian government aspired to help President-elect Trump's election chances whenever possible by discrediting Secretary Clinton and publicly contrasting her unfavorably to him.

- † Moscow's influence campaign followed a Russian messaging strategy that blends covert intelligence operations – such as cyber activity – with overt efforts by Russian government agencies, state-funded media, third-party intermediaries, and paid social media users or "trolls."

A year later, then Director of National Intelligence – and, as such, the leader of the United States' 17 intelligence agencies – Dan Coats confirmed to the Senate Intelligence Committee that "the United States is under attack" and that Russia is attempting to "degrade our democratic values and weaken our alliances."

Director Coats also warned that the intelligence agencies "expect Russia to continue using propaganda, social media, false-flag personas, sympathetic spokespeople and other means of influence to try to exacerbate social and political fissures in the United States."

Months later, Coats continued to warn that "the warning lights are blinking red again. Today, the digital infrastructure that serves this country is literally under attack." Then National Security Adviser H.R. McMaster called the evidence of Russian interference in the 2016 presidential election "incontrovertible."

According to a 37-page federal indictment of thirteen Russian nationals issued by special counsel Robert S. Mueller III, these Russians stole Americans' identities, created fake drivers' licenses, bank accounts, and PayPal accounts in the names of fictitious Americans, faked social media accounts, created and distributed inflammatory digital ads and images, organized political rallies on U.S. soil, and even had two operatives on the ground in America. The pair traveled to at least nine states posing as tourists to gather information for their bosses back in Russia.

When the infamous Mueller Report was finally released to the public in April 2019, it made clear from the very beginning: "The Russian government interfered in the 2016 presidential election in sweeping and systematic fashion."

The report continued, "Russia's Internet Research Agency (IRA) < a Russian company engaged in online influence operations on behalf of Russian business and political interests > carried out the earliest Russian interference operations identified by the investigation, a social media campaign designed to provoke and amplify political and social discord in the United States. The Office determined that Russia's two principal interference operations in the 2016 U.S. presidential election – the social media campaign and the hacking-and-dumping operations – violated U.S. criminal law."

In July 2019, the Republican-controlled Senate Intelligence Committee released a report that revealed all fifty states were targeted by Russia in 2016. The report says that "the Russian government directed extensive activity, beginning in at least 2014 and carrying into at least 2017, against U.S. election infrastructure at the state and local level."

Although the Committee "has seen no evidence that any votes were changed or that any voting machines were manipulated...Russia may have been probing vulnerabilities in voting systems to exploit later."

In August 2020, the Senate Intelligence Committee released its final report (the fifth in a series) regarding 2016 Russian election interference. The report, which totals almost 1,000 pages and includes information from over a million documents and 200 interviews, confirms that "the Russian government engaged in an aggressive, multi-faceted effort to influence, or attempt to influence, the outcome of the 2016 presidential election."

The report continues, "Russian President Vladimir Putin ordered the Russian effort to hack computer networks and accounts affiliated with the Democratic Party and leak information damaging to Hillary Clinton and her campaign for president."

The report also confirms that Konstantin Kilimnik – a close business associate of Paul Manafort, Donald Trump's original campaign chairman – was indeed a Russian intelligence officer, and that Donald Trump's campaign accepted help from Russians who were trying to get him elected. To that end, the campaign provided Russians with polling data and coordinated the leak of stolen internal emails from the Democratic National Committee.

Two non-governmental studies clarify even further how exactly Russia exploited data provided by social media firms in 2016.

A study by the University of Oxford and Graphika – a company that analyzes complex online networks – explains the Russia's Internet Research Agency (IRA) attack this way:

> "IRA activities were designed to polarize the U.S. public and interfere in elections by: campaigning for African American voters to boycott elections or follow the wrong voting procedures in 2016, and more recently for Mexican American and Hispanic voters to distrust U.S. institutions; encouraging extreme right-wing voters to be more confrontational; and spreading sensationalist, conspiratorial, and other forms of junk political news and misinformation to voters across the political spectrum.
>
> The analysis found that between 2013 and 2018, the Russian Internet Research Agency's Facebook, Instagram, and Twitter campaigns reached tens of millions of users in the

United States; over 30 million users, between 2015 and 2017, shared the IRA's Facebook and Instagram posts with their friends and family, liking, reacting to, and commenting on them along the way; peaks in advertising and organic activity often correspond to important dates in the U.S. political calendar, crises, and international events; IRA activities focused on the U.S. began on Twitter in 2013 but quickly evolved into a multi-platform strategy involving Facebook, Instagram, and YouTube among other platforms; and the most far reaching IRA activity is in organic posting, not advertisements.

Surprisingly, these campaigns did not stop once Russia's IRA was caught interfering in the 2016 election. Engagement rates increased and covered a widening range of public policy issues, national security issues, and issues pertinent to younger voters.

The highest peak of IRA ad volume on Facebook is in April 2017 – the month of the Syrian missile strike, the use of the Mother of All Bombs on ISIS tunnels in eastern Afghanistan, and the release of the tax reform plan; IRA posts on Instagram and Facebook increased substantially after the election, with Instagram seeing the greatest increase in IRA activity; the IRA accounts actively engaged with disinformation and practices common to Russian 'trolling.'"

Indeed, Mueller's 37-page federal indictment mentions Facebook and Instagram 41 times. Facebook finally admitted that divisive, Russian-placed political content reached 146 million Americans on their platform alone.

The second study, from New Knowledge (now Yonder) – a company that specializes in information integrity – revealed in part the following:

"The most prolific IRA efforts on Facebook and Instagram specifically targeted Black American communities and appear to have been focused on developing Black audiences and

> recruiting Black Americans as assets; the IRA created an expansive cross-platform media mirage targeting the Black community, which shared and cross-promoted authentic Black media to create an immersive influence ecosystem; the IRA exploited the trust of their Page audiences to develop human assets, at least some of whom were not aware of the role they played…This tactic was substantially more pronounced on Black-targeted accounts; the degree of integration into authentic Black community media was not replicated in the otherwise right-leaning or otherwise left-leaning content."

Ноах? Я так не думаю
(that's *I don't think so*, in Russian)

WE'RE GOING MENTAL, LITERALLY

The *2019 World Happiness Report* – a publication from the Sustainable Development Solutions Network that uses data from the Gallup World Poll – actually had an entire chapter called *The Sad State of Happiness in the United States and the Role of Digital Media.* That title alone is enough to drop our state of happiness a few points.

> "The years since 2010 have not been good ones for happiness and well-being among Americans. Even as the United States economy improved after the end of the Great Recession in 2009, happiness among adults did not rebound to the higher levels of the 1990s, continuing a slow decline ongoing since at least 2000 in the General Social Survey.
>
> Happiness and life satisfaction among United States adolescents, which increased between 1991 and 2011, suddenly declined after 2012. Thus, by 2016-17, both adults and adolescents were reporting significantly less happiness than they had in the 2000s. In addition, numerous indicators of low psychological well-being such as depression, suicidal ideation, and self-harm increased sharply among adolescents since 2010, particularly among girls and young women.
>
> Depression and self-harm also increased over this time period among children and adolescents in the UK. Thus, those in iGen (born after 1995) are markedly lower in psychological well-being than Millennials (born 1980-1994) were at the same age.
>
> This decline in happiness and mental health seems paradoxical. By most accounts, Americans should be happier now than ever. The violent crime rate is low, as is the unemployment rate. Income per capita has steadily grown over the last few decades. This is the Easterlin paradox: As the

standard of living improves, so should happiness – but it has not."

Gallup's own latest annual update on the world's emotional state reenforces this. "Americans were more likely to be stressed and worried than much of the world. In fact, the 55 percent of Americans who experienced stress was one of the highest rates out of the 143 countries studied and it beat the global average (35 percent) by a full 20 percentage points. The U.S. even ties statistically with Greece, which has led the world on this measure every year since 2012."

Over 40 million adults in America (19.1 percent) have an anxiety disorder: "Even as the economy roared, more Americans were stressed, angry and worried last year than they have been at most points during the past decade. Asked about their feelings the previous day, the majority of Americans (55 percent) in 2018 said they had experienced stress during a lot of the day, nearly half (45 percent) said they felt worried a lot and more than one in five (22 percent) said they felt anger a lot. Each of these figures matches or tops previous highs in the U.S."

Researchers from the University of Nebraska reveal that "a large number of Americans believe their physical health has been harmed by their exposure to politics and even more report that politics has resulted in emotional costs and lost friendships."

The American Psychological Association's (APA) report *Stress in America 2020* discovered that "nearly 2 in 3 adults (65 percent) say the amount of uncertainty in our nation causes them stress. Further, 3 in 5 (60 percent) say the number of issues America faces currently is overwhelming to them."

The report continues, "More than 3 in 4 adults (77 percent) say the future of our nation is a significant source of stress, up significantly from 2019 when 66 percent of adults said the same. And more than 7 in 10 Americans (71 percent) say this is the lowest point in our nation's history that they can remember. In 2019, only 56 percent of Americans shared this sentiment."

Americans are obviously super stressed out, but way too many are also really, really sad. Too many Americans are silently suffering, strangled by depression and emotional trauma – without the support they so desperately need.

The APA also reports that, "61 percent of adults say they could have used more emotional support than they received over the prior twelve months, with more than 8 in 10 Gen Z adults saying the same."

It should come as no surprise that the chaos we all endured in 2020 blew out every single statistic in regard to mental health. Domestic violence charges, suicides, and drug overdoses soared, as did alcohol sales. There was a 1,000 percent increase in calls to the federal government's disaster distress hotline in April 2020 alone.

At the same time, many states had to reconfigure mental health care facilities – including psychiatric and detox/drug rehab facilities – to treat Covid cases, which only exacerbated the problem.

The University of Chicago found that "in the midst of the coronavirus outbreak, the public's happiness is at a five-decade low." The report went on to say that "42 percent of Americans believe that their children's standard of living when they are older will be better than their own standard of living – a sharp decline from 57 percent in 2018 and the lowest level of optimism for the next generation since first measured in 1994."

But even before lockdowns and quarantines, things in the mental health department were heading in the wrong direction.

The Henry J. Kaiser Family Foundation reports that, before Covid-19, "nearly one in five of U.S. adults (47 million) reported having a mental illness in the past year, and over 11 million had a serious mental illness, which frequently results in functional impairment and limits life activities. In 2017-2018, more than 17 million adults and an additional three million adolescents had a major depressive episode in the past year."

Also prior to the pandemic, the Pew Research Center found that "in 2017, 13 percent of U.S. teens ages 12 to 17 (or 3.2 million) said they had experienced at least one major depressive episode in the past year, up from 8 percent (or 2 million) in 2007. One-in-five teenage girls – or nearly 2.4 million – had experienced at least one major depressive episode."

Plus, a report from the National College Health Association found that over 65 percent of college students reported they had "felt overwhelming anxiety" within the past year. Over 70 percent reported to have "felt very sad." Over 45 percent said they had "felt so depressed that it was difficult to function."

According to a December 2021 report from the U.S. surgeon general Dr. Vivek H. Murthy, "Even before the Covid-19 pandemic, mental health challenges were the leading cause of disability and poor life outcomes in young people, with up to 1 in 5 children ages 3 to 17 in the U.S. with a reported mental, emotional, developmental, or behavioral disorder. In 2016, of the 7.7 million children with treatable mental health disorder, about half did not receive adequate treatment."

That's concerning enough, but the report also warns that "since the pandemic began, rates of psychological distress among young people, including symptoms of anxiety, depression, and other mental health disorders, have increased. In early 2021, emergency department visits in the United States for suspected suicide attempts were 51 percent higher for adolescent girls and 4 percent higher for adolescent boys compared to the same time period in early 2019."

Suicide rates were already at crisis level. After decreasing for almost two decades, the suicide rate among Americans aged 10 to 24 increased a whopping 56 percent in just ten years (2007 to 2017). It is still the second leading cause of death for people 10 to 34 years of age.

According to the U.S. Centers for Disease Control and Prevention, suicide is the 10th leading cause of death in the United States, claiming the lives of over 48,000 Americans in 2018. That's one death every 11 minutes. That same year, 10.7 million Americans seriously contemplated suicide but didn't go through with it, while 1.4 million actually attempted it.

It shouldn't be this way. Not in the United States of America. Looking back over this entire chapter, it feels like we've been on a collision course for a while now.

So, where does this all lead?

Democracy on the Line

It all leads here: Angry and disillusioned Americans crash through security barricades, climb scaffolding, and scale walls to breach the United States Capitol. A furious and frantic mob shatter windows, splinter doors, and carry Tasers, guns, baseball bats, tear gas, truncheons, zip-tie handcuffs, and American flags with sharpened poles.

Members of the United States Congress, duly elected by *We the People*, crouch behind benches and lock themselves in bathrooms, terrified for their lives. The vice president of the United States of America and his family hide in a closet while trying to coordinate some sort of rescue. Enraged men pull a journalist down a flight of stairs, past graffiti that screams "Murder the Media," then throws him over a ledge, screaming "We'll f---ing kill you."

Flags portray Donald Trump as Rambo and others have him astride a Tyrannosaurus rex, carrying a rocket-propelled grenade launcher. Flags honor QAnon, some with the favored abbreviation "WWG1WGA" (Where We Go One, We Go All).

Inflammatory flags reach as far as the eye can see. Confederate battle flags and American flags with stars replaced by the Roman numeral III, a symbol of the Three Percenters. Green-and-white flags of Kekistan, an alt-right fictional god of chaos and darkness. Flags with Nazi imagery and flags with the skull-like symbol of the Punisher. A yellow banner from the time of the American Revolution that has a rattlesnake along with the phrase *Don't Tread on Me*.

Nooses, crusader crosses, fur and horns, and Pepe the Frog masks illuminate the scene. Chants of *Stop the Steal* and *Trust the Plan*; patches that read Oath Keepers and Zombie Outbreak Response Team; Camp Auschwitz sweatshirts; and t-shirts that say MAGA Civil War, Jan. 6, 2021, RWDS (Right-Wing Death Squad), and 6MWE (Six Million Wasn't Enough), referring to the number of Jews murdered in the Holocaust, pretty much tell the story.

Five people dead, over 100 police officers injured, and four law enforcement officers who responded to the riot have died by suicide.

§§§

Guys, these are words that never in a million years would I have thought I would write, but there is no other way to say it: A sitting United States president actually tried to overthrow a democratically held, perfectly legal election.

Donald Trump tried to overthrow the election in the courts. He tried to overthrow it by sweet talking, shaming and threatening members of the Electoral College. He tried to overthrow it by harassing and bullying election officials, Department of Justice employees, members of Congress, state legislators and governors. And, in the big finale, he tried to overthrow it by inciting his loyal followers to stop the constitutionally mandated congressional electoral vote count.

One might even call Donald Trump and his enablers and supporters' actions a failed coup d'état (i.e., defined as a sudden, violent, and illegal seizure of power from a government).

You may think my likening the events surrounding January 6th to a coup is hyperbolic – and that I am being overly dramatic – but am I? Seriously, just stop and really think about this for a second.

"Seditious conspiracy," as defined by the U.S. criminal code is an effort by two or more people to "conspire to overthrow, put down, or to destroy by force the Government of the United States, or to levy war against them, or to oppose by force the authority thereof, or by force to prevent, hinder or delay the execution of any law of the United States, or by force to seize, take or possess any property of the United States contrary to the authority thereof."

That was exactly what these people were trying to do that day. Don't confuse what went down that day as "free speech." These people were actively trying to prevent our government from functioning, by preventing, hindering, and delaying the execution of a law of the United States.

As U.S. District Judge Timothy Kelly, who was appointed by Donald Trump, said of the Proud Boys: "No matter defendants' political motivations or any political message they wished to express, this alleged conduct is simply not protected by the First Amendment. Defendants are not, as they argue, charged with anything like burning flags, wearing black armbands, or participating in mere sit-ins or protests."

Regardless of how hard certain Republicans and conservative media outlets try to rewrite history, the attack on the United States Capitol on January 6th – and the events leading up to it – were seditious (i.e., conduct or speech inciting people to rebel against the authority of a state). As Americans, it is really hard for us to wrap our minds around this concept, but the assault on the Capitol was an insurrection (i.e., a violent uprising against an authority or government.) When you look at the evidence, listen to their words, and see the images, there is really no doubt about it.

In fact, we now know that the U.S. Department of Justice views January 6th as sedition as well. Almost a year to the day – January 13, 2022 – eleven members and/or associates of the Oath Keepers were charged with *seditious conspiracy*, including the group's founder and leader Stewart Rhodes.

The 725+ people charged with various crimes from that fateful day must take personal responsibility for their own actions (more on this in a minute). But many people present that day were nothing more than chess pieces in a game they didn't know they were playing. As District Judge Amit B. Mehta said to a man named John Lolos as he was sentencing him to jail for entering the Capitol that day, "I think you are a pawn. You are a pawn in a game that's played and directed by people who should know better."

As Mehta put it, "People like Mr. Lolos were told lies, falsehoods, told the election was stolen when it really wasn't."

Although the attack on the Capitol was obviously planned and groups like the Oath Keepers and Proud Boys coordinated in the weeks before the attack, there is no denying that Donald Trump was the driving force behind the entire disgusting episode, both before and on January 6th. The causation is clear: *But for* Donald J. Trump, the revolt on January 6th would not have happened.

If you really think about it, he had been grooming his army of insurrectionists for years. It started in earnest the minute he descended that escalator: The incendiary language, the constant undermining of the media and government institutions, the subtle racist undertones and the not-so-subtle nod to White supremacists – to the point where, after the domestic terrorist event in Charlottesville, former KKK leader David Duke gushed on Twitter: "Thank you President Trump for your honesty & courage to tell the truth about #Charlottesville & condemn the leftist terrorists in BLM/Antifa."

As a result, the treasonous events on January 6th couldn't come fast enough for the Proud Boys, Three Percenters, Oath Keepers, and other anti-government militias and far-right extremists, plus QAnon whackos and other violent conspiracy theorists who had been waiting for this "storm" for years. None of them could believe their luck! Finally, there was someone in power who validated their delusions.

Once forced to hide in the darkest corners of the Internet, Donald Trump gave these people permission. He gave them legitimacy. He gave them cover. He gave them orders: Stand back and stand by you very fine, very special people…we love you… "Big protest in D.C. on January 6th. Be there, will be wild!"

The morning of January 6th, Donald was on a roll: Remember, Joe Biden is being controlled by "people in dark shadows" so "we're going to have to fight much harder…You have to show strength, and you have to be strong…When you catch somebody in a fraud, you are allowed to go by very different rules…We will never give up. We will never concede. It doesn't happen. You don't concede when there's theft involved…Our country has had enough…We will not take it anymore, and that is what this is all about."

If we don't fight "you will have an illegitimate president. That is what you will have, and we can't let that happen. These are the facts that you won't hear from the fake news media. It's all part of the suppression effort. They don't want to talk about it; We fight like hell, and if you don't fight like hell, you're not going to have a country anymore." "It's just bullshit." "Bullshit! Bullshit!" repeated his adoring crowd. Then the chants turned to "Invade the Capitol."

The ex-president's inflammatory language that morning reflected the exact same themes his little army had been hearing from him for years. And they answered the call, some well before that fateful day.

An FBI situation report, released on January 5th, warned: "An online thread discussed specific calls for violence to include stating 'Be ready to fight. Congress needs to hear glass breaking, doors being kicked in, and blood from their BLM and antifa slave soldiers being spilled. Get violent. Stop calling this a march, or rally, or a protest. Go there ready for war. We get our President or we die. NOTHING else will achieve this goal.'"

The FBI also found social media posts directing people to the multiple rally points across the country: "MAGA Cavalry to Connect Patriot Caravans to Stop the Steal in D.C." There were maps of the U.S. Capitol building showing how the various tunnels were connected. The maps had the heading: "CREATE PERIMETER."

In the days after Donald Trump lost the presidential election, one of the leaders of the Oath Keepers, the now criminally charged Stewart Rhodes, said the group was ready for a "bloody fight." Another one of their leaders, Thomas Edward Caldwell, said, "This kettle is set to boil. It begins for real Jan 5 and 6 on Washington D.C. when we mobilize in the streets. Let them try to certify some crud on capitol hill with a million or more patriots in the streets."

A QAnon supporter tweeted: "It was a rigged election but they were busted. Sting of the Century! Justice is coming!" Naturally, Donald quickly retweeted the message.

On the day of the assault, inside the Senate chamber, one devout Trump follower said, "While we're here, we might as well set up a government." Another one reminded his fellow insurgents, "You are executing citizen's arrest. Arrest this assembly; we have probable cause for acts of treason, election fraud."

In May 2020, Couy Griffin, a county commissioner in New Mexico who also leads the group Cowboys for Trump, said on a video, "The only good Democrat is a dead Democrat." Naturally, Donald Trump wasted no time promoting the video adding, "Thank you Cowboys. See you in New Mexico!"

Later that month, Mr. Griffin told *The Daily Beast* that Democratic governors who shut down their states because of the coronavirus could be guilty of treason and could get the death penalty: "You get to pick your poison: You either go before a firing squad, or you get the end of the rope." When the reporter asked Mr. Griffin if violence may be necessary, he said, "I'll tell you what, partner, as far as I'm concerned, there's not an option that's not on the table."

Cut to January 7th, the day after the Capitol riot. Once again on video, Mr. Griffin said of Joe Biden's inauguration: "We could have a Second Amendment rally on those same steps that we had that rally yesterday. You know, and if we do, then it's going to be a sad day, because there's going to be blood running out of that building."

If you are not convinced that Donald Trump's words incited the riot at the U.S. Capitol – both before and on January 6th – just ask the very people whom he incited.

The leader of the Florida Oath Keepers, Kelly Meggs, made it clear he was answering Donald Trump's call when he posted on Facebook, "He called us all to Capitol and wants us to make it wild!!! Sir yes Sir!!! Gentlemen we are heading to DC." Kelly has since been charged with conspiracy.

QAnon loyalist Kenneth Grayson said, "I'm there for the greatest celebration of all time after Pence leads the Senate flip!! OR IM THERE IF TRUMP TELLS US TO STORM THE FUKIN CAPITAL IMA DO THAT THEN!" Kenneth has since been charged with 5 felonies.

A bodybuilder named Samuel Fisher who, for some odd reason also goes by the name Brad Holiday, posted that "at 1 when congress certifies the election…Trump just needs to fire the bat signal…deputize patriots…and then the pain comes." Samuel (a.k.a. Brad Holiday) is facing multiple charges for his role in the Capitol riot and was arrested with over 1,000 rounds of ammunition, a tactical vest plus another vest with ballistic plates and a knife, two machetes, a shotgun, and, of course, a copy of the Daily News with Donald Trump's face on the cover and an American flag.

Oath Keeper Jessica Watkins sent messages in advance of the 6th that said, "Trump wants all able bodied patriots to come" and "if Trump activates the *Insurrection Act*, I'd hate to miss it." The day of the assault, Jessica – dressed, as the rest of her group was, in tactical gear including bulletproof vests and helmets – posted a message that said, "Trump's been trying to drain the swamp with a straw. We just brought a shop vac."

Incidentally, this is also the gal that said, "If (Biden) is (sworn in), our way of life as we know it is over. Our Republic would be over. Then it is our duty as Americans to fight, kill and die for our rights…If Biden get the steal, none of us have a chance in my mind. We already have our neck in the noose. They just haven't kicked the chair yet."

Two other ladies (I use that term loosely all the way around) in red MAGA hats, Dawn Bancroft and Diana Santos-Smith, recorded a video for Bancroft's children (these poor kids) documenting their big day which was later confiscated by the FBI: "We broke into the Capitol…We got inside, we did our part."

But Bancroft, who is obviously not the brightest bulb in the chandelier, wasn't finished. "We were looking for Nancy to shoot her in the friggin' brain, but we didn't find her." Thereby threatening to kill the fourth highest ranking person in the United States government. On tape.

In other parts of the Capitol that day, insurrectionists can be heard on camera yelling at law enforcement, things like: "Our president wants us here; Stand down. You're outnumbered. There's a f---ing million of us out there, and we are listening to Trump – your boss; We wait and take orders from our president; We were invited here by the president of the United States…"

Interestingly enough, many of these Trump loyalists were pretty quick to throw him right under the bus once they got arrested. For instance, Jessica Watkins' attorney wasted no time in saying that Jessica was there that day "not to overthrow the government, but to support what she believed to be the lawful government. She fell prey to the false and inflammatory claims of the former president, his supporters, and the right-wing media."

Dominic Pezzola, a once proud Proud Boy, said that, despite all appearances, he had "honorable intentions" that day and was only "protecting his country." However, he "now realizes he was duped into these mistaken beliefs" and "is consumed with guilt."

There are plenty of other people who are complicit in this attempted hostile takeover, including the eight Republican senators and 139 Republican members of the House of Representatives who voted on at least one of the objections made during the Electoral College vote count.

...as are Donald Trump's adult children, his laughable attorneys, his increasingly small staff, and anyone else who amplified his election fraud lies – particularly, as I mentioned earlier, conservative media outlets.

< As I write this, I still can't believe any American would jeopardize our country in this way. All of this feels almost like an out-of-body experience. It makes me physically nauseous...and really, really sad. >

I have spoken to, and listened to, hard core Trump supporters throughout this ugly debacle. To me, the scariest and most destructive part of the entire thing is this: I'm pretty certain many of them actually believe what I'm saying to be true. They just don't care.

We have reached a point in our fractured politics where they feel completely justified doing anything it takes to keep the Democrats and their "Socialist" agenda out of power. They truly believe, on authority from God above, that they and they alone have the power to choose the president of the United States. Constitution be damned.

The implications of this reality are breathtaking. In Russia, Hungary, Poland, Turkey and the Philippines, populist leaders, much like their buddy Donald Trump, have made lying and corruption an artform. Because these countries don't have strong, independent legal systems and autonomous news media outlets, the lies of these leaders know no bounds.

Luckily, we do have these things, and more. The United States of America was protected from this assault on our democracy by honorable judges, heroic election officials, steadfast state legislatures, and the brave American citizens who stayed true to the constitutionally mandated Electoral College process. *God Bless Them All.*

But still, all of this feels way too close for comfort. In their outstanding book *How Democracies Die*, Steven Levitsky and Daniel Ziblatt, both Harvard professors, warn:

> "During the Cold War, coup d'état accounted for nearly three out of every four democratic breakdowns.

Democracies in Argentina, Brazil, the Dominican Republic, Ghana, Greece, Guatemala, Nigeria, Pakistan, Peru, Thailand, Turkey, and Uruguay all died this way. More recently, military coups toppled Egyptian President Mohamed Morsi in 2013 and Thai Prime Minister Yingluck Shinawatra in 2014. In all these cases, democracy dissolved in spectacular fashion, through military power and coercion.

But there is another way to break a democracy. It is less dramatic but equally destructive. Democracies may die at the hands not of generals but of elected leaders – presidents or prime ministers who subvert the very process that brought them to power. Some of these leaders dismantle democracy quickly, as Hitler did in the wake of the 1933 Reichstag fire in Germany. More often, though, democracies erode slowly, in barely visible steps."

On February 1, 2021, Myanmar's military, known as the Tatmadaw, declared a state of emergency and took control of the country – in what amounted to a military coup.

The Myanmar (Burma) military detained the head of state Aung San Suu Kyi and other leaders of the National League for Democracy, who had been reelected by a landslide in November 2020, in only the second democratically held election since the country moved to a democracy from almost fifty years of military rule.

The military announced that power would be transferred to the commander in chief, Min Aung Hlaing, then handed to Myint Swe, the military-backed vice president. The violence is escalating. In late March 2021, security forces killed over 100, including seven children.

What reason did the Myanmar military give for this coup d'état? Well, election fraud, of course! The fact that the country's election commission continues to insist there was no evidence to support this claim doesn't seem to matter a damn bit.

Meanwhile, before the Taliban takeover, there had been four democratically held presidential elections in Afghanistan in the two decades since the United States arrived on the scene. Three of them were disputed.

On March 9, 2020, Ashraf Ghani and Abdullah Abdullah both took the oath of office as the rightful president of Afghanistan – at the exact same time. The incumbent, Ashraf Ghani, was declared the rightful winner of the election, but Abdullah insisted that the election was…wait for it…stolen. Incredibly, the media dutifully did the split screen thing as both men simultaneously gave their acceptance speeches.

As this was taking place, rockets rained down over the presidential palace in Kabul. I can practically hear Abdullah's people shouting…

أوقف السرقة
(this means "Stop the Steal" in Arabic)

Really, America? We're in the exact same place in our democracy as Myanmar is? And Afghanistan? …which, as a reminder, was just taken over by terrorists. Really? This is what we're gonna do now?

I am not overreacting. Who among us cannot visualize Donald Trump staging the split screen acceptance speech deal? In fact, he's probably down at Mar-a-Lago kicking himself for not trying it.

If you are *still* not convinced Donald Trump's words incited the riot at the U.S. Capitol – both before and on January 6th – just ask leaders from around the world, many of whom know a thing or two about rebellions (shout out to *Axios* for compiling these):

† European Union foreign policy chief Josep Borrell Fontelles: "In the eyes of the world, American democracy tonight appears under siege. This is an unseen assault on U.S. democracy, its institutions and the rule of law. This is not America. The election results of 3 November must be fully respected."

† German Foreign Minister Heiko Maas, translated: [The enemies of democracy will find out about these incredible images #WashingtonDC looking forward. Insurgent words turn into violent acts – on the steps of the Reichstag, and now in the #Capitol. The disdain for democratic institutions is devastating.]

- † German Chancellor Angela Merkel: "These images made me furious and also sad, and I'm quite sure I feel like most friends of the United States, like millions of people who admire America's democratic tradition. And I regret very much that President Trump since November has not conceded his defeat, and not yesterday either."

- † French President Emmanuel Macron: "When, in one of the world's oldest democracies, supporters of an outgoing president take up arms to challenge the legitimate results of an election, that one idea – that of 'one person, one vote' – is undermined."

- † United Kingdom Prime Minister Boris Johnson: "Disgraceful scenes in U.S. Congress. The United States stands for democracy around the world and it is now vital that there should be a peaceful and orderly transfer of power."

- † Canadian Prime Minister Justin Trudeau: "Canadians are deeply disturbed and saddened by the attack on democracy in the United States, our closest ally and neighbor. Violence will never succeed in overruling the will of the people. Democracy in the US must be upheld – and it will be."

- † NATO Secretary-General Jens Stoltenberg: "Shocking scenes in Washington, D.C. The outcome of this democratic election must be respected."

- † Indian Prime Minister Narendra Modi: "Distressed to see news about rioting and violence in Washington DC. Orderly and peaceful transfer of power must continue. The democratic process cannot be allowed to be subverted through unlawful protests."

- † Ukrainian Foreign Minister Dmytro Kuleba: "Concerning scenes in Washington, D.C. I'm confident American democracy will overcome this challenge. The rule of law & democratic procedures need to be restored as soon as possible. This is important not only for the U.S., but for Ukraine and the entire democratic world as well."

† Dutch Prime Minister Mark Rutte: "Horrible images from Washington D.C. Dear [Donald Trump], recognize [Joe Biden] as the next president today."

† Italian Prime Minister Giuseppe Conte: "I am following what is happening in #Washington with great concern. Violence is incompatible with the exercise of democratic rights and freedoms. I am confident in the strength and robustness of the institutions of the United States."

† First Minister of Scotland Nicola Sturgeon: "The scenes from the Capitol are utterly horrifying. Solidarity with those in [the United States] on the side of democracy and the peaceful and constitutional transfer of power. Shame on those who have incited this attack on democracy."

† Norwegian Prime Minister Erna Solberg: "Unbelievable scenes from Washington D.C. This is a totally unacceptable attack on democracy. A heavy responsibility now rests on President Trump to put a stop to this."

This is so embarrassing. But even worse were the delighted reactions from people who don't want us to succeed in the first place. For example, Jürgen Elsässer, the editor of a German far-right magazine, gleefully said, "We were following it like a soccer match."

A Russian foreign ministry spokesman said, "The events in Washington show that the U.S. electoral process is archaic, does not meet modern standards, and is prone to violations," while the president of Zimbabwe said the riot "showed that the U.S. has no moral right to punish another nation under the guise of upholding democracy."

The annual report from Freedom House – a U.S. government-funded nonprofit non-governmental organization that conducts research and advocacy on democracy, political freedom and human rights –

called *Freedom in the World* evaluates the state of freedom in 210 countries and territories. Each country/territory is assigned between 0 and 4 points on a series of 25 indicators, for an aggregate score of up to 100.

In 2018, the theme of the report was *Democracy in Crisis*, and it said, "Political rights and civil liberties around the world deteriorated to their lowest point in more than a decade in 2017, extending a period characterized by emboldened autocrats, beleaguered democracies, and the United States' withdrawal from its leadership role in the global struggle for human freedom."

The report continues, "A long list of troubling developments around the world contributed to the global decline in 2017, but perhaps most striking was the accelerating withdrawal of the United States from its historical commitment to promoting and supporting democracy."

We received a score of 86 out of 100, which was well below France, Germany and the United Kingdom. This represented an 8-point drop since our score of 94 in 2009. In 2019, the theme of the report was *Democracy in Retreat*, and it said,

> "The great challenges facing U.S. democracy did not commence with the inauguration of President Donald Trump. Intensifying political polarization, declining economic mobility, the outsized influence of special interests, and the diminished influence of fact-based reporting in favor of bellicose partisan media were all problems afflicting the health of American democracy well before 2017.
>
> Previous presidents have contributed to the pressure on our system by infringing on the rights of American citizens. Surveillance programs such as the bulk collection of communications metadata, initially undertaken by the George W. Bush administration, and the Obama administration's overzealous crackdown on press leaks are two cases in point.
>
> At the midpoint of his term, however, there remains little question that President Trump exerts an influence on American politics that is straining our core values and testing the stability of our constitutional system. No president in living memory

has shown less respect for its tenets, norms, and principles. Trump has assailed essential institutions and traditions including the separation of powers, a free press, an independent judiciary, the impartial delivery of justice, safeguards against corruption, and most disturbingly, the legitimacy of elections. Congress, a coequal branch of government, has too frequently failed to push back against these attacks with meaningful oversight and other defenses."

Yet again we received a score of 86. The 2020 report, called *A Leaderless Struggle for Democracy*, may have been the most depressing of all. We again received a score of 86, which was below Italy, Greece, Slovakia, Latvia and Mauritius (a country in East Africa). This one says:

"Democracy and pluralism are under assault. Dictators are toiling to stamp out the last vestiges of domestic dissent and spread their harmful influence to new corners of the world. At the same time, many freely elected leaders are dramatically narrowing their concerns to a blinkered interpretation of the national interest. In fact, such leaders – including the chief executives of the United States and India, the world's two largest democracies – are increasingly willing to break down institutional safeguards and disregard the rights of critics and minorities as they pursue their populist agendas. As a result of these and other trends, Freedom House found that 2019 was the 14th consecutive year of decline in global freedom.

Those in the United States and elsewhere who doubt the value of a foreign policy designed to advance human freedom should realize that no one's rights are safe when tyranny is allowed to go unchecked. History has shown that the chaotic effects of authoritarian misrule abroad are not confined by national borders, and that authoritarian powers will seek to expand their control by subverting the democratic sovereignty of other states. The same is true in domestic affairs: attacks on the rights of specific groups or individuals in a given country ultimately imperil the liberty of the entire society."

In the 2021 report, *Democracy Under Siege*, we finally broke our three-year-in-a-row score of 86, but unfortunately not in the right direction. This year, we received a score of 83. I take back what I said earlier. This is by far the most depressing assessment yet:

> "The final weeks of the Trump presidency featured unprecedented attacks on one of the world's most visible and influential democracies. After four years of condoning and indeed pardoning official malfeasance, ducking accountability for his own transgressions, and encouraging racist and right-wing extremists, the outgoing president openly strove to illegally overturn his loss at the polls, culminating in his incitement of an armed mob to disrupt Congress's certification of the results. Trump's actions went unchecked by most lawmakers from his own party, with a stunning silence that undermined basic democratic tenets.
>
> Only a serious and sustained reform effort can repair the damage done during the Trump era to the perception and reality of basic rights and freedoms in the United States. The year leading up to the assault on the Capitol was fraught with other episodes that threw the country into the global spotlight in a new way. The politically distorted health recommendations, partisan infighting, shockingly high and racially disparate coronavirus death rates, and police violence against protesters advocating for racial justice over the summer all underscored the United States' systemic dysfunctions and made American democracy appear fundamentally unstable.
>
> Even before 2020, Trump had presided over an accelerating decline in U.S. freedom scores, driven in part by corruption and conflicts of interest in the administration, resistance to transparency efforts, and harsh and haphazard policies on immigration and asylum that made the country an outlier among its Group of Seven peers.

But President Trump's attempt to overturn the will of the American voters was arguably the most destructive act of his time in office. His drumbeat of claims – without evidence – that the electoral system was ridden by fraud sowed doubt among a significant portion of the population, despite what election security officials eventually praised as the most secure vote in US history. Nationally elected officials from his party backed these claims, striking at the foundations of democracy and threatening the orderly transfer of power.

The exposure of U.S. democracy's vulnerabilities has grave implications for the cause of global freedom. Rulers and propagandists in authoritarian states have always pointed to America's domestic flaws to deflect attention from their own abuses, but the events of the past year will give them ample new fodder for this tactic, and the evidence they cite will remain in the world's collective memory for a long time to come."

There is also this thing called the *Social Progress Index*, released annually by the Social Progress Imperative, a global nonprofit that provides data on the social and environmental health of societies. The Index assesses 50 metrics of well-being from 163 countries across the globe, everything from nutrition and basic medical care to personal freedom and choice.

We currently rank 28th…behind the Czech Republic. In fact, the United States is only one of three countries that is worse off than when the index began in 2011. We share that honor with Brazil and Hungary. We are ranked 91st in access to quality basic education and 97th in access to quality health care.

These reports really, really irritate me. Now, you might ask why *these* particular reports aggravate me so much. I'm not 100% sure, but I think the answer is that they put an actual score on our present circumstances. I am a highly competitive person and I'll be damned if my spectacular country is going to get a score of 83 and be ranked 28th in *anything*. It's just not going to happen.

…which means we have some serious work to do. And we'll do it. In the wise words of Abraham Lincoln:

"We know how to save the Union. The world knows we do know how to save it. We, even we here, hold the power and bear the responsibility...We shall nobly save or meanly lose the last best hope of earth...The way is plain, peaceful, generous, just – a way which if followed the world will forever applaud and God must forever bless."

Chapter Four

For Policy Geeks Like Me

Seismic Shifts

Clearly, there are many challenges we have to address, and most all of them – along with possible solutions – are covered in these books.

As you read the solutions, some things will seem like really big shifts away from what we are currently doing, while others will seem more like minor modifications.

Without question, the really big shifts can feel overwhelming, if not impossible, to achieve. But I believe there is a secret to pulling them off: We will be more successful if we do some of the really big shifts in coordination with one another, because the aggressive actions we need to take to shift one of the big challenges can sometimes soften the negative consequences that are caused by shifting the other.

Okay, that sounds like a lot, so let's walk through an example. Take two of our most looming policy issues: Our national defense strategy and our energy policy.

Whether we like it or not – and regardless of what our personal opinions are on these two issues – major shifts in both areas are coming. Unfortunately, the difficult changes we need to make in our national defense and energy strategies have the potential to have a negative effect on many American lives and livelihoods.

Politicians are often dishonest about this inevitability – and most are masters at postponing the unpleasant – but, given the way both the basic facts and the world are evolving, these two shifts are going to happen sooner rather than later. It's just the way it is.

The great news is that, if we are proactive, we can make the landing as soft as possible for those who may face hardships because of these changes. Believe me, it is far better to endure a little pain now – while we still have control over how to absorb it – than to live in denial until the music just stops and there aren't enough chairs.

Up first, our national defense strategy. The United States of America should never be forced to forgo the critical military capabilities that we need to protect ourselves. America must have a cutting-edge military that has the fortitude to fully protect this country, regardless of where the threat comes from or in what form it comes in. And, the United States should never be in a position where we are forced to pick and choose between the most dangerous regions of the world.

– the 1787 Recommendations for
National Security are in *The Policy Guide* –

Given China's rise and the importance of nurturing relationships with other Asian countries, ensuring stability in the Asia-Pacific region is increasingly critical to our economic and national security. At the same time, it's dangerous to fixate solely on that region of the world, particularly when the Middle East – and now, thanks to Vladimir Putin's highly illegal and decidedly destructive invasion of Ukraine, Eastern Europe – remain so unstable (more on these in the *Foreign Policy* section of this book).

The bottom line is that we must be able to sustain security simultaneously in Russia, Africa, South and East Asia, the Middle East, and Europe – and have everything we need to operate successfully in the traditional theatres of land, sea, air, cyberspace and outer space.

Because of the sheer scope of these operational and geographical realities, our national security must be forward-thinking, innovative, and dare I say, crafty.

War has evolved, big time. This means we must evolve as well – and do what five-star Army general and former president of the United States Dwight D. Eisenhower once advised: "Learn how to compose differences not with arms, but with intellect and decent purpose."

This is not to say that diplomacy can solve everything. It clearly cannot. But the "intellect" part of President Eisenhower's advice is convicting. The harsh truth is that throwing a bunch of money at a million different things to see what sticks – as we have done since the 9/11 terrorist attacks – is not going to cut it anymore.

Neither is relying on the threat of a ridiculously gigantic arsenal of big, scary bombs. The "my bomb is bigger than your bomb" strategy we have depended on for decades now seems lazy and terribly inadequate.

Russia and China figured this out years ago. Sure, they still rely on the bomb thing to a certain degree. Even though the entire world now knows that the Russian military is completely inept (more on this later), they announced in December 2019 that they had deployed Avangard, a new hypersonic weapon that flies at lightning-fast speeds, allowing it to evade American missile defense systems. They are also working on stealth submarines and torpedoes. And, as we all well know, since the day his troops illegally entered Ukraine, Putin has made sure nuclear war is never far from our minds.

China now has the wealth necessary to heavily upgrade its military and make a move for East Asia. China's DF-21D anti-ship ballistic missile is a game changer, as is their intermediate-range missile called the DF-26 that threatens our naval forces and bases in the Pacific.

Already, China and Russia both have weapons that jeopardize our assets in space, through everything from cyberattacks to radio jamming to destroying them altogether.

The 2019 *Worldwide Threat Assessment of the U.S. Intelligence Community* said our intelligence agencies expect:

> "Foreign governments will continue efforts to expand their use of space-based reconnaissance, communications, and navigation systems – including by increasing the number of satellites, quality of capabilities, and applications for use. China and Russia are seeking to expand the full spectrum of

their space capabilities, as exemplified by China's launch of its highest-resolution imagery satellite, Gaofen-11, in July 2018."

Plus, "China and Russia are training and equipping their military space forces and fielding new anti-satellite (ASAT) weapons to hold U.S. and allied space services at risk, even as they push for international agreements on the non-weaponization of space. Both countries recognize the world's growing reliance on space and view the capability to attack space services as a part of their broader efforts to deter an adversary from or defeat one in combat."

– the 1787 recommendations for
Space and Counterspace are in *The Policy Guide* –

These advancements by China and Russia are all the more frustrating because we did a lot of the heavy lifting for them by developing superior military technologies (like long-range precision-strike, electromagnetic-spectrum warfare, and hypersonic warfare) – and then just letting them copy us.

But beyond all of that, the most significant advancements China and Russia have made have little to do with space or military hardware at all. While we were busy fighting wars in the Middle East, China and Russia were busy closely examining our weak spots and developing new tactics to exploit our vulnerabilities.

Yes, by far, the most impressive part of their strategy to challenge the United States falls under the "crafty" category.

For example, both countries have developed anti-access/area denial (A2/AD) networks and designed smart asymmetric-warfare strategies (asymmetric -warfare is essentially a conflict between two countries that have significantly uneven military capabilities, like the United States versus either China or Russia).

These hybrid warfare tactics are designed to significantly raise the risk and cost of retaliation, and to keep potential adversaries guessing. This creates a kind of gray zone between war and peace, where things don't necessarily escalate into military conflict, but where adversaries know the threat exists nonetheless.

China has unlawfully used the disputed waters of the South and East China Seas as their gray zone battlefield, building militarized artificial islands and occupying disputed reefs and shoals to keep our naval forces out deep in the Pacific.

Stephen Biddle and Ivan Oelrich, global security experts, explain it this way:

> "For more than a generation, China has been fielding a series of interrelated missile, sensor, guidance, and other technologies designed to deny freedom of movement to hostile powers in the air and waters off its coast. As this program has matured, China's ability to restrict hostile access has improved, and its military reach has expanded. Many now believe that this anti-access, area denial capability will eventually be highly effective in excluding the United States from parts of the Western Pacific that it has traditionally controlled.
>
> Some even fear that China will ultimately be able to extend a zone of exclusion out to, or beyond, what is often called the 'Second Island Chain' – a line that connects Japan, Guam, and Papua-New Guinea at distances of up to 3,000 kilometers from China."

For its part, Russia demonstrated hybrid warfare in the annexation of Crimea and in their effort to destabilize Ukraine (before the physical invasion) by using cyber warfare, extortion, and incredibly effective and destabilizing propaganda.

Now that Putin has started a full-fledged war in Ukraine, the propaganda has gone into overdrive. To justify his invasion, Putin told the Russian people that he started the war to "demilitarize and denazify" the Ukrainian government. He perpetuated the lie that Kyiv has been carrying out "genocide" against the Russian-speaking people who live in the Donetsk and Luhansk regions of Ukraine (known as the Donbas).

Since the war started, the *New York Times* reports that "the Kremlin has cycled through a torrent of lies to explain why it had to wage a 'special military operation' against a sovereign neighbor. Drug-addled neo-Nazis. Genocide. American biological weapons factories. Birds and reptiles trained to carry pathogens into Russia. Ukrainian forces bombing their own cities, including theaters sheltering children."

An analysis by the RAND Corporation – a nonprofit policy think tank partially funded by the U.S. government – "characterizes the contemporary Russian model for propaganda as 'the firehose of falsehood' because of two of its distinctive features: high numbers of channels and messages and a shameless willingness to disseminate partial truths or outright fictions. In the words of one observer, 'new Russian propaganda entertains, confuses and overwhelms the audience.'"

Russia's guerilla-style brand of asymmetric-warfare has been targeting America for decades. Moonlight Maze, Russia's three-year covert operation to hack into U.S. governmental agencies, started in 1996 and penetrated both NASA and the Pentagon. In fact, Moonlight Maze is the reason the U.S. Cyber Command center was created in the first place.

James Andrew Lewis, Senior Vice President of the Center for Strategic and International Studies, explains that "Russia is a haven for the most advanced cybercrime groups and no clear line delineates the criminal world from the government. The Kremlin sees Russian cybercriminals as a strategic asset, and one of the most difficult problems for reducing cybercrime is that Russia, along with North Korea, will not cooperate with Western law enforcement. High-end cybercriminal groups in Russia have hacking capabilities that are better than most nations for both criminal and intelligence purposes."

– the 1787 Recommendations for
Online Influence Operations are in *The Policy Guide* –

– the 1787 Recommendations for
Cybersecurity are in *The Policy Guide* –

Unfortunately for us, Russia has just gotten better and better at cyberwarfare through the years, so much so that we now are engaged in an ongoing and unrelenting cyberconflict.

This battle reached deep into the good 'ol USA when the Russians significantly intervened in the 2016 presidential election, then yet again in 2020 when they unleashed the mother of all cyberattacks against us.

In Spring 2020, as Americans were settling into Covid lockdown and the U.S. cyber-defense agencies were obsessively focused on protecting the upcoming presidential election, Russian hackers known as APT29 and Cozy Bear – the pride of the Foreign Intelligence Service of the Russia Federation (SVR) – launched a massive cyber hack against the United States of America.

A large portion of the hack was facilitated by software called Orion, which is made by SolarWinds, a company that makes network monitoring software used by at least 425 of the Fortune 500 companies, media companies, and most of our governmental agencies.

For years, SolarWinds has been accused of having insufficient security for its products, but for some reason the U.S. government and large corporations kept using them anyway.

In the end, thousands of people, both inside and outside of the U.S. government, downloaded the corrupted software, giving the Russians a way to create hidden back doors in order to access each user's network. The hack is believed to have reached at least 250 United States federal agencies and American corporations, including Microsoft and Amazon.

In my mind, this went way beyond spying, which most every country does to some degree. Instead, this was a global espionage supply chain attack that compromised U.S. intelligence agencies; nuclear laboratories; Fortune 500 companies; companies that monitor and protect critical domestic infrastructure; the National Institutes of Health; and the U.S. departments of State, Treasury, Commerce and Energy. The Department of Defense adamantly denies that the attacks penetrated its systems, although we have yet to see proof of that.

The National Nuclear Security Administration, which oversees our nuclear stockpile, was also breached, as was the Los Alamos National Laboratory, where most of our nuclear weapons are designed.

The Federal Energy Regulatory Commission (FERC) was compromised, which may not seem like a big deal until you find out that FERC is responsible for *Black Start*, the United States' strategy for restoring power if we ever experience a disastrous national blackout (which you can bet is already on Russia's attack checklist).

The Department of Homeland Security and the Pentagon were also hit, which is ironic given they are the very departments tasked with protecting our networks. All of this, despite the fact that the United States has thrown billions after billions after billions of dollars to prevent this from happening.

The National Cybersecurity Protection System (NCPS) is, according to its website, "an integrated system-of-systems that delivers a range of capabilities, including intrusion detection, analytics, intrusion prevention, and information sharing capabilities that defend the civilian federal government's information technology infrastructure from cyber threats and includes the hardware, software, supporting processes, training, and services that the program develops and acquires to support DHS's cybersecurity mission."

These capabilities, known as EINSTEIN, "provide a technological foundation that enables the Department of Homeland Security to secure and defend the federal civilian government's information technology infrastructure against advanced cyber threats."

Not to sound bitchy, but we should probably give EINSTEIN a new name since it completely missed hundreds of Russians stealthily digging around our governmental networks for months.

This is even more frustrating given that, in December 2018, the Government Accountability Office (GAO) warned of this exact thing happening: "The 23 civilian agencies covered by the *Chief Financial Officers Act of 1990* have often not effectively implemented the federal government's approach and strategy for securing information systems. Until agencies more effectively implement the government's approach and strategy, federal systems will remain at risk."

As if all of that is not humiliating enough, two other facts make it even worse: First, the United States government may have never discovered the hack at all. A private cybersecurity firm named FireEye actually discovered it and informed U.S. intelligence agencies, calling the attack "top-tier operational tradecraft."

Second, the Russians facilitated the attack from servers *inside* the United States. Some of the servers were actually in the same city as their intended targets. This was actually the most brilliant part of the plan because this allowed them to exploit rules that prohibit U.S. federal agencies from conducting domestic surveillance.

The Russian assault was so sophisticated – and so flawlessly executed – that experts were reportedly "stunned" by its scope and impact. It will be months – if not years, or maybe never – before we know how much damage has been done, but it is already apparent that the harm is significant and severe.

As a point of reference, the 2017 WannaCry fiasco – a hack perpetrated by North Korea that exploited a vulnerability in the Microsoft Windows operating system – reached 300,000 computer systems in 150 countries. The estimated global loss caused by the attack is over $4 billion.

From all angles, it's clear that China and Russia are ready to test the international order that America has ruled for decades, through military capabilities, hybrid warfare, and (in China's case) increasingly positive diplomatic relations around the world. (more on China and Russia in the *Foreign Policy* section of this book)

These countries are all the more dangerous because they view pesky things like human rights and the rule of law as nothing more than nuisances – and that philosophy can easily spread across the globe.

The bottom line is that China and Russia's crafty tactics are working, so we better find ways to nip them in the bud. And fast.

§§§

Hopefully, most of us can agree with the two statements I made earlier: 1) The United States of America should never be forced to forgo the critical military capabilities that we need to protect ourselves, and 2) The United States must have a cutting-edge military that has the fortitude to fully protect this country, regardless of where the threat comes from or in what form it comes in.

Plus, we must be able to sustain security simultaneously in Russia, Africa, South and East Asia, the Middle East, and Europe – and have everything we need to operate successfully in the traditional theatres of land, sea, air, cyberspace and outer space.

Now the question becomes: How can we best achieve this? Contrary to what some in Washington believe, we don't have a bottomless bank account when it comes to military spending and national security.

– the 1787 Recommendations for
Defense Spending are in *The Policy Guide* –

The Pentagon should never be immune to thoughtful spending and strict fiscal accountability – and that statement does not make me soft on defense, disloyal to the military, or unpatriotic in any way. What it makes me is a responsible realist.

We spend more on military expenditures – by far – than anyone in the entire world. In fact, we spend about as much on our military as the next ten largest-spending countries *combined.* Our military spending reached $766.58 billion in 2020, and it just keeps increasing every year. In December 2021, President Biden signed into law $777.7 billion worth of military spending.

With that level of spending – surprise, surprise – here come the lobbyists. The defense sector – which includes defense aerospace, defense electronics and other miscellaneous defense companies – spent a whopping $117,431,129 to lobby Congress in 2021 alone.

Since 9/11, the defense sector has spent well over $2.5 billion to lobby Congress. Does this sound like a good idea to you? It's pretty clear who is actually writing our national security strategy, and it ain't the people we elect.

Now, more than ever, we need to heed yet another piece of advice from President Dwight D. Eisenhower: "In the councils of government, we must guard against the acquisition of unwarranted influence, whether sought or unsought, by the military-industrial complex. The potential for the disastrous rise of misplaced power exists, and will persist."

Listen, I believe in free market enterprise, but I also believe we have to watch our defense suppliers like hawks because they have billions of reasons to fight us on this.

In 2019, Lockheed Martin held contracts with the Department of Defense worth $47 billion, with an additional $4.4 billion for "Missile Defense." The company also had contracts with NASA ($1.36 billion), the Army ($9.6 billion); the Air Force ($10.9 billion), and the Navy ($20 billion).

The United States is by far Boeing's largest customer, making up 31 percent of the company's annual revenue. In 2019, this equaled $28.6 billion. In fact, deals with Boeing account for 21 percent of the Department of Defense's entire procurement budget.

Relying on defense lobbyists to write our national security strategy guarantees that our national security strategy will be all about bombers, helicopters, Super Hornets, Phantom Eyes, Growler, Prowler, B-2, PAC-3, F-15s, ICBMs, MEADS, B-52s, MHTK – and a lot of other cool weapons and bombs that ensure America's arsenal has all the latest, greatest hardware.

It also guarantees that innovative, forward-thinking strategic planning will be discouraged. After all, if all you have is a hammer, everything looks like a nail, right?

The most dangerous part of abdicating our national security strategy to the defense lobby is that it lets the United States Congress off the hook from asking the truly critical questions. Questions like: Given the changing nature of war, how many armored brigade combat teams do we need to keep active and what exactly will their role be going forward?

How can we redesign our aging fleet of aircraft carriers since they are now sitting ducks thanks to China's new anti-ship missiles? Should we replace the F-35 and/or the F-22 with longer-range strike bombers since the Joint Concept for Access and Maneuver in the Global Commons (JAM-GC) calls for weapons that can hit distant targets to better retaliate against China's new anti-access/area-denial capabilities?

And what is up with the Conventional Prompt Strike (CPS) – a program that the United States has been working on for almost two decades – and why in the hell does it cost so much money?

According to the Congressional Research Service, the Conventional Prompt Strike (CPS) "allows the United States to strike targets anywhere on Earth in as little as an hour. This capability may bolster U.S. efforts to deter and defeat adversaries by allowing the United States to attack high-value targets or 'fleeting targets' at the start of or during a conflict. CPGS weapons would not substitute for nuclear weapons but would supplement U.S. conventional capabilities. They would provide a 'niche' capability, with a small number of weapons directed against select, critical targets."

That all sounds pretty good, but then this: "The Pentagon's FY2021 budget request continues to show significant increases in funding for the Navy's CPS program."

"In FY2019, this program received $278 million. The Navy received $512 million for this program in FY2020 and requested $1.008 billion for FY2021. The budget request shows continuing increases in funding over the next five years, with $5.3 billion allocated to the program between FY2021 through FY2025."

This is an obscene amount of money. What due diligence is being done to justify this program? What is the end game, or do we even have one? Who are the players involved in making these decisions? Are strategies like these even the best way forward?

The questions just keep coming: Should we endorse submarine- and sea-launched low-yield weapons and/or a nuclear modernization program like the one outlined in the 2018 *Nuclear Posture Review* and the most recent *Assessment and Recommendations of the National Defense Strategy Commission*?

Or do we really even need the New START limit of 700 deployed intercontinental ballistic missiles (ICBMs), deployed submarine-launched ballistic missiles (SLBMs), and deployed heavy bombers equipped for nuclear armaments?

Do we really need 1,550 nuclear warheads on deployed ICBMs, deployed SLBMs, and deployed heavy bombers equipped for nuclear armaments, or 800 deployed and non-deployed ICBM launchers, SLBM launchers, and heavy bombers equipped for nuclear armaments – when it takes a fraction of that to blow any country off the face of the earth?

Really think about that last sentence for a second. There are 195 sovereign countries in the entire world. Our estimated total nuclear inventory is 5,428 (this includes warheads in the military stockpile as well as retired, but still intact, warheads in queue for dismantlement).

If you take only the 1,964 active warheads in our Military Stockpile – defined as warheads that are in the custody of the military and earmarked for use by commissioned deliver vehicles – we could literally blow up every single country on earth 10 times!

The Congressional Budget Office (CBO) estimates that "if carried out, the plans for nuclear forces delineated in the Department of Defense's and the Department of Energy's fiscal year 2019 budget requests would cost a total of $494 billion over the 2019–2028 period, for an average of just under $50 billion a year."

That's just the money it takes *going forward*, but this outrageous spending has been going on for eight decades.

The Brookings Institution, a research group, found that: "From 1940 through 1996, we spent nearly $5.5 trillion on nuclear weapons and weapons-related programs, in constant 1996 dollars." Just imagine what that number would be in today's dollars, 25 years later!

The report continues, "If we could represent $5.8 trillion as a stack of dollar bills, it would reach from the Earth to the Moon and nearly back again, a distance of more than 459,000 miles."

This has gotten out of hand. It's high time we have a serious conversation about our nuclear program because it's bleeding us dry.

– the 1787 Recommendations for
Nuclear War/WMD Proliferation are in *The Policy Guide* –

A world without nuclear weapons would be wonderful. Sadly, the reality of our current geopolitical environment doesn't support that at this point (as Vladimir Putin is clearly illustrating).

That said, we have made great strides in reducing the number of nuclear weapons in the past few decades. There are still too many, but there are far less than during the Cold War. In fact, there has been an 85 percent reduction since the *Nuclear Non-Proliferation (NPT) Treaty* was enacted in 1970.

The *Nuclear Non-Proliferation (NPT) Treaty* was followed by the I*ntermediate-Range Nuclear Forces (INF) Treaty*, which was signed by President Ronald Reagan and Soviet leader Mikhail Gorbachev in 1987 to eliminate intermediate- and shorter-range missiles (or those with ranges between 300 to 3,400 miles); the *Strategic Arms Reduction Treaty*, signed in 1991 by President George H.W. Bush and Gorbachev; and the *New START Treaty*, signed in 2010, again by the presidents of Russia and the United States, Barack Obama and Dmitry Medvedev (on January 26, 2021, Presidents Biden and Putin agreed to extend the *New START* Treaty through February 4, 2026).

After such a good run, I'm sorry to report that this remarkable international progress hit a major speed bump during the Trump administration, when the U.S. formally withdrew from the *Intermediate-Range Nuclear Forces (INF) Treaty* on August 2, 2019.

This reversal could not have come at a worse time, and that was true even *before* Putin invaded Ukraine. The latest *Nuclear Posture Review* (NPR), the latest available, says, "The United States remains committed to its efforts in support of the ultimate global elimination of nuclear, biological, and chemical weapons. It has reduced the nuclear stockpile by over 85 percent since the height of the Cold War and deployed no new nuclear capabilities for over two decades."

But the review continues with a more ominous tone: "Nevertheless, global threat conditions have worsened markedly since the most recent 2010 NPR, including increasingly explicit nuclear threats from potential adversaries…The United States now faces a more diverse and advanced nuclear-threat environment than ever before, with considerable dynamism in potential adversaries' development and deployment programs for nuclear weapons and delivery systems."

To make matters even more precarious, the threat of cyberattacks, cyber-terrorism and cyber-espionage is obviously increasing, which directly compromises nuclear command-and-control systems. For example, these attacks could signal false alarms and cause hair trigger-type retaliation responses.

This is super scary stuff, but this type of thing is where true leadership and skilled negotiation must come into play. Our tricky nuclear position requires we remain calm and make smart decisions about how to move forward, not hyperventilate and just arbitrarily start pulling the United States out of proven treaties that have taken decades to cultivate – an approach that is amateurish and reeks of fear. Not to mention the profoundly mixed message it sends to aspiring nuclear states like North Korea and Iran.

It's an approach that is also dangerous, destabilizing and, if not reversed immediately, will eventually put us squarely back in an unconstrained arms race.

Short-sighted people like Donald Trump welcome a new arms race. They seem to think that if Russia, for example, is not complying with existing nuclear treaties, the United States must need a bigger arsenal to scare them into submission, right?

This logic, if you can even call it that, is absurd. Our arsenal is already as big as Russia's. If Russia is indeed not complying with existing treaties, arsenal size obviously has nothing to do with it.

There are still around 12,700 nuclear weapons in the world. The last thing we need is more, especially if the number is increasing without international arms control agreements.

As we navigate this, it's important to remember that, although Russia is certainly a huge player in this game – roughly 90 percent of all nuclear warheads are owned by Russia and the United States – the threat of nuclear, biological, and chemical weapon attacks lies more with proliferation, rogue nations, and terrorist organizations than with other countries.

This is a perfect example of why we need strong international allies. The United States needs to lead a united coalition that penalizes proliferators and ensures multilateral enforcement of those penalties. Preventing this very real threat should be priority one in our dealings with the United Nations and other international bodies.

Likewise, the United States must – starting right this second – exercise true global leadership and, together with allies, hold other nations accountable for developing things like the intermediate-range missile called the DF-26 that threatens our naval forces and bases in the

Pacific (China) or a ground-launched cruise missile (GLCM) called the SSC-8 that the U.S. has declared is in violation of the Intermediate-Range Nuclear Forces (INF) Treaty (Russia).

There are plenty of ways for a global alliance to hold noncompliant countries responsible, including restoring the extensive on-site inspection clause in the – now cancelled – INF.

Committing to international agreements and forming strong alliances are no-brainers. Not only do they make us safer, but they can also save us a ton of money by helping us replace the "my bomb is bigger than your bomb" lunacy with "intellect and decent purpose."

In reality, we don't really have a choice because we are spending <u>WAY</u> too much money on our nuclear arsenal and it needs to stop.

Let's cut to the chase: It's past time to shift our entire national defense strategy. To achieve this monumental task, the United States needs to start with three things:

† Increase our commitment to arms control diplomacy and decrease our commitment to more nuclear weapons.

† Transition from a military strategy that relies on aging conventional weapons systems and platforms to one that is better equipped to confront the new high-tech nature of war.

† Stop producing military weapons and equipment we no longer need.

These three things alone will save hundreds of billions of dollars. The crazy thing about the third one – stop producing military weapons and equipment we no longer need – is that no one knows this better than our military leaders.

For years, the Army has tried to make Congress understand that the Army doesn't need money to, for example, upgrade and/or purchase more tanks.

At one point, Army Chief of Staff General Raymond Odierno told the Senate Armed Services Committee, "We are still having to procure systems we don't need." (The Army) spends hundreds of millions of dollars on tanks that we simply don't have the structure for anymore."

Nevertheless, even though this four-star general told Congress point blank they were wasting millions and millions and millions of dollars and to please reallocate the funds, they appropriated $120 million for Abrams tank upgrades anyway. And not for the first time. Three years earlier, General Odierno made the exact same plea to Congress, which resulted in $183 million for tanks.

In fact, in 2019, the Army announced that it would spend around $714 million to upgrade M1A1 Abrams tanks at the Joint Systems Manufacturing Center (a.k.a. the Lima Army Tank Plant) in Lima, Ohio.

There is no doubt that this, at least in part, is Congress completely selling us out to lobbyists. But there is also another reason: Jobs. The production of tanks and bombers directly and indirectly supports hundreds of thousands of jobs across America. And those hundreds of thousands of jobs represent hundreds of thousands of votes.

Members of Congress want to be reelected by their constituents. Happy, employed voters have reliable jobs and reward their congressional representative with their vote. Unhappy, unemployed voters will throw their congressional representative right out the door.

This is not a criticism. It actually makes perfect sense. *Of course* members of Congress want to keep their jobs and *of course* people in their districts want to keep their jobs. It would be strange if they didn't.

However, what most politicians are too lazy or corrupt to figure out is that this doesn't have to be a zero-sum game. Most politicians never even consider bringing a major shift like this to the table because they cannot get past visions of shuttered factories and decimated communities.

This is yet another seriously short-sighted and irresponsible approach. I hate to break it to the members of Congress who choose to bury their heads in the sand but, in former manufacturing towns anyway, shuttered factories and decimated communities are already a reality – and it's just going to get worse if we don't do something fast.

According to the United States Bureau of Labor Statistics, "The manufacturing sector is projected to lose 444,800 jobs [by 2029], the most of any sector over the projections decade. This sector also contains

12 of the 20 industries projected to have the most rapid employment declines."

Already, our manufacturing sector has taken an absolute beating. In the 1940s, more than a third of Americans worked in a factory. In 1990, that number was 17.2 percent. In 2018, manufacturing accounted for just 8.5 percent of the jobs in the private sector.

Then there are manufacturing wages, which have fallen. The U.S. Bureau of Labor Statistics reports that "in 1990, average hourly earnings of production workers in manufacturing ($10.78) were about 6 percent greater than those of production or nonsupervisory workers in the total private sector ($10.20). By 2018, however, manufacturing workers were earning approximately 5 percent less ($21.54) than their total private sector counterparts ($22.71)."

"On an annualized basis, hourly earnings of manufacturing workers rose by 2.5 percent per year from 1990 to 2018, while private sector average earnings rose by 2.9 percent. As a result of this disparity in the rate of growth over the period, the level of the two data series converged in July 2006. Since then, earnings in manufacturing have remained below those of private sector workers, on average."

Donald Trump and his trade wars certainly did not improve things for the manufacturing sector, although you would never know it by listening to him.

During his failed reelection campaign, he told the crowd at a Michigan rally, "You better vote for me, I got you so many damn car plants. And we're going to bring you a lot more!" Nope. In truth, Michigan's manufacturing sector lost 66,500 workers from July 2019 to 2020 alone. As you can see from the dates, this was already happening *before* Covid.

On the 2020 campaign trail in Ohio, Donald said, "Over the last six months, we've witnessed one manufacturing miracle after another." Nope. Ohio's manufacturing sector lost 48,000 workers from July 2019 to 2020.

The manufacturing sector was in a technical recession – which is triggered when output falls for at least six months – for the entirety of 2019 (I'm excluding 2020 from this discussion because of the outliers inherent to the Covid disruption). In 2019, U.S. factory production decreased 1.3 percent, making it the worst year for manufacturing since 2015.

The PMI, or the Purchasing Managers' Index – the most common way to measure the health of manufacturing – plummeted. In December 2019, another popular gauge of the manufacturing sector's health – a survey of purchasing managers from the Institute for Supply Management – fell to its lowest level since the Great Recession.

These numbers point to a troubling trend, to say the least, which is why we have no time to waste. Artificially propping up pockets of manufacturing by making things we don't need will only make the long-term problem worse. It's not a solution; it's a band-aid that will soon be ripped off to reveal a wound that has gotten progressively more infected. Wouldn't it make more sense to just proactively solve the problem instead of trying to constantly camouflage it?

We CAN solve this. The fact is that many of the plants that make old-school military weapons and equipment can shift into making something *we actually do* need! Imagine that!!

The timing is perfect. For one, the Covid-19 crisis has proven that the United States is far too dependent on China and other countries for our essential and nonessential goods. The fact that we did not have – nor could quickly produce – things like masks and ventilators is just unacceptable. The United States *invented* the dang ventilator for goodness' sake! What is going on here?

Without question, the United States can once again be a global leader in manufacturing – and both save and create jobs – but our strategy to revitalize manufacturing must be smart and aggressive because we face stiff competition in automation alone. < read more about how we can pay for this later in this chapter >

In a July 2020 survey, Honeywell, a Fortune 100 technology company, found that American companies are planning to increase automation investments, in large part because of the fallout from Covid-19. The survey found that the e-commerce (66 percent); grocery, food and beverage (59 percent); and logistics (55 percent) industries are the most interested in doing this.

Tyson, the second largest processor of chicken, beef, and pork in the entire world, is moving toward robot butchers, and the car manufacturer BMW is beginning to use automation for its quality control.

To succeed, we need to look forward, not backward. The McKinsey Global Institute – the business and economics research arm of the management consultant firm McKinsey & Company – reminds us that:

> "A successful U.S. manufacturing revitalization will not restore 1960s-style mass employment on assembly lines. But it can raise manufacturing GDP by more than $500 billion annually above the current trend, spurring income growth, new jobs, local investment, and ripple effects across other industries.
>
> The decline of U.S. manufacturing is not solely the result of technology and globalization – and it is not inevitable. The United States can make policy and investment decisions to change the current trajectory. But this effort has to be focused on competing in the future rather than recreating the past."

So, where do we even begin? Even though we have shipped an unprecedented amount of production overseas, the United States remains the second-largest manufacturer in the world, and we still have a lot of the infrastructure and personnel we need to reclaim the <u>number one</u> position. There are <u>**five**</u> ways to jump start this effort:

† Stop relying on "just in time" supply chains by bringing vital ones back from overseas. Before the pandemic, the U.S. generally considered only things like weapons and semiconductors "vital," but we need to expand that definition to include things like pharmaceuticals and medical equipment. Currently, around 80 percent of the ingredients in our pharmaceuticals come from overseas.

† To reposition our supply chain, we need to heavily invest in advanced manufacturing for things like 5G, lasers, innovative computer chips and software engineering, as well as investment in

emerging technologies like artificial intelligence, high-performance computing, and synthetic biology.

We also need to respond to the vast shortage of semiconductors that revealed itself during the pandemic. In January 2022, a survey conducted by the U.S. Commerce Department revealed that "median demand for chips highlighted by buyers was as much as 17 percent higher in 2021 than 2019, and buyers aren't seeing commensurate increases in the supply they receive. This is a major supply and demand mismatch." The report continued, "The median inventory of semiconductor products highlighted by buyers has fallen from 40 days in 2019 to less than 5 days in 2021. These inventories are even smaller in key industries.

Today, the United States manufactures only 12 percent of the world's semiconductors, which – for what should be the world's most competitive country – just makes zero sense. Since semiconductors are used in everything from vacuum cleaners to space shuttles, the current semiconductor shortage is unsustainable because it forces car companies and other manufactures to cut or stop production altogether. This is also a national security issue because most of the existing plants are near China. For instance, just <u>one</u> Taiwanese company manufactures <u>70 percent</u> of all microcontrollers, a chip used in most every vehicle in the world.

And get this. In a very ironic twist, a lot of the international factories that build advanced weapons systems for China *use American chip technology*. So, essentially, China is acquiring deadly missiles that can one day threaten our military – and they are using OUR OWN TECHNOLOGY TO DO IT! Say what?

Advanced manufacturing factories are complex and take time to build – and are really, really, really expensive – but that's all the more reason to begin the process, like yesterday. On this, we have some awesome news from the private sector. In October 2021, Micron Technology announced plans to invest over $150 billion in memory chip research and development globally, with the United States being a significant part of their plan. One month later, Samsung, a South Korean company, announced plans to build a $17 billion semiconductor plant in Texas.

One month after *that*, General Motors said they plan to spend over $4 billion to increase electric vehicle and battery production in Michigan, and just days later, Toyota answered with its own plan to spend $1.3 billion for a battery plant in North Carolina. Intel, a U.S. chip maker, kicked off 2022 with an announcement that they will spend $20 billion to build two new factories in Ohio. Yay!

† Expand relationships with organizations like Fraunhofer-Gesellschaft, the leading organization for applied research and development based in Germany. Partnerships like these can drive scientific progress and economic development. We can build on the already six Fraunhofer centers scattered throughout the United States.

† When we begin to manufacture all of these things stateside, we have to make sure there is enough demand for them. We can't force Americans to buy American, but we can force the federal government to. We need to demand that the federal government commit to targeted procurement of our newly manufactured items and incentivize state and local governments to do the same. We also need to view the entire world as our customers. (read more about this in the *Trade* section)

† Although we can't force Americans to buy American, we can certainly entice them to. The main reason all this stuff moved overseas is the cost structure, but I bet Americans would happily pay a few cents more at the register to see our manufacturing sector roar back. We just need to convince them that the extra money is for the greater good, as well as for their own safety. The difference in the quality of pharmaceuticals, for example, varies widely around the world.

To this end, we should launch a massive marketing campaign to underscore the importance of this effort. Plus, we should require that all manufactured items sold in the United States include where the item – and each component of the item – were manufactured. We will speak directly to the American public's patriotism!

Together, these five things kill two birds with one stone: 1) Saves the jobs that would otherwise be lost by the shift in our national security strategy, and 2) Helps revitalize our manufacturing sector.

As we redesign our future, it's important to remember that the American manufacturer worker doesn't need (or want) to be coddled. In truth, they are much more resilient than condescending politicians often give them credit for.

These workers – the very backbone of America – have proven over and over that they are as flexible as they are committed. Beginning in World War II, when the auto industry changed its line to make tanks and bombers for the war effort, American enterprise and its work force has absorbed major shifts brilliantly.

Likewise, the communities around these workers have the most fabulous ability to adapt as well. It's actually remarkable. Even cities that completely lost their leading industry have shown they can thrive.

Pittsburgh is a perfect example. Pittsburgh, as their football team proudly champions, used to be the gold standard for steel production. But as the world turned, the city proactively and cleverly broadened its focus.

Pittsburgh now has five leading industries: health care, energy, advanced manufacturing, financial and business services, and information technology. This vibrant city also attracts emerging industries like Robotics and Artificial Intelligence, Cyber Security, and Additive Manufacturing.

All that said, the federal government still needs to provide a financial backstop for these families and communities, just in case there is any gap between winding down old jobs and beginning new ones. This should include temporary income replacement, strong protections for pensions, and retraining and relocation support. (more on this in the *U.S. Works* section later in this chapter)

§§§

Our mission is to save every single job compromised by our national security shift, and bringing some of our vital supply chains back from overseas will definitely help move us closer to our goal.

But the even greater news is that there is another sector that not only has the ability to close any remaining employment gaps that may exist because of our defense shift, but that can actually get us over the finish line with plenty of jobs to spare: clean energy.

Yippee! We made it! We have finally arrived at the intersection of our two coordinated big shifts (national defense and energy).

As we <u>*decrease*</u> our production of old-school weapons and other conventional military equipment, we can <u>*increase*</u> our production of things like electric vehicles, heat pumps and batteries, as well as solar panels, wind turbines, fuel cells, and hydrogen combustion turbines.

This kills two birds with one stone: 1) Helps save jobs that would otherwise be lost by the shift in our national security strategy, and 2) Escalates our transition from fossil fuels to cleaner energy alternatives – and saves jobs that the big shift in our energy policy may put at risk.

Our mission with our energy shift is the same as it is for the one in national security: Save every single job that may be potentially compromised. And we can! Get this, a study by the *Costs of War Project* based at Brown University found that:

> "While defense spending is indeed a source of job creation, other areas create many more jobs for any given level of spending. Education and health care create more than twice as many jobs as defense for the same level of spending, while clean energy and infrastructure create over 40 percent more jobs.
>
> War-related spending at a level of $230 billion per year supported about 1.5 million defense-related jobs on an annual basis, not an insignificant amount of employment. However, if that same level of spending had been channeled to other domestic purposes, it could have supported over 2 million jobs

in clean energy or infrastructure, over 3 million in health care, and over 4 million jobs in primary and secondary education.

If we look at the average job creation potential of health care, education, clean energy, and infrastructure, $230 billion could have created about 2.8 million jobs instead of the 1.5 million created through war spending, thus the average opportunity cost is about 1.3 million jobs annually."

That's crazy, right? Putting aside 2020 because of the Covid economic interruption, the Energy Efficiency (EE) sector is the fastest-growing energy industry in the United States. Energy Efficiency jobs include things like making buildings more efficient; retrofitting homes; converting heating, ventilation, and air conditioning equipment; manufacturing appliances; and conceiving and constructing high-performance buildings.

The EE sector now employs over 2.3 million American workers and is responsible for one out of every four jobs in the energy industry. In fact, it employs more Americans than the entire fossil fuel industry in 41 states and the District of Columbia, and twice as many nationwide.

Worldwide, there were around 11.5 million renewable energy jobs in 2019, up from 7.3 million just seven years earlier.

According to *Forbes* magazine (written in April 2019, before Covid hit), "renewable energy jobs are booming across America, creating stable and high-wage employment for blue-collar workers in some of the country's most fossil fuel-heavy states, just as the coal industry is poised for another downturn."

The article continued, "Economics are driving both sides of this equation: Building new renewable energy is cheaper than running existing coal plants and prices get cheaper every year. By 2025, almost every existing coal plant in the United States will cost more to operate than building replacement wind and solar within 35 miles of each plant."

An economic impact study of new offshore wind leases by Wood Mackenzie, a global consultancy group, found that "the growth of U.S. offshore wind will not only deliver clean energy in the U.S., but also generate significant near-term, mid-term and long-term economic benefits."

If the Bureau of Ocean Energy Management (BOEM) grants leases as expected, "a significant near-term benefit will be $2 billion in U.S. Treasury revenue. Even more significant is the mid-term development and construction of offshore wind farms created by these leases would support 80,000 jobs annually and generate hundreds of billions of dollars of investment into construction, transportation and port-related development. Long-term, these projects will provide sustainable green energy to 20 million households and support 20,500 jobs annually beyond 2035 that continues for decades."

It's been a long road, but it's finally time for our energy policy to make the big shift. We must move from a high-carbon to low-carbon energy system to better protect our environment and health, as well as secure an energy source that is less economically volatile and more diversified both geologically and technologically – two things that will greatly strengthen our national security.

All the indicators are very promising but, just like in the manufacturing sector, the federal government needs to provide a financial backstop for families and communities in the coal and oil and gas industries, just in case there is any gap between winding down old jobs and beginning new ones. This should include temporary income replacement, strong protections for pensions, and retraining and relocation support. Plus, communities dependent on the coal and oil and gas industries need additional funds to reclaim and repurpose land. (more on this in the *U.S. Works* section later in this chapter)

This is an emotionally charged topic. Building pipelines, fracking, and offshore drilling evoke reactions from enthusiasm to discomfort to complete hostility, and I completely understand the entire spectrum of emotions.

This topic is understandably emotional because it affects our health and the air we breathe, and our children's health and their children's health and the air *they* will all breathe. It's emotional because how we get our energy directly affects the wildlife we love, this beautiful land we love, the communities we love, the people we love.

Okay, Republicans. I can practically see you rolling your eyes, but please just hear me out on this. Remember, I'm from East Texas. I started my career in the energy business. I have clients, friends and family whose livelihoods depend on the energy business. Believe me, I get it. The oil patch is not just a job, it's a way of life.

To these clients, friends, family, and everyone else freaking out that I even uttered the words "cleaner energy alternatives," I promise I would never leave you hanging out to dry. On the flip side, I will always fight to protect our natural resources and, for that matter, the entire planet.

Let's just get this out of the way now: I will not debate anyone on whether global warming is a real thing. I simply refuse to waste my time arguing about this because the highly agenda-driven, volatile arguments are a complete waste of time.

This is a common sense issue. Period. To suggest that global warming is some sort of elaborate deception is absurd. I don't need a study to tell me that when billions of people live on a planet, they have a profound effect on it. I don't need a study to tell me that fewer toxins in the air are better than more.

I don't need a study to tell me that we can't continue to act like our natural resources will last forever. I don't need a study to tell me that taking no environmental action poses a dangerous risk to our planet, our health, and our international strength. < even though I don't need studies to tell me these things, there are several included in *The Policy Guide* :) >

Call me crazy, or a bleeding-heart liberal, or anything else, but I actually care about the tens of thousands of dolphins, whales and other marine animals that have been harmed by the Trump administration's approval of deafening seismic surveys off the Atlantic coast. I actually care about the sage grouse that is now endangered in the American West. < If you are making fun of me, Google a picture of this precious little thing and I promise you will care too! >

I actually care that, in the spring of 2020, California, Arizona, New Mexico, Oregon and Idaho had to suffer through the first megadrought in over 1,200 years. I actually care that two Antarctic glaciers are breaking free, perhaps initiating the collapse of the entire West Antarctic ice sheet.

I mean, seriously, how in the world could anyone *not* care about these things? Especially Christians. Do you really think God created the heavens and the earth – and designed that adorable little sage grouse – just to have a bunch of ungrateful jerks destroy it? Is that being a good steward of God's blessings?

– The Recommendations for
Energy and the Environment are in *The Policy Guide* –

§§§

Although energy is a volatile issue, it's also a sexy one – "blood for oil," shady international cartels, billion-dollar lobbying efforts, ferocious environmental debates…this is an issue that has it all.

It also offers a perfect example of how we constantly work against ourselves in the quest for sustainable solutions.

The way lobbyists, hard-core activists, and politicians portray it, this appears to be a black and white issue: fossil fuels v. renewable energy. This is generally where the argument gets incredibly heated and people on both sides get really ticked off. This is also where, as in most arguments, everyone develops tunnel vision and stops listening.

We can avoid this drama if, from the jump, all sides understand that a successful outcome depends on cooperation, collaboration, and a bit of patience. Everyone should keep in mind that even the most aggressive carbon action plans call for zero emissions by 2050. That's <u>30</u> years from now, so obviously this is a process.

It's important to keep in mind that fossil fuels and renewable energy sources are not mutually exclusive, at least at this point in the process. Picture a large brass scale similar to the scales of justice. The left side of the scale represents fossil fuels and the right side represents renewable energy.

Currently, the scale is tipped significantly toward fossil fuels because renewable energy sources don't yet provide a significant amount of energy. Combined, these sources contribute just 12.6 percent of our total energy needs. However, as we begin to implement an intelligent energy shift, the scales will slowly begin to balance, then begin tipping toward renewable energy.

Given how screwed we were, energy wise, not even ten years ago, it's remarkable we can even contemplate a big shift.

Ever since George H.W. Bush's 1990 Gulf War – and even way before – people both inside and outside of America have accused the U.S. government of fighting wars over nothing more than oil. Did these "blood for oil" believers have a point?

They probably did on some level but, back then, the question was largely irrelevant. Like it or not, we had forced ourselves into a position where we had to ensure stability in the Persian Gulf.

Let the Sunni and Shia civil war in Iraq escalate into a regional war? No chance. Kiss up to the Saudis? Have to. Be new best friends with Angola's insanely corrupt leaders? You better believe it.

For decades, energy was the main driver of our foreign policy agenda because, until fairly recently, foreign nations were in absolute control of our energy survival. The undisputed truth was that U.S. supply did not meet U.S. demand.

It wasn't even close. The grim reality was that 49 percent of the petroleum consumed in the United States was imported from foreign countries, with crude oil comprising 78 percent of gross petroleum imports. We were basically stuck.

This is something I witnessed first-hand. My early years in the energy business gave me a front row seat to the very basics of domestic and international policy. When I graduated from college, I was blissfully unaware of our national energy situation. When I needed gasoline, I would stop at a gas station and never question if the pump would be dry. When I entered a room, I turned the lights on and never questioned if I would spend the evening in darkness.

When the Texas summer grew unbearably hot, I relied heavily on my air conditioner and never questioned the imminent relief it would surely bring. After working on an energy trading floor, I no longer harbored such certainty. Day after day, I witnessed the scramble, often times bordering on panic, to procure enough natural gas to ensure uninterrupted electricity generation.

Fast-forward to today. Practically everything about our energy supply situation has changed…dramatically.

The International Energy Agency (IEA) is an intergovernmental organization established within the Organization for Economic Co-operation and Development (OECD). Its 2018 *World Energy Outlook* revealed:

> "The shale revolution continued to shake up oil and gas supply, enabling the United States to pull away from the rest of the field as the world's largest oil and gas producer…In the New Policies Scenario, the United States accounts for more than half of global oil and gas production growth to 2025 (nearly 75 percent for oil and 40 percent for gas). By 2025, nearly every fifth barrel of oil and every fourth cubic meter of gas in the world come from the United States."

The U.S. Energy Information Administration (EIA) reported it this way: "In February 2018, U.S. crude oil production exceeded that of Saudi Arabia for the first time in more than two decades. In June and August, the United States surpassed Russia in crude oil production for the first time since February 1999."

In its 2022 report, the EIA reported that "by 2050, approximately 25 percent more natural gas will be produced than consumed in the United States." Already, in 2021, "U.S. natural gas exports reached a record high."

This is an astonishing turnaround that was only achievable because we tapped into fields like the Permian Basin, which is located in western Texas and southeastern New Mexico and currently provides one out of every three barrels of American oil.

Wow! All this sounds pretty great, right? Well, not so fast. Our energy self-sufficiency came at a big cost. We were only able to access fields like the Permian Basin because of the F Word: Fracking.

Fracking is a process that shoots water mixed with chemicals and sand into shale rock to break it up. This releases oil and natural gas that would otherwise be trapped in tight formations.

One of the major concerns regarding fracking, among many, is the associated contaminated water issues, which include the removal of the polluted water that is created by the fracking process as well as the protection of nearby groundwater and aquifers (more on this later).

In addition to accessing a ton of oil, the combination of fracking and directional drilling has made domestic natural gas cheap and plentiful. On one hand, this is good news because natural gas releases only half as much greenhouse gas as coal when combusted, so it can help balance the scales by replacing oil as a transportation fuel. On the other hand, natural gas is still a fossil fuel.

So, here is where the conversation ratchets up a notch. In the continued quest for American "energy dominance," as they put it, the Trump administration wildly slashed energy restrictions and regulations, and heavily promoted drilling and mining on our public lands.

This included opening nine million acres of federal lands in Wyoming and across the West, opening the Arctic National Wildlife Refuge to oil and gas exploration, and allowing new offshore oil and gas drilling in a large part of our coastal waters (including off California – which had been off-limits for decades – and along the Eastern Seaboard).

The Trump administration also authorized the largest rollback of federal land protections in U.S. history by significantly reducing the size of two national monuments in Utah: Bears Ears National Monument by 85 percent and the size of the Grand Staircase-Escalante by around half. Together, this is around two million acres.

I take issue with many of these actions, and my commitment to fighting back against them is reflected in the Energy & Environment recommendations (located in *The Policy Guide*). That said, let's put a pin in bad policy decisions and environmental irresponsibility for a minute. The most problematic issue with the Trump administration's actions is that they only served to perpetuate the severe crisis that the American energy industry finds itself in.

What the Trump administration interpreted as American "energy dominance" was really nothing more than feverish drilling that led to a massive glut in the global energy markets. It is this development, more than any other, that makes the timing perfect to start our big energy policy shift.

In the old days, the debate surrounding our energy future came down to this: Building pipelines and fracking on one side, protecting against harmful carbon emissions and environmental damage on the other. Both sides were extremely passionate about their position, and the arguments sometimes got really ugly.

When confronted with an issue where both sides equally believe they are right, and the antagonistic arguments from each camp grow increasingly circular, one of my favorite sayings is "let go of your end of the rope." After all, when you let go of your end of the rope, there's nothing for the other side to fight against. I don't view this advice as surrender in the least; rather, it often lowers the temperature and creates room to find common ground.

That's pretty much where we find ourselves now, except most oil and gas companies have not only let go of their end of the rope; they have no rope left.

< Note to Self: You may want to start looking for new clients because several of yours will probably stop speaking to you after reading this. Also, you may need to find somewhere else to go for Thanksgiving this year. >

In many ways, the American energy industry is a victim of its own success. Simply put, the breakneck energy production in the United States not only outpaced our own energy needs; it outpaced the entire world's.

This was true even before the pandemic but made far worse because of it. At one point in April 2020, oil prices went negative, which means that traders were actually *paying buyers* to take their oil (one unfortunate thing about trading oil is that, when your futures contract expires, you have to take physical possession of it. And if there is no storage capacity, as was the case in April 2020, the oil barrels will get dumped on your doorstep. That almost happened to me once!).

Shocking but not surprising, many of these energy companies forgot the basics of Economics 101, which tells us that too much output (production/supply) pushes prices down (consumption/ demand). This is no secret, it's just math.

I've seen it my entire career. Energy companies want to drill, baby, drill…right this second. With little regard for tomorrow. Just churn and burn until the next bust.

But this bust feels different. The international law firm Haynes and Boone found that, since 2015, over 500 bankruptcies have been filed by oilfield services companies and producers. The total amount of debt, secured and unsecured, associated with oilfield services bankruptcies alone is roughly $111 billion, and the equity lost is incalculable.

In 2020, nine oilfield services companies filed bankruptcies in excess of $1 billion. Texas was home to 69 percent of the oilfield services companies that filed bankruptcy in 2020.

Moody's, the credit rating company, reports that oil and gas companies "accounted for a hefty 91 percent of total U.S. corporate debt that defaulted in the third quarter of 2019." *Before* Covid.

On March 9, 2020, the price of oil dropped 25 percent, the largest one day drop in almost thirty years. This caused the Dow Jones Industrial Average to experience its worst single-day point drop in U.S. market history, followed by another record drop three days later and yet another one four days after that.

Many people assumed this collapse was because of fears of a recession or the coronavirus pandemic lockdowns, but those factors were only part of the story. In truth, Russia and Saudi Arabia got into a pissing match over the price of oil.

Four years earlier, faced with an oil boom in the United States, Russia agreed to join the Organization of the Petroleum Exporting Countries (OPEC) in their quest to manage the price of oil by at times limiting production. They cleverly named this alliance OPEC Plus.

This relationship worked for a while, but when demand for oil drastically decreased because of the pandemic, Russia and Saudi Arabia couldn't agree on which country would reduce its production and by how much (I mean, seriously. Who couldn't see this coming a mile away?)

So, predictably, Saudi Arabia announced price discounts on their oil without first notifying Russia. Then, the kingdom followed that unexpected move up with announcing an increase in their production, again with no warning. In retaliation, Russia did the same, which caused oil supply to overwhelm the market and the price of oil to tumble.

These countries are not new to this. In the 1980s, Saudi Arabia increased its oil production from two million to ten million barrels a day, which led to the collapse of oil prices and, ultimately, the end of the Soviet Union itself. (more on OPEC in a minute)

This is a marginally interesting story, but the reason I tell it is not because Saudi Arabia and Russia acted exactly how we assumed they would. Rather, I tell it because March 9, 2020 finally exposed the unsustainability of the shale business model and revealed the house of cards America's energy industry had become.

The predicament of the big guys tells part of the story. ExxonMobil has lost 60 percent of its value since 2013 and was sent packing from the Dow Jones Industrial Average, ending a ninety-year relationship with the exchange. The once hugely profitable and highly valued energy company was replaced with a software company.

But the real mess centers around shale oil, where getting to the goods requires fracking. Currently, around 65 percent of American crude oil production requires fracking. Still keeping a pin in the environmental issues for the moment, there are **three** problems with this:

† Fracking is expensive…*really* expensive. In fact, on average, fracking doesn't hit the green until oil prices reach $50 a barrel – which is obviously a huge problem when oil prices average $28 per barrel for an entire quarter, like they did in the second quarter of 2020. < Note: Breakeven oil prices can vary widely depending on the location, the type of deposit, and even the operator. >

† The rate of production of "tight" wells, or those that must be fracked, declines sharply. When I say sharply, I'm talking like up to 70 percent by the end of the first year. That's about TEN TIMES the decline rate of conventionally drilled wells.

† Thanks to #1 and #2, most companies that rely almost exclusively on shale gas seldom, if ever, make a profit (although, naturally, that doesn't extend to the executives). Thanks to the steep decline curve, shale-focused energy companies are forced to keep chasing the next expensive well…meaning they burn tons and tons of cash.

This game plan is risky enough when the market is high, but when prices fall it causes big time trouble. Ultimately, this creates a self-fulfilling prophecy for cash-poor companies already operating on a shoestring: prices fall, leading to less revenue, leading to a slashing of capital expenditures, leading to stalled production, etc. etc. etc.

That said, for well over a decade, energy companies have had plenty of help keeping the shale charade going. Some private equity guys (certainly not all) who only care about pocketing their 2 percent management fee have spent $125 billion since 2008 on shale gas plays. As a result of the industry being artificially propped up by outside money, energy companies failed to make the hard but responsible business decisions necessary to survive long term.

Now, that money is drying up quickly as private equity firms, tired of chasing their tail, are shifting to clean energy investments. In July 2020, *The Wall Street Journal* reported that "holdings of oil-and-gas stocks by active money managers are at a 15-year low."

§§§

I hate for this to happen to any industry, even if it does bring it on itself. But, more distressing, this puts the United States in a major bind because, at least for now, we need these guys to keep finding and producing oil and gas.

I've made it clear that I believe it's time to begin the big shift from fossil fuels to renewable energy sources, and we must do absolutely everything in our power to advance renewable forms of energy as quickly as possible. And we will. (more on this in a minute)

But remember, this is a *process* and facts are facts. We're just not there yet. Because it will take time for renewable energy solutions to fully materialize, fossil fuels remain a necessary part of our energy portfolio. The numbers just don't work otherwise.

That in no way means we just keep doing business as usual. As we shift, there must be strong protections in place to protect the environment (you can find 1787's recommendations in *The Policy Guide*). That said, environmental concerns are not the only consideration. This is also a national security issue of the highest order.

It's critical that we remain as self-sufficient as possible through this transition. We cannot ever put ourselves back in the position where we are held captive to any one country or region for our energy needs (just consider the havoc the war in Ukraine is wreaking on the global energy markets). Our economic and national security depend on our energy sovereignty, regardless of the form it comes in.

I would never suggest that fear dictate policymaking or that relationships with Middle Eastern countries be discouraged. However, it would be incredibly naïve and irresponsible to disregard the national security part of this conversation.

Even though the United States is now one of the world's largest energy producers, we are 9th when it comes to proven oil reserves (or oil that has already been discovered and that can be recovered under current technologies and prices). Venezuela, Saudi Arabia, Canada, Iran, Iraq, Russia, Kuwait, and the United Arab Emirates all clock in ahead of us.

Almost 80 percent of the world's proven crude oil reserves are controlled by members of the Organization of the Petroleum Exporting Countries (OPEC). The current OPEC members are Algeria, Angola, Congo, Equatorial Guinea, Gabon, Iran, Iraq, Kuwait, Libya, Nigeria, Saudi Arabia, United Arab Emirates, and Venezuela.

To put our reserve situation into perspective, Venezuela, the country with the largest oil reserves, has 303 billion barrels of proven reserves to our 50 billion barrels. Saudi Arabia has 266 billion barrels. This is yet another reason that the "drill, baby, drill…right this second, even if we don't need it" approach is incredibly shortsighted and irresponsible.

< Note: One of the best things about renewable energy – which includes sources like the sun, wind, water, and biomass – is that it's a naturally replenishing source of energy. Unlike with fossil fuels, which companies have to go out and physically find, the only constraints for renewable energy are economic and technological. Although the energy output (per unit of time) is more limited than with fossil fuels, renewable energy sources are virtually inexhaustible, meaning there is no need for what we conventionally think of as "reserves." >

Because of OPEC's vast amounts of oil reserves and production, the cartel still enjoys a huge amount of control over the global market by manipulating how much oil reaches consumers, which leaves the rest of us vulnerable to supply interruptions and price fluctuations. This largely explains why, according to *The Economist*, the price of oil has "swung by over 30 percent in a six-month period 62 times since 1970."

< Note: That said, even these countries are not immune to volatile energy markets, which is why they were forced to act in the first place. Saudi Arabia's government revenue fell by 49 percent in the second quarter of 2020 because of the energy crash >.

Just consider January 5, 2021, ten months after the Russia/Saudi Arabia oil price spat (that I mentioned earlier) sent prices plummeting. On January 5th, OPEC Plus agreed to reduce oil production, which instantly caused a 4 percent increase in oil prices – to a price level not seen since February 2020.

Through the years, the oil riches and investment capabilities of the Persian Gulf states have empowered them to, among other things, greatly affect worldwide interest and exchange rates. Multiple times, they have deemphasized holdings priced in U.S. dollars and invested heavily in alternative markets like China and Asia.

§§§

So, this brings us back full circle to the beginning of this section, where I said that energy companies are in major crisis and that their woes put the United States in a major bind, because we need domestic oil and gas until we can transition to renewable energy sources.

In my mind, our options are limited here because we certainly cannot give the energy industry one more dime in fossil fuel subsidies. In fact, we need to start significantly scaling back the astronomical subsidies they already get – which have only served to enable their poor management practices.

According to the International Monetary Fund (IMF), global fossil fuel subsidies were $4.7 trillion (6.3 percent of global GDP) in 2015, with the United States being the second largest subsidizer, behind China, at $649 billion. < Fossil fuel subsidies are defined here as fuel consumption times the gap between existing and efficient prices (i.e., prices warranted by supply costs, environmental costs, and revenue considerations). > By the way, that's just the most recent number I could find. There is no telling what that number was during the Trump administration.

However, we can absolutely help these companies help themselves. There are several ways we can achieve this, but I'll offer at least one.

Included in my energy recommendations (which you can find in *The Policy Guide*) is one that increases the federal royalty rate for oil and gas drilling on public lands from 12.5 percent to 20 percent and the federal royalty rate for drilling in federal waters from 18.75 percent to 20 percent. < I know this sounds extreme, but Texas charges 25 percent. One thing about us Texans, we damn sure know our value! >

The federal government can then offer discounts on federal royalty rates to incentivize energy companies to make smart environmental decisions.

For example, instead of using water for fracking, companies can use gel made from propane. Or they can clean and recycle the wastewater on site using new technologies that utilize membrane distillation. Or they can replace diesel-powered drilling equipment with alternatives that run on natural gas or solar energy, replace gas-powered chemical injection pumps with solar-powered ones, or use infrared cameras that locate methane leaks.

But wait…wouldn't that just be raising the rate only to discount it back down to where it was before? Isn't that just a wash? Kind of, but this does protect energy companies from our new higher rates and protects the environment. Plus, in my opinion, the new discounted rate should not be as low as 12.5 percent, which is just a joke of a rate. These guys have been vastly underpaying us for years.

Beyond this type of incremental help, the only thing that can realistically happen here is this: Energy companies need to pull themselves together and start properly managing their business, without leaning on private equity money and government subsidies.

I personally know a lot of these guys and it's so funny to hear them bash "socialism" and "welfare" – until, of course, it benefits their own bottom line.

To become and stay healthy, these companies < after, of course, the global energy markets settle from the turmoil caused by the war in Ukraine > not only need to tweak their near-term output to stop decimating market prices, but they also need to read the tea leaves and be proactive about aligning their capital expenditures with the goals of coalitions like the *Paris Climate Agreement.*

They should also focus on drilling conventional wells, meaning wells that don't have to be fracked, because of the now proven unsustainability of the shale model. This takes more work, but the long-term financial benefits make it worth the effort.

Before the fracking frenzy, American oil production had peaked on the mainland in 1970 and in Alaska in 1988, meaning that these conventional reservoirs are now in a state of terminal decline. Since these sources are depleting, we need to get busy looking for new ones because, regrettably, finding conventional oil and gas is not quite as easy as Jed Clampett made us believe.

Because our big energy shift is a *process*, these companies have plenty of time to adjust – but they need to start now if they don't want to get stuck holding the bag.

For example, one major challenge that countries and energy companies will face during this big shift involves something called *stranded assets*. Stranded assets, as defined by the International Energy Agency are "investments which have already been made but which, at some time prior to the end of their economic life, are no longer able to earn an economic return."

In this case, if countries and energy companies don't properly prepare, they could still have oil and gas underground toward the *end* of the big shift – which means these assets would be *stranded.* This would be a huge financial loss for these countries and companies because these assets reflect huge investments on their part.

This is one reason why global treaties like the *Paris Climate Agreement* are such a threat to them. The goal of the Paris agreement is to limit the rise in temperatures to at least 2 degrees Celsius above pre-industrial levels, although preferably to 1.5 degrees Celsius. The agreement was adopted by 196 parties in 2015 (this is the agreement that Donald Trump pulled the U.S. out of on June 1, 2017 but that the Biden administration rejoined in February 2021).

Analysis from Carbon Tracker, a nonprofit think tank based in London, shows that "between 60-80 percent of coal, oil and gas reserves of publicly listed companies could be classified 'unburnable' if the world is to achieve emissions reductions that mean an 80 percent probability of not exceeding global warming of 2°C."

This means that, according to the *Financial Times*, around $900 billion of value – or one-third of the current value of big oil and gas companies – could simply vanish.

< Note: Another challenge here is that, already, estimating and valuing reserves is a tricky business. ExxonMobil has been under investigation by the Securities and Exchange Commission (SEC) as well as New York attorney-general Eric Schneiderman for its methods of valuing reserves.

ExxonMobil has resisted adjusting the value of its reserves on its balance sheet, a move that some in the accounting industry call fraud.

To be fair, the volatility of the price of oil makes it exceedingly difficult to value reserves, but experts estimate that the amount of Exxon's adjustment could equal some $56 billion. >

In any event, regardless of how countries and companies feel about the goals of the Paris agreement, this is the way the ball is bouncing whether they like it or not. In 2019, United States renewable energy consumption exceeded coal for the first time since 1885, when the only renewable sources were wood and water.

This is happening, fellas – regardless of what you still have in the ground or what you originally paid for it. The bottom line is that, if you don't get on board *right now*, you are only going to exacerbate your future financial pain.

The good news is that, if companies and countries are proactive, there are ways to manage reserve capacity to mitigate the stranded asset trap. Net-Zero America, a comprehensive analysis led by Princeton University that outlines pathways to achieve net-zero greenhouse gas emissions by 2050, says that "oil production to 2050 in net-zero scenarios exceeds current proven reserves but is less than projected reserves based on recent growth rates."

An impressive few already get it. Some kicking and screaming, but still. Shell – a global group of energy and petrochemical companies –

> "Strongly supports the goals of the *Paris Climate Agreement* to limit the rise in the average global temperature well below 2° Celsius. The *Paris Climate Agreement* also said the world should pursue efforts to limit the temperature increase to 1.5° Celsius. For society to achieve a 1.5° Celsius future, the world is likely to need to stop adding to the stock of greenhouse gases in the atmosphere – a state known as net-zero emissions – by around 2060. That is why Shell has set itself an ambition to become, by 2050 or sooner, a net-zero emissions energy business. This is accompanied by our ambition, by 2030, to provide a reliable electricity supply to 100 million people in the developing world."

In 2020, BHP Billiton (BHP) – a global resources company based in Melbourne, Australia that extracts and processes minerals – published its *Climate Change Report 2020* that says,

> "Warming of the climate is unequivocal, the human influence is clear and physical impacts are unavoidable. We will: Continue to take action to reduce our operational greenhouse gas emissions in line with our public targets; Support emissions reductions in our value chain, and the economy-wide transitions necessary to meet the Paris Agreement goals, by working with customers and suppliers to achieve sectoral decarbonization; Partner with others to accelerate the transition to a low carbon future and in the development of low emissions and negative emissions technologies, including natural climate solutions; Adapt to the potential physical impacts of climate change by building the resilience of our operated assets and investments and contributing to community and ecosystem resilience; and seek to enhance the global response to climate change by engaging with governments, maintaining a commitment to climate change advocacy and continuing to promote market mechanisms to reduce global emissions at least cost."

BlackRock – a multinational investment management corporation based in New York City that has around $7 trillion assets under management – recently announced a huge transition in their investment strategy: "Because sustainable investment options have the potential to offer clients better outcomes, we are making sustainability integral to the way BlackRock manages risk, constructs portfolios, designs products, and engages with companies. We believe that sustainability should be our new standard for investing."

Barclays, Morgan Stanley, and JPMorgan Chase have also announced plans to remove emissions from loans and other deals they structure.

With support from three of the largest pension funds in the United States, a group of ExxonMobil shareholders has announced their intention to vote against ExxonMobil's current management and replace them with more climate-friendly board members. In late May 2021, the shareholders initiated their plan, installing two new independent directors – an outcome ExxonMobil spent millions to prevent. One week later, the activist investors secured yet another seat on the board.

The Net Zero Asset Managers Initiative – a group of international asset managers – has committed to a goal of net zero greenhouse gas emissions by 2050 or before. There are currently 30 signatories that collectively have $9 trillion in assets under management.

The fact that these asset managers are making commitments like this is a cataclysmic development. These are the money guys. This is actually way more of a game changer than anything any government or international body could possibly achieve.

These verbal commitments are already turning into reality. In the year leading to October 2020, the S&P Global Clean Energy Index – an index that provides liquid and tradable exposure to thirty clean energy companies worldwide – outperformed the S&P 500, an index that tracks the stock performance of 500 large American companies.

General Motors announced its intention to sell only zero-emission cars and trucks by 2035, blindsiding fellow automakers and upending the entire industry. Putting its money where its mouth is, GM committed $27 billion to produce 30 electric vehicle models by 2025. The company is building a new plant in Ohio to produce batteries, and I already mentioned their plan to spend over $4 billion to increase electric vehicle and battery production in Michigan.

True, it doesn't hurt that companies like Tesla, the electric vehicle and clean energy company, are worth a fortune. As of April 2022, Tesla's market capitalization shot over ONE <u>TRILLION</u> DOLLARS. It is now the 6th most valuable company by market cap in the entire world and is considered to be the most valuable automaker by far. In fact, investors value Tesla more than General Motors, Toyota, Volkswagen, and Ford *combined.*

Elon Musk, who bought 14 percent of Tesla for $6.5 million in 2004, is now one of the richest people in the world. In fact, Elon is now $100 BILLION richer that Jeff Bezos.

< Interesting fact: In 2021, while many old-school automakers shuttered factories as they waited for computer chips to arrive from overseas, Tesla enjoyed record sales. By the end of the year, Tesla had sold almost twice as many vehicles as they had the year before. They achieved this by not only understanding their technology, but by magnificently managing their own supply chain.

The *New York Times* reports: "When Tesla couldn't get the chips it had counted on, it took the ones that were available and rewrote the software that operated them to suit its needs. Larger auto companies couldn't do that because they relied on outside suppliers for much of their software and computing expertise. In many cases, automakers also relied on these suppliers to deal with chip manufacturers. When the crisis hit, the automakers lacked bargaining clout.

Just a few years ago, analysts saw Mr. Musk's insistence on having Tesla do more things on its own as one of the main reasons the company was struggling to increase production. Now, his strategy appears to have been vindicated." >

Amazon has backed five climate-related tech firms, and Bill Gates has put together Breakthrough Energy Ventures (BEV). BEV brought together 20 uber rich people – including the richest man of three countries, America (Jeff Bezos), China (Jack Ma), and India (Mukesh Ambani) – to back 40 firms for 20 years.

So far, it appears that investors learned important lessons from the first go-round of clean energy investment, when the industry experienced a huge boom that resulted in a huge bust. This time, it seems investors are willing to be more patient and invest in a broader portfolio beyond energy and transport.

Lucky for them, there are already a ton of new green technologies to invest in, and even more in development. This includes advanced geothermal; agricultural technology such as high yield bioenergy crops; synthetic fuels; hydropower; advanced nuclear reactors; battery powered ships and aircrafts; advanced bioenergy conversion processes; and carbon removal technologies.

Until recently, I wasn't really aware of how far these technologies have come, but they are super cool. Honestly, it blows me away how smart people are.

In Colorado, Aspen Skiing Company converted a dirty coal mine – owned by the Koch brothers, no less – into a power plant fueled by the coal mine's methane. The company's latest progress report says that the project has "prevented the emission of 250 billion cubic feet of methane annually into the atmosphere."

"This is equivalent to over 3 million hot air balloons full of methane destroyed annually; 2,392,000 tons of CO2; emissions sequestered by over three million acres of U.S. forest in one year; and removing 517,000 passenger vehicles from the road for a year." Wow!

Several companies are working to replace hydrocarbon aviation fuel with hydrogen. A British company has already reconfigured a six-seat Piper M-class plane to be a fuel-cell-powered aircraft, and a German company has done something similar with a motorized Pipistrel glider. A U.S. electric-motor manufacturer, magniX, has partnered with Los Angeles-based Universal Hydrogen to convert a 40-seat de Havilland Canada Dash 8-300 to be powered by fuel cells.

Airbus, a European multinational aerospace corporation, recently introduced a project called ZEROe with the goal of designing the first zero-emission commercial aircraft: "All three ZEROe concepts are hybrid-hydrogen aircraft. They are powered by hydrogen combustion through modified gas turbine engines. Liquid hydrogen is used as fuel for combustion with oxygen. In addition, hydrogen fuel cells create electrical power that complements the gas turbine, resulting in a highly efficient hybrid-electric propulsion system. All these technologies are complementary, and the benefits are additive."

Dominion Energy – a power and energy company headquartered in Richmond, Virginia – has also invested in green hydrogen, a stable source of carbon-free power that can reduce emissions from power plants and pipelines.

While old-school hydrogen is largely produced from coal or natural gas (which essentially cancels out any benefit hydrogen may ultimately bring), green hydrogen is made when renewable energy is used to split hydrogen atoms from oxygen through a process called electrolysis. This is a major breakthrough because green hydrogen can be stored, unlike the excess energy produced from wind or solar that is often wasted.

Dominion also has high hopes for offshore wind farms and has launched the Coastal Virginia Offshore Wind (CVOW) project. The utility constructed two initial wind turbines off Virginia Beach and, if the project shows early success, intends to install 200 more.

In preparation for its shift to a cleaner footprint, Dominion has shut down six coal power plants, announced the closure of two more, and has converted five coal plants to natural gas. They, along with their partner Duke Energy, recently pulled the ripcord on the Atlantic Coast Pipeline, a project that caught tons of heat for crisscrossing the Appalachian Trail.

General Electric has produced a wind turbine that is longer than the length of two football fields. Although still in the testing phase in the Netherlands, GE plans to use these turbines to produce power offshore. These turbines each have the capacity to produce 13 megawatts of power, which can keep the lights on in approximately 12,000 homes.

Altogether, worldwide investment in the clean energy sector totaled $2.6 trillion between 2010 to 2019. Across the globe, *government-funded* clean energy research and development reached $25.4 billion in 2019, increasing for the third year in a row.

This level of research & development and investment will make key technologies cheaper and more scalable, which only accelerates our progress.

The Wall Street Journal reports that China has invested heavily in both green hydrogen and associated refueling stations in its quest to industrialize big trucks that run on something called hydrogen proton-exchange membrane cells. A Canadian company called Ballard is a leading producer of these cells, which have already powered Chinese trucks over 50 million kilometers. Heads-up America! Around 75 percent of Ballard's cells have been sold to China.

Chinese companies produce 72 percent of the solar modules, 69 percent of the lithium-ion batteries, and 45 percent of the wind turbines that are used around the world. China also has a heap of cobalt and lithium, two minerals that are essential to producing clean energy.

Additionally, the Chinese have launched *Made in China 2025*, a plan that makes massive investments in key green technologies and advanced technologies in rail, shipping and aviation. (more on this later)

Even Middle Eastern countries invest in green technologies – and have been doing so for years. As far back as 2009, the crown prince of Abu Dhabi invested $15 billion in renewable energy.

At the time, Khaled Awad – a director of a project called Masdar, a zero-carbon city and research park in Abu Dhabi – said, "Abu Dhabi is an oil-exporting country, and we want to become an energy-exporting country, and to do that we need to excel at the newer forms of energy. We know we can't continue with this carbon footprint. We have to change. This is why Abu Dhabi must develop new models – for the planet, of course, but also so as not to jeopardize Abu Dhabi." Come on, America! Even Abu Dhabi got the memo! :)

At around the same time, the government of Qatar invested over $220 million in a British low-carbon technology fund, and the King Abdullah University of Science and Technology in Saudi Arabia gave a scientist from Stanford $25 million to develop research on solar power. Egypt just unveiled Benban, one of the world's largest solar farms. Benban generates enough power to keep the lights on in over one million homes.

All in, renewable energy capacity in the Middle East doubled in the past ten years and is set to double again in the next four.

Back stateside, Silicon Valley is highly optimistic about the reemergence of geothermal energy, a technique that locates and taps into hot water or hot rocks trapped in fractures three or more miles underground in order to produce electricity.

The United States is the largest producer of geothermal energy and The Geysers, owned by the utility Calpine and located in the Mayacamas Mountains in California, is the largest single geothermal field. Geothermal energy produces roughly one-sixth of the CO^2 that even the cleanest natural gas-fired power generation produces, and unlike wind or solar, it doesn't depend on natural elements to produce electricity.

Mirrors now convert sunlight into heat oil which can then be used to produce electricity. Arizona Public Service used this technology to build a solar trough power plant, and similar technology was used to build Nevada Solar One, one of the largest concentrated solar power plants in the world. Replacing a conventional power plant with a solar power plant is the equivalent to taking 20,000 cars off the road every single year.

§§§

The entire world is making amazing progress, and I certainly appreciate the urgency to introduce renewable energy sources as quickly as possible.

However, it's a good thing this is a *process* because these new technologies and their government oversight need time to properly evolve. Subsidies and tax credits can be useful in terms of research and development, but they can also encourage quantity over quality.

For example, depending on how they are generated, biofuels can emit as much pollution as fossil fuels. There is no real reduction in carbon dioxide emissions if coal is used to convert wheat into ethanol or if rapeseed is grown using fertilizer made from natural gas. Presently, it's difficult to distinguish good biofuel from bad, but often they both receive the same breaks from the government.

Subsidies also tend to make companies less mindful of long-term strategy and costs. The *American Recovery and Reinvestment Act of 2009*, the stimulus package passed by Congress after the 2007-2009 Financial Crisis, offered to pay wind-farm developers up to 30 percent of the capital investment costs of new wind projects.

However, as subsidies increased, thoughtful due diligence at times decreased. After the federal money was offered, for example, wind-power projects were built in areas with 16 percent less wind than a decade before. That doesn't sound like the smartest move.

There are global implications to consider as well. In the 2005 energy bill, the U.S. government mandated the use of ethanol in gasoline and, two years later, significantly increased the original quota.

These government mandates and their corresponding subsidies unleashed a construction frenzy to build ethanol plants.

Not long after, it became clear that the boom in American ethanol was a major contributor to a severe spike in worldwide food prices, which had risen 75 percent since the U.S. energy legislation passed (ethanol is generally made from biomass like sugar or corn). This was devastating for poor countries, where people could barely keep food on the table under normal conditions. As a consequence, there were food riots in Mexico, Egypt, Haiti and many other countries.

Very little concern was shown when the international community was damaged by rising food prices, but that changed when it hit closer to home. Elevated corn prices eventually came back to bite American ethanol producers in the britches because their product was now much more expensive to produce.

Shaken by record high prices, many ethanol producers hedged their future corn price to protect against additional increases. However, banner harvests and a significant drop in commodity prices across-the-board led to a nosedive in corn prices, leaving the ethanol producers with a $7 a bushel price tag in a $4 a bushel market.

These factors, combined with the economic fallout from the 2007-2009 Financial Crisis, left the industry crippled. Many ethanol producers filed for bankruptcy protection and construction plans for new ethanol plants were postponed or abandoned entirely.

As we see over and over, good intentions can have unintended consequences if we don't pay attention. #TheButterflyEffect

§§§

Without question, an appropriate balance between fossil fuels and renewable energy calls for significant concessions on all sides, but over time the scales will steadily shift.

More than anything else, shifts like these depend on the support and sacrifice of the American people. We, as consumers, can't be naïve. At times, environmentally responsible energy may mean money, and that may mean rate increase. But if we truly value national security and environmental stewardship, we have to be willing to pay the price.

Being responsible caretakers of our environment is a perfect example of how we tend to wait for *someone else* to do something or for *someone else* to change. We can debate long-term energy strategies until the cows come home, but quite frankly, it seems pretty superficial when our national consumption is at an all-time high and has no sign of waning.

It's pretty difficult to take ANY of the outrage seriously when very few of us have energy efficient homes or engage in simple things like using fluorescent light bulbs (especially given the fact that if every family in the U.S. replaced just one incandescent light bulb with a compact fluorescent bulb, greenhouse gas emissions would decrease by over 90 billion pounds – the equivalent of removing 7.5 million cars from our roads).

We vow to be as green as the Jolly Green Giant when oil hits $147, but then we're struck with environmental amnesia when it drops back down to a comfortable $40. The United States covers less than 7 percent of the world's land surface and has only 4 percent of the world's people, but we account for 17 percent of the world's total energy consumption.

That said, I believe in us, America! We can do this! After all, environmental responsibility is certainly not a new concept in the United States.

The first comprehensive environmental legislation was signed by President Richard Nixon. The *Clean Air Act of 1970* addressed air pollution, water pollution and toxic waste. The law established the National Ambient Air Quality Standards to protect public health and to regulate emissions of harmful air pollutants. It also created State Implementation Plans, New Source Performance Standards and National Emission Standards for Hazardous Air Pollutants. President Nixon also established the Environmental Protection Agency.

In response to the 1973 oil crisis – when the Organization of Arab Petroleum Exporting Countries declared an oil embargo because of America's supply commitment to the Israeli military – Congress adopted the Corporate Fuel Economy Standards which required higher fuel-economy standards for cars and trucks.

In 1975, Congress passed and President Gerald Ford signed the *Energy Policy and Conservation Act* with broad bipartisan support. The legislation established the Strategic Petroleum Reserve which required a petroleum reserve of up to 1 billion barrels. It also put into place a corporate average fuel economy standard – 27.5 miles per gallon – for new passenger vehicles.

President Ronald Reagan championed the *Montreal Protocol on Substances That Deplete the Ozone Layer*, a historic international treaty crafted to protect the high-altitude, or stratospheric, ozone layer by slowly eliminating the production of chemicals that deplete it.

During the George H.W. Bush administration, the *Clean Air Act Amendments of 1990* proposed emissions trading and created a national permits program. It also addressed acid rain, ozone depletion and toxic air pollution. The legislation established auto gasoline reformulation requirements and set Reid Vapor Pressure standards to control evaporative emissions from gasoline.

We have made tremendous progress in the past five decades. The time has come to write the next – and most critical – chapter.

Fiscal Strategy

Red Flags & Ticking Time Bombs

– the 1787 Recommendations for
the Economy are in *The Policy Guide* –

Does no one in Washington understand the wise saying *make hay while the sun shines*?

In July 2019, the United States economic expansion entered its 10th year, making it the longest on record. At the time, according to *The Wall Street Journal*, "more than 20 million jobs had been created so far in the expansion that started in mid-2009, and the net worth of American households – the value of assets such as stocks and housing minus debts such as mortgages and credit cards – had increased by $47 trillion."

Unemployment was low and job creation seemed solid. In fact, the labor market had experienced an astonishing recovery from the 2007-2009 Financial Crisis. In January 2020, the seasonally adjusted official unemployment rate was 3.6 percent.

Although there is debate among economists about the magic unemployment target, this is a great number. Some would even say that America had reached its full productive capacity – meaning we were finally at a point where almost everyone who wanted a job actually had one and that our workforce was producing at near to full speed. By many measures, the U.S. economy looked strong.

But, as always, here is where we got ourselves into trouble. During our claw back from the 2007-2009 Financial Crisis, it was impossible to know how long the economic expansion was going to last. After all, the U.S. economy looked great *before* the Financial Crisis also, to the point where practically no one saw it coming. In other words, everything was great – until it wasn't.

Therefore, while we were fortunate enough to be in an expansion, the smart, responsible course of action would have been to use those critical years to solidify our financial stability; spend money on investment in our future through cutting-edge research and development and intelligent infrastructure projects; and finally tackle the root causes of the financial Apocalypse that is quickly bearing down on us (a.k.a. Social Security, Medicare, Medicaid and pensions).

Instead, Congress and the Trump administration drowned us in debt, passed extremely expensive tax cuts, started trade wars, restricted legal immigration, eviscerated regulation, and allowed our workforce to remain in denial and ill-prepared for the harsh realities of the 21st century workplace.

Trump supporters, I know you may be thinking that I am, once again, unfairly bagging on your guy but, I promise you, I'm not saying this just because I don't like him. Trust me, that's not it. I would have been thrilled to see him be a successful president and, if he had been, I would be the first to give him credit for it. That's the God's honest truth.

I'm only saying this because – while things like tax cuts, trade, immigration and regulation provide great one-liners at campaign rallies – taken together, many of the Trump administration's actions were incredibly reckless and devastating for our long-term economic outlook. And I'm going to prove it to you in the following pages, with actual facts straight from the United States government, not cable news nonsense.

§§§

America's fiscal course is unsustainable, and we all know it. Year after year our spending has increased while our revenues have fallen short. But instead of tackling this shortfall head-on and jeopardizing their re-election bids, our leaders have chosen to borrow enormous amounts of money to cover it.

Let's take a closer look at **three financial bombs** that started ticking during the Trump presidency – the ones that then exploded when Covid-19 hit.

Financial Bomb One

During the Trump presidency, he and the Republicans took America straight down the dangerous road of trickle down, supply-side economics by encouraging domestic investment through tax cuts and less regulation – even though history pretty much tells us this approach doesn't work.

< Please don't misunderstand, all this negative talk about trickle down, supply-side economics in no way means that the better way is massive tax-and-spending, which may even be worse. There will be more on this this later in this chapter. >

Here is the Republican fantasy about supply-side economics in a nutshell: Cutting corporate taxes and rich people's taxes, plus minimizing regulation, will give corporations and rich people the chance to create so many fabulous opportunities that the benefits will "trickle down" to everyone else and the economy will flourish beyond anyone's wildest dreams!!!

Obviously, a tax cut means that less money is being collected by the federal government, but supply-side Republicans believe that this tangible loss is more than compensated for by the level of economic growth that the tax cuts will surely bring.

They believe this fairytale because forty years ago, President Reagan unleashed "Reaganomics" when he signed the *Economic Recovery Tax Act of 1981.*

What these Republicans seem to forget is, although the U.S. economy did indeed experience a boost during this time period – including a net gain of 2 million jobs per year during Reagan's two terms (which, incidentally, is less than the 2.6 million jobs per year under President Jimmy Carter) – it was more a function of the Paul

Volcker-led Federal Reserve's significant interest rate cuts <u>and</u> increased spending for defense and construction projects.

They also forget that, when President Reagan took office, the economy was in recession, interest rates were 19 percent, unemployment was in the double digits, and inflation was almost 10 percent (which are all reasons why the Federal Reserve's interest rate cuts made such a huge impact). Also, the top marginal income tax rate was 70 percent.

All of us can probably agree that a top marginal income tax rate of 70 percent was waaaaay too high and, at the time, substantial reform of the tax code was long overdue.

To that end, the *Economic Recovery Tax Act of 1981* reduced the marginal tax rate from 70 percent to 50 percent. From the beginning, President Reagan and his team recognized that the tax cuts would not pay for themselves, but their expectation was that spending cuts would help balance everything out. Typically, the spending cuts never came.

But even back then – with an economy that had negative markers across the board – supply-side economics didn't work. Soon after the 1981 tax cut, federal revenues dropped like a rock and the deficit blew out, making it clear that the tax reduction was too aggressive.

As a result, President Reagan and Congress had to *raise* taxes in 1982 (a rollback of some of the 1981 tax cuts), 1983 (a payroll tax on Social Security and Medicare), 1984 (a closure of tax loopholes) and 1987 (a closure of more loopholes and an extension of a telephone excise tax). President George H.W. Bush was forced to raise taxes again in 1990 – violating his "read my lips, no new taxes" campaign pledge, which cost him a second term – as was President Bill Clinton in 1993.

In 2010, tax historian Joseph Thorndike put it this way, "Reagan was certainly a tax cutter legislatively, emotionally and ideologically. But for a variety of political reasons, it was hard for him to ignore the cost of his tax cuts." Together, the tax legislation that passed in 1982 and 1984 "constituted the biggest tax <u>*increase*</u> ever enacted during peacetime."

After two years of intense analysis by the U.S. Treasury Department, President Reagan signed the *Tax Reform Act of 1986*, a bipartisan bill with the stated goal of "fairness, simplicity and economic growth." This legislation reduced the marginal income tax rate from 50 percent to 28 percent and reduced the corporate tax rate from 46 percent to 34 percent.

But this didn't really have an impact either. As Bruce Bartlett – a domestic policy adviser to President Reagan and one of the architects of the *Economic Recovery Tax Act of 1981* – explains:

> "Today, Republicans extol the virtues of lowering marginal tax rates, citing as their model the *Tax Reform Act of 1986*, which lowered the top individual income tax rate to just 28 percent from 50 percent, and the corporate tax rate to 34 percent from 46 percent. What follows, they say, would be an economic boon.
>
> Indeed, textbook tax theory says that lowering marginal tax rates while holding revenue constant unambiguously raises growth. But there is no evidence showing a boost in growth from the 1986 act. The economy remained on the same track, with huge stock market crashes – 1987's 'Black Monday,' 1989's Friday the 13th 'mini-crash' and a recession beginning in 1990. Real wages fell.
>
> Strenuous efforts by economists to find any growth effect from the 1986 act have failed to find much. The most thorough analysis, by economists Alan Auerbach and Joel Slemrod, found only a shifting of income due to tax reform, no growth effects: 'The aggregate values of labor supply and saving apparently responded very little,' they concluded."

This is more of what Auerbach and Slemrod had to say:

> "Of course, saying that a decade of analysis has not taught us much about whether the *Tax Reform Act of 1986* was a good idea is not at all the same as saying it was not in fact a good idea. We think it was.
>
> The theoretical case remains valid for a tax system with a broad and clean base which minimizes the reward to tax-driven

economic activity. Advocates of this kind of tax system will, however, be frustrated that a retrospective analysis of the most comprehensive attempt in history to achieve this goal offers little hard evidence of the fruits of this effort."

"Reaganomics" didn't work as advertised because of those damn unintended consequences, and no one knew that better than Ronald Reagan himself. In his farewell address to the nation, he said, "I've been asked if I have any regrets. Well, I do. The deficit is one." #The Butterfly Effect

That said, it probably made sense to give supply-side economics a shot back in 1981, given the dire state of the economy and before we had actual *evidence* of its ineffectiveness.

But, even speaking theoretically, supply-side economics made absolutely ZERO sense for an economy that had been on a healthy trajectory in terms of stable growth and low unemployment for over eight years. Essentially, the Republican *Tax Cuts and Jobs Act of 2017* (TCJA) acted as a fiscal stimulus when we didn't need one.

This was a double-whammy because, not only are the Republican tax cuts costing this nation a fortune, but the Federal Reserve Bank of San Francisco reports that "many recent studies have found that fiscal stimulus has a smaller impact when the economy is strong, implying that the near-term boost to GDP growth could be two-thirds or less of that from previous tax cuts."

There is an additional huge red flag here: Even with the Republican tax cuts acting as a stimulus, the annual gross domestic product (GDP) growth rate was only 3 percent in 2018, then fell to 2.2 percent in 2019. Hardly a boon. (we'll talk more about this and other consequences of the Republican tax cuts in a minute)

The Congressional Research Service – Congress' public policy research group – reported that, "on the whole, the growth effects [of the Republican 2017 tax cuts] tend to show a relatively small (if any) first-year effect on the economy. Although growth rates cannot indicate the tax cut's effects on GDP, they tend to rule out very large effects particularly in the short run."

They concluded that "the growth patterns for different types of assets do not appear to be consistent with the direction and size of the supply-side incentive effects one would expect from the tax changes."

Financial Bomb Two

The decision to add hundreds of billions of dollars to the federal budget just weeks after the Republicans rammed through their very costly tax cuts is just mind-boggling in its irresponsibility. The bipartisan agreement responsible for this raised the debt ceiling as well as the spending caps that were placed on military and domestic spending during the Obama presidency. Now, the spending caps were increased by around $300 billion.

Just one month later, Congress approved a 2,232-page $1.3 trillion appropriations bill, which covered federal funding for only six months. Of the bill, Senator Ben Sasse (R-NE) said, "Every Republican would vote against this disgusting pork bill if a Democrat were president. This spending kegger is a wildly irresponsible use of the taxpayers' money, and the president should not sign it." Just hours before the bill passed, Representative Jim McGovern, (D-MA) said, "In all honesty, none of us know what is actually in this bill."

But wait! There's more! In August 2019, Congress and the Trump administration followed all of this up by approving a two-year $2.7 trillion budget agreement, a move that required the debt ceiling be suspended until the end of July 2021. This was the fourth time Congress had voted to ignore the spending limits established by the 2011 *Budget Control Act*.

We have to fund the federal government of course, but not one penny of this $2.7 trillion went to fund federal agencies. Say what? Yep, funding for that was finally passed – after two stop gap spending bills were passed to keep the government afloat while Congress continued to duke it out – on December 19, 2019.

This is so irresponsible and foolish. For one, this level of spending acted like yet another fiscal stimulus. Bomb #1 and Bomb #2 amounted to taking lighter fluid and pouring it over an already roaring fire.

But here's the most dangerous part: Thanks to the lingering effects of the 2007-2009 Financial Crisis, we already have fewer financial weapons in our arsenal to combat a financial crisis than we have had in the past. What if we need the boost of that lighter fluid down the road, like if a scary worldwide virus starts to spread and shuts down a large part of our economy, or war breaks out in Eastern Europe?!? Did anyone in Washington even consider that possibility? Of course not.

Which, of course, is exactly what happened. As of May 2021, the United States of America had appropriated over SIX TRILLION DOLLARS to respond to "Covid-19 and its economic fallout." I use quotation marks because every single one of the associated Covid-19 bills was jammed with things that have nothing at all to do with Covid-19 and its economic fallout. (we'll talk more about this in a few minutes)

Financial Bomb Three

Separately, Bomb #1 and Bomb #2 are disastrous but, taken together, they drastically widened our deficit and blew our debt out of the water.

Less than one year after the Republican tax bill passed, the U.S. Treasury Department reported that the federal budget deficit increased by 17 percent – to $779 billion – from FY2017 to FY2018 (the budget deficit is the difference between government spending and tax revenue).

According to the Committee for a Responsible Federal Budget, an independent, bipartisan public policy organization, "Over one-third of the 2018 deficit and 234 percent of the increase in deficits, $264 billion, was due to legislation enacted by Congress over the past year. The largest portion was the tax law, estimated to cost $164 billion in FY2018, followed by the *Bipartisan Budget Act of 2018* which was estimated to cost $68 billion in 2018."

The next year, Treasury reported that the deficit had grown to $984 billion from FY2018 to FY2019, a 26 percent increase. From FY2019 to FY 2020, our budget deficit reached $3.1 trillion. This was by far the largest one-year gap in history.

Meanwhile, at the end of December 2019 and right before the pandemic hit, the United States' total public debt outstanding was $23.2 trillion. By July 2021, it hit $28.4 trillion. (Tip: I know this can be confusing. It sometimes helps to think of the federal debt as the sum of our past deficits.)

By September 2020, the Congressional Budget Office (CBO) was reporting that, for the first time since World War II, our nation's debt now equaled the size of the entire American economy and would surpass that threshold in 2021. (Spoiler Alert: That's not good.)

In March 2021, the CBO released a report that said: "At an estimated 10.3 percent of gross domestic product (GDP), the deficit in 2021 would be the second largest since 1945, exceeded only by the 14.9 percent shortfall recorded last year. In CBO's projections, deficits decline as the effects of the 2020–2021 coronavirus pandemic wane. But they remain large by historical standards and begin to increase again during the latter half of the decade. Deficits increase further in subsequent decades, from 5.7 percent of GDP in 2031 to 13.3 percent by 2051 – exceeding their 50-year average of 3.3 percent of GDP in each year during that period."

Regarding federal debt, the same CBO report said that "by the end of 2021, federal debt held by the public is projected to equal 102 percent of GDP. Debt would reach 107 percent of GDP (surpassing its historical high) in 2031 and would almost double to 202 percent of GDP by 2051. Debt that is high and rising as a percentage of GDP boosts federal and private borrowing costs, slows the growth of economic output, and increases interest payments abroad. A growing debt burden could increase the risk of a fiscal crisis and higher inflation as well as undermine confidence in the U.S. dollar, making it more costly to finance public and private activity in international markets."

We're well on our way. The United States federal government spent $927 billion dollars in March 2021, which was $660 billion more than we received in tax revenue. This monthly deficit was the third largest in history, beaten only by April and June of 2020. Our budget deficit surpassed $1.7 trillion in the first six months of FY2021 alone.

§§§

So, let me get this straight. We went from the longest economic expansion in history to a $3.1 trillion deficit and so much debt that it exceeds our entire gross domestic product. How does that wise saying *make hay while the sun shines* sound right about now?

That this happened during Donald Trump's presidency comes as no surprise since he obviously has no problem accruing massive debt (nor a problem with just walking away from it and leaving others, like hard-working Americans who built his casinos, holding the bag).

But clearly, between 2017 and 2020 the rest of our leaders got lulled into the false sense of security they always seem to find in-between inevitable economic calamities. They fell right back into their destructive habit of reacting to negative outcomes as opposed to proactively anticipating and preparing for them.

I've heard some people argue that, since interest rates are so low right now, it's no big deal to borrow whatever and whenever we want. This is a preposterous thing to say. Even if we paid <u>zero</u> interest on borrowed money – heck, even if China and Japan *paid us* to borrow from them – we still have to pay the money back.

It would be one thing if we borrowed money to buy ourselves state-of-the-art airports, subways, railways and ports; sophisticated fiber-optic lines, bandwidth and wireless networks; modern schools, roads, bridges, levees, dams and water systems; hi-tech electricity-distribution grids; or extensive high-speed rail systems.

But that's not what we have spent our money on. We have borrowed for consumption, not investment. Our infrastructure is still crumbling, and we don't have squat to show for our trillions of dollars of debt. Nothing. Nada.

You and I don't have to be Nobel Prize-winning economists to understand that continued borrowing for consumption rather than investment is not good. We don't need a Ph.D. in economics to understand that there is a significantly negative relationship between crushing debt and economic growth.

Let me quickly paint a picture that ain't pretty. If we allow this to continue, our government will eventually become basically paralyzed. The United States of America will be unable to borrow money to respond to short-term financial emergencies such as wars, recessions, or economic calamities like the 2007-2009 Financial Crisis (when we desperately needed our public balance sheets to offset the enormous de-leveraging of private ones) or things like the economic fallout caused by the Covid-19 pandemic (when American families were in dire straits).

If we keep borrowing for consumption rather than investment, we will eventually be unable to find financing for our long-term productive capacity, where borrowed money can be repaid with actual income. Interest rates will likely increase, which will exponentially increase the pain of our indebtedness and make it more expensive, if not impossible, to raise capital, invest in innovation, and create jobs.

We will be at the mercy of foreign creditors, who even now own a third of our public debt (as of January 2022, Japan owns 1.3 trillion and China owns $1 trillion). Investors will eventually lose confidence that we can repay our debts or have the political will to, which could initiate a debt crisis and worldwide panic. Next comes a run on the dollar.

Then comes this little issue known as inflation, a phenomenon everyone seemed to completely forget until it blew in like a hurricane in 2021. Before the last few months, "inflation" sounded like an antiquated word from the past. That's because many economists thought it was. But they have been proven quite wrong. This is exactly the kind of thinking I'm talking about when I say we get lulled into a false sense of security and, as a result, fall right back into the destructive habit of reacting to negative outcomes as opposed to proactively anticipating them.

While it's true that, after significantly increasing our federal debt coupled with the drastic measures the Fed took after the 2007-2009 Financial Crisis, the anticipated higher inflation did not come to pass. But that in no way meant it was dead and buried forever.

Even before the Covid-19 stimulus packages, the evidence was not nearly strong enough to believe that inflation was no longer a potential threat to our economy. Fast forward to December 2021, when prices shot up 7 percent, the largest spike in almost 40 years. By March 2022, inflation was still surging – by 8.5 percent. This was the largest increase since 1981.

We have got to get a handle on this because this reality is already causing serious short-term pain for many American households. Longer-term, high inflation strikes at the very heart of the financial security of the middle class, affecting savings accounts, pensions, and home ownership.

Thanks to years of financial irresponsibility, there are additional challenges. If higher inflation persists, it will be more dangerous than ever since both federal and corporate debt is so high and the balance sheet of the Federal Reserve is so bloated. These factors alone could greatly diminish the effectiveness of a reduction in bond purchases or higher interest rates, tools the Fed uses to address inflation.

Fear should not dictate policymaking, but this is not unjustified fear. I'm not being hyperbolic…this could very well be our future if we don't do something fast. Being a happy-go-lucky gal, I absolutely hate being a buzz kill. But the time has come where there is really no choice: This has got to stop. We <u>must</u> be more fiscally responsible.

How Will 1787 Pay for Everything?

You have my word, I will always fight hard to make sure 1787 is fiscally responsible – exhibiting transparency, leveraging assets, and exercising discipline.

To me, the goal is to enhance the quality of life for *every* American by greatly improving federal programs and the way our government operates while, at the same time, significantly reducing our debt and closing the ever-widening gap of our deficit. Initially, 1787 has a **two-part** fiscal strategy and we will live by it faithfully.

Fiscal Strategy: Part One

No New Non-Emergency Spending, Just a Reallocation of Existing Resources

All of 1787's non-emergency policies will be cost neutral for at least two years, then we will reevaluate. No new money is necessary, just a reallocation of existing resources.

Don't worry! None of our important federal programs will suffer – they will just be run much more efficiently (I will explain how we will achieve this in Part II). Without a doubt, we can make serious headway in our national funding crisis – full stop – if we: stop wasting resources and get a bigger bang for our buck by taking a comprehensive approach.

Fiscal Strategy: Part Two

Significantly Reduce Our Debt and Close the Gap on Our Deficit

We will begin to reduce our astronomical debt and deficit in **two steps**:

Step One

Step one is to end the massive inefficiency and waste that infects every level of our federal government and use these found funds solely for the purpose of reducing our debt and closing the gap on our deficit. The 1787 initiative that leads this effort is called *Operation Overhaul.*

Step Two

Fairly readjust the tax code.

Significantly Reduce Our Debt and Close the Gap on Our Deficit

Step One Explained

Waste. The word that comes to mind over and over when I think of our governmental policies is waste. Billions after billions are just wasted. Seriously wasted. Like just flush-it-down-the-toilet wasted.

Why does this happen? Because our government has become a bureaucratic Behemoth monster that will eventually strangle our ability to advance on any level. This is not a Republican-esque rant about the size of government, because theirs is a misguided argument.

Contrary to their belief, size does not necessarily correlate to efficiency. Just because the federal government is smaller doesn't mean it will automatically run more effectively. Some of the largest of companies run like a well-oiled machine while some of the smallest of companies are management disasters.

It's not about *size.* It's about *efficiency.* If we focus on being efficient, our government will be exactly the size it needs to be.

Walmart tops the Fortune 500 list with $549 billion in annual revenue, and Amazon is second with $348 billion. Meanwhile, the U.S. federal government collected $3.4 trillion in receipts in FY2020.

The portion of that figure squandered is off the chain. From the F-35 Joint Strike Fighter – which is on track to cost American taxpayers over $1 trillion over its 60-year life span, leading Chairman of the House Armed Services Committee Representative Adam Smith (D-WA) to call it a "rathole" – to things like the Internal Revenue Service (IRS) having to pay taxpayers $3 billion in interest because refunds were late – waste permeates our federal government.

And those type of things are just the tip of the iceberg. For example, the rampant fraud, waste, and abuse within the Centers for Medicare & Medicaid Services (CMS) is staggering. The U.S. Government Accountability Office (GAO) – a government agency that provides auditing, evaluation, and investigative services for the U.S. Congress – says that:

> "CMS, which administers Medicare, faces many challenges related to implementing payment methods that encourage efficient service delivery, managing the program to serve beneficiaries well, and safeguarding the program from loss due to fraud, waste, and abuse. Medicare has been designated as a *High Risk* program because its complexity and susceptibility to improper payments, in addition to its size, have led to serious management challenges. Addressing these challenges requires improvements to payment methods, program management, and program safeguards."

A follow-up report from the GAO revealed that:

> "Improper payment estimates for fiscal year 2019 totaled about $175 billion, based on improper payment estimates reported by federal programs, an increase from the fiscal year 2018 total of $151 billion. Of the $175 billion, about $121 billion (approximately 69 percent) was concentrated in three

program areas: (1) Medicaid, (2) Medicare, and (3) Earned Income Tax Credit.

Improper payments – payments that should not have been made or that were made in incorrect amounts – continue to be an area of fiscal concern in the federal government. Improper payments have been estimated to total almost $1.7 trillion government-wide from fiscal years 2003 through 2019."

SAY WHAT? 1.7 TRILLION DOLLARS? Is this a joke? And the Chinese and Japanese governments say, "Thank you, America!"

Unfortunately, this is not a one-off. It's actually the modus operandi for practically every single department of our federal government, and it's been happening for decades.

Let's look to FY2012 for another example. I know this is a few years back, but it's one of the craziest examples and you and I both know it hasn't gotten any better. If anything, it's gotten much worse.

In FY2012, there were at least 92 federal programs designed to help lower-income Americans, for a combined cost of $799 billion to the American taxpayer. This included 28 education and job-training programs ($94.4 billion), 17 different food-aid programs ($105 billion), and over 22 various housing programs ($49.6 billion). There were seven federal agencies involved in "Education and Job Training" and seven involved in the category called "Social Services."

There are many glaring issues in that last paragraph, but the most obvious one is that this process is incredibly inefficient. Inefficient is not even the right word – we need an entirely new word for what this is.

Seven separate federal agencies that administer 28 different employment and training programs, with practically zero coordination between them? This is beyond absurd. It is imperative that we reorganize this mess and use our resources more effectively. The overlap alone is wasting so, so, so much money.

It's this lack of coordination that leads to things like this: A 2019 report called *Asleep at the Wheel*, published by the nonprofit group Network for Public Education, did a deep dive into the federal Charter School Program (CSP), which began in 1994 under the U.S. Department of Education.

The report revealed that over 1,000 grants had been given to charter schools that were forced to close due to mismanagement, poor performance, or fraud, or charters that never formally opened at all. These wasted grants equaled roughly $1 billion. The report also says that the U.S. Department of Education does not verify the information on charter school applications, nor appropriately monitors even the valid grants.

Worse, the report found "troubling examples of charter management organizations (CMO's) that received massive grants that engaged in practices that push-out low-performing students, violate the rights of students with disabilities and cull their student bodies through policies, programs and requests for parental donations."

The conclusion of the analysis was that the "U.S. Department of Education has not been a responsible steward of taxpayer dollars in its management of the Charter School Program." Ya think?

The examples of waste are endless. Earlier, we talked about the Pentagon so let's take a peek under that hood. In 2015, the Defense Business Board – a group that provides the Secretary of Defense and Deputy Secretary of Defense along with other senior leaders within the Department of Defense with independent advice on business management issues – found that the Department of Defense (DoD) could save $125 billion over five years...an assertion that inherently implies there is $125 billion being wasted at the DoD.

The internal report said that this could be achieved not through civil servant or military personnel layoffs, but by focusing on streamlining bureaucracy, offering early retirements, reducing the number of high-priced contractors, and embracing information technology.

According to the Government Accountability Office (GAO), "In 2014, Congress authorized the creation of the *Iraq Train and Equip Fund* (ITEF) to provide equipment and other assistance to Iraq's security forces, including the Kurdistan Regional Government forces, to counter the expansion of the Islamic State of Iraq and Syria…As of December 2016, DoD had disbursed about $2 billion of the $2.3 billion Congress appropriated for ITEF in fiscal years 2015 and 2016 to purchase, for example, personal protective equipment, weapons, and vehicles for these forces."

However, the Pentagon has no idea where many of these shipments ultimately landed: "DoD cannot fully account for ITEF-funded equipment transfers because of missing or incomplete transfer documentation. Without timely and accurate transit information, DoD cannot ensure that the equipment has reached its intended destination, nor can program managers conduct effective oversight of ITEF-funded equipment."

But wait! Of course, there's more. A special report from *Reuters* says that "pay errors in the military are widespread."

> "*Reuters* found multiple examples of pay mistakes affecting active-duty personnel and discharged soldiers. Some are erroneously shortchanged on pay. Others are mistakenly overpaid and then see their earnings drastically cut as the Defense Finance Accounting Service (DFAS) recoups the money...Precise totals on the extent and cost of these mistakes are impossible to come by, and for the very reason the errors plague the military in the first place: The Defense Department's jury-rigged network of mostly incompatible computer systems for payroll and accounting, many of them decades old, long obsolete, and unable to communicate with each other.
>
> The DFAS accounting system still uses a half-century-old computer language that is largely unable to communicate with the equally outmoded personnel management systems employed by each of the military services.
>
> The department's authorized 2013 budget, after sequester, totaled $565.8 billion – by far the largest chunk of the annual federal budget approved by Congress. Yet the Pentagon is literally unable to account for itself. As proof, consider that a law in effect since 1992 requires annual audits of all federal agencies – and the Pentagon alone has never complied. It annually reports to Congress that its books are in such disarray that an audit is impossible.
>
> In its investigation, *Reuters* found that the Pentagon is largely incapable of keeping track of its vast stores of weapons,

ammunition and other supplies; thus, it continues to spend money on new supplies it doesn't need and on storing others long out of date. It has amassed a backlog of more than half a trillion dollars in unaudited contracts with outside vendors; how much of that money paid for actual goods and services delivered isn't known. And it repeatedly falls prey to fraud and theft that can go undiscovered for years, often eventually detected by external law enforcement agencies.

In its annual report of department-wide finances for 2012, the Pentagon reported $9.22 billion in 'reconciling amounts' to make its own numbers match the Treasury's, up from $7.41 billion a year earlier.

It said that $585.6 million of the 2012 figure was attributable to missing records. The remaining $8 billion-plus represented what Pentagon officials say are legitimate discrepancies. However, a source with knowledge of the Pentagon's accounting processes said that because the report and others like it aren't audited, they may conceal large amounts of additional plugs and other accounting problems."

This *Reuters* investigation was in 2013, so one would hope that there had been at least small improvements over the years. Nope. The Department of Defense's financial management practices have been on the GAO's *High-Risk List* since 1995. Yes, you did the math right. That's 26 years.

The GAO's latest report notes the following:

"DOD's financial management continues to face long-standing issues – including its ineffective processes, systems, and controls; incomplete corrective action plans; and the need for more effective monitoring and reporting.

Although DOD's spending makes up about half of the federal government's discretionary spending, and its physical assets represent more than 70 percent of the federal government's physical assets, it remains the only major agency that has never been able to accurately account for and report on its spending or physical assets. DOD's financial management issues extend beyond financial reporting as long-standing control deficiencies adversely affect the economy, efficiency, and effectiveness of its operations." Oh, for the love of #@^%.

This last example is also the most recent. On March 27, 2020, Donald Trump signed into law the *Coronavirus Aid, Relief, and Economic Security Act* (a.k.a. the *CARES Act*). This economic stimulus legislation provided $2.2 trillion in response to the financial fallout caused by the Covid-19 pandemic.

One of the signature programs in the *CARES Act* was the *Paycheck Protection Program* (PPP), a loan program enacted during the pandemic to provide an incentive for small businesses to keep workers on the payroll. The $525 billion program offered up to $10 million in loans and, if certain rules are followed, doesn't have to be repaid (the rules include, for example, that the number of employees and their compensation must stay consistent and at least 60 percent of the money must be spent on payroll costs).

The amount of PPP money that was misused, misappropriated, and even flat out stolen is shameful. Okay, I get it. We had to do something really fast, and if we didn't the American economy would crater, and on and on and on. I get that, and I believe that.

This is not a commentary on the *concept* of PPP. It's an indictment of how haphazard this country continually conducts business.

At what point did our government decide to not prepare for ANYTHING? EVER?!? Being in a rush IS NOT AN EXCUSE for gross negligence. We have had over a decade since the last financial crisis to get our s%@# together. Did not one person in Washington think it was wise to draft even the most rudimentary plan of action for the next one? Guys, seriously. We can't go on like this.

We almost didn't find out about how badly the PPP was mismanaged because the Trump administration tried everything under the sun to keep the information from seeing the light of day – including sidelining inspectors general and refusing to hand over information to watchdog agencies like the Government Accountability Office, even though the *CARES Act* mandates the information be released.

The Washington Post and ten other news organizations were finally forced to sue the Small Business Administration (SBA) under the *Freedom of Information Act* to get information about the PPP.

What they found is even more disturbing than I originally assumed. The first problem is how the loans were distributed. Instead of targeted relief based on need, the program was essentially a first-come, first-served deal, which threw everything off from the jump.

Large companies, including those backed by private equity and/or otherwise well capitalized, headed to the front of the line, despite the fact that the PPP application required borrowers to verify the money was "necessary to support ongoing operations."

Because outside lenders across the nation processed these loans, business owners with long-term banking relationships – which tend to be larger companies – had a tremendous advantage. Businesses with fewer employees and less revenue were put at an additional disadvantage because, since banks were allowed to establish their own lending criteria, the lenders were inherently incentivized to select large businesses over smaller ones.

The fact that the program allowed multiple subsidiaries of the same owner to apply for loans separately further increased the advantage for larger businesses while amplifying the disadvantage for smaller ones. < All of these factors disproportionally hurt businesses of color, which we will discuss in detail in Part Two of this book series. >

The lenders that processed these loans won big. Combined, they collected between $13.7 billion and $20.9 billion in fees (these numbers had to be extrapolated because the SBA still refuses to release the exact number, which is telling in and of itself). The University of Massachusetts Amherst's Political Economy Research Institute estimates the lenders, together, collected around $19 billion in fees.

By their math, JPMorgan Chase earned just over a billion in fees, with Bank of America right on their heels. Both firms originally said they would donate any profits they made from processing the loans but are now saying their expenses were so high there probably won't be any money left over after all. Dang! That's some expensive paperwork those guys did.

< That said, Citi has donated at least $25 million that it earned in fees, and Wells Fargo is donating around $400 million to support Community Development Financial Institutions (CDFIs), which are lenders that focus on underserved communities (more on these in Part Two of this book series). >

A month into the PPP program, almost 300 publicly traded companies had received over $1 billion in PPP money that was meant for small businesses. Several of these companies had executives who were paid at least $2 million a year. An artificial intelligence tech firm named Veritone, for example, received $6.5 million after paying its chief executive $18.7 million and the company president, his brother, $13.9 million in 2018.

Around 600 large entities – including chain restaurants, hotels, law firms, horse tracks and even churches – received a $10 million loan, the maximum allowed. In fact, the run on the PPP was so aggressive by these larger entities that the program ran out of money in just 13 days, leaving over 80 percent of applicants with no funding.

In the end, although 87 percent of the PPP loans were for $150,000 or less, these loans made up less than 30 percent of the total amount dispersed. ONE PERCENT of the 5.2 million borrowers received a FULL QUARTER of the $523 billion distributed. Twenty-seven companies that enjoy annual sales of $1 billion+ received loans, as did 2,068 that reported over $100 million in sales just a year before.

Providence Health Systems, for example, is a multibillion-dollar institution and one of the largest hospital chains in the country. Although Providence had $12 billion in its coffers, the company received at least $509 million in federal assistance. Dr. Rod Hochman, Providence's chief executive, made over $10 million in 2018.

In addition to Providence, nineteen other large hospital chains received over $5 billion – even though, combined, these hospitals had over $108 billion in cash. The Cleveland Clinic received $199 million, then paid investment consultants $28 million to manage the windfall. It's worth noting that most of these organizations are established as nonprofit organizations, which exempts them from paying federal income tax.

On the flip side, 2,000 rural hospitals didn't have enough money to survive for even a month. The $3 million St. Claire HealthCare in Kentucky received only paid for two-weeks of payroll, forcing them to lay employees off and cancel vendor contracts.

How in the world did this get so twisted? The answer will not surprise you. Yep, good 'ol lobbying. Yum! Brands spent $460,000 on lobbying efforts in the first quarter of 2020, and one of its executives contributed $200,000 to Donald Trump's joint fundraising committee.

The National Restaurant Association and the International Franchise Association lobbied hard to make sure large hotels and restaurants were eligible for "small business" loans. Combined, they spent over $1 million on lobbying efforts in the first quarter of 2020, plus tens of thousands of dollars in political contributions.

Their clients got even more bang for their buck. For years, the retail, restaurant, and hotel industries have been pushing hard to allow quick write offs for renovation costs. Even though this has nothing – NOTHING – to do with the pandemic, the provision was put in the *CARES Act* at a cost to the U.S. government of $15 billion.

There are other shady things about this legislation. For one, unbelievably, foreign firms were eligible to apply. Korean Air, for example, received a loan between $5 million and $10 million.

For another, Congress gave a "blanket approval" that allowed lawmakers, government officials, and members of their families to apply for PPP funds, without the conflict-of-interest reviews that are usually conducted by the Standards of Conduct Committee.

For example, the shipping company owned by the family of then Transportation Secretary Elaine Chao – who happens to be married to Senator Mitch McConnell – received a loan of between $350,000 and $1 million. At least seven members of Congress and/or their spouses also received loans.

The law firm founded and still operated by Donald Trump's longtime personal lawyer Marc E. Kasowitz received loans totaling $10 million. A restaurant located in the Trump International Hotel received between $2 million and $5 million, and the restaurant in the Trump hotel in Washington D.C. received between $150,000 to $350,000.

Almost 100 tenants of a Trump-owned skyscraper in New York City received a combined $34 million in federal help. Despite the fact that executives of Atane Engineers – which pays $2.5 million a year in rent to the Trump organization – recently pled guilty to paying bribes for NYC infrastructure contracts, the company received a $7.6 million loan.

Companies that received loans despite bad behavior didn't stop there. For-profit nursing homes that have previously been sued by the government for Medicare fraud and other violations received over $300 million.

That's all sketchy enough, but this next example wins the Super Shady Swamp award. Claiming it was "critical" to national security, the U.S. Treasury Department, at the request of Senator Jerry Moran of Kansas, gave a $700 million+ loan (at a reduced interest rate) to one of the largest trucking companies in North America in exchange for a 30 percent stake in the company.

The company, YRC Worldwide, was on the verge of bankruptcy *before* the Covid crisis, after losing over $100 million in 2019 alone, and was actively being sued by the Justice Department for committing fraud against the United States government over a seven year period. Shockingly, YRC has close ties to former Trump administration officials.

Then there is the straight-up fraud. On July 28, 2020, the SBA inspector general released a report with the very long title *Serious Concerns of Potential Fraud in Economic Injury Disaster Loan Program Pertaining to the Response to Covid-19.* It says, in part, "our preliminary review reveals strong indicators of widespread potential fraud in the program."

"Additionally, we have found indications of deficiencies with internal controls related to disaster assistance for the Covid-19 pandemic. Our review of SBA's initial disaster assistance response has identified $250 million in economic injury loans and advance grants given to potentially ineligible recipients. We have also found approximately $45.6 million in potentially duplicate payments."

The Wall Street Journal reports that several hundred investigations into PPP loans have been opened by the FBI, involving almost 500 suspects and hundreds of millions of dollars.

In reality, none of this should come as surprise since businesses applying for PPP loans were allowed to self-report their eligibility with practically zero vetting. Among those arrested were people who spent the money on personal luxury items; those who applied for multiple loans, which was not allowed; and people who faked documents and even entire companies.

The Wall Street Journal also reports this: "Researchers at the Massachusetts Institute of Technology in July 2020 compared payroll data at PPP-eligible companies to ineligible ones and estimated the program had boosted employment by about 2.3 million jobs. At that rate, the PPP would have cost about $224,000 per job supported." In other words, we could have just handed the people in those 2.3 million jobs $224,000.

And that's just the misuse, misappropriation, and fraud in the PPP program. The U.S. Government Accountability Office found that the federal government sent stimulus payments to nearly 1.1 million dead people, a mistake that totaled $1.4 billion.

§§§

This has to stop. I know that putting the genie back in the bottle seems overwhelming – if not impossible – but it can absolutely be done. As promised, I'd like to introduce you to *Operation Overhaul*!

Operation Overhaul reduces costs, maximizes value and improves performance by strengthening operational strategies, building an effective organizational structure and demanding accountability. The policy removes redundancy, unlocks hidden value by eliminating waste, establishes clear channels of reporting and responsibility and gets the most out of government employees.

Operation Overhaul brings private sector principles into government to transform the current bureaucratic mentality.

Historically, entrepreneurship and government have been largely viewed as mutually exclusive, mainly because they have been. However, there is absolutely nothing that prevents us from bringing an entrepreneurial spirit into government. It would be enormously helpful if government would embrace bold innovation, strategic vision and tenacious problem-solving techniques.

The hallmark of *Operation Overhaul* is that it demands tough but fair accountability. After the departments and programs are streamlined, strict review processes will keep them on track. Every program and agency will be continually evaluated and measured. Plus, the federal departments must make a strong case for their value every single year. Departments must prove that they narrowly define their challenges, conduct in-depth due diligence, formulate smart and timely plans of action, assess the risks and develop responsible budgets.

To facilitate this process, a non-connected Efficiency Review Board will oversee the federal departments, acting as a new line of financial defense. Currently, the Office of Management and Budget (OMB) receives each department's yearly budget request, communicates with them about the requests and makes budget recommendations before the president's budget is sent to Congress. The new Efficiency Review Board will assess each department's programs and approve their budgets *before* they are presented to the OMB.

To get started, *Operation Overhaul* will:

† Design an overall strategy for the entire U.S. government instead of viewing each department as a sum of its parts.

† Address organizational design and management infrastructure to create a more agile culture.

† Implement strict review processes. Establish a new, non-connected Efficiency Review Board.

† Define the U.S. government's core strengths and values and ensure that federal employees are empowered by them.

- † Create an environment where working for the United States of America is as prestigious as working for a Fortune 500 company.

- † Guarantee U.S. digital strategies are far ahead of the speed of digital innovation.

- † Do not "Starve the Beast." Rather, implement a smart reduction strategy in order to tighten the cost structure.

You can find detailed information on each of these on the 1787 website, but a quick word on *Starving the Beast.* This is a political strategy that chokes the amount of revenue going into the government's bank account by cutting taxes.

The theory is that by cutting taxes Congress will be forced to cut spending. I think some Republicans genuinely thought they were employing the *Starve the Beast* strategy with their 2017 tax cuts, but if they still believe that they are completely delusional.

They certainly got the tax cut part of the strategy down but just like in the Reagan administration, they forgot the other – and most important – half of the equation. Clearly, not having enough revenue means nothing to the United States Congress. Lack of revenue hasn't slowed that bunch down one bit.

Significantly Reduce Our Debt and Close the Gap on Our Deficit

Step Two Explained

I try really hard to always remain positive. I try hard to give people the benefit of the doubt, and to not point fingers and constantly play the blame game.

But there are times when there is simply no option but to call people out: The *Tax Cuts and Jobs Act of 2017* that congressional Republicans passed – and Donald Trump signed, on December 22, 2017 – is outrageous in its irresponsibility.

To be clear, I am not against tax cuts as a rule. There is a time and place when they are absolutely appropriate. But this particular tax cut is one of the largest financial heists in U.S. history – the crazies have officially taken over the asylum and they have your checkbook. Once again, a Republican-led Congress passed a tax bill that ensures the wealthiest Americans and already flush corporations win. Bigly.

Every Single Thing That Was Promised to Middle Class America by Donald Trump and Congressional Republicans Regarding Their 2017 Tax Cut Has Proven To Be 100% False.

Strike One: Tax Rates
Strike Two: Household Income
Strike Three: Gross Domestic Product (GDP)
Strike Four: Deficit and Debt
Strike Five: Wall Street v. Main Street
Strike Six: Repatriation
Strike Seven: Increased Investment

Strike One: Tax Rates

The Claim:

The taxes for Middle Class America – who Donald Trump repeatedly called the "forgotten men and women" – are going down and rich people's taxes are staying the same or may even go up.

† DJT on September 28, 2015 at a news conference: "[The tax bill] is going to cost me a fortune."

† DJT on May 7, 2016 on *Meet the Press*: "For the wealthy, I think, frankly, it's going to go up. And you know what? It really should go up."

† DJT on September 13, 2017 at a meeting with members of Congress: "The rich will not be gaining at all with this plan. I think the wealthy will be pretty much where they are.... If they have to go higher, they'll go higher, frankly."

† DJT on September 29, 2017 at an event for small businesses: "By eliminating the tax breaks and special interest loopholes that primarily benefit the wealthy, our framework ensures that the benefits of tax reform go to the middle class, not the highest earners."

† DJT on November 29, 2017, at a speech in St. Charles, Missouri: "[The tax cuts] are not good for me. Me, it's not so – I have some very wealthy friends. Not so happy with me, but that's OK. You know, I keep hearing Schumer: 'This is for the wealthy.' Well, if it is, my friends don't know about it."

† DJT on November 29, 2017, the same speech in St. Charles, Missouri: "Our focus is on helping the folks who work in the mailrooms and the machine shops of America. The plumbers, the carpenters, the cops, the teachers, the truck drivers, the pipe fitters. The people that like me best."

† DJT on December 16, 2017, at the White House: [The tax cuts] are "one of the great Christmas gifts to middle-income people."

THE TRUTH:

Every single one of these statements is complete b.s. It makes my blood boil because Donald Trump – over and over and over – just bald faced lied to the very people who never wavered in their loyalty to him. Millions of Americans root for him and trust him, and he repays them by blatantly lying to their faces. It's just not right.

The truth is that wealthy Americans got a windfall from the tax bill (and were going to from the very beginning), a fact Donald Trump acknowledged when he walked into dinner at Mar-a-Lago after the bill passed and said to the entire room, "You all just got a lot richer."

The alternative-minimum tax was slashed, the estate tax was weakened, and the top two tax brackets saw the largest reductions by percentage than any of the others – which is fine if that's what you want to do, but at least be man enough to be honest with the "forgotten men and women" who fervently believe in you and count on you to tell them the truth.

The United States Joint Economic Committee (JEC) – one of four joint committees of the U.S. Congress, this one responsible for reporting the current economic condition of the country – reports this: "The personal income tax cuts were heavily weighted to the very wealthy, with the top 1 percent of households – those with average incomes of almost $2 million – projected to receive an average tax break of nearly $50,000 in 2020. Their tax cuts alone are worth more than the entire average annual income of households in the bottom 40 percent."

The Tax Policy Center, a joint venture of the Urban Institute and Brookings Institution, found that, in 2018 – the first year the tax bill went into effect – "the lowest income households (those making less than about $25,000) got an average tax cut of about $40. Middle-income households (who made between about $48,000 and $86,000) paid about $800 less."

<u>But here's the most dishonest part of all</u>: The tax bill was booby-trapped with built-in, automatic tax increases that are triggered every two years beginning in 2021. By 2027, Americans with incomes of $100,000 and under – which is roughly three-quarters of American taxpayers – will have a higher tax bill in 2027 than in 2019. <u>Essentially,</u>

the tax "cut" was a delayed *tax increase* for most Americans. Naturally, this is not the case for corporations and wealthy Americans, because tax cuts for corporate profits, investment income, estate tax, etc. were made permanent.

Does the timing of this seem suspicious to anyone but me? The booby-traps triggered in 2021, just months *after* the 2020 presidential election. Hmmm…

Strike Two: Household Income

The Claim:

Household incomes will increase between $4,000 to $9,000 a year, or maybe even more. This will happen because, thanks to the corporate tax cut, the money corporations will save will "trickle-down" to the American worker.

† DJT on October 11, 2017 at a speech in Harrisburg, Pennsylvania (but he also said it a zillion times elsewhere): Speaking to hundreds of truck drivers, he said that the average American family would get "a $4,000 pay raise." He also said that his wealthy friends told him they don't want anything from the tax bill, and that he should just "give it to the middle class."

† 2018 Economic Report from the President: "The corporate tax changes alone are expected to increase annual income for families by an average of $4,000."

The Truth:

According to the U.S. Joint Economic Committee (JEC), "Annual household income growth in the first year the tax cuts took effect lagged far behind the previous three years. It grew only $550 in 2018, compared to $850 in 2017, $1,900 in 2016 and $2,900 in 2015. The growth curve of real median income became flatter."

The Wall Street Journal reported it this way (remember, the tax cuts went into effect on January 1, 2018): "American incomes remained essentially flat in 2018 after three straight years of growth…in recent weeks, the government has revised downward its estimates for job gains, economic output and corporate profits at various points in time since early last year."

Strike Three: Gross Domestic Product (GDP)

The Claim:

The tax cuts will boost gross domestic product (GDP) growth to between 4 and 6 percent.

† DJT on December 16, 2017 at the White House: "The economy now has hit 3 percent. Nobody thought we'd be anywhere close. I think we can go to 4, 5, and maybe even 6 percent ultimately. Each percentage point is $2.5 trillion. We are back. We are really going to start to rock. We need this as our final push and you're going to see some numbers that are really great. You're going to see great jobs numbers. Jobs are going to come pouring back into this country, which we need very much."

The Truth:

After experiencing a two-quarter "sugar high," GDP growth fell to the same average growth rate as before. The growth rate increased from 2.3 percent in 2017 to 3 percent in 2018 but fell to 2.2 percent in 2019.

< In 2020, the growth rate was -3.5 percent but, remember, I'm leaving 2020 out of this discussion because, thanks to the pandemic, the entire year is an outlier. >

Strike Four: Deficit and Debt

The Claim:

The tax cuts will pay for themselves. Not one penny will be added to the debt and will probably help reduce it. The deficit gap will not widen, but probably shrink.

† DJT on July 27, 2018 on *The Sean Hannity Show*, "We have $21 trillion in debt. When [the 2017 tax cut] really kicks in, we'll start paying off that debt like it's water."

He said things like this repeatedly. As far back as his campaign, Donald Trump insisted that the federal debt and deficit would not increase from his tax cuts and the economy would "take off like a rocket ship."

Then Treasury Secretary Steven Mnuchin proclaimed that "not only will this tax plan pay for itself, but it will pay down debt." Two years later, when this clearly had not happened, Mnuchin stuck with his prediction: "I'll stick with my projections that the tax deal will pay for itself."

The Truth:

The Trump administration blew out our deficit and vastly increased our debt. We covered this earlier, but here is how *ProPublica*, an independent, nonprofit newsroom that produces investigative journalism in the public interest, put it:

"The national debt has risen by almost $7.8 trillion during Trump's time in office. That's nearly twice as much as what Americans owe on student loans, car loans, credit cards and every other type of debt other than mortgages, combined, according to data from the Federal Reserve Bank of New York. It amounts to about $23,500 in new federal debt for every person in the country.

The growth in the annual deficit under Trump ranks as the third-biggest increase, relative to the size of the economy, of any U.S. presidential administration, according to a calculation by a leading Washington budget maven, Eugene Steuerle, co-founder of the Urban-Brookings Tax Policy Center. And unlike George W. Bush and Abraham Lincoln, who oversaw the larger relative increases in deficits, Trump did not launch two foreign conflicts or have to pay for a civil war."

Strike Five: Wall Street v. Main Street

The Claim:

For most of 2018 and 2019 – time after time and tweet after tweet – Donald Trump pointed to the hot stock market as proof that the tax cuts were working.

The Truth:

First of all, THE STOCK MARKET IS NOT THE U.S. ECONOMY!! Hyping a hot stock market as proof that the tax cuts are working is a false premise and shows a complete misunderstanding of what life is like for many Americans – as well as how the stock market actually works.

Responsible people recognize markets are not an accurate reflection of the overall economy, and it's certainly not a reflection of what is happening in the homes of the vast majority of Americans. That whole Wall Street vs. Main Street adage is overused, but the truth is that Wall Street and Main Street live in two completely separate (terribly unequal) universes.

In any event, the stock market didn't do better after the tax cuts anyway. We already talked about the fact that the stock market returns during the Trump administration rank 8th when compared to other presidents. Behind, in order, Bill Clinton, Barack Obama, Dwight Eisenhower, Ronald Reagan, Harry Truman, George H.W. Bush, and Lyndon Johnson. But let's dig a little deeper.

Fortune magazine reports that "on October 31st of Obama's third year in office, the S&P 500 (the 500 largest public companies on either the New York Stock Exchange or Nasdaq exchange, measured by market capitalization) hit 156 percent of the value it had on President Obama's first day in office, which means the index increased by 56 percent."

In that same timeframe, "under Donald Trump the increase was 34 percent, or 22 percentage points lower than the gain under Obama."

Ouch. Let's check the other exchanges. Using the same timeframe, on the Dow – which is 30 large capitalized ("large cap") companies that are chosen specifically by Dow Jones & Company in an attempt to represent the broader economy – "the percentage change under Obama was roughly 150 percent, meaning a 50 percent increase over the initial value. Under Donald Trump, the 136 percent change, or 36 percent gain in value, was 14 percentage points less." Interesting.

Well, surely the Nasdaq was better for the super-duper stock market wrangler Donald Trump? Nope. During the Trump administration, "the Nasdaq saw a 149 percent change for an increase of 49 percent. At the same point under Obama, it was a change of 186 percent – an increase of 86 percent, or 37 percentage points more than for Donald Trump." Double ouch.

Strike Six: Repatriation

The Claim:

Trillions of dollars will quickly find their way back to America as U.S. multinational enterprises bring their foreign profits home.

† DJT on December 16, 2017, at the White House: "We think $4 trillion is going to be flowing back into the country. That's money that's overseas that's stuck there for years and years."

† DJT on August 7, 2018 at a meeting with business leaders: "We expect to have in excess of $4 trillion brought back very shortly." Actually, he revised, "close to $5 trillion."

The Truth

Repatriations didn't reach anywhere close to $4 trillion. Not even remotely close.

What is repatriation anyway? Great question! Most countries tax corporations only on economic activity that happens within their borders. This is called a territorial system.

However, before the Republican tax bill, the United States taxed all of the profits of U.S. multinational enterprises – even if the money was earned overseas – but only if the money was repatriated (or, brought home). As a result, most American multinational firms simply kept their profits abroad. This income was kept on corporate balance sheets and was deferred until the income made its way back to the American parent company.

The Republican tax bill gave corporations a break on the foreign profits they brought home to America and changed the way U.S. multinational companies are taxed going forward. The law shifted our system to a quasi-territorial system, and now profits are taxed only where they are earned.

To help U.S. multinational companies transition to this new system, the federal government gave companies a tax "holiday" on foreign earnings that were brought back to America. During this holiday, multinational companies paid a one-time tax on cash and assets held overseas, whether or not money was repatriated (this removed any incentive for companies to keep the cash overseas). They were allowed to spread out this one-time tax over eight years.

I'm all for a territorial system because I believe it will ultimately increase our global competitiveness. But it was delusional to believe these changes would immediately cause floods and floods of dollars to rain down on America. That's just not how it works in the real world.

According to *The Wall Street Journal*, although "U.S. companies more than quadrupled the amount of foreign earnings they sent home in 2018 following enactment of a tax-law overhaul in late 2017," the "repatriations declined after an initial spike."

The Journal continues, "Companies sent $664.91 billion of their foreign earnings back to the U.S. in the form of dividend payments in 2018, up from $155.08 billion the year before. However, repatriations fell steadily through 2018 to $85.9 billion in the fourth quarter, from $100.74 billion in the third quarter, $183.58 billion in the second quarter and $294.69 billion in the first quarter."

But even the money that did come back was not spent the way the Trump administration promised, and certainly did not land in the pockets of America's "forgotten men and women." Which brings us to strike seven…

Strike Seven: Increased Investment

The Claim:

The corporate tax cut will entice corporations to increase business investment with all their new cash. This will lead to millions of new jobs.

† DJT on January 31, 2018 in the Oval Office: "I think expensing is the unsung phrase within our bill. That's going to be fantastic. People are going to really go out and do something."

The Truth:

The U.S. Joint Economic Committee reports that: "Since the enactment of the tax cuts, growth of business investment has averaged just 3.5 percent, substantially below the 4.6 percent average growth of the previous seven quarters. Although there was a slight bump in business investment in the first two quarters after the tax cuts took effect, it subsequently fell below its long-term trend and has contracted in the most recent quarters."

The Federal Reserve Bank of Cleveland reports that "business investment grew more slowly after the tax reform than before it…The average quarterly growth rate of business investment was 2.8 percent in 2018–2019, lower than the rates in 2016–2017 (4.0 percent), 2013–2017 (3.9 percent), or 2010–2017 (5.5 percent). Even taking into account that other economic factors, such as changes in trade policy and a global economic slowdown, may have held investment down, these data suggest that the stimulus provided by the tax reform was not large."

This should come as no surprise because, even before the bill passed, it was pretty apparent companies weren't planning to increase investment.

Major companies including Cisco, Pfizer, and even Coca-Cola made it clear that they would use any new windfall not for investment, but to buy back stocks – which would pass any gains to their shareholders, not employees.

Hey, don't blame them! They were completely honest about their intentions from the start. In fact, at a meeting of *The Wall Street Journal* CEO Council in November 2017, the CEOs in attendance were asked to raise their hands if they intended to use their new fortune for investment. Gary Cohn, who at the time was Donald Trump's top economic adviser, seemed perplexed that very few hands were raised. "Why aren't the other hands up?" he asked.

The Federal Reserve Bank of Atlanta periodically surveys business executives. According to the results of their survey after the tax bill passed, "roughly two-thirds of respondents indicated that tax reform hasn't enticed them into changing their investment plans for 2018."

The survey also asked the respondents about their investment plans for 2019: "The results were not statistically different from their 2018 response. Roughly three-quarters of firms don't plan to change their capital expenditure plans in 2019 as a result of the [tax cuts]."

Then, what *are* businesses doing with all this newfound cash? Well, instead of increasing wages or making investments, corporations have indeed bought back their own shares – which, again, only benefits shareholders and executives.

Essentially, what happens in a stock buyback (a.k.a. share repurchase) is that a company buys back its shares from the marketplace with any accumulated cash they might have. They do this, in part, to reduce the number of shares that are available on the open market, which ultimately increases the value of those shares (i.e., supply and demand). Buybacks can also increase equity value, make a company look more financially sound, and allow a way for money to be returned to investors.

According to the S&P Dow Jones, "In Q4 2018, S&P 500 stock buybacks, or share repurchases, set a fourth consecutive record of $223 billion. This displaced the previous record of $203.8 billion, set during Q3 2018 and is a 62.8 percent increase from the $137 billion reported for Q4 2017. For the year 2018, buybacks set an annual (and

12-month) record of $806.4 billion, up 55.3 percent from the prior year's $519.4 billion, and up 36.9 percent from the prior annual record set in 2007, of $589.1 billion."

The following year, they reported that: "Buybacks for the full year 2019 were $728.7 billion. Apple continued to lead, spending $22.1 billion – up from last quarter's $17.6 billion, and ranking as the 3rd highest expenditure historically."

The National Bureau of Economic Research (NBER) reveals that "the average annual inflation-adjusted amount paid out through dividends and repurchases by public industrial firms is more than three times larger from 2000 to 2019 than from 1971 to 1999."

This buyback strategy is dubious, and I'm being generous. Companies do this for all of the reasons I mentioned earlier, but executives in particular have millions of incentives to buy back stock.

According to Robert J. Jackson Jr., a former commissioner of the U.S. Securities and Exchange Commission appointed by Donald Trump, "There is clear evidence that a substantial number of corporate executives today use buybacks as a chance to cash out the shares of the company they received as executive pay. We give stock to corporate managers to convince them to create the kind of long-term value that benefits American companies and the workers and communities they serve. Instead, what we are seeing is that executives are using buybacks as a chance to cash out their compensation at investor expense."

What's really infuriating is that many of the companies that benefited mightily from the corporate tax cut (only to buy back shares) went crawling to the federal government for help during the Covid economic crisis – with their hand firmly out.

After telling his investors, "I don't think we're ever going to lose money again" after their big tax cut, the chief executive of American Airlines gladly accepted a $5.48 billion loan from the U.S. Treasury and could receive up to $2 billion more before everything is said and done. This is on top of the $5.8 billion they had already received.

§§§

The *Tax Cuts and Jobs Act of 2017* was the most significant change in the United States tax code since Ronald Reagan's *Tax Cuts and Jobs Act of 1986*.

Without question, some sort of corporate tax reform was desperately needed. For decades, the U.S. corporate tax code had been ridiculously complicated and inefficient, and the statutory tax rate was much higher than in other Organization for Economic Cooperation and Development (OECD) economies. < Note: Even though the statutory tax rate was higher on paper, relentless lobbying efforts, complex deductions, and loopholes brought the effective marginal tax rate closer to our international competition, but that only caused even greater confusion and inconsistency. >

Our previous system incentivized corporations to borrow too much money, leave money in overseas subsidiaries, and/or potentially move operations overseas altogether. Yes, we definitely needed reform, but the Republican bill went way too far.

Analysis by *The New York Times* discovered that "in the 2017 fiscal year, FedEx owed more than $1.5 billion in taxes. The next year, it owed nothing...FedEx reaped big savings (from the tax cut), bringing its effective tax rate from 34 percent in fiscal year 2017 to less than zero in fiscal year 2018, meaning that, overall, the government technically owed it money."

This is probably not as bad as it sounds, because surely FedEx expanded their payroll and increased investment in new equipment and other assets in the years after its big windfall (or, as Alan Graf, FedEx's chief financial officer, called it, "a mighty fine Christmas gift"), right!?!

Nope. "The company spent less in the 2018 fiscal year than it had projected in December 2017, before the tax law passed. It spent even less in 2019. Much of its savings has gone to reward shareholders: FedEx spent more than $2 billion on stock buybacks and dividend increases in the 2019 fiscal year, up from $1.6 billion in 2018, and more than double the amount the company spent on buybacks and dividends in fiscal year 2017."

The New York Times analysis "of data compiled by Capital IQ shows no statistically meaningful relationship between the size of the tax cut that companies and industries received and the investments they made. If anything, the companies that received the biggest tax cuts increased their capital investment by less, on average, than companies that got smaller cuts."

> "FedEx's use of its tax savings is representative of corporate America. [As of November 2019,] companies had already saved upward of $100 billion more on their taxes than analysts predicted when the law was passed. Companies that make up the S&P 500 index had an average effective tax rate of 18.1 percent in 2018, down from 25.9 percent in 2016, according to an analysis of securities filings. More than 200 of those companies saw their effective tax rates fall by 10 points or more. Nearly three dozen, including FedEx, saw their tax rates fall to zero or reported that tax authorities owed them money.
>
> From the first quarter of 2018, when the law fully took effect, companies have spent nearly three times as much on additional dividends and stock buybacks, which boost a company's stock price and market value than on increased investment."

A study by the Institute on Taxation and Economic Policy, a non-partisan tax policy organization, reveals that, in 2020, 55 corporations had <u>zero</u> federal tax liability on over $40 billion in profits. <u>Zero</u>. These companies include Nike, Dish Network, and FedEx. Not only did these companies not have to pay federal income taxes, they actually *received* tax rebates of $3.5 billion, giving them an effective tax rate of roughly negative 9 percent.

Twenty-six of these companies have paid <u>zero</u> federal income tax on over $77 billion in profits since the Republican tax cut. Yet they have *received* almost $5 billion in rebates, making their effective three-year tax rate negative 6 precent. Seriously, they have got to be kidding me with this.

It cannot be denied that the Republican tax cuts cost far too much for far too little. By passing this law, the Trump administration and congressional Republicans sold the vast majority of Americans out. Straight up. Worse, it's not like they didn't know they were selling Americans a bill of goods. At the time, plenty of people were waving huge red flags. They knew.

A report from the Tax Policy Center at the time said that "the new tax law will raise deficits and make the distribution of after-tax income more unequal...The new tax law simplifies taxes for some people, but also adds complexities and exacerbates compliance issues in other areas."

The Penn Wharton Budget Model (PWBM), a nonpartisan, research-based initiative located at the Wharton Business School, was more specific: "The Tax Cuts and Jobs Act of 2017 increases debt by between $1.9 trillion to $2.2 trillion over the next decade."

The Center on Budget and Policy Priorities, a progressive think tank that analyzes the impact of federal and state government budget policies, had this to say: "The evidence indicates that the bulk of the benefits from a corporate rate cut will go to those at the top, with only a small share flowing to low and moderate-income working families."

This, on top of the fact that the United States has been losing significant revenue from tax breaks for the wealthy for years. Another report from the Institute on Taxation and Economic Policy says that "since 2000, tax cuts have reduced federal revenue by trillions of dollars and disproportionately benefited well-off households."

The report continued, "From 2001 through 2018, significant federal tax changes have reduced revenue by $5.1 trillion, with nearly two-thirds of that flowing to the richest fifth of Americans. The cumulative impact on the deficit during this period is $5.9 trillion, including interest payments. By the end of 2025, the tally of tax cuts will grow to $10.6 trillion. Nearly $2 trillion of this amount will have gone to the richest 1 percent. By then, the total impact on the deficit will be $13.6 trillion, including interest payments."

The researchers also point out that their "analysis does not include hundreds of billions of dollars in so-called tax cut 'extenders' for corporations and other businesses that Congress has periodically enacted under each administration."

Congressional Republicans and Donald Trump absolutely knew their promises would not be kept. They just didn't care. As usual, they decided to listen to lobbyists instead.

Corporations, trade associations and special interest groups spent $9.6 million to lobby Congress on issues related to taxes in the first three quarters of 2017 alone. But the fourth quarter said hold my beer. In that one quarter alone, the National Association of Realtors spent $22.2 million, the Business Roundtable spent $17.3 million, and the U.S. Chamber of Commerce spent $16.8 million.

Public Citizen, a nonprofit consumer rights advocacy group and think tank, found that "6,243 lobbyists were listed on lobbying disclosure forms as working on issues involving the word 'tax' through the first three quarters of 2017. That is equal to 57 percent of the nearly 11,000 people who have reported engaging in any domestic lobbying activities at all in 2017. Put another way, this equals more than 11 lobbyists for every member of Congress."

I'm fairly certain that when that many hands are in the cookie jar, the cookies are going to be badly crumbled. So, did corporations get their money's worth from all of this lobbying? You betcha!

In fact, poor Corporate America didn't feel they got quite enough in the original tax bill, so they continued their lobbying efforts full blast even after it passed. And boy, did that work out for them! In fact, those lobbyists worked so hard that large companies got even more tax breaks in the *CARES Act*. Yes, you read that correctly.

Big business – and wealthy Americans – got an additional $174 billion in tax relief in the initial economic rescue package. These breaks include increasing the amount of deductions companies can take on the interest of their debt, allowing net operating losses to reduce tax liabilities, and another slash in capital gains taxes (which can be applied retroactively, for up to two years! Yay!).

And then there is this: Another *New York Times* analysis found that "through a series of obscure regulations, the U.S. Treasury carved out exceptions to [the *CARES Act*] that mean many leading American and foreign companies will owe little or nothing in new taxes on offshore profits, according to a review of the Treasury's rules, government lobbying records, and interviews with federal policymakers and tax experts. Companies were effectively let off the hook for tens if not hundreds of billions of taxes that they would have been required to pay...One of the most effective campaigns, with the greatest financial consequence, was led by a small group of large foreign banks, including Credit Suisse and Barclays."

Let me get this straight. These banks don't like paying taxes for some odd reason, so Donald Trump's Treasury Secretary Steven Mnuchin unilaterally decided to exempt these banks from paying them? Where can I sign up for that deal?

The *New York Times* again: "Officials at the Joint Committee on Taxation have calculated that the exemptions for international banks could reduce (their tax burden) by up to $50 billion."

Set aside for a moment that the U.S. Treasury in no way has the unilateral power to do such a thing – making this whole move unconstitutional – but we should probably question why Steven Mnuchin was so hell-bent on protecting foreign banks.

The answer to that question came on February 23, 2021, when *The Washington Post* reported that Steven Mnuchin is starting an investment fund that is raising money from Persian Gulf sovereign wealth funds and other international sources. As a matter of fact, when the Capitol riots broke out on January 6th, Mnuchin was on a "diplomatic" trip to the Middle East and Africa – a trip paid for by American taxpayers – meeting with Egypt, Israel, Qatar, Sudan, the United Arab Emirates, and Saudi Arabia. These pricks have some nerve.

§§§

So, where do we go from here? Conversations about taxes usually focus on *who gets what* and *who pays what*, but we need to start thinking much broader than that. We should design a tax system that matches our ambitious vision for America's future. < The 1787 tax code recommendations are in *The Policy Guide*. >

The time has come to change the American growth model completely. Adam Smith, the author of *The Wealth of Nations*, once said taxes should be efficient, predictable and convenient. Our current method is the exact opposite.

The U.S. tax code is still arbitrary and ridiculously complicated, which makes the entire mess inefficient, unfair and outdated. It's also super easy to cheat.

A hard-to-believe report from the Internal Revenue Service (IRS) revealed that: "The gross tax gap is the amount of true tax liability that is not paid voluntarily and timely [The tax gap provides a rough gauge of the level of overall noncompliance and voluntary compliance.] The estimated gross tax gap is $441 billion. The net tax gap is the gross tax gap less tax that subsequently will be paid, either paid voluntarily or collected through IRS administrative and enforcement activities; it is the portion of the gross tax gap that will not be paid. It is estimated that $60 billion of the gross tax gap eventually will be paid resulting in a net tax gap of $381 billion."

Additionally, the IRS estimates that the American public reports less than half of income that doesn't require third-party verification (i.e., a W-2). *The New York Times* puts it this way: "Unreported income is the single largest reason that unpaid federal income taxes may amount to more than $600 billion this year, and more than $7.5 trillion over the next decade. It is a truly staggering sum – more than half of the projected federal deficit over the same period."

To start, we need to simplify the tax code in order to promote fairness and encourage economic growth. Within the current system, there are numerous tax expenditures which are, in reality, just more spending (a tax expenditure is revenue that the federal government does not receive because of a special exclusion, exemption, deduction, special credit, preferential rate of tax, or deferral of tax liability).

Tax expenditures cost us a fortune. For example, in late December 2020, Congress finally came to an agreement on a second stimulus package in response to the economic fallout from the coronavirus pandemic. The 5,593-page spending bill contained numerous tax breaks for various industries. The Joint Committee on Taxation estimates these "tax extenders" – which are made to look temporary but are actually renewed year after year – will cost <u>$100 billion over the next ten years</u>.

The Tax Policy Center reports that "the value of the tax breaks for homeownership, although reduced by the 2017 tax act, still exceeds total spending by the U.S. Department of Housing and Urban Development (HUD)."

The thirteen largest tax expenditures – which range from tax exclusions for employer-sponsored health insurance TO reduced rates of tax on dividends and long-term capital gains TO credit for children and other dependents – will cost the United States over a TRILLION DOLLARS in 2021. That's trillion, with a T.

Really think about that for a second. That's more than the annual budget of every single department in the United States government besides the Department of Health and Human Services and the Social Security Administration.

In Defense of Rich People

I realize rich people got a little shrapnel in that last section, but we need to cut them some slack. It seems like lately they have been demonized for things that are realistically not their fault. I get that many Americans are frustrated, especially now, but taking it out on rich people seems petty, bitter and jealous, and that's just not the American way.

Personally, I know some super uber duper rich people. Several of them are jerks, but most are some of the greatest people I have ever known.

Two jerks in particular come to mind – one is a guy I went to college with who is now a millionaire several times over, and the other is now a billionaire I worked with at the very beginning of my career. I knew them both when they were eating beanie weenies out of a can and guess what!?! They were total jerks back then too (although, to be fair, slimy, cold beanie weenies don't bring out the best in people).

I also know a lot of people who are not super uber duper rich and guess what!?! Several of them are jerks, but most are some of the greatest people I have ever known.

It's not difficult to see why super uber duper rich people are sometimes villainized in today's America. For one thing – although it's an entirely unfair thought – it's easy to believe it impossible to make that much money without some sort of moral deficiency or shady behavior.

Plus, it's not easy to reconcile social justice and capitalism. On one hand, you have the promise of the American Dream, where every American has the opportunity to achieve success and prosperity, regardless of their originating circumstances. On the other hand, you have statistics that reveal a shocking level of income inequality in the United States. < we will talk much more about this in Part Two of this book series >

It can also be maddening when money seems to make life so much easier, at least in the short-term, for people who do bad things (à la

Jeffrey Epstein) or super entitled things (college admissions bribery scandal).

I have seen people born in the most devastating conditions imaginable work four jobs just to pay the bare minimum of their bills. I have also seen plenty of people raised with a ton of money and opportunity who have crashed and burned.

However – from my experience and with minor exceptions – this last group seems to miraculously rebound virtually unscathed from their mistakes and bad decisions. Redemption seems to come much easier when you can afford rehab and qualified attorneys. It's funny how prosperity can hide a multitude of sins.

But these are separate issues that seem to get unfairly wound up in one another. The truth is that most rich Americans not only greatly enhance our society and democracy, but they are also incredible public relations ambassadors for the United States on a global scale. As a nation, they make us all look really, really good.

Over a billion people worldwide have emerged from poverty in the past two decades. There is no question that Bill Gates and Melinda French Gates deserve a ton of the credit for this. Over the past two decades, their foundation has spent over $54 billion on everything from American education and health care to increasing economic opportunities and providing emergency relief overseas.

Dolly Parton, already a national treasure, gave $1 million to the Vanderbilt University Medical Center in early 2020 to help fund research efforts for Covid-19. Her contribution helped lead to the Moderna vaccine. Plus, Dolly's Imagination Library charitable organization has sent over 150 million books to children since 1995. She's just a gem.

Over 200 of the world's wealthiest individuals and families from 23 countries have signed The Giving Pledge. The Giving Pledge was introduced by Bill Gates, Melinda French Gates and Warren Buffett in 2010 to "help address society's most pressing problems by inviting the world's wealthiest individuals and families to commit more than half of their wealth to philanthropy or charitable causes either during their lifetime or in their will."

That is just an extraordinary thing for these people to do. < although, I must admit, I probably wouldn't feel as good about it if I were one of their kids :) >

MacKenzie Scott – who is just a stone-cold bad ass – donated around $6 billion in 2020 alone. Most of that money went to places like Meals on Wheels, food banks, and other organizations that greatly helped Americans survive the Covid-19 crisis. Other funds went to organizations like the NAACP, Easterseals, Goodwill, the United Way, and over 100 separate YMCA and YWCA organizations.

Ms. Scott also gave money to schools like Morgan State University ($40 million) and Prairie View A&M ($50 million), both Historically Black Colleges and Universities (HBCUs). This was by far the largest private gift in both of their histories. Just a few months later, she gave another $2.74 billion to 286 different organizations.

As of March 2022, this incredible human being had given $12 billion and announced she would be giving to Ukraine relief efforts and organizations that support women's groups around the globe. She ended her announcement with this: "Helping any of us can help us all."

In addition to giving over $300 million to help disadvantaged students throughout the last two decades, billionaires Bruce and Martha Karsh gave $10 million to Howard University, a HBCU, in 2020 to fund scholarships in science, technology, engineering and math (STEM) fields.

After the domestic terrorist incident in Charlottesville, the couple turned their attention to the protection of the rule of law and democracy. In 2018, they gave $43.9 million to the University of Virginia law school to promote programs to that end. In early June 2021, largely in response to the election lies circulating around the 2020 election and the January 6th attack on the U.S. Capitol, the couple gave an additional $50 million – which the university will match – to establish the Karsh Institute of Democracy.

One question I've heard repeatedly, asked in response to these huge donations, is: While the generosity is greatly appreciated, why do we live in a country where this is even possible? How can these people even have that much money to give when many others can't even put food on their table?

Again, I understand the frustration behind this question, and we really dig into this and other social justice issues in Part Two of this book series. But for now, maybe we should show a little more gratitude. All in, Americans donated $427.7 billion to charity in 2018 alone. The year before, that number was $410.02 billion, which was 2.1 percent of America's then gross domestic product (GDP).

These numbers are enormous. It's a shame there is no line item for this on the federal Balance Sheet because it's nearly impossible to quantify exactly how much this generosity boosts the entire American economy – but there is no question it has a significant impact.

This is not to say that rich people don't need to pay their fair share, because they certainly do. *ProPublica* was recently sent, by an anonymous source, thousands of federal tax documents that cover over fifteen years.

In what the president of *ProPublica* Richard Tofel calls "the most important story we have ever published," the organization revealed that:

> "In 2007, Jeff Bezos, then a multibillionaire and now the world's richest man, did not pay a penny in federal income taxes. He achieved the feat again in 2011. In 2018, Tesla founder Elon Musk, the second-richest person in the world, also paid no federal income taxes. Michael Bloomberg managed to do the same in recent years. Billionaire investor Carl Icahn did it twice. George Soros paid no federal income tax three years in a row."

In their words, *ProPublica*'s investigation "demolishes the cornerstone myth of the American tax system: that everyone pays their fair share and the richest Americans pay the most. The IRS records show that the wealthiest can – perfectly legally – pay income taxes that are only a tiny fraction of the hundreds of millions, if not billions, their fortunes grow each year."

Okay, this news is definitely aggravating, to say the least. But, in reality, if the uber rich don't pay their fair share that's technically not their fault. As Warren Buffett, consistently one of the richest men in the world, said in a 2011 article titled *Stop Coddling the Super-Rich*:

"Our leaders have asked for 'shared sacrifice.' But when they did the asking, they spared me. I checked with my mega-rich friends to learn what pain they were expecting. They, too, were left untouched. While the poor and middle class fight for us in Afghanistan, and while most Americans struggle to make ends meet, we mega-rich continue to get our extraordinary tax breaks.

Some of us are investment managers who earn billions from our daily labors but are allowed to classify our income as 'carried interest,' thereby getting a bargain 15 percent tax rate. Others own stock index futures for 10 minutes and have 60 percent of their gain taxed at 15 percent, as if they'd been long-term investors.

These and other blessings are showered upon us by legislators in Washington who feel compelled to protect us, much as if we were spotted owls or some other endangered species. It's nice to have friends in high places."

That's a pretty solid point, don't ya think?

Domestic Policy

Finding Balance on a Tightrope

My congressional campaign was one of the best times of my life. Obviously, I experienced first-hand all that is wrong with our political system. But I also had a unique opportunity to see everything that is right with this country, and it is truly magnificent.

I know the commercials with politicians shaking hands, kissing babies and eating at diners may seem cheesy, but it really was an honor to meet so many amazing people and talk with them about their hopes and dreams for the future (okay, I can practically hear *The Battle Hymn* of *the Republic* playing in the background, so I'll stop now).

The experience was even more special because I had it in East Texas, back where it all began for me. In my early years, I was "fiscally conservative." In high school, I regarded the conservative trinity of small government, low taxes and less regulation as the answer to everything.

Now, if you had asked me *why* I believed these things, I would not have had the first clue. Since I had engaged in zero research, I believed these things probably for the same reason I eat mustard on my hamburgers and order my steak medium well: Because my dad did.

Over time, common sense waged war with these beliefs – if not always with the belief itself, then certainly with the inflexibility.

How, I wondered, can lower taxes always be the right thing in a dynamic economy? If we cut government spending at the expense of investing in our future, won't our national growth slow and our infrastructure eventually fall apart? If we slash social safety nets, won't income inequality just get worse? If we always put the needs of the individual over the needs of the collective, won't we enable a divided, narcissistic society that will ultimately sabotage civil civilization?

My questions were bipartisan. But if we don't curb spending, won't we soon face a monumental deficit? If we implement too many financial regulations, won't we potentially choke the free market? If we expand the federal government too much, won't we end up with a runaway budget and paralyzed bureaucracy?

And then it hit me: The only way to operate at the most optimal level is to reject the liberal's fallacy that the government is always our savior and Wall Street is always the enemy and the conservative's fallacy that individualism, tax cuts and smaller government are the miraculous solutions to everything.

A mature democracy requires a robust and thriving private sector and a strong and stable government, working together to stimulate the economy, promote innovative development, and enrich the public interest.

It's all about *balance*. As we work to find a healthy balance, we also need to move past three debilitating misconceptions.

The **first misconception** is that clear, intelligent solutions to our challenges don't exist. This is categorically false. Exhaustive research conducted by think tanks, colleges and universities, nonprofit organizations, private foundations, and even our federal government directly address our policy challenges.

Many questions have been answered on someone else's dime, but politicians have very little incentive to acknowledge or accept them. After all, it would be political suicide if a Democrat learned of overwhelming evidence that proves school vouchers work, or for a Republican to be faced with data that unequivocally supports a public option in health care. They have way too much to lose because they have way too many people to repay.

As I said before, I think we'll be shocked by how straightforward the answers actually are when we drown out the noise of special interest groups, ideological labels, and the paralyzing backlash of a hard-core base.

The **second misconception** is that, because there are only two major political parties, there are only two distinctive – but extremely divergent – options, and we are required by some invisible law to strictly adhere to one of their outdated, one-size-fits-all bullet point platforms.

No. Just no. There is no way to craft intelligent policy when your solutions are confined to these ridiculously constricting labels.

Leo Tolstoy said, "The most difficult subjects can be explained to the most slow-witted man if he has not formed any idea of them already; but the simplest thing cannot be made clear to the most intelligent man if he is firmly persuaded that he knows already, without a shadow of doubt, what is laid before him."

It's wildly irresponsible to address dynamic policy issues with boilerplate solutions. Take regulation, for example. As hard as people try, this is an issue that can't be wrapped up in a nice, tidy bow.

When speaking on this topic, people – mainly those leaning to the conservative side of things – often ask, "Are you for more regulation or less?" They seem to want a one-word answer, but it's way more complicated than that.

In reality, the only reply to that question should be, "Am I for or against regulation *for what*?" Are we speaking about small businesses or Wall Street? Or social media, food safety, environmental protection, or the oil and gas industry? Or condo buildings in Florida?

One of the most irresponsible ideas the Trump administration had – enacted by executive order naturally – was the "one in, two out" regulation requirement. This meant that, whenever a federal agency issued one regulation, it was required to take at least two regulations away.

This approach is ridiculous. And, quite frankly, more than a little lazy. Without question, there are outdated and burdensome regulations, but these should be dealt with specifically, not as part of some big monolithic exorcism.

Besides, this strategy didn't work in the first place. The Penn Program on Regulation (PPR) is located at the University of Pennsylvania – incidentally, Donald Trump's alma mater – and conducts balanced analysis on regulatory policy.

In an analysis titled *Deregulatory Deceptions: Reviewing the Trump Administration's Claims About Regulatory Reform*, they conclude that,

> "Deregulation has been celebrated as one of the Trump Administration's most important economic accomplishments. The Administration suggested both that the magnitude of its

deregulatory efforts far outpaced those of prior years and that the economic gains from these efforts were drivers of historic economic and jobs growth, delivering an increase in real income of over $3,000 to each American household.

This report investigates these claims in turn. We find that they are a mix of exaggerated, cherry-picked, and indefensible. Stated simply, the Administration did not roll back regulations at anything close to the rates it has claimed, and households have not gained thousands of dollars annually from these efforts.

Overall, we find that every claim we examine about the Trump Administration's deregulatory efforts is either wrong or exaggerated. The reality is that the Trump Administration has done less deregulating than regulating, and its deregulatory actions have not achieved any demonstrable boost to the economy.

The positive economic trends that the Administration likes to give deregulation credit for – such as increases in the gross domestic product and decreases in unemployment – had their roots in policies predating the Administration. If anything, the pace of overall growth in GDP has actually slowed somewhat during the pre-Covid years of the Trump Administration relative to the last three years of the Obama Administration.

The Trump Administration has not only exaggerated the positive effects of deregulation, it too often has ignored or downplayed its negative consequences. These adverse effects could be substantial. Although it is too early to assess the overall impact of the Trump Administration's deregulatory efforts, our research suggests that the Administration may be more effective at deceiving the public about its achievements than in actually using deregulation to boost the economy."

In my mind, there is a different level of acceptable regulation for almost everything. < the 1787 regulation threshold for each policy issue can be found in each issue's section of *The Policy Guide* or on the 1787 website >

For example, some state and local governments create onerous barriers to upward mobility by making occupational licenses ridiculously difficult to obtain. On the other hand, large corporations, banks and financial institutions could use a little more regulation, as we will discuss later in this chapter.

Let's look closer at two more examples. An excellent one at the moment is the electricity fiasco that transpired in Texas in February 2021. Now, I have to warn you, this section may sound somewhat hostile because I am, at this very moment, sitting at my computer in Texas. Because of the ice storm, my house has been without power for days and days – in fact, it's only been back on for one day – and I have not taken a shower in seven days. That's right…my water is *still* not on, and probably won't be for a while.

I'm not going to act like a big baby and whine about the cold because I realize northern states go through frigid temperatures every year. But the past week has been, in Heidi Cruz's infamous word, FREEZING. I've lived in places that get cold, but this seemed next level. I have never been so freak'n miserable in my entire life.

So, you can well imagine what my mood has been like for the past week. I was already cranky because I was FREEZING, but then came the posts on my Facebook feed that blamed the Texas power outages on windmills. Never mind that wind power makes up less than 10 percent of the state's generation mix this time of the year. After months and months of election lies and conspiracy theories, this idiotic, politically motivated garbage sent me over the edge.

Texas Governor Greg Abbott – who desperately needs to be voted out of office for his horrible pandemic response alone – said on *The Sean Hannity Show*: "This shows how the Green New Deal would be a deadly deal for the United States of America," while the Fox News scroll at the bottom of the screen declared "Green Energy Failure." Another Fox News host, Tucker Carlson, chimed in on his show: "The windmills froze so the power grid failed." I mean, what? These statements are just laughable.

Tucker also told his audience that "global warming is no longer a pressing concern here," suggesting that, because it was so cold outside, the earth is obviously not warming – yet another idiotic theme on my Facebook feed last week.

< Allow me to let Tucker in on a little secret: Global warming refers to earth's *overall temperature*, which is rising. That's just a fact. Global warming, in turn, causes the *climate* to *change*. Climate change causes extreme weather patterns, rising sea levels, shifting jet streams, and plenty of other things that are really bad. As a result of *climate change*, floods, droughts, ice storms and heat waves become more frequent and way more intense. Essentially, the extremes become even more extreme. So, when Tucker uses the fact that Texas had historic cold and icy weather this year as proof that there is no global warming, he is inadvertently proving the exact opposite. >

Back to Texas. Yes, non-winterized wind turbines froze. But because they were also not properly winterized, so did power plants, oil and gas wells, gas pipelines, oil rigs, piles of coal, and even a nuclear reactor water pump.

People trying to blame this on windmills is just nonsensical (I originally used another two words here but finally thawed out, calmed down, and changed them). Two-thirds of the winter electricity demand in Texas is generated by natural gas. One of the main culprits in the Great Texas Blackout of 2021 was the interruption of natural gas getting to power plants…and no amount of spin on Fox News is going to change that fact.

The truth is this. The energy catastrophe in Texas was caused by two things and two things only: Texas hubris and energy deregulation.

First up, Texas hubris. Never has a state loathed regulation or government intervention as has my beloved Texas. In the midst of the crisis, former Texas governor (and former Secretary of Energy) Rick Perry actually said that "Texans would be without electricity for longer than three days to keep the federal government out of their business." Speak for yourself dude. WE'RE FREEZING!

Texas Republicans hate federal government intervention so much (or I should say, they hate federal government intervention until they happily take $11.24 billion from the *CARES Act* and God only knows how much more after this massive leadership failure) that 90 percent of Texas' electric grid is not connected to interstate grids. This means that

Texas can largely avoid any oversight by the Federal Energy Regulatory Commission (FERC). But is also means that Texas can't rely on other states to help when its electric grid fails. #texasproud

Second up, deregulation. My first job out of college was with an energy company started solely to take advantage of FERC Order 888. Order 888 promoted wholesale electricity competition through open access, non-discriminatory transmission services. In simple terms, companies could now "rent" electric transmission lines and move electricity through them, regardless of who owned the lines.

Unsurprisingly, Texas went all in! The state embraced this new opportunity and shifted a great deal of control over the state's electric delivery system to the private sector.

At the same time, electric generation entities were given permission to do pretty much whatever they want in terms of reserve margins for backup power and generation planning, which was another major culprit in the February 2021 disaster. Want to take your power plant offline for maintenance in the middle of February? No problem! Go for it!

In the beginning, and maybe even still today, Texas leadership naïvely believed that market forces would correct for just about anything, making energy shortages and service disruptions virtually impossible in their minds.

But here's the inevitable problem: Although competition has kept Texas energy prices low through the years, smaller profit margins and practically no regulation and/or oversight also tempted energy companies to cut corners on necessary capital investments...like say, oh I don't know, WINTERIZATION PROTECTIONS THAT INCLUDE PROPER INSULATION, HEATERS AND DE-ICING MACHINES.

What happened in February is all the more irritating because it has happened before. In 2011, Texas experienced a very similar winter blackout that affected over 4 million people. In the aftermath, the Texas Public Utility Commission demanded that Texas power generators submit annual winterization plans, but that doesn't seem to have worked out that well.

Thad Hill, the chief executive of Calpine Corporation, admitted that during the 2021 freeze "two of [Calpine's] power plants failed because of winterization...That's my fault." Yep, it sure is Thad, because you knew full well what could happen. After all, two of Calpine's plants also failed during the 2011 freeze. NRG, another generation company, experienced power failures at its coal-fired plant in Limestone County and another at Greens Bayou, the same exact two plants that failed in 2011.

At the end of the day, Texas Republicans chose ideology over reliability. Then, naturally, blamed everyone else when the price of electricity skyrocketed during the crisis. When I say skyrocketed, I'm not exaggerating. Some consumer electric bills reached well over $16,000.

Texas Lieutenant Governor Dan Patrick – who desperately needs to be voted out of office just for consistently saying stupid things – said, "the people who are getting those big bills are people who gambled on a very, very low rate…going forward, people need to read the fine print in those kinds of bills."

Another regulation example that sticks in my mind maybe more than any other is attorney Rob Bilott's courageous fight to regulate polyfluoroalkyl substances (PFAS) in American drinking water. < FYI, cutie-pie Mark Ruffalo plays Rob in the movie *Dark Waters*. >

It all started when an angry farmer noticed bubbling green water in his creek and blood running out of the noses of his cattle not long after DuPont, the chemical company, began operating a waste landfill near his property.

Rob Bilott watched a video the farmer provided, where he "saw cows with stringy tails, malformed hooves, giant lesions protruding from their hides and red, receded eyes; cows suffering constant diarrhea, slobbering white slime the consistency of toothpaste, staggering bowlegged like drunks."

In a study funded by DuPont (lest you think they were acting responsibly, they were pretty much forced to conduct one thanks to the lawsuit Bilott filed), scientists discovered there was a "probable link'" between PFOA and kidney cancer, testicular cancer, thyroid disease, high cholesterol, pre-eclampsia and ulcerative colitis.

According to the Congressional Research Service, "PFAS include thousands of diverse chemicals, some of which have been used for decades in an array of industrial, commercial, and U.S. military applications. The chemical characteristics of PFAS have led to the use of various PFAS for an array of purposes such as fighting fuel-based fires and for processing and manufacturing numerous commercial products (e.g., stain-resistant and waterproof fabrics, nonstick cookware, and food containers)."

In 2016, the U.S. Environmental Protection Agency (EPA) reported that "PFOA and/or PFOS were detected in at least one public water system in 24 states. Four other PFAS were also detected in some systems."

Rob Bilott started his fight in 1999. On February 20, 2020, the EPA announced preliminary decisions to develop *Safe Drinking Water Act* (SDWA) regulations for the two most frequently detected PFAS, perfluorooctanoic acid (PFOA) and perfluorooctane sulfonate (PFOS) – <u>TWENTY-ONE YEARS</u> after Bilott filed his first federal suit against DuPont chemical company.

Now, I have a question for the people who ask, "are you for more regulation or less?" Are <u>*you*</u> cool with this poison in <u>*your*</u> drinking water? Because I am most certainly not.

The **<u>third debilitating misconception</u>** is the delusion that we can have our cake and eat it too. Although it would be fantastic to solve our problems with little effort or send the bill to someone else, those are unrealistic fantasies.

Unfortunately, we don't live in the Candyland board game. Don't get me wrong, I desperately wish we did.

> I wish that we could all sit in a colorful field of Pixy Stixs, singing Kumbaya and licking lollypop flowers under a marshmallow sky filled with Skittle rainbows.
>
> Little elves, who make delicious cookies, live in sugarplum trees that will never be harvested, you really do get $200 every time you pass Go, and an extraordinarily handsome prince will gallop in to gently kiss the sleeping princess, saving her from a lifetime of kissing good for nothing frogs (okay, that last one sounds bitter).
>
> The words coronavirus, riots, recession, fiscal cliff, police brutality and inequality are banned, and never again are we

forced to eat all of our vegetables because there really aren't kids starving in Africa after all.

We breathe air as pure as those oxygen bars in L.A., while we drive our environmentally responsible Hummers as oil gushes from our unpolluted earth like a chocolate fountain.

We not only have free tuition but actually get paid to go to college, are given a comprehensive and universal health care plan for our birthdays and get a bright and shiny national infrastructure for Christmas. The Oompa-Loompas at Treasury will print money 24/7 to pay for our goodies and we are taxed only 2% of our earnings thanks to several permanent tax cuts. Oh, happy day!!

We know better. We know that it's impossible to sustain freedom and liberty without sacrifice. To abandon this basic truth will only create a deeper and deeper hole for all of us. You know what they say when you're digging yourself further into a hole don't you? Stop digging!

Eight Bad Habits We Need to Break

So, we have established that we need to find balance plus get past three debilitating misconceptions. There are also eight destructive habits we need to break (policy examples of each will follow):

Bad Habit One	Refusing to learn from history. Example: The 2007-2009 Financial Crisis
Bad Habit Two	Making legislation cumbersome, complicated and jam packed, which does nothing but increase costs and inefficiency and create confusion and uncertainty. Example: Infrastructure
Bad Habit Three	Hitting the bulls-eye on the wrong target. Example: Education
Bad Habit Four	Constantly reacting to negative outcomes as opposed to proactively anticipating them. Example: Global Trade
Bad Habit Five	Getting stuck in ideology instead of just doing the math. Example: Health Care
Bad Habit Six	Allowing past prejudices and preconceived notions to prevent potential progress. Example: Health Care, again

Bad Habit Seven	Foolishly believing the promises made by politicians who have zero intention of keeping them and, as a result, allowing our problems to get progressively worse. Example: Immigration
Bad Habit Eight	Tolerating shady shenanigans from our leaders. Example: Government Reform

"When the situation was manageable it was neglected, and now that it is thoroughly out of hand we apply too late the remedies which then might have effected a cure.

There is nothing new in the story.

It is as old as the Sibylline books. It falls into that long, dismal catalogue of the fruitlessness of experience and the confirmed unteachability of mankind. Want of foresight, unwillingness to act when action would be simple and effective, lack of clear thinking, confusion of counsel until the emergency comes, until self-preservation strikes its jarring gong. These are the features which constitute the endless repetition of history."

– Winston Churchill

Bad Habit One

Refusing To Learn From History

...the endless repetition of history. Although history is always there for us, patiently waiting to impart its hard-earned knowledge, we continue to stubbornly disregard it.

It's fascinating how soon we forget disasters. From hurricanes to wars to financial crises, it seems we have little interest in examining cause and effect – which is unfortunate because that is one of the best ways to stop bad history from repeating itself.

When the fallout from the 2007-2009 Financial Crisis was finally in our rearview mirror, for example, it seemed like people believed yet again that the good times would roll forever. *Laissez les bons temps router*!

Throughout the 2007-2009 Financial Crisis, the term *moral hazard* was widely used in reference to the government "bailouts." Moral hazard is the concept that people take riskier risks if they are not the ones who directly feel the consequences of their actions. What has happened since 2007 proves that those concerned about moral hazard had a very valid point.

In the years leading to the 2007-2009 global catastrophe, there was a multitude of events – the savings and loans fiasco, the dot-com bubble burst, the Asian currency crisis, the Russian government bond default, massive accounting scandals, and blatant fraud – that presented cautionary tales.

But the lessons were not learned because, miraculously, the fallout from those events had little long-term significance. Any one of these should have brought our economy to a screeching halt but somehow, as a nation, we recovered virtually unscathed. Yet someday, if we're not diligent, the music will stop and there won't be enough chairs.

I am the first to admit that, before the 2007-2009 Financial Crisis, my self-interest had started to overshadow my self-sacrifice. I had become so seduced by the glitter of the American Dream that I lost sight of its glory.

But then the wakeup call came. The first few days of the crisis felt like the last day of a four-day Vegas trip. You know the one – where you live daring and carefree and throw all caution to the wind…the one where, although you really don't know what the heck you're doing, you throw that dice like a high roller and double down and hit 18 like the gambler you are.

The trip where, on the final morning, you suddenly feel irresponsible and reckless as you mentally calculate the little cash you have left as you fearfully check for a wedding ring.

After a few days, fear quickly turned into anger and frustration because most of us felt blindsided by the financial disappearing acts in the markets. But then, unexpectedly, something else started to tug at our subconscious. Although it would be far easier to ignore the rude intrusion and continue to blame uncontrolled traders and corrupt executives, feelings of regret, responsibility and guilt crept in as we tried to answer a question that in *retrospect was as inevitable as it was disturbing: Why* did we allow things to get this out of control?

It would have been painful enough to look at our 401(k) statements if we were unaware that a day of reckoning was coming, but many of us had a gut feeling that a debt far costlier than our Visa bill was about to come due – the nagging sensation that most of us had tilted more toward the glitter than the glory.

We knew it was rampant on Wall Street where a few bad apples showed blatant disregard for responsible governance and basic morality. We knew it dominated Congress, where our leaders used our tax dollars as their very own re-election fund. But we also knew that the trend extended beyond Washington and Wall Street.

From the edge of the abyss – where an international crisis of confidence crashed into a citizen's crisis of conscious – it was impossible to ignore that we all needed to make changes.

But did we? Here's a fun little story for you.

Inadequately regulated banking systems experience severe boom and bust cycles, where the enormous risks taken during the boom times inevitably lead to tremendous losses during the busts. From the early

1800s until 1929, the U.S. financial system experienced banking panics every five to ten years. These events culminated in the disastrous collapse of U.S. stock market prices on October 29, 1929 – Black Tuesday – which signaled the beginning of the Great Depression.

After the Wall Street Crash of 1929, tight regulations were put into place to prevent another catastrophe. These included the formation of the Securities and Exchange Commission and the enactment of the *Banking Act of 1933*, commonly known as the Glass-Steagall Act.

Glass-Steagall prevented banks from engaging in risky investment banking activities and prohibited any one institution from acting as any combination of an investment bank, commercial bank or insurance company. After these firewalls were established, the U.S. enjoyed over 40 years of economic growth without one major financial crisis.

Over time, many of the significant protections that were put into place between traditional commercial banking, investment banking and brokerage industries were systematically dismantled. Meanwhile, banks were required to keep fewer cash reserves on hand and the government, banks and rating agencies all lowered their mortgage standards to entice more Americans to purchase homes.

Financial deregulation was a bipartisan endeavor. In the late 1970s, savings & loans (S&Ls) were in crisis, hit hard by high interest rates and inflation (S&Ls are cooperative financial institutions that accept deposits and make mortgage, auto and other personal loans to members).

Although interest rates at that time spiked as high as 21.5 percent, S&Ls could only offer a 5.25 percent interest rate, a number established by the government.

In an effort to help S&Ls compete, Congress passed – and President Jimmy Carter signed into law – the *Depository Institutions Deregulation and Monetary Control Act*, which gave S&Ls broader authority and phased out limits on what S&Ls and banks could pay out for consumer deposits.

Although the S&L crisis was in full swing when President Ronald Reagan took office, he for some reason signed the *Garn-St. Germain Depository Institutions Act*, which only accelerated S&L deregulation. In fact, this action basically deregulated S&Ls entirely. Of the bill,

Reagan said, "This bill is the most important legislation for financial institutions in the last 50 years…All in all, I think we hit the jackpot."

Yeah, he hit the jackpot all right! S&Ls were now freer than ever to make riskier investments with depositors' money. Essentially, they were allowed to operate like banks without being regulated like them. Because there was little oversight, fraud spun out of control. In the end, over 1,100 bankers were prosecuted by the Justice Department in response to the S&L scandal and, unsurprisingly, many imploded. Ultimately, 1,043 savings & loans failed at a cost of $124 billion to the American taxpayer.

Even still, President Bill Clinton doubled down on financial deregulation. In 1998 Citicorp, a commercial bank holding company and Travelers Group, an insurance company, merged to form Citigroup. Citigroup instantly became the largest financial services company in the world combining banking, securities and insurance services. However, the merger violated the Glass-Steagall Act.

No worries! Congress simply passed – and President Clinton signed into law – the *Financial Services Modernization Act*, commonly known as the Gramm-Leach-Bliley Act.

Although Glass-Steagall had been diminished over the years, it was gutted with this legislation that allowed commercial banks, investment banks, securities firms and insurance companies to consolidate. In the absence of Glass-Steagall, financial institutions could grow larger, become more entangled and take far greater risks…and boy did they ever!

The financial sector soon consolidated into just a few huge firms, any one of them so large and interconnected that their individual failure would threaten the entire system. In other words, they became <u>too big to fail.</u>

Meanwhile, derivatives – financial instruments based on some underlying asset such as mortgages – were a multi-trillion unregulated market and Washington and Wall Street fought hard to keep it that way. In December 2000, Congress passed – and President Clinton signed into law – the *Commodities Futures Modernization Act*, which prevented the Commodity Futures Trading Commission from regulating almost all over-the-counter derivative contracts. Stay tuned for the destruction this eventually caused.

By the end of the 1990s, shiny happy market optimism and venture capitalist cash had fueled a massive bubble in Internet stocks. By 2001, the dot-com bubble burst losing over $8 trillion in paper and actual wealth.

Afterward, several regulators launched an investigation into allegations that analysts issued biased opinions in order to increase their investment banking business. A main source of evidence in the investigation were internal e-mails that showed financial analysts privately denouncing stocks they publicly praised.

During the 2000's there were tons of shenanigans going on. Enron Corporation repeatedly used fraudulent accounting practices to hide tens of billions of dollars of debt, a colossal scandal that cost shareholders $11 billion.

The Federal National Mortgage Association (Fannie Mae), established by the government to boost the housing market, engaged in what federal officials called "extensive financial fraud" by overstating earnings by around $10.6 billion in order for executives to collect hundreds of millions of dollars in bonuses. CEO Franklin Raines made over $52.8 million in bonuses based on the fraudulent numbers.

The Federal Home Loan Mortgage Corporation (Freddie Mac), also established by the government, paid $125 million to settle charges of fraudulent accounting practices, which involved underreporting earnings by $5 billion.

A Senate investigation found that Riggs Bank laundered money for former Chilean dictator Augusto Pinochet, helping him conceal millions of dollars in assets from international authorities. American International Group (AIG) agreed to pay $1.64 billion to settle charges involving improper accounting, manipulated bids, and unethical portfolio practices.

Credit Suisse paid a $536 million fine to settle claims it violated U.S. sanctions by helping other countries launder hundreds of millions of dollars through American banks. They even facilitated transactions for Iran's Atomic Energy Organization and the Aerospace Industries Organization, both of which were proliferators of weapons of mass destruction. UBS paid a fine of $780 million when they were caught helping wealthy Americans evade taxes.

These are all despicable acts to be sure, but it's hard to get worse than the vile behavior exhibited in the years leading to the 2007-2009 Financial Crisis, the largest financial disaster since the Great Depression.

This international catastrophe resulted in the collapse of large financial institutions; the government takeover of Fannie Mae, Freddie Mac and the nation's largest insurance company; an astronomical government intervention; and a massive crash in the U.S. housing market.

In the end, the United States financial system was stabilized only through significant injections of taxpayer capital, together with additional guarantees and lending facilities provided by the Federal Reserve, the Department of the Treasury, and the Federal Deposit Insurance Corporation (FDIC).

Although many intangible consequences of the fiasco cannot be precisely measured, the Federal Reserve Bank of Dallas "conservatively estimates" that "$6 trillion to $14 trillion – or the equivalent of $50,000 to $120,000 for every U.S. household – was foregone due to the 2007-09 recession."

A few additional things that can't be precisely measured – but make a huge impact on society – include psychological trauma, skill atrophy from prolonged unemployment, the loss of citizen trust in government institutions and the overall financial system, and the unintended consequences of substantial government intervention.

According to the U.S. Government Accountability Office, "The 2007-2009 Financial Crisis has been associated with large economic losses and increased fiscal challenges. Studies estimating the losses of financial crises based on lost output (value of goods and services not produced) suggest losses associated with the crisis could range from a few trillion dollars to over $10 trillion."

In the years before the crash, many Wall Street banks began to operate far differently than they had in the past. Instead of just making a loan and keeping it on the books, lending became all about loan origination and securitization, which supposedly spread the risk of a loan among hundreds of parties.

During this time, a new lending channel emerged. This "shadow" banking system consisted of non-depository banks and other financial entities such as investment banks, hedge funds, money market funds and insurers. Enormous amounts of risk were moved from the more regulated parts of the banking system to this shadow system, where there was little oversight and low capital requirements.

The risk involved in these transactions was generally considered caveat emptor, the Latin term for *let the buyer beware*. The thinking was that the parties involved in these deals were sophisticated and well-funded and therefore didn't need to be saved from themselves. However, what became crystal clear in the aftermath is that losses sustained in the shadow banking system weren't limited to the parties that made the deals. In truth, no one was isolated from the destruction.

Meanwhile, Wall Street was busy engineering new, nefarious financial instruments. After all, the possibilities were endless thanks to derivatives being unregulated…thanks President Clinton!

The deadliest of these was an extremely complex security called the collateralized debt obligation (CDO). Originally the CDO mirrored a mortgage bond, which aimed to redistribute risk associated with home mortgage lending and make the financial markets more efficient.

In a mortgage bond, thousands of home loans are gathered together and then resold in bits and pieces to investors. The assumption is that it's extremely unlikely all of the home loans grouped together will repay or default at the same time.

This structure depends largely on securitization, with thousands of loans being divided into what are called tranches (generally, the riskiest loans are in the bottom tranche and receive the highest interest rate, whereas the loans in the top tranche are the least risky and receive the lowest interest rate).

In this new world, the CDO gathered one hundred mortgage bonds and used them to create an entirely new pyramid of bonds. The bonds used in this set-up were usually Triple-B-rated bonds, some of the riskiest of the bunch. Not only were these bonds risky, at times they weren't even tied to actual home mortgages.

Financial firms soon discovered they didn't need an actual home loan as the origination. Like Vegas, they only needed someone to take the other side of their bet. In these "synthetic CDOs," short-sellers – pessimists who believed the CDO market would eventually crash and therefore bet against it – happily served as the counter party. This new market made the risk associated with subprime mortgage lending endless.

To make matters far worse, many financial firms borrowed heavily against these securities to increase their returns. This is known as leverage (using borrowed money as a source of financing). This multiplied the pain exponentially when the market collapsed.

The next little trick is where Wall Street got either really creative or really criminal depending on your take (my take is really criminal). Instead of carrying over the Triple-B-rating to the new tranches, financial firms simply got the low-rated bonds re-rated as Triple-A.

Who in the world would do this for them? Answer: Nationally Recognized Statistical Rating Organizations (NRSROs) named Moody's, Standard and Poor's and Fitch Ratings. With just one word from these agencies, the risk of these horrid loans simply disappeared – that is, on paper anyway.

NRSROs are agencies that rate the creditworthiness of a company or a financial product. Because they help investors determine the risk of a security, they are extremely influential in the financial markets. At the time, an epic conflict of interest existed in their model. For years, investors paid the bill for the risk assessments given by the rating agencies, but this changed over time. Eventually the issuers of the securities were responsible for paying for their own ratings.

To say this arrangement was lucrative for the credit agencies is quite an understatement. When Moody's went public, its stock multiplied by six and its earnings increased 900 percent. During the mortgage boom, Moody's rated $4,700 billion of residential mortgage-backed securities and $736 billion of CDOs in just seven years.

Yet over and over they completely missed – or, more accurately, blatantly overlooked – enormous risks being taken by those who paid them huge amounts of money.

Ten years after the crisis, Moody's finally reached an agreement with the "U.S. Department of Justice and the attorneys general of 21 U.S. states and the District of Columbia to resolve pending and potential civil claims related to credit ratings that Moody's Investors Service assigned to certain structured finance instruments in the financial crisis era."

They agreed to pay a $437.5 million civil penalty to the Department of Justice, and $426.3 million to the participating states and the District of Columbia.

The house of cards finally came crashing down on February 27, 2007, when Freddie Mac announced it would no longer buy the riskiest subprime mortgages and the stock market dropped 416 points. For the next eighteen months, as hundreds of billions of dollars in mortgage-related investments vanished, government regulators made desperate attempts to contain a widespread virus that ultimately metastasized into a global financial panic.

The total cost of the government intervention wasn't revealed until years later, when Bloomberg LP won a court case against the U.S. Federal Reserve and a group of the largest U.S. banks. As a result, the Federal Reserve was forced to release 29,000 pages of documents under the *Freedom of Information Act.*

Because the level of the Fed's financial commitment had been such a closely held secret, citizens, shareholders and even Congress had been unaware of the full scale of the financial rescue – which enabled many of the distressed banks to hide the magnitude of their fiscal predicament.

For example, on November 26, 2008, Bank of America CEO Kenneth Lewis sent a letter to shareholders that said the bank was "one of the strongest and most stable major banks in the world." However, at the time his bank owed the Federal Reserve $86 billion. In just one day alone – December 5, 2008 – the Federal Reserve loaned the still deeply troubled banks a combined $1.2 trillion.

As the dust settled and Americans learned more about the backroom negotiations between the government and Wall Street, public outrage grew.

AIG's initial $85 billion support from taxpayers eventually grew to $182 billion. It was discovered that shortly after their rescue, millions of dollars in bonuses had been paid to AIG executives. To add insult to injury, less than a week after the government committed the initial funds, AIG executives attended a retreat at a luxury resort and spa. AIG paid over $440,000 for the event.

Just before his firm's liquidity crisis, Merrill Lynch CEO John Thain spent $1.22 million of company money redecorating his office (he spent $35,115 on his toilet!). It was also discovered that Merrill had paid its employees billions of dollars in bonuses right before their sale to Bank of America was finalized. Also, before the deal closed, Merrill's trading losses increased to $15.31 billion and the firm had to take additional write-downs on its weakening assets.

However, none of these game-changing developments were made public before the merger was approved by the shareholders of both companies. When Bank of America made these disclosures after the deal closed, the bank's stock fell by more than 60 percent, equaling a market value loss of over $50 billion.

The Securities and Exchange Commission (SEC) sued Bank of America for allegedly concealing huge losses at Merrill Lynch to ensure that shareholders would approve the merger. The suit was settled for $150 million, although the judge himself said the agreement was "half-baked justice at best." Shareholders also sued Bank of America. That case was settled for $2.43 billion.

In August of 2013, the Justice Department finally sued Bank of America, but not because of the Merrill Lynch deal. Bank of America stood accused of lying to investors in the years leading to the financial crisis and defrauding them by vastly minimizing the risks of $850 million in securities. The suit claims that then-CEO Kenneth Lewis referred to the wholesale mortgages his firm was actively selling as "toxic waste." One year later, Bank of America agreed to a settlement of $16.65 billion. Bank of America has paid a total of $76.1 billion in fines.

I don't mean to pick on Bank of America. In August of 2013, JP Morgan Chase finally admitted that the firm faced criminal and civil investigations into whether the firm sold sketchy mortgage securities in the years before the crisis. JP Morgan Chase has paid a total of $43.7 billion in fines. Citigroup $19 billion; Deutsche Bank $14 billion; Wells

Fargo $11.8 billion; RBS $10.1 billion; BNP Paribas $9.3 billion; Credit Suisse $9.1 billion; Morgan Stanley $8.6 billion; Goldman Sachs $7.7 billion; and UBS $6.5 billion.

All in, banks have been fined $243 billion from the fall-out of the 2007-2009 Financial Crisis. But as *Market Watch* reminds us, "It's important to note that the banks don't just send a check for their fines to federal and state governments. Many times, they get credit by making loans and supporting debt restructuring. For example, a Goldman Sachs commitment for $1.8 billion of loan forgiveness and financing for affordable housing was considered as part of a $5.1 billion 'fine' the bank had to pay."

§§§

The 2007-2009 Financial Crisis was avoidable. And so is the next one, but only if we learn from the past.

The underlying elements of the mortgage crisis – inadequate financial regulation, shockingly awful corporate leadership, uncontrolled risk-taking, excessive borrowing by Wall Street and the American public, federal officials who were unprepared for such a crisis and, therefore, inconsistent in their decisions and practically zero accountability for anyone – must be examined and fixed. For good.

< The recommendations for this are outlined in *The Policy Guide*. >

In reality, little has changed over the past ten years. Banks are bigger than ever. Combined, the top 15 largest banks in the United States hold $12.54 trillion in assets. The ratings agencies are still up to shady shenanigans.

Insanely reckless trading, foreclosure abuse, the rigging of foreign exchange markets, the enabling of tax evasion and money laundering, and the exploitation of the London Interbank Offered Rate (LIBOR), the key global interest rate, are just a few examples of Wall Street's continued hubris and lack of repentance. Derivatives are still all the rage – to the tune of over 15 trillion.

This is frustrating because we actually acted responsibly for a while after the 2007-2009 Financial Crisis. In fact, for several years, our financial system was much safer than it was before.

On July 21, 2010, President Obama signed the *Dodd-Frank Wall Street Reform and Consumer Protection Act* into law. This legislation was far from perfect – for example, it put too much regulation on smaller community banks, and it was far too cumbersome, which we'll get to in a minute – but it did make sure the nation's largest banks were operating with substantially higher levels of capital than they did before and that banks were no longer making risky, speculative bets for their own profit.

Dodd-Frank also established the Financial Stability Oversight Council, the Volcker Rule, and stress tests for banks; created both the Orderly Liquidation Authority (OLA) and the Consumer Financial Protection Bureau (CFPB); and strengthened the regulation of credit agencies as well as whistleblower protections.

These were positive steps but, almost immediately, congressional Republicans went to work on chipping away the safety measures that were enacted – big surprise! – and some rules were never finalized in the first place. Davis Polk, a law firm that closely tracked the progress of Dodd-Frank, reported that, as of July 19, 2016 – a full six years after Obama signed the legislation – only 70.3 percent of the rulemaking requirements had been finalized.

Naturally, the Republicans had plenty of help dismantling the law from their buddies, the lobbyists. Yet again our destiny was sold to the highest bidder. Since 2010, the Finance, Insurance and Real Estate sector has contributed $3,652,531,988 to the political process, and it appears their onslaught worked beautifully.

For example, on the eve of a December 2014 continuing resolution omnibus bill – which was jammed through Congress to stop yet another government shutdown – an unrelated provision was slyly stuck in the down-to-the-wire spending package.

Written by the financial services corporation Citigroup, the random provision repealed a central part of Dodd-Frank – banks can once again use insured deposits and other taxpayer subsidies to play in the derivatives market.

Meanwhile, remember that deadly, extremely complex security called the collateralized debt obligation (CDO)?

Today, we have the CLO (collateralized loan obligation), which are loans once again being made to risky borrowers with little oversight. This time around, instead of risky homeowners the target is risky companies. The estimated size of the CLO market is $900 billion.

...the endless repetition of history.

Bad Habit Two

Making Legislation Cumbersome, Complicated and Jam Packed, Which Does Nothing But <u>Increase</u> Costs and Inefficiency and <u>Create</u> Confusion and Uncertainty

The importance of financial reform in the wake of the 2007-2009 Financial Crisis cannot be overstated, as President Obama knew when he signed the *Dodd-Frank Wall Street Reform and Consumer Protection Act* into law.

Although Dodd-Frank has been successful by many measures – despite the Republican's fierce sabotage efforts (see Consumer Protection in *The Policy Guide* as an example) – from the beginning it was too cumbersome and complicated...which is a practice our politicians have taken to an art form.

Dodd-Frank started out being 848 pages long but, within five years, 22,296 pages of rules and regulations related to the legislation had been published in the Federal Register.

To put this into perspective, the *National Bank Act of 1864*, a law that helped establish our entire banking system, was 29 pages long. The *Federal Reserve Act of 1913*, which created the Federal Reserve system, was 32 pages, and the *Banking Act of 1933* (a.k.a. Glass-Steagall), the law that separated commercial banking from investment backing and created the Federal Deposit Insurance Corporation (FDIC), was just 37 pages.

Jonathan Macey of Yale Law School put it this way: "Laws classically provide people with rules. Dodd-Frank is not directed at people. It is an outline directed at bureaucrats and it instructs them to make still more regulations and to create more bureaucracies." To which *The Economist* brilliantly replied: "Like the Hydra of Greek myth, Dodd-Frank can grow new heads as needed."

I don't imagine there were many tiny violins playing for Wall Street in the wake of the financial crisis, but between 2010 and 2016, implementing Dodd-Frank cost financial institutions an estimated 73 million hours in paperwork and $36 billion in actual dollars.

Behold, one of the most fundamental problems in Washington, D.C.! Even though the atmosphere in politics is already toxic – or probably *because* of that – politicians decide the best way to proceed with their legislative agenda is to cram as many issues (and earmarks) as possible into a bill, which does nothing but increase costs and inefficiency and create confusion and uncertainty.

The examples are endless. Take the *Patient Protection and Affordable Care Act* (a.k.a. Obamacare), legislation that ended up being thousands of pages of text essentially written in Klingon. The sheer breadth and depth of the bill led former Senator Jay Rockefeller (D-WV), one of the primary authors of the legislation, to say it's "probably the most complex piece of legislation ever passed by the United States Congress" and "just beyond comprehension."

It's tricky to pin down exact numbers, but *USA Today* estimates that, within three and a half years of the ACA being signed into law, almost 11,000 pages of regulations had been added.

Unsurprisingly, at the time, Republicans claimed the number of pages of regulations in the Democrat-backed bill was much higher. Representative Richard Hudson (R-NC) proclaimed, "We've got 33,000 pages of regulations that they've already written. If we stacked it up here, it would be seven feet tall" (he later revised the number of pages down to 13,000).

Meanwhile, Senator Mitch McConnell (R-KY) said that "implementation had become a bureaucratic nightmare, with some 159 new government agencies, boards and programs busily enforcing the roughly 20,000 pages of rules and regulations already associated with this law."

Whether there are 11,000, 13,000 or 20,000 pages, I think we can all agree there are a lot! My point is that, to make significant progress, there is one thing we must do before all else: Simplify. Legislation needs to be clear, precise and uncomplicated, the exact opposite of what happens today.

Steve Jobs, the co-founder of Apple, once said, "We tried to make something much more holistic and simple. When you first start off trying to solve a problem, the first solutions you come up with are very complex, and most people stop there. But if you keep going and live with the problem and peel more layers of the onion off, you can often arrive at some very elegant and simple solutions. Most people just don't put in the time or energy to get there."

...but we must get there, fast! Especially in light of President Biden's *Build Back Better Plan.* The *Build Back Better Plan* was originally divided into three parts. The *American Rescue Plan*, a Covid-19 relief bill that President Biden signed into law in March 2021, the *American Jobs Plan*, which was essentially a physical infrastructure bill, and the *American Families Plan*, which focused on social services. The entire *Build Back Better* agenda called for trillions and trillions of dollars in spending.

Elements of the *American Jobs Plan* were rolled into the *Infrastructure Investment and Jobs Act,* which was signed into law by President Biden on November 15, 2021. However, I am still going to use the original *American Jobs Plan* and *American Families Plan* as examples – because they make really good ones! These two policy proposals are counterproductive for **three reasons**:

"No" On These Two Plans: Reason One

As usual, these two bills were cumbersome, complicated and jam packed. For example, the *American Jobs Plan* (phase one) was sold as the physical infrastructure piece of the plan, served with a heaping side of investment in research and development.

First, let me say unequivocally that I am all for spending money on our deteriorating infrastructure. The U.S. transportation system has 12,971,484 miles of highway; 19,639 airports; 181 ports; 8,238 cargo handling docks; 114,244 miles of railroad; 11,607 miles of public transit; 2,558,007 miles of pipeline; 616,096 bridges; and 25,000 miles of navigable waterways.

Every year, this labyrinth carries passengers over 5 trillion miles in their vehicles, 722 billion miles in the air, and almost 39 billion miles by rail. It also transports, literally, a boatload of merchandise. In 2018, the U.S. transportation system moved over 18 billion tons of freight, valued at almost $19 trillion. By 2045, that number is expected to be $37 trillion.

Practically every one of these categories have been neglected for years, and it shows. Big time! It's bad enough that things are about to collapse, but our outdated infrastructure also makes us look bush-league. We all know you can't exactly be the *shining city upon the hill* if everything is falling down.

The American Society of Civil Engineers gives U.S. infrastructure an overall grade of C- and estimates it will take an investment of $2.59 trillion over the next ten years to even get us a B. The group also warns that, if we continue to underinvest in infrastructure, by 2039 the costs to society will equal $10 trillion in GDP, over 3 million jobs, and $2.24 trillion in exports.

Our C- infrastructure is yet another textbook example of the importance of being proactive versus reactive. This is happening. We can't twitch our noses and wish a new bridge to appear, and we can't afford to keep slapping Band-Aids on gaping wounds. We must mobilize our resources to get these things done...immediately.

We're not talking about a third world country; we're talking about the United States of America!

There is no excuse for the world's largest national economy to lack state-of-the-art airports, subways, railways and ports; sophisticated fiber-optic lines, bandwidth and wireless networks; modern schools, roads, bridges, levees, dams and water systems; hi-tech oil and gas pipelines and electricity-distribution grids; and extensive high-speed rail systems.

– the 1787 Recommendations for
Infrastructure are in *The Policy Guide* –

Modernizing our infrastructure creates a safer nation, helps revitalize hard-hit sectors like construction and heavy manufacturing, and makes our economy more productive and efficient.

Investment in infrastructure also produces jobs, both directly (jobs involved in the actual projects) and indirectly (jobs created by the need for supplies and support for the projects). This, in turn, sparks a cycle of growth that will eventually create even more jobs – employed people spend money in the economy so more people will be needed to handle the higher demand. #TheButterflyEffect

Additionally, we cannot ignore the fact that our infrastructure is integral to our global competitiveness. These two are intricately intertwined because infrastructure is one of the main things domestic and international companies evaluate when they choose locations for their business operations, not to mention the absolute necessity of safely and swiftly moving the people, goods and services that are already here. Time is money, people! :)

Hence President Biden's *American Jobs Plan.* In the original proposal, money was allocated for roads and bridges; airports; public schools; the U.S. freight system; public transit; Amtrak and other railways; port and airports; universal broadband; the electric grid; electric vehicle chargers; lead pipe replacement; affordable housing improvements; the modernization of community colleges, Department of Veterans Affairs hospitals and clinics and child-care facilities; and even the electrification of 20 percent of our yellow school buses.

But wait! There's more! This one bill also covered investments in the manufacturing sector; the improvement of working conditions; increasing road safety for cyclists and pedestrians; worker training; refilling our Strategic National Stockpile; and expanding home or community-based care for older and disabled Americans.

Good grief! I mean, where's the kitchen sink?

Now, I know some of you may think I'm being hypocritical because I have used the word "comprehensive" a thousand times in this book, and Lord knows Biden's bill was comprehensive in the truest sense of the word.

Yes, I have used the word *comprehensive* quite a bit, but only as it pertains to looking at our *entire* policy agenda to ensure that seemingly disparate policies work together for the biggest bang for our buck, not as a mechanism for loading so much into a bill that there is zero chance for smooth implementation and proper oversight. (we'll circle back to this point in a minute)

Plus, these massive bills tend to be Trojan Horses heavily influenced by lobbyists. For example, if the *American Jobs Plan* was really meant to address our physical infrastructure, why was only 5 percent of the funding allocated to roads and bridges but almost 20 percent allocated for expanding elderly and disabled care?

Let me be clear: I'm certainly not against our elderly and disabled getting the very best care – I assure you, I'm very much for protecting our elderly and disabled – but $400 billion for their "home or community-based care" being in a bill supposedly focused on physical infrastructure is suspicious. As was the Biden administration's explanation, after being grilled over these semantics, that elderly and disabled Americans are indeed infrastructure, just in human form – which is just a ridiculously silly thing to say and makes the entire thing even more questionable.

Another part of the Biden administration's explanation was that the jobs involved in taking care of our elderly and disabled are disproportionally filled by women of color, and they should be making more money…something that, again, I agree with 100%. But this justification instantly lost credibility with me when I learned that the $400 billion allocated for "home or community-based care" – which constitutes a fifth of the cost of the entire bill – was included mainly because special interest organizations like the Service Employees International Union (SEIU) lobbied hard for it to be.

Of course, it makes perfect sense that the SEIU would get special treatment from a Democrat-led White House and Congress since the organization has given $136,075,857 in political contributions since 1990 and spent $22,950,291 on lobbying since 1998. This is in addition to spending $74,920,001 in so-called outside spending, which are political expenditures made “independent” of candidates’ committees (i.e., party committees, Super PACS and 501(c) “dark money” groups.) The SEIU contributed $27,992,765 during the 2020 election cycle alone.

What is that brilliant phrase that the wise sage Sarah Palin used about lipstick and pigs?

“No” On These Two Plans: Reason Two

The second reason these two original policy proposals would have been at best counterproductive and, at worst, disastrous for this country is that the cost of these proposals was astronomical and, no, taxing rich people and corporations wouldn’t even begin to cover the tab.

President Biden’s original *Build Back Better Plan* had a combined price tag of over $6 trillion. As a comparison, the United States spent just over $4 trillion (in 2021 dollars) to fight the entire Second World War, which lasted four years.

< Commercial Break: I would like to take this opportunity to remind everyone that we are already $29.7 trillion in debt, a fact that, as far as I can tell, has been ignored by the Biden administration throughout these discussions. Who are they going to tax to pay for *that*? >

Now, let’s circle back to my earlier point about loading so much into a bill that there is zero chance for smooth implementation and proper oversight.

I’m not naïve. Infrastructure is super expensive, and I get that. In fact, we already know that the American Society of Civil Engineers estimates it will take an investment of $2.59 trillion for even a grade of

B. And there is no question that we have an enormous challenge on the horizon regarding the care of our rapidly aging population.

But the sad, unfortunate truth is this: It's not so much the *amount* of money I have a problem with; it's *who* we are entrusting the money *to*.

It's funny how these massive bills never include any sort of detail beyond an obscene dollar amount. I mean, wouldn't it be helpful to know who is ultimately in charge of each of these infrastructure categories? Who will manage them? What is the bidding process and the bidding parameters? What is each of their budget, scope, targets, timelines, risks, and expected outcomes? Who will authorize funding, contracting, or changes to the original scope? Is this going to be one of those deals like we talked about in the *Operation Overhaul* section, where seven separate federal agencies administer 92 different programs, with practically zero coordination between them?

After the implementation of the *American Recovery and Reinvestment Act of 2009* – President Obama's stimulus package that was passed in the wake of the 2007-2009 Financial Crisis – Congress passed the *Digital Accountability and Transparency Act of 2014* (the *DATA Act*), partly in response to a severe deficit of proper oversight and transparency. The goal of the legislation was to require agencies to prepare and submit clear, standardized information on the money they spend.

In 2020, six years after the *DATA Act* passed, the U.S. Government Accountability Office (GAO) found that "47 (out of 51) offices of inspectors general (OIGs) reported control deficiencies related to system limitations, quality control procedures, data from external systems, and other issues. Further, 44 OIGs made recommendations for agencies to help improve data quality." Does it really seem like these agencies are ready to properly account for the trillions of dollars set to be thrown on the pile?

We already discussed the colossal amount of money and resources our federal government wastes in the *Operation Overhaul* section. Now we are being asked to fork over $400 billion to the Centers for Medicare & Medicaid Services (CMS), an agency that we *already know* is rife with rampant fraud, waste, and abuse?

The following was covered earlier, but I don't think we can read/hear about it enough. The U.S. Government Accountability Office (GAO) says that:

> "CMS, which administers Medicare, faces many challenges related to implementing payment methods that encourage efficient service delivery, managing the program to serve beneficiaries well, and safeguarding the program from loss due to fraud, waste, and abuse. Medicare has been designated as a *High Risk* program because its complexity and susceptibility to improper payments, in addition to its size, have led to serious management challenges. Addressing these challenges requires improvements to payment methods, program management, and program safeguards."

A follow-up report from the GAO revealed that:

> "Improper payment estimates for fiscal year 2019 totaled about $175 billion, based on improper payment estimates reported by federal programs, an increase from the fiscal year 2018 total of $151 billion. Of the $175 billion, about $121 billion (approximately 69 percent) was concentrated in three program areas: (1) Medicaid, (2) Medicare, and (3) Earned Income Tax Credit.
>
> Improper payments – payments that should not have been made or that were made in incorrect amounts – continue to be an area of fiscal concern in the federal government. Improper payments have been estimated to total almost $1.7 trillion government-wide from fiscal years 2003 through 2019."

And we can just forget about proper oversight at this point. The latest example is the "oversight" of the $2.2 trillion 2020 stimulus legislation, which still has no centralized supervision and is being tracked by a huge, uncoordinated web of congressional panels, departments and agencies.

In a quarterly report from Brian D. Miller, the U.S. Treasury Department's special inspector general for pandemic recovery programs, he describes epic turf wars between the agencies and said, in a nutshell, that "things are not working well."

The U.S. Government Accountability Office (GAO) concurs, finding that, among many other atrocities, there has been numerous fraud-related cases associated with the *Paycheck Protection Program* (PPP) and *Economic Injury Disaster Loans* (EIDL) program and over $3.6 billion in *Pandemic Unemployment Assistance* (PUA) overpayments from March 2020 through January 2021.

The GAO classifies the Small Business Administration (SBA) a *High Risk* area that has "deficiencies within all components of internal control." The report states that "SBA's failures to provide data and documentation on a timely basis for PPP and EIDL have impeded efforts to ensure transparency and accountability for the programs. This includes delays in obtaining key information from SBA, such as detailed oversight plans and documentation for estimating improper payments."

§§§

President Biden pledged that the original *American Jobs Plan* ($2.3 trillion) and the *American Families Plan* ($1.8 trillion) would not add a penny to the national debt. He insisted that raising taxes on corporations and taxing anyone who makes over $400,000 would pay for both plans.

This is simply not true. There's just not enough money there. For example, the largest tax slice of both proposals is taxing multinational corporations but, by the administration's own calculations, that piece is estimated to only bring in $1 trillion.

The Penn Wharton Budget Model (PWBM) projected that the *American Families Plan* (AFP) alone "would spend $2.5 trillion, about $700 billion more than the White House's estimate, over the 10-year budget window, 2022-2031. They estimate that AFP would raise 1.3 trillion in new tax revenue over the same period. By 2050, the AFP would increase government debt by almost 5 percent and decrease GDP by 0.4 percent."

The final Congressional Budget Office (CBO) report on the matter, released in November 2021, concluded that the *American Families Plan* would increase the budget deficit by $160 billion over the next decade.

At best, the Biden administration was doing the fuzziest of fuzzy math. At worst, they were being straight-up disingenuous.

To pay for the *American Jobs Plan*, the Biden administration planned to raise the corporate tax rate from 21 percent to 28 percent; increase the global minimum tax from 10.5 percent to an average of 21 percent (the exact calculation on this is country specific); impose a 15 percent tax on "book-incomes," or the amount of income corporations publicly report; end federal tax breaks for fossil fuel companies; crack down on U.S. corporations claiming to be foreign companies; stop deductions for moving jobs overseas; and offer tax credits for bringing jobs back home to America.

But here's the catch, and it's a big one (and I think it's super shady they even tried this subterfuge). The Biden administration said that the $2.3 trillion worth of spending in the *American Jobs Plan* would take place over the next 8 years, but that it will take the next 15 years of higher taxes on corporations to pay for it. Sorry to break it to you, Mr. President, but that ain't what I call apples to apples. Do you think no one is going to look into this stuff? C'mon man!

Another super shady gimmick the Biden administration used to artificially reduce the cost of the legislation lies in the way the programs in the bill were to be structured and accounted for in the budget. For one, the Democrats declared many programs in the bill *temporary* as opposed to *permanent* because, if a program is considered temporary, the CBO doesn't calculate it over the requisite ten-year period – which obviously lowers the overall cost impact of the legislation.

Problem is, these programs are not truly considered temporary by anyone. Programs in Washington rarely get cancelled, they get renewed – adding huge additional costs. For example, let's look at four of the "temporary" policies in the original *American Families Plan:* an increase in the Child Tax Credit; an expansion of the Earned Income Tax Credit; support for childcare and pre-k; and an expansion of the *Affordable Care Act.*

If these four programs were renewed, it would add $2.18 trillion to the bottom line. This means that the cost of the bill would actually be $4.29 trillion instead of the officially stated cost of $2.43 trillion. Therefore, the total deficit impact is actually $2.7 trillion. I told you. Shady.

There are three additional problems with this pie-in-the-sky payment plan.

Pie-In-the-Sky Payment Plan: Problem One

The "spend for 8 years, tax for 15 years" plan can't even *logistically* work because Joe Biden has zero control over what happens in 15 years. He only has "control" for the next 4, possibly 8, years, and even that's a stretch given his polarized political party and our practically dead even Congress.

Meanwhile, the funding strategy for the *American Families Plan* was no more realistic. This plan allocated money for universal pre-K, free childcare, two years of free community college for all, a paid family and medical leave program, *Affordable Care Act* subsidies, scholarships for teachers, increased Pell Grants, expanded nutrition programs, among many, many more things. It also claims to help solve climate change and racial inequities, end child poverty, and ensure world peace (okay, I made that last one up).

For this phase of the plan, President Biden intended to impose new taxes on rich people.

This included almost doubling the capital gains tax to 39.6 percent for people earning over $1 million a year (this would be the highest capital gains tax in a hundred years). Plus, the top marginal income tax rate would increase from 37 percent to 39.6 percent (effectively rolling back Donald Trump's tax cut).

An additional part of the payment strategy called for the Internal Revenue Service (IRS) to crack down on legally owed but uncollected taxes. The U.S. Treasury's Office of Tax Analysis claims this increased enforcement would raise $700 billion in new revenue over 10 years, plus $1.6 trillion in the following ten. The Biden Administration reckoned it would take giving the IRS at least $80 billion and doubling the size of the agency to achieve this threshold.

Unfortunately, the Congressional Budget Office (CBO) found that Biden's IRS crackdown plan would only yield around $120 billion over the next ten years, far (far!) less than the Biden Administration was banking on.

Setting aside the $80 billion and increase in the size of the IRS for a moment, this is not necessarily a bad thought process. In fact, 1787's thought process for *Operation Overhaul* – where we will end the massive inefficiency and waste that infects every level of our federal government and use these found funds solely for the purpose of reducing our debt and closing the gap on our deficit – is somewhat similar on paper. But 1787's outcomes rely on finding and improving the endless wasteful practices *within* the U.S. government, not a big Easter Egg hunt in the Cayman Islands.

Plus, it is highly doubtful that, as originally proposed, this effort would bring in anywhere close to $700 million in 10 years...especially when the Treasury Department, in the very same breath as saying how much money they plan to recoup, assures everyone earning less than $400,000 per year that audit rates "will not rise relative to recent years." Say whaaaat? That leaves out over 40 percent of all taxpayers and relies solely on the audits of, by far, the most complicated returns. That doesn't even make sense.

Five former U.S. Treasury secretaries from both Republican and Democratic administrations – Timothy F. Geithner, Jacob J. Lew, Henry M. Paulson Jr., Robert E. Rubin and Lawrence H. Summers – said in a *New York Times* guest essay that unpaid taxes are a $600 billion per year problem that could total over $7 trillion over the next ten years if left unaddressed. They write, in part, that:

> "Over the past 25 years, IRS resources have been steadily cut, with the ratio of enforcement funding to returns filed falling by around 50 percent. Today, the IRS has fewer auditors than at any time since World War II. Faced with resource constraints, it is no surprise that the agency is not able to appropriately focus scrutiny on complex returns, where noncompliance is greatest. Of about four million partnership returns filed in 2018, the IRS audited only 140 of them. It did not pursue 300 high-income taxpayers who together cost the agency $10 billion in unpaid taxes over a three-year period when they failed to even file returns. And audit rates of those in the top 1 percent have fallen most staggeringly over the course of the past decade, such that rural counties in the Deep South have some of the highest rates of examination in the country."

They believe that doing more to retrieve uncollected taxes is possible but will require a very comprehensive overhaul, including significant information technology (IT) advancements and better customer service. These are all super smart guys who have seen the deficiencies in the IRS firsthand.

But as Biden's plan was originally written, the Penn Wharton Budget Model estimated that enhanced IRS tax collection enforcement would actually bring in "almost $480 billion in additional revenue" over the next 10 years, which is a far cry from $*700 billion in new revenue over 10 years, plus $1.6 trillion in the following ten.*

Analysis from the Congressional Budget Office (CBO) is perhaps the most telling assessment of all:

> "The difference between the amount of taxes owed and the amount collected each year – often called the tax gap – is estimated periodically by the IRS. The gross tax gap is the amount that taxpayers do not pay by their filing deadline. As such, it measures the extent of noncompliance with the tax code. In its most recent report, the IRS estimated that the annual gross tax gap was $441 billion, on average, between

2011 and 2013. The IRS ultimately collects some of that amount. The net tax gap, which is the gross tax gap reduced by the amount that the IRS collects through its enforcement activities, was an estimated $381 billion annually over that period.

On the basis of its analysis of the effects that different funding levels have had on IRS enforcement, CBO estimates that increasing the IRS's funding for examinations and collections by $20 billion over 10 years would boost revenues by $61 billion, resulting in a $41 billion decrease in the cumulative deficit; increasing such funding by $40 billion over 10 years would boost revenues by $103 billion, resulting in a $63 billion decrease in the deficit."

Pie-In-the-Sky Payment Plan: Problem Two

Which brings us to the second problem with Biden's payment plan. He forgets that, although it makes good television to say that huge taxes on rich people and corporations will solve every single cash crunch in this country, in reality all that happens – as we learned from the *ProPublica* tax exposé – is that uber rich people find ways to wiggle around tax law…especially when, although the administration talks a big game about "closing loopholes" and the like, so far there is no meaningful tax reform to accompany these tax hikes.

So, until that happens, uber rich people and their team of financial wizards will keep finding loopholes to exploit. As will corporations, as they also pass through any new tax expense to consumers and employees through higher prices and lower wages.

Pie-In-the-Sky Payment Plan: Problem Three

Biden's *American Jobs Plan* gave away the benefits that public-private partnerships can bring to the table. All of our policy challenges require money and, because there is only so much of it to go around, we have to prioritize. But in the case of infrastructure, there are several ways to mitigate our cost and leverage our investment.

One of the best ways is through public-private partnerships. These partnerships usually have lower costs and greater efficiency, and the private sector can often assume risks that government entities are unable to take.

These partnerships, together with a national infrastructure bank – a bank, funded with seed capital from the government then leveraged by our capital markets, that can provide low-interest loans, issue bonds, provide insurance for the bonds of state and local governments, streamline the construction process, and coordinate and prioritize the rebuilding efforts – are a fabulous way to achieve our infrastructure goals.

But, instead of leveraging the private sector and getting more bang for our buck, Biden's *American Jobs Plan* freely gave them what amounts to corporate welfare, which ultimately throws the expense back onto the American taxpayer. This is all the weirder because Biden is giving companies subsidies while, at the same time, significantly increasing their taxes. Does that make sense to you?

The *American Jobs Plan* allocated $100 billion for broadband, $100 billion for electric utilities, $174 billion for electric vehicles, and $180 billion for something generically called "research." Supposedly, this money was meant to incentivize private sector companies toward a certain outcome – like building manufacturing plants in the Rust Belt, for example. < note: yet a *separate* piece of legislation called the *United States Innovation and Competition Act* appropriates $250 billion to specifically counteract China's economic and military progress. For example, $52 billion is allocated for subsidizing domestic computer-chip manufacturing. >

But many companies are doing things like this anyway. We talked earlier about corporate America's huge investment in clean energy. Likewise, Elon Musk and SpaceX are creating a lightning-fast broadband network to cover the *entire world.* SpaceX's project, Starlink, already has over 1,200 working satellites in orbit, and plans to have 42,000 operational by 2027.

Intel, which still designs and manufactures its own chips, announced that it would open its factories to outside auto chip companies as well as build new factories. Companies like AT&T, Comcast, and CenturyLink are also investing heavily in broadband because, after all, it's *their business*.

In 2018, Apple announced a $350 billion investment in the United States, in the form of buildings and jobs, among other things. In April 2021, Apple increased that investment by $80 billion, to include 20,000 new jobs, over the next five years. One of the first projects is a new campus located near Raleigh, North Carolina.

These companies don't need our money. They are doing just fine on their own.

"No" On Biden's Two Plans: Reason Three

The third reason President Biden's *American Jobs Plan* and its follow-up, the *American Families Plan* would be at best counterproductive and, at worst, disastrous for this country leads us to another bad habit we need to break…

Bad Habit Three

Hitting the Bulls-Eye on the Wrong Target

Note: The entirety of Part Two is dedicated to
social justice issues and how to help solve them.

Since we don't tackle social justice issues until Part Two – and, therefore, you may not yet know my position on these issues – you might think that I'm being cold-hearted and unempathetic by not supporting President Biden's *American Families Plan.* It sounds like such a nice thing to do for people!

To the contrary it's my passion for social justice that leads me to my verdict on phase two of Biden's plan. Out of everything the two major political parties have gotten terribly wrong, vulnerable American families are the number one tragedy.

As our leaders in Washington increasingly shift their strategy to poisonous politics, our most imperative systems – everything from health care to education to those that help lower-income Americans – have slipped further into total chaos.

I honestly can't decide which is worse: Democrats who act like they give a damn but fail to appropriately act or Republicans who don't even pretend to give a damn. Both major parties have proven to be consistently inept at confronting these challenges.

For decades, the damaging consequences of our national social service policies – which forced an already struggling population into a devastating cycle of perpetual, long-term dependence – have mounted. Many Americans remain captive to our misaligned social systems, ones that establish detrimental patterns that are virtually impossible to unilaterally break.

The plight of these Americans reminds me of that Whack-A-Mole game, where the little moles randomly pop up only to be whacked down by a big fat mallet. Every time compromised families get their heads somewhat above ground to establish a semblance of control over their life and destiny, they get whacked down again by cycles heaped on them nine decades ago.

Certainly, there was an enormous need for social and economic programs after the Great Depression. President Franklin Roosevelt's *New Deal* provided relief for the poor and unemployed, greatly aided economic recovery, and established reforms to prevent another depression. But some of these programs ignited a devastating cycle of generational poverty.

When poverty goes generational – meaning a family has lived in poverty for at least two generations – it becomes about far more than how much money they have in the bank. Every single day that someone has no job, for example, they experience a tremendous loss of hope and self-esteem, along with increased stress and depression.

There is also accumulated damage caused by increased emotional instability, declining physical health, entrenched cultural customs, and a severe lack of social support and appropriate role models. This reinforces the crushing feeling of inferiority, reignites frustration and low expectations, and decimates any sense of self-worth.

It's just wrong. And excruciatingly unfair. And exceedingly unjust.

But then, suddenly, we hear about a trillion dollar+ plan to help. Wow! Finally, someone is paying attention! Thank goodness! Surely appropriating $1.8 trillion for things like our poverty, inequality and racial crises proves we mean serious business, and will most definitely help solve all of our social challenges, right?

Unfortunately, no. It's not that I think Joe Biden has nefarious intentions. I sincerely don't think that and believe 100% that he is doing what *he thinks* is the right thing for people. But history tells us that throwing a huge amount of money at deeply entrenched, pervasive challenges with no clear strategy on how to fix it does not work and wastes time we just don't have.

Our federal government is absolutely genius at hitting the bulls-eye on the wrong target. Why do we, time after time and issue after issue, keep going back to failed policies and political philosophies that don't work? Answer: Because that's the easy thing to do.

It's easy to vote yes to $1.8 trillion in funding. It's easy to hand someone a school voucher, or give them free housing, college, and health care. It's easy to attend meeting after meeting to discuss tweaking existing, but failing, programs. But all this does is lull us into a false sense of security that allows us to foolishly believe that things are actually getting better. *At least*, we tell ourselves, *we're doing something*!

But we're not. The only way things will truly get better is if we learn from past mistakes, then roll up our sleeves and do the really, really hard work of developing a clear, thorough and accountable plan of action – *before* we spend $1.8 trillion on it.

Let's look at education reform as an example. < Note: you can read more about education reform, as well as see 1787's proposed policy recommendations, in the *America's Best Chance* section in Part Two. >

Without question, the future security of our country will be determined by far more than tightening our borders, fighting terrorists, or attaining technological superiority. In truth, the success or failure of our educational system is the prime determinate in our ability to preserve supremacy within the international power structure.

The way we educate our children – all our children – has increasingly historic implications for every single one of us. In this new era of world interdependence, an uneducated, unskilled, and unprepared work force equals an unparalleled disaster for this country. To that end, we must do whatever it takes to ensure a flexible, dynamic labor market and a well-educated, adaptable workforce.

Combined, globalization and technology make drastic alterations to our educational curriculum an urgent priority. Although low-skilled workers have always been at a disadvantage, a deficit of skilled labor is now even more ominous as America continually expands its free trade policies and companies become more multinational.

And make no mistake, despite the campaign promises and rally cries you have heard – and will continue to hear over the next few years – America's dedication to worldwide commerce will not likely change any time soon because the overall financial benefit to our nation greatly outweighs the negatives (read more about this in the *Trade* section of this book). Temporary financial assistance for displaced workers may help in the short term, but at the end of the day it's education and education alone that will be the great equalizer.

And we're failing at it, miserably. The National Assessment of Educational Progress (NAEP) – commonly referred to as *The Nation's Report Card* – reveals that only 40 percent of 4th graders and 34 percent of 8th graders perform at or above the *Proficient* level in Math, a level that represents "solid academic performance." Only 8 percent of fourth graders and 10 percent of eighth graders perform at the *Advanced* level.

Breaking the numbers down by race is absolutely devastating. In 4th grade math, there is a 32-point score gap between White and Black students (51 percent to 19 percent) and a 25-point score gap between White and Hispanic students (51 percent to 26 percent). In 8th grade math, there is a 31-point score gap between White and Black students (44 percent to 13 percent) and a 24-point score gap between White and Hispanic students (44 percent to 20 percent).

Only 37 percent of 4th graders and 36 percent of 8th graders perform at or above the *Proficient* level in reading. Only 9 percent of fourth graders and 4 percent of eighth graders perform at the *Advanced* level.

In 4th grade reading, there is a 27-point score gap between White and Black students (47 percent to 20 percent) and a 24-point score gap between White and Hispanic students (47 percent to 23 percent). In 8th grade reading, there is a 27-point score gap between White and Black students (45 percent to 18 percent) and a 22-point score gap between White and Hispanic students (45 percent to 23 percent).

Clearly, yet another generation of Americans is receiving substandard education and that is COMPLETELY UNACCEPTABLE in a nation as prosperous as ours. It's not only unacceptable…it's downright embarrassing.

The Program for International Student Assessment (PISA) is an international assessment that measures the reading, mathematics and science literacy of 15-year-old students in 76 international education systems. Unlike other modern-day assessment tests, PISA questions do not measure memorization of facts. Instead, the questions measure real-world problem solving and critical thinking skills.

Highlights from the latest PISA report:

† The United States ranks 18th in science, 13th in reading, and 37th in mathematics.

† China was first in all three categories.

† The trend lines of United States' mean performance in reading since 2000, mathematics since 2003, and science since 2006 are stable, with no significant improvement or decline.

† The United States spends more on education per student from age 6 to 15 than all but four Organization for Economic Cooperation and Development (OECD) countries, yet scored no better than, and in some cases, below, countries that spend between 10 percent and 30 percent less.

That last one hits hard. Bad outcomes for our students are all the more frustrating given that total expenditures for public school education for the 2020-21 school year was $709 billion, or $14,000 per public school student.

Luckily, our universities are still considered to be the best in the world. Eighteen of the top 25 universities on the Shanghai Ranking Consultancy's list of the world's best universities are located in the United States. From 2015-2019, 66 percent of the Nobel Prize winners in the science categories (Physics, Economic Sciences, Chemistry, and Physiology/Medicine) were affiliated with an American university at the time of their big win, and 56 percent received their graduate degree(s) at a U.S. university.

However, our continued success in higher education depends on the skill level of future American students. If the talent of our graduating seniors diminishes, our institutions of higher learning will have to progressively rely on foreign students to maintain their superiority (and we already rely on them heavily!).

To make matters worse, our politicians half-assed educational efforts have been frighteningly inadequate for decades. In the face of devastating evidence, Congress consistently refuses to challenge failed policies or champion innovative ones.

In 2010, the U.S. Department of Health and Human Services (HHS) released an impact study on the effectiveness of the *Head Start* program, which was established in 1965 as part of President Lyndon Johnson's *War on Poverty*.

According to HHS, *Head Start* "promotes school readiness for children in low-income families by enhancing their social and cognitive development through educational, nutritional, health, social and other services." There are "1,600 public and private nonprofit and for-profit agencies that provide *Head Start* services in local communities. *Head Start* and *Early Head Start* grantees provide services to over a million children every year, in every U.S. state and territory, in farm worker camps, and in over 155 tribal communities."

The results of the 2010 study were alarming. Although "providing access to *Head Start* has a positive impact on children's preschool experiences" and "access to *Head Start* has positive impacts on several aspects of children's school readiness during their time in the program," the "advantages children gained during their *Head Start* and age 4 years yielded only a few statistically significant differences in outcomes at the end of 1st grade for the sample as a whole."

Two years later, a follow-up HHS report said this: "There were initial positive impacts from having access to *Head Start*, but by the end of 3rd grade there were very few impacts found for either cohort in any of the four domains of cognitive, social-emotional, health and parenting practices. The few impacts that were found did not show a clear pattern of favorable or unfavorable impacts for children."

The report continued, "No significant impacts were found for math skills, pre-writing, children's promotion, or teacher report of children's school accomplishments or abilities in any year."

This analysis was disheartening to say the least, but more disturbing was the reaction of the Obama Administration and the U.S. Congress – which both decided to just throw more money at the problem.

Despite the discouraging evidence in the 2010 study, Congress authorized $8.2 billion for *Head Start* in 2011, almost a billion more than they allocated in 2010. Combined, from 1970 to 2000, the budgets for *Title I* and *Head Start* grew in inflation-adjusted dollars from $1.7 billion to $13.8 billion. The combined budget for 2010 for both was $21.7 billion.

"*Head Start* remains a key part of the Obama Administration's strategic focus on early learning," said HHS Secretary Kathleen Sebelius at the time. She continued, "Still, for *Head Start* to achieve its full potential, we must improve its quality and promote high standards across all early childhood programs."

Ya think? Ms. Sebelius, with all due respect, that was the understatement of the year. When you made that statement, *Head Start* had already had 47 years and nine presidents to prove its effectiveness.

What happened next was, of course, no big surprise. Ten years later, in April 2019, researchers from Brown University released a study that replicated and extended Harvard professor David Deming's 2009 evaluation of *Head Start's* life-cycle skill formation impacts, a study that found attending a *Head Start* program had lasting positive impacts into early childhood.

The researchers from Brown found that "extending the measurement interval for Deming's adulthood outcomes, we found no statistically significant impacts on earnings and mixed evidence of impacts on other adult outcomes. Applying Deming's sibling comparison framework to more recent birth cohorts born to CNSLY mothers (mothers who participated in the National Longitudinal Survey of Youth 1979 Children and Young Adults) revealed mostly negative *Head Start* impacts. Combining all cohorts shows generally null impacts on school-age and early adulthood outcomes."

< Note: There are earlier studies that identify some positive effects derived from *Head Start* programs, including one from the Brookings Institute. Given the scope and parameters of the various research, I find the HHS and Brown studies to be more accurate than the others but

want you to have the opportunity to judge for yourselves. You can find the links to the other studies in the *America's Best Chance* section of the 1787 website. >

In any event, potentially damaging data about *Head Start* wasn't even a speed bump for the Trump administration and Congress. For FY2020, Congress appropriated $10.6 billion for programs under the *Head Start Act,* and $10.7 billion for FY2021.

§§§

When is everyone going to wake-up and realize the status quo is not good enough anymore! I'll ask the question again: Why do we, time after time and issue after issue, keep going back to failed policies and political philosophies that don't work? Answer: Because that's the easy thing to do.

The hard part of education reform is addressing *what* we teach in programs like *Head Start* and schools across the nation, *how* we teach it, and *how* we measure our progress. This is a much scarier proposition for school administrators and politicians because it requires some serious soul searching and some significant changes.

The brutal truth is this: It doesn't matter how much money you spend or how many early education programs you modify or how many qualified teachers you recruit or how many charter schools you open. Every effort toward education reform will fail without a complete overhaul of our misguided curriculum; a change in how it is presented; a reevaluation of what we value in education; and how we define what success actually means. We will also continue to fail if we have zero understanding how our kids *think.* America, it's high time we start riding this horse in the direction it's going.

In his book *Frames of Mind: The Theory of Multiple Intelligences*, renowned Harvard psychologist Howard Gardner suggests there is a collection of intelligences that exists in each of us. Because everyone exhibits these intelligences on various levels, each individual has a distinctive cognitive profile.

Gardner initially identified seven intelligences: verbal-linguistic, logical-mathematical, spatial, bodily-kinesthetic, musical, interpersonal and intrapersonal (Gardner later concluded naturalist intelligence should be added to the list and insinuated two others may be worthy of inclusion: spiritual intelligence and existential intelligence).

According to Gardner, the child who masters math is not necessarily more intelligent overall than the child who struggles with it; rather, s/he is stronger in that *particular* intelligence.

I love this guy. The conventional American method of assessing what is and is not "intelligent" is insane. When it was time to take my *Assessment of Intelligence* class for my psychology degree, I was stunned when my professor passed out these black briefcases that held the standard psychometric instruments we would use to test our patient's "level" of intelligence.

The contents inside the briefcase were an absolute joke. Are we really so simple in this country that we think intelligence and individual capabilities can be evaluated by items that fit into a 10" x 15" piece of luggage? Traditional IQ tests and our current educational assessment tests fail miserably to adequately assess the wide array of aptitude each human being distinctly exhibits.

We have gotten to the point where much of what happens in our schools doesn't even resemble education at all. Somewhere down the line we forfeited vital knowledge for trivial test scores. A high school sophomore recently told me that most of her school day in the Spring semester revolves around memorizing test questions and learning testing strategies.

Ugh.

Hell on earth is to sit in an uncomfortable chair, memorizing material that you know has <u>zero</u> relevance to your life's ambition. High-stakes testing has reduced American education to nothing more than a regurgitation of facts that will be forgotten the minute the bell rings.

This is the main reason we do so badly on the PISA assessment. Real-world problem solving, deep deliberation, and critical thinking are out – right and wrong answers to questions that out-of-touch administrators deem important are in. This approach is beyond lazy and completely strangles the construction of knowledge. What a wasted opportunity and what a waste of everyone's time.

Okay, so I may be a little defensive on this point, but I know from firsthand experience that this is true. Recently I read a SAT prep question – "If there are 8 x 1012 hydrogen molecules in a volume of 4 x 104 cubic centimeters, what is the average number of hydrogen molecules per cubic centimeter?" – and immediately went into the fetal position.

I consistently received horrendous scores on these tests and quite frankly I'm still ticked off about it. Maybe I can't tell you within three seconds how much faster Train A got to the station than Train B, but I always knew I was smart in a unique way. I never understood why I had to suffer through advanced equations in high school when I could be writing short stories, studying history, or learning a foreign language.

Advanced math was not my thing back then and it's not my thing now. I vividly remember sitting in Algebra thinking I might actually die before the bell rang. Just as I suspected, and as I told my math teachers many times, there isn't one math challenge I'm confronted with today that requires more than what a calculator will fix. I'm certainly not pulling out a protractor and determining the circumference of a freak'n circle on a daily basis.

This I can say with certainty: If I would not have been grounded for weeks and weeks by my parents, I would have cut Algebra II every day. And, if I hadn't been born with a supercharged superego, my consistent inability – fueled by a complete lack of interest – to grasp difficult mathematical concepts would have completely depleted my confidence.

Most of our kids experience this feeling every single school day. Our across-the-board approach to curriculum is a fossilized tactic and an enormous contributor to our kids being bored and unprepared. Those who have interests in careers that don't require advanced science or math sit in class questioning what the heck any of this has to do with their *futures*. And, if they happen to have parents who will not ground them for weeks and weeks, they get bored, disenchanted, and simply leave.

Of course, there are certain skills everyone needs to be exposed to. Math, for example, is a critical element in learning how to formulate complex thought, and its fundamentals are an absolute necessity.

Certainly, everyone needs to master basic arithmetic, multiplication, division, decimals, fractions, percentages, ratios, probability, exponents and how to calculate area, volume and surface area – even I can do all of this (kind of). And some masochists (just kidding, kind of) will master concepts far beyond these.

But the fact remains that we have advanced in the preparation for a chosen few but have still not learned how to properly empower those who continue to be left behind. As a four-year college education has increasingly become the be-all and end-all in America, we seem to completely miss the immense value of high-quality vocational schools, junior colleges, on-the-job training, and apprenticeships – which are often the best ways to train (and retrain) for many of today's jobs.

Forget more money; it's our entire paradigm that must change.

When asked near the end of his life what schools should emphasize in the teaching process, Albert Einstein said, "Accumulation of material should not stifle the student's independence."

Children don't develop in a straight line. Therefore, our focus must shift from blanket education to a more personalized approach. Embracing individualized learning styles enables children to learn the most advantageous way possible for their aptitude.

Kids will be far more engaged if they learn material relevant to their individual skills, interests and aspirations – material actually relevant to their futures. When students are exposed to meaningful material, they will be able (and much more willing) to tackle more rigorous, academically challenging curriculum. #TheButterflyEffect

It may seem that this approach would take a tremendous amount of additional money, time and effort, but that's not necessarily true. Switzerland's dynamic educational system provides an excellent example. Switzerland has created a system that embraces innovative thinking and open learning, ensuring their position among the global elite in education.

A key element of the Swiss system is the student's ability to choose their educational path according to their abilities and interests. The initial decision is made early, but students can alter their course if they choose.

To begin, students attend primary and lower secondary school, which provide a basic general education as well as encourages a balanced relationship with social, personal, and technical abilities.

Then, the students enter the upper secondary level, which offers a "dual" vocational education and training system. If the vocational path is chosen, students can enhance their education by learning both in school and within a workplace setting. Over 70 percent of Swiss students choose to participate in this Vocational Education and Training (VET) program.

A report called *Gold Standard: The Swiss Vocational Education and Training System* from the Center on International Education Benchmarking explains that the VET program "prepares a broad cross-section of students including high achievers for careers in a range of occupations – high-tech, human service, health, as well as traditional trades and crafts, so white-collar as well as blue-collar."

The report also describes how, in Switzerland, the entire country takes ownership of the educational process, with around 30 percent of Swiss companies participating in the VET program: "The Swiss VET system is well supported by employers who see it as their obligation to help prepare young people for productive and meaningful employment.

Apprenticeships also make economic sense for employers, providing them with an incentive to continue to participate in the system. The apprenticeships provide hands-on and applied learning opportunities, giving students real work responsibilities with plenty of coaching and adult support.

Small and large companies, state of the art factories, insurance agencies, banks, hospitals, retail stores, and childcare centers host 16- to 19-year-old apprentices who serve customers, work on complex machines, carry out basic medical procedures, and advise investors – in short, they do everything an entry level employee would do, albeit under the wings of credentialed trainers within the company."

The final step for Swiss students is the Tertiary level, or higher education, where students again choose between technical or vocational schools, or higher university degrees which include universities of art and music as well as universities of teacher education.

It's surely no coincidence that Switzerland tops the list on the World Economic Forum's *Global Competitiveness Report* in the categories of Basic Skills, Skills of Current Workforce, Extent of Staff Training, Skillset of Graduates, Digital Skills Among Active Population, Active Labor Market Policies, Workers' Right, and Government's Ensuring Policy Stability.

It's also no coincidence that, according to the United Nations' *World Happiness Report*, Switzerland is the third happiest country in the world, behind only Finland and Denmark. Interestingly enough, Denmark and Finland also hold the #1 and #2 spots in NJ MED's 2021 *World Best Education Systems*. Hmmm....

Speaking of Finland, the country has a truly unified school system, where kids stay at the same school until they are sixteen. Then, Finnish education is divided into two systems – vocational and academic. There are special programs where adults receive additional training, all students learn to speak English, free hot meals are provided to all students, and free health and psychological services are offered to all students.

When asked how many children don't complete school in her city, one Finnish school official said there are so few that she could "tell you their names if you want."

Teachers in Finland have wide professional discretion and autonomy, and have the freedom to teach how they want. The only external testing is done solely on a sampling basis and is designed to provide information on the functioning of the overall school system. Therefore, it is the teachers' responsibility to regularly assess their students using national assessment guidelines. Students are expected to take an active role in their learning, and, in upper grades, even design their own individualized programs.

The Preamble of Finland's *National Core Curriculum for Basic Education* states,

> "The learning environment must support the pupil's growth and learning. It must be physically, psychologically, and socially safe, and must support the pupil's health. The objective is to increase pupils' curiosity and motivation to learn, and to promote their activeness, self-direction, and creativity by offering interesting challenges and problems. The learning environment must guide pupils in setting their own objectives and evaluating their own actions. The pupils must be given the chance to participate in the creation and development of their own learning environment."

I've said it before and I'll say it a thousand more times before we are through: We can no longer expect half-measures and incremental ideas to work in systems that have collapsed; rather, we must embrace an unprecedented full and fundamental restructuring. It's way past time that we move to crisis mode and thoroughly alter the way we approach the education of our children to prevent an all-out disaster.

Simply appropriating more funding for failed programs is not going to cut it anymore. It's time to make substantial and sustaining improvements in the way we educate our children, and boldly approach the challenges from a completely new perspective, making our resolution both wide and deep for <u>every</u> child. **...and that has little to do with <u>*more*</u> money**.

§§§

Ironically, the one part of President Biden's multi-trillion-dollar trilogy – the *American Rescue Plan*, *American Jobs Plan* and *American Families Plan* – that I agreed with (albeit with a few modifications) is the part Congress let expire in January 2022.

The *American Rescue Plan* – the Covid relief package that passed in March 2021 – converted the existing annual *Child Tax Credit* into a more frequently issued "child allowance," amounting to $3,600 for children 5 and under and a $3,000 credit for those aged 6 to 17 (equaling $300 or $250 per month). The legislation also made the benefit "fully refundable," meaning, even if the parents of lower-income families make too little money to pay federal income taxes, they would still get the money.

In my mind, Senator Mitt Romney (R-UT) improved the fundamentals of this plan by increasing the benefit to $4,200 a year for children under six, then eliminating the *Temporary Assistance to Needy Families* (you'll better understand why I say this about TANF in a minute). However, I didn't agree with Senator Romney's plan to partially pay for this increase by ending the *State and Local Tax Deduction* (SALT), which would effectively raise taxes on families who have no children.

The problem is that the *American Rescue Plan* only authorized this change in the *Child Tax Credit* for one year. Beyond that, additional legislation would have to be passed by Congress – and, in his *American Families Plan,* President Biden asked Congress to only extend these changes until 2025 instead of making the change permanent.

This is a real bummer because making this change permanent is something we really needed to get done. In America, according to the Organization for Economic Cooperation and Development (OECD), "more than one child in five lives in income poverty. This is almost <u>seven times</u> higher than the rate in Denmark." Ouch.

Making the *Child Tax Credit* permanent is a smart move because, instead of being a *cost* to society, research shows that the *Child Tax Credit* is truly an *investment* in our future.

For one, poverty can literally shrink the brain. One study, led by neuroscientists from Columbia University and Children's Hospital Los Angeles, found that children in households earning less than $25,000 per year had, on average, a brain surface area 6 percent smaller than those from families earning more than $150,000.

The study also discovered that children in the poorest households not only had lower scores on tests measuring cognitive skills (i.e., reading and memory ability), there were significant differences in the actual structure of the brain, particularly in areas of the brain that handle language and decision-making skills.

Research conducted for the *Proceedings of the National Academy of Sciences* uncovered the "causal impact of a poverty reduction intervention on early childhood brain activity." Using data from the *Baby's First Years* study – a randomized control trial – the numbers "show that a predictable, monthly unconditional cash transfer given to low-income families may have a causal impact on infant brain activity. In the context of greater economic resources, children's experiences changed, and their brain activity adapted to those experiences. The resultant brain activity patterns have been shown to be associated with the development of subsequent cognitive skills."

But wait! There's more! Analysis from The Center on Poverty and Social Policy at Columbia University found that "the value to society that flows from these impacts is equal to over eight times the annual costs" and that "cash and near-cash benefits increase children's health, education, and future earnings and decrease health, child protection, and criminal justice costs."

The Center on Budget and Policy Priorities, a think tank, revealed that "the current *Child Tax Credit* and *Earned Income Tax Credit* (EITC) together lift more children above the poverty line, 5.5 million, than any other economic support program. This level of poverty reduction was achieved through multiple expansions of the EITC and *Child Tax Credit* since their respective enactments in 1975 and 1997. This one significant change to the *Child Tax Credit* would lift another 4.1 million children above the poverty line, cutting the remaining number of children in poverty by more than 40 percent."

Indeed, after the *Child Tax Credit* expired, child poverty shot up 41 percent (from 12 percent to 17 percent), according to the Center on Poverty and Social Policy at Columbia. That translates to an additional 3.7 million children.

This is a perfect example of how we can learn from history. In 1996, Congress passed – and President Bill Clinton signed – the *Personal Responsibility and Work Opportunity Reconciliation Act of 1996*, a bill that would, in President Clinton's words, "end welfare as we know it" and make welfare "a second chance, not a way of life."

The main goal of the legislation was to repeal Title IV of the *Social Security Act of 1935*, the program then known as *Aid to Families with Dependent Children* (AFDC). The new version of AFDC is called *Temporary Assistance for Needy Families* (TANF). TANF assistance has a maximum benefit of two consecutive years (with a five-year lifetime limit) and requires recipients to find work within two years of receiving assistance.

There is no question that changes to the welfare system needed to be made in 1996, but the miscalculation was in *how* the legislation was originally implemented. For some Americans, the transition was a disaster from which they and their families never recovered.

The **first** misstep was that the final version of the bill was much more stringent than President Clinton had originally proposed. Clinton initially recommended that, since the legislation had a work requirement, the federal government should act as an employer of last resort.

Unfortunately, this pivotal idea did not make it to the final bill, which ultimately ended cash welfare with little transitional help like job training, etc. Essentially, the final version pushed welfare recipients to find work without a backstop, and eventually cut off almost all cash benefits (although there was an expansion of non-cash benefits like food stamps and housing vouchers to supposedly compensate).

This speaks to the **second** misstep, which continues today: The way TANF is funded, which is in the form of a "block grant" to states. The amount is a fixed sum that has never been adjusted for inflation, which is obviously yet another issue.

Clinton's legislation gave states broad flexibility to carry out their own programs, including how the programs were designed, the amount of assistance recipients received, and the state's rules for determining who was eligible for benefits. Because states are given few restrictions on how they spend the money, they can spend it for things other than the original intent.

As a result, many states routinely channel the money toward things that barely have anything to do with easing the chokehold of poverty. The Pew Charitable Trusts puts it this way: "TANF has devolved into a kind of candy store that many states are raiding to plug budget holes and pay for programs that have little to do with moving poor people into the workforce."

If you judge solely by the numbers, President Clinton's law worked. The number of Americans on welfare fell by half within four years (some states fudged their numbers by shifting people from the welfare rolls to disability insurance, but still). Of the 1.6 million parents who were still receiving assistance four years in, almost one-third were working.

Jump to 2019, when there were just over two million people receiving *Temporary Assistance for Needy Families* (TANF), which was less than one-fifth of the number the year Clinton signed the bill. Fourteen years later, in 2010, 16.3 million children under age 18 (22 percent) were living in poverty. By 2019, that number was down to 10.5 million (14.4 percent).

That said, the Butterfly Effect caught up with many American families, who paid – and continue to pay – a steep price. In 1996, Americans living in "deep poverty" (meaning, those who have a family income of below one-half of their poverty threshold) represented 32 percent of those living in poverty. That number jumped to 39 percent four years later.

A report from sociologists Luke Shaefer (University of Michigan) and Kathryn Edin (Johns Hopkins University) underscores that, although poverty has been reduced overall, the number of Americans living in deep poverty has increased:

> "More aid is now available to working poor families via refundable tax credits and expanded eligibility for the *Supplemental Nutrition Assistance Program* (SNAP). But the amount of assistance for non-working families has decreased, and what remains has shifted away from cash and toward in-kind benefits.
>
> In 2010, Kathryn Edin – who had spent years talking with welfare recipients in the period just prior to welfare reform – began to encounter something markedly different from

anything she had seen previously: families with no visible means of cash income from any source: 'What was so strikingly different from a decade and a half earlier was that there was virtually no cash coming into these homes.'

We first tested this hypothesis using the *Survey of Income and Program Participation* (SIPP), where we saw a striking spike in the number of households with children reporting cash incomes of no more than $2 per person, per day over a month, calendar quarter, and year. We have further found that families most affected were single-mother households and minority families – those most likely to have been affected by welfare reform – and that families in $2-a-day poverty were more likely to live in parts of the country where TANF was the least accessible, particularly the Appalachian region and the Deep South. And our research and that of others finds that families in $2-a-day poverty and deep poverty more broadly face higher rates of material hardship than other poor families that are higher up the income ladder."

Just FYI, analysis from the Manhattan Institute, a think tank, takes issue with the $2 per person, per day claim:

"The reality of poverty after welfare reform is not that portrayed by critics – including, most recently, Edin and Shaefer. Children – in particular, those in single-mother families – are significantly less likely to be poor today than they were before welfare reform. This is because income and poverty trends are poorly conveyed by official statistics and by most analyses of poverty data. Household surveys underestimate the cash income of these families and do not count as income a variety of valuable non-cash benefits, including food stamps, housing subsidies, and Medicaid (the receipt and value of which are also underestimated). Meanwhile, the rise in the cost of living tends to be overestimated, pulling up poverty trends over time."

< Note: Edin and Shaefer acknowledge that “findings from household surveys should be scrutinized carefully because some people may not want to reveal all their sources of income, others may forget some of their income, and still others may misunderstand the questions,” but they say they account for this in their analysis. >

Regardless, we can all probably agree that everyone needs a little cash in their pocket because it’s virtually impossible to live in this world without it. If you don’t believe me, just try it for a week (which I have, and it did not go well).

Beyond those stuck in deep poverty, other disturbing statistics persist. For example, even though we currently have the lowest poverty rate since 1959, 34 million Americans remain shackled by poverty, which is still way too many Americans if you ask me. Think about that…34 million people. As usual, it gets shockingly worse when you break the poverty numbers down by race.

The U.S. Census Bureau puts it this way: “Looking at poverty more closely, there are disparities in the distribution of poverty among the different race groups. In 2019, non-Hispanic Whites accounted for 59.9 percent of the total population and 41.6 percent of the people in poverty. Blacks accounted for 13.2 percent of the total population and 23.8 percent of the people in poverty.”

Boiling those numbers down further, 7.3 percent of non-Hispanic, White Americans lived in poverty compared to 18.8 percent of Black Americans. Thirty-one percent of Black children lived in poverty compared to 10 percent of non-Hispanic White children. That’s just extraordinary.

§§§

We need to begin doing things differently, starting right now …which is why I have such deep concerns about President Biden’s *American Families Plan*. In my mind, it feels way too much like the old Democratic habit of throwing money at a massive, multi-dimensional challenge with no specifics, which is a lazy, ineffective approach that does nothing more than waste precious time, as our vulnerable families are now so painfully aware.

You may be wondering what I have in mind when I say, "the only way things will truly get better is if we learn from past mistakes, then roll up our sleeves and do the really, really hard work of developing a clear and thorough plan of action – before we spend $1.8 trillion on it."

Let's walk through it. In President Biden's plan, $20 billion is allocated to help communities of color "reconnect" to economic opportunities that were stripped from them decades ago. I agree this is a great way to reverse bad policy decisions and right past wrongs.

We talked earlier about redlining being one of the very first bricks that built the impermeable wall that has prevented Black Americans from having the chance to fully participate in American capitalism.

But other bricks that helped build that impermeable wall were massacres like the one that happened in the Greenwood district of Tulsa, Oklahoma – often called the "Black Wall Street" – on May 31, 1921. That fateful day, a White mob not only attacked Black people and their homes, but also their businesses.

A report by the *Oklahoma Commission to Study the Tulsa Race Riot of 1921* describes it this way: "As the Whites moved north, they set fire to practically every building in the African American community, including a dozen churches, five hotels, 31 restaurants, four drug stores, eight doctor's offices, more than two dozen grocery stores, and the Black public library. By the time the violence ended, the city had been placed under martial law, thousands of Tulsans were being held under armed guard, and the state's second-largest African American community had been burned to the ground."

These types of atrocities started well before Tulsa. On September 22-24, 1906, during the *Atlanta Race Riot of 1906*, White mobs murdered numerous Black men and women and destroyed many of their businesses. In the years before the riot, the Black population had become increasingly educated and successful, building strong communities and networks along with thriving, competitive businesses. Naturally, this shift in dynamics threatened the White elite class in Atlanta, so they responded by expanding Jim Crow segregation laws, which only served to heighten tensions even more.

The death and destruction in Atlanta led W.E.B. Du Bois – a sociologist, historian, civil rights activist, and one of the founders of the National Association for the Advancement of Colored People (NAACP) – to write his unforgettable *A Litany of Atlanta*:

> "A city lay in travail, God our Lord, and from her loins sprang twin Murder and Black Hate. Red was the midnight; clang, crack and cry of death and fury filled the air and trembled underneath the stars when church spires pointed silently to Thee. And all this was to sate the greed of greedy men who hide behind the veil of vengeance! Bewildered we are, and passion-tost, mad with the madness of a mobbed and mocked and murdered people."

In the *East St. Louis Race War of 1917*, a White mob brutally murdered Black men and women over what began as a labor dispute. When White workers at the Aluminum Ore Company went on strike, Black workers were hired to replace them.

Dhati Kennedy, the founder of the Committee for Historical Truth, told *Smithsonian Magazine* the story of his father, who lived through the massacre:

> "We spent a lifetime as children hearing these stories. It was clear to me my father was suffering from some form of what they call PTSD. He witnessed horrible things: people's houses being set ablaze, people being shot when they tried to flee, some trying to swim to the other side of the Mississippi while being shot at by White mobs with rifles, others being dragged out of street cars and beaten and hanged from streetlamps.
>
> Thousands of Blacks were streaming across that bridge when what they called the 'race war' got into full swing. When that happened, the police shut down the bridge, and no one could escape. Some, in desperation, tried to swim and drowned."

Carlos F. Hurd, a reporter, wrote a first-hand account of the mayhem in the *St. Louis Post-Dispatch*: "The East St. Louis affair, as I saw it, was a man hunt, conducted on a sporting basis, though with anything but the fair play which is the principle of sport. There was a horribly cool deliberateness and a spirit of fun about it. 'Get a n*****' was the slogan, and it was varied by the recurrent cry, 'Get another!'"

Another journalist, Hugh L. Wood, wrote in the *St. Louis Republic*:

> "A Negro weighing 300 pounds came out of the burning line of dwellings just north and east of the Southern fright home. 'Get him!' they cried. So, a man in the crowd clubbed his revolver and struck the Negro in the face with it. Another dashed an iron bolt between the Negro's eyes. Still another stood near and battered him with a rock. Then the giant Negro tumbled to the ground. A girl stepped up and struck the bleeding man with her foot. The blood spurted onto her stockings and men laughed and grunted."

The consequences of these unthinkable tragedies extend far beyond death, destruction, and property damage. These events literally smashed and burned the prosperity that Black men and women had – against all odds and with zero advantages – worked so hard to build.

Unsurprisingly, in all of these instances, most of the victims were unable to recover and rebuild, which, along with policies like redlining, contributed heavily to the astonishing racial wealth gap that exists in this country today.

As I said earlier, the latest *Survey of Consumer Finances* released by the Federal Reserve revealed that wealth of typical White households is <u>eight</u> <u>times</u> the wealth of typical Black households and <u>five</u> <u>times</u> that of typical Hispanic households.

The median wealth (the number squarely in the middle of all the numbers) of White households is $188,200, compared to $24,100 for Black households and $36,100 for Hispanic households. The mean wealth (the average) of White households is $983,400, compared to $142,500 for Black households and $165,500 for Hispanic households.

We dig much deeper into the racial wealth gap in Part Two, Chapter Two, but I'll give you a quick preview: My obsession with closing this gap is not just a bleeding-heart call for compassion or charity.

If we fail to properly address this inequality, we are leaving money – lots of money – on the table. My overriding argument is not that we address these disparities simply to be nice to our fellow man (although that would, in and of itself, be a splendid thing to do!). Rather, rising inequality is increasingly strangling our economy and impeding our economic growth – big time!

We have arrived at a point where empathy must be applied as an intellectual exercise. If I can't appeal to your heart, let me appeal to your wallet. Analysis by McKinsey & Company – a global management consulting firm – found that the racial wealth gap has a "dampening effect on consumption and investment" and will "cost the U.S. economy between $1 trillion and $1.5 trillion between 2019 and 2028 – 4 to 6 percent of the projected GDP in 2028." That's a lot.

Redlining and things like mob destruction at the hands of White people are perfect examples of how the staggering inequity that exists in this country – in everything from wealth to incomes to education to criminal justice – did not just happen organically.

The uncomfortable, harsh truth is that the disparities that infect practically every one of our systems and institutions is a direct result of decades of irresponsible and, at times, downright racist public policy decisions.

< Note: I'm pretty sure this is the spirit of what people mean when they use the term "systemic racism." I'm not a huge fan of this term because it fails to convey the multidimensional challenges of racism in this country. Inanimate entities – like systems – *reveal* racist cycles and *uncover* the consequences of racism, they don't *cause* it. Systems in and of themselves aren't the problem; the human-driven decisions made within those systems are. >

From the beginning, these decisions – made both intentionally and unintentionally – initiated and perpetuated pervasive, deep-rooted division and inequality. They just did. This is not my opinion. It's a well-documented fact.

Debating whether or not this is true is an unnecessary waste of time because numbers don't lie. All we have to do is read the astonishingly unequal statistics in Part Two to know that these inequalities not only exist, but they are not healing on their own. For example, McKinsey's report says that "almost 70 percent of middle-class Black children are likely to fall out of the middle class as adults."

The way I see it, thanks to very clear data and statistics, you can only believe one of the following two things:

That the grave injustices Black Americans have been shackled to for centuries are now intricately woven into the fabric of our nation, perpetuating division, desolation, and damaging cycles and patterns.

OR

Grossly uneven statistics exist because Black people are lazy and/or bad parents and/or a less intelligent underclass that thrives on self-destructive patterns of behavior.

Realistically, these are the only two options because the lopsided statistics are overwhelming. If you don't believe that these are the only two options, take a few seconds to try and think of a third alternative. You won't be able to.

To all of my fellow White people: Re-read those two options and do a quick gut check. Are you certain you are on the right side of this issue? Have you been thinking about this correctly?

As we search for solutions, we all need to understand that chronic inequality is not something that those trapped in its relentless grip can work – or even at times educate – themselves out without a hand...and it is highly insulting to act like they can, or even should. In truth, the only way to close these persistent gaps is to enact policies that actively work to counteract the original ones…

… like the effort in Biden's plan to reconnect communities of color to economic opportunities.

After Biden announced his original proposal, he added that he would also strengthen the *Fair Housing Act* and give more help to minority small businesses and entrepreneurs, which is great! But these few ideas, however admirable, are just a drop in the bucket compared to what we must do to confront and conquer the miasma of entrenched inequality that exists in this country. It's not just one thing…it's *everything*.

1787 has designed a plan of action that fights all of these issues *together at once* in order to make the biggest impact:

1787's Solution
The Six Pillars

- † Provide Job/Skills Training & Push Wages Higher
- † Government Investment in Low-Wealth Americans
- † Guidance for Optimal Financial Inclusion
- † Boost Opportunities for Wealth Creation
- † Block Policies that Sabotage Advancement
- † Ensure Fair and Equitable Education

Pillar One:

Provide Job/Skills Training & Push Wages Higher

First up…jobs! So, if we convert the existing annual *Child Tax Credit* into a more frequently issued "child allowance" and make it permanent, does that mean we will just give money to people so they can have a bunch of kids and not work?

Not in the 1787 plan, no. Although President Biden's proposal does not have a work requirement, I believe that encouraging work is an incredibly important piece of the puzzle. In fact, I'll go even further and say that *not* having a work requirement attached to these benefits does a tremendous disservice to the very people they are designed to help and perpetuates devastating cycles that we already know set people up to fail. < 1787's work requirement for receiving benefits does not extend to Medicaid. Read more about this in *The Policy Guide*. >

There are many obvious benefits to people having jobs, earning more money being one, but other considerations are not so obvious – the devastating effects of generational poverty and the psychological impact of being unemployed or underemployed, for example.

The longer a person is out of work, the more unemployable they are. Not to mention the mental health consequences of people being unemployed or underemployed. It is well documented that these states of being drastically increase depression, domestic violence, alcohol abuse and suicide.

The United States has just experienced a major shock to the system. In many ways, our economy has made a remarkable recovery, but we still have a way to go.

The official U.S. unemployment rate in March 2022, seasonally adjusted, was 3.6 percent. That's still 6 million people. A more accurate measure of our employment situation is the U-6 unemployment rate, which includes the unemployed, people working part-time because they can't find full-time work and those who have just given up. In March 2022, that number was 6.9 percent.

Another instructive number to look at is the labor force participation rate, a measure of the economy's active workforce that adds the number of all workers who are employed or actively seeking employment, then divides that number by the total number of the civilian working-age population.

In March 2022, the labor force participation rate was 62.4 percent. Compare that to 2000, when that number was 81.9 percent. The labor force participation rate is an interesting number because it signals that there are possibly millions of people who still are in prime working years who may be enticed back into the work force if it was worth their while.

Although the Covid-19 crisis put a spotlight on our jobs and wage situation, the need for a new paradigm began long before. Going forward, we need to not only create 21st century jobs, but we also need to create ones that pay better. Plus, we need to make certain that the new jobs we create don't replace middle-class jobs with low-paying ones.

The great news is that the timing couldn't be better! Fact: We have a high U-6 unemployment rate. Fact: We essentially need an entirely new infrastructure. Fact: We need to get serious about lifting people out of poverty. Do we not have the perfect opportunity here? 1 + 1 + 1 = Progress.

Stabilizing and strengthening our work force requires an all-out blitz that will take every magic trick we've got. Therefore, since this is truly a multi-dimensional challenge, both the private sector and the federal government must be part of the solution.

The contribution of the private sector, as always, is significant. Private sector employment increased by 742,000 jobs in April 2021 alone. Small businesses contributed 235,000 of that number, medium businesses 230,000, and large businesses 277,000.

Analysis by the Congressional Research Service found that even though "high-impact" businesses (defined as "having sales that have doubled over the most recent four-year period and have an employment growth quantifier of two of more over the same time period") only account for between 5-6 percent of all businesses, they "account for 'almost all [net] job creation in the economy.'" That's crazy!

Despite the Covid-19 disruption, entrepreneurship and the nation's startup sector were on fire in 2020. A report from PitchBook, a data delivery company, and the National Venture Capital Association (NVCA) revealed that "investors deployed $156.2 billion into startups" and closed a "record 321 mega-deals in 2020, with late-stage companies contributing 265 to that sum. For perspective, just 242 mega-deals closed in 2019. In 2011, less than a decade ago, just 46 mega-deals closed. The closed mega-deals in 2020 accrued a total of $70.9 billion, surpassing the previous highwater mark of $64.6 billion set in 2018, and constituted 45.4 percent of total US VC deal value."

The federal government must play a significant role too. To that end, 1787's jobs program, *U.S. Works*, includes a federal jobs program that not only creates near-term jobs to help restore our economic health, but also helps secure our long-term economic future by appropriately developing our nation's human capital. The program is a simple, straightforward way to leverage our spending by not only providing Americans short-term work, but also valuable training for the long-term. This jobs program ensures we don't make the miscalculation that President Clinton did when he called for a work requirement for those who receive federal assistance but then didn't have the government act as employer of last resort.

I can literally hear the splash from Tea Partiers jumping into Boston Harbor. No doubt the term "federal jobs program" will completely freak some conservatives out. They will surely argue that we don't need a big government, "Socialist" program because our unemployment and wage issues will eventually be fully corrected by market forces.

But there is certainly no guarantee that will happen. In reality, I believe a federal jobs program is actually a conservative-minded approach because, done correctly, it replaces a no-strings-attached check with actual jobs – and we all know how much Republicans hate handing out checks to people! :)

America will never be a country that abandons citizens in need and thank God for that. Therefore, we need to design smart programs that make sense because *we're spending the money anyway*. The United States has paid almost $413 billion in *Temporary Assistance for Needy Families* (TANF) state block grants since the program started in 1996.

Why not leverage those dollars by not only providing Americans short-term work, but also valuable training for the long-term? We can at least *try* to start doing things that make sense.

Here are the basics of the *U.S. Works* federal jobs program:

Anyone who is capable of work and applies for federal assistance in any way must register with an *Empower Society* and work or be engaged in the education/training programs provided for at least 20 hours a week. < the *Empower Society* is a 1787 policy initiative that helps ensure long-term financial stability for families and communities by providing for their basic needs while, at the same time, offering them the knowledge and tools necessary to establish a long-term financial plan. You can read more about the *Empower Society* in Part Two. >

The *Empower Society* has mechanisms in place for childcare, transportation, and other access issues. The goal is to provide income for people while they look for long-term employment and/or allow them to gain specialized training or a learned skill set for their future success.

Empower Society clients first meet with case managers who assess their skills, then help them create an in-depth profile for potential employers. The profile includes standard information like work history and education, plus provides an opportunity for the applicant to share his or her professional goals, a personal statement, and even an introductory video.

A website, facilitated by the U.S. Department of Labor, will serve as a clearinghouse of job listings, searchable by category, skill set, and location. This already exists but needs to be modernized.

Two new categories will be added to the existing site. The first consists of jobs generated by the projects funded by the National Infrastructure Bank. As a reminder, the National Infrastructure Bank is a bank, funded with seed capital from the government then leveraged by our capital markets, that can provide low-interest loans, issue bonds, provide insurance for the bonds of state and local governments, streamline the construction process, and coordinate and prioritize the rebuilding efforts. The other new category is the cornerstone of *U.S. Works*.

One of the main criticisms of the *Civil Works Administration* – a work-relief program established by FDR's *New Deal* to provide temporary jobs for over 4 million Americans – was that people were just on the government payroll and not really doing anything...just pushing leaves around if you will. That won't be the case here. These will be real jobs.

Although many infrastructure projects are vast in scope and require mid-skill and/or experienced labor, this country has many projects that can benefit from unskilled labor as well. *U.S. Works* creates these jobs – landscaping, street maintenance, pressure washing, litter removal, trash collection/recycling, graffiti removal, hospitality, retail, warehousing, construction, janitorial services etc. – and offers these services at a discounted rate to the general public, from individuals to businesses to municipalities.

The revenue *U.S. Works* receives by charging for these services greatly reduces the cost of the program, and the services offered provide an excellent way for businesses and communities to receive low-cost, quality labor while making a positive impact in their community. Plus, it allows workers to gain skills, self-confidence, a recent work history and references.

Pillar Two:

Government Investment in Low-Wealth Americans

You can find detailed information
on each of these at www.1787forAmerica.org

Facilitate Financing

- † Fully and wholeheartedly support Community Development Financial Institutions (CDFIs).
- † Encourage more banks to conduct *Community Reinvestment Act* (CRA) lending.
- † Encourage Fannie Mae and Freddie Mac to partner with banks that conduct *Community Reinvestment Act* (CRA) lending.
- † Fully and wholeheartedly support microlending impact funds.
- † Encourage states to start social innovation funds.

† Overhaul the *Opportunity Zone* program. Add public reporting, terminate high-income zones, and prohibit casinos, stadiums, and luxury apartments.
† Lobby corporations to commit 2 percent of their annual profits to capitalize financial institutions that service Black-owned businesses and entrepreneurs.
† Lobby banks to commit 2 percent of their annual profits to capitalize financial institutions that service Black-owned businesses and entrepreneurs.
† Lobby corporate America to invest in banking, telecom, technology, education, and health care infrastructure to benefit the Black community.
† Lobby banks to invest in banking, telecom, technology, education, and health care infrastructure to benefit the Black community.
† Extend the Federal Reserve's Term Asset-Backed Securities Loan Facility to leverage loans from banks and corporate America.

Enhance Jobs & Wages

† WAGES! WAGES! WAGE! We have to get wages up!
† Implement a federal policy that guarantees workers paid time off to care for their new babies or for a sick family member.
† Provide a job of last resort for Americans who use social services, as described above.
† Offer all the necessary ingredients for a successful job search. Use technology to connect workers with jobs.
† Provide relevant, world-class workforce training programs.
† Organize high-quality registered apprenticeships and mentor opportunities.
† Support new small business owners and entrepreneurs.

- † Work hard to solve the gender pay gap.
- † Provide significant transitional assistance to workers displaced by advances in technology and/or globalization.
- † Provide unconscious bias/cultural competency coaches to consult with U.S. management teams.
- † Protect low-income workers from monopsony and collusion.
- † Modernize labor laws through waivers from federal law to allow state experimentation.
- † Call on state and local governments to dismantle unjustified barriers to upward mobility caused by occupational licensing.

Leverage the Tax Code

- † Expand the *Saver's Credit* and make it refundable, which will create more accessibility for more low-wage families.
- † Create a refundable housing credit that would allow more taxpayers to enjoy the housing benefits of the tax code.
- † Reduce poverty by providing an enhanced minimum benefit for low-wage workers.
- † Reinstate the *First-Time Homebuyer Tax Credit* and make it permanent.
- † Overhaul the *Opportunity Zone* program. Add public reporting, terminate high-income zones, and prohibit casinos, stadiums, and luxury apartments.

Promote Savings

- † Reboot the *My Retirement Account* (myRA) to provide a safe and portable savings accounts for workers with low wages.
- † Establish universal *Children's Savings Accounts* (a.k.a. baby bonds) for every American child at birth.
- † Allow families who participate in public benefit programs to have at least three month's income in savings.
- † Expand the *Saver's Credit* and make it refundable, which will create more accessibility for more low-wage families.

Broaden Home Ownership

- † Champion the *Family Self-Sufficiency* (FSS) program to increase incomes and reduce dependency on government assistance and rental subsidies.
- † Encourage and support programs like the *Moving to Opportunity* (MTO) initiative.
- † Create a refundable housing credit that would allow more taxpayers to enjoy the housing benefits of the tax code.
- † Create a matched-savings program for down-payments.
- † Reinstate the *First-Time Homebuyer Tax Credit* and make it permanent.
- † Encourage the Senate to pass the *Housing Voucher Mobility Demonstration Act*.
- † Overhaul the *Opportunity Zone* program. Add public reporting, terminate high-income zones, and prohibit casinos, stadiums, and luxury apartments.

† Fully and wholeheartedly support Community Development Financial Institutions (CDFIs).
† Encourage more banks to conduct *Community Reinvestment Act* (CRA) lending.
† Encourage Fannie Mae and Freddie Mac to partner with banks that conduct *Community Reinvestment Act* (CRA) lending.
† Incentivize cities and states to ease up on land use restrictions and other undue regulations, which is decimating housing affordability.
† Incentivize cities and states to provide a broader and more affordable range of housing options to alleviate tight housing market conditions.
† Incentivize cities and states to modernize zoning laws and code requirements and to streamline permitting processes.

Pillar Three:

Guidance for Optimal Financial Inclusion

† Provide personalized financial counseling to include debt management, credit counseling, and budget advice.
† Re-enforce financial literacy, a critical life skill that is the foundation for the development of financial security and independence.
† Begin a broad dialogue on the importance of personal retirement savings.

Pillar Four:

Boost Opportunities for Wealth Creation

Build Assets

- † Find a balance between overly restrictive credit requirements and giving under-served borrowers the opportunity for sustainable homeownership.
- † Do everything possible to protect unscorable and credit invisible consumers.
- † Demand that credit-scoring mechanisms be fair to protect consumers from abusive and harmful lending practices.
- † Incentivize cities and states to ease up on land use restrictions and other undue regulations, which is decimating housing affordability.
- † Incentivize cities and states to provide a broader and more affordable range of housing options to alleviate tight housing market conditions.
- † Incentivize cities and states to modernize zoning laws and code requirements and to streamline permitting processes.
- † Reinstate the *First-Time Homebuyer Tax Credit* and make it permanent.
- † Create a refundable housing credit that would allow more taxpayers to enjoy the housing benefits of the tax code.
- † Create a matched-savings program for down-payments.
- † Encourage the Senate to pass the *Housing Voucher Mobility Demonstration Act.*

Partner with Banks and Corporate America

- † Lobby corporations to commit 2 percent of their annual profits to capitalize financial institutions that service Black-owned businesses and entrepreneurs.
- † Lobby banks to commit 2 percent of their annual profits to capitalize financial institutions that service Black-owned businesses and entrepreneurs.
- † Encourage endowment chiefs to demand diversity from the firms that manage their money. Thanks for the example, Yale!
- † Fully and wholeheartedly support Community Development Financial Institutions (CDFIs).
- † Encourage more banks to conduct *Community Reinvestment Act* (CRA) lending.
- † Encourage Fannie Mae and Freddie Mac to partner with banks that conduct *Community Reinvestment Act* (CRA) lending.
- † Lobby corporate America to invest in banking, telecom, technology, education, and health care infrastructure to benefit the Black community.
- † Lobby banks to invest in banking, telecom, technology, education, and health care infrastructure to benefit the Black community.
- † Extend the Federal Reserve's Term Asset-Backed Securities Loan Facility to leverage loans from banks and corporate America.
- † Break down geographic and affordability challenges.
- † Increase diversity in the financial system.
- † Explore innovative, inclusionary credit decisioning.
- † Alleviate financial pressure through supportive employee policies.

Promote Savings

- † Reboot the *My Retirement Account* (myRA) to provide a safe and portable savings accounts for workers with low wages.
- † Establish universal *Children's Savings Accounts* (a.k.a. baby bonds) for every American child at birth.
- † Allow families who participate in public benefit programs to have at least three month's income in savings.
- † Expand the *Saver's Credit* and make it refundable, which will create more accessibility for more low-wage families.

Pillar Five:

Block Policies That Sabotage Advancement

Reduce Bureaucracy

Equitable Housing

- † *Honor the Fair Housing Act*: Reinstate the Affirmatively Furthering Fair Housing Rule
- † *Honor the Fair Housing Act*: Protect the Small Area Fair Market Rent Rule
- † *Honor the Fair Housing Act*: Protect the Disparate Impact Rule
- † Champion the *Family Self-Sufficiency* (FSS) program to increase incomes and reduce dependency on government assistance and rental subsidies.

- † End redlining and lending discrimination once and for all. Improve credit access for persons and neighborhoods of color.
- † Put an end to unfair property assessments, which cause widespread over-taxation of Black Americans' homes.
- † Expand the protected classes to protect people against discrimination on the basis of sexual orientation, gender identity, and marital status.
- † Stop predatory land contract practices. Demand that all contracts for deed be appropriately recorded.
- † Continue to go after tech companies that restrict access to housing ads based on characteristics like race, religion, or national origin.

Consumer Protection

Lending

- † Rebuild the Consumer Financial Protection Bureau (CFPB). Protect the Office of Fair Lending and Equal Opportunity.
- † Reinstitute strict restrictions on payday lenders. Balance the interests of borrowers and lenders to ensure fair access to beneficial credit.
- † As payday lending gains restrictions, watch the "consumer installment loan" market closely for potential predatory lending.

Financial Institutions

- † Ban fixed fee overdraft programs. Banks can instead charge reasonable interest rates as they do for any small loan.

- † Enforce high standards and accountability for credit rating agencies and Nationally Recognized Statistical Rating Organization (NRSROs). Eliminate the conflicts of interest that exist in their models.
- † Ensure that investor protection is paramount as the Securities and Exchange Commission (SEC) works to approve a Bitcoin (BTC) Exchange-Traded Fund (ETF).

Debt Collection

- † Require that debt-buying companies provide proof that they own a debt before they can sue a debtor.
- † Stop debt collectors from harassing consumers and collecting on "zombie" debts.

Credit Scoring

- † Do everything possible to protect unscorable and credit invisible consumers.
- † Demand that credit-scoring mechanisms be fair to protect consumers from abusive and harmful lending practices.

Pillar Six:

Ensure Fair and Equitable Education

See *America's Best Chance* in the Part Two, Chapter Three.

Bad Habit Four

Constantly Reacting to Negative Outcomes as Opposed to Proactively Anticipating Them

– the 1787 Recommendations for
Global Trade are in *The Policy Guide* –

It all began with solar panels ($2.7 billion) and washing machines ($861.7 million). The next shot in Donald Trump's tariff war took aim at steel and aluminum. Naturally, countries struck back hard. China initially retaliated with $3 billion of tariffs on U.S. products. The European Union threatened the U.S. with tariffs on $7.1 billion worth of U.S. goods. Canada retaliated with $12.8 billion of tariffs as did Mexico with over $3 billion worth on, among other things, steel, pork and cheese.

Then Donald hit China with another $50 billion worth of tariffs. Then China hit America with $50 billion in tariffs. Then Donald threatened China with another $200 billion of additional tariffs, and $200 billion more on top of that. Then China threatened an additional 25 percent tariff on another 106 U.S. products.

Then, in May 2019, Donald Trump imposed 25 percent tariffs on $250 billion worth of Chinese products, to which the Chinese responded by raising tariffs from 10 percent to 20-25 percent on nearly $60 billion worth of American goods. The Dow Jones Industrial Average fell 617 points.

In mid-August 2019 it really hit the fan. Two years after the first shot, Donald Trump announced that he would impose an additional 10 percent tariff on $300 billion of Chinese imports. In response, Beijing allowed its currency to weaken in order to offset some of the pain of the tariffs.

Almost immediately, the U.S. Treasury Department formally labeled China a currency manipulator. Great. This meant that now this idiotic trade war could suddenly escalate into a currency war. The very idea of this insanity sent the Dow plummeting a jaw-dropping 800 points in just one day.

Unsurprisingly, on August 23rd Beijing announced that it would impose new tariffs on $75 billion in goods to which, in a tweet, Donald Trump responded that the U.S. would raise the rate of all tariffs on China by 5 percentage points. The Dow Jones Industrial Average fell another 600 points.

At the time, Donald Trump's tariffs affected over 50 percent of Chinese imports, but that wasn't the worst of it. Tariffs also affected 9.6 percent of imports from South Korea, 7.3 percent from Canada, 3.8 percent from Japan, and 2.5 percent from the European Union. These are our allies! This was just not cool.

The most disturbing – and confusing – example to me from that time is Canada. From the beginning, Donald Trump's obsession with Canada "ripping us off" was weird because they are actually one of our best trading partners. < I swear Donald's main problem with Canada is that Justin Trudeau is younger, smarter, thinner and looks uber hot in a suit, but I can't prove it. >

Take cars, for example. At the beginning of the Trump administration, we were buying more cars from Canada than they were buying from us. But Canada buys the *individual parts* that make those cars from us. So, all told, our automotive trade with Canada was then about even.

U.S. goods and services trade with Canada totaled an estimated $714.1 billion in 2018: Exports were $360.5 billion and imports were $353.6 billion. Our northern neighbor was our largest goods export market, and our second largest goods trading partner with $617.2 billion in total (two way) goods trade.

The U.S. goods and services trade surplus with Canada was $7 billion. Canada's Foreign Direct Investment in America was $453.1 billion in 2017, up 19 percent from the year before. According to the U.S. Department of Commerce, U.S. exports of goods and services to Canada supported an estimated 1.6 million American jobs in 2015. I'm not seeing the problem. Overall, this looks pretty solid to me.

Donald Trump obviously didn't share my opinion, because his Canadian obsession lasted right through the end of his presidency. In August 2020, he slapped 10 percent tariffs on aluminum from Canada. He said it was because there was a surge in aluminum coming from Canada, but that just wasn't true. < It's Trudeau in that suit, I'm telling you! >

Naturally, Canada retaliated against these new tariffs with tariffs of their own, which included bicycles, golf clubs, refrigerators, and other items that contain aluminum.

Contrary to what Donald Trump seems to think, trade deficit doesn't equal *we're getting screwed.* Trade deficits are not scorecards that keep track of who is winning and who is losing or if trade deals are good or bad. This is not a zero-sum game.

Let's say that China really loves American tractors. They just can't get enough of our tractors over there! So, China buys $100 worth of our tractors. We, in turn, love us some Chinese fortune cookies. We just can't get enough of Chinese fortune cookies! So, we buy $200 worth of Chinese fortune cookies.

The difference between these two purchases is the trade deficit (i.e., the gap between how much in goods and services we import from other countries, and how much we export to them). As it stands now in our example, China has a $100 trade surplus and America has a $100 trade deficit.

You'll notice that no one is winning or losing in this scenario. Remember, we didn't just write China a check for nothing...we got a lot of cookies for our money!

Although the formal definition of deficit includes one that says the amount of something is too small (which makes us feel like we lost somehow), in practice it's not a bad thing. It's true that trade deficits are subtracted from the Gross Domestic Product (GDP). Therefore, on paper at least, if one country is selling less stuff, they are likely producing less, which means there are potentially less jobs.

But in reality, that is not necessarily true. The United States had a large trade deficit in 2009 when the unemployment rate was 10 percent but had an even larger trade deficit in 2006 when the unemployment rate was just 4.4 percent. The trade deficit is actually more a function of the value of the U.S. dollar...more on this in a minute...

Isn't this fun!?! Now, there is a flip side to all of this that many people fail to take into account, and it's major. When we last left our tractor/fortune cookie trade, China had a $100 trade surplus. So, what are they going to do with that $100?

Well, they can do one of two things: 1) They can do nothing and just keep the money in their back account. However, this will just increase the value of their currency and ultimately push their domestic prices upward…OR…They can 2) Take the $100 and invest it back in America through stocks, bonds, or direct investment (i.e., plants, equipment and real estate).

I know this is confusing, but *The Economist* explains it way better: "It is as if container ships arrived at American ports to deliver furniture, computers and cars, and departed filled with American stocks and bonds. Over time, those assets yield returns in the form of interest, dividends and capital gains."

This is a really positive development because foreign investment is critical to our economic growth. When you read this next part, don't forget that in this scenario, China is investing the money we pay them for their goods back into America through stocks, bonds, or direct investment.

The Economist continues, "To the extent that trade deficits thus represent borrowing from abroad there is some truth to the idea that they could erode American wealth. But that is to ignore a crucial point about the debt incurred: it comes cheap. America has run current-account deficits – which are substantially driven by the balance of trade – almost every year since 1982. As a result, foreigners own American assets worth $8.1 trillion more than the assets Americans own overseas, a difference equivalent to 43 percent of America's GDP."

Now, back to what I mentioned earlier about the trade deficit being more a function of the value of the U.S. dollar:

One of the most important things to keep in mind is that trade deficits are a little different for the United States than other countries because our currency is the dominant global reserve currency – meaning the U.S. dollar is used in many transactions that the United States has nothing to do with.

Many countries trade with one another – and borrow and lend – using the U.S. dollar. This increases the demand for our dollar on foreign exchange markets which, in turn, makes it stronger. A stronger U.S. dollar, in turn, makes our exports more expensive and imports less expensive – which ultimately makes our exports less competitive and leads to an overall trade deficit.

Not to get uber dorky, but this is called the Triffin Dilemma: "Incessant foreign demand for a reserve currency forces its issuing country to run persistent current account deficits. The United States, for example, enjoys the consumption benefit of running a trade deficit, while the rest of the world benefits from the additional liquidity, which helps facilitate trade. The cost comes from the declining value and credibility of any currency which runs a persistent trade deficit – eventually leading to a reluctance of creditors to hold the reserve currency."

I know this can get confusing – and this Triffin Dilemma thing sounds tricky – but as a country we want this role. It gives us unparalleled power in global finance, not to mention lower interest rates and a strong stock market. And, lucky for us, foreign investors have no reluctance to hold our currency at this point (this is another reason why being fiscally responsible is so important). In fact, United States Treasuries are still one of the safest bets in the world.

Because of our currency's position in the world, the United States running a trade surplus could actually upend the entire global market. That sounds dramatic but remember that, in the past four decades, the United States has had current account surpluses in only three years – 1980, 1981 and 1991 – and each of those years was tied to a recession.

As long as the American economy is growing faster than those around the world, our trade deficit will likely increase. Strong domestic growth increases America's demand for imports while, at the same time, weaker foreign growth decreases the world's demand for America's exports.

§§§

The Trump administration's populist trade "strategy" was completely inconsistent, unpredictable and unstable.

Corporate America can survive bad policy as long as it is *consistent*. Companies that are responsible to shareholders, customers, employees and the communities they serve don't have the luxury of playing chicken. They have to make decisions based on the facts as they are today. They have to decide how to deploy capital *today*.

The executive vice president of Columbia Sportswear, Peter Bragdon, summed it up when he said that companies are used to weathering bad public policy, but that "nobody is used to navigating public policy that is this horrible. It's chaotic and incoherent. It's not surprising that investments have slowed in the United States because of the chaos."

In the very beginning of the Trump presidency, players in industries like steel, aluminum, and lumber were generally supportive of his tariffs because of what they viewed as unfair competition from companies that received subsidies from their governments (like China). Some of these companies believed that the U.S. tariffs would give them breathing room and more confidence to invest in their futures.

After all, if the volume of imports from countries imposed with U.S. tariffs is lower there should be more room for production in America to increase, right? Steelmakers were only using 78 percent of their capacity, and some mothballed plants have been brought back online to fill the void.

But – uh oh! – here comes that dang Butterfly Effect again. Those who did see an increase in production, thanks to the trade war, also saw higher prices thanks to (you guessed it) the same trade war!

This was particularly true for businesses that use metals – and those businesses account for many American jobs. So, these peeps got a double whammy: As their prices increased their global competitiveness decreased.

As a result, things like this started happening pretty quickly: *The New York Times* reported that "Century Aluminum, one of the few aluminum makers left in the United States, applauded Mr. Trump's 10 percent tariff on aluminum when it was introduced. The company said the tariffs had made it possible to invest over $150 million to more than double output at its smelting plant in Hawesville, Kentucky."

"Yet Century posted a $66 million loss last year, compared with a $49 million profit in 2017. A big reason for the loss was a sharp spike in the price of alumina, the substance that is smelted to produce aluminum. A major cause of the increase: Authorities in Brazil ordered a huge alumina producer to operate at half capacity after a spill."

As of August 2020, Century had reported losses for nine straight quarters. The company hadn't enjoyed an annual profit since 2017. In February 2021, Century reported a "net loss of $123.3 million for the full year 2020, a $42.5 million decline from the full year 2019."

Soon after the Trump administration imposed the first steel and aluminum tariffs, Milwaukee-based Harley-Davidson announced it was shifting more production overseas, explaining that a rise in the price of their motorcycles "would have an immediate and lasting detrimental impact," and that moving production overseas was "the only sustainable option to make its motorcycles accessible to customers in the EU and maintain a viable business in Europe."

The Chief Executive Officer of Pittsburgh-based Alcoa, the country's largest aluminum maker and importer, called the tariffs on imported aluminum a "significant" headwind. Alcoa then estimated that its operating earnings could take as much as a $100 million hit in 2018 alone. Indeed, six months later Alcoa's aluminum division reported a fourth-quarter loss.

Caterpillar, the largest global machinery producer and a huge purchaser of metal, revealed it may have lost over $100 million in 2018 because of the tariffs.

In the quarter after the initial tariffs were announced, General Motors reported a $300 million increase in commodity costs, and Ford revealed that the tariffs resulted in $145 million in increased costs, an amount they estimated could reach as high rise as $600 million for the entire year.

General Motors said in a statement that there would be "less investment, fewer jobs and lower wages" for its employees. Less than six months later, GM announced it would close five North American facilities, as well as eliminate an estimated 14,700 jobs.

The trade war eventually caught up with Whirlpool, who originally loved the Trump administration's tariffs on imported washing machines. Six months later, after their first quarter net income was down $64 million from the year prior thanks to the steel and aluminum tariffs, Whirlpool's chief executive warned, "There continues to be uncertainty regarding potential future tariffs and trade actions. We'll continue to monitor, evaluate and take the right action for our business."

In the end, Donald Trump did the exact opposite of his promise to "negotiate fair trade deals that create American jobs, increase American wages, and reduce America's trade deficit." Trade is just one more example of Donald Trump ripping things apart without being ready with a successful solution.

The few trade deals he did try to cut haven't exactly set the world on fire. The North American Free Trade Agreement (NAFTA) went into effect on January 1, 1994. The U.S. State Department reports that "exports under NAFTA support more than three million American jobs. In NAFTA's first ten 10 years, trade in goods among the three countries more than doubled from approximately $293 billion in 1993 to nearly $627 billion in 2003. In 2016, goods-trade between the U.S. and the two NAFTA trading partners totaled nearly $800 billion."

In October 2018, the Trump administration announced that the United States, Canada and Mexico had reached a new trade agreement. Donald Trump signed the agreement on January 29, 2020.

This new agreement is called the United States-Mexico-Canada Agreement or USMCA (how creative!). The new agreement does include stronger labor provisions and new rules for auto parts; updates rules for patents and intellectual property; and modernizes trade rules for e-commerce, digital products, and financial services – which is all positive. But, otherwise, the agreement is pretty much NAFTA.

Ditto with the bilateral trade agreements negotiated with Japan and South Korea, which were both so close to the existing agreements that many people didn't even consider them new trade deals.

And then there's China. Always China. Ultimately, Donald's trade war with China did nothing but give China a huge trade surplus. In

November 2020, China hit a record trade surplus of $75.43 billion, with 46.1 percent of that number – $51.98 billion – coming from America. Which was also a new record.

The Wall Street Journal reports that "the tariffs did succeed in reducing the trade deficit with China in 2019, but the overall U.S. trade imbalance was bigger than ever that year and has continued climbing, soaring to a record $84 billion in August as U.S. importers shifted to cheaper sources of goods from Vietnam, Mexico and other countries. The trade deficit with China also has risen amid the pandemic and is back to where it was at the start of the Trump administration."

In addition, the WSJ reports that the trade war with China "didn't achieve the central objective of reversing a U.S. decline in manufacturing, economic data show, despite tariffs on hundreds of billions of dollars of Chinese goods to discourage imports." Nor did the trade war "achieve the central objective of reversing a U.S. decline in manufacturing, economic data show, despite tariffs on hundreds of billions of dollars of Chinese goods to discourage imports."

Although the WSJ acknowledged that, as former U.S. Trade Representative Robert Lighthizer continually pointed out, there was a net gain of 400,000 U.S. manufacturing jobs from November 2016 until March 2020, they reported that "about 75 percent of the increase in manufacturing jobs occurred before the first tranche of tariffs took effect against China in July 2018, when annual growth in manufacturing jobs peaked and then began to decline. By early 2020, even before the pandemic reached the U.S., manufacturing job growth had stalled out, and factories shed workers in four of the six months through March."

"An industry-by-industry analysis by the Federal Reserve showed that tariffs did help boost employment by 0.3 percent, in industries exposed to trade with China, by giving protection to some domestic industries to cheaper Chinese imports. But these gains were more than offset by higher costs of importing Chinese parts, which cut manufacturing employment by 1.1 percent. Retaliatory tariffs imposed by China against U.S. exports, the analysis found, reduced U.S. factory jobs by 0.7 percent."

After all of the fits and tantrums and disruption and chaos, Donald undoubtably felt compelled to get something on paper with China, even if the deal ended up being a complete capitulation on his part (which it absolutely was).

On January 15, 2020, he and China's Vice Premier Liu He, also their chief negotiator, signed the *Economic and Trade Agreement Between the United States of America and the People's Republic* of *China: Phase One.*

In the deal, China "promised" to buy lots of stuff from us, but there is virtually no way to enforce this loose commitment. By the end of 2020, China's purchases only reached 59 percent of the agreed upon target. There is the pandemic to consider, but the more likely scenario is that the United States never had the productive capacity to reach the very inflated targets in the first place.

Also, per the agreement, China isn't required to buy U.S. products if "market conditions" are unfavorable or if they don't approve of the quality, which makes the entire deal a virtual no deal. How do you say "gigantic loophole" in Chinese?

Worse, this deal still does nothing to address currency manipulation and/or China's industrial policy. So, to recap, American businesses are still unprotected from Chinese unsavory trade practices; Chinese imports from the United States are lower than they were before the trade war started; and our trade deficit with China the day Donald Trump left office was exactly the same as it was when he was sworn in.

§§§

The word proactive has already been used a million times in this book, but I cannot stress enough how critical it is that, as a nation, we start being proactive as opposed to reactive.

Somewhere down the line, we got into the horrible habit of constantly reacting to negative outcomes as opposed to proactively anticipating them. This approach lends itself to overreaction and overcompensation, which causes even greater chaos.

It reminds me of the Popeye cartoon where the mighty Sailor Man and his beloved Olive Oyl are in a boat that, thanks to dozens of leaks, is rapidly sinking. Every time they manage to plug one of the leaks with their fingers, toes and Olive Oyl's pointy nose, a brand new leak springs making it impossible to catch them all.

America, we don't have time for this. Perpetually being on defense rather than playing offense accomplishes nothing. We have to – for once and for all – solve the roots of our problems instead of continuing to treat the symptoms. This means a more proactive approach, which will minimize potential problems before they escalate into full-scale catastrophes.

Trade offers an excellent example. Globalization – or the worldwide interaction and integration among people, companies and governments – has brought the world together in unprecedented ways. We are living in an unmatched era of global interdependence, multilateralism and competition. Love it or hate it, there is no escaping it.

Make no mistake, despite the campaign promises and rally cries you may hear, America's dedication to global commerce will not likely change any time soon because the overall financial benefit to our nation greatly outweighs the negatives. If the past four years have taught us anything, it's this.

The fabulous news is that, if we proactively make smart adjustments, we can all successfully evolve within this rapidly changing landscape. This will allow us to maintain control over our future instead of being vulnerable to forces beyond our control.

The number one misconception about globalization is that there have to be winners and losers. This is a false premise.

There is no question that global trade has hit certain sectors of our economy hard and, as I said earlier in this chapter, the federal government needs to provide a financial backstop for these families and communities, just in case there is any gap between winding down old jobs and beginning new ones. This should include temporary income replacement, strong protections for pensions, and retraining and relocation support.

That said, globalization is not wholly responsible for the displacement of the American worker. Even if we halt all progression toward globalization, including imports and outsourcing, vast advancements in technology alone would cause certain jobs within industries such as steel, textile and automobiles to eventually become obsolete.

The coolest thing about a capitalist economy, however, is that it offers everyone the opportunity to make adjustments as the demands of the economy evolve (which was clearly illustrated by the seismic shifts in our defense and energy policies).

...and everything evolves eventually. In his book *Clashing Over Commerce*, Dartmouth College economics professor Douglas A. Irwin explains that the main purposes of U.S. trade policy can be summed up with what he calls the three Rs – revenue, restriction, and reciprocity.

Before the Civil War, food and raw materials (like wheat and cotton) made up about two-thirds of our exports. Manufactured goods (like clothing and metal goods) made up about two-thirds of our imports.

Back then, tariffs (or taxes imposed by governments) were super high – some up to 62 percent – because taxing imports was the primary source of **revenue** for our early government.

From the Civil War to the Great Depression, in an effort to protect domestic production, the **restriction** of imports was the order of the day. This trend came to an end thanks to the disaster that was the *Smoot-Hawley Tariff of 1930*, which was supposed to protect U.S. businesses and farmers by raising import duties but instead accelerated the Great Depression.

Since the Great Depression, multilateral trade agreements, or **reciprocity,** has been the focus. After World War II, the United States represented nearly half of global production, which gave us enormous economic leverage because everyone else desperately needed U.S. goods and investment.

Expanded global trade saved a crippled Europe and Japan, and the United States helped rebuild many economies from afar by importing their goods. This not only rebuilt the global order to our advantage, but also repaired and strengthened alliances around the world. The global rules, institutions, and alliances that emerged from this period are the foundation of our modern-day international structure – a structure that still significantly benefits the United States.

Certainly, there are instances when America should embrace unilateralism and sovereignty, but it is essential that we reject isolationism at all costs. We do not have such an embarrassment of riches in this country that we can afford to abandon the golden opportunity of globalization solely out of misperception and fear.

There are many misguided assumptions that fueled Donald Trump's failed foreign policy approach, but one of the worst was his incredibly naïve and 100% false belief that, if America disengages from the rest of the world, the rest of the world will just somehow disappear – leaving America in a gloriously isolated bubble of nothing but fabulous health and wealth.

This thought process reminds me of the mythical ostrich that sticks his head in the sand to avoid danger. If I can't see them, they can't see me, right? Well, not exactly.

The Trans-Pacific Partnership (TPP) was an ambitious free trade agreement among twelve Asia-Pacific countries designed to eliminate trade barriers and establish new market-oriented trade rules. The original member countries were Australia, Brunei, Canada, Chile, Japan, Malaysia, Mexico, New Zealand, Peru, Singapore, the United States, and Vietnam. Combined, these counties comprise around 40 percent of global GDP.

After grueling – and quite astonishing, given the significant concessions many countries were willing to give to make TPP a reality – negotiations, TPP was signed by the member countries on February 4, 2016. However, because it got turned into a political football in the 2016 presidential campaign, the TPP was never ratified by the United States Congress.

According to the U.S. International Trade Commission, American trade with these eleven countries totaled more than $1.5 trillion in merchandise in 2015 and more than $276 billion in services in 2014. In 2014, U.S. foreign direct investment into these countries totaled $61 billion, while these countries invested almost $59 billion in the United States.

The TPP's thirty chapters provided greater access to markets for service providers, and addressed tariffs on goods and services, discrimination protections, investor protections, e-commerce rules, intellectual property rights, worker's rights, environmental safety and stewardship, dispute resolution mechanisms, and restrictions on state-owned enterprises.

The TPP also significantly lowered tariffs and other trade barriers on a vast range of goods. America alone would have seen 18,000 individual tariffs be reduced to zero.

The Peterson Institute for International Economics, a think tank, estimated that the TPP would "increase annual real incomes in the United States by $131 billion, or 0.5 percent of GDP, and annual exports by $357 billion, or 9.1 percent of exports, over baseline projections by 2030, when the agreement is nearly fully implemented."

The U.S. International Trade Commission (USITC) said that "among broad sectors of the U.S. economy, agriculture and food would see the greatest percentage gain relative to the baseline projections."

< Note: There is at least one study that shows negative effects for the United States from joining the TPP. I disagree with the models used by the researchers but want you to have the opportunity to judge for yourselves. It is from Tufts University and you can find the link in the Trade section of the 1787 website. >

On January 23, 2017, three days into his presidency, Donald Trump signed an executive order withdrawing the United States from the TPP.

Wow, what a gutsy move! "America First" baby…we showed them! There had to be weeping and gnashing of teeth by the other eleven countries when we left, right? They probably went into a fetal position because they had nowhere else to turn!!

Ummm…nope. Not even close. Now known as the TPP-11, they just carried right on without us, signing a new agreement called the Comprehensive and Progressive Trans-Pacific Partnership (CPTPP), an agreement that moved them all toward expanded international trade and investment, increased economic growth, lower consumer prices, and new domestic jobs.

As an added bonus, our exit from TPP gave China even more room to solidify their increasingly dominant presence in Asia, which is the last thing we need.

To illustrate my point, look no further than the China-led Regional Comprehensive Economic Partnership (RCEP), an agreement signed in

November 2020 by China and 14 other nations, including Australia, Brunei, Cambodia, Indonesia, Japan, Laos, Malaysia, New Zealand, Myanmar, the Philippines, Singapore, South Korea, Thailand, and Vietnam. Covering 30 percent of the global population – 2.2 billion people – and 30 percent of global GDP, the RCEP is the largest regional free trade agreement in the world.

Donald Trump made a huge mistake when he pulled us out of the TPP, and he seemed to realize it pretty quickly. One year after our withdrawal, he indicated during a television interview that he would be willing to get back in the TPP. In April 2018, he officially ordered his top administration officials to look into rejoining the partnership.

Two years after the Trump administration pulled us out, in a stunning absence of self-awareness, our Ambassador to Japan William Hagerty simply could not believe the nerve of Japan to forge an economic partnership agreement with the European Union and their nerve to continue with the CPTPP, which by now had both taken effect.

"By implementing these agreements before addressing our bilateral trade relationship, Japan is effectively redistributing market share away from its strongest ally, the United States...Given the strength of our security and diplomatic relationships, our view is that we should have an equally strong economic relationship."

Is he serious with this? Sorry boys, that's just not the way real life works. Has Ambassador Hagerty never heard the phrase *what's good* for *the goose is good for the gander*? My guess is that Japan decided that, since America decided to stop being a global leader, they should just Make Japan Great Again! I bet that would look great on a red hat!

If there is an upside to Donald Trump's dreadful trade policy, it's that we now know what *doesn't* work. Tweeting insults, being a bully, the laughable mob boss routine – it just didn't work. Period.

In the end, the Trump administration's trade policies alienated our allies, slowed business investment in the U.S., imposed import taxes on American citizens, bankrupted farmers, and caused a recession in U.S. manufacturing – and we have the signed, sealed and delivered numbers to prove it.

One of Donald's measures of "winning" or "losing" in trade is the size of our trade deficit, which he called "unacceptable" when he became president and vowed to "start whittling it down as fast as possible."

This is another misguided assumption, which we'll get into in a minute, but let's use his own favorite barometer to measure his own success. By his own preferred measure his trade policy was a complete failure.

The United States trade deficit completely blew out under his watch. In 2018, our overall trade deficit (for goods and services) grew 12.5 percent from the year before, to $621 billion. That's about 25 percent *larger* than it was in 2016, President Obama's final year in the White House.

Even though we had a trade surplus in services in 2018, we recorded a $891.3 billion trade deficit in merchandise. This is the largest in American history. Interestingly enough, although Donald Trump hit China the hardest by far, the trade gap between the two countries reached $419 billion in 2018, which is also the highest in history.

To sum the entire episode up, in January 2017, when Donald Trump took the reins, the U.S. trade deficit was $43 billion. In October 2020, a month before he lost a second term, it was $63 billion.

I'm sure he has plenty of people and/or things to blame for this, including Covid-19. But blaming the pandemic is not going to work. There are historic examples of recessions where our trade deficit actually contracted.

"America First" may make for a great chant at campaign rallies but, in the real world, it's reckless and just bad business. Donald was convinced that playing his version of hardball would bring everyone – with their tails between their legs – to the table. That's just not the world we live in anymore.

I'm not saying we don't need to put America and American workers first. We absolutely do! But that can be achieved without completely withdrawing from global commerce and pissing off the entire world. In fact, handled correctly, these agreements can be one of the best ways to <u>protect</u> our workers.

This isn't a fake boardroom filled with D-level celebrities who all read from a pre-written script. This is the real world, where real people can get really hurt…and where real people are the ones who pay for incompetence.

American consumers paid the tab for Donald Trump's trade war, full stop. The Chinese people didn't pay, nor did the people of Mexico. Americans paid. Period. He kept denying this and denying this (in this rare case, I actually don't think he was lying. He just clearly doesn't understand how trade works).

Finally, someone in his administration sort of admitted that Americans paid the price for this trade debacle. After facing tough questions from Fox host Chris Wallace, National Economic Council Director Larry Kudlow acknowledged that U.S. consumers, not China, pay the tariff bill.

On Fox News Sunday, Wallace pressed, "It's not China that pays tariffs. It's the American importers, the American companies that pay what, in effect, is a tax increase and oftentimes passes it on to U.S. consumers." To which Kudlow replied, "Fair enough."

Wallace kept pushing until Kudlow finally admitted that, "no," China doesn't pay for the tariffs, but "the Chinese will suffer GDP losses and so forth with respect to a diminishing export market" – which is also true but entirely different than Donald Trump's completely wrong

assertion that China foots the bill for the tariffs.

In May 2019, the Federal Reserve Bank of New York issued a report on the impact of tariffs on $200 billion of U.S. imports from China. Before, these imports were subject to 10 percent levies but, after a breakdown in trade negotiations, that increased to 25 percent.

From their report: "As a result of this expenditure switching, we estimate that the annualized deadweight loss increases from $132 to $620 per household, bringing the total annual cost of the new round of tariffs to the typical household to $831."

Another study from the Federal Reserve Bank of New York – by economists Mary Amiti of the New York Fed, Stephen Redding of Princeton University and David Weinstein of Columbia University – found that "the full incidence of the tariff falls on domestic consumers, with a reduction in U.S. real income of $1.4 billion per month by the end of 2018."

The report continues, "The trade war also caused dramatic adjustments in international supply chains, as approximately $165 billion dollars of trade ($136 billion of imports and $29 billion of exports) is lost or redirected in order to avoid the tariffs. We find that the U.S. tariffs were almost completely passed through into U.S. domestic prices, so that the entire incidence of the tariffs fell on domestic consumers and importers up to now, with no impact so far on the prices received by foreign exporters. We also find that U.S. producers responded to reduced import competition by raising their prices."

Aaron Flaaen of the Federal Reserve Board, and Ali Horta and Felix Tintelnot of the University of Chicago found that "in response to the 2018 tariffs on nearly all source countries, the price of washers rose by nearly 12 percent; the price of dryers – a complementary good not subject to tariffs – increased by an equivalent amount. Factoring in the effect of dryers and price increases by domestic brands, our estimates for the 2018 tariffs on washers imply a tariff elasticity of consumer prices [or, the costs that pass-through to consumers] of between 110 and 230 percent."

Then there are the American farmers, whose businesses just have gotten hammered by Donald's contentious approach to trade. The American Farm Bureau reports that debt in the farm sector reached an estimated $434 billion in 2020, the highest on record, and farm bankruptcies have steadily increased.

Again, this is due to bad trade policies, not the Covid-19 disruption. To help them through the pandemic, farmers received lots of federal funds through the *CARES Act*, including the Coronavirus Food Assistance Program and Paycheck Protection Program loans. But this just brings up another point.

Over the course of the Trump administration, well before the pandemic, American farmers were forced to become increasingly dependent on government aid. While I'm sure they appreciate the help, American farmers don't want handouts, they want to compete.

All in, retaliatory tariffs (i.e., a tax that one government charges another government to punish it for imposing tariffs on its own exports) hit our farmers so hard that the Trump administration had to give them an additional $12 billion in aid in 2018, and another additional $16 billion in May 2019. The federal subsidies that cotton farmers received in 2019, for example, were 33 times the income they lost because of the trade war.

Federal assistance to farmers reached an estimated $51.2 billion by Donald Trump's last year in office, which means that government support constituted 40 percent of their total net cash income. Who's the socialist now?

It's just baffling that no one in the Trump administration could see what a nightmare this was going to be for our farmers. Already contending with significant challenges before the trade war, including oversupply and extreme weather, American farmers were all of the sudden forced to deal with retaliatory tariffs on everything from soybeans to pigs.

According to the U.S. International Trade Administration, American agricultural exports to China fell from $15.8 billion in 2017 to $5.9 billion in 2018 (63 percent).

In farming, if you lose global market share in things like soybeans, pork, beef and poultry, you will have a heck of a time getting it back, if you even can at all. Almost immediately after Donald's first trade tantrum, China happily started buying soybeans from Brazil, who happily increased its soybean production to fill our void.

This is a major problem because soybeans happen to be the second-biggest crop in America. Before this fiasco, soybean farmers exported around half of what they produce, and over one-third of all American soybeans went to China at a price tag of around $12.4 billion.

After the trade war commenced, soybean exports fell to just $3.1 billion in 2018, before rebounding a little to $8 billion in 2019. But still well below $12.4 billion.

Meanwhile, in Montana, a Chinese company agreed in 2017 to purchase $200 million worth of beef from Montana ranchers, as well as build a $100 million slaughterhouse in the state. Unfortunately, thanks to the toxic trade relationship between the Trump administration and China, three years later neither had happened.

Pre-trade war, wheat farmers exported 46 percent of their crop. The Department of Agriculture actually gave them a bit of good news in

2018 when it said: "Grain and feed exports are forecast up $700 million to $33.8 billion, driven by higher corn and wheat volumes."

That was obviously a relief, so imagine how deflating it was to wake up to this *Bloomberg* headline six months later in the midst of the escalating U.S.-China trade war: "Trump Trade Tweets Send Grain Markets Diving to 42-Year Low." Wow. It's almost like he was sabotaging them on purpose.

Words – and tweets – matter. Mexico imported ten times more corn from Brazil in 2017 because of Trump's negative, aggressive rhetoric about NAFTA. This is really bad because Mexico had always been the top importer of American corn and was the second largest buyer of American soybeans.

Think about all of this in terms of the Butterfly Effect. Rural America was already in trouble. Farm country in particular is experiencing huge demographic shifts. In Iowa, for example, a record high 35 percent of farmland owners are aged 75 years or older and 60 percent are over the age of 65. Smaller farming operations were already having a difficult time competing, so Donald's trade war was most likely the final death knell for many.

But the fallout doesn't stop there. Once smaller farms are folded into larger operations or are gone altogether, they won't need local credit anymore. As a consequence, community banks, which help drive economic growth in rural towns, will find it difficult to stay afloat. People will be forced to find work elsewhere and as people relocate, the viability of hospitals, clinics, and other social services will be in jeopardy…and so on and so forth.

And it's not just rural America. Mid-sized, export-dependent cities also took the brunt of barriers to trade. For example, in Columbus, Indiana over half the economy is dependent on exports which, according to the Brookings Institution, makes it the most export-reliant city in the entire country (ironically, Columbus is former Vice President Mike Pence's hometown).

Many in the state of Indiana, which leads the country in manufacturing, felt the heat. Carmel, a suburban city north of Indianapolis, is home to Telamon Corporation, a private company that operates on three continents. Thanks to increased tariffs, the company now pays 30 percent more for the components it needs to manufacture its products.

In 2019, Telamon's chief executive Stanley Chen said, "That's a big hit. We don't have a lot of warm fuzzies that (the trade dispute) gets resolved in the near term...We see risk long term to revenue."

This nonsense is all the more frustrating because these tariffs did not even remotely find a solution to what many American companies were complaining about in the first place: The fact that, thanks to their state-run model, their Chinese counterparts get an unfair advantage.

Without question, China's state-owned firm model, nontransparent government subsidies, dumping (where the price of a product when sold in the importing country is less than the price of that product in the market of the exporting country), and outright theft of intellectual property have distorted markets and must stop immediately.

China needs to be held accountable and forced to be transparent, modernize its trading practices, protect intellectual property, and allow better access for foreign business.

When China joined the World Trade Organization (WTO) in 2001, the expectation was that they would bend toward Western-style capitalism. In exchange for international access, China committed to being open and transparent. Unfortunately, that never happened.

Although originally there were high hopes for China, the country remains an economy of state-subsidized enterprises and shady trade practices. For example, for years China has heavily subsidized its steel makers which artificially lowers the price of imported steel to the U.S. and causes gluts in the steel supply. To leverage exports, they hold down the value of their currency.

This hurts American consumers because most of our trade deficit with China is consumer goods, meaning most of the things that we buy at Walmart.

More disturbing, China requires foreign companies investing there to enter into joint ventures with domestic partners. Because of this, American companies are forced to disclose proprietary technology in order to participate in the Chinese market. Often, the domestic partners end up just ripping off the ideas.

No company knows this better than Micron Technology, a company based in Boise, Idaho that designs and builds advanced memory and semiconductor technologies, including state-of-the-art microchips.

Several years ago, Micron turned down a multi-billion offer from a state-controlled Chinese company. China subsequently launched lawsuits and investigations against Micron while, at the same time, continued to buy around half of their products. Then China escalated the attacks by just outright stealing Micron's technology.

Clearly, this is unacceptable behavior and China must be stopped. But, without a doubt, these issues are best handled by the WTO.

The WTO provides a multilateral rules-based system that governs international trade, including a process for resolving disputes. The WTO trading system applies in 164 countries and to 98 percent of worldwide trade. The agreements cover agriculture, textiles and clothing, banking, telecommunications, government purchases, industrial standards and product safety, food sanitation regulations, and intellectual property.

The WTO is the "only global international organization dealing with the rules of trade between nations. At its heart are the WTO agreements, negotiated and signed by the bulk of the world's trading nations and ratified in their parliaments. The goal is to ensure that trade flows as smoothly, predictably and freely as possible."

One of the most important features of WTO membership is the "most-favored-nation" clause, which guarantees that countries cannot normally discriminate between their trading partners. In other words, if a country grants someone a special favor, they must do the same for all other members. < Note: Non-discrimination among trading partners is one of the core principles of the WTO; however, regional trade agreements – or reciprocal preferential trade agreements between two or more partners – are also authorized under the WTO, subject to a set of rules. >

Two other benefits of WTO membership are that 1) Other WTO members must grant us lower tariffs at WTO-agreed rates, and 2) The dispute-resolution process, which provides a mechanism to challenge unfair trade practices.

One study that analyzed the effects of the WTO and other trade agreements since World War II found that "the WTO substantially increased trade for countries with institutional standing, and that other embedded agreements had similarly positive effects. Moreover, international trade agreements have complemented, rather than undercut, each other."

There are absolutely ways the WTO can control China. For example, there is nothing stopping the WTO from setting rules on how to detect market distortion, along with how to properly monitor and punish it. Same goes with state subsidies. The WTO can do this through "plurilateral" agreements which have a narrower group of signatories, in this case a group of the larger WTO economies.

They could also do something similar to the Trade Facilitation Agreement (TFA), which has been ratified by two-thirds of the WTO membership. The TFA "contains provisions for expediting the movement, release and clearance of goods, including goods in transit. It also sets out measures for effective cooperation between customs and other appropriate authorities on trade facilitation and customs compliance issues. It further contains provisions for technical assistance and capacity building in this area."

That said, the challenge with China is obvious: Why would they return to the negotiation table when the talks are clearly geared toward curtailing the very practices they benefit from exploiting?

The answer is equally obvious: Because that's the beauty of the WTO. There is strength in numbers, pure and simple. Which underscores why being a member of the WTO is a great thing for America and is essential to our continued international economic strength.

The United States and other WTO members, particularly the European Union and Japan, must apply significant pressure and unite against China. This will create a unified block so significant that China will have no choice but to come around. If not, they will be completely isolated and that simply does not work for their ambitious international plans.

China's ambitious international plans are the main source of leverage for the United States and our allies. If China is locked-out from the rest of the world, their *Made in China 2025*, for example, will obviously not succeed (*Made in China 2025* is a national initiative to strengthen their manufacturing sector – more on this later).

Although Donald Trump consistently railed against the WTO, United States membership remained safe since leaving the organization requires the approval of Congress.

Donald's tirades often include the claim the WTO is "rigged" against the United States, despite the fact that a report from his own administration revealed that "the United States has won 85.7 percent of the cases it has initiated before the WTO since 1995, compared with a global average of 84.4 percent. In contrast, China's success rate is just 66.7 percent."

Another report found that the "ad hoc nature of WTO panels, judicial hierarchy, and panelists' concern for compliance create a set of incentives that encourage panelists to moderate rulings against the most powerful WTO members. Analysis shows that WTO dispute settlement panels limit the negative effects of judgements against the United States and the European Union by reducing the scope of such verdicts through the use of judicial economy."

Despite this, Donald tried hard to do significant damage to our relationship with the WTO with the small amount of unilateral control he had (or thought he had). For example, he tried to get around WTO rules when he imposed tariffs on steel and aluminum imports by claiming Section 232 of the *Trade Expansion Act of 1962*. Section 232 is a provision that allows the U.S. president to bypass Congress and levy tariffs on the grounds of national security.

Donald's using Section 232 in imposing these tariffs was absurd. There was absolutely no national security threat that justified his actions.

This was just flat unconstitutional. Article I, Section 8, Clause 3 of the United States Constitution (a.k.a. The Commerce Clause) says: "The Congress shall have power...To regulate commerce with foreign nations, and among the several states, and with the Indian tribes."

It's true that, under Article II of the Constitution, the president has the "power, by and with the Advice and Consent of the Senate, to make Treaties, provided two thirds of the Senators present concur."

However, that only means that the president has the authority to negotiate international trade agreements. HE DOES NOT HAVE AUTHORITY OVER INTERNATIONAL COMMERCE AND/OR TRADE. The United States Congress is THE ONLY body that has authority to regulate foreign commerce and impose tariffs. But Congress refused to do what Trump wanted, so voilá. We all of a sudden have a completely fabricated national security situation.

This is yet another example of presidential power getting completely out of whack (which we'll talk more about in the next section). Congress should pass legislation immediately to limit presidential trade authority. The legislation should require a congressional review whenever a president invokes Section 232 and should be retroactive for at least two years.

Beyond being unconstitutional, invoking Section 232 was a complete violation of WTO rules, which clearly state that if a country has a valid national security concern, Article XXI of the WTO treaty is a security exception that allows member countries to take "any action which it considers necessary for the protection of its essential security interests." But that's only in the case of true emergencies.

Donald also blocked the appointment of judges to the WTO Court of Appeals. WTO members must unanimously approve judges, but the Trump administration refused to fill vacancies. At the end of his term there were still not enough sitting judges to hear cases.

To be sure, the WTO does need certain reforms. After fourteen years, the Doha Round of talks, the most recent trade negotiations between the WTO membership, have stalled indefinitely. The goal of these negotiations was to agree on major reforms of the international trading system, including revised trade rules.

One of the main challenges of these talks was that developed or developing economies (i.e., the United States, European Union, China and India) weren't super motivated to make concessions that would encourage development in poorer nations...things like more protection for their farmers, for example.

The failed Doha talks not only led to many countries pursuing bilateral and regional trade deals but has also left the WTO with outdated mechanisms to handle issues like patents and copyrights – and largely unable to handle modern-day complaints about unfair competition.

This is a major problem at a time when, as I said earlier, China's state-owned firm model, nontransparent government subsidies, and theft of intellectual property continue to distort markets. But there is no doubt we can get there.

It is incredibly important that the United States honor these international rules. We have to see the bigger picture here. Americans are nice people, but the actions we took after World War II were not just about the United States being nice to our fellow man. America has received significant and substantial returns on the global investments we made.

Far beyond peace and security – which, alone, would have made our efforts worth it – we solidified new markets which guaranteed we would have more countries to trade with. We gained the gratitude and respect of loyal friends...allies who are now more than willing to share our burdens and who have our back in times of peace and war.

History tells us that, for our long-term economic and national security, the United States must take full advantage of the world market. It is foolish to believe that we even have a choice.

According to Credit Suisse's 2018 *Global Wealth Report*, a report that provides information on global household wealth, "aggregate global wealth rose by $14 trillion to $317 trillion, representing a growth rate of 4.6 percent." But here's the disturbing part: "China was the main beneficiary of the newly recorded wealth." Uh oh.

"China is now clearly established in second place in the world wealth hierarchy...China overtook Japan with respect to the number of ultra-high net worth individuals in 2009, total wealth in 2011, and the number of millionaires in 2014."

The following year, the same report revealed that "China's progress has enabled it to replace Europe as the principal source of global wealth growth and to replace Japan as the country with the second-largest number of millionaires. More tellingly, China overtook the United States this year to become the country with most people in the top 10 percent of global wealth distribution."

China is the largest export economy in the world, and the Chinese bought more Cadillacs than Americans did in 2018 and 2019. In a new twist, these Cadillacs were made at a General Motors plant *in China*.

Chinese foreign direct investment in the European Union skyrocketed from below $840 million in 2008 to $42 billion in just eight years. In 2014, total annual trade between China and Latin America increased from practically zero to over $200 billion. Over the past fifteen years, the China Development Bank and China Export-Import Bank have loaned over $137 billion to Latin American and Caribbean countries.

Already, around 40 percent of the sales made by the companies on the S&P 500, an index that tracks the stock performance of 500 large American companies, come from overseas.

Although the entire planet hit a brick wall in 2007, in the 17 years before the 2007-2009 Financial Crisis, the worldwide economy grew from $23 trillion to $53 trillion, and global trade increased by 133 percent. Developing nations were responsible for over half of that new growth.

From 2001 to 2007, emerging equity markets were on fire. In that time, the value of Brazil's market increased by 369 percent, India by 499 percent, Russia by 630 percent, and China by 201 percent.

Although they have faced challenges in the past few years, from 1990 to 2014 the combined share of global GDP of Brazil, Russia, India, China and South Africa – otherwise known as the BRICS countries – rose from 11 percent to almost 30 percent. Together, these countries represent over 40 percent of the global population, control around 30 percent of the world's land, hold over $4 trillion in reserves, and account for around 18 percent of global trade. They were responsible for 50 percent of the world's economic growth in 2017.

According to the World Bank – an international financial institution that provides loans and grants to the governments of low and middle-income countries for the purpose of pursuing capital projects – before the pandemic, "two-thirds of the increase in energy demand and two-fifths of the rise in food consumption came from seven countries: Brazil, China, India, Indonesia, Mexico, Russia and Turkey. This group now exceeds the Group of Seven industrial nations in consumption of coal and all base and precious metals, as well as of rice, wheat and soybeans."

The Brookings Institution, a nonprofit public policy organization, reports that "just over 50 percent of the world's population, or some 3.8 billion people, live in households with enough discretionary expenditure to be considered 'middle class' or 'rich'."

Why does this matter, you might ask? Because "the middle class is already the largest segment of demand in the global economy. What makes it interesting for business is that it is also the most rapidly growing segment, projected to reach some 4 billion people by end 2020 and 5.3 billion people by 2030."

The report continues, "By our calculations, the middle-class markets in China and India in 2030 will account for $14.1 trillion and $12.3 trillion, respectively, comparable in size to a U.S. middle-class market at that time of $15.9 trillion."

That's a lot of people to sell stuff to, America! This dovetails nicely with our plan to invest in advanced manufacturing for things like 5G, lasers, innovative computer chips and software engineering, as well as investment in emerging technologies like artificial intelligence, high-performance computing and synthetic biology. Gooooo America!!

Bad Habit Five

Getting Stuck in Ideology Instead of Just Doing the Math

&

Bad Habit Six

Allowing Past Prejudices and Preconceived Notions to Prevent Potential Progress

Health care provides the perfect example for two bad habits we need to break. The first bad habit is getting stuck in ideology instead of just doing the math, which we will get to in a few minutes. But first, let's talk about the second bad habit: Allowing past prejudices and preconceived notions to prevent potential progress.

The highly controversial and heated debate over the public option and single-payer health care is always immediately shut down by Republicans, mainly because of the "Socialist" connotation associated with them. The inherent laziness in this approach drives me C R A Z Y!

Over the past few years, I have taken a hard look at both the public option and single-payer health care. In my opinion, this is definitely not the direction to go (more on this later).

That said, although these are not solutions I ultimately landed on, I learned a ton about the health care system from researching them, and I'm convinced this newfound knowledge made my health care plan stronger and much more comprehensive than it would have been otherwise.

Why in the world would we take *any* potential solution off the table without fully checking it out, simply because the supposed philosophy behind it makes us uncomfortable?

I admit that, before my research, I always associated the public option and single-payer health care with the Soviet Union and, being a good capitalist, both concepts made me plenty nervous. But this reaction *had* to be based on a preexisting bias because, until a few years ago, I didn't know what the heck they even were.

Let's please, please, please not allow past prejudices and preconceived notions to prevent potential progress. We have lost the luxury of making uninformed, snap judgments about pivotal issues. I don't know about you, but I'd rather be called a Socialist than stupid.

§§§

Let's start this section off with a bang! Is health care a *right* or a *privilege*? In my mind it is neither. It's a means (the best way to deliver high-quality, low-cost health care) to an end (living the healthiest life possible). Whether we get good health care or bad health care is a vital component of <u>all</u> of our lives...and I want <u>every</u> American to get excellent care.

But the *right v. privilege* debate misses the point. If you go straight to the founding documents, health care is not a *right.* Sure, the Declaration of Independence says that we all have "unalienable Rights, that among these are Life, Liberty and the pursuit of Happiness," but that's not the U.S. Constitution, and using that phrase to say we all have a right to health care is a stretch anyway.

Although the purpose of the actual U.S. Constitution is to "promote the general Welfare" – the word used is *promote*, not *provide.*

The two documents that inch health care more toward being an actual right are the *United Nations Universal Declaration of Human Rights* ("everyone has the right to a standard of living adequate for the health and well-being of himself and of his family, including food, clothing, housing and medical care") and the World Health Organization resolution 58.33 (which speaks to equity in access, plus financial-risk protection to ensure that the cost of health care does not put people at risk of financial catastrophe).

But those still don't get us to *every single American has the right to free health care*, which is pretty much what people mean when they say health care is a right (meaning, people who say this typically don't mean the government should simply acknowledge that health care is one of our Constitutional rights – they mean the government should be responsible for *giving* health care to each of us).

It is 1000% understandable this issue sparks heartbreaking emotions because, at its core, it is about our loved ones who have life-threatening cancer, heart disease, or things like high-blood pressure that can cause massive strokes.

It's about our children who have severe asthma or diabetes or other potentially debilitating health issues. It's about desperately wanting the ones we love to have the highest quality of health care, and to be with us – pain free – for as long as they possibly can.

As a reminder, before people start putting words in my mouth, I desperately want every American to have the very best health care. However, when speaking of *how* to best deliver high-quality, low-cost health care, the stronger argument is one that moves beyond emotions and goes straight to dollars and cents.

The principle at the heart of the health care policy debate is not about our *rights*. It's about the very *best way* to provide universal health coverage – which means that, as the World Health Organization puts it, "all people and communities can use the promotive, preventive, curative, rehabilitative and palliative health services they need, of sufficient quality to be effective, while also ensuring that the use of these services does not expose the user to financial hardship."

On this point, I am an emphatic YES!! One thing the U.S. Constitution definitely provides us is the freedom to build a country we can all be proud of. America will never be a country that abandons citizens in need and thank God for that. Because of this gift, we need to design smart programs that give us the biggest bang for our buck. Because – hear this – we are spending the money anyway.

According to *The Economist,* in an article written in 2018, "America is the only rich country to lack universal coverage. Even in a booming economy, 12 percent of American adults remain uninsured. Though the best care they receive is world-beating, the system as a whole has high costs and disappointing results. America spends 17 percent of gross domestic product (GDP) on health care, the highest of any rich country, but in return achieves an average life expectancy no better than that of the formerly communist countries of eastern Europe." Ouch.

That pretty much sums up our bleak situation. If we allow emotions to get in the way of common sense, we will lose our way. The challenges we face in health care are linked in intricate ways and, therefore, our solutions must be developed collectively as opposed to individually.

When it comes to this topic, we all have an ultimate bond of common fate. I realize that we Americans cherish our individual freedoms but, when it comes to health care, our fortunes are completely tied to one another. For good or ill, we are all in this together.

§§§

As we move forward, it is absolutely critical that we forget ideology and just do the math. First, let's address the elephant (or, in this case, donkey, ha ha, get it?) in the room: Medicare for All, single-payer, and/or a public option.

Let's get our terms squared away.

† Medicare for All – All Americans would be covered under the government-sponsored insurance program that currently serves Americans 65 and over.

† Single-Payer – A term typically used to describe a system run by the federal government: Everyone gets health care from one insurer, and the system is generally paid for by taxes.

† Public Option – This is sort of a mix between single-payer and what we have now (where only certain citizens qualify for programs run by the government). With a public option, more people could qualify for government-run programs (i.e., Medicare or Medicaid) if they wanted to. These could replace private insurance plans for people, but private insurance plans would still exist.

None of these are the way to go for at least **four reasons**:

† Every one of these alternatives demand massive middle-class tax increases. Anyone who says differently is just being dishonest. Very few things in this world are free, and health care certainly isn't. If you are getting "free" health care, you are paying for it through increased taxes. That's just a fact. Taxing the rich is not enough to cover this divide. Not even close.

† The reason taxes would have to increase is that these options are insanely expensive. According to a study led by Charles Blahous –

who was a senior economic adviser to former President George W. Bush and a public trustee of Social Security and Medicare during the Obama administration – the Medicare for All plan Senator Bernie Sanders released in 2018 would increase federal spending by around $32.6 trillion over its first 10 years. That's TRILLION, with a T.

In 2016, the Urban Institute looked at then-presidential candidate Sanders' proposal and found that: "In total, federal spending would increase by about $2.5 trillion (257.6 percent) in 2017. Federal expenditures would increase by about $32.0 trillion (232.7 percent) between 2017 and 2026." To put this into perspective, overall spending in the FY2019 U.S. Budget – literally everything we spend money on – was $4.4 trillion.

† These options would disrupt private insurance contracts, which would affect employer coverage for over 156 million people.

† Patient choice would decrease big time, and doctors' salaries and hospital revenue would drop significantly.

Believe me when I say that we do not want this to happen without careful thought and bringing everyone into the conversation. There is no question that we must control costs, and payments to doctors and hospitals are certainly not immune from hard choices. But these decisions must be strategic and part of a much broader plan. The last thing we want to do is unleash a slew of unintended consequences by pulling the rug out from underneath everyone all at once.

For example, cutting doctors' pay incentivizes them to choose higher-paid specialties over lower-paying jobs in primary care. This one act alone could lead to fewer available doctors for the sickest patients, plus would mean longer wait times for appointments and less time with the doctor when you finally get one. A reduction in doctors' pay is certainly not off the table. We just need to be super careful that issues like these are part of a smart strategy...and be very mindful of #TheButterflyEffect!

§§§

So, what should we do? It's no secret that the American health insurance markets are in complete disarray. The rising costs of health care are not only decimating many American families; they are stifling our economic growth by being just another thing that increases our long-term deficit. We have to do something – and fast!

From the jump, we all need to understand that, if we want to keep covering things like pre-existing conditions, there must be some sort of individual mandate in our plan (meaning we all get insurance or pay a penalty).

Anyone who says differently is just lying or does not understand how an insurance model works at all. From a financial perspective, you can't have one without the other. Period. Healthy people have to counterbalance people who are not as healthy. There's just no way around it.

But that's okay! Because the end result is that costs go down for all of us! To be clear, I'm not suggesting that without the individual mandate the health insurance markets would come crashing down. In fact, we already know they won't. In 2017, Congress set the penalty to zero – effectively repealing the individual mandate provision in the ACA – and the markets survived. My point is that, without the individual mandate, the markets will not operate at optimal efficiency and we will never get costs down.

A quick word to all the healthy people out there: This may be annoying to you *today*, but keep in mind that there will probably come a day, if only temporarily, that *you* get sick, or someone in *your* family gets sick. See, it goes both ways!

Our Goal is to Get Quality Up and Costs Down!

We Can Achieve This In a Two-Step Process:

Step One: Strengthen the *Affordable Care Act* (ACA)
Step Two: Get Spending Under Control

Get Quality Up and Costs Down: Step One
Strengthen the Affordable Care Act (ACA)

The time for debate on whether the *Affordable Care Act* is "Socialist" or the work of the devil or whatever else (blah blah blah) has passed. We already have it – it is here, it is a reality, and American companies have spent billions to comply with it – so let's make it the strongest, smartest health care policy we possibly can.

I'm well aware that the ACA has major issues that must be solved. The final version of the legislation ended up being a complex hodgepodge of private insurance and government-funded care, and there are many, many ways it needs to be improved. But the bottom line is that we have the architecture of something that can work, so starting from scratch makes no sense.

Besides, we have little choice anyway, because no one in Washington can seem to come up with a viable alternative. We've already gone over the fact that the plans being pushed by progressive Democrats are just too expensive and unrealistic, and it is quite obvious that the Republicans have no idea how to solve this (remember "repeal and replace?").

We can absolutely strengthen the ACA but, unfortunately, thanks to the Trump administration and congressional Republicans, we have way more work to do now than we did four years ago. Throughout the Trump administration, the petty, lazy sabotage efforts to destroy the ACA by the Republicans have exacerbated our challenge big time.

They clearly had no idea what to do, so to substitute for substance and compensate for incompetence, they reduced complex issues to dirty tricks and inflammatory dogma.

For the final two years of Obama's presidency, Republicans had a solid platform to outline their solutions for the nation's health care challenge, and after Donald Trump's election to the presidency, their power became absolute.

Even with a vast amount of time and influence available to them, Republicans were unable to craft an intelligent health care agenda. So instead, they decided to just dismantle the ACA piece by piece. Essentially, it was the "repeal" without the "replace."

Their efforts included canceling the all-important individual mandate; blocking reimbursements to insurers who sell ACA health plans; establishing new rules that allow states to opt-out of the ACA's most important provisions; cutting the open enrollment period in half; limiting the operating hours of HealthCare.gov, the enrollment platform; slashing funding for Navigators, individuals or organization that are trained to help consumers, small businesses, and their employees look for health coverage and complete eligibility/enrollment forms; and killing an outreach program that helps people sign up for health insurance.

Even though Republicans continually vilify "Obamacare," they never really articulate what their objections are beyond it being "Socialist." It seems like their real objection to the ACA is that Obama's name is attached to it, which I think we can all agree is an idiotic and incredibly juvenile response.

< And, not for nothing, but for those worried that our health care system is getting more "Socialist," that ship sailed long ago. We already have single-payer systems. They are called Medicare, Medicaid, and the Veterans' Administration. >

The narrative that the ACA is some sort of "Socialist" government takeover of the health care system is just not true. In fact, in its purest form, the ACA draws on market-based ideas. It's actually a conservative-minded approach because, done correctly, it keeps health care in the hands of the people rather than as a handout by the government – and we all know how much Republicans hate handing out things to people. :)

The centerpiece of the original ACA was competition which, in theory, should keep costs low and the level of service high. That's a pretty conservative concept, right?

To this end, the ACA established government-run marketplaces, or "exchanges." The legislation also limited discrimination (i.e., insurers must accept all applicants, regardless of their health or other factors such as the applicant's sex, pre-existing conditions, or occupation).

§§§

In truth, I do have empathy for members of Congress because solving our health care challenge cannot happen without coming to terms with some super brutal realities – which is not what voters generally want to hear.

What lawmakers need to understand, however, is that it just wastes valuable time to try to disguise these facts or sugarcoat the uphill battle we face. These are tough pills to swallow, but it is what it is.

From the very beginning, the ACA challenges were an example of the Butterfly Effect in action: Low enrollment in the exchanges LED TO private insurers leaving the exchanges which LED TO a lack of competition in the marketplaces.

To solve this, we have no choice but to drive people toward the exchanges. There are several ways we can achieve this, but the most obvious is that – brutal reality alert – we must make the penalty for not having health insurance harsh enough so people will choose insurance over the penalty.

The Trump administration cancelled the Individual Shared Responsibility Payment (a.k.a. the penalty for not having health insurance). Not only must we reinstate the penalty; we have to raise it. I know this is about as popular as a skunk at a church picnic, but it's just the truth.

Before it was cancelled, the penalty was only $695 a year or 2.5 percent of yearly household income, whichever was higher. That is not high enough. Too many people just chose to pay the fine, which undercut the entire premise of the ACA.

Another major thing we have to address are the subsidies involved. Because the ACA does not exclude coverage for pre-existing conditions, it has greatly benefited the least healthy Americans. However, this has come at a higher cost for healthy, higher-earning Americans (healthy, low earners receive their own subsidies, so they are not as affected).

The RAND Corporation, a nonprofit policy think tank partially funded by the U.S. government, sums up the problem this way:

> "One of the key challenges addressed by the *Affordable Care Act* is to make health insurance affordable for uninsured Americans without harming those who are already insured – and without increasing federal spending. To address this challenge, the ACA provides tax subsidies for qualified individuals purchasing health insurance in the ACA marketplaces and retains the existing tax exemptions for employer and employee contributions to employer-sponsored insurance.
>
> However, the two subsidy structures are quite different: Low-income individuals are eligible for the largest ACA marketplace subsidies, while higher-income workers benefit most from subsidies for employer-sponsored insurance."
>
> RAND "examined three alternatives for expanding insurance and lowering premiums, using tax revenue recovered by eliminating tax exemptions for employers and the employees who buy health insurance through their workplaces."

They found that "of the three alternatives, extending the *Affordable Care Act's* subsidies to all consumers and placing a floor on subsidies would have the greatest benefit: coverage for an additional 4 million people, premiums that would be 10 percent lower, and $14 billion saved annually in federal spending."

There are plenty of ways our health care challenge can be solved if we all cooperate, remain disciplined, and exercise a little patience. We just have to decide if we really want to.

So, how in the world do we actually strengthen the *Affordable Care Act*? Let's break this down.

You can find detailed information on each of these recommendations at www.1787forAmerica.org.

First, Protect the Basics!

† Under no circumstance can pre-existing conditions be excluded from health insurance coverage.

† If a parent's plan covers children, they can add or keep their children on their health insurance policy until they turn 26 years old.

† Pressure the states that are hold-outs to expand Medicaid. Give them the same federal funding as those that previously expanded.

† Do not raise the 3-to-1 rate band (premiums for those 55+ cannot be more than three times higher than those for younger people).

† Protect the ban on yearly or lifetime dollar limits on essential health benefits.

† Protect the cap on out-of-pocket spending. For 2021, these amounts are $8,550 for individuals and $17,100 for families.

† Protect the ACA ban on gender-based premiums and the requirement that all insurers cover preventive health services without co-pays.

- † Retain the Cadillac health insurance tax, which is instrumental in funding the ACA and keeping health care costs down.

Next, Be Proactive About the Potential Spoilers

Spoiler: Low Enrollment (i.e., Not Enough Healthy People in the Exchanges)

- † Extend the *Affordable Care Act's* subsidies to all consumers and place a floor on subsidies.
- † Reinstate and raise the *Individual Shared Responsibility Payment*, and strictly enforce the penalty. Garnish wages if necessary.
- † No longer require businesses to offer insurance to their employees.
- † Give states more flexibility to implement automatic enrollment programs.

Spoiler: Private Insurers Leaving the Exchanges

- † STABILIZATION: Make the risk corridor permanent.
- † STABILIZATION: Resume and protect the insurers' disbursements guaranteed under the risk adjustment program.
- † STABILIZATION: Encourage states to start reinsurance programs.
- † Protect the ability of insurance companies to "silver load."
- † Do not restrict narrowed network products.
- † Eliminate the ACA coverage mandate.

Spoiler: Lack of Competition in Many of the Online Insurance Marketplaces

- † Open contracts for government programs (i.e., Medicaid) only to insurers that participate in the exchanges.
- † Strengthen competition and market incentives to control costs.
- † Require insurers to participate in broad regions.
- † Don't waste time on selling insurance across state lines. It's not worth the trouble.

Get Quality Up and Costs Down: Step Two Get Spending Under Control

- † Establish a long-term global budget for total health care spending.
- † Encourage insurers to explore value-based insurance design in order to minimize overuse without discouraging necessary care.
- † Allow Americans to legally access lower-cost prescription drugs from Canada, including biologics and insulin.
- † Give Medicare the ability to negotiate prices with drug companies, but not the power to determine the drugs it must provide by law.
- † Modernize the 340B Drug Pricing Program, which effectively raises costs for patients and Medicare.
- † Encourage competition among drug manufacturers. Do not allow monopolistic pricing beyond what patent/exclusivity sets forth.
- † Do not allow drug manufacturers to offer financial assistance to persuade a patient to buy their product unless a generic version is not available.

- † Reverse Donald Trump's executive order requiring price transparency. It allows collusion to happen in plain sight.
- † Retain the Cadillac health insurance tax, which is instrumental in funding the ACA and keeping health care costs down.
- † Protect consumers from unfair balance billing. Encourage states to limit hospital prices for out-of-network emergency care.
- † Protect consumers from unfair balance billing in regard to air ambulances, helicopters, and ambulances that travel by road.
- † Instruct the Federal Trade Commission to crack down on monopoly providers in local health care markets.
- † Support public-private initiatives that develop superior drugs, vaccines and diagnostic tests.
- † Support tech firms that are working on innovative ways to deliver medical care to patients.
- † Embrace digital communication and analytics, as well as remote and computer-assisted diagnosis and treatment.

Bonus! These Are Other Health Care Recommendations

- † An ounce of prevention is worth a pound of cure. Let's get healthy, America!
- † Implement a federal policy that guarantees workers paid time off to care for their new babies or for a sick family member.
- † Confront the mental health challenges plaguing our nation, including an increase in the suicide rate and frequent mental distress.
- † Enforce the *Mental Health Parity and Addiction Equity Act of 2008.*
- † Require all doctors, dentists, nurse practitioners and other prescribers to receive training in the management of opioids and their misuse.

- † Ensure that our public health system has the wherewithal to cope with the physical and psychological consequences of any type of attack.
- † Address the lack of affordable long-term care and housing for middle-income seniors, which is quickly turning into a crisis.
- † Reinstate harsh fines against nursing homes that harm residents or place them in positions that put them at risk of injury.
- † Ensure that the National Institutes of Health is properly funded and supported.
- † Address the massive shortage we face in specialists who have the ability to diagnose and treat Superbugs (antibiotic-resistant microbes).

Why This Matters: Health Care

According to the Centers for Medicare and Medicaid Services, national health expenditures continued to grow in 2019 to $3.8 trillion and accounted for 17.7 percent of Gross Domestic Product (GDP). National health spending is projected to grow at an average rate of 5.4 percent per year for 2019-28 and to reach nearly $6.2 trillion by 2028. The health share of GDP is expected to rise from 17.7 percent in 2018 to 19.7 percent by 2028. To put this all into perspective, the GDP of France – the world's sixth largest economy – is $2.8 trillion.

§

According to *The Economist*, "Drugs are more expensive in America than anywhere else. A month's supply of Harvoni, which cures hepatitis C, costs $32,114 in America and $16,861 in Switzerland. Some cancer drugs can cost more than $150,000 a year."

§

A report from *Axios* found, "A majority of the health care industry's profits in the first three months of 2019 went to the top 10 companies, and 9 of those 10 companies were pharmaceutical manufacturers...12 of the most profitable drug companies in the first quarter (Q1) collectively reported more than $29 billion in profits."

§

Our federal spending on our major health care programs accounts for 27 percent of our non-interest spending. That number jumps to 40 percent by 2048, thanks to rising costs and an aging population. Already, almost half of our health care spending comes from government sources and is predominately for older Americans. As baby boomers continue to retire this is going to get a heck of a lot worse.

According to the Congressional Budget Office (CBO), "The number of people age 65 or older is now more than twice what it was 50 years ago. Over the next decade, as members of the baby-boom generation age and as life expectancy continues to increase, that number is expected to rise by about one-third...The costs of health care (adjusted to account for the aging of the population) are projected to grow faster than the economy over the long term. Although growth in health care spending has slowed in recent years, it still has grown faster than the economy, on average."

§

A tracking poll by the Kaiser Family Foundation, a nonprofit organization focused on national and global health issues, revealed that: "Among those currently taking prescription drugs, one-fourth of adults (24 percent) and seniors (23 percent) say it is difficult to afford their prescription drugs including about one in ten (overall and among seniors) saying it is 'very difficult.' Certain groups are much more likely to report difficulty affording medication, including those who are spending $100 or more a month on their prescriptions (58 percent), those who report being in fair or poor health (49 percent), those who take four or more prescription drugs (35 percent), and those with incomes less than $40,000 annually (35 percent). In addition, three in ten of all adults (29 percent) report not taking their medicines as prescribed at some point in the past year because of the cost and one in ten (8 percent) say their condition got worse as a result of not taking their prescription as recommended."

Bad Habit Seven

Foolishly Believing Promises Made by Politicians Who Have Zero Intention of Keeping Them, Allowing Our Problems to Get Progressively Worse

One of the worst habits we must break is foolishly believing the promises made by politicians who have zero intention of keeping them and, as a result, allow our problems to get progressively worse.

Sure, maybe hearing some of the pie-in-the-sky b.s. our politicians throw at us may help us sleep better *tonight*, but the perpetual charade of political theatre in this country depletes us of two things we simply do not have: time and money.

We have a decision to make, America, and we need to make it right now: Either we can continue to believe empty promises, or we can start intelligently solving our challenges once and for all. I strongly suggest the latter. We have to start clearing the deck on some of this stuff!

The last major immigration bill to pass Congress was the *Immigration Reform and Control Act of 1986*. Well over 30 years ago! Meanwhile, year after year, politicians act like they are gung-ho about tackling comprehensive immigration reform on the campaign trail but avoid it like the plague in-between elections – while billions and billions of dollars fall through the cracks.

This should come as no surprise. Immigration has always been the poster child of our nation's fly-swatting-policymaking approach. For decades, this topic has given our politicians the perfect opportunity to pander to their base with flawed terrorist rhetoric and fearmongering.

Instead of constructing intelligent and thoughtful ideas, many in Washington have repeatedly lobbed a rhetorical Molotov cocktail of anger, frustration, blame, and fear (I'm looking at you, Republicans).

Because they have zero ideas – beyond making America a cement-walled compound – they try to make the issue as complicated as possible by adding domestic disorder, national security, and America's "rule of law" into the mix. This is an effective means for them to gain support, because between cultural chaos, terrorism, and "illegal" aliens, almost every fear that Americans harbor can be exploited.

This tactic is extremely dangerous, however, because it prevents accurate, independent definitions of the prevailing challenges and further distorts the already blurry line that exists between them. The more tangled and convoluted these problems get, the more impossible they seem to solve.

But, believe me, they can be solved! Once we untangle all of the concerns, we can appropriately break down the elements of each and finally assign them achievable solutions. In this case especially, doing *something* cannot possibly be worse than never doing anything at all.

When it comes to immigration, it doesn't really matter what we believe *should* happen. Or even what is *fair.* We have a majorly complicated challenge on our hands, and the only way to truly find sustainable solutions for majorly complicated challenges is to build strategies within the context of the realities of the situation, *not what we wish the realities were*.

As we come up with solutions to this challenge, let's please not lose the essence of who we are. We are the country that welcomes the poor, the tired and the huddled masses. We are the country that celebrates life, liberty and justice for all. We are the country that perfected the right to peaceful assembly, freedom of speech and the free exercise of religion. We are the United States of America!

Not everyone can live here, and I totally get that. And there are people who will vehemently disagree with these recommendations – and I get that too. At the end of the day, even with the most open-armed proposals, there is simply no choice but to turn many people away from this glorious country....

.... but we don't have to be jerks about it. At our best, we're just not that kind of country. And, deep down, we all know it.

§§§

Okay everybody. Take a deep breath and don't immediately flip out when you read this section. Just please hear me out on this. I recognize this issue is one of our country's most heated and that some of these ideas are particularly flammable. All I ask is that you keep an open mind.

It's time to stop the nonsense and get realistic about this situation. Immigration is one of those issues where we desperately need to move beyond ideology and just do the math.

I think we can skip the *build a wall* v. *let everyone in* debate, because it's largely irrelevant at this point. I didn't cause this problem, nor did you. But, nevertheless, we have an estimated 10.5 million unauthorized immigrants living in America and they are not going anywhere – that's just a fact. I don't care what politicians promise or what cable news hosts say. It's just a fact.

The Pew Research Center tells us that "about two-thirds of unauthorized immigrants (66 percent) had lived in the U.S. for more than 10 years as of 2017, up from 41 percent 10 years earlier. The vast majority (83 percent) of unauthorized immigrants from Mexico have been in the country more than 10 years."

Love it or hate it, this is the reality of our situation. It is ludicrous to believe that we can round-up 10.5 million unauthorized immigrants and deport them all. Anyone who tries to convince you otherwise is just full of s^%#.

Don't believe me? Then consider this: Donald Trump – Mr. "Kick Everyone Out" himself – didn't even make a dent.

< Note: The numbers below can get confusing, so we need to really watch our terms here. The U.S. Department of Homeland Security defines removal as the "expulsion of an alien from the United States, based on grounds of inadmissibility or deportability" and apprehension

as "the arrest of a removable alien by the Department of Homeland Security. An administrative arrest is a civil arrest in the interior of the country, made when a person violates U.S. immigration laws. >

Despite Donald the Deporter's campaign promise to remove millions of undocumented immigrants immediately after his inauguration – – "What we are going to do is get the people that are criminal and have criminal records, gang members, drug dealers, where a lot of these people, probably 2 million, it could be even 3 million, we are getting them out of our country or we are going to incarcerate." – – the U.S. Customs and Border Patrol (CBP) and U.S. Immigration and Customs Enforcement (ICE) combined carried out only 288,093 removals in FY2017; 337,287 removals in FY2018; and 360,000 removals in FY2019.

The 288,093 removals in FY2017 were much lower than the removals in every single year of the Obama presidency, and the number of removals in FY2018 and FY2019 were lower than six of the eight years under President Obama. Plus, most of these removals were people trying to get *in*, not people who were already here. In FY2019, for example, 68 percent of removals were a consequence of an apprehension at the border.

ICE reported that they made 143,470 administration arrests in FY2017, which is less than half of the 297,898 made in 2009, the year President Obama took office. ICE made 158,581 administrative arrests in FY2018 and 143,099 in FY2019. Hmmm.... let's see...143,099 is only 1.4 percent of the 10,500,000 unauthorized immigrants in these United States. 1.4 percent. Are you getting my drift yet?

The CBP reported 851,508 apprehensions at the southwest border in FY2019, the highest number since 2007 but still far less than apprehensions under Presidents George H.W. Bush and Bill Clinton, and the first six years of George W. Bush's presidency (the peak was 1,643,679 in 2000, under Clinton). Fifty-six percent of those apprehended in FY2019 were traveling in families, and 71 percent were from El Salvador, Guatemala and Honduras (the "Northern Triangle" countries).

And let's be honest, despite what they say publicly, it doesn't appear that anyone in Washington even really *wants* to round-up unauthorized immigrants and deport them – even if we had the logistical capacity to do it, which we don't.

In its 2019 *Enforcement and Removal Operations* report, ICE reported its operations were "significantly impacted" by the "high volume of migration, including unprecedented numbers of family unit and Unaccompanied Alien Children (UAC) arrivals." This "stretched both Enforcement and Removal Operations (ERO) resources and those of the entire U.S. government to the breaking point and created a severe humanitarian crisis and border security crisis that continues to cripple the immigration system."

Does anyone honestly believe we can add 10.5 million more people to this turmoil?

§§§

There are Two Very Distinct Immigration Issues Here:

Immigration Issue One: Authorized Immigration
Immigration Issue Two: Unauthorized Immigration

Immigration Issue One: Authorized Immigration

Let's deal with authorized immigration first. Immigrants have always greatly enhanced America, both culturally and economically, and they continue to add tremendous value to our country. Immigrants strengthen America's academic communities, lead in scientific and technological innovation, and elevate our economic development by starting new businesses, creating new jobs, and patenting intellectual property.

To ensure our long-term economic health and to remain globally competitive, we should offer a Permanent Resident Card (Green Card) to every single foreign student that receives a science, technology, engineering or mathematics (STEM) degree from an American university.

We are just leaving money on the table if we don't. Why in the world would we educate smart, talented people over here, then send them away to use their skills and knowledge to compete with us?

The number of these visas will change on a yearly basis but, as an example, in the 2019-20 school year there were 1,075,496 international students in higher education in the United States: 220,542 studied Engineering; 205,207 studied Math and Computer Science; 84,440 studied Social Sciences; 81,971 studied Physical and Life Sciences; and 13,134 studied Agriculture.

Whatever visas we extend to STEM international graduates will go against the new yearly national limit we set for all immigration categories. (Please re-read that sentence! This is a huge point.)

Which brings us to the next step: finding a rational balance. Immigration is just like Goldilocks and those bowls of porridge. Too little immigration will stunt our economic growth and global competitiveness. Too much immigration will increase inequality, stress our social systems, and ultimately become counterproductive. Therefore, we have to find the balance that is *just right* (you will find my recommendations for the perfect balance later in this section).

As you'll see when you look at the new limits, our system will now be a merit-based system, which means no more random lottery. Only U.S. citizens can sponsor a foreign spouse, parent, unmarried child 25 years of age or younger, or an adopted orphan (or to be adopted). No other family member can be sponsored, and Lawful Permanent Residents (LPR) can no longer provide sponsorship. The naturalization process will stay the same as it is now.

There are many, many reasons why this approach is critical for our economic future, but here are a few:

§

Immigrants to the United States have been awarded 35 percent of the Nobel Prizes won by Americans in chemistry, medicine and physics between 1901 and 2020. In 2016, six Americans won the Nobel Prize in economics and scientific fields, and all six were immigrants to the U.S.

§

New American Economy, a bipartisan research fund, found that, in 2019, "44.6 percent, or 223 companies, in the Fortune 500 were founded by immigrants or their children. Of those companies, 101 were founded directly by foreign-born individuals while another 122 were founded by the children of immigrants." These companies "brought in $6.1 trillion in revenue. To put it in context, that figure is greater than the GDP of many developed countries – including Japan, Germany, and the United Kingdom. In fact, a country with a GDP equal to the revenues of the New American Fortune 500 firms would be the third largest economy in the world, behind only the United States and China."

The report continues: "These companies are a strong driver of job creation." Together, these companies employ over 13.5 million people – a population that would rank as the fifth largest state in the country, just after New York but easily beating Pennsylvania." All told, 3.2 million immigrants run their own businesses.

§

A study from the National Bureau of Economic Research, a private nonprofit research organization, shows that "immigrant inventors are especially productive and that the technology areas in which they are active exhibit higher levels of growth over the long run." Their evidence is "consistent with the view that immigrant inventors had a substantial positive macroeconomic impact through their influence on U.S. inventiveness."

§

Another study, from two researchers at the London School of Economics, found that American cities/regions that had more immigrants in the past are much better off in terms of income, unemployment, poverty, and education than those with less: "Counties with a more heterogeneous population composition over 130 years ago are significantly richer today, whereas counties that were strongly polarized at the time of the migration waves have endured persistent negative economic effects."

§

According to a comprehensive report by The National Academies of Sciences, Engineering and Medicine – which was established by an Act of Congress as a private, nongovernmental institution to advise the nation on issues related to science and technology – "Immigrants influence the rate of innovation in the economy, which potentially affects long-run economic growth. While research in this area is very recent, literature on the topic as a whole indicates that immigrants are more innovative than natives; more specifically, high-skilled immigrants raise patenting per capita, which is likely to boost productivity and per capita economic growth. Immigrants appear to innovate more than natives not because of greater inherent ability but due to their concentration in science and engineering fields."

§

A study from the National Foundation for American Policy, a nonprofit, non-partisan research organization, found that "without international students, the number of students pursuing graduate degrees (master's and PhD) in fields such as computer science and electrical engineering would be small given the size of the U.S. economy. In 2015, at U.S. universities there were only 7,783 full-time U.S. graduate students in electrical engineering, compared to 32,736 full-time international students. Similarly, in computer science, in 2015, there were only 12,539 full-time U.S. graduate students compared to 45,790 international graduate students at U.S. universities."

Immigration Issue Two: Unauthorized Immigration

To clear a pathway for this new merit-based system, we must aggressively deal with unauthorized immigration.

Sometimes we are confronted with a problem that has no great solution. Therefore, we simply have to do the best we can under extremely challenging circumstances. So it is with our unauthorized immigration situation. Is it ideal to give millions of people amnesty in one fell swoop? No. Is it the most practical solution we have out of a list of really bad ideas? Yes.

< Note: I'm not going to insult you by trying to disguise amnesty in a less objectionable phrase like "pathway to citizenship." We are all adults here and you are no fool. We all know these are essentially the same thing – so let's just cut the innuendo and political double-speak and save everyone time by just being honest and upfront. >

This is a Two-Part Process:

Unauthorized Immigration Part One: Mitigate the Current Situation by Clearing the Deck

Unauthorized Immigration Part Two: Put Mechanisms in Place to Prevent History from Repeating Itself

Before anything else, we have to clear the deck. The best way – actually, the only way – to achieve this is to offer a one-shot amnesty deal (à la President Ronald Reagan) to every unauthorized, non-criminal person who is already here.

In 1986, Congress passed – and President Reagan signed – the *Immigration Reform and Control Act*. This is a great template to follow. If unauthorized immigrants can establish that they have resided in the United States for five continuous years, they will be granted temporary resident status. This status will allow previously unauthorized immigrants to live, work and travel in the United States legally. The status moves from temporary resident status to permanent residency status after eighteen months and then to citizenship five years later.

Every individual will undergo a thorough background check to identify any criminals to be deported (individuals with convictions for a felony or three misdemeanors are ineligible for the program and will be deported right away). Those deemed eligible are required to register for military selective service and will be granted amnesty, which forgives their acts of illegal immigration and other related illegal acts such as driving and working with false documents.

Unlike Reagan's 1986 plan, those granted temporary resident status will not be required to pay back taxes, learn English, take a medical exam or pay any fines. These requirements are just not realistic. We are not doing this for the fun of it – we are trying to solve a problem. We *want* people to take advantage of this program and the majority of them simply cannot afford back taxes and fines. For now, the only cost associated with the new status should be the actual cost involved to process the applications.

This offer is a one-shot deal. After we implement the amnesty program, we have to drastically crack down on any remaining undocumented individuals who live and work in this country, which will be much easier because there will be fewer people to deal with.

Those who choose not to participate will be deported immediately when identified, and they will never again be given the chance to receive legal status in America.

It is critical that we don't get into this position again and we need to take extensive measures to ensure that we won't. To this end, we will implement strict prevention mechanisms, including harsh financial fines on employers who employ unauthorized immigrants, and a smart, comprehensive border security strategy (more on this in a minute).

Since amnesty is such a turbo-charged, super controversial issue, let's untangle the prevailing concerns and false premises:

Concern One: National Security

Protecting our borders is a high priority and an amnesty plan will only help that endeavor. Many of the people coming back and forth from Mexico are not new to our country – they are going back and forth to see their families. If they were legally allowed to travel, it would *increase* our level of national security because they could travel without fear and in broad daylight through established borders.

This also frees up resources to fix the current humanitarian crisis at the border, as well as help us keep unauthorized immigrants from entering America after our amnesty program is in place.

Concern Two: Domestic Disorder

There is a deep, pervasive fear in some Americans. The fear that something really bad is going to happen if we allow people into our country that speak, dress, worship or look different – and it speaks directly to our unease of the unknown. But in the context of unauthorized immigration, it makes no sense.

Lest we forget, 10.5 million undocumented immigrants already live here, and things are going pretty smoothly between us.

Obviously, this is not the narrative that many Republican politicians sling – when they find the one man from Mexico who murdered someone in the Midwest, then plaster the horrific story all over the television in election years. Okay, maybe that one man did murder someone but, in a broader sense, this narrative is just not true.

A study conducted jointly by four universities, published in the *Journal of Ethnicity in Criminal Justice*, discovered this:

> "Research has shown little support for the enduring proposition that increases in immigration are associated with increases in crime. Although classical criminological and neoclassical economic theories would predict immigration to increase crime, most empirical research shows quite the opposite.
>
> We investigate the immigration-crime relationship among metropolitan areas over a 40-year period from 1970 to 2010. Our goal is to describe the ongoing and changing association between immigration and a broad range of violent and property crimes. Our results indicate that immigration is consistently linked to decreases in violent (e.g., murder) and property (e.g., burglary) crime throughout the time period."

The Marshall Project, a nonprofit journalism organization, extended the study's data up to 2016, showing "that crime fell more often than it rose even as immigrant populations grew almost across the board...In general, the study's data suggests either that immigration has the effect of reducing average crime, or that there is simply no relationship between the two."

Another study by two prominent sociologists, published in the journal *Criminology*, confirms those findings:

> "Undocumented immigration does not increase violence. Rather, the relationship between undocumented immigration and violent crime is generally negative, although not significant in all specifications. Using supplemental models of victimization data and instrumental variable methods, we find little evidence that these results are due to decreased reporting or selective migration to avoid crime. We consider the theoretical and policy implications of these findings against the backdrop of the dramatic increase in immigration enforcement in recent decades."

The Cato Institute, a think tank, found that "all immigrants are less likely to be incarcerated than natives relative to their shares of the population. Even illegal immigrants are less likely to be incarcerated than native-born Americans."

In another report, they found that "the homicide conviction rate for illegal immigrants was 16 percent below that of native-born Americans in Texas in 2015. The conviction rates for illegal immigrants were 7.9 percent and 77 percent below that of native-born Americans for sex crimes and larceny, respectively. For all criminal convictions in Texas in 2015, illegal immigrants had a criminal conviction rate 50 percent below that of native-born Americans. Legal immigrants had a criminal conviction rate 66 percent below that of native-born Americans."

In his presidential announcement speech, Donald Trump famously said: "When Mexico sends its people, they're not sending their best...They're sending people that have lots of problems, and they're bringing those problems...They're bringing drugs. They're bringing crime. They're rapists."

This is just complete b.s. Out of the 404,142 apprehensions by U.S. Border Patrol agents along the border in FY2018, 6,698 of the people arrested by U.S. Customs and Border Patrol had been convicted of one or more crimes, whether in the United States or abroad, before being intercepted by U.S. Border Patrol. That's just 1.7 percent.

It's also important to remember that the criminal records of these people include both violent and nonviolent offenses, including illegal entry or reentry into the United States – which 59 percent of these people had been arrested for.

Oh! And while we're on the subject, although we definitely need to keep a close eye on them, there is also no "infestation" of the street gang Mara Salvatrucha (MS-13) coming through our borders, or even terrorists for that matter.

In FY2018, U.S. Border Patrol agents arrested 808 non-Americans at the border who were affiliated with *any* gang, 413 of whom were supposedly affiliated with MS-13. There are around 33,000 violent street gangs, motorcycle gangs, and prison gangs criminally active in America today, with an estimated 10,000 of them being members of MS-13. But most people who join MS-13 in the United States are not migrants, but rather young kids who were born here.

In regard to terrorists, the U.S. State Department says that "there was no credible evidence indicating international terrorist groups established bases in Mexico, worked directly with Mexican drug cartels, or sent operatives via Mexico into the United States…the U.S. southern border remains vulnerable to potential terrorist transit, although terrorist groups likely seek other means of trying to enter the United States."

Ironically, the State Department is more concerned with our border with Canada, which has been known to be the home of "violent extremists inspired by terrorist groups such as ISIS and al-Qaida and their affiliates and adherents." Although the numbers are still small, the U.S./Canadian border has been a more prevalent gateway for suspected terrorists, although most still come to the United States by air.

Analysis by the Cato Institute found that "zero people were murdered or injured in terror attacks committed on U.S. soil by special interest aliens who entered illegally from 1975 through the end of 2017. However, seven special interest aliens who initially entered illegally have been convicted of planning a terrorist attack on U.S. soil. They all entered illegally from Canada or jumped ship in American ports before the list of special interest countries even existed. None of them successfully carried out their attacks and none illegally crossed the Mexican border."

FALSE PREMISE ONE: IMMIGRANTS TAKE OUR JOBS AND LOWER OUR WAGES

The American people are my number one priority. So, as we figure out the best way to navigate the realities of globalization and immigration, it is super important that we thoroughly understand the impact each of these have on *every* American.

To that end, what effect do immigrants truly have on the American workforce? Two studies from IZA World of Labor, a German-based economic research institute, address the question of whether immigrants take the jobs of native-born workers.

The first, conducted jointly with George Washington University and Temple University, found that "immigrants – of all skill levels – do not significantly affect native employment in the short term and boost employment in the long term."

It goes on to say: "Immigrants who are self-employed or entrepreneurs directly create new jobs. Immigrant innovators create jobs indirectly within a firm, leading to long-term job growth. New immigrants fill labor shortages and keep markets working efficiently. High-skilled immigrants contribute to technological adaptation and low-skilled immigrants to occupational mobility, specialization, and human capital creation; both create new jobs for native workers. By raising demand, immigrants cause firms and production to expand, resulting in new hiring."

The second study, conducted jointly with University of California, Davis, says:

> "Politicians, the media, and the public express concern that immigrants depress wages by competing with native workers,

> but 30 years of empirical research provide little supporting evidence to this claim. Most studies for industrialized countries have found no effect on wages, on average, and only modest effects on wage differentials between more and less educated immigrant and native workers. Native workers' wages have been insulated by differences in skills, adjustments in local demand and technology, production expansion, and specialization of native workers as immigration rises.
>
> Immigration has a very small effect on the average wages of native workers. There is little evidence of immigration lowering wages of less educated native workers. In the long term, immigration, especially of high-skilled workers, increases innovation and the skill mix, with potentially positive productivity effects. In many countries, the share of graduate workers is higher for immigrants than for native workers. Firms have absorbed immigrants by adopting appropriate technologies, expanding production, and moving native workers into more communication-intensive jobs."

Another study by the National Bureau of Economic Research shows that "H-1B-driven increases in STEM workers in a city were associated with significant *increases* in wages paid to college educated natives. Wage increases for non-college educated natives are smaller but still significant. (The researchers) did not find significant effects on employment. They also found that STEM workers increased housing rents for college graduates, which eroded part of their wage gains. Together, these results imply a significant effect of foreign STEM on total factor productivity growth in the average U.S. city between 1990 and 2010."

In yet another study from the National Bureau of Economic Research, Britta Glennon, an Assistant Professor at the Wharton School of Business at the University of Pennsylvania, discovered that:

> "Skilled immigration restrictions may have secondary consequences that have been largely overlooked in the immigration debate: multinational firms faced with visa

> constraints have an offshoring option, namely, hiring the labor they need at their foreign affiliates. If multinationals use this option, then restrictive migration policies are unlikely to have the desired effects of increasing employment of natives, but rather have the effect of offshoring jobs. Combining visa data and comprehensive data on US multinational firm activity, she found that restrictions on H-1B immigration caused foreign affiliate employment increases at the intensive and extensive margins, particularly in Canada, India, and China."

This is a huge potential landmine because "U.S. multinational firms are responsible for 80 percent of U.S. research and development and employ about one-fourth of U.S. private employees."

According to a comprehensive report by The National Academies of Sciences, Engineering and Medicine, "when measured over a period of more than ten years, the impact of immigration on the wages of natives overall is very small."

> "While many studies conclude that, economy wide, the impact of immigration on average wages and employment is small, a high degree of consensus exists that specific groups are more vulnerable than others to inflows of new immigrants. Theory predicts that the workers already in the receiving labor market who are the closest substitutes for immigrants are most likely to experience immigration-induced wage declines.
>
> Some studies have found sizable negative short-run wage impacts for high school dropouts, the native-born workers who in many cases are the group most likely to be in direct competition for jobs with immigrants. Even for this group, however, there are studies finding small to zero effects, likely indicating that outcomes are highly dependent on prevailing conditions in the specific labor market into which immigrants flow or the methods and assumptions researchers use to examine the impact of immigration. The literature continues to

> find less favorable effects for certain disadvantaged workers and for prior immigrants than for natives overall."

False Premise Two: Immigration Costs the United States Way More Than It Benefits Us

Drilling down on the numbers involved in this analysis is a super complex, unsatisfying task. For example, both critics and supporters of immigration use the exact same comprehensive report by The National Academies of Sciences, Engineering and Medicine to defend their positions. This is a perfect illustration of how intricate the issue is, and how there are costs and benefits on both sides.

For instance, the report from the National Academies of Sciences, Engineering and Medicine found that lower-income households benefit from lower consumption costs (i.e., clothing, housing, food) that exist because of immigrant labor. But, at the same time, these same people are the most affected by any negative wage impact that may occur because of immigrant labor. In the end, one of the report's double-edged conclusions was that "through lower prices, low-skilled immigration created positive net benefits to the U.S. economy during the last two decades of the 20th century, while also generating a redistribution of wealth from low- to high-skilled native-born workers."

That said, on balance the report determines that "immigration is integral to the nation's economic growth." The report continues:

> "Immigration supplies workers who have helped the United States to avoid the problems facing stagnant economies created by unfavorable demographics – in particular, an aging (and, in the case of Japan, a shrinking) workforce. Moreover, the infusion by high-skilled immigration of human capital has boosted the nation's capacity for innovation, entrepreneurship, and technological change. The literature on immigrants and

> innovation suggests that immigrants raise patenting per capita, which ultimately contributes to productivity growth. The prospects for long-run economic growth in the United States would be considerably dimmed without the contributions of high-skilled immigrants."

One of the stronger points of the report is that, while first generation immigrants add a certain amount of cost to the system, this is balanced by the following generations. By the second generation, America sees a net positive result, thanks to an increase in education levels and, as a result, wages.

The Cato Institute researched the issue of immigrants and social welfare programs and discovered that:

> "Immigrant consumption of welfare benefits through means-tested or entitlement programs is a complex issue as myriad programs have different eligibility requirements that vary by state. All immigrants consume 39 percent fewer welfare benefits relative to all natives, largely because they are less likely to receive Social Security retirement benefits and Medicare. Immigrants consume 27 percent fewer benefits relative to natives with similar incomes and ages...the per capita cost of providing welfare to immigrants is substantially less than the per capita cost of providing welfare to native-born Americans."

The Institute on Taxation & Economic Policy, a nonprofit, nonpartisan think tank, took a look at undocumented immigrants' state and local tax contributions. They found:

† Undocumented immigrants contribute significantly to state and local taxes, collectively paying an estimated $11.64 billion a year. Contributions range from almost $2.2 million in Montana with an estimated undocumented population of 4,000 to more than $3.1 billion in California, home to more than 3 million undocumented immigrants.

† Undocumented immigrants nationwide pay on average an estimated 8 percent of their incomes in state and local taxes (this is their effective state and local tax rate). To put this in perspective, the top 1 percent of taxpayers pay an average nationwide effective tax rate of just 5.4 percent.

† Granting legal status to all undocumented immigrants in the United States as part of a comprehensive immigration reform and allowing them to work legally would increase their state and local tax contributions by an estimated $2.1 billion a year. Their nationwide effective state and local tax rate would increase to 8.6 percent.

False Premise Three:

Amnesty is a Magnet that Will Increase the Number of Undocumented Workers

Critics of President Reagan's amnesty program say his actions led to the quadruple-the-size problem we face today. Their logic is that Reagan's decision made us look soft on undocumented workers and, therefore, enticed a brand-new wave of them to flood through our borders.

Although the number of undocumented workers did significantly increase in the years after Reagan's plan, it was not due to the amnesty component of the plan. The main flaw in the 1986 amnesty plan was this: Companies continued to hire undocumented workers and were not appropriately penalized. Simply put, the law was not enforced.

After Reagan's law passed, it quickly became clear that corporations had become dependent on Mexican migrant labor and continued to have a huge appetite for undocumented workers and their low pay scale.

Unfortunately – and for a variety of reasons, including heavy lobbying by powerful industries like hospitality, agriculture and construction – law enforcement on every level chose to look the other way. Basically 2.9 million unauthorized immigrants were granted amnesty without a serious plan to stop history from repeating itself. That cannot happen again.

We have to hold individuals and companies who use undocumented workers accountable. Two obvious ways to do this is to demand mandatory E-Verify and enforce super harsh financial fines on these employers.

Not only are companies that hire them for below-market wages breaking the law, but they are also committing unfair trade practices against their competition. They are cheating – straight up. Which brings up an interesting point…I wonder why the leaders of these companies aren't called ugly names by Republicans and being accused of violating the U.S. "Rule of Law." After all, they are actually Americans breaking American laws.

This crackdown will go a long way in solving this problem. It's true that many people are coming to America because they are fleeing the terror of their own country, but many are coming for the same reason they always have: Economics.

A 2018 analysis of the migration patterns of people from Guatemala, El Salvador and Honduras – conducted by the Inter-American Development Bank (IDB), the region's central development bank – found that "seven of every 10 migrants list economic reasons as one of the main motivations behind their decision (74 percent)." For Guatemalans, that number was 87 percent. Guatemalans also tend to regard migration to the United States as temporary. Only 34 percent said they intended to stay in the United States.

To me, this next discovery is fascinating: "In 2018, international remittances < or, money migrants send back home > to the region exceeded $19 billion, which is more than a fifth of total remittances in Latin America and the Caribbean (LAC). These remittances accounted for 20.7 percent of the Gross Domestic Product (GDP) in El Salvador, 20.1 percent in Honduras, and 12.1 percent in Guatemala, compared to less than 2 percent for LAC and 1 percent worldwide." Sixty-eight percent of this money was sent back to parents.

Have you ever wondered why we don't have immigration issues with Canada? Canadians just sit up there, calmly behaving themselves.

Easy answer: Unlike Mexico, 42 percent of the Canadian population doesn't live in poverty.

One thing is for certain, as long as a poorer country with willing, cheap labor borders a richer country that provides a market for that labor, workers will cross the border. It's just that simple. If jobs are available, workers come to fill them. If jobs are not available, workers stay home. It's no coincidence that apprehensions at our border started to decline significantly in 2007 – the very same year the 2007-2009 Financial Crisis hit the United States.

Even though living in America is wonderful, many of those who cross the border would probably prefer to create a comfortable life in their own countries, with their own families. Believe it or not, America is not the only country that embraces nationalism.

False Premise Four:
Undocumented Workers Violate Our "Rule of Law"

Critics argue that since it is against American law to be an undocumented worker in this country, these workers are inherently criminals.

This argument is absurd. It's time we demonstrated a little empathy and a lot of compassion. Many Americans out there are undoubtably against the amnesty idea, but that doesn't mean those same people cannot, or should not, have sympathy for our southern neighbor. Sometimes we forget, but it is entirely possible to hold two ideas in our heads at the same time.

Universally, our deepest desire is to create the best life possible for our families. Answer this question, truthfully: If you were born in Mexico and your children were living in abject poverty [and, by the way, you make $6.85 a day (the minimum wage in Mexico), are feeding your family rice and beans for the second month in a row, living in a house with no running water, all while dodging bullets from dangerous drug cartels], what would you do to create a better life for them?

Easy answer: Every single one of us would do anything – anything – necessary to provide them a better future. Build a wall…we would dig a tunnel. That would not make us criminals.

Don't make me break out *The New Colossus*, the poem that is mounted on the Statue of Liberty:

Not like the brazen giant of Greek fame,
With conquering limbs astride from land to land;
Here at our sea-washed, sunset gates shall stand
A mighty woman with a torch, whose flame
Is the imprisoned lightning, and her name
Mother of Exiles. From her beacon-hand
Glows world-wide welcome; her mild eyes command
The air-bridged harbor that twin cities frame.
"Keep, ancient lands, your storied pomp!" cries she
With silent lips.
Give me your tired, your poor,
Your huddled masses yearning to breathe free,
The wretched refuse of your teeming shore.
Send these, the homeless, tempest-tost to me,
I lift my lamp beside the golden door!

§§§

So often, when controversial topics are raised, our deeply ingrained, robotic reflexes kick in and inhibit the constructive, open-minded conversations that are essential to finding creative, sustainable solutions.

We need to fight against this instinct because, with issues like immigration, nonconventional alternatives that get us the biggest bang for our buck – such as offering financial and governance help to countries destabilized by violence and poverty and, as a result, improving the lives of people within their *own* countries – are key to our success. This type of idea would not only slow the flow of immigrants coming to America and strengthen our national security, but the United States would reap countless benefits of being surrounded by strong, stable economies.

I can practically hear the outrage this suggestion is causing across America. Those knee-jerk reactions are kicking in so fast that people are practically tripping over themselves. Why in the world would we give money to Mexico, El Salvador, Honduras and Guatemala when we have tons of our own troubles over here? We've got our own problems lady!

The argument is valid, but think about it: At a time when the number of Central Americans crossing the southwest U.S. border continues to increase due to horrific conditions in their own countries, is it smart to *cut* their foreign aid? Which only makes the problem in those countries *worse*? Which will surely send *even more* people our way? Does that make sense to you? #TheButterflyEffect

Creating a better and safer environment for people within their own countries is not a new, earthshattering concept. We can build on existing programs like the Central America Regional Security Initiative (CARSI), a program the U.S. government has supported in Central America since 2008.

The Congressional Research Service (CRS) explains that CARSI "provides the seven nations of the isthmus (El Salvador, Costa Rica, Belize, Guatemala, Honduras, Nicaragua and Panama) with equipment, training, and technical assistance to support immediate law enforcement operations. CARSI is also designed to strengthen the long-term capacities of Central American governments to address security challenges and the underlying social and political factors that contribute to them."

CARSI has mixed reviews, but it's a pretty good start. In FY2018, the Department of State reported on the program:

CARSI "enhanced local economies by boosting private sector exports and domestic sales by more than $73 million and helping businesses generate more than 18,000 new jobs; strengthened the rule of law through support to more than 1,200 civil society organizations, training to more than 1,700 human rights defenders, improving case management in more than 300 local courts, and training more than 15,000 judicial personnel: and contributed, with host government and other donor efforts, to dramatic decreases in homicide rates in El Salvador and Honduras, including through cutting-edge crime and violence prevention programming, such as after-school and pre-employment services and support to more than 140,000 at-risk youth across the region.

Since 2015, there have been dramatic decreases in homicides in communities that pair the United States Agency for International Development's (USAID) citizen security programs with the Department of State's law-enforcement efforts. In several of these locations, where violence is driving out-migration, homicide rates have dropped between 40 and 73 percent since 2015. Additionally, in FY 2018, the migration rates for beneficiaries of a USAID agriculture program in Honduras were approximately half that of the surrounding population."

This is vital to our national security. The CRS warns: "Absent such efforts, conditions are likely to remain poor in several Central American countries, contributing to periodic instability that – as demonstrated by the increasing number of migrants, asylum seekers, and refugees from the region arriving at the U.S. border – is likely to affect the United States."

Regardless of whether a potential solution is ultimately implemented or not, it's never a bad idea to at least consider adventurous alternatives as opposed to consistently going back to ideas that continually fail.

Just think about Donald Trump's beloved "Wall." To me, "The Wall" is nothing more than a mean, racist dog whistle that is offensive and annoying. But even if you're all in on "The Wall," you must admit that it wasn't that difficult to dream up. That concept is one of the first things preschool kids figure out with their Legos.

But beyond that, "The Wall" is ridiculous in its ineffectiveness. During the Trump administration, we spent billions and billions and billions on this damn thing, never mind that smugglers have repeatedly cut through it with a basic saw that you can buy at Walmart.

In fact, U.S. Customs and Border Patrol report that, as of the beginning of March 2022, "The Wall" had been breached by Mexican smugglers 3,272 over the previous three years. In that time, we Americans paid over $2.6 million to repair the various breaches.

At one point, engineers noticed that a section of "The Wall" that was meant to be a showcase model for future projects – built for $42 million by a private company that had been awarded around $1.7 billion in federal contracts for border wall construction – had erosion at its base and may yet fall into the Rio Grande river.

Better still, this particular "Wall" design requires hundreds of storm gates be installed to prevent flash floods from literally knocking it over. Because of weather patterns, these storm gates must be left open for practically the entire summer. Which kind of defeats the purpose, don't ya think?

Have I mentioned that this proposed Swiss cheese of a "Wall" was estimated to cost over $30 million per mile? Is this where we want our tax dollars to go? As of the summer of 2020, the Trump administration had already spent $15 billion on the project – of American (not Mexican) taxpayer money.

Of this fabulous plan, the Government Accountability Office (GAO) released a report that says: "Department of Homeland Security (DHS) plans to spend billions of dollars developing and deploying new barriers along the southwest border. However, by proceeding without key information on cost, acquisition baselines, and the contributions of previous barrier and technology deployments, DHS faces an increased risk that the Border Wall System Program will cost more than projected, take longer than planned, or not fully perform as expected."

Well, that's just perfect, isn't it?

§§§

My recommendations for our immigration challenges are at the end of this section, and I think they are pretty solid, if I do say so myself. However, as with every other issue, we need to watch carefully for any unintended consequences our fabulous ideas may bring.

#TheButterflyEffect

For example, one of the recommendations is to help Mexico secure its porous 570-mile border with Guatemala.

Mexico knows how to keep people out of their country because they have done it before. According to a 2015 report by the Migration Policy Institute, a think tank, "The United States and Mexico apprehended nearly 1 million Salvadoran, Guatemalan, and Honduran migrants from 2010-2015, deporting more than 800,000 of them, including more than 40,000 children."

The report continues, "While the United States led in pace and number of apprehensions of Central Americans in 2010-2014, Mexico pulled ahead in 2015. Amid increasingly muscular enforcement by Mexico, U.S. apprehensions of Central Americans for fiscal 2015 to date have fallen by more than half compared to the prior year. Many of those who previously would have made it to the U.S. border and been apprehended by the Border Patrol now are being intercepted by Mexican authorities."

This rise of apprehensions in Mexico was a result of *Programa Frontera Sur* (PFS), a.k.a. the *Southern Border Program*, which then-president of Mexico Enrique Peña Nieto implemented in 2014 under intense pressure from the United States.

Sounds like a promising way to decrease the number of unauthorized Central Americans who pass through Mexico on their way to America, right?

Not so fast. There was a huge downside to this crackdown: Many migrants simply sought alternative, but much more dangerous, routes. As a result, risk, bribes and smugglers fees significantly increased.

Much more concerning, this also led to massive breaches in humanitarian protection. *Reuters* reported that "in the year through June 2015, Mexico's National Commission on Human Rights (CNDH) logged 567 complaints of abuse by officials at the National Migration Institute (INM), up by 39 percent from the previous 12-month period."

Three years after the implementation of *Programa Frontera Sur* (PFS), the Washington Office on Latin America (WOLA), a research and advocacy organization, reported that:

> "Crimes and abuses against migrants traveling through Mexico continue to occur at alarming rates, and shelters have noted a more intense degree of violence in the cases they document.
>
> While Mexico's major organized criminal groups do not operate heavily in the Tenosique corridor, smaller criminal bands and Central American gang affiliates routinely rob, kidnap, and sexually assault migrants along this portion of the migration route. Migrant rights organizations in southern Mexico documented an increase in cases of migration and police authorities' abuse of migrants as a result of the *Southern Border Program*, including recent accounts of migration agents, who are supposed to be unarmed, using pellet guns and electrical shock devices."
>
> Five years on, WOLA found that "migrants transiting through southern Mexico continue to suffer assault, robbery, rape, and kidnapping at the hands of organized crime or common criminals…migrant rights defenders in Tenosique, Tabasco did report an alarming uptick in serious crimes against migrants, such as sexual violence and brutal kidnappings. Shelters and organizations that support victims who have filed criminal complaints before prosecutor's offices reported to us that prosecutors have taken little action to investigate these crimes or combat these criminal trends."

As we move forward, we desperately need to learn from past mistakes. In this case, it's literally a matter of life and death.

In 2000, President George W. Bush gave Mexico $1.4 billion to fight drug trafficking. The allocation of those funds looked somewhat promising on paper, with initiatives ranging from cutting-edge technological equipment to training for the Mexican police force, but the plan was ultimately ineffective in its isolation. After all, couldn't the same cutting-edge equipment used to stop drug smuggling also help greatly in keeping unauthorized immigrants out of the U.S.?

But, true to form, instead of getting the biggest bang for our buck by creating coordinated plans that work in conjunction with one another, the result was largely unproductive because we continued to develop them separately.

This uncoordinated approach guaranteed that our efforts to stop the flow of drugs from Mexico – the country that is still the primary source of heroin and methamphetamine in the United States – would be as wildly unsuccessful as our *War on Drugs* was in Colombia, where the U.S. spent 16 years and $10 billion.

Plan Colombia took aim at Colombian drug cartels and the left-wing insurgents, the Revolutionary Armed Forces of Colombia (FARC). The United States provided foreign, military, and diplomatic aid.

From one angle, *Plan Colombia* was a success. Colombia is now one of our greatest allies and active trading partners, and its economic growth increased to 3.3 percent in 2019. However, when you look at the outcome from the *production of drugs* angle, *Plan Colombia* failed miserably. Colombia's cocaine production and trafficking business still brings in over $4.5 billion a year, and Colombia is still the primary source of cocaine supply in the United States.

In a nutshell, our infusion of cash to Colombia made practically zero impact on diminishing drug production, although it made Colombia a safer place to vacation. So, in effect, the primary result of our effort is that the largest narcotic kingpins in the world have a much safer environment to manufacture their product.

And then there are those dang unintended consequences. Through it all, those who endured the greatest suffering in Colombia – as is almost always the case – were Colombia's people. Over 200,000 people died in the conflict between the Colombian government and the FARC, four million were displaced, and thousands simply disappeared.

At one point, three Colombian generals and over twenty Colombian officers and soldiers were fired over the alleged killing of innocent civilians. Evidently, to satisfy rebel body count quotas to earn promotions, time off, and additional pay, security forces murdered innocent people, planted weapons on their bodies and/or dressed them in guerilla fatigues to make them appear to be leftist insurgents, and then left them in unmarked graves. The commander of Colombia's army resigned over the scandal.

A joint study conducted by Amnesty International and the Fellowship of Reconciliation found that 47 percent of the reported civilian killings involved Colombian units financed by the United States.

And the examples just go on and on. In November 2005, the Department of Homeland Security launched the *Secure Border Initiative* (SBI), a comprehensive multi-year plan to secure America's borders and reduce illegal migration. Between FY2005 and FY2010 the SBI received around $4.5 billion in funding. $4.5 billion. With a B.

The original intent of the initiative was to provide more agents to patrol our borders; secure our ports of entry and enforce immigration laws; expand detention and removal capabilities to eliminate "catch and release" once and for all; implement a comprehensive and systemic upgrade of the technology used in controlling the border, including increased manned aerial assets, expanded use of Unmanned Aerial Vehicles (UAVs), and next-generation detection technology; increase investment in infrastructure improvements at the border – providing additional physical security to sharply reduce illegal border crossings; and to greatly increase interior enforcement of our immigration laws, including more robust worksite enforcement.

The results of the SBI were bleak. Actually I'm being generous. It was a complete failure. One major element of SBI was SBInet, which included a technology-based "virtual fence" to be constructed on the Southwestern border of the U.S. and Mexico.

Ultimately, an ill-equipped contractor (Boeing) mismanaged the oversight, used untested technology, and blew through budget after budget. After major delays, DHS ultimately cancelled the program.

Unfortunately, this move came after we had already spent over a billion dollars on the "virtual fence" alone.

According to the Government Accountability Office (GAO), "in January 2010, the number of new system defects identified over a 17-month period while testing was underway was generally increasing faster than the number of defects being fixed, not indicative of a maturing system. Given the program's shortcomings, in January 2010, the Secretary of Homeland Security ordered an assessment of the program, and in March 2010, the Secretary froze a portion of the program's fiscal year 2010 funding."

A billion here, a billion there. It is absolutely insane that we let them get away with this.

AMERICA!! WE HAVE GOT TO LEARN FROM THESE EXTREMELY EXPENSIVE MISTAKES AND GET SERIOUS ABOUT HOLDING PEOPLE ACCOUNTABLE!!

…especially now, because in July 2020 the Trump administration awarded a massive border security contract to a California technology start-up that claims it will use artificial intelligence to achieve yet another "virtual wall."

I agree that this *concept* should be part of our border security, but we need to watch this very, very closely so that it won't be another disaster like SBI.

So, let's review. The Trump administration authorized (well, actually stole it from the Department of Defense, but whatever) billions and billions and billions of dollars on a meager 317 miles of bollard, replacement, and/or secondary fencing. Our government spent 16 years and $10 billion making practically zero difference in Colombian drug production. We also blew billions on the now defunct *Secure Border Initiative*, with zero repercussions.

This nation has got to learn that just because our leaders approve the money for their lamebrain ideas, we are not suddenly on the fast track to resolution. In fact, it usually means just the opposite. Throwing good money after bad is a habit this country can no longer afford.

We Have to Find a Rational Balance for Authorized Immigration

It's just like Goldilocks and those bowls of porridge! Too little immigration will stunt our economic growth and global competitiveness. Too much immigration will increase inequality, stress our social systems, and ultimately become counterproductive. We have to find the balance that is *just right.*

1787 Proposes:

Permanent Resident (Green Card)

- † Allows you to live and work permanently in the United States.
- † You must have worked legally in the United States at least five years before applying. Requires 3 references from non-family, U.S. citizens.
- † First come, first served – with the exception of family members of U.S. citizens only, who have priority but still must follow the above rule.

The Yearly Number:

1,000,000 MINUS the number of STEM graduates MINUS the number of H-2A & H-2B Visas awarded MINUS the number of Refugees & Asylum-Seekers Visas given

Currently, around a million immigrants receive U.S. green cards each year. Fewer than half are new arrivals from other countries.

Permanent Workers (EB1 – EB5)

EB-1

Persons of extraordinary ability in the sciences, arts, education, business, or athletics; outstanding professors or researchers; and multinational executives and managers.

EB-2

Persons who are members of the professions holding advanced degrees or for persons with exceptional ability in the arts, sciences, or business.

EB-3

Professionals, skilled workers, and other workers.

EB-4

Certain religious workers, employees of U.S. foreign service posts, retired employees of international organizations, alien minors who are wards of courts in the United States,

EB-5

Business investors who invest $1 million or $500,000 (if the investment is made in a targeted employment area) in a new commercial enterprise that employs at least 10 full-time U.S. workers.

The Yearly Number: Unlimited, but all categories will now require a Labor Certification (i.e., a job offer from U.S. sponsor or, for EB-5, proof of investment and at least 10 full-time U.S. workers).

STEM Graduates

This is a new, separate category that will open up space in the EB categories for other important disciplines.

The Yearly Number: Unlimited

The number of these visas will change on a yearly basis but, as an example, in the 2019-20 school year there were 1,075,496 international students in higher education in the United States: 220,542 studied Engineering; 205,207 studied Math and Computer Science; 84,440 studied Social Sciences; 81,971 studied Physical and Life Sciences; and 13,134 studied Agriculture.

Temporary Worker

H-1B	Person in Specialty Occupation
H-1B1	Free Trade Agreement
H-3	Trainee or Special Education
L	Intracompany Transferee
O	Individual with Extraordinary Ability or Achievement
P-1	Individual or Team Athlete, or Entertainment Group
P-2	Artist or Entertainer (Individual or Group)
P-3	Artist or Entertainer (Individual or Group)
Q-1	Participant in an International Cultural Exchange Program

The Yearly Number: Unlimited, but all categories will now require a Labor Certification (i.e., job offer or specific event).

H-2A Temporary Agricultural Worker

† For temporary or seasonal agricultural work. Limited to citizens or nationals of designated countries, with limited exceptions, if determined to be in the United States interest.

† U.S. employers or U.S. agents who meet specific regulatory requirements can bring foreign nationals to the U.S. to fill

temporary agricultural jobs. A U.S. employer, a U.S. agent, or an association of U.S. agricultural producers named as a joint employer must petition on a prospective worker's behalf.

The Yearly Number: 225,000/year, up from 200,000/year

H-2B Temporary Non-Agricultural Worker

- † For temporary or seasonal non- agricultural work. Limited to citizens or nationals of designated countries, with limited exceptions, if determined to be in the United States interest.
- † U.S. employers or U.S. agents who meet specific regulatory requirements can bring foreign nationals to the U.S. to fill temporary nonagricultural jobs. A U.S. employer or U.S. agent must petition on a prospective worker's behalf.

The Yearly Number: 100,000/year, up from a cap of 66,000/year

Refugees & Legitimate Asylum Seekers

The Yearly Number: 100,000/year. This goes against the annual limit.

† Before applying for a visa, students and exchange visitors must be accepted by their schools or program sponsors.
† For Temporary Business and Tourism & Visit visas, begin using the same process as the Visa Waiver Program.

The Yearly Number: As Needed

Immigration
Plan of Action

You can find detailed information on each of these recommendations at www.1787forAmerica.org.

Protect

† Top Priority: Protect the American Worker!

† Secure Our Border! Implement a smart, comprehensive border security strategy. See the next section for details.

† Noncitizen veterans should never be removed from this country without careful, extensive review.

† Fix the family separation nightmare at the border – one of the vilest, most outrageous atrocities that has happened in our lifetimes.

† Lift our lamp beside the golden door once again: Support and protect refugees and legitimate asylum seekers.

† Offer financial and governance help to countries destabilized by violence and poverty. Improve and protect their lives in <u>their</u> <u>own</u> countries.

† Reform our overwhelmed immigration courts. Provide funding to help reduce the backlog.

† Support "sanctuary" jurisdictions as long as they do not actively interfere with federal immigration enforcement efforts.

† Fight hard against laws that blatantly violate the United States Constitution.

† The multiculturalism v. assimilation debate is silly. A person can adjust to a new culture without abandoning their own.

† Implement a hard-core vetting process to identify all unauthorized individuals with convictions for a felony and/or three misdemeanors.

Prosper

† Offer a one-shot amnesty deal (à la President Ronald Reagan) to every unauthorized, non-criminal person who is already here.

† Reinstate DACA immediately, just in case amnesty takes a while to pass.

† Offer a green card to every foreign student who receives a STEM degree from a U.S. university (this number goes against the yearly limit).

† Stop using "The Wall" as a metaphor, which is really just a mean, racist dog whistle.

Prevent

† Reorganize the yearly limits on authorized immigrants in all categories. No more lottery. Change the rules for sponsorship. (see the new limits directly after these recommendations)

† Enforce harsh financial fines on employers who employ unauthorized immigrants.

† Help Mexico secure its porous 570-mile border with Guatemala.

† Establish the federal immigration court as an "Article I" court outside the Justice Department.

† Pass a federal mandate requiring states to use E-Verify.

- † Implement a biometric entry-exit tracking system. Convene a bipartisan commission to decide how best to regulate facial recognition technology.
- † Expand the Visa Waiver Program (VWP) to the appropriate partners and allies.
- † Use of safety-net programs can be considered for citizenship, except those used "for a relatively short duration." All refugees exempt.

Secure Borders
Plan of Action

You can find detailed information on each of these recommendations at www.1787forAmerica.org.

- † Stop using "The Wall" as a metaphor. It's really just a mean, racist dog whistle that is offensive and annoying.
- † ...but build fencing where necessary.
- † After assessing and correcting past mistakes, utilize cutting-edge technology to strengthen border security and infrastructure.
- † Implement a biometric entry-exit tracking system. Convene a bipartisan commission to decide how best to regulate facial recognition technology.
- † Pass a federal mandate requiring states to use E-Verify.
- † Implement a hard-core vetting process to identify all unauthorized individuals with convictions for a felony and/or three misdemeanors.
- † Support and protect the Mérida Initiative & strengthen bilateral partnerships between Mexican and U.S. law enforcement agencies.
- † Enforce the Strengthen Opioid Misuse Prevention (STOP Act), which facilitates international interdiction efforts. Provide the USPS the funding necessary to achieve their objective.
- † Strengthen the Bureau of International Narcotics and Law Enforcement Affairs (INL).
- † Disrupt transnational crime and enforce strong criminal penalties against transnational criminal networks.
- † Help foreign governments build effective law enforcement institutions that counter transnational crime.

- † Combat corruption by helping governments and civil society build transparent and accountable public institutions.
- † Establish and implement international treaties for combating crime and provide tools for legal cooperation in criminal cases among countries.
- † Work with international partners to develop effective approaches to border and maritime security.
- † Disrupt and dismantle human trafficking networks before migrants reach the United States.
- † Support the International Law Enforcement Academy (ILEA).
- † Work with Canada to increase joint law enforcement efforts and strengthen cross-border security operations.
- † Promote economic prosperity along the southern border and STOP THIS TRADE WAR NONSENSE.
- † Continue to ensure that the border cities are among the safest in the country.
- † Continue to ensure a seamless process of sharing information between our intelligence agencies and other law enforcement.

Bad Habit Eight

Tolerating Shady Shenanigans From Our Leaders

– the 1787 Recommendations for
Government Reform are in *The Policy Guide* –

America, there are some seriously shady shenanigans going on. For the most part, I believe the best way to fight corrupt practices within our government is to just change the rules of the political game, like we're doing with 1787. After all, these corrupt practices are not the root of our problems…most are just unfortunate consequences of a severely broken system.

Unfortunately, there are certain things that are simply too destructive to our democracy to wait out. Every issue we face is important, but we have to get a handle on these things quickly because a strong, fair, healthy government is the bedrock of everything else we do.

Sorting through all of the government reform issues requires its own book so, with this section especially, I encourage you to take a look at the recommendations in *The Policy Guide*, then go to the 1787 website to read about the details of each.

However, there is room here for me to rant about three examples of government rot that are particularly insidious: the Citizens United decision, earmarks and lobbying.

The Citizens United decision is a disgrace to our democracy. C*itizens United v. Federal Election Commission* is a 2010 Supreme Court case that involved the regulation of political campaign spending by organizations. The Court made a grave error with the Citizens United decision, and we should work hard to see it overturned.

In the decision, the U.S. Supreme Court held, in a 5–4 vote, that the F*ree Speech* clause of the First Amendment prohibits the government from restricting independent expenditures for communications by nonprofit corporations, for-profit corporations, labor unions, and other associations – meaning these organizations can now spend unlimited amounts of money on political activities as long as they don't give money directly to political candidates and their spending is not coordinated with any candidate (a prohibition that is a total joke).

This decision – combined with another awful federal court decision, *SpeechNow.org v. Federal Election Commission* – have given rise to so-called super PACs. Super PACs, or "independent expenditure only" committees, can raise unlimited sums of money from corporations, unions, associations and individuals, then spend unlimited amounts of money to advocate for or against political candidates.

The Citizens United decision is deeply flawed mainly for its unintended consequences. The Federal Election Commission's (FEC) interpretation of it has caused even more damage than the decision itself.

The Supreme Court held that independent expenditures should be "totally independent" of candidates and made it clear that corporate spending should be fully disclosed. However, neither is being properly enforced. Because they are allowed to be shady, Super PACs – in conspiracy with their candidates – have taken political warfare to a new level.

The Supreme Court's ruling included this statement: "We now conclude that independent expenditures, including those made by corporations, do not give rise to corruption or the appearance of corruption." Let's check to see if that's actually true.

A report by Issue One, a nonpartisan nonprofit organization, found that "twelve political megadonors – at least eight of whom are billionaires – are responsible for $1 of every $13 in federal elections since Citizens United and 25 percent of all giving from the top 100 ZIP codes – a total of $3.4 billion." I don't know about you, but that sure doesn't sound right to me.

Now on to another gross topic, the earmark. An earmark is a line-item in congressional legislation that allocates a specified amount of money for a specific project, program, or organization. Conveniently for lawmakers, the American taxpayer dollars that are allocated for these specific purposes bypass customary budgetary procedures and often the American people never hear of them. You may know this better as “pork.”

Congress’ exploitation of the earmark is so shady that it often borders on criminal – and sometimes it is actually criminal (I’m looking at you, Representative Duke Cunningham and lobbyist Jack Abramoff).

This entire topic is just vomit. Instead of intelligent compromise and altruistic collaboration, Congress uses American tax dollars as their very own re-election fund, exchanging their vote for money to fund their local pet projects (remember the infamous “Bridge to Nowhere?”).

The highly corrupt process ensures that the funding of these projects is based on power instead of merit, and they clearly exemplify one of the most fundamental problems with our government: a lack of transparency that leads to a significant absence of accountability.

There is no other way to say it: These special projects, regardless of their worthiness, are straight up bribery. It is absolutely flabbergasting that we let them get away with this.

Please forgive me if this section comes across angry, but this topic makes my head explode. Because our dysfunctional two-party system has completely broken down, Congress has decided to pass legislation by simply paying one another off. Paying. One. Another. Off.

…in the United States of America. Not Colombia, not Mexico, not Guatemala, not Ghana. The United States of America.

The crazies have officially taken over the asylum and they have our checkbook. This is how the world’s greatest democracy legislates? This is the level of corruption, malpractice and irresponsibility that we have decided to accept?

No. Just no. No! No! No! No! Remember when I said earlier that we could significantly reduce our deficit and balance our budget through little more than eliminating waste? This is exactly the kind of b.s. I was talking about. Earmarks alone are reason enough to bust up the little party our members of Congress are having in Washington.

This is not the way to govern. This snake oil, smoke and mirrors, sideshow approach to governing is absurd.

< Okay, I’m taking a break and going for a run before I have a heart attack. >

I'm back, in a much better state of mind (not for nothing, but when I said "run" in that last sentence, I actually meant "beer"). I will now calmly walk through the ways of the evil earmark.

Earmarks were technically "banned" in 2011, but that was pretty much a joke. In fact, Citizens Against Government Waste's annual *Congressional Pig Book* (is it just the beer or is that the greatest name of anything, ever?) reveals that the cost of the earmarks members of Congress have crammed into spending bills has set a new record three years in a row.

Yes, you read that right. Even though there was an actual law prohibiting Congress from adding earmarks to legislation, they just completely ignored it and did it anyway. I guess laws just don't apply to them. In any country and in any language, that is the very definition of corruption.

In FY2020, Congress included $15.9 billion (that's BILLION, with a B) of earmarks, which is only 3.6 percent less than the cost of earmarks in 2010, the year before the "ban." This number is a 133.8 percent increase from FY2017.

Examples of FY2020 earmarks include $2.1 billion for twenty-two F-35 Joint Strike Fighter (JSF) aircraft that, by the way, the Pentagon didn't even request (plus, doesn't the Pentagon have their own astronomical budget already?); wild horse and burro management ($25.8 million); money to get rid of the poor little brown tree snake ($663,000); and $65,000,000 for Pacific coastal salmon recovery.

Listen, I've made it clear that I want to protect the sage grouse and dolphins – and I love the Pacific coastal salmon as much as the next guy – but could whoever is in charge of their recovery not get it done with the $65,000,000 they received in <u>both</u> FY2018 AND FY 2019? I'll do the math for you. In just three years, the United States spent $195,000,000 on this one fish.

I mean, seriously? People, we have eighth graders <u>*who can't read*</u>.

"Underwater pests" – whatever the hell that means – should be really jealous of the Pacific coastal salmon, because they only got $39,325,000 in FY2020. But all the other fishies shouldn't worry, they didn't forget them entirely! "Fish passage" and "fish screens" – again, whatever the heck that means – were funded in FY2020 with $11,400,000 of American taxpayer money.

< my head just literally exploded again. I'm going to have to go out for another "run" soon. >

Even though the so-called earmarks "ban" didn't stop lawmakers, members of the House of Representatives decided in March 2021 to forgo the charade and bring earmarks back legitimately.

The writing was on the wall not long into the Trump presidency, when he said to members of Congress, "Maybe all of you should start thinking about going back to a form of earmarks. Our system lends itself to not getting things done, and I hear so much about earmarks – the old earmark system – how there was a great friendliness when you had earmarks."

Hey, I would be friendly too if someone handed me $65,000,000 to recover salmon. But let's be honest, coming from the most transactional human being to ever sit in the Oval Office, that statement alone is evidence enough that earmarks are bad news.

Some people (mainly in Washington, naturally) would say that my animosity toward earmarks is a disproportionate response. After all, earmarks accounted for less than 2 percent of President Obama's $410 billion spending bill, signed less than two months after he took office.

Overlooking the fact that earmarks were less than 2 percent of an exceptionally bloated budget – and that the projects included thirteen that were driven by a lobbying firm accused of passing illegal campaign contributions to congressmen – when did $7.7 billion become inconsequential?

In fact, though the $410 billion was to fund the government for less than seven months, the earmarks in the bill equaled 16.5 percent of the entire 2010 budget for the Department of Education, 29 percent of the Department of Energy's budget, and 32 percent of the budget for the Department of Justice.

It's also important to remember that this particular transgression occurred right after the 2007-2009 Financial Crisis, at a time when we had just spent billions on an unprecedented financial bailout. Because the purpose of the congressional rescue was to stabilize our financial system and to strengthen it, one would hope that Congress would have been extra careful with our money.

Ha! Even in a time of crisis, they just couldn't help themselves. In the midst of the largest financial calamity in decades, and when the only concern should have been the protection of our economic future, our leaders crammed billions of dollars-worth of tax breaks into the bill at the very last minute – to the tune of $6.6 billion.

These included $6 million for the manufacturers of wooden arrows for children, $192 million for Puerto Rico and Virgin Islands rum producers, and $128 million for auto racetrack owners.

Representative John Murtha (D-PA), who himself included projects totaling $111 million, was quick to explain that people really shouldn't be annoyed with the clandestine add-ons, because the $6.6 billion in earmarks were just an itty-bitty percentage of "what the administration wants to bail out those rich guys in New York."

That is just a gross thing to say. Everyone in Washington knows full well that Americans are suspicious of earmarks in the very best of times. But in a time of economic crisis, when we are already on the hook for billions and billions of dollars, shoving *even more* billions of dollars-worth of earmarks into a spending bill feels like nothing less than a slap in the face.

If our leaders will blatantly squander billions against strong public dissent, how can we possibly feel confident that they make any prudent decisions on our behalf?

The oink-oink in President Obama's spending bill was all the more frustrating given that he promised multiple times during his presidential campaign to finally correct the egregious practice.

Although Senator Obama requested 112 earmarks totaling more than $330 million in 2007, presidential candidate Obama declared, "We can no longer accept a process that doles out earmarks based on a member of Congress' seniority, rather than the merit of the project. The entire earmark process needs to be re-examined and reformed."

On the campaign trail, Obama specifically said, "I've pledged to slash earmarks by more than half when I am president of the United

States." He went on to say, "I will go through the entire federal budget, page by page, line by line, and eliminate programs that don't work and aren't needed."

To be fair, I guess he eventually (kind of) tried with the toothless "ban," but not before he allowed $7.7 billion to slip through the net.

It was difficult even back then to find a congressman who would publicly defend earmarks – despite the fact that almost all of them jammed them into legislation – but those who did publicly defend them claimed earmarks are simply a harmless way to fund worthy projects in their districts.

Senator Dan Inouye (D-HI), then chairman of the Senate Appropriations Committee, came out swinging after critics slammed the number of earmarks in President Obama's inaugural spending bill.

He cited the creation of programs like the F-22, the C-17, and the Predator Unmanned Aerial Vehicle: "I dare anyone to suggest these are evil projects. It has helped to shorten the war. It has helped to save lives. It will bring back the brave men and women from Iraq. I think these few should remind us that earmarks are not evil."

Again, Senator, I will remind you that the Department of Defense has its own enormous budget. Why didn't you just transparently appropriate money for these not-evil projects in that? In addition to the military bonanza, other earmarks attached to the bill involved swine odor, tattoo removal, Mormon crickets, and lighthouses.

Whether these projects sound ridiculous to me or not, this is not about judging the merit of them. Not every earmark is evil, wasteful or crooked. I have had three tattoos removed and know how liberating it can be.

But, again, at the risk of sounding like a broken record, what's with the secrecy?

If members of Congress are so proud of their decisions, why not openly share the worthiness of their hometown projects with those of us who pay for them instead of covertly attaching them to unrelated legislation? As we discussed in the last section, why not be completely transparent, eliminate earmarks, and pass standalone legislation to fund all of these goodies?

Back in 2010, Senator Mel Martinez (R-FL) agreed: "At a time when families are struggling to balance their budgets, when workers are concerned about losing their jobs, when states are struggling to maintain service levels, it's unconscionable Congress won't end its addiction to earmarks."

That would have been a heroic stance if Senator Martinez's earmarks in the spending bill hadn't totaled $106.7 million.

When asked about his hypocrisy, Senator Martinez's spokesman said, "Florida taxpayers are federal taxpayers and until all earmarks are stripped, Florida deserves its fair share." Which pretty much sums the entire problem up in a nutshell.

And the examples just go on and on and on. Before Obama, one of President George W. Bush's spending bills, worth $555 billion and signed at the end of 2007, passed with over 9,000 earmarks, at the time the second largest number in U.S. history.

Addressing his spending bill, President Bush said, "These projects are not funded through a merit-based process and provide a vehicle for wasteful government spending." But, of course, he signed it anyway.

Not only did President Bush sign the bill, he also requested thousands of earmarks of his very own, including $6.5 million for research on the "fundamental properties of asphalt" and $330 million to eradicate plant pests like the light brown apple moth and the sirex woodwasp.

All in, President Bush and Congress had a huge year in 2007. In the *Iraq Emergency Supplemental Appropriations Act* – a 2007 emergency appropriations bill to address military spending in Iraq – they covertly attached $21 billion (House) and $18 billion (Senate) of non-war spending.

This nonsense included $100 million for the Democratic and Republican national conventions, $3.5 million to fund tours of the Capitol, $13 million for ewe lamb replacement and retention, $74 million for peanut storage, $95 million for dairy producers, and $24 million for sugar beet growers.

These all, of course, were buried deep, deep, deep within the bill. The $100 million given for the conventions was included in a section called "Katrina recovery, veterans' care and for other purposes." Interesting.

I would certainly never diminish the importance of the sugar beet, but the funding of what I can only assume is some sort of plant should be addressed elsewhere, not hidden in a bill whose sole concern should be the safety and care of our military. And screw the national conventions. I'm sure Congress has other ways to pilfer our money for those. I cannot imagine a more insulting tribute to our troops.

§§§

Earmarks are definitely evil, but then there are the lobbying shenanigans on Capitol Hill – which possibly make my head explode even faster than earmarks. Most lobbying practices have become so detrimental to our nation that they too can no longer be tolerated.

Corporations, labor unions, trade associations, and other special interest groups have spent a whopping $71.28 billion to lobby Washington since 1998.

This is not an anti-union commentary or an indictment of special interest groups or lobbyists on their merit. All voices in this country have an equal right to be heard, and these groups have as much of a right as anyone to contribute to the conversation.

These groups should not be demonized. In fact, many of the leaders of these organizations do an incredible job of giving their issue a heartbeat. Sure, some lobbyists are sleazy, but it's the politicians that sell out to them who cause the problem.

Within the brokenness of our current two-party political atmosphere, the problematic dilemma with special interest groups is that there is no appropriate counterbalance to their control, which ensures them disproportionate influence that allows them to essentially own Congress.

In theory, a lobbyist is an expert in governmental policy that provides useful information to policymakers. In its purest form, lobbying can provide lawmakers with valuable knowledge of our nation's challenges and, sometimes, the exchange can even lead to plausible solutions.

Unfortunately, the potentially productive act of sharing information has morphed into the decidedly destructive practice of people buying access and influence.

It is absolutely imperative that we have significant lobbying reform that protects the right of Americans to have a voice, but that puts an end to the modern-day corruption that exists among lobbyists, lawmakers, and the almighty dollar.

America, seriously, enough is enough.

§§§

There are many more topics that fall under government reform – things like the Electoral College, the filibuster, gerrymandering, and the conduct of presidents and members of Congress – and you can find them and their recommendations in *The Policy Guide* (along with recommendations for policing earmarks and lobbying).

However, before we end this section, I would like to address an extremely dangerous phenomenon that we must resolve immediately: Our system of checks and balances has gotten completely out of whack.

Checks and balances are fundamental to our democracy and rule of law. The United States Constitution is crystal clear: The Legislative Branch (Article 1), the Executive Branch (Article 2), and the Judicial Branch (Article 3) each have separate and independent powers, and each branch is given equal weight. There is <u>ZERO</u> question about this.

Except that's not how it's currently playing out. We have an increasingly political judiciary, a power-hungry executive branch, and an impotent Congress that won't do a damn thing about either.

Please believe me when I say this is an incredibly dangerous path we are on, America. We cannot be like that frog in the pot who, because the temperature is raised ever so slowly, doesn't realize he is getting boiled to death until it's too late. A United States without healthy checks and balances is not somewhere you want to be. We need to get this back under control. Right now.

Let's start with the Executive Branch. Although Donald Trump pushed executive power to unfathomable levels, the Lone Wolf mentality of the Executive Branch has been inappropriately increasing for decades.

One mechanism that presidents use to abuse their power is the executive order. Executive orders were designed as a way for presidents to establish directives, communicate priorities, and provide guidance within the bounds of existing law.

A great example of the true intention of the executive order is the very first one, issued in 1789 by President George Washington to those in charge of the federal departments. In part, his order said:

> "I am desirous of employing myself in obtaining an acquaintance with the real situation of the several great Departments, at the period of my acceding to the administration of the general Government. For this purpose, I wish to receive in writing such a clear account of the Department, at the head of which you have been for some years past, as may be sufficient (without overburdening or confusing the mind which has very many objects to claim its attention at the same instant) to impress me with a full, precise, and distinct general idea of the affairs of the United States, so far as they are comprehended."

In other words, President Washington used the executive order kind of like a management tool, which makes sense because the U.S. Constitution says that "the executive power shall be vested in a President of the United States of America" and that s/he may "require the opinion, in writing, of the principal officer in each of the executive departments, upon any subject relating to the duties of their respective offices."

Today, however, executive orders are being used as a substitute for actually having to build consensus in Congress to legislate. This approach is somewhat understandable given our two-party system has severely limited the ability to get things done, but the fact remains that the way executive orders are being used is **straight-up unconstitutional.**

It's true that, since George Washington's time, Congress has given the president a certain degree of additional discretionary power, but the U.S. Supreme Court has also ruled that every executive order must adhere to Article II and/or by statutes that Congress has *already* legislated. In other words, Congress still makes laws, not the president.

A great example of presidential overreach by executive order is President Abraham Lincoln's Proclamation 95 (a.k.a. the *Emancipation Proclamation*). This 1862 proclamation was an executive order/ presidential proclamation that changed the legal status of over 3.5 million slaves. To me, this remains the most brave, noble and powerful action in American history.

However, since the *Emancipation Proclamation* essentially overturned the *Fugitive Slave Act of 1850* – a law that forced slaves to be returned to their "owner" if captured – it fell outside Constitutional presidential action.

Of course, no one recognized this better than President Lincoln, who quickly followed the *Emancipation Proclamation* up with a demand that southern states include abolition in their plans for Reconstruction, as well as a hard push for the passage of the Thirteenth Amendment – which finally ended slavery for good.

President Lincoln's actions *after* the *Emancipation Proclamation* are the most instructive when it comes to executive orders. In their essence, executive orders are nothing more than theatre because they are temporary. They provide a way for presidents to look like they are doing something – and they actually may be for three or four years – but in the end they achieve nothing because they can simply be rescinded by the next president.

Imagine if Lincoln had just stopped after he made his initial proclamation by executive order. Andrew Johnson was the next president. Andrew Johnson, one of the most hideous, racist presidents in American history. Andrew Johnson who opposed Reconstruction, the *Civil Rights Act of 1866*, and the Fourteenth Amendment.

Imagine if President Lincoln had just gotten lazy and simply left the freedom and protection of enslaved African Americans to the fate of an executive order. Imagine if Andrew Johnson could have just repealed the *Emancipation Proclamation*? …which under the rules he most certainly could have.

This is a perfect example of why it's worth the time and effort to actually pass legislation. It's harder, no doubt. But it's lasting.

Beyond the constitutionality of executive orders, one of the most damaging things they do is create chaos and uncertainty. Take DACA, for example. The *Deferred Action for Childhood Arrivals* (DACA) is a policy that allows kids who are not U.S. citizens but were brought here as children to receive a two-year period of deferred action from deportation. They also may be eligible for a U.S. work permit. President Obama established DACA through an Executive Branch memorandum on June 15, 2012.

The kids protected by DACA – also referred to as "Dreamers" – were ecstatic and started to make plans for their unencumbered future in the United States. That is, until five years later when Donald Trump announced plans to phase DACA out. Four years after *that*, President Biden issued an executive order reinstating DACA.

Although Dreamers are surely relieved about DACA's revival, their lives are still subject to political whiplash. Although the prevailing sentiment favors them *today,* they continue to live in a perpetual state of limbo about *tomorrow.*

DACA is just one example. Although Democrats threw a fit when Donald Trump used executive orders to move his agenda forward, naturally their side did the exact same thing the minute they resumed power.

Within hours of taking the oath of office, President Biden had already signed 15 executive orders and two additional actions to rescind Trump-era policies, including ones regarding immigration, the pandemic response, and climate change. Within 16 days, Biden had signed three times the number of executive orders than past presidents had at the same point in their presidencies.

Among other things, he ended the bans on Muslim travel and transgender military service; revoked the abortion "global gag rule," the "1776 Commission," and the permit for the Keystone XL pipeline; plus stopped construction on "The Wall." He also rejoined the *Paris Climate Agreement* and reiterated U.S. support for the World Health Organization.

The most destructive consequence of an overly empowered Executive Branch is that, as the power of the presidency has grown, the power of Congress has equally diminished. Worse, Congress just sits there like lap dogs and lets it happen.

For example, the U.S. Constitution gives Congress the power to protect civilian control of the military by setting forth congressional war powers (Article I, Section 8). This is critical not only to protect our rule of law, but also to ensure that the United States has solid national security objectives and a smart, thoughtful foreign policy strategy. Most importantly, our troops must be certain that the dangerous missions we ask them to engage in are fully warranted and vetted.

However, for almost two decades, Congress has avoided tough votes on military action, which has essentially given the U.S. president unlimited power to unilaterally make military decisions…**which is straight-up unconstitutional**. < Read more about this in the Authorization for Use of Military Force (AUMF) section in *The Policy Guide.* >

Another one of Congress' main responsibilities is inquiry and oversight (Article I, Section 8), a congressional responsibility that Donald Trump felt empowered to completely ignore… **which is also straight up unconstitutional**.

The U.S. Supreme Court has already ruled on this: "The power of the Congress to conduct investigations is inherent in the legislative process. That power is broad. It encompasses inquiries concerning the administration of existing laws, as well as proposed or possibly needed statutes. It includes surveys of defects in our social, economic or political system for the purpose of enabling the Congress to remedy them. It comprehends probes into departments of the Federal Government to expose corruption, inefficiency or waste."

This high court ruling is in addition to a judgement by the U.S. Court of Appeals for the District of Columbia Circuit nineteen years earlier which found "a legislative inquiry may be as broad, as searching, and as exhaustive as is necessary to make effective the constitutional powers of Congress."

As the Executive Branch's power has inflated, so too has the assertion of *executive privilege.* Among many other things, Donald Trump invoked executive privilege to try to block Congress from receiving the entire Mueller Report and other important documents related to the investigation and to block key witnesses from testifying before Congress.

In other words, he invoked *executive privilege* to try to stop Congress from conducting their constitutionally mandated oversight responsibilities.

This is absolutely outrageous. The term *executive privilege* is not even in the U.S. Constitution. The U.S. Supreme Court did finally address this in the Richard Nixon case in 1974, acknowledging "the President's need for complete candor and objectivity from advisers." However, in that instance the Court was speaking specifically to judicial subpoenas.

In any event, the closest comparison we have to Donald Trump's behavior on this point is, in fact, Nixon, who infamously tried to invoke *executive privilege* in order to not turn over the infamous White House tapes. In the same case referenced above, the Court unanimously ruled against him.

Do we need any more examples? What the heck, let me give you a couple more. As you know by now, this kind of s@#t really, really gets me going. I hope it does you too because our constitution is *everything.*

Article I, Section 9, Clause 7 of the U.S. Constitution says: "No Money shall be drawn from the Treasury, but in Consequence of Appropriations made by Law." Which means Congress, and Congress alone, has control of spending policy. The Constitution is pretty clear, right?

In the Federalist Papers: No. 58 (uh oh! I'm bringing out the big guns!), James Madison called this "the power of the purse," as in "this power over the purse may, in fact, be regarded as the most complete and effectual weapon with which any constitution can arm the immediate representatives of the people."

Donald Trump tried to circumvent this mandate a thousand different ways although, to be fair, so did practically every president before him.

For example, President Obama did when he paid for cost-sharing subsidies after the *Affordable Care Act* passed, while Donald Trump decided to reallocate $44 million from the Federal Emergency Management Agency (FEMA) to bolster Covid-19 unemployment benefits – which may have actually been a sweet gesture if it weren't **completely unconstitutional**.

By far, the most disturbing Donald Trump attempt was, naturally, tied to his beloved border wall. On February 15, 2019, Donald Trump declared a "national emergency" at the U.S-Mexico border, which gave him more authority to reallocate taxpayer money from other accounts to fund more than 230 miles of barriers along the U.S.-Mexico border. At the risk of sounding like a broken record, yes, this too is blatantly **STRAIGHT-UP UNCONSTITUTIONAL**.

At the time, there was no national emergency at the border and certainly not one that could have waited for an entire border wall to be constructed. Were there issues at the border that we needed to address? Certainly. Were they national emergencies? Certainly not.

To be fair, one reason this gets a little confusing is the *National Emergencies Act* passed by Congress in 1976, which significantly weakens Article 1, Section 9, Clause 7. This legislation allows the president to essentially declare a national emergency at his or her discretion. However, the legislation offers no specific definition of "emergency" – which is a recipe for total disaster.

Although Congress can reverse an emergency declaration by passing a resolution through both Houses, this specific example proves that is not an effective counterbalance. Even if both Houses pass a resolution, presidents can simply veto it.

A better way would be to pass legislation that automatically terminates an emergency declaration within 30 days unless Congress votes to extend the order and also requires strong reporting requirements of the president.

There are plenty of ways to stop this madness, and we must. Check out the recommendations in the Government Reform section of *The Policy Guide*.

Foreign Policy

Although it sometimes seems there is an avalanche of problems in America, let's begin this section from a place of profound gratitude. Yes, we face challenges. But in the whole scheme of history, we're in pretty great shape.

The United States of America is not a flimsy, fragile country. America has overcome horrific atrocities, from the horrors of slavery, to brothers fighting brothers in the Civil War, to the nightmare of the Depression, to the unfathomable murders of Kennedys and King. Our incredibly resilient country survived two horrific World Wars, one very hot war in Asia, and one very cold one.

Above all, every single one of us should be profoundly grateful to live in this extraordinary country. The fact that I can write this book – and have unlimited freedom to even suggest a new political party with the comforting knowledge that not one single person in this country can stop us – is remarkable. It's just awesome.

Please don't get the wrong impression. Surely you know by now that I'm not minimizing the struggles and stress that American families feel on a daily basis, nor am I downplaying the magnitude of the problems we need to fix. But it's really – really! – important that we all remember exactly what we are fighting to save.

Our fortunes were never more apparent to me than when I traveled to Ecuador in 2002. For days, I had been curious about the unending line of people that twisted around the city blocks in Quito, Ecuador's capital, twenty-four hours a day.

A local finally explained to me that all Ecuadorian bank accounts were frozen by the government and these people, in line for days at a time, were waiting for their turn inside the banks. At the time, Ecuador was in the process of dollarization, or changing their national currency from the Ecuadorian sucre to the American dollar to stabilize its heavily inflated currency. Although converting to the dollar was, on balance, a positive long-term decision for Ecuador's economy, the years of transition were difficult, to say the least.

During the transition, the banks would distribute a certain amount of money to a certain number of customers every day. When the daily limit was reached, the banks would shut their doors and the people outside would be left waiting another day.

WhaaaWhaaaWHAT? Wait a second. The *government* froze people's bank accounts?!? And they had to wait in long lines to get whatever amount of money the *government* decided they could have? As an American, this concept truly blew my mind.

To add insult to injury, because of the exchange rate, their money was temporarily worth far less than before, a bitter pill to swallow in a country where, at the time, over 47 percent of the people were unemployed and two-thirds of those who did work earned less than $30 a month.

Can you imagine how Americans would react if this occurred in the United States? You think having to wear a mask is an outrage! I suspect a battle cry would be sounded from sea to shining sea, making it crystal clear to politicians that this behavior was *completely* unacceptable and that they had no authority to withhold *our* money!

Any politician associated with such a treacherous act would not even bother to run for re-election. The response would be so swift and severe that their heads would spin – and roll. How great is it that something like this is just unthinkable to us?

And this is just one small example. To see firsthand the reality of what people around the world face every day of their lives has been life changing. According to the World Health Organization (WHO), "Some 2.2 billion people around the world do not have safely managed drinking water services, 4.2 billion people do not have safely managed sanitation services, and 3 billion lack basic handwashing facilities…Globally, at least 2 billion people use a drinking water source contaminated with feces."

The U.S. State Department reports that in Saudi Arabia,

> "Significant human rights issues include: unlawful killings; executions for nonviolent offenses; forced disappearances; torture and cases of cruel, inhuman, or degrading treatment of

prisoners and detainees by government agents; harsh and life-threatening prison conditions; arbitrary arrest and detention; political prisoners or detainees; serious restrictions on free expression, the press, and the internet, including threats of violence or unjustified arrests or prosecutions against journalists, censorship, site blocking, and engaging in harassment and intimidation against Saudi dissidents living abroad; substantial interference with the freedom of peaceful assembly and freedom of association; severe restrictions of religious freedom; restrictions on freedom of movement; inability of citizens to choose their government peacefully through free and fair elections; violence and discrimination against women, although new women's rights initiatives were implemented; trafficking in persons; and criminalization of consensual same-sex sexual activity."

The Kingdom has also been incessantly bombing the Houthi rebels in Yemen, which has quickly turned into the largest humanitarian crisis in the entire world. This bloody military conflict started in 2015 and has decimated the lives of over 24 million people and caused the deaths of well over 18,000 civilians. (read more about this in *The Policy Guide*)

Human Rights Watch reports that "roughly 80 percent of Yemen's population requires humanitarian aid, including over 12 million children."

The United Nations Children's Emergency Fund (UNICEF) reports that the number of Yemeni children under the age of 5 who suffer from acute malnutrition could rise to 2.4 million. UNICEF also reveals that 7.8 million of the children have no access to education following Covid-19-related school closures and nearly 10 million do not have adequate access to water and sanitation. The International Committee of the Red Cross (ICRC) reports that 50 percent of the children in Yemen are experiencing irreversible stunted growth.

What has happened in Myanmar (Burma) is an absolute abomination. Thousands of Rohingya Muslims have been subjected to a ruthless campaign of murder, arson, human burnings and beatings, gang rape and other mass brutalities – essentially amounting to ethnic cleansing by genocide.

This vicious conflict has forced over 700,000 Rohingya Muslims to flee Myanmar into Bangladesh, causing a massive humanitarian crisis as hundreds of thousands of people, at least half of them children, now live in ill-equipped and tattered refugee camps along the border.

China is just one big human rights catastrophe. The U.S. State Department reports that in China,

> "Significant human rights issues include: arbitrary or unlawful killings by the government; forced disappearances by the government; torture by the government; harsh and life-threatening prison and detention conditions; arbitrary detention by the government, including the mass detention of more than one million Uyghurs and other members of predominantly Muslim minority groups in extrajudicial internment camps and an additional two million are subjected to 're-education' training; political prisoners; politically motivated reprisal against individuals outside the country; the lack of an independent judiciary and Communist Party control over the judicial and legal system; arbitrary interference with privacy; pervasive and intrusive technical surveillance and monitoring; serious restrictions on free expression, the press, and the internet, including physical attacks on and criminal prosecution of journalists, lawyers, writers, bloggers, dissidents, petitioners, and others as well as their family members, and censorship and site blocking; interference with the rights of peaceful assembly and freedom of association, including overly restrictive laws that apply to foreign and domestic nongovernmental organizations; severe restrictions and suppression of religious freedom; substantial restrictions on freedom of movement; refoulement of asylum seekers to North Korea, where they have a well-founded fear of persecution; the inability of citizens to choose their government; restrictions on political participation; serious acts of corruption; forced sterilization and coerced abortions; forced labor and trafficking in persons;

severe restrictions on labor rights, including a ban on workers organizing or joining unions of their own choosing; and child labor."

Then there is this. On November 9th and 10th, 1938 – known as the *Kristallnacht (a.k.a. Night of Broken Glass, November Pogrom)* – Nazi forces damaged and/or destroyed multiple Jewish hospitals and schools, 267 synagogues, and over 7,000 Jewish businesses. Approximately 30,000 Jewish men were arrested and confined to concentration camps. These horrific acts were the beginning of the nightmare that was the Holocaust.

Today – right this second – another *Kristallnacht* is underway, and it has been going on for not days, but years. In Xinjiang, an ethnic minority region of China, thousands of Muslim religious sites have been destroyed, over one million Muslim ethnic minorities – including the Uyghurs and Kazakhs, both Turkish ethnic groups – have been detained in camps, and around 500,000 children have been separated from their families.

In Tibet, China has built military style "training centers," mandating hundreds of thousands of people be trained for what will ultimately be forced labor. These camps also engage in forced assimilation and ideological indoctrination.

§§§

The examples of worldwide heartbreak, injustice and abuse are endless, but let's just leave it at this: We are incredibly fortunate to live in the United States of America. Above all, let's be profoundly grateful to live in this exceptional, one-of-a-kind place.

We are the country that welcomes the poor, the tired and the huddled masses. We are the country that celebrates life, liberty and justice for all. We are the country that perfected the right to peaceful assembly, freedom of speech and the free exercise of religion.

Lately, there have been evil forces that have tried to divert us from these ideals, but we will not allow them to win this battle. Our greatest responsibility as Americans is to preserve and protect the very reasons that America is so great, and to make sure America's light shines far beyond our shores once again.

Notice I said we *should let our light shine*, not arrogantly try to dominate the entire world by acting superior and bossing everyone around. It's unnecessary for America to be a bully. It's unnecessary for America to be threatening and hostile. It's unnecessary for America to be arrogant or petty or unwelcoming. America does not need to overtly flaunt our strength because *we are actually strong*.

Instead, I like the idea of the United States being *partners* with other countries. This does not mean we should give up our title of being a global leader (actually, still the global leader if we don't screw it up), but mutually beneficial partnerships will only strengthen our position.

Just look at what a collaborative, compassionate, and supportive America has achieved around the globe. We are the country that initiated the Lend-Lease policy, which helped defeat Germany, Japan and Italy in World War II by providing weapons, food, oil, and other supplies to the United Kingdom, China, the Soviet Union and France.

We are the country that enacted the Marshall Plan, which enabled Europe to rebuild after years of devastating war. With our support, South Korea evolved from an extremely poor, vulnerable autocracy to a vibrant, healthy democracy – as did Japan. China was able to integrate into the global economy, which helped reduce poverty for billions.

Around the globe, our security and support have provided countries the opportunity to foster democratic governments *and* strong economies. We were instrumental in creating international organizations like the United Nations, the International Monetary Fund, and the World Bank.

We crushed the Cold War and stopped communism in its tracks. We spent billions to fight HIV in developing countries, which provided almost 10 million people antiviral drugs and prevented hundreds of thousands of infants from being infected with HIV at birth.

High five, America!!

Compare these honorable, spectacular successes to Donald Trump's isolationist, transactional, and conditional approach to foreign policy. Instead of strengthening and solidifying our position on the world stage, the Trump administration was hell-bent on just tearing everything down without replacing it with anything more substantial than disrespectful Tweets and insults.

It's not just the policies he initiated or failed to initiate – see examples of each in *The Policy Guide* – it's also the mixed signals, the reversals, the inconsistencies and contradictions, the trashing of our intelligence agencies, the dismantling of key international agreements, the breakdown of our relationships with European partners, and the outright lies that caused so much harm. It's the complete absence of risk versus reward analysis, serious deliberation with experts, or even the most rudimentary inquiry into potential consequences.

It cannot be denied that the four years of the Trump administration – and now, thanks to the absolute tragedy that unfolded in Afghanistan, at least the first months of the Biden administration – shook the world's fundamental assumptions about American exceptionalism and called into question the special role we have played in foreign affairs for decades.

From the day he took office, Donald Trump wasted no time trying to abdicate our unique position. He withdrew the United States from the I*ntermediate-Range Nuclear Forces Treaty*, the *Open Skies Treaty*, the *Paris Climate Accord,* the *Trans-Pacific Partnership,* and the *Joint Comprehensive Plan of Action* (a.k.a. the Iranian nuclear deal), plus several organizations within the United Nations system including the UN Human Rights Council, the UN Educational Scientific and Cultural Organization, and the UN Relief and Works Agency.

He constantly undermined – and threatened to withdraw from – the North Atlantic Treaty Organization (NATO); started trade wars with half the globe; authorized a Muslim travel ban; and engaged in full-fledged love fests with authoritarian leaders like Kim Jong-un, Vladimir Putin, Rodrigo Duterte and Recep Tayyip Erdoğan…to the point that he sold out our intelligence agencies in front of the entire world by siding with Putin in Helsinki and shared highly classified information with the Russian foreign minister and Russian ambassador in the Oval Office.

All of this would be bad enough if Donald Trump's authoritarian, tough guy approach worked, but it didn't. His mode of operation only served to alienate our allies and empower and embolden our potential adversaries, handing authoritarians around the world – whether Chinese, Turkish, Saudi, Russian, Syrian or North Korean – almost all of America's leverage without getting *anything* of consequence in return.

China called his bluff on trade and Kim Jong-un is essentially shooting us the bird as North Korea fires short-range ballistic missiles and rockets, conducts ground tests at its nuclear test sites, and increases production of long-range missiles and the fissile material used in nuclear weapons.

Iran has not only resumed its nuclear program, it's scarier than ever. Soon after the U.S. withdrew from the *Joint Comprehensive Plan of Action* (JCPOA), Iran increased the number of its centrifuges enriching uranium and its stockpile of low-enriched uranium and, as a result, has gotten much closer to obtaining fissile uranium, another ingredient needed for nuclear weapons.

The "peace" deal the Trump administration signed with the Taliban may be the worst agreement in the history of agreements. Basically, the United States capitulated to every single one of the Taliban's unimageable, outrageous demands…to the point where, in our final days in Afghanistan, the *Taliban* were giving *us* – THE UNITED STATES OF AMERICA – orders, like we were their - - - - (my mom said I had to take this description out, but I can't think of another way to say it so I'm leaving it blank). More on the worst agreement in the history of agreements in a few minutes.

Venezuela, Turkey, Syria and Russia have gotten in the habit of pretty much ignoring anything we have to say. In addition to China and Russia investing in new strategies and technologies to exploit our vulnerabilities, which we covered earlier, they have both carefully cultivated military and diplomatic alliances around the world – all while actively undermining the United States at every turn.

They have also made it a priority to boost their geopolitical standings through increased outreach as well as providing vulnerable countries with things like medical supplies and vaccines. "Gracias China!!!," Mexico's foreign minister Marcelo Ebrard posted to Twitter after China – now the second-largest trading partner in Latin America – sent a planeload of masks, testing kits, and ventilators.

§§§

Being a world leader is an enormous responsibility and sometimes costly, but it gives us a tremendous advantage.

That we have taken this privilege for granted – and have been inadequate stewards of our rare position in this world – are colossal understatements. Somewhere down the line, we started taking American exceptionalism for granted, believing that we are somehow *owed* this honorable distinction instead of understanding that we have to continually *earn* it.

No more, America! Anyone who thinks we can keep our superpower status without humility, meticulous attention to detail, and tremendous foresight needs to think again. That is exactly what the Greeks, Spanish and Romans thought, and they are now named in history books as failed empires. We better stop thinking this can't happen to us, because it absolutely can.

But here's the great news! The Covid-19 crisis has given us the perfect opening to reset our approach to foreign policy, and we need to take advantage of this opportunity without delay.

In many ways, our current state of foreign affairs feels like it probably did after World War II, when world events put President Franklin Roosevelt, followed by President Truman, in a perfect position to create a new world order.

When the United States helped save a crippled Europe after the war, we not only rebuilt the global order to our advantage, but also repaired and strengthened alliances around the world. The global rules, institutions, and alliances that emerged from this period are the foundation of our modern-day international structure – a structure that still significantly benefits the United States.

To seize such a moment today, we need to evaluate our standing in the world, assess what we have gotten right and what we have gotten wrong, then realistically define what we want our role to be going forward.

My vote is that we make America the Gold Standard again…for America to be a country that has unimpeachable integrity and one that causes no harm…for America to be a country that takes tremendous pride in our accomplishments but that is empathetic and supportive of those with less opportunity…for America to be a country that is committed to the rules-based international world order that has successfully governed peace, security, democracy and prosperity since World War II…for America to be a country that is once again the go-to nation during an international crisis, not to foot the bill for everyone, but to offer bold solutions and coordinate multilateral responses.

My vote is for America to be a country that champions human rights around the world…one that works to improve the factors that enable violent extremism such as poverty, inequality and repression by creating economic advancements for those around the world who do not have the opportunities we are blessed with…one that always strives to honor the motto of the U.S. Special Forces: De Oppresso Liber…*To Free the Oppressed.*

But as much as anything else, my vote is for America to be a country that is a reliable and trustworthy partner…one that is fiercely loyal to our allies. The way our friends were treated during the Trump administration and in the first months of the Biden administration is unacceptable.

This is not a zero-sum game. Being a trustworthy ally and putting "America First" do not have to be mutually exclusive endeavors. We can absolutely be faithful to America without pissing off (and abandoning) the entire world.

Believe it or not, we need our allies as much as they need us. These relationships are, in the words of the military, *force multipliers* – meaning, our allies and multilateral institutions can magnify our strengths and allow us to leverage our investments and advancements regarding climate change, global pandemics, cybersecurity and cyber-warfare and in our continued fight against nuclear proliferation and terrorism – which, despite what some people say, remains a serious threat. *America First* doesn't have to mean *America Alone.*

– you can find detailed information on over
sixty foreign policy topics in *The Policy Guide* –

It's important for 1787 to have a general philosophy regarding foreign policy, but a philosophy is just words until it's tested. In the real world, you, as a voter, need to understand what the 1787 philosophy would look like in action. As five-star Army general and former president of the United States Dwight D. Eisenhower once advised: "Plans are nothing; planning is everything."

To that end, let's look at three examples:

† *Semper Fidelis* (Always Faithful)
(Example: Afghanistan, Syria and Turkey)

† Speak softly…
(Example: China)

† …and carry a big stick.
(Example: Russia)

Semper Fidelis (Always Faithful)

In early 2014, ISIS – also called the Islamic State of Iraq and the Levant (ISIL) or Daesh, its name in Arabic – captured the Syrian city of Raqqa to establish a caliphate (a "political-religious state comprising the Muslim community and the lands and peoples under its dominion in the centuries following the death (632 CE) of the Prophet Muhammad").

In his book *Caliphate: The History of An Idea*, professor of Arabic at the University of London Hugh Kennedy makes the concept a little easier to understand:

"You can choose what you want to take from this tradition, but the choice is yours. If you want a caliphate which is aggressive and fiercely controlling of the Muslim population, you can find precedents in the vast historical records.

If you want a caliphate which is generous and open to different ideas and customs while, of course, remaining true to its vision of God's will and purpose, then you can find that in the historical tradition too.

The past bears many different messages. There are those who see caliphate as a vehicle for imposing their particular and often very narrow view of Islam on the umma (i.e. the whole community of Muslims bound together by ties of religion); there are others who see caliphate as a justification for aiming at world conquest; but there are equally those who see caliphate as simply providing a framework in which Muslims can strive to live a godly life and make up their own minds about the best way to this."

Unfortunately, the aggressive, fiercely controlling type is what ISIS had in mind in Syria in 2014. Through the next few months, ISIS stampeded across eastern Syria and northwestern Iraq gaining territory – including Mosul, Iraq's second largest city. ISIS finally declared its self-styled caliphate in June. At its peak, ISIS had engaged over 40,000 recruits from 100 countries.

Almost five years later, in March 2019, the Syrian Democratic Forces (SDF) – the Syrian Kurdish militia led by the Kurdish YPG (People's Protection Units) – declared victory over ISIS and their so-called caliphate.

Serving as America's primary ground ally, the SDF liberated five million people from terrorism and 52,000 square kilometers of Syrian territory at the cost of 11,000 of their soldiers' lives. Although ISIS was not entirely defeated, the collapse of the caliphate was a massive victory for the SDF and the United States.

Meanwhile, in Turkey, President Recep Tayyip Erdoğan was on a tyrant roll, increasingly favoring more radical versions of Islam and becoming a growing threat to Israel; meeting with guys like Ismail

Haniyeh and Saleh al-Arouri, Hamas leaders on pretty much every terrorist watch list, including ours; providing comfort, aid and support – and arming – the Muslim Brotherhood in Africa; and expanding Turkey's military presence into thirteen countries, including Libya where he unilaterally claimed large natural gas deposits.

Erdoğan was also busy taunting important friends of America. He was fighting with Greece, a U.S. NATO ally, over gas reserves and maritime rights; he was taunting France, another U.S. NATO ally, by violating an arms embargo against Libya; and he was threating the United Arab Emirates because they normalized ties with Israel.

But the biggie was that, for years, Erdoğan had been threatening to invade northern Syria as tensions increased over 1) a "safe zone" between the Syrian Democratic Forces and southern Turkey, as well as the Syrian town of Manbij, and 2) Turkey's acquisition of a $2.5 billion Russian-made missile system – the S-400 air defense system – that the West sees as a threat to NATO security. The main problem with the S-400 is that it's not fully compatible with the broader NATO air defense system, which several member countries believe would weaken the entire NATO defense framework.

Erdoğan claimed he was forced to buy the missile system from Russia because the Obama administration would not sell him Patriot missiles, but that was a lie. Both the Obama and Trump administrations approved weapons sales to Turkey.

As a consequence of Erdoğan's S-400 deal with Russia, the United States kicked Turkey out of our F-35 fighter jet program over safety concerns (the F-35 is an advanced aircraft that is going to be used in several NATO-member air forces). Essentially, American officials thought the new Russian system would compromise U.S. stealth technology – or more to the point, that the Russians implementing the new S-400 defense system on the ground in Turkey would *steal* our stealth technology, which was probably a good bet.

This move by the United States prompted Erdoğan and his people to tell anyone with a microphone that, if the U.S. showed aggression toward Turkey in any way, they would not hesitate to retaliate. This was not just talk. Erdoğan had been amassing troops along the borders of northern Syria and northern Iraq for over a year.

It was against this volatile backdrop that, reportedly bored in the White House on a random Sunday in October, Donald Trump decided to insert himself into the drama – which, as we all know, was always super helpful.

Nine months earlier, in December 2018, Donald announced that the United States was going to pull 2,000 troops from Syria – a proclamation that came as such an offense to some high in his government that two of them resigned (Defense Secretary Jim Mattis and Special Presidential Envoy to the Coalition Fighting the Islamic State Brett McGurk). The primary reason for the adamant dissent was the immense danger our faithful allies, the Syrian Democratic Forces (SDF), would face if America abruptly left Syria.

Thankfully, Donald was talked out of this monumentally terrible idea and around 1,000 U.S. Special Operations forces remained.

Fast forward to that boring October Sunday in the White House. In typical schizophrenic fashion, Donald Trump again announced that U.S. forces would withdraw from the border between Syria and Turkey – an out of the blue, unilateral announcement that, without question, is one of the single most ill-informed, irresponsible, and shameful foreign policy failures of Donald Trump's presidency (and that's saying something).

It cannot be overstated what an amateur move this was. Clearly, Donald Trump knew nothing about the situation on the ground in Syria and cared about nothing more than making his role-model Erdoğan happy, which he certainly did by handing Erdoğan exactly what he had always longed for – American allies and soldiers be damned.

Donald Trump's Sunday Surprise also gave Syrian President Bashar al-Assad and his Iranian and Russian allies – who had already proven they would go to any lengths necessary to regain total control of Syria – free rein to continue committing mass murder and other vicious war crimes.

But, BY FAR, the absolute worst – and most heartbreaking – part of this insanely irresponsible decision was the danger our loyal allies, the Syrian Democratic Forces, were immediately put in by Donald Trump.

It's impossible to imagine how betrayed they felt by his actions. It physically makes me sick to my stomach to think that my beloved

United States of America could do this to such dedicated and faithful allies. < Note: At the time, I thought this was one of the most disgraceful days in American history, at least in my lifetime. However, it gave me a measure of peace to know that – hopefully sooner rather than later – Donald Trump would no longer be the U.S. president, which would surely put an end to this type of egregious behavior. I never imagined that this shameful episode would be eclipsed by the actions of the very next American president, who outright abandoned many of our dedicated and faithful allies in Afghanistan with what seemed like zero conscious or compassion. More on this in a few minutes. >

… now, back to the epic betrayal of the Syrian Democratic Forces. To make matters worse, U.S. troops were standing right next to SDF forces when they all learned of Donald Trump's decision, placing our service members squarely in the crosshairs of an incredibly hostile and dangerous situation. The entire episode is just outrageous.

Almost immediately – and entirely predictably – the Islamic State started murdering local SDF leaders, and within three days, Turkey launched air and ground operations against them. To protect themselves – and given pretty much no other choice by the United States – the SDF, one of the most loyal allies America has even known, was soon forced to announce a partnership with the Russian and Iran-backed government in Damascus.

To add insult to injury, over 100 highly trained, highly dangerous ISIS fighters being held by the SDF escaped, an outcome that SDF leadership had long warned of in the event of a Turkish invasion.

Well, my fellow Americans, by this point in the Trump presidency we all could have guessed where this was leading. After creating colossal chaos, his specialty, Donald Trump – under enormous domestic pressure and international outrage – suddenly changed his mind and reversed course yet again.

Within two months of his October troop-withdrawal announcement, the U.S. military had resumed large-scale counterterrorism missions against the Islamic State in northern Syria…but not before Syria and Russia, emboldened by America's whiplash strategy, initiated brutal attacks in the northern province of Idlib, an area located on the Turkish border in northwest Syria.

This out-and-out slaughter of innocent civilians eventually led to the displacement of over 100,000 people. This, in addition to the over 5 million Syrians who had already been forced to leave the country and the more than 6 million who were already internally displaced.

Although there had been a long-standing truce between Turkey and Russia that would ostensibly protect Idlib (signed in 1992, called the Sochi agreement), the almost three-decade truce was shattered when Hayat Tahrir al-Sham (HTS), al-Qaeda's former Syrian affiliate, attacked, prompting Assad, with help from Russia, to resume bombing everyone and everything in sight. Thankfully, Turkey and Russia reached a new ceasefire agreement in March 2019. However, the Syrian and Russian reign of terror within Syria didn't slow down one bit. Amnesty International reports:

> "The Syrian government, backed by its ally Russia, subjected civilians in opposition-held areas in northwest Syria to a new wave of horrors. In an all-too-familiar pattern, attacks from the air and the ground repeatedly struck residential areas and crucial infrastructure. Yet even by the standards of this calamitous nine-year crisis, the resulting displacement and humanitarian emergency were unprecedented.
>
> In towns and villages in Idlib and western Aleppo governorates, the barrage of attacks emptied out entire communities; the escalation was evidently a continuation of an offensive that began in April 2019 targeting the last pocket under the control of armed opposition groups. Cornered, and with nowhere left to go, civilians flooded already overstretched displacement camps, pitched tents in farms and schools, or ended up in the open in brutal weather.
>
> Amnesty International documented a total of 18 attacks on medical facilities and schools that happened between May 5, 2019 and February 25, 2020 in Idlib, northwestern Hama and western Aleppo governorates. Of those, Syrian government forces carried out three ground attacks and two-barrel bomb attacks. The remaining 13 attacks were air strike attacks: two

by Syrian government forces, seven by Russian government forces, and four by Syrian or Russian government forces.

A doctor who survived one of the documented attacks – three air strikes in the vicinity of al-Shami hospital in Ariha on January 29, 2020 – told Amnesty International how the strikes flattened at least two residential buildings around the hospital, killed 11 civilians including one of his colleagues, and injured more than 30 others. 'I felt so helpless. My friend and colleague dying, children and women screaming outside… We were all paralyzed,' he said. 'It took the civil defense two days to remove the bodies' from underneath the rubble of one the flattened buildings, he added.

Based on corroborating witness statements and other credible information, particularly observations by flight spotters, Amnesty International concluded this unlawful attack was carried out by Russian government forces.

A teacher who witnessed an attack on a school in Idlib city on February 25, 2020 described to Amnesty International how a cluster munition explosion injured her and killed a student before her eyes. As soon as she had finished teaching the first period that day, the principal ordered everyone to evacuate the school due to a wave of attacks on the city.

She and others who evacuated were walking past another nearby school when it was hit by a cluster munition. 'A bomblet exploded close to my feet, blowing the flesh off… The pain was unbearable… Two students were walking in front of me. One died instantly and the other one, miraculously, survived… I know the sound of a cluster munition attack very well. You hear a series of small explosions. As if the sky were raining shrapnel instead of water,' she said. In total, three people were killed, and five others injured.

Amnesty International concluded this unlawful attack was carried out by Syrian government forces; it identified the remnant as a surface-fired, 220mm 9M27K cargo rocket, manufactured in Russia and transferred to the Syrian army,

> containing 9N210 or 9N235 cluster munitions, which are prohibited under international law.
>
> Evidence shows that, in their entirety, the documented attacks by Syrian and Russian government forces entailed a myriad of serious violations of international humanitarian law. To name a few, the attacks were not directed at a specific military object and they violated the immunity from direct attack of civilians and civilian objects, as well as the special protection afforded to specific persons and objects, particularly medical facilities, medical personnel and children.
>
> These violations amount to war crimes. The attacks must also be viewed in the context of the well-established pattern of Syrian government forces targeting civilian infrastructure and civilians in areas under the control of armed opposition groups as part of a widespread and systematic attack on the civilian population, therefore constituting crimes against humanity."

Today, ten years after the Syrian people began to openly protest the horrendous treatment they suffered at the hands of their government – a move that prompted Bashar al-Assad to unleash the holy hounds of hell on them – Assad still rules the two-thirds of the country he controls like the murderous tyrant that he is.

Three million terrified, displaced Syrians remain stranded in the northwestern province of Idlib. Assad is literally starving them to death, using food as an instrument of war, while continuing to rain bombs down on them.

His henchman Vladimir Putin is now threatening to close off access to Bab al-Hawa, a cross-border humanitarian aid route that brings food and critical medical supplies to the one-third of Syria not under Assad's rule. This, at a time when the United Nations World Food Program reports that 12.4 million Syrians – 60 percent of the population – cannot survive without food assistance.

< Giving credit where credit is due, Turkish President Erdoğan and his government have been instrumental in protecting displaced Syrians from Assad and his Russian allies. First, Turkey came through in Idlib, providing Syrians not only clothes, blankets, and food, but military

protection as well. Now, in Afrin, a district of northwestern Syria that borders Turkey, the Turks have provided electricity, cell phone service, education, and health care services for the Syrian people. This is in addition to already hosting 3.6 million Syrian refugees *inside* Turkey. With Erdoğan, nothing is purely altruistic. But still, that's good work. >

Under the heading of *when it rains, it pours*, the fallout from stiff international sanctions and the pandemic has been brutal in Syria. The economy is basically in shambles. Syria's currency collapsed, causing food and fuel to skyrocket and wages to plummet. Medical doctors there make less than $50 *a month*.

The New York Times reports that a Syrian mother of three recently told the story of having to sell her hair: "'I had to sell my hair or my body.' Her husband, a carpenter, was ill and only sporadically employed, she said, and she needed heating oil for the house and winter coats for her children. With the $55 she got for her hair, which will be used to make wigs, she bought two gallons of heating oil, clothes for her children and a roast chicken, the first her family had tasted in three months."

Because of their own economic crises, Russia and Iran are unable to help Assad financially as much, so he has resorted to kidnapping and blackmail. When an Israeli woman inadvertently found herself in Syria, the Assad regime arrested her and blackmailed Israel, eventually releasing the woman in exchange for two Syrian shepherds and 60,000 doses of the coronavirus vaccine (which Israel was forced to buy from Russia for $1.2 million).

Another serious consequence of the idiotic decision made on that boring October Sunday in the White House was that Donald Trump enabled and empowered the resurgence of the Islamic State, a point that was underscored on November 15, 2019 by the U.S. Department of Defense Inspector General (DoD OIG):

> "The Defense Intelligence Agency (DIA) reported to the U.S. Department of Defense Inspector General (DoD OIG) that ISIS exploited the Turkish incursion and subsequent drawdown of U.S. troops to reconstitute capabilities and resources within Syria and strengthen its ability to plan attacks abroad. The

DIA also reported that without counterterrorism pressure, ISIS will probably be able to more freely build clandestine networks and will attempt to free ISIS members detained in SDF-run prisons and family members living in internally displaced persons (IDPs) camps.

Additionally, according to the DIA, ISIS will likely have the 'time and space' to target the West and provide support to its 19 global branches and networks. In the longer term, ISIS will probably seek to regain control of some Syrian population centers and expand its global footprint." < we'll go deeper into the state of global terrorism in the next section >

Despite all of this, thankfully, we have discovered a successful light-footprint, low-cost operation formula for Syria. Around 900 U.S. troops and Special Forces remain to support and advise the Syrian Democratic Forces, who are still bravely fighting the Islamic State.

Adding to that support, we should increase our diplomatic presence there to continue facilitating talks between rival Kurdish factions and to address the massive humanitarian crisis that still exists.

These actions are critical to our national security. Beyond fighting terrorism, a huge benefit of having U.S. troops in Syria is that we can keep a close eye on Russia and Iran, making sure that Russia stays away from the oil fields and other valuable resources in the northeast region and that Iran doesn't get a chance to develop a passageway to deliver weapons to Syria.

Likewise, a solid relationship with Iraq is critical to our national security. For the past four years, the relationship between the United States and the Iraqis has been rocky, to say the least. Although the tension had been increasing for years, the assassination of Iranian Maj. Gen. Qassim Suleimani – who was killed by a U.S. drone strike in Iraq on January 3, 2020 – was the final straw for Iraq.

After the attack, the Iraqi Parliament voted to expel all U.S. forces from the country. However, ten days later, the American and Iraqi militaries resumed joint operations against the Islamic State.

Thank goodness, because there is no question that Iraq is an incredibly important component of our national security strategy in the

Middle East. We need Iraq to help establish safe and reliable trade, provide security for our allies, and navigate our way forward with our nemesis, but their friend and neighbor, Iran.

The good news is that, as in Syria, we can achieve our objections in Iraq with a relatively light presence. In late July 2021, President Biden and Iraqi Prime Minister Mustafa al-Kadhimi agreed to end the U.S. combat mission in Iraq on paper but, in reality, nothing is really changing on the ground.

For well over a year now, the U.S. role in Iraq has been, not to fight in combat, but to train and support the Iraqis who are still fighting the Islamic State. There are 2,500 U.S. troops and Special Forces still stationed there, gathering intelligence and coordinating airstrikes, and this is not expected to change anytime soon.

Our continued presence in Syria and Iraq is a huge relief because, if the United States leaves either country a second too soon, we will be forced to eventually return to far worse and more dangerous conditions than ever before. We should know this from our earlier experience in Iraq, where we pulled out based on an arbitrary deadline as opposed to conditions on the ground. Our premature exit enabled the Islamic State to regroup and expand, which eventually forced our return to Iraq.

…which brings us to Afghanistan.

§§§

Before we begin this section, please know that to me – above all else – the wellbeing of our troops is always the number one concern. Please also know that I completely understand some may consider my giving an opinion on military matters the height of arrogance.

After all, it's easy for me to sit here in an air-conditioned room, with no sand flying in my face and no bullets flying past my head – and with no military experience beyond watching *Restrepo* over and over – to wax poetic about what we should have done differently and how we should move forward.

Believe me, if I could go back in time, I would choose to serve my country in the Armed Forces. Not doing so is one of the greatest regrets of my life. But since that ship has sailed, all I can do is listen carefully to those who do (and did) serve; learn as much as possible about the complex history of the region, religion, people and cultures involved; gather all of the intel I can about the realities on the ground; then apply a little common sense. I don't claim to know anything beyond that.

American boots hit the ground in Afghanistan (again) on October 19, 2001. The war that ensued cost the United States trillions of dollars and thousands of lives. At one point, over 100,000 U.S. troops were stationed there.

Then came August 15, 2021, the day the Taliban captured Kabul, the capital of Afghanistan.

In the last section, I shared with you my heartbreak over Donald Trump's betrayal of our faithful allies, the Syrian Democratic Forces. And now, in Afghanistan, we have one of the worst foreign policy disasters in American history.

Over that long first weekend after the Taliban takeover, it was extremely upsetting to see/hear the relentless images/stories coming out of Afghanistan, but then came Joe Biden's speech on the following Monday, which made my head explode.

…you know, the speech where he said, "I am the President of the United States of America, and the buck stops with me," but then proceeded to blame everyone and everything else for the chaos and drama, from the Trump administration to American intelligence agencies to Afghan President Ashraf Ghani and leader of the Afghan High Council for National Reconciliation Abdullah Abdullah to the Afghan people themselves.

Biden also blamed the Afghan military forces, which he claimed had 300,000 active troops but, according to the International Institute of Strategic Studies, really had less than 178,800 (Biden's number evidently included the Afghan National Police, whose responsibilities are very different from those of the military). The Center for Strategic and International Studies had been warning for months that, of those less than 178,800 troops, only a "small fraction" could be used "effectively" – an assessment that certainly came as no surprise to our military brass, who had known this for a very long time.

Sadly, the manipulation of this very important fact fit a pattern that the Biden administration fell into while desperately trying to deflect responsibility for the latest tragedy to befall Afghanistan. In the months before the Taliban takeover, for example, Biden administration officials gave at least nine different explanations for the excruciatingly slow – and now deadly – process of the evacuation of our faithful Afghan partners.

< Commercial Break: I'm sure by now everyone is familiar with the nightmare I am about to describe, but just in case…

Throughout the past two decades, hundreds of thousands of Afghans risked their lives to serve alongside us, whether it be cooking, driving, providing security, or serving as journalists, interpreters, or cultural advisers.

In exchange for their invaluable help, the United States promised these brave men and women that we would not leave them behind to suffer for their loyalty to us. And suffer they would. Terribly. Even as they were negotiating their joke of a "peace" agreement with the Trump administration, the Taliban made it crystal clear that anyone who helped the U.S. during the war would be put to death, and they wasted no time acting on that threat.

The Norwegian Center for Global Analyses, an organization supported by the United Nations to supply the organization with rapid response capacity, reported well before America's final withdrawal deadline that the Taliban had been "intensifying the hunt-down of all individuals and collaborators with the former regime," going door-to-door to find and kill our faithful partners. If their original target wasn't around, they just harassed and/or harmed their target's family members until they arrived to face their fate.

When the United States withdrew from Afghanistan, we sealed the fates of these loyal allies – and essentially signed many of their death certificates.

This happened even though American veterans, refugee advocates, members of Congress, and human rights organizations had been sounding the warning – loudly – for months that these faithful Afghans were in danger of being left for dead.

I guess we shouldn't be surprised, because it's not like we haven't done this to our allies before, multiple times. After we left Vietnam, for example, the North Vietnamese communists put 300,000 of our South Vietnamese partners in prison, subjecting them to horrendous treatment, including starvation, torture and, of course, death.

After the first Gulf War we abandoned the Kurds, leaving them to be slaughtered by Saddam Hussein. Likewise, in 2011 when our combat troops exited Iraq, our government failed to issue even a fraction of the U.S. visas authorized for the loyal allies who helped us. After we left, an estimated 1,000 Iraqi interpreters were murdered in retribution. >

Not to toot my own horn, but long ago I devised a failsafe solution to our predicament in Afghanistan: Have Elon, Jeff or Richard invent a time machine and travel back to 2001.

Once there, make the decision to significantly limit U.S. ground forces in Afghanistan and instead focus on air strikes on al-Qaeda and Taliban forces – in partnership with the Northern Alliance, Pashtun and other anti-Taliban forces – much like we did at the very beginning of *Operation Enduring Freedom*.

Meanwhile, U.S. Special Forces and the CIA will focus on hunting down Osama bin Laden and the others responsible for the 9/11 attacks, keeping a laser-focus on terrorists and those who harbor them (much like our Special Forces and CIA actually did). Under no circumstance will we go into Iraq, which would only divide our resources and focus.

Diplomatically, we will absolutely help Afghanistan stabilize and become a civil society, but we will not tolerate corruption on any level from the new Afghan government. On. Any. Level. We will have a smart fiscal strategy and not waste billions and billions of dollars.

But, unfortunately, even Elon, Jeff and Richard can't invent time machines so, like it or not, we have no choice but to play the hand we were dealt by those who came before us. The bottom line is that we did go – full on – into Afghanistan and with that lethal decision comes responsibility.

To help break this disaster down, let's take a closer look at the head-exploding speech President Biden gave that Monday after the Taliban takeover:

> Joe Biden: "So I'm left again to ask of those who argue that we should stay: How many more generations of America's daughters and sons would you have me send to fight Afghanistan's civil war when Afghan troops will not? How many more lives – American lives – is it worth? How many endless rows of headstones at Arlington National Cemetery?"

Setting aside the fact that, at the time of this speech, Americans weren't freaking out because of the decision to withdraw from Afghanistan but because of the total incompetence of *how* it was being handled, this is a completely disingenuous argument.

For one, American military casualties in Afghanistan have been steadily declining for years (the U.S. Department of Defense reports there were 13 U.S. combat deaths in 2018, 17 U.S. combat deaths in 2019, 4 combat deaths in 2020, and zero combat deaths in 2021, until the unspeakable tragedy on Thursday, August 26th when we lost 13 of our brave soldiers).

For another, we weren't in Afghanistan just to "fight Afghanistan's civil war." We were there to prevent terrorism from once again rising to the point where it can harm America and our allies.

Before the American withdrawal, I once wrote, "Having no U.S. troops in Afghanistan is just not feasible unless we are cool with a resurgence of terrorism and the Taliban slaughtering people as they overthrow the Afghan government to establish Sharia law – which is exactly what we found when we stormed into Afghanistan twenty years ago. Not to mention that, because we will no longer have a CIA presence in Afghanistan, we will lose all ability to gather intelligence and carry out counterterrorism strikes – a decision that I promise we will live to regret."

I stand by those words 1000%. There are two distinct questions involved in this discussion and, even though the Biden administration has tried hard to muddy the waters by merging the two, we must keep them separate: 1) Should the United States have completely withdrawn from Afghanistan in the first place, and 2) After the decision was made to leave, how and why did our withdrawal go so horribly wrong.

First up, should we have completely withdrawn from Afghanistan in the first place? My answer is a resounding NO for TWO reasons.

Before I honor you by sharing my stellar reasoning, let's clear something up: Maintaining an American presence in Afghanistan IS NOT analogous with America continuing to fight an "endless war." This is a false choice.

Over the past few years, our Afghan war strategy has transitioned from a conventional "troops on the ground" mission to one that relies heavily on U.S. Special Forces and missile and drone strikes. Our presence in Afghanistan was finally beginning to resemble the light-footprint, low-cost operation formula that has been successful in Syria and Iraq.

I recognize these are all very different places – and I don't pretend to know exactly how many U.S. troops it would take to maintain order in Afghanistan, however uneasy and fragile it may be – but, in Syria, 900 U.S. troops have been able to successfully help hold back Russians, Turks, Iranians and ISIS.

American troops being stationed around the world to maintain stability in certain regions is nothing new for the United States. I mean, that's kind of what we do, right? After all, this is the strategy we followed in South Korea and Western Europe after World War II (except, in those cases, we left *way* more troops than what I'm suggesting).

After World War II, we left almost 30,000 troops in South Korea and almost 40,000 troops in Western Europe. To this day, the United States has 35,486 troops in Germany, 53,938 in Japan, and 26,326 in South Korea. Obviously, we have not been "at war" in any of these places for decades, but we still have a vested interest in maintaining peace and prosperity in those regions.

At some point during the withdrawal process, I heard an American veteran of the Afghan war say that this post-World War II example doesn't make sense in terms of Afghanistan; rather, a more appropriate comparison is our experience in Vietnam. With the greatest respect, I disagree with his assessment.

Although the entire debacle devolved into a deadly mess, the U.S. mission in Vietnam was to ostensibly prevent the spread of communism, a problem relatively contained to just a few clearly identified countries.

The challenge we face today is completely different. The United States continues to battle a <u>*global*</u> war on terror, a fact President Biden acknowledged when he said in his speech, "Today, the terrorist threat has metastasized well beyond Afghanistan: al Shabaab in Somalia, al Qaeda in the Arabian Peninsula, al-Nusra in Syria, ISIS attempting to create a caliphate in Syria and Iraq and establishing affiliates in multiple countries in Africa and Asia."

Biden's position is that leaving Afghanistan was necessary, in part, because these new threats "warrant our attention and our resources."

My position is the exact opposite. Given these emerging threats around the world, doesn't it make sense to have a relatively small number of troops hold what we've got in Afghanistan – especially since we have already invested trillions of dollars and thousands of precious lives – instead of giving the Taliban a wide-open net to turn Afghanistan back into a cornerstone of terror?

A cornerstone of terror, by the way, that we will most certainly be forced to return to, finding it in far worse and more dangerous shape than ever before. This just doesn't make sense – which brings me back to my two-point stellar reasoning for why the United States should <u>not</u> have completely withdrawn from Afghanistan.

The <u>**FIRST REASON**</u> is the inevitable reemergence of terrorism.

> Joe Biden: "We went to Afghanistan almost 20 years ago with clear goals: Get those who attacked us on September 11, 2001, and **make sure al-Qaeda could not use Afghanistan as a**

> **base from which to attack us again.** We did that. We severely degraded al-Qaeda in Afghanistan. We never gave up the hunt for Osama bin Laden, and we got him. That was a decade ago…our only vital national interest in Afghanistan remains today what it has always been: **preventing a terrorist attack on American homeland**."

Exactly, Mr. President! That's why we should maintain a residual presence there. Does anyone really believe for one second that empowering the freak'n *Taliban* is going to move us *closer* to *preventing* a terrorist attack on the American homeland? Seriously?

Months before our withdrawal, CIA Director William J. Burns told the Senate Intelligence Committee that there is "significant risk" associated with withdrawal. "The U.S. government's ability to collect and act on threats will diminish. That's simply a fact."

As Marc Polymeropoulos, a veteran intelligence officer who served as a CIA base chief in Afghanistan told *The Washington Post*, "The counterterrorism posture went from problematic with the U.S. withdrawal to extraordinarily bad with the Taliban in full control. Suddenly one wonders if we will go entirely dark. It's like a bad dream."

The Washington Post also reports that another intelligence officer, who withheld his/her name over safety concerns, said the successful Taliban takeover "is encouraging many jihadists to think about traveling to Afghanistan now instead of Syria or Iraq." Indeed, one al-Qaeda fighter named Abu Khaled said, "God willing, the success of the Taliban will be also a chance to unify mujahideen movements like al-Qaeda and Daesh."

Well, that's just awesome, isn't it?

A senior counterterrorism official in the Trump administration, Nathan Sales, added this piece of good news: "We are now back to 1998, where the Clinton administration was launching missiles at desert camps and hoping to hit something. That wasn't enough to prevent 9/11 and returning to that is not a recipe for success."

Seriously, guys. Whiskey. Tango. Foxtrot.

Without question, it is great news that over a decade after we finally got Osama bin Laden, the threat from terrorism has weakened around the world. In the Institute for Economics & Peace's 2020 *Global Terrorism Index*, they report that, "In 2019, deaths from terrorism fell for the fifth consecutive year, after peaking in 2014. The total number of deaths fell by 15.5 percent to 13,826. The fall in deaths was mirrored by a reduction in the impact of terrorism, with 103 countries recording an improvement on their Global Terrorism Index (GTI) score, compared to 35 that recorded a deterioration (the full GTI score takes into account not only deaths, but also incidents, injuries, and property damage from terrorism, over a five-year period.)"

This was actually good news! And it's also my entire point. The momentum was *finally* going in our direction! We should have taken the opportunity to *diminish* terror organizations even more, not give them a golden opportunity to regroup and thrive. Why in the world would we let up on the gas *now*?

There are several interesting ways we can take advantage of this momentum. One involves a concept I rarely hear anyone talk about: Counter-Ideological Warfare.

For decades, the United States has allowed terrorist organizations to frame America's image for a large part of the Muslim world. Seizing every opportunity, terrorists have done a masterful job of making sure their audience knows all about the "evil" that is America: The brutal, wealthy bully that uses power, might and military strength to repress and oppress Muslims around the world. Naturally, in their version, the terrorists are the good guys, who fight bravely and unselfishly to protect Islam and Muslims on a global scale.

These groups often base their pitch on half-truths or outright lies, then fill in the blanks with our actual failures like the catastrophes of U.S. torture, Guantánamo and Abu Ghraib – and now, of course, our humiliating capitulation to the Taliban.

Conspiracy theories like *The Protocols of the Meetings of the Learned Elders of Zion* (a fraudulent document that served as a pretext and rationale for anti-Semitism in the early 20th century) and the 9/11

Truth movement (a conspiracy theory that disputes the conventional wisdom of the 9/11 accounts, specifically the part where al-Qaeda terrorists hijacked four airliners and crashed them into the Pentagon and Twin Towers) are exploited mightily.

Terrorist groups have achieved great success with their *America is Evil* narrative primarily through Information Warfare, or "using truth, intelligence, propaganda, psychological warfare, and media in a unified effort to control the way an enemy's own ideology or policies are perceived by the global public."

In the past, terrorists have waged their extremist propaganda war by using everything from CDs to television to radio. Now they have the enormous benefit of the Internet, which gives them the opportunity to reach into unlimited parts of the world.

A smart counter-ideological warfare strategy goes way beyond the standard "winning hearts and minds" campaign. In a weird twist, Abu Yahya al-Libi, a senior al-Qaeda leader, scholar, and strategist, once laid out the outlines of a successful campaign in an interview. His advice:

> "Start a social epidemic of rejection. Create a social epidemic of personal revulsion against the "cult;" Identify the criminality to al-Qaeda's target audience. Appeal to the universal value placed on stability, law and order, and justice; Make al-Qaeda answer publicly for killing innocents, particularly children; Make the terrorists' community and families fear for the spiritual safety of recruits; Make people remember they can't depend on terrorists; Reframe al-Qaeda as political opportunists; Encourage positive ideological fitna (civil war). Support former militants who recant terror and speak out against it; and Demand al-Qaeda pay blood debts (wrongful deaths they have caused) to Muslims and Non-Muslims, as proscribed in the Qur'an."

Okay, I realize this may be a much heavier lift for America after what happened in Afghanistan but, otherwise, the timing for this approach is pretty great – especially when the Muslim world is as concerned about Islamic extremism as we are.

Even as far back as 2013, the Pew Research Center found that "concern about Islamic extremism remains widespread among Muslims from South Asia to the Middle East to sub-Saharan Africa. Across 11 Muslim publics surveyed, a median of 67 percent say they are somewhat or very concerned about Islamic extremism. In five countries – Pakistan, Jordan, Tunisia, Turkey and Indonesia – Muslim worries about extremism have increased in the past year."

The report continues, "In many of the countries surveyed, clear majorities of Muslims oppose violence in the name of Islam. Indeed, about three-quarters or more in Pakistan (89 percent), Indonesia (81 percent), Nigeria (78 percent) and Tunisia (77 percent), say suicide bombings or other acts of violence that target civilians are <u>never</u> justified."

In 2019, *The Economist* revealed that:

> Across Arab countries, "The share of people expressing much trust in political parties, most of which have a religious tint, has fallen by well over a third since 2011, to 15 percent. (The share of Iraqis who say they do not trust parties at all rose from 51 percent to 78 percent). The decline in trust for Islamist parties is similarly dramatic, falling from 35 percent in 2013, when the question was first widely asked, to 20 percent in 2018.
>
> The doubts extend to religious leaders. In 2013 around 51 percent of respondents said they trusted their religious leaders to a 'great' or 'medium' extent. When a comparable question was asked last year, the number was down to 40 percent. The share of Arabs who think religious leaders should have influence over government decision-making is also steadily declining."

Employing strategies like Counter-Ideological Warfare is super important because, although the threat level of terrorism is down, it's certainly not gone. Without question, the demise of their caliphate was a major blow to ISIS, as was the death of Islamic State leader Abu Bakr al-Baghdadi in October 2019. But these should be viewed as events that provided a temporary disruption to the terrorist group's activities, not as absolute victory for those of us who have been fighting them.

After al-Baghdadi's death, for example, the Defense Intelligence Agency (DIA) concluded that "ISIS is 'postured to withstand' al-Baghdadi's death, and will likely maintain 'continuity of operations, global cohesion, and at least its current trajectory.'"

Indeed, very soon after their caliphate collapsed, ISIS militant fighters were reorganizing in Syrian bunkers, the Badia desert, areas around the disputed border between the Kurdistan region and the rest of Iraq, and other areas controlled by Kurdish and Iraqi forces – devising guerrilla warfare tactics to make a comeback.

In some areas – like Raqqa and the Deir al-Zour province in Syria, the province of Diyala in northeastern Iraq, and Afghanistan – the group was soon back to carrying out bombings, assassinations, ambushes, and firing mortar rounds.

One thing we learned or should have learned from this episode is that there are plenty of menacing groups chomping at the bit to fill the vacuum created by the exit of United States forces from the region.

Iran, for one, is just waiting for the moment when it can call down the Hezbollah militias under its control in western and southern Syria to gain control over the major oil fields in Deir al-Zour.

The United States Institute of Peace – a federal institution founded by Congress that is tasked with promoting conflict resolution and prevention worldwide – reminds us that:

> "To a certain extent we have been here before, back in 2007 following the 'Anbar Awakening' in Iraq. And we have seen how the Islamic State in Iraq, as it was then called, was able to rebuild itself and reach even greater heights. The Islamic State's strategy is based on a staged approach – not dissimilar from the Maoist strategy of protracted warfare – and after their defeat in the Anbar Awakening they simply returned to a lower stage, went underground and re-grouped in the countryside. They expect to oscillate between stages before eventual victory. It is important to remember that it is this strategy that is arguably its primary export to global affiliates.

If we are not careful and vigilant, the Islamic State is more than capable of re-emerging and rising in strength once again.

Already, "the decline of ISIS's core has been coupled with the rise and expansion of ISIL provinces and affiliates around the world – now stretching across Europe, Russia, Eurasia, Asia, and Africa…the central trend has been the displacement of activity away from the Middle East and North Africa, with a global presence becoming an increasing part of the Islamic State's operations. In 2019, Islamic State provinces and affiliates accounted for 74 percent of all the deaths from the group's acts of terrorism. In particular, the African continent has become a focus of affiliates' growth and increasing activity, with sub-Saharan Africa by itself now accounting for 41 percent of deaths."

Then there was this warning from a United Nations report, released on June 1, 2021:

"A significant part of the leadership of al-Qaida resides in the Afghanistan and Pakistan border region, alongside al-Qaida in the Indian Subcontinent. Large numbers of al-Qaida fighters and other foreign extremist elements aligned with the Taliban are located in various parts of Afghanistan.

The primary component of the Taliban in dealing with al-Qaida is the Haqqani Network (an officially listed terrorist group). Ties between the two groups remain close, based on ideological alignment, relationships forged through common struggle and intermarriage.

The Islamic State in Iraq and the Levant-Khorasan remains diminished from its zenith, following successive military setbacks that began in Jowzjan in summer 2018. However, since June 2020, it has had an ambitious new leader, Shahab al-Muhajir, and it remains active and dangerous, particularly if it is able, by positioning itself as the sole pure rejectionist group in Afghanistan, to recruit disaffected Taliban and other militants to swell its ranks."

In his speech, Biden, in defense of his opting for a full withdrawal, said, "We conduct effective counterterrorism missions against terrorist groups in multiple countries where we don't have a permanent military presence. If necessary, we will do the same in Afghanistan."

Wait, what? Mr. President, what do you mean by "if necessary?" Less than one week after the Taliban captured Kabul, your own national security adviser Jake Sullivan said that the threat of the Islamic State "is real. It is acute. It is persistent."

Wake-up! Anyone with eyes and a television could see that U.S. counterterrorism missions in Afghanistan were already needed right then. That Very Day! In fact, the Islamic State Khorasan (ISIS-K) – the Islamic State's Afghanistan and Pakistan arm – had just killed 13 of our soldiers. Plus, ISIS-K considers the Taliban an enemy also, which means that, even if the Taliban wanted to, they cannot control them.

Worse, ISIS-K aside, it was clear even then that the Taliban remain thicker than thieves with other terrorist groups, and they have been from the moment the Trump administration started the sham negotiations with them for a "peace" agreement.

In truth, these terrorists were ten steps ahead of the United States government the entire time. Being outfoxed by a bunch of radical fanatics is embarrassing enough but, to make matters worse, by then terrorists had become so indifferent to the United States that they didn't even try to disguise the cozy relationships between themselves.

The February 2020 "peace" agreement that Trump administration officials signed in Doha, Qatar was countersigned by an organization led by the Haqqani Network. In fact, at the time, the Haqqani Network's leader, Sirajuddin Haqqani, was the Taliban's deputy leader and military commander. After the Taliban takeover, he was announced as their new Interior Minister.

The Haqqani Network is designated as a foreign terrorist group by the United States, and Sirajuddin Haqqani – who has a $5 million U.S. bounty on his head – is wanted for questioning in conjunction with, among other murderous acts, a hotel bombing in Kabul, a failed assassination attempt on former Afghan President Hamid Karzai, and attacks on the Afghanistan U.S. embassy and NATO bases.

Because of their close ties to the Haqqani Network, al-Qaeda were on hand to coach the Taliban throughout the negotiations, even though part of the Taliban's agreement with the United States was that they would sever all ties with them. Yeah, right.

Several points of agreement were established between the Trump administration and the Taliban, but the essence of the deal was this: Taliban insurgents assured U.S. officials that Afghanistan will never again be a harbor for international terrorism in exchange for a full withdrawal of American troops. Yeah, right.

It's understandable that war weary Americans were encouraged by this "groundbreaking" agreement, but not so fast. Setting aside the fact that we should never believe a word that comes out of these murderers' mouths, to close the deal, the United States capitulated on practically *everything*. The United States even agreed to drop the word "terrorist" when describing al-Qaeda, which is just a jaw-dropping concession.

The U.S. also agreed to help convince the Afghan government to release 5,000 Taliban prisoners, while the Taliban was only required to release 1,000 and agreed to what the Taliban called a "reduction in violence" instead of the total cease-fire that the United States had demanded at the beginning of the negotiations.

The United States also agreed to support the gradual removal of Taliban leaders from international sanctions blacklists, including the lists of the United States and United Nations. Zalmay Khalilzad, the Afghan American diplomat leading the negotiations for the Americans, consistently said that the United States was not looking for a withdrawal agreement but "a peace agreement that enables withdrawal."

Give me a ### break. This entire episode is humiliating enough. Let's at least have the dignity to call this what it really is: Surrender.

The Taliban certainly had no problem calling it what it was. At the Doha Sheraton hotel where the United States and Taliban signed the February 2020 agreement, the Taliban's press guy gleefully called the agreement "the defeat of the arrogance of the White House in the face of the white turban." Hmmm…catchy!

At one point, Sirajuddin Haqqani proudly said that "no mujahid ever thought that one day we would face such an improved state, or that we will crush the arrogance of the rebellious emperors and force them to admit their defeat at our hands."

These statements undoubtably sent chills up and down the spine of every Afghan. Keep in mind, the Afghan government didn't even attend the February negotiations because the Taliban refused to negotiate with them. If ever there was a flaming red flag, this was it. How in the world could anyone believe that peace and cooperation were possible between the Afghan government and the Taliban after our exit if the Taliban wouldn't even sit at a table with them?

Of course, the incendiary statements from the Taliban came as no surprise to the Afghans, who have seen this play before. Afghanistan and her people have already lived through at least one brutal civil war, which is the reason they were living under the tyrannical rule of the Taliban when U.S. forces arrived in 2001 to stop the ruthless Islamic regime.

In September 2020 – after multiple delays over the terms of a prisoner swap the U.S. had negotiated with the Taliban without the input of the Afghan government – the Afghans and Taliban did finally sit down at the same table to engage in "peace" talks.

This was a historic moment to be sure, but it's important to remember what happened *between* the signing of the peace agreement in February 2020 and the September joint "peace" talks.

Between these two meetings, the Taliban conducted multiple targeted attacks on Afghanistan's security forces, members of the government and judiciary, activists, journalists and religious leaders. They also attacked Afghanistan's National Directorate of Security – an Afghan intelligence complex located in the northern city of Aybak – killing 11 people and injuring over 60 more. On March 9, 2020, Afghanistan's presidential inauguration day, the Taliban unleashed a barrage of mortar shells.

Meanwhile, the Islamic State Khorasan (ISIS-K) continued its suicide bombing routine, including one at a funeral for a local police commander in the province of Nangarhar that killed 25 people and injured 68 more.

There were other mass casualty attacks – both before and after the meeting between the Taliban and Afghan government – like the one at a tutoring center that murdered 44 people, one at Kabul University that killed 21, a truck bomb that killed 27 people in Kabul, and an attack on a Kandahar airfield.

Then there was this: Sayed Ul-Shuhada, an Afghan high school in Kabul, was bombed, killing at least 90 civilians and injuring almost 150 more – during the holy month of Ramadan, no less. Most of the victims were teenage girls innocently leaving class.

There was also a mass casualty event so evil that even the Taliban or ISIS-K wouldn't take credit for it: An attack on a maternity ward supported by *Doctors Without Borders* that killed brand new mothers, their newborn babies, medical staff, and a police officer.

On June 16, 2021, at least 24 members of an Afghan elite force and five police officers were killed by the Taliban in Faryab Province. Ferdous Samim, whose best friend – a major in the Afghan security forces – was killed in the attack, spoke for many Afghans when he said: "We mourn. The Taliban celebrate. And it hurts too much."

The United Nations Assistance Mission in Afghanistan (UNAMA) reported 1,783 civilian casualties between January 1, 2021 and March 31, 2021 alone. This was a 29 percent increase from the same period in 2020. The number of women casualties increased by 37 percent and child casualties were up 23 percent. There was a 38 percent increase in civilian casualties in the six months after the beginning of the Afghanistan "peace" negotiations in September 2020 compared to the same period the year prior.

President Biden has tried to distance himself from the hell that was unleashed in Afghanistan after the U.S. announced its withdrawal because, after all, he "inherited a deal that President Trump negotiated with the Taliban."

While it is true that the Trump administration signed a ridiculously flawed, joke of a deal with the Taliban, the Biden administration didn't have to abide by its terms because the Taliban was in breach of practically every provision of the agreement.

By now, you know how important it is to me for the United States to honor our commitments, even bad ones that are passed from one presidential administration to the next. But the Taliban's egregious actions – happening in real time and in plain sight – were in such violation of the agreement that, in my mind, it was void practically from the beginning. The Taliban's failure to reduce violence and refusal to sever ties with al-Qaeda alone justifies this view.

The **SECOND REASON** we should not have completely withdrawn from Afghanistan: We had already spent a fortune there in blood and treasure. Even a modest American presence would have helped protect the enormous investment we have made.

As none other than Imran Khan, the prime minister of Pakistan, said months before the Taliban takeover of Kabul, "All those who have invested in the Afghan peace process should resist the temptation for setting unrealistic timelines. A hasty international withdrawal from Afghanistan would be unwise. We should also guard against regional spoilers who are not invested in peace and see instability in Afghanistan as advantageous for their own geopolitical ends. Like the United States, we do not want the blood and treasure we have shed in the war against terrorism to be in vain."

John Sopko, the Special Inspector General for Afghanistan Reconstruction (SIGAR) for the Obama and Trump administrations, put it this way in January 2019:

> "Afghanistan is our nation's longest war. Our investment there is unprecedented. To date, the U.S. has provided over $132 billion for Afghanistan's reconstruction, a number that does not include the significantly higher cost of war-fighting, which the Pentagon estimates to have cost as much as $800 billion. Adjusting for inflation, we have spent more on Afghanistan's reconstruction than we spent on the entire *Marshall Plan* to rebuild western Europe after World War II." (an October 2021 SIGAR report now puts the dollar figure at $146 billion)

The *Costs of War* project located at the Watson Institute of International Affairs at Brown University has a team of fifty scholars, legal experts, human rights practitioners, and physicians who began their work in 2010.

< Note: The *Costs of War* project explains that their numbers "differ substantially from the Pentagon's estimates of the costs of the post-9/11 wars because it includes not only war appropriations made to the Department of Defense – spending in the war zones of Iraq, Syria, Afghanistan, Pakistan, and in other places the government designates as sites of 'overseas contingency operations' – but also includes spending across the federal government that is a consequence of these wars. Specifically, this is war-related spending by the Department of State, past and obligated spending for war veterans' care, interest on the debt incurred to pay for the wars, and the prevention of and response to terrorism by the Department of Homeland Security." >

The *Costs of War* project says this regarding the financial costs:

> "Through Fiscal Year 2020, the United States federal government has spent or obligated $6.4 trillion dollars on the post-9/11 wars in Afghanistan, Pakistan, Iraq, and elsewhere. This figure includes direct Congressional war appropriations; war-related increases to the Pentagon base budget; veterans care and disability; increases in the homeland security budget; interest payments on direct war borrowing; foreign assistance spending; and estimated future obligations for veterans' care.
>
> This total omits many other expenses, such as the macroeconomic costs to the U.S. economy; the opportunity costs of not investing war dollars in alternative sectors; future interest on war borrowing; and local government and private war costs.
>
> The current wars have been paid for almost entirely by borrowing. This borrowing has raised the U.S. budget deficit, increased the national debt, and had other macroeconomic effects, such as raising consumer interest rates. Unless the U.S. immediately repays the money borrowed for war, there will also be future interest payments. We estimate that interest payments could total over $8 trillion by the 2050s.
>
> Spending on the wars has involved opportunity costs for the U.S. economy. Although military spending does produce

jobs, spending in other areas such as health care could produce more jobs. Additionally, while investment in military infrastructure grew, investment in other, nonmilitary, public infrastructure such as roads and schools did not grow at the same rate.

Finally, federal war costs exclude billions of dollars of state, municipal, and private war costs across the country – dollars spent on services for returned veterans and their families, in addition to local homeland security efforts."

The *Costs of War* project says this regarding the human costs:

"At least 800,000 people have been killed by direct war violence in Iraq, Afghanistan, Syria, Yemen, and Pakistan. The number of people who have been wounded or have fallen ill as a result of the conflicts is far higher, as is the number of civilians who have died indirectly as a result of the destruction of hospitals and infrastructure and environmental containment, among other war-related problems.

Thousands of United States service members have died in combat, as have thousands of civilian contractors. Many have died later on from injuries and illnesses sustained in the war zones. Hundreds of thousands of soldiers and contractors have been wounded and are living with disabilities and war-related illnesses. Allied security forces have also suffered significant casualties, as have opposition forces. However, the vast majority of people killed are civilians. More than 310,000 civilians have been killed in the fighting since 2001."

A *Costs of War* report released in November 2018 included this:

"Nearly 7,000 United States soldiers and sailors have been killed post-9/11. But deaths do not tell the entire story. Since 2001, more than 53,700 U.S. soldiers and sailors have been officially listed as wounded in the major post-9/11 war zones wars. Many other U.S. soldiers have become amputees. From

> the start of the wars through mid 2015, there were 1,645 major limb amputations for U.S. service members associated with battle injuries in the major war zones.
>
> The Congressional Research Service has stopped releasing regular updates on U.S. military casualty statistics. In its most recent report, issued in 2015, the Congressional Research Service found that more than 300,000 troops have suffered traumatic brain injuries.
>
> Suicide is also an urgent and growing problem among the veterans of the post-9/11 wars. Although it is difficult to tell how many of these suicides are by post-9/11 war Veterans, because the VA does not disaggregate by war, there were more than 6,000 Veteran suicides each year from 2008-2016, a rate that is 1.5 times greater than that of the non-Veteran population.
>
> Between 480,000 and 507,000 people have been killed in the United States' post-9/11 wars in Iraq, Afghanistan, and Pakistan. This tally of the counts and estimates of direct deaths caused by war violence does not include the more than 500,000 deaths from the war in Syria, raging since 2011, which the U.S. joined in August 2014....The wars are ongoing, although the wars in Afghanistan, Pakistan and Iraq are less intense than in recent years. Still, the number of civilians killed in Afghanistan in 2018 is on track to be one of the highest death tolls in the war."

Before the U.S. withdrawal, I once wrote, "If our politicians don't wise up fast, every single dime we have spent in Afghanistan will be wasted and any progress on the ground we have made in the past twenty years will simply vanish." Regrettably, Joe Biden didn't wise up and that's exactly what has happened. It's sickening.

> Joe Biden: "Our mission in Afghanistan was never supposed to have been nation building. It was never supposed to be creating a unified, centralized democracy."

You know, maybe nation building wasn't supposed to be one of America's key roles in Afghanistan, but it sure was a damn nice side effect. Listen, I get it. There are many, many, many things that were handled horribly in Afghanistan, including unprecedented waste and corruption.

And, thanks to the Afghanistan Papers – a set of interviews relating to the war in Afghanistan prepared by the Special Inspector General for Afghanistan Reconstruction (SIGAR) – we now know the American people were blatantly lied to, over and over.

There will be plenty of time to sort all of this out as we muddle through court cases and congressional hearings, but none of this should diminish the incredibly great things that we had achieved for Afghanistan and her people.

We helped Afghanistan build schools and a health care system, a security force, infrastructure like roads and airports, and institutions like parliament and a justice system.

Albeit slowly, Afghanistan *was* becoming a civil society, finally on the right path in areas like education, health, communications, and improved living conditions.

Although, before the Taliban takeover, Afghanistan was still looking for sustainable sources of growth – and was still heavily dependent on foreign aid – the country's GDP before the pandemic was $19.3 billion and the economy grew by 3.9 percent in 2019 according to the World Bank, an international financial institution that provides loans and grants to the governments of low- and middle-income countries for the purpose of pursuing capital projects.

The World Bank alone had committed over $4.7 billion for development projects, and the bank administered the Afghanistan Reconstruction Trust Fund which had raised over $12.27 billion.

Reflecting on the chaotic and deadly U.S. withdrawal, the loss of our soldiers and innocent civilians and the betrayal of our steadfast Afghan partners is crushing. But add to that the devastating future we solidified for the girls and women of Afghanistan.

Over the past two decades, the U.S. spent $780 million to promote the rights of Afghan females. In 2006, First Lady Laura Bush was on hand to open the American University of Afghanistan (AUAF). The

AUAF – established by a $100 million grant from the United States – became the country's only coeducational school of higher education.

As a result of our efforts, 40 percent of all students were female, and many had gone on to be government officials, doctors, lawyers, engineers, computer scientists, police officers, teachers, artists, small business owners and professional athletes.

There was an Afghan female soccer team and mountaineering team, not to mention the Afghan Girls Robotics Team – made up of 25 girls, ranging in age from 12 to 18, who had captured the hearts of entire countries around the world.

These hopeful little girls, inspired teens and empowered women trusted us. They all believed in America and the principles we convinced them we stood for.

Afghan females fought hard for their freedom. On August 24, 2016, the Taliban, armed with guns and explosives, attacked the AUAF. The ten-hour attack killed 15 people, ten of them students. Just weeks earlier, the Taliban had kidnapped two of the school's English teachers, one from America and one from Australia (the teachers were finally released, in exchange for Taliban leaders, three years later).

But the AUAF would not be denied! The resilient students and staff refused to cower in the face of terror and reopened, better than ever, less than one year later.

Now, we have stripped these girls, teens and women of their hope and freedom and sentenced them to a life of draconian rules and abject misery. Within days of the takeover, the girls on the robotics team could not leave their homes without a male escort, women's health clinics were forced to close, and females of all ages were turned away from what was once their schools and universities. In some provinces, women were already back in head-to-toe burqas.

The United States left at least 600 AUAF students behind. After several attempts were made to escape the country, their fates were sealed with a final email: "I regret to inform you that the high command at HKIA in the airport has announced there will be no more rescue flights."

After the students were told their names had been given to the Taliban, a 24-year-old sophomore named Hosay, who was studying business administration, told *The New York Times*, “We are all terrified. There is no evacuation, there is no getting out.” Hosay’s plan before the Taliban took control of her life was to get an M.B.A. and start an all-female engineering firm.

Statistically speaking, Hosay won’t make it out of this alive, and I’m not being overdramatic. For obvious reasons, AUAF students are at the top of the Taliban’s death list.

At an emergency meeting of the United Nations Security Council right after the Taliban takeover, the UN secretary general António Guterres said he was already “receiving chilling reports of severe restrictions on human rights” in Afghanistan and was “particularly concerned by accounts of mounting human rights violations against the women and girls of Afghanistan.”

Taliban spokesman Zabihullah Mujahid didn’t make anyone feel better when he released a statement saying that women should stay at home because the Taliban was “worried our forces who are new and have not been yet trained very well may mistreat women.”

This entire thing is just surreal to me. Did we really relinquished 20 years of admirable progress to the Taliban for them to destroy in an instant? The realization that we have done exactly that makes me sick to my stomach.

Biden remarked in his infamous speech that “we have to be honest: our mission in Afghanistan has taken many missteps over the past two decades…I will not mislead the American people by claiming that just a little more time in Afghanistan will make all the difference.”

But the truth is, MORE TIME *WOULD* HAVE MADE A DIFFERENCE. A REALLY, REALLY BIG ONE. I’ll say again, without question the United States and the Afghan government have both made countless missteps over the past two decades. Not many people, if any, deny that.

However, we were JUST arriving at the point where the first generation of Afghans who were born into a world with freedom and without fear were coming of age. THEY are the ones who would have made all the difference.

Think of this: At the time of the U.S. withdrawal, the average Afghan was 18 years old and almost two-thirds of the country was under 25. Living under the protection of America and NATO forces are all this generation has ever known. Now, we have ripped the rug out from under them, never even giving them the chance to lead.

Now for the second question involved in this conversation: After the decision was made to leave Afghanistan, how and why did the withdrawal go so horribly wrong?

When I first saw the horrifying images of the withdrawal coming out of Afghanistan, my initial thought was that the Biden administration was caught flatfooted, completely unprepared for what was an easily predicable event. Now that time has passed, it's clear that it was far worse than being unprepared, it was total incompetence.

The defensive, accusatory and angry reaction of Joe Biden and his administration made them look far worse, and their theme of "*no one* could have seen this coming" is downright absurd.

> Joe Biden, July 2, 2021, when asked about Afghanistan at a White House Press Briefing, where he called the journalists questions "negative": "I want to talk about happy things, man. Look, it's Fourth of July. I'm concerned that you're asking me questions that I will answer next week, but it's the holiday weekend. I'm going to celebrate it. There's great things happening."

> Joe Biden, August 16, 2021: "The truth is: This did unfold more quickly than we had anticipated."

> Joe Biden, August 22, 2021: "Let me be clear: The evacuation of thousands of people from Kabul is going to be hard and painful no matter when it started or when we began. It would have been true if we started a month ago or a month from now. There is no way to evacuate this many people without pain and loss – of heartbreaking images you see on television."

What? No, seriously, *what*? Forget classified briefings and tactical strategy reports, does anyone in the White House even bother to read a newspaper?

It brings me no pleasure to say this, but if Joe Biden really believes that the only way to evacuate Afghanistan was through complete chaos and inflicting unavoidable "pain and loss," he should not be our Commander in Chief.

Watching and/or reading media coverage alone provided all the knowledge necessary to figure out that the Taliban had zero intention of playing it straight and never did. These terrorists had been on a murderous warpath through Afghanistan for months – capturing government military bases and entire command centers – and it's not like they were trying to keep it a secret.

Following his playbook of passing the buck, Biden essentially blamed his senior military advisors for the mess, saying "no one" that he "can recall" advised him to keep at least some troops in Afghanistan until all Americans were evacuated. This is just more insulting spin.

In April 2021, *The New York Times* reported that, after Biden announced to his advisors that he wanted all U.S. troops to be out of Afghanistan by September 11, 2021, this happened:

> "Over two decades of war that spanned four presidents, the Pentagon had always managed to fend off the political instincts of elected leaders frustrated with the grind of Afghanistan, as commanders repeatedly requested more time and more troops.
>
> The current military leadership <Defense Secretary Lloyd J. Austin III and Gen. Mark A. Milley, the chairman of the Joint Chiefs of Staff> hoped it, too, could convince a new president to maintain at least a modest troop presence, trying to talk Mr. Biden into keeping a residual force and setting conditions on any withdrawal. But Mr. Biden refused to be persuaded.
>
> There would be no conditions put on the withdrawal, Mr. Biden told the men, cutting off the last thread – one that had worked with Mr. Trump – and that Mr. Austin and General Milley hoped could stave off a full drawdown."

Four months later, *The Wall Street Journal* recounted the same scene, saying that, according to several administration and defense officials, Biden's decision to bring home U.S. troops was "made against the recommendations of his top military generals and many diplomats, who warned that a hasty withdrawal would undermine security in Afghanistan." The article continued:

> "The president's top generals, including Chairman of the Joint Chiefs of Staff Army Gen. Mark Milley, urged Mr. Biden to keep a force of about 2,500 troops, the size he inherited, while seeking a peace agreement between warring Afghan factions, to help maintain stability. Defense Secretary Lloyd Austin, who previously served as a military commander in the region, said a full withdrawal wouldn't provide any insurance against instability.
>
> In a series of meetings leading up to his decision, military and intelligence officials told Mr. Biden that security was deteriorating in Afghanistan, and they expressed concerns both about the capabilities of the Afghan military and the Taliban's likely ability to take over major Afghan cities.
>
> Other advisers, including Secretary of State Antony Blinken and national security adviser Jake Sullivan, raised the possibility of Taliban attacks on U.S. forces and diplomats as well as the Afghans who for two decades worked alongside them. Ultimately, neither disagreed with the president, knowing where he stood."

The Wall Street Journal also reported that, according to a U.S. official and a person familiar with the document, a July 2021 internal State Department memo, sent to Secretary of State Antony Blinken and Director of Policy Planning Salman Ahmed "warned top agency officials of the potential collapse of Kabul soon after the United States' August 31 troop withdrawal deadline in Afghanistan."

The memo also "warned of rapid territorial gains by the Taliban and the subsequent collapse of Afghan security forces and offered recommendations on ways to mitigate the crisis and speed up an evacuation."

On August 18, 2021, *The New York Times* revealed that there were "drumbeats of warnings" over the summer: "Classified assessments by American spy agencies over the summer painted an increasingly grim picture of the prospect of a Taliban takeover of Afghanistan and warned of the rapid collapse of the Afghan military, even as President Biden and his advisers said publicly that was unlikely to happen as quickly, according to current and former American government officials."

The article continues, "By July, many intelligence reports grew more pessimistic, questioning whether any Afghan security forces would muster serious resistance and whether the government could hold on in Kabul."

In yet another piece of outstanding journalism, *The New York Times* reported that: "In early May, a Taliban commander telephoned Muhammad Jallal, a tribal elder in Baghlan Province in northern Afghanistan, and asked him to deliver a message to Afghan government troops at several bases in his district. 'If they do not surrender, we will kill them,' Mr. Jallal said he was told."

In the article, Antonio Giustozzi, a research fellow at the Royal United Services Institute in London who has written multiple books about Afghanistan, explained the Taliban's strategy: "They contacted everyone and offered the chance to surrender or switch sides, with incentives, including money and rewarding people with appointments afterward. A lot of money changed hands."

Unsurprisingly, Mr. Jallal and the other tribal elders ultimately complied, and the Taliban moved on to capture the next district, all the while gobbling up more weapons, ammunition, food and fuel. By the way, the Taliban was doing this with volunteer and financial support from Pakistan, Russia and Iran…which is just perfect, isn't it?

The result, *The New York Times* explains, was a "lopsided fight between an adaptable and highly mobile insurgent juggernaut, and a demoralized government force that had been abandoned by its leaders and cut off from help. Once the first provincial capital city surrendered this month, the big collapses came as fast as the Taliban could travel."

Even if the Biden administration didn't fully grasp the totality of the destruction happening in Afghanistan – which, after what we just covered is in and of itself disqualifying – there was certainly enough evidence to know that troops had to stay until, at a bare minimum, we had a solid plan for the evacuation of American citizens and our Afghan allies; keep Bagram air base open until everyone was out; make sure humanitarian efforts were coordinated between the U.S. and nongovernmental organizations (NGOs); and make sure the CIA had time to plan for new ways to gather intelligence and initiate counterterrorism strikes.

> Joe Biden: "And here's what I believe to my core: It is wrong to order American troops to step up when Afghanistan's own armed forces would not…the Afghan military collapsed, sometimes without trying to fight. If anything, the developments of the past week reinforced that ending U.S. military involvement in Afghanistan now was the right decision. American troops cannot and should not be fighting in a war and dying in a war that Afghan forces are not willing to fight for themselves."

This is a despicable thing to say. Really, Mr. President? Are you really going to stand in front of the entire world and essentially call Afghan soldiers cowards?

It is obvious you deeply love your children and grandchildren. What would <u>you</u> do if <u>you</u> were stuck out in the middle of nowhere – vastly outnumbered – and <u>your</u> wife, <u>your</u> parents and <u>your</u> children were looking down the barrel of a terrorist's gun? Are you really blaming these people for handing over their weapons to stop the slaughter of their families?

Certainly, no one would mistake the Afghan military for a mighty fighting force, but this is just incredibly unfair.

Since I am neither an Afghan nor a soldier on the ground in Afghanistan, it's far more appropriate that you hear from someone who is both. General Sami Sadat, a three-star commander in the Afghan

National Army, explained it this way in a guest essay in *The New York Times*:

> "For the past three and a half months, I fought day and night, nonstop, in southern Afghanistan's Helmand Province against an escalating and bloody Taliban offensive. Coming under frequent attack, we held the Taliban back and inflicted heavy casualties. Then I was called to Kabul to command Afghanistan's special forces. But the Taliban already were entering the city; it was too late. I am exhausted. I am frustrated. And I am angry.
>
> President Biden said last week that 'American troops cannot and should not be fighting in a war and dying in a war that Afghan forces are not willing to fight for themselves.' It's true that the Afghan Army lost its will to fight. But that's because of the growing sense of abandonment by our American partners and the disrespect and disloyalty reflected in Mr. Biden's tone and words over the past few months. The Afghan Army is not without blame. It had its problems – cronyism, bureaucracy – but we ultimately stopped fighting because our partners already had."

General Sadat went on to explain the reasons why the Afghan military – one that has lost over 66,000 troops in the war – collapsed, including political divisions in both Kabul and Washington and the February 2020 "peace" deal – which, as reminder, the Afghan government was completely left out of. In fact, the General says the deal "doomed" him and his men by pinpointing a date certain for withdrawal.

General Sadat also laments the corruption in the Afghan government (then led by Ashraf Ghani, who blew town early on in this mess), which he acknowledges is significant. He explains that most of the leaders in the Afghan government were there because of personal relationships, not experience:

"These appointments had a devastating impact on the national army because leaders lacked the military experience to be effective or inspire the confidence and trust of the men being asked to risk their lives. Disruptions to food rations and fuel supplies – a result of skimming and corrupt contract allocations – destroyed the morale of my troops."

The final nail in the coffin – and every American should really pay attention – was the sudden loss of logistical and maintenance support from America. Funny, in his condescending speech that dissed the Afghan military, Biden conveniently left this part out:

> "Still, we kept fighting. But then Mr. Biden confirmed in April he would stick to Mr. Trump's plan and set the terms for the U.S. drawdown. That was when everything started to go downhill.
>
> The Afghan forces were trained by the Americans using the U.S. military model based on highly technical special reconnaissance units, helicopters and airstrikes. We lost our superiority to the Taliban when our air support dried up and our ammunition ran out.
>
> Contractors maintained our bombers and our attack and transport aircraft throughout the war. By July, most of the 17,000 support contractors had left. A technical issue now meant that aircraft – a Black Hawk helicopter, a C-130 transport, a surveillance drone – would be grounded.
>
> The contractors also took proprietary software and weapons systems with them. They physically removed our helicopter missile-defense system. Access to the software that we relied on to track our vehicles, weapons and personnel also disappeared. Real-time intelligence on targets went out the window, too.
>
> The Taliban fought with snipers and improvised explosive devices while we lost aerial and laser-guided weapon capacity. And since we could not resupply bases without helicopter support, soldiers often lacked the necessary tools to fight. The Taliban overran many bases; in other places, entire units surrendered. Mr. Biden's full and accelerated withdrawal only exacerbated the situation. It ignored conditions on the ground. The Taliban had a firm end date from the Americans and

feared no military reprisal for anything they did in the interim, sensing the lack of U.S. will.

And so the Taliban kept ramping up. My soldiers and I endured up to seven Taliban car bombings daily throughout July and the first week of August in Helmand Province. Still, we stood our ground."

It is just unfathomable to me that the United States of America handled things this...well...this *un-American*. This entire episode is truly shameful.

General Sadat ended his essay with this: "We were betrayed by politics and presidents. This was not an Afghan war only; it was an international war, with many militaries involved. It would have been impossible for one army alone, ours, to take up the job and fight. This was a military defeat, but it emanated from political failure."

So, here is where things stood mere weeks after the Taliban takeover: The United States snuck out of Bagram Airfield in the middle of the night, without even telling General Mir Asadullah Kohistani, Bagram's new commander.

We left an estimated 5,000 to 7,000 prisoners at Bagram – including many hard-core Taliban fighters and senior al-Qaeda operatives – whom the Taliban promptly released after they captured Bagram from the Afghan government without a fight.

Meanwhile, Afghan President Ashraf Ghani fled the country with a reported $169 million in cash, and Americans lowered our flag at the U.S. Embassy in Kabul, leaving it empty.

In one of its last communications, the Embassy issued a Security Alert warning that "the United States government could not ensure safe passage to the Hamid Karzai International Airport," making Afghanistan a Level 4 security risk because of "civil unrest, armed conflict, crime, terrorism, kidnapping and Covid-19."

This warning turned into a devastating reality when 13 of our brave soldiers and scores of Afghan civilians were killed by dual explosions set by ISIS-Khorasan, making Thursday, August 26, 2021, the deadliest day in Afghanistan since 2011.

Soon thereafter, in northwestern Kabul, ten civilians from the same family – eight of them under the age of 18 – were killed in a U.S. drone strike meant for the Islamic State. The family's neighbor described the scene: "The bodies were covered in blood and shrapnel, and some of the dead children were still inside the car."

A relative of the victims, Ahmad Fayaz, put it this way: "The United States 'always says they are killing [the Islamic State], al-Qaeda or the Taliban, but they always attack civilian people and children. I don't think they are good people.'"

When asked about the deaths, the chief Pentagon spokesman, John F. Kirby, said, "We're not in a position to dispute it."

And remember the American University of Afghanistan? The Taliban promptly took over the entire campus and started the hunt for the students who dared attend there. The school's vice president of academic affairs Victoria Fontan told the radio network *FranceInfo* that, before school officials and faculty left, they "burned the university's servers [and] all the documents we were able to take before leaving, such as the lists of professors, students."

Practically overnight, images started to emerge of women and children who had very obviously been beaten. An incredibly brave group of women who staged a protest for women's rights were reportedly attacked with rifle butts and metal clubs.

The few Afghans who were successfully evacuated before the U.S. withdrawal were taken to places like our military base in Doha, Qatar, where they sat sweltering, starving, and without proper sanitation. A leaked email sent from a member of the State Department's Diplomatic Security Service to officials at the Pentagon and States Department – obtained by *Axios* – detailed "a life-threatening humanitarian disaster" caused by "conditions that are of our own doing."

The email included assessments from members of the Doha U.S. Embassy staff, with one reporting this: "Where the Afghans are housed is a living hell. Trash, urine, fecal matter, spilled liquids, and vomit cover the floors."

The Taliban stole millions – if not billions – worth of military equipment that the United States provided Afghan forces, including Black Hawk helicopters, armored vehicles and drones. There was also highly informed speculation that the Taliban was in possession of biometric devices that could identify our Afghan partners.

The Taliban started building their "government" – or what they call an "Islamic Emirate" – which initially included only hard-core Taliban hardliners. The prime minister is Mullah Mohammad Hassan Akhund, who is on the United Nations blacklist, and their new Interior Minister is Sirajuddin Haqqani – the terrorist I mentioned earlier that has a $5 million U.S. bounty on his head and who is on our foreign terrorist list.

Even though, in his speech, Biden said that "our true strategic competitors, China and Russia, would love nothing more than the United States to continue to funnel billions of dollars in resources and attention into stabilizing Afghanistan indefinitely," it's actually just the opposite. China and Russia are thrilled by our withdrawal.

A spokeswoman for China made clear that her country is ready to foster a "friendly and cooperative" relationship with Afghanistan. "The Taliban have repeatedly expressed their hope to develop good relations with China, and that they look forward to China's participation in the reconstruction and development of Afghanistan. We welcome this. China respects the right of the Afghan people to independently determine their own destiny and is willing to continue to develop... friendly and cooperative relations with Afghanistan."

For his part, Vladimir Putin took the opportunity to scold us, saying this is even more proof that the West needs to stop its "irresponsible policy of imposing someone's outside values from abroad."

Our allies around the world were, at best, shaken and, at worst, super pissed off…particularly Britain, the country that had been the second-largest supplier of troops to Afghanistan and the one that has had the second-most casualties from the war. Despite that, the Biden administration kept Britain largely in the dark as to how and when the U.S. would leave Afghanistan.

Rory Stewart, a former British cabinet minister with lengthy experience in Afghanistan, put it this way, "(Biden) hasn't just humiliated America's Afghan allies. He's humiliated his Western allies by demonstrating their impotence." Ben Wallace, Britain's defense secretary who also served as a captain in the British Army, "I'm a soldier. It's sad that the West has done what it's done."

Conservative member of Parliament and head of the British Foreign Affairs Committee Tom Tugendhat said that the actions by the United States were the "biggest foreign policy disaster" since the 1956 Suez crisis. He wasn't finished: "We need to think again about how we handle friends, who matters and how we defend our interests."

The chairman of the Defense Committee in the British Parliament Tobias Ellwood perhaps put it the most succinctly, "Whatever happened to 'America is back'?"

The chairman of the German Parliament's Foreign Relations Committee said the U.S. withdrawal was "a serious and far-reaching miscalculation by the (Biden) administration" and that these actions have done "fundamental damage to the political and moral credibility of the West." The head of Germany's conservative party Armin Laschet called the withdrawal "the greatest debacle that NATO has experienced since its foundation."

Even Latvia's defense minister weighed in: "This kind of troop withdrawal causes chaos…unfortunately, the West, and Europe in particular, are showing they are weaker globally."

§§§

This is where things stand less than a year after the American withdrawal from Afghanistan.

Almost immediately, the Taliban started hanging the bloody corpses of executed "criminals" in town squares, this after the Taliban announced they would bring back not only public executions but amputations as well.

Less than four months after the Taliban takeover, the Afghan economy was in shambles and 23 million Afghans were experiencing extreme food insecurity. In fact, according to United Nations Secretary General António Guterres, "Ninety-five percent" of the country "does not have enough to eat." He also said that Afghan families have resorted to selling some of their children to feed the rest of the family.

As 2021 ended, over 60,000 interpreters who supported the United States during the war were still in Afghanistan, even though at least 33,000 of them had already been vetted and approved for evacuation. Seven months after, the Taliban reopened high schools for girls, only to close them indefinitely hours later. The drug trade has exploded.

Meanwhile, Human Rights Watch reports that Taliban forces have been systematically executing or forcibly "disappearing" former police and intelligence officers, and thousands upon thousands of Taliban fighters have swarmed into Afghanistan from Pakistan at the urging of clerics and commanders.

But the scariest thing is the persistent threat of terrorist activity. The latest *Annual Threat Assessment*, released by the Office of the U.S. Director of National Intelligence on February 2022, warns: "Foreign Racially or Ethnically Motivated Violent Extremists (REMVE) very likely will continue to pose a threat to the United States and its allies. These actors continue to rely on transnational ties and adapt violent extremist narratives around current events, including the U.S. and coalition departure from Afghanistan last August."

"Speak Softly and Carry a Big Stick."
– Theodore Roosevelt –

Speak Softly...

Often when people read this quote from President Theodore Roosevelt, they focus on the big stick part. I believe we should heed the *entire* piece of advice.

President Roosevelt said that "nine-tenths of wisdom is to be wise in time, and at the right time." He described his own approach to foreign policy as an "exercise of intelligent forethought and of decisive action sufficiently far in advance of any likely crisis to make it improbable that we would run into serious trouble."

This approach won him the 1906 Nobel Peace Prize for negotiating a peace treaty that ultimately ended the Russo-Japanese War.

The U.S.-China relationship is one of the most important bilateral relationships in the world. When you listen to politicians and foreign policy "experts," it often seems like our approach to China must be framed in either one of two ways: We can either take a super hard line with Beijing or become apologists for them, essentially capitulating to everything they want.

Neither one of these extremes is ideal. We need to approach our relationship with China with a calm and steady hand, understanding that China's fortunes will only enhance America's economy and national security if we take a *sensible* and *proactive* approach. We need to find an appropriate balance between competing with China, holding them accountable for their military, trade and human rights transgressions, and cooperating with them on mutually beneficial issues.

Navigating the choppy waters between China and the United States has always been tricky, but the Trump presidency made the waters even rougher. From big things like starting a trade war and a tech war, to petty things like cancelling the Peace Corps and Fulbright scholarship programs in China and using racist and stigmatizing tropes like "kung flu" and "China virus" to insult them, the Trump years caused our relationship with China to deteriorate to the lowest point since the two countries re-established diplomatic relations over forty years ago.

It is critical that we stop this downward spiral before we have another Cold War on our hands. China's foreign minister, Wang Yi, underscored this point in July 2020: "The current China policy of the United States is based on ill-informed strategic miscalculation and is fraught with emotions and whims and McCarthyist bigotry. It seems as if every Chinese investment is politically driven, every Chinese student is a spy and every cooperation initiative is a scheme with a hidden agenda."

As we envision our future relationship with China, it's important that we *honestly* assess both the strengths and the weaknesses that we have in our negotiation arsenal.

Let's start with our weaknesses (actually, there is just one). Some people say that America's position on human rights abuses around the world is inconsistent. For example, the United States hasn't done unrestricted business with Cuba for decades because the Cuban government refuses to make steps toward "democratization" or commit to having a "greater respect for human rights," yet China, a country far more egregious in their violation of human rights, is consistently one of our largest trading partners.

The inconsistency is obvious but, in the real world, even the smallest victories in high-stakes negotiations come down to one thing: *leverage*. Think of it this way: We give Egypt $1 billion a year in military aid, which we can use as *leverage* when we finally do the right thing and support Egyptians throwing President Abdel Fatah al-Sissi – a brutal tyrant who came to power through a violent coup against a democratically elected government and continues to repress his people, and terrorize, torture and imprison thousands of journalists, humanitarian aid workers, and human rights activists – out of office.

As another example, since Israel is the largest cumulative recipient of U.S. foreign assistance since World War II (and counting), we have a certain amount of *leverage* that we can use when we try to initiate direct peace negotiations between the Israelis and the Palestinians.

At the end of the day, sovereign countries like Egypt and Israel can, of course, do whatever they want, but that doesn't mean the United States has to financially support their actions and/or decisions.

We don't have this type of financial leverage with China, to say the least. Thanks to Congress borrowing obscene amounts of money from them, China's holdings of U.S. Treasuries (bonds, notes and bills) is now $1 trillion, making them the second largest non-U.S. holder of debt behind Japan…which puts us in the exact opposite position of having financial leverage.

< Note: A word about sanctions as leverage. In late August 2020, the Trump administration imposed sanctions on 24 Chinese companies in retaliation for Beijing's illegal activities in the South China Sea. For example, one of the firms, China Communications Construction, builds artificial islands in the disputed waters on China's behalf. Next up, in March 2021, the Biden administration, together with the European Union, the United Kingdom and Canada, placed sanctions on Chinese officials for their roles in the human rights abuses against the Uyghurs.

When people ask for my opinion on whether sanctions work, I always respond, "It depends on what, when and where" – which, given the vast spectrum of outcomes over the years, is realistically the only answer a person can truthfully give.

In the case of these last two rounds of sanctions on China, I feel it's a split decision. Without question, the visa restrictions the U.S. State Department put on the top executives of those 24 Chinese companies will sting.

That said, China isn't Russia. Unlike in Putin's government, where governmental officials stash cash overseas, Chinese officials that simply do the bidding of the Communist Party of China (CPC) don't likely have tons of hidden foreign assets. And, although China is home to 373 billionaires, they operate far differently than the kleptocrats have in Russia.

My main concern about using sanctions to punish China is the danger that the sanctions will push China even further toward partnerships with Iran, Venezuela and, of course, Putin – who now positions everything we do as "Beijing & Moscow v. The West" in an effort to provide an alternative to Western, liberal world order. >

I assure you, none of what I've said so far means we are forced to kowtow to Beijing and Xi Jinping, but it does mean that we have to approach the relationship a little differently. So.... drumroll please... this is where having allies comes in handy, big time! When it comes to China, building a worldwide coalition to deal with them is *everything*. This coalition doesn't have to just be nation states. We should also include Corporate America, which may be an even more effective source of pressure.

There is strength in numbers, pure and simple. When we all create a unified block, China will have no choice but to come around. If they don't, they will be completely isolated and that simply does not work for their ambitious international plans (more on this in a few minutes).

China is a perfect illustration of why the United States must fully re-engage with the world and start being better friends to our allies, immediately. Thankfully, we and the entire world only had to suffer through four years of Donald Trump's isolationist foreign policy because, if he had won another four years, I'm afraid this would have gotten away from us completely.

It would be hard for America to survive too many other "Trans-Pacific Partnership-type withdrawal" episodes, where we saw first-hand that the world has no problem moving right along without us and what China is capable of when we give them room to solidify their increasingly dominant presence in Asia.

The end result of the TPP catastrophic mistake was that Beijing won two huge victories. Not only did its biggest competitor lose out on greater access to markets and lower tariffs/trade barriers on a vast range of goods, China went on to shepherd deals like the *Regional Comprehensive Economic Partnership* (RCEP) – an agreement signed by China and 14 other nations that covers 30 percent of the global population (2.2 billion people) and 30 percent of global GDP, making it the largest regional free trade agreement in the world.

And it didn't stop there. As the United States retreated from the world, China was also busy gaining ground and building influence in what has historically been Western-led multilateral institutions like the World Health Organization, the United Nations, the World Bank, and the International Monetary Fund.

In an extremely eye-opening (and very frightening) April 2020 article for *Politico*, Kristine Lee, an associate fellow in the Asia-Pacific Program at the Center for a New American Security, wrote:

> "Over the past several years, Beijing has systematically positioned Chinese nationals at the head of a wide range of United Nations (U.N.) agencies. Since 2019, the U.N. Food and Agriculture Agency has been led by Qu Dongyu, formerly China's vice minister of agriculture. This followed the 2018 reinstatement of Zhao Houlin, who began his career in China's Ministry of Posts and Telecommunications, for a second four-year term as the secretary-general of the International Telecommunication Union, a crucial body that sets technical standards for communications networks; Zhao has used his position to advance Huawei's standing as a vendor of 5G telecommunications equipment worldwide.
>
> The previous year, U.N. Secretary-General António Guterres appointed Liu Zhenmin, formerly China's vice minister for foreign affairs, to a key position in the U.N.'s Department of Economic and Social Affairs – a body tasked with advancing the U.N.'s hallmark program to promote development, combat climate change and reduce inequality. Even the International Civil Aviation Organization, the U.N. agency that regulates global air travel headed by Fang Liu, a Chinese national, has been accused of keeping Taiwan out of the loop on Covid-19 protocols.
>
> In part this dominance of Chinese nationals in key U.N. agencies reflects Beijing's savvy diplomatic maneuvering as a rising power, and its position as the world's second-largest economy. But it's also possible because of a void left by the United States, which under Trump has repudiated its previous leadership role in international organizations.
>
> As Beijing tries to retool the U.N. and other international institutions to its advantage, it is leaving in its wake a global system that has been knocked off balance by the absence of the steadying leadership of the United States. Even amid a global

pandemic, Washington continues to send equivocal signals about its commitment to multilateralism.

In this context, Trump's decision to defund the World Health Organization (WHO) isn't just petty or reactive – it literally plays into China's hands. If the U.S. downgrades its participation in the WHO and other U.N. organizations, it will cede even more ground, and influence, to the Chinese – which is what they want."

Kristine then just nails it with this question: "So, Americans who now blame the World Health Organization for failing to do a better job against Covid-19 have an important question to answer – if you want international organizations to perform to U.S. standards and reflect U.S. values, how much global leadership are you ready to take back on?"

The bottom line is that for four valuable years – in practically every way possible – the United States gave China a wide-open net to run up the score.

It's not like we didn't know better. China has been on a hot roll for years. According to the World Bank, "Since China began to open up and reform its economy in 1978, GDP growth has averaged almost 10 percent a year, and more than 800 million people have been lifted out of poverty. There have also been significant improvements in access to health, education, and other services over the same period."

In fact, trade agreements and high-level United Nations appointments were just the cherry on top for Beijing. Chinese leadership had already been making serious strides across the planet since 2013, when President Xi Jinping announced what would become the multibillion-dollar *Belt and Road Initiative* (BRI). *One Belt, One Road*, as it's known in China, extends low-cost loans and builds infrastructure – including roads, ports, railways, power plants, 5G networks and fiber-optic cables – for countries around the globe. Many consider this initiative to be the most ambitious infrastructure project in the world, for good reason.

Thirty-seven heads of state headed to Beijing for the *Belt and Road* forum in April 2019. Between 2013 and 2018, China signed 173 cooperation documents with 125 countries and 29 international organizations. Pre-Covid, trade between China and the countries involved with the *Belt and Road Initiative* had exceeded $6 trillion, with an average annual growth of 4 percent. And, despite the pandemic, Beijing continues to cut deals. At the end of 2020, the European Union and China struck a deal that allows Beijing to make larger investments in E.U.-based companies.

China is also, unsurprisingly, aligning with other autocrats. For example, China recently committed to invest $400 billion in Iran over the next 25 years. The plan calls for improvements in everything from banking and telecommunications to physical infrastructure. In return, China will receive Iranian oil at a heavy discount. The agreement also includes greater military cooperation between the two countries, including weapon development and the sharing of intelligence.

China has been wooing Russia for a while now, to the point where Presidents Vladimir Putin and Xi Jinping made pancakes together at a joint military drill. Just weeks before Putin's invasion of Ukraine, Putin and Xi Jinping signed an agreement during the Beijing Winter Olympics that rejected NATO expansion and framed Western democracy as some sort of evil plot.

How deep into the global economy does China's reach extend thanks to *One Belt, One Road*? The Kiel Institute – an independent, nonprofit economic research institute and think tank based in Kiel, Germany – analyzed "a total of 1,974 Chinese loans and 2,947 Chinese grants to 152 countries from 1949 to 2017."

The analysis revealed that "China's direct loans and trade credits have climbed from almost zero in 1998 to more than 1.6 trillion, or close to 2 percent of world GDP in 2018. These loans mostly go to low- and middle-income countries. In total, estimates suggest that the Chinese state now accounts for a quarter of total bank lending to emerging markets. This has transformed China into the largest official creditor, easily surpassing the IMF or the World Bank."

Although these are huge numbers, the real numbers are actually much larger because "about one half of China's large-scale lending to developing countries is 'hidden' and not recorded in the main international databases used by researchers and practitioners alike."

Okay, I admit that China's progress is a little disconcerting, but Beijing's ambition provides us exactly the leverage we need! Oddly enough, China's thirst for world domination is the very thing that can ultimately keep them in line. If China is locked-out from the rest of the world, strategies like *One Belt, One Road* and *Made in China 2025* – a national initiative to strengthen China's manufacturing sector – would be seriously jeopardized.

There are also several new forces at play that puts even more wind at our back. For one, America is getting our mojo back at the exact same time that China has reminded the world of its dark side.

Although at the beginning of the coronavirus crisis Beijing was quick to provide medical equipment and vaccines to vulnerable countries in need, President Xi Jinping and company were also secretive, nontransparent, and quick to bully other countries – like when they threatened Australia with punitive tariffs for demanding an investigation into the coronavirus's origins.

And, ironically, because of the economic fallout from the coronavirus crisis, many *One Belt, One Road* nations have asked Beijing to renegotiate, delay or forgive altogether billions of dollars of loans, which puts China in a super tight spot.

On one hand, acquiescing to these requests would be financially devastating (the Kiel Institute estimates China has loaned at least $520 billion), not to mention the fury it would undoubtably ignite in the Chinese people, who are also struggling. Even though their leaders are throwing money at other countries, 40 percent of Chinese households – over 600 million people – lived on just $1,621 in 2019 (that's $135/month).

Specifically, Beijing surely understands that provoking China's youth any further would be a big mistake. These young people – who, until now, have been content to live with limited freedoms as long as there are jobs and a chance for upward mobility – have been activated by the pandemic. They are particularly angry about Beijing's lack of transparency and efforts to conceal any culpability China may have. Unfortunately for Chinese leadership, these concerns have sparked larger conversations about censorship, the treatment of whistleblowers, and the need for financial accountability – which is obviously a very dangerous can of worms for Beijing to be forced to open.

On the other hand, not being agreeable to the requests of the *One Belt, One Road* nations – especially at a time when China is under fire for not being forthcoming about the origins of the coronavirus as well as how it was handled – could significantly damage China's reputation as the world's friendliest banker/partner, which would completely undermine the reason they lent the money in the first place.

And there is one last thing a-brewin'. Unlike in the wake of the 2007-2009 Financial Crisis, when China was the primary engine that drove the worldwide recovery, this time we are. According to Oxford Economics, the United States is poised to make a larger contribution to worldwide growth than China for the first time since 2005. For China – the world's second largest economy with a value of $14 trillion – the year 2020 marked the end of an almost half-century-long run of growth.

Things are heading in the right direction, America! The nightmares from the Trump presidency are receding and our longtime allies are as happy and relieved about it as we are. Take Germany, for example. The Pew Research Center found that only 34 percent of Germans say the relationship between their country and the United States is *good,* with a paltry 2 percent saying the relationship is *very good.* That doesn't seem all that great, although these numbers are much more positive than they were in 2018, when only 24 percent of Germans said the relationship with the United States was *good.*

However, the more interesting numbers in terms of this section are these: "Germans are about twice as likely to say they prefer a close relationship to the U.S. over China (50 percent to 24 percent)." Clearly, we still have work to do to rebuild trust with our allies, but without question, the tide has finally turned back in our favor.

This is great news because we don't have a second to waste! The list of transgressions against China is long: The sabotaging of democracy in Hong Kong; an increasingly antagonistic military posture toward Taiwan; the continued repression and forced labor of the Tibetan people; the blatant violation of international law in the South China Sea; cyberwarfare and sinister influence campaigns against the United States, coordinated through the Chinese Communist Party's (CCP) *United*

Front Work Department; unfair trade practices; and the ethnic cleansing of the Uyghurs and other Muslim minorities, among the other epic human rights atrocities that I mentioned earlier.

Together with our allies, we can work through these issues toward a productive working relationship with China. The start of a strong coalition was evident during President Biden's first international trip in June 2021. At the Group of Seven (G7) meeting, the members agreed to jointly counter China's economic rise, then at the North Atlantic Treaty Organization (NATO) meeting, the 30-nation alliance agreed that China's increasingly aggressive military tactics must be addressed immediately.

While Russia was deemed a "threat" to NATO, China was described more as a country presenting "challenges," due to the fact that "China's stated ambitions and assertive behavior present systemic challenges to the rules-based international order."

NATO Secretary General Jens Stoltenberg, said it this way, "China is not our adversary, but the balance of power is shifting. And China is coming closer to us. We see them in cyberspace, we see China in Africa, but we also see China investing heavily in our own critical infrastructure. We need to respond together as an alliance."

We can start with issues that greatly affect all of us. For instance, what Secretary General Stoltenberg was likely referring to when he said that China was "investing heavily in our own critical infrastructure" was Huawei, the Chinese telecommunications goliath. If Huawei moves forward with its plan to install 5G networks across Africa, the Middle East and Europe, the company could possibly be in a position to control the communications infrastructure that NATO itself needs.

Joining with China's Southeast Asian neighbors and our other allies, we can also unite against China's aggressive, unlawful actions in the South China Sea. We already have a starting point. In 2016, in a case brought by the Philippines, the Permanent Court of Arbitration in The Hague unanimously ruled that China had no sovereignty over the waters of the South China Sea and, therefore, was violating international law by militarizing artificial islands and occupying disputed reefs and shoals.

Unsurprisingly, the Chinese rejected this ruling because Beijing ostensibly believes that roughly 90 percent of the South China Sea has belonged to them since "ancient times," pointing to waters within a "nine-dash line" that appears only on official Chinese maps. < I wonder if Xi Jinping would like to borrow Donald Trump's Sharpie? :) >

And then there is North Korea. China has been North Korea's most important ally, largest trading partner and primary source of food, arms, and fuel for over six decades. Beijing not only financially supported the late Kim Jong-Il's regime – and now Kim Jong-un's – it has also protected Pyongyang against harsh international economic sanctions to prevent the government's collapse and to avoid a flood of refugees across the shared border.

Lately, President Xi Jinping seems to be doubling down on his relationship with North Korea. In late March 2021, Xi Jinping called North Korea a "valuable asset" and committed to provide even more humanitarian aid. In response, Kim Jong-un embraced "unity and cooperation" with China in the face of a "hostile" new U.S. administration.

As things stand now, Xi Jinping has little incentive to help us control Kim Jong-un, but our new "ally leverage strategy" can help change that. The first order of business is to pressure China to stop allowing oil tankers to use its territorial waters to provide oil and other petroleum products to North Korea which, because of active sanctions, is a violation of international law (China supported these very U.N. Security Council sanctions in 2017).

The world also needs Beijing's cooperation in tackling climate change. Chinese annual greenhouse gas emissions now account for 27 percent of emissions worldwide, which is more than those of all developed countries combined. < the United States accounts for 11 percent >

Last but certainly not least, we need to vigorously protect human rights, which is the most important thing we can all do together. After Tiananmen Square – when, in 1989, Beijing executed an estimated 10,000 civilians protesting for democracy – the United States and the rest of the world let Beijing off with little more than a slap on the wrist. At the time, the thinking was that, although the Tiananmen Square massacre was abhorrent, China was on the verge of turning things around through more transparency and substantial reforms. It has become clear that has not happened – and most likely will not without significant pressure. We cannot repeat that mistake.

…and Carry a Big Stick

Vladimir Putin is on a brutal, bloody, psychotic rampage, on a level not seen since the terrorizing reign of Josef Stalin. And why not? He has become accustomed to getting away with murder – literally – ever since he found his soul mate in the 45th president of the United States.

It's no mystery why Don and Vlad fell in love with one another: 1) They both love politics as theatre, and 2) they both operate from a place of low self-esteem and, as a result, profound weakness (really, does anyone with a high self-esteem emerge from scuba-diving, in front of television cameras, holding two very rare ancient Greek urns he "found" on his dive or ride around shirtless on a horse like Putin does?)…and Donald Trump's weaknesses and insecurities could fill an entire book.

It's safe to say that no foreign state benefited more from the Trump administration's antics than Russia and, for Putin, the timing could not have been better. When Donald Trump took the oath of office, Russia's economy was shrinking – strangled by slow growth and depressed wages – and the war in Syria was becoming more costly every day. Putin was also having to navigate between increasingly demanding factions within Russia, like the Russian Orthodox Church, oligarchs, and the security forces.

The Russian people were demanding more freedom, and more of them than ever believed their politicians were corrupt. The standard of living was falling and Russia was more repressed than it had been since the days of the Soviet Union. Even super rich people were getting twitchy.

Enter Donald Trump, his authoritarian tendencies, and the complete chaos that his administration inflicted on practically every aspect of

American life. For Putin, an unreliable, divided, angry America fed perfectly into the narrative he had been trying to sell about the United States for years. It was more than he could have ever hoped for when he long dreamed of discrediting American democracy: a U.S. president who insulted American allies and threatened the free press; ditched international agreements; maligned NATO; and smeared America's institutions, military, judicial system and intelligence agencies.

Putin delighted in this (hopefully) once-in-a-lifetime opportunity to undermine trust in the United States and question our moral authority. He lived for moments like that fateful news conference during the 2018 Russia–United States summit in Helsinki, Finland, when the president of the United States stood right beside him and chose to publicly believe his obviously bogus denial of Russian interference in our elections over the exhaustive investigation of U.S. intelligence agencies.

That said, even with this new ammunition against America, Putin still saw his popularity continue to decline. In fact, in 2020 anti-government protests began to swell across Russia – even in small towns 4,000 miles away from Moscow. The economic fallout from the pandemic and global collapse in oil prices certainly weren't helping matters, as many Russian families came close to losing everything.

Putin's solution? To double-down on authoritarianism. By the end of 2020, Putin's regime had passed laws that severely cracked down on opposition in any form, including peaceful protests, as well as laws that curtail certain Internet sites including Twitter, Facebook and YouTube. Putin now enjoys immunity from prosecution for the rest of his life, and almost all information, however trivial, regarding members of his family, friendship circle, and government is now considered classified.

Meanwhile, the Kremlin was busy poisoning opposition figures, including former Russian military officer Sergei Skripal and his daughter, and Alexei Navalny, Russia's most visible opposition figure who, having survived his assassination attempt, is now locked in a Russian prison.

Navalny's message particularly resonates with many Russian people because it focuses on Putin's – or as Navalny so perfectly describes him, the "little thieving man in the bunker" – corruption. Putin is so threatened by Navalny's political movement that he had a

Russian court designate the group an "extremist network." This means that the group's organizers, donors and supporters can arbitrarily be arrested, prosecuted and imprisoned at any time.

And now, Putin is committing the most heinous of war crimes in Ukraine, an unprovoked assault on a level not seen since 1939. Kharkiv and Mariupol have been destroyed, and the threat of Putin using chemical weapons on innocent civilians gets louder every day. That said, Putin's invasion of Ukraine has uncovered some seriously massive cracks in Putin's armor.

Far from Putin's picturesque delusion of restoring the glory of the Russian empire, his military has been exposed as decrepit, inept, unprepared, undersupplied, and unmotivated – to the point that the Ukrainians held Kyiv, forcing Russia's humiliating retreat from the north of the country. Thousands and thousands of Russian troops have already been killed.

Meanwhile, crippling sanctions have wrecked the Russian economy and the Ukrainians have proven to be fierce and fearless adversaries, which makes Russia's military look even worse. Instead of dividing the rest of the world – another one of Putin's delusions – his misguided war has inspired unwavering unity among European countries and strengthened the NATO security alliance. This cohesiveness is forcing Putin to increasingly rely on China for its trade options and financial security – a path that may eventually also close to him.

Although Xi Jinping has shown extraordinary patience with Putin this round – China highly values national sovereignty and territorial integrity, a position they made known when Putin raided Georgia and Crimea – Russia, with its 11th largest economy, is relatively small potatoes for China. Even though Xi Jinping has his own delusions of walking a fine line between Putin and the West, the threat of secondary sanctions may eventually convince him that his best bet is to cut his losses with Russia.

Vladimir Putin must be stopped and his invasion of Ukraine provides the perfect opportunity. Taken separately, Russia's war crimes in Ukraine; his interference in our elections; the cyberattacks they have waged and sanctioned against us; the poisoning of pro-democracy opposition leaders; bullying behavior in places like Moldova, South

Ossetia, Montenegro, and the Balkan; the annexation of Crimea; and the slaughtering of innocent civilians in opposition-held areas in northwest Syria with his buddy Syrian President Bashar al-Assad would each independently warrant brutal consequences. Together, they are just completely unacceptable and cannot go unanswered.

Enough is enough with this guy.

Epilogue

I remember well the night I drove back to my grandmother's house from Nacogdoches, Texas after seeing *Charlie Wilson's War*. At the end of the movie, Gust Avrakotos, the CIA agent who helped the congressman arm the Afghan mujahideen, told Charlie the cautionary tale of a village's Zen Master and one of the local boys in the town.

Although their covert war in Afghanistan appeared to be successful at the time, Gust understood that the best of intentions can have unintended consequences if awareness is abandoned. Events never occur in isolation – nothing in this life is random and everything is interconnected. Based on the events that have occurred in the Middle East since that time, history has proven Gust correct.

Once upon a time, a young boy got a horse as a present for his 12th birthday. It was a coveted gift and his entire village cheered and said, "Isn't this wonderful!" "We'll see," replied the wise Zen master who lived in the village.

Two years later, the boy was violently thrown off of his horse, shattering his leg and causing great dismay throughout the town. The villagers all cried, "How unfortunate this is for the boy!" "We'll see," replied the wise Zen master.

Shortly after the boy's fall, a brutal war broke out near the village, but the boy could not fight because of his broken leg. Relieved that the boy would remain safe, the whole village said, "This is so fortunate for the boy!" "We'll see," replied the Zen master. And so the story unfolds.

Highway 21 is lonely in the daylight, but at night it becomes downright desolate. The towering pine trees successfully block out all of the light from the moon and stars, creating a mood that demands reflection.

Memories of a childhood lived in these woods come flooding back; the very heart of America where neighbors are family, you always get a return smile, and friends last a lifetime. I remember vividly my first day of kindergarten, when I stood in my knee socks and pigtails and pledged allegiance to the flag that I already deeply believed in.

Nothing could be better than those sacred nights, when my parents would come to kiss me goodnight and we would read together, laugh together, and pray together. I was confident in all of my hopes and aspirations and I could not wait to spread my wings and fly, because I knew that I lived in a country where no dream was too big and that anything was possible.

As I grew, my belief in America grew with me. Not because we do everything right, but because I know deep in my heart that we will always be ultimately led by the core values that make this country great. I recently attended the symphony and was struck by the intricacies involved in the performance. Collectively, the music is perfectly synchronized and flawlessly executed.

As they played, I watched the individual sections seamlessly enter and exit the songs as the score dictated. Possessing absolutely zero musical ability, I am always amazed by the immense talent of those who do. I am also overwhelmed when I think of the years of perseverance and commitment that every single person on that stage endured to develop the skills necessary to contribute to the overall endeavor.

A violinist's path may have started in elementary school and eventually taken her to Juilliard, while a guy in the percussion section might have started his journey in high school or as a member of a garage rock band. Regardless of the road taken, everyone on that stage spent countless hours, at great personal sacrifice, to perfect their individual talent.

That's us, America. Every single one of us has an extremely important contribution to make to the betterment of our country, and we have all been preparing for our role for years. Whatever our individual pursuits may be, we must all resolve to contribute our unique voice and commit to participate with a serving heart.

The time has come for all of us to honestly question our commitment to the future of this nation. I'll ask again: Will our legacy be something we are proud of, or will we forever be known as the former superpower that recklessly relinquished our prominence because we lack the will to protect it?

I have the deepest confidence that we will come together and pull this off. But we'll see.

Emily Mathews
San Augustine, Texas

I'll meet you at www.1787forAmerica.org.

Sources

Chapter One
The Butterfly Effect

1. From George Washington to Henry Knox, Mount Vernon, 25 February 1787
2. Bob Dylan. “The Times They Are A-Changin’.” The Times They Are A-Changin’. Columbia Records, 1964.

Chapter Two
Let’s Get This Party Started

We Now Know

1. Henry David Thoreau. “Civil Disobedience.” 1849
2. Associated Press. “Trump: Pentagon Leaders Want War To Keep Contractor’s ‘Happy’.” ABC News. 8 Sept 2020
3. Warren Buffett. “1992 Shareholder Letter.” Chairman of the Board, Berkshire Hathaway Inc. 1 Mar 1993
4. Sun Tzu. “The Art of War.” 5th Century BC. Public Domain.

Obliterating the Game of Politics

1. United States. Treasury Department. “The Debt to the Penny and Who Holds It.” 17 Mar 2021
2. United States. Congressional Budget Office. “The Budget and Economic Outlook: 2021 to 2031.” 11 Feb 2021
3. United States. Census Bureau. “Income and Poverty in the United States: 2019.” 15 Sept 2020

4. John Mayer. “Waiting On the World to Change.” Continuum Sony. 2006

1787 National Committee

1. David McCullough. “1776.” New York: Simon & Schuster, 2005
2. “Republic.” Merriam-Webster Online.
3. Suzy Platt. “Respectfully Quoted: A Dictionary of Quotations.” Barnes & Noble Books, 1993
4. George Washington. “Farewell Address.” Independent Chronicle. 26 Sept 1796
5. Walt Whitman. “I Hear America Singing.” Leaves of Grass, 1867 edition. 6 vols. Nov 1866
6. “Our Movement.” The American Israel Public Affairs Committee. 17 Mar 2021
7. “About NEA.” National Education Association. 17 Mar 2021
8. “NRA Membership” National Rifle Association. 17 Mar 2021
9. United States Census Bureau. “National Population by Characteristics: 2010-2019 - Population Estimates by Age (18+).” 17 Mar 2021

The Gang Who Can’t Shoot Straight

1. Daniel Cox and Robert P. Jones, Ph.D. “America’s Changing Religious Identity.” Public Religion Research Institute.
2. Katherine Schaeffer. “The Most Common Age Among Whites in U.S. is 58 – More Than Double That of Racial and Ethnic Minorities.” 30 July 2019
3. “National Exit Polls: How Different Groups Voted.” New York Times. 18 Mar 2021
4. “Exit Polls.” CNN. 18 Mar 2021
5. Kim Parker, Juliana Menasce Horowitz, Anna Brown, Richard Fry, D’Vera Cohn and Ruth Igielnik. “Demographic and Economic Trends in Urban, Suburban, and Rural Communities.” Pew Research Center. 22 May 2018

6. Jeffrey Jones. “Quarterly Gap In Party Affiliation Largest Since 2012.” Gallup. 7 Apr 2021
7. Natalie Martnez. “In the Past 24 hours, Alex Jones and Laura Loomer Have Taken to Instagram to Promote White Nationalism.” Media Matters. 11 April 2019
8. Eric Hananoki. “The Republican Party of Florida is Backing Laura Loomer, a “Proud Islamophobe” Who Said She’s in Favor of “More” Migrant Deaths.” Media Matters for America. 19 Aug 2020
9. Brett Samuels. “Trump Calls QAnon GOP Primary Winner a 'Future Republican Star’.” The Hill. 12 Aug 2020
10. Colbert King. “The GOP Once Knew What To Do About Problems Like Marjorie Taylor Greene.” Washington Post. 1 Feb 2021
11. Matthew Rosenberg. “Pushing QAnon And Stolen Election Lies, Flynn Re-Emerges.” New York Times. 6 Feb 2021
12. Jack Brewster. “All The Times Trump And His Allies Winked At QAnon Before Its Followers Stormed The Capitol.” Forbes. 19 Jan 2021
13. Simon van Zuylen-Wood. “QAnon Goes To Washington.” New York Magazine. 28 Sept 2020
14. Steven Sebelius. “Nye County GOP Chairman Spins Conspiracies Online.” Las Vegas Review-Journal. 10 Jan 2021
15. Perry Bacon Jr. “The Trumpiest Republicans Are At The State And Local Levels – Not In DC.” FiveThirtyEight. 16 Feb 2021
16. “Trump Praises QAnon Supporters: ‘I Understand They Like Me Very Much.” Axios. 20 Aug 2020
17. Editorial Board. “House Republican Reckoning.” Wall Street Journal. 2 Feb 2021
18. Nick Corasaniti, Annie Karni and Isabella Grullón Paz. “There’s Nothing Left’: Why Thousands Of Republicans Are Leaving The Party.” New York Times. 10 Feb 2021
19. United States. Federal Bureau of Investigation. “Anti-Government, Identity Based, and Fringe Political Conspiracy Theories Very Likely Motivate Some Domestic Extremists to Commit Criminal, Sometimes Violent Activity.” Phoenix Field Office. 30 May 2019
20. Nicholas Riccardi. “Democrats Keep Winning the Popular Vote. That Worries Them.” Associated Press. 13 Nov 2020

21. Stef W. Kight. "Exclusive Poll: Young Americans Are Embracing Socialism." Axios. 10 Mar 2019
22. Mohamed Younis. "Four in 10 Americans Embrace Some Form of Socialism." Gallup. 20 May 2019
23. Tom Bonier. "A Tool To Analyze The Most Diverse Electorate In History." 20 Apr 2021
24. Robert A. Pape. "What An Analysis Of 377 Americans Arrested Or Charged In The Capitol Insurrection Tells Us." Washington Post. 6 Apr 2021
25. Jeffrey M. Jones. "LGBT Identification Rises to 5.6% in Latest U.S. Estimate." Gallup. 24 Feb 2021
26. Adam McCann. "Tax Burden by State." WalletHub. 31 Mar 2021
27. John S. Kiernan. "States With the Best and Worst Taxpayer ROI." WalletHub. 23 Mar 2021
28. "State Partisan Composition." National Conference of State Legislatures." 13 May 2021
29. "Cost of Living Index By State 2021." World Population Review. 27 June 2021

Chapter Three
The Truth Will Set Us Free

Some Perspective on our Political Division

1. United States. Census Bureau. "U.S. and World Population Clock." 13 Mar 2021
2. United States. Census Bureau. "FAQs for Faith Based Communities." 13 Mar 2021
3. United States. Census Bureau. "Table 75. Self-Described Religious Identification of Adult Population: 1990, 2002, and 2008." 30 Sept 2011
4. United States. Census Bureau. "Language Use: Frequently Asked Questions." 13 Mar 2021

5. United States. Federal Bureau of Investigation. “2019 Crime in the United States.” 28 Sept 2020

Truth Matters

1. Proverbs 12:19. New International Version.

The Total Distortion of Economic Accomplishments

1. “Business Cycle Dating Committee Announcement June 8, 2020.” National Bureau of Economic Research. 8 June 2020
2. United States. Department of Commerce. Bureau of Economic Analysis. “Table 1.1.5. Gross Domestic Product.” 13 Mar 2021
3. United States. Department of Commerce. Bureau of Economic Analysis. “Table 1.1.1. Percent Change From Preceding Period in Real Gross Domestic Product.” 13 Mar 2021
4. Sergei Klebnikov and Halah Touryalai. “We Looked At How The Stock Market Performed Under Every U.S. President Since Truman – And the Results Will Surprise You.” Forbes. 23 July 2020
5. Chuck Jones. “Obama’s Last Three Years of Job Growth All Beat Trump’s Best Year.” Forbes. 7 Feb 2020

The Election Fraud Lie

1. “In Four Years, President Trump Made 30,573 False or Misleading Claims.” Washington Post. 21 Jan 2021
2. Nicole Perlroth. “Election Security Experts Contradict Trump’s Voting Claims.” New York Times. 16 Nov 2020
3. United States. Cybersecurity and Infrastructure Agency. “Joint Statement from Elections Infrastructure Government Coordinating Council and the Election Infrastructure Sector Coordinating Executive Committees.” 12 Nov 2020
4. Ali Swenson and Amanda Seitz. “AP Fact Check: Trump Tweets a Tall Tale of ‘Deleted” Votes.” Associated Press. 12 Nov 2020

5. Michael M. Grynbaum and Jonah Bromwich. “Fox News Faces Second Defamation Suit Over Election Coverage.” New York Times. 26 Mar 2021
6. Colleen Long. “Dominion Voting Systems Sues Giuliani Over Election Claims.” Associated Press. 25 Jan 2021
7. “Dominion Files Defamation Suit Against Rudy Giuliana.” Dominion Voting. 25 Jan 2021
8. “Dominion Sues Trump Lawyer Sidney Powell for Defamation.” Associated Press. 8 Jan 2021
9. Alexa Corse. “Pro-Trump Lawyer Sidney Powell Seeks to Dismiss Defamation Suit Over Election Claims.” Wall Street Journal. 22 Mar 2021
10. Steve Karnowski and David Bauder. “Dominion Voting Systems Sues ‘My Pillow Guy’ for $1.3 Billion.” Associated Press. 22 Feb 2021
11. 60 Minutes. CBS. 29 Nov 2020
12. Matthew Brown. “Trump Campaign Lawyer Stirs Outrage By Saying Ex-Cyber Chief Should Be ‘Taken Out At Dawn and Shot.” USA Today. 1 Dec 2020
13. Kevin Johnson. “Ex-Election Security Chief Christopher Krebs Sues Trump Campaign, Lawyer for Defamation.” USA Today. 8 Dec 2020
14. Michael Balsamo. “Barr: No Evidence of Fraud That’d Change Election Outcome.” Associated Press. 1 Dec 2020
15. Michael Balsamo. “Disputing Trump, Barr Says No Widespread Election Fraud.” Associated Press. 1 Dec 2020
16. Josh Gerstein. “Another Law Firm Bails Out On Trump Campaign.” Politico. 13 Nov 2020
17. Bradford Betz. “Chris Christi Rips Trump’s Legal Team As ‘National Embarrassment.” Fox News. 22 Nov 2020
18. Elise Viebeck, Emma Brown, and Rosalind Helderman. “Judges Turn Back Claims by Trump and His Allies in Six States as the President’s Legal Effort Founders.” Washington Post. 4 Dec 2020
19. Rosalind Helderman and Elise Viebeck. “‘The Last Wall’: How Dozens of Judges Across the Political Spectrum Rejected Trump’s Efforts to Overturn the Election.” Washington Post. 12 Dec 2020

20. Alison Burkee. “Trump Campaign Lawyers Quit Pennsylvania Lawsuit – Again.” Forbes. 16 Nov 2020
21. Ian MacDougall. “The Trump Campaign Can’t Find a Judge Who Will Ignore Facts – But It’s Trying.” ProPublica. 13 Nov 2020
22. Aaron Blake. “Trump’s Own Lawyers Keep Undermining His Voter Fraud Claims.” Washington Post. 19 Nov 2020
23. Tessa Berenson. “Donald Trump And His Lawyers Are Making Sweeping Allegations of Voter Fraud In Public. In Court, They Say No Such Thing.” Time. 20 Nov 2020
24. Lisa Lerer. “Giuliani in Public: ‘It’s a Fraud.’ Giuliani in Court: ‘This Is Not a Fraud Case.’” New York Times. 18 Nov 2020
25. Jan Wolfe and Tom Hals. “U.S. Judge Calls Trump Claim Challenging Biden Win in Pennsylvania 'Frankenstein's Monster'.” Reuters. 21 Nov 2020
26. Tom Hals. “In Fresh Blow to Trump, U.S. Court Rejects Pennsylvania Election Case.” Reuters. 27 Nov 2020
27. Elise Viebeck. “Pennsylvania Supreme Court Dismisses Lawsuit Against Mail Ballots With Prejudice in Another Defeat For Trump.” Washington Post. 28 Nov 2020
28. Jacob Bogage and Shawn Boburg. “Postal Service Finds No Evidence Of Mail Ballot Fraud In Pa. Case Cited By Top Republicans.” Washington Post. 17 Mar 2021
29. Ken Ritter. “Nevada Judge Won’t Block Certifying Election, Rejects Revote.” Associated Press. 20 Nov 2020
30. Alan Feuer.” “Federal Judge in Wisconsin Deals Trump Another Court Defeat.” New York Times. 7 Jan 2021
31. Aaron Blake. “Trump Lawyers Suffer Embarrassing Rebukes From Judges Over Voter Fraud Claims.” Washington Post. 11 Nov 2020
32. “Someone’s Going to Get Killed: GA Official Blasts GOP Silence On Election Threats.” NPR. 1 Dec 2020
33. Amy Gardner. “’I Just Want to Find 11,780 Votes’: In Extraordinary Hour-Long Call, Trump Pressures Georgia Secretary of State to Recalculate the Vote in his Favor.” Washington Post. 3 Jan 2021
34. Miriam Marini. “Protesters Descend on Secretary of State Jocelyn Benson’s Home After Dark.” Detroit Free Press. 6 Dec 2020

35. Brett Samuels. “Michigan Lawmakers Say They Will Follow ‘Normal’ Process’ Following Trump Meeting.” The Hill. 20 Nov 2020
36. “Donald J. Trump and Donald J. Trump for President, Inc.’s Objections to Dr. Jill Stein’s Recount Petition.” In re. Petition for Recount for the Office of President of the United States of America.” State of Michigan, Board of State Canvassers.
37. “Application to Dismiss by the Republican Party of Pennsylvania All Pennsylvania Electors of President-Elect Donald J. Trump and Vice-President Elect Michael Pence, President-Elect Trump, Vice-President Elect Pence, and Donald J. Trump for President, Inc.” In re. to Matter of the 2016 Presidential Election. In the Commonwealth Court of Pennsylvania.
38. David Daley. “Kobach and Trump’s Spectacular Voter-Fraud Failure.” Excerpted from “Unrigged: How Americans Are Battling Back to Save Democracy.” Rolling Stone. 27 Apr 2020
39. Marina Villeneuve. “Report: Trump Commission Did Not Find Widespread Voter Fraud.” Associated Press. 3 Aug 2018
40. Gary Fineout. “2012 Election: Nearly 200,000 Florida Voters May Not Be Citizens.” 11 May 2012
41. Alexa Ura. “Someone Did Not Do Their Due Diligence: How an Attempt to Review Texas’ Voter Rolls Turned Into a Debacle.” Texas Tribune. 1 Feb 2019
42. “Florida Says No Evidence of Fraud in 2018 Mail Vote Fraud Probe.” Tampa Bay Times. 21 May 2020
43. James Pindell. “N.H. Says Once and For All That No One Was Bused in to Vote.” Boston Globe. 1 June 2018
44. Editorial Board. “Trump’s Dangerous Vote-Fraud Claims in N.H.” Boston Globe. 1 Sept 2019
45. Kristina Torres. “Georgia AG Gets 53 Forms in Fraud Probe of Stacey Abrams’ Voter Registration Group.” 20 Sept 2017
46. Ben Nadler. “Voting Rights Become A Flashpoint In Georgia Governor’s Race.” Associated Press. 9 Oct 2018
47. Shannon Van Sant. “Judge Rules Against Georgia Election Law, Calling It A 'Severe Burden' For Voters.” 3 Nov 2018
48. “Kansas Official Kris Kobach Claims Law Halted Up to 18K Noncitizen Votes.” Associated Press. 6 Mar 2018

49. Jane C. Timm and Adam Edelman. “Illegal Voting? Not Much in Kobach’s Home State.” NBC News. 19 July 2017
50. Jennifer Calfas. “Pew Study Author: ‘Zero Evidence of Fraud’ in 2016 Election.” The Hill. 24 Jan 2017
51. Justin Levitt. “The Truth About Voter Fraud.” Brennan Center for Justice at New York University School of Law. 2007
52. Lorraine C. Minnite, Ph.D. “The Politics of Voter Fraud.” Columbia University.
53. Lorraine C. Minnite, Ph.D. “The Misleading Myth of Voter Fraud in American Elections.” Rutgers University-Camden. January 2014
54. Natasha Khan and Corbin Carson. “Comprehensive Database of U.S. Voter Fraud Uncovers No Evidence That Photo ID Is Needed.” 12 Aug 2012
55. Sami Edge and Sean Holstege. “Voter Fraud is Not a Persistent Problem.” News21. 20 Aug 2016
56. Rosalind S. Helderman. “Our Democracy Is Imperiled’: Maricopa County Officials Decry 2020 Recount As A Sham And Call On Arizona Republicans To End The Process.” Washington Post. 17 May 2021
57. Taylor Goldenstein. “Ken Paxton’s Beefed-Up 2020 Voter Fraud Unit Closed 16 Minor Cases, All in Harris County.” Houston Chronicle. 22 Dec 2020
58. Karoun Demirjian and Matt Zapotosky. “New Emails Detail Trump’s Efforts To Have Justice Department Take Up His False Election-Fraud Claims.” Washington Post. 15 June 2021
59. Amy B. Wang. “Georgia Judge Dismisses Most of Lawsuit That Alleged Fraudulent Absentee Ballots in Fulton County.” Washington Post. 25 June 2021
60. Senators Edward McBroom, Lana Their, Jeff Irwin and John Bizon. “Report On The November 2020 Election in Michigan.” Michigan State Senate.

The Perfect Scapegoat: antifa

1. Ben Collins, Brandy Zadrozny and Emmanuelle Saliba. "White Nationalist Group Posing As Antifa Called for Violence on Twitter.” NBC News. 1 June 2020

2. "Demonstrations And Political Violence in America." ACLED. September 2020
3. Josh Margolin. "Intelligence Bulletin Warning of Protest-Related Violence Makes Little Mention Of 'Antifa'." ABC News. 9 June 2020
4. Neil MacFarquhar, Alan Feuer and Adam Goldman. "Federal Arrests Show No Sign That Antifa Plotted Protests." New York Times. 11 June 2020
5. United States. Department of Justice. "Over 300 People Facing Federal Charges For Crimes Committed During Nationwide Demonstrations." 24 Sept 2020
6. Ryan Lucas. "No Sign Of Antifa So Far In Justice Department Cases Brought Over Unrest." NPR. 9 June 2020
7. Jan Wolfe. "U.S. Attorney General Barr Says Antifa 'Flying Around' U.S. To Incite Violence." Reuters. 2 Sept 2020
8. Davey Alba. "F.B.I. Says There Is No Evidence Antifa Participated In Storming The Capitol." New York Times. 8 Jan 2021
9. Daniel A. Cox. "After The Ballots Are Counted: Conspiracies, Political Violence, And American Exceptionalism." Survey Center on American Life, American Enterprise Institute. 11 Feb 2021
10. Spencer S. Hsu. "N.M. Official Who Warned Of 'Blood Running Out Of' U.S. Capitol Jailed Pending Trail In Jan. 6 Riot Case." Washington Post. 1 Feb 2021
11. Michael M. Grynbaum, Davey Alba and Reid J. Epstein. "How Pro-Trump Forces Pushed A Lie About Antifa At The Capitol Riot." New York Times. 1 Mar 2021
12. Teo Armus. "Rep. Matt Gaetz And Other GOP Politicians Baselessly Suggest Antifa Is To Blame For Pro-Trump Mob Rioting Into Capitol." Washington Post. 7 Jan 2021
13. Davey Alba. "Antifa Falsehood Tops List Of Misinformation After Capitol Rampage." New York Times. 8 Jan 2021
14. Craig Silverman. "A Facial Recognition Company Says That Viral Washington Times 'Antifa' Story Is False." Buzz Feed. 7 Jan 2021
15. Aaron Blake. "Wray Delivers A Big Blow To Jan. 6 Baseless Claims About Antifa, But The GOP Keeps Feeding Them." Washington Post. 2 Mar 2021

16. Olivia Beavers. "Wray: Racially Motivated Violent Extremism Makes Up Most of FBI's Domestic Terrorism Cases." The Hill. 17 September 2020
17. Eric Tucker and Ben Fox. "FBI Director Says Antifa Is An Ideology, Not An Organization." Associated Press. 17 Sept 2020
18. Rachel Weiner and Spencer S. Hsu. "Actions By Proud Boy At Capitol Show 'Planning, Determination, And Coordination." Washington Post. 29 Jan 2021
19. Adam Goldman, Katie Benner and Zolan Kanno-Youngs. "How Trump's Focus On Antifa Distracted Attention From The Far-Right Threat." New York Times. 30 Jan 2021
20. Rachael Levy and Warren P. Strobel. "Extremists Pose A Violent Threat, FBI And DHS Officials Say." Wall Street Journal. 24 Sept 2020
21. "ADL Report: Right-Wing Extremists Killed 38 People In 2019, Far Surpassing All Other Murderous Extremists." Anti-Defamation League. 26 Feb 2020
22. Luke Mogelson. "Among the Insurrectionists." New Yorker. 15 Jan 2021
23. "White Supremacy Extremism: The Transnational Rise of the Violent White Supremacist Movement." The Soufan Center. September 2019
24. Charles Kurzman. "Muslim-American Involvement With Violent Extremism, 2001-2020." Triangle Center on Terrorism and Homeland Security, Duke Sanford. 14 Jan 2021
25. Katrin Bennhold and Michael Schwirtz. "Capitol Riot Puts Spotlight On 'Apocalyptically Minded" Global Far Right." New York Times. 24 Jan 2021
26. United States. Department of Homeland Security. "Rightwing Extremism: Current Economic and Political Climate Fueling Resurgence in Radicalization and Recruitment." 7 Apr 2009
27. Peter Beinart. "Trump Shut Programs To Counter Violent Extremism." Atlantic. 29 Oct 2018
28. United States. Department Of Homeland Security And Federal Bureau of Investigation. "White Supremacists Extremism Poses Persistent Threat Of Lethal Violence." 10 May 2017

29. United States. Federal Bureau Of Investigation. "Counterterrorism Policy Directive And Policy Guide." 1 Apr 2018
30. Tom Dreisbach and Meg Anderson. "Nearly 1 in 5 Defendants In Capitol Riot Cases Served In The Military." NPR. 21 Jan 2021
31. Rachel Weiner and Sepncer S. Hsu. "Former FBI Official, A Navy Veteran, Is 'Key Figure" In Jan. 6 Riot, Prosecutors Allege." Washington Post. 11 Feb 2021
32. Will Carless and Michael Corey. "To Protect And Slur." Reveal. 14 June 2019
33. Emily Hoerner and Rick Tulsky. "Cops Across The U.S. Have Been Exposed Posting Racist And Violent Things on Facebook. Here's the Proof." BuzzFeed and Injustice Watch. 1 June 2019.
34. Kristine Phillips. "DOJ Inspector General Finds Weaknesses In How The FBI Identifies Homegrown Terrorists." USAToday. 4 Mar 2020
35. Alexander Mallin. "DOJ Watchdog Faults FBI Investigations Into 'Homegrown Violent Extremists." ABC News. 4 Mar 2020
36. United States. Office Of The Director of National Intelligence. "Domestic Violent Extremism Poses Heightened Threat in 2021." 1 Mar 2021
37. Drew Harwell, Isaac Stanley-Becker, Razzan Nakhlawi And Craig Timberg. "QAnon Reshaped Trump's Party and Radicalized Believers. The Capitol Siege May Just Be the Start." Washington Post. 13 Jan 2021
38. Robert O'Harrow Jr., Andrew Ba Tran and Derek Hawkins. "The Rise Of Domestic Extremism In America." Washington Post. 12 Apr 2021
39. Feng Zhang, Maxwell Cohen and Aaron Barr. "Economic Impact Study Of New Offshore Wind Lease Auctions By BOEM." Wood Mackenzie. August 2020
40. "Peaceful Gathering In Southeast - Destructive Crowd Downtown." Portland Police Bureau. 26 May 2021
41. Scott Wilson. "Anarchists and an Increase in Violent Crime Hijack Portland's Social Justice Movement." Washington Post. 31 May 2021
42. Mark Hosenball. "U.S. Prosecutors Do Not Charge Portland Protesters With Antifa Ties." 4 Aug 2020

43. United States. Federal Bureau of Investigation Department of Homeland Security. "Strategic Intelligence Assessment and Data on Domestic Terrorism." May 2021
44. United States. Department of Justice. "Over 300 People Facing Federal Charges For Crimes Committed During Nationwide Demonstrations." 24 Sept 2020
45. Alanna Durkin Richer, Colleen Long and Michael Balsamo. "AP Finds Most Arrested in Protests Aren't Leftist Radicals." Associated Press. 20 Oct 2020
46. "DA Mike Schmidt Announces 10 People Charged Following Civil Unrest Incidents." Multnomah County District Attorney. 3 June 2021
47. "DA Mike Schmidt Provides Community Update Following Downtown Riot." Multnomah County District Attorney. 26 May 2021
48. "Finally, Portland Antifa Is Being Brought To Justice For Its Violence." New York Post. 7 June 2021
49. Alastair Reed and Kateira Aryaeinejad. "2020 Trends in Terrorism: From ISIS Fragmentation to Lone-Actor Attacks." United States Institute of Peace." 8 Jan 2021

Tinfoil Hats to Red Hats: The Conspiracy Theory Trap

1. Shawn Boburg, Dalton Bennett, Neena Satija and Ken Hoffman. "Ex-Cop Hits Truck Thinking It Held 750,000 Fraudulent Ballots, Police Say. It Held Air Conditioning Parts." Washington Post. 21 Dec 2020
2. Shaila Dewan and Kay Nolan. "Pharmacist Accused Of Tampering With Vaccine Was Conspiracy Theorist, Police Say." New York Times. 4 Jan 2021
3. Amanda Robb. "Anatomy Of A Fake News Scandal." Rolling Stone. 16 Nov 2017
4. Sheera Frenkel and Davey Alba. "Misleading Virus Video, Pushed by the Trumps, Spreads Online." New York Times. 28 July 2020
5. Will Sommer. "Trump's New Favorite COVID Doctor Believes in Alien DNA, Demon Sperm, and Hydroxychloroquine." Daily Beast. 28 July 2020
6. Shawn Boburg and Dalton Bennett. "The Troll: A Fake Flag Burning

At Gettysburg Was Only His Latest Hoax." Washington Post. 17 July 2020

Social Media

1. Davey Alba. "Misinformation About George Floyd Protests Surges on Social Media." New York Times. 1 June 2020
2. Sheera Frenkel, Ben Decker and Davey Alba. "How The 'Plandemic' Movie And Its Falsehoods Spread Widely Online." New York Times. 21 May 2020
3. Martin Enserink and Jon Cohen. "Fact Checking Judy Mikovits, the Controversial Virologist Attacking Anthony Fauci in a Viral Conspiracy Video." 8 May 2020
4. Jonathan Jarry. "The Doctor Carl Sagan Warned Us About." McGill. 8 Jan 2021
5. Elizabeth Dwoskin and Craig Timberg. "Misinformation Dropped Dramatically the Week After Twitter Banned Trump and Some Allies." Washington Post. 16 Jan 2021
6. "Mail-In Voter Fraud: Anatomy of a Disinformation Campaign." Berkman Klein Center for Internet & Society, Harvard University. 1 Oct 2020
7. "Repeat Offenders: Voting Misinformation on Twitter in the 2020 United States Election." Election Integrity Partnership. 29 Oct 2020
8. Sarah Evanega, Mark Lynas, Jordan Adams, and Karinne Smolenyak. "Coronavirus Misinformation: Quantifying Sources and Themes in the COVID-19'Infodemic.'" Cornell University.
9. Sheera Frenkel. "How Misinformation 'Superspreaders' Seed False Election Theories." New York Times. 23 Nov 2020
10. Alex Thompson. "Why the Right Wing Has a Massive Advantage on Facebook." Politico. 26 Sept 2020
11. Steven L. Johnson, Brent Kitchens and Peter Gray. "Facebook Serves as an Echo Chamber, Especially for Conservatives." New York Times. 26 Oct 2020
12. United States. "Cyberspace Solarium Commission." March 2020

13. Jeff Horwitz and Deepa Seetharaman. "Facebook Executives Shut Down Efforts to Make the Site Less Divisive." Wall Street Journal. 26 Mar 2020
14. Greg Bensinger. “Does Zuckerberg Understand How the Right to Free Speech Works?” New York Times. 8 July 2020
15. “Who Controls the Conversation.” Economist. 24 Oct 2020
16. “The Great Clean-Up.” Economist. 24 Oct 24
17. Kate Kelly, Emily Flitter and Shane Goldmacher. “Companies Pull Back Political Giving Following Capitol Violence.” New York Times. 11 Jan 2021
18. United States. Federal Trade Commission. Lesley Fair. "FTC’s $5 billion Facebook Settlement: Record-Breaking and History-Making." 24 July 2019
19. Gordon Pennycook, Adam Bear, Evan T. Collins, and David G. Rand. “The Implied Truth Effect: Attaching Warnings to a Subset of Fake News Headlines Increases Perceived Accuracy of Headlines Without Warnings.” 2020
20. Katherine Clayton, Spencer Blair, Jonathan A. Busam, Samuel Forstner, John Glance, Guy Green, Anna Kawata, Akhila Kovvuri Jonathan, Martin Evan Morgan, Morgan Sandhu, Rachel Sang, Rachel Scholz-Bright, Austin T. Welch, Andrew G. Wolff, Amanda Zhou, and Brendan Nyhan. “Real Solutions for Fake News?: Measuring the Effectiveness of General Warnings and Fact-Check Tags in Reducing Belief in False Stories on Social Media.”
21. “Ants in a Web.” Graphika. May 2021

Media

1. Rebecca Tan, Peter Jamison, Carol D. Leonnig, Meagan Flynn, and John Woodrow Cox. “Trump Supporters Storm U.S. Capitol, With One Woman Killed And Tear Gas Fired.” Washington Post. 6 Jan 2021
2. Roy Peter Clark. “Telling It Like It Is: When Writing News Requires a Distance From Neutrality.” Poynter. 23 Jan 2021
3. Celine Castronuovo. “James Murdoch Predicts ‘A Reckoning’ For Media After Capitol Riots.” The Hill. 15 Jan 2021

4. Michael M. Grynbaum, Tiffany Hsu, Katie Robertson and Keith Collins. "How Right-Wing Radio Stoked Anger Before The Capitol Siege." New York Times. 10 Feb 2021
5. Brian Klaas. "He Worked In Russia Media. He Recognizes The Same Tactics At Fox News." Washington Post. 23 Mar 2021
6. Peter Pomerantsev. "Sean Hannity's Learned Helplessness." The American Interest. 27 Apr 2018
7. Christopher Rufo. Twitter.
8. Mike Hixenbaugh. "A Viral Video Forced a Wealthy Texas Suburb To Confront Racism. A 'Silent Majority' Fought Back." NBC News. 22 Jan 2021
9. Nikole Hannah-Jones. "The 1619 Project." New York Times. August 2019
10. Lexi Nahl. "'Critical Race Theory' Now Banned in Florida Public Schools." CBS 12 News. 10 June 2021
11. Jeremy Barr. "Critical Race Theory is the hottest topic on Fox News. And it's only getting hotter." Washington Post. 24 June 2021
12. Zselyke Csaky. "Nations in Transit: Dropping the Democratic Facade." Freedom House.
13. Anna Lührmann, Juraj Medzihorsky, Garry Hindle, and Staffan I. Lindberg. "New Global Data on Political Parties: V-Party." Varieties of Democracy. October 2020

Online Influence Operations

1. George Washington. Farewell Address. 1796
2. United States. National Intelligence Council. "Foreign Threats To The 2020 U.S. Federal Elections." 16 Mar 2021
3. United States. Office of the Director of National Intelligence. "Statement by NCSC Director William Evanina: Election Threat Update for the American Public." 7 Aug 2020
4. United States. Department of the Treasury. "Treasury Sanctions Russia-Linked Election Interference Actors." 10 Sept 2020
5. Jack Date and John Santucci. "Treasury Department Says Ukrainian Linked to Rudy Giuliani is 'Russian Agent.'" ABC News. 10 Sept 2020

6. United States. Intelligence Community Assessment. “Assessing Russian Activities and Intentions in Recent U.S. Elections.” 6 Jan 2017
7. Desmond Butler and David Rising. "Trump Adviser: Russian Meddling ‘Incontrovertible’.” Associated Press. 18 Feb 2018
8. Kevin Johnson. “’The United States is Under Attack’: Intelligence Chief Dan Coats Says Putin Targeting 2018 Elections.” USA Today. 13 Feb 2018
9. “Russia: U.S. Intelligence Chief.” Reuters. 13 Feb 2018
10. “Transcript: Dan Coats Warns The Lights Are 'Blinking Red' On Russian Cyberattacks.” NPR. 18 July 2018
11. Patricia Zengerle and Doina Chiacu. “U.S. 2018 Elections ‘Under Attack’ By Russia: U.S. Intelligence Chief.” Reuters. 13 Feb 2018
12. Special Counsel Robert S. Mueller, III. “Report On The Investigation Into Russian Interference In The 2016 Presidential Election.” Volume I of II. March 2019
13. Special Counsel Robert S. Mueller, III. “Report On The Investigation Into Russian Interference In The 2016 Presidential Election.” Volume II of II. March 2019
14. Jessica Guynn. “Facebook Expands Scope of Russian Influence on Americans for Second Time.” USA Today. 1 Nov 2017
15. United States. Senate. “Report of the Select Committee on Intelligence On Russian Active Measures Campaigns and Interference in the 2016 U.S. Election. Volume 4: Review of the Intelligence Community Assessment.”
16. United States. Senate. “Report of the Select Committee on Intelligence On Russian Active Measures Campaigns and Interference in the 2016 U.S. Election. Volume 5: Counterintelligence Threats and Vulnerabilities.”
17. Philip N. Howard, Bharath Ganesh, Dimitra Liotsiou, John Kelly, and Camille François. “The IRA, Social Media and Political Polarization in the United States, 2012-2018.” University of Oxford and Graphika. Computational Propaganda Research Project.
18. Renee DiResta, Dr. Kris Shaffer, Becky Ruppel, David Sullivan, Robert Matney, Ryan Fox, Dr. Jonathan Albright and Ben Johnson. “The Tactics & Tropes of the Internet Research Agency.”

19. James Andrew Lewis. "After the Breach: The Monetization and Illicit Use of Stolen Data," Statement Before the House Committee on Financial Services Subcommittee on Terrorism and Illicit Finance. 15 Mar 2018

Mental Health

1. John F. Helliwell, Richard Layard and Jeffrey D. Sachs. "World Happiness Report." 2019
2. John F. Helliwell, Richard Layard, Jeffrey D. Sachs, and Jan Emmanuel De Neve. "World Happiness Report." 2020
3. John F. Helliwell, Haifang Huang, Shun Wang and Max Norton. "World Happiness Report." 2021
4. Nirmita Panchal, Rabah Kamal, Kendal Orgera, Cynthia Cox, Rachel Garfield, Liz Hamel, Cailey Muñana and Priya Chidambaram. "The Implications of COVID-19 for Mental Health and Substance Use." Henry J. Kaiser Family Foundation. 21 Aug 2020
5. "Stress in the Time of COVID-19." American Psychological Association. June 2020
6. "Stress in America 2020" American Psychological Association.
7. "National College Health Assessment." American College Health Association. Spring 2019
8. Paige Winfield Cunningham. "The Health 202: Texts to Federal Government Mental Health Hotline Up roughly 1,000." Washington Post.
9. "Historic Shift in American's Happiness Amid Pandemic." NORC, University of Chicago. June 2020
10. "America's Health Rankings: 2018 Annual Report." United Health Foundation.
11. "America's Health Rankings: 2019 Annual Report." United Health Foundation.
12. United States. Centers for Disease Control and Prevention. "Leading Causes of Death Reports, 1981 - 2017." 1 Aug 2019
13. United States. Centers for Disease Control and Prevention. "Preventing Suicide." 16 Nov 2020

14. “Anxiety Disorders.” National Alliance on Mental Illness. 19 Jan 2020
15. “Global Emotions Report.” Gallup. 2019
16. Kevin B. Smith, Matthew V. Hibbing, and John R. Hibbing. “Friends, Relatives, Sanity, and Health: The Costs of Politics.” 25 Sept 2019

Democracy on the Line

1. Charlie Savage, Adam Goldman and Neil MacFarquhar. “’This Kettle Is Set To Boil’: New Evidence Points to Riot Conspiracy.” New York Times. 22 Jan 2021
2. Alan Feuer. “Justice Dept. Links Oath Keepers And Proud Boys Ahead of Capitol Riot.” New York Times. 24 Mar 2021
3. Morgan Chittum, Stephen Rex Brown and Graham Rayman. “Man Arrested On Upper East Side With SUV Loaded With Ammo, Shotgun In Aftermath Of Capitol Siege.” Daily News. 20 Jan 2021
4. Rachel Weiner and Spencer S. Hsu. “Capitol Riot Defendants Facing Jail Have Regrets. Judges Aren’t Buying It.” Washington Post. 26 Feb 2021
5. Devlin Barrett and Matt Zapotosky. “FBI Report Warned of ‘War’ at Capitol, Contradicting Claims There Was No Indication of Looming Violence.” Washington Post. 12 Jan 2021
6. Meryl Kornfield. “Women Charged in Capitol Riot Said She Wanted To Shoot Pelosi ‘In the Friggin’ Brain.’” Washington Post. 29 Jan 2021
7. Devlin Barrett, Spencer S. Hsu and Aaron C. Davis. “’Be Ready to Fight’: FBI Probe of U.S. Capitol Riot Finds Evidence Detailing Coordination of an Assault.” Washington Post. 30 Jan 2021
8. Stella Cooper, Ben Decker, Anjali Singhvi and Christiaan Triebert. “Tracking the Oath Keepers Who Attacked the Capitol. New York Times. 29 Jan 2021
9. Steven Levitsky and Daniel Ziblatt. “How Democracies Die.” Crown Publishing. 2018
10. Jacob Knutson. “’Disgraceful Scene’: World Leaders Condemn Chaos At U.S. Capitol.” Axios. 7 Jan 2021

11. "Freedom in the World 2018: Democracy in Crisis." Freedom House.
12. "Freedom in the World 2019: Democracy in Retreat." Freedom House.
13. "Freedom in the World 2020: A Leaderless Struggle for Democracy." Freedom House.
14. "2020 Social Progress Index." Social Progress Imperative.

Chapter Four
For Policy Geeks Like Me

Seismic Shifts

1. President Dwight D. Eisenhower. "Farewell Radio and Television Address to the American People." 17 Jan 1961
2. Stephen Biddle and Ivan Oelrich. "Future Warfare in the Western Pacific." International Security. 9 Aug 2016
3. Christopher Paul and Miriam Matthews. "The Russian 'Firehose of Falsehood' Propaganda Model." RAND Corporation. 2016
4. United States. Department of Homeland Security. "Russian Government Cyber Activity Targeting Energy and Other Critical Infrastructure Sectors." United States Computer Emergency Readiness Team. 15 Mar 2018
5. United States. "Final Report." Cyberspace Solarium Commission." March 2020
6. United States. "Cybersecurity Lessons From the Pandemic." White Paper One. Cyberspace Solarium Commission. May 2020
7. Octavian Manea. "Russia Is Practicing a Form of Geopolitical Guerrilla War Against the West." Defense Matters. 14 Dec 2017
8. United States. Government Accountability Office. "Information Security: Agencies Need to Improve Implementation of Federal Approach to Securing Systems and Protecting Against Intrusions." December 2018

9. "U.S. Defense Spending Compared To Other Countries." Peter G. Peterson Foundation. 13 May 2020
10. Jonathan Ponciano. "Senate Averts Shutdown, Passes $741 Billion Defense Bill With Veto-Proof Majority, Buying Time For Stimulus And Budget Bill." Forbes. 11 Dec 2020
11. "Budget Basics: National Defense." Peter G. Peterson Foundation. 11 Jan 2021
12. "Sector Profile: Defense." OpenSecrets.org. 29 Mar 2021
13. Dan Auble. "Capitalizing On Conflict: How Defense Contractors And Foreign Nations Lobby For Arm Sales." Center for Responsive Politics. 25 Feb 2021
14. Erin Duffin. "Value of U.S. Government Contracts of Lockheed Martin in 2019, by Department." Statista. 15 May 2020
15. Trefis Team. "How Much of Boeing's Revenues Comes From The U.S. Government." Forbes. 2 Jan 2020
16. Abraham Maslow, Maslow's Golden Hammer
17. Amy F. Woolf. "Conventional Prompt Global Strike and Long-Range Ballistic Missiles: Background and Issues." Congressional Research Service. 6 April 2018
18. Amy F. Woolf. "Conventional Prompt Global Strike and Long-Range Ballistic Missiles: Background and Issues." Congressional Research Service. 14 Feb 2020
19. United States. Office of the Secretary of Defense. "Nuclear Posture Review." February 2018
20. United States. "Providing for the Common Defense: The Assessment and Recommendations of the National Defense Strategy Commission."
21. United States. Department of State. "New START Treaty." 30 Mar 2021
22. "How Many Countries Are There In The World?" World Atlas. 4 Jan 2018
23. "Fact Sheet: The United States' Nuclear Inventory." Center for Arms Control and Non-Proliferation. 2 July 2020
24. United States. Congressional Budget Office. "Projected Costs of U.S. Nuclear Forces, 2019 to 2028." January 2019

25. Stephen I. Schwartz. "The Hidden Costs Of Our Nuclear Arsenal: Overview of Project Findings." The Brookings Institution. 30 June 1998
26. "Report of the United States of America Pursuant to Actions 5, 20, and 21 of the NPT Review Conference Final Document." 2015 Review Conference of the Parties to the Treaty on the Non-Proliferation of Nuclear Weapons. New York City. April 27 - May 22, 2015
27. "Nuclear Weapon Modernization Continues But The Outlook For Arms Control Is Bleak." Stockholm International Peace Research Institute. 15 June 2020
28. Matthew Cox. "Pentagon Tells Congress to Stop Buying Equipment It Doesn't Need." Military.com. 28 Jan 2015
29. Aaron Gregg. "Military-Industrial Complex Finds A Growth Market In Hypersonic Weaponry." Washington Post. 21 Dec 2018
30. United States. "Worldwide Threat Assessment." Office of the Director of National Intelligence Daniel R. Coats. 13 Feb 2018
31. United States. "Worldwide Threat Assessment." Office of the Director of National Intelligence Daniel R. Coats. 29 Jan 2019
32. United States. Memo from Air Force Lt. Gen. David Goldfein, the Pentagon's Joint Staff Director. 8 Jan 2015
33. Hans M. Kristensen and Robert S. Norris. "Status of World Nuclear Forces." Federation of American Scientists. 11 Mar 2022
34. United States. Bureau of Labor Statistics. "The Relative Weakness In Earnings Of Production Workers in Manufacturing." December 2019
35. "Making It In America: Revitalizing U.S. Manufacturing." McKinsey & Company. November 2017
36. Eleanor Mueller. "Trump Hails 'Manufacturing Miracle' As Factories Bleed Jobs." Politico. 16 Sept 2020
37. "Companies Planning To Increase Automation Investments Due To Covid-19, Honeywell Study Shows." Honeywell. 7 July 2020
38. United States. Bureau of Labor Statistics. "Employment Projections – 2019-2029." 1 Sept 2020
39. United States. Federal Reserve. "Part 1: Recent Economic and Financial Developments." 7 Feb 2020

40. Heather Long and Andrew Van Dam. "U.S. Manufacturing Was In A Mild Recession During 2019, A Sore Spot For The Economy." Washington Post. 17 Jan 2020
41. Jeanne Whalen, Reed Albergotti and David J. Lynch. "Biden Can't Fix The Chip Shortage Any Time Soon. Here's Why." Washington Post. 1 Mar 2021
42. Jeanne Whalen, Jeff Stein and Reed Albergotti. "Growing Computer-Chip Shortage Alarms Biden And Congress." Washington Post. 23 Feb 2021
43. Heidi Garrett-Peltier. "Job Opportunity Cost of War." Costs of War, Brown University. 24 May 2017
44. "Number of Renewable Energy Jobs Worldwide from 2012 to 2019." Statista. 1 Jan 2020
45. "Energy Efficiency Jobs in America: 2019." E2. September 2019
46. Silvio Marcacci. "Renewable Energy Job Boom Creates Economic Opportunity As Coal Industry Slumps." Forbes. 22 Apr 2019
47. United States. Energy Information Administration. "Renewable Energy Explained." 28 Dec 2020
48. United States. Energy Information Administration. "Oil and Petroleum Products Explained." 28 Dec 2020
49. United States. Energy Information Administration. "How Much Petroleum Does the United States Import and Export?" 28 Dec 2020
50. International Energy Agency. "World Energy Outlook 2018." 13 Nov 2018
51. International Energy Agency. "World Energy Outlook 2019." November 2019
52. United States. Energy Information Administration. "Annual Energy Outlook 2019." 24 Jan 2019
53. United States. Energy Information Administration. "U.S. Petroleum Product Exports Set Record High in 2018." 23 Apr 2019
54. United States. Energy Information Administration. "The United States Is Now the Largest Global Crude Oil Producer." 12 Sept 2018
55. Patti Domm. "This Texas Area Is Expected To Double Oil Output to 8 Million Barrels In Just Four Years, Boosting U.S. Exports." 8 Mar 2019

56. United States. Energy Information Administration. "How Much Shale (Tight) Oil Produced In The United States." 4 Apr 2021
57. "Oilfield Services Bankruptcy Tracker." Haynes and Boone, LLP. 31 Dec 2020
58. "Energy Defaults Are On The Rise Again, Clouded Economic Outlook Calls For A Higher U.S. Speculative-Grade Default Rate." Moody's. 31 Oct 2019
59. Christopher M. Matthews. "Exxon Posts Third Consecutive Quarterly Loss for First Time." Wall Street Journal. 30 Oct 2020
60. Tom Kirkman. "Private-Equity Firms Fueled the U.S. Shale Revolution With $125 Billion. Now They Face A Reckoning Of Epic Proportions As The Oil Market Melts Down." OilPrice.com. 30 Apr 2020
61. "Power in the 21st Century." Economist. 19 Sept 2020
62. Christopher M. Matthews. "Big Oil Companies Lose Billions, Prepare For Prolonged Pandemic." Wall Street Journal. 31 July 2020
63. Michael D. Plante and Kunal Patel. "Breakeven Oil Prices Underscore Shale's Impact On The Market." Federal Reserve Bank of Dallas. 21 May 2019
64. "Production And Royalty Declines In A Natural Gas Well Over Time." Geology.com. 31 Mar 2021
65. "Lex in Depth: The $900bn Cost Of 'Stranded Energy Assets.'" Financial Times. 3 Feb 2020
66. "Wasted Capital And Stranded Assets Press Release." Carbon Tracker. 4 Dec 2013
67. "Net-Zero America." Princeton University. 15 Dec 2020
68. "America's Zero Carbon Action Plan." The Zero Carbon Consortium. 2020
69. David Coady, Ian Parry, Nghia-Piotr Le, and Baoping Shang. "Global Fossil Fuel Subsidies Remain Large: An Update Based on Country-Level Estimates." International Monetary Fund. 2 May 2019
70. "How To Deal With Worries About Stranded Assets." Economist. 24 Nov 2016
71. United States. Energy Information Administration. "U.S. Renewable Energy Consumption Surpasses Coal For the First Time In over 130 Years." 28 May 2020

72. “Arab States Are Embracing Solar Power.” Economist. 7 May 2020
73. “Coastal Virginia Offshore Wind.” Dominion Energy. 1 Jan 2021
74. “Climate Change and Energy Transition.” Shell. 2 Jan 2021
75. “Climate Change Report 2020.” BHP Billiton.
76. “Our 2021 Stewardship Expectations.” BlackRock.
77. “Sustainability as BlackRock’s New Standard for Investing.” BlackRock. 2 Jan 2021
78. “Net Zero Asset Managers Initiative.” 2 Jan 2021
79. “Tesla Market Value Crosses $800 Billion For The First Time.” Reuters. 8 Jan 2021
80. “Counting the Carbs.” Economist. 12 Dec 2020
81. “If At First You Don’t Succeed.” Economist. 12 Dec 2020
82. Neal E. Boudette and Coral Davenport. “G.M. Announcement Shakes Up U.S. Automaker’s Transition to Electric Cars.” New York Times. 29 Jan 2021
83. Rochelle Toplensky. “Investors Have a Local Route Into China’s Hydrogen Plans.” Wall Street Journal. 1 Oct 2020
84. Stanley Reed. “A Monster Wind Turbine Is Upending An Industry.” New York Times. 1 Jan 2021
85. “Greenbacks for Greenery.” Economist. 31 Oct 2020
86. United States. Environmental Protection Agency. “Power Sector Programs: 2017 Progress Report.”
87. “Can American States Slow Global Warming on Their Own?” Economist. 29 June 2019
88. Michael Hiltzik. “No Longer Termed a ‘Failure,’ California’s Cap-and-Trade Program Faces a New Critique: Is it Too successful?” Los Angeles Times. 12 Jan 2018
89. “California Climate Investments Using Cap-and-Trade Auction Proceeds.” March 2019
90. Samuel Stebbins. “These 15 Countries, As Home To Largest Reserves, Control the World’s Oil.” USA Today. 22 May 2019
91. “Share of World Crude Oil Reserves.” Organization of the Petroleum Exporting Countries (OPEC). 28 Dec 2020
92. Elizabeth Rosenthal. “Gulf Oil States Seeking A Lead in Clean Energy.” New York Times. 13 Jan 2009

93. Will Mathis. “Clean Energy Investment Is Set To Hit $2.6 Trillion This Decade.” Bloomberg. 5 Sept 2019
94. “Wind Energy in the United States.” American Wind Energy Association. 31 July 2019
95. “ERCOT Expects Record Electric Use, Increased Chance of Energy Alerts.” ERCOT. 8 May 2019
96. “Clean Energy Investment Exceeded $300 Billion Once Again in 2018.” Bloomberg NEF 16 Jan 2019
97. “The End of Cheap Food.” Economist. 6 Dec 2007
98. United States. U.S. Department of Energy. “U.S. Installed Wind Capacity.”
99. “ERCOT Breaks Peak Demand Record Third Time.” ERCOT. 3 Aug 2011
100. United States. US Government Accountability Office. Crude Oil: Uncertainty About Future Oil Supply Makes it Important to Develop a Strategy for Addressing a Peak and Decline in Oil Production. Feb 2007
101. Clifford Krauss. “New Technologies Redraw the World’s Energy Picture.” New York Times. 25 Oct 2011
102. “The Power and the Glory.” Economist. 19 June 2008
103. United States. Central Intelligence Agency. The World Factbook 2021
104. United States. Central Intelligence Agency. The World Factbook 2021
105. United States. Energy Information Administration. “What Is The United States’ Share Of World Energy Consumption?” 10 Apr 2021
106. United States Congress. America’s Climate Security Act of 2007. S 2129. 1st Session, 110th Congress. The Library of Congress (THOMAS). 18 Oct 2007
107. Allan Sloan. “The Ethanol Cure’s Side Effects.” Washington Post. 29 April 2008
108. Kate Galbraith. “Economy Shifts, and the Ethanol Industry Reels.” New York Times. 5 Nov 2008
109. United States. Clean Air Act Extension of 1970. Public Law 91-604. 31 Dec 1970

110. United States. Energy Policy and Conservation Act. Public Law 94-163. 94th Congress. S 622. 22 Dec 1975
111. Steven Mufson. "The Fight For the Soul – and the Future – Of ExxonMobil." Washington Post. 21 May 2021
112. "Turning Polluting Methane Into Clean Energy: A Progress Report From Aspen Skiing Company." Aspen Snowmass. Winter 2021

Red Flags & Ticking Time Bombs

1. Jon Hilsenrath. "After Record-Long Expansion, Here's What Could Knock the Economy Off Course." Wall Street Journal. 3 June 2019
2. Alan J. Auerbach and Joel Slemrod. "The Economic Effects Of The Tax Reform Act Of 1986." Journal of Economic Literature.
3. Jeanne Sahadi. "Taxes: What People Forget About Reagan." CNN Money. 12 Sept 2010
4. Glenn Kessler. "Rand Paul's Claim That Reagan's Tax Cuts Produced 'More Revenue' And 'Tens Of Millions Of Jobs.'" Washington Post. 10 Apr 2015
5. Bruce Bartlett. "I Helped Create the GOP Tax Myth. Trump is Wrong: Tax Cuts Don't Equal Growth." Washington Post. 28 Sept 2017
6. Tim Mahedy and Daniel J. Wilson. "Fiscal Policy in Good Times and Bad." Federal Reserve Bank of San Francisco. 9 July 2018
7. Jane G. Gravelle and Donald Marples. "The Economic Effects of the 2017 Tax Revision: Preliminary Observations." Congressional Research Service. 7 June 2019
8. Thomas Kaplan. "Senate Leaders Reach Budget Deal To Raise Spending Over Two Years." New York Times. 7 Feb 2018
9. Thomas Kaplan. "Trump Signs Budget Deal To Raise Spending And Reopen Government." 8 Feb 2018
10. Thomas Kaplan. "Congress Approves $1.3 Trillion Spending Bill, Averting A Showdown." New York Times. 22 Mar 2018
11. Deirdre Shesgreen and Eliza Collins. "What's In – And What's Out – Of The $1.3 Trillion Spending Bill." USA Today. 21 Mar 2018
12. Caitlin Emma. "Trump Signs 2-Year Budget Deal." Politico. 2 Aug 2019

13. Emily Cochrane. "Congress Approves Spending Package To Avoid Shutdown, Clearing It For Trump." New York Times. 19 Dec 2019
14. "Are Defense and Disasters Causing the Deficit Increase?" Committee for a Responsible Federal Budget. 18 Oct 2018
15. United States. Department of the Treasury. "Final Monthly Treasury Statement of Receipts and Outlays of the United States Government." 13 Nov 2018
16. United States. Department of the Treasury. "Final Monthly Treasury Statement of Receipts and Outlays of the United States Government." FY2019
17. United States. Department of the Treasury. "Mnuchin and Vought Release Joint Statement on Budget Results for Fiscal Year 2019." 25 Oct 2019
18. United States. Department of the Treasury. "Monthly Statement of the Public Debt of the United States." 31 Dec 2019
19. United States. Congressional Budget Office. "The Budget and Economic Outlook: 2018 to 2028." 9 Apr 2018
20. United States. Congressional Budget Office. "An Update to the Budget and Economic Outlook: 2019 to 2029." August 2019
21. United States. Congressional Budget Office. "The Budget and Economic Outlook: 2021 to 2031." 11 Feb 2021
22. United States. Congressional Budget Office. "The 2021 Long-Term Budget Outlook." March 2021
23. United States. Office of Management and Budget. "An American Budget: Mid-Session Review." Fiscal Year 2019. 13 July 2018
24. Jeff Stein. "U.S. Government Spent $660 Billion More In March Than It Collected In Revenue, The Third-Largest Monthly Deficit on Record." Washington Post. 12 Apr 2021
25. United States. Department of the Treasury. "The Debt to the Penny and Who Holds It." 17 Mar 2021
26. United States. Department of the Treasury. "Major Holders Of Treasury Securities." 15 Mar 2021
27. "The World's Consumers Are Sitting On Piles Of Cash. Will They Spend It?" Economist. 13 Mar 2021

28. “Track the Covid Money.” Committee for a Responsible Federal Budget. 14 May 2021

How Will 1787 Pay for Everything?

1. The Editorial Board. “The Fighter Jet That’s Too Pricey To Fail.” New York Times. 12 Mar 2021
2. Adam Twardowski. “A Conversation With HASC Chairman Adam Smith.” Brookings. 16 Mar 2021
3. Michelle Singletary. “The IRS Paid $3 Billion In Interest To Taxpayers Because It Failed To Get Refunds Out On Time.” Washington Post. 2 Mar 2021

Operation Overhaul

1. “Fortune 500.” Fortune. 13 Apr 2021
2. United States. Department of the Treasury. “Mnuchin and Vought Release Joint Statement on Budget Results for Fiscal Year 2019.” 25 Oct 2019
3. United States. Government Accountability Office. “Payment Integrity: Federal Agencies’ Estimates of FY 2019 Improper Payments.” March 2020
4. United States. “The War on Poverty: 50 Years Later.” House Budget Committee Report. 3 Mar 2014
5. “Transforming DoD’s Core Business Processes for Revolutionary Change.” Defense Business Board. 22 Jan 2015
6. United States. Government Accountability Office. “Iraq: DOD Needs to Improve Visibility and Accountability Over Equipment Provided to Iraq’s Security Forces.” May 2017
7. United States. Government Accountability Office. “DOD Financial Management.” 13 Apr 2021
8. Scot J. Paltrow and Kelly Carr. “How the Pentagon’s Payroll Quagmire Traps America’s Soldiers.” Reuters. 2 July 2013
9. Scot J. Paltrow. “Behind the Pentagon’s Doctored Ledgers, A Running Tally of Epic Waste.” Reuters. 18 Nov 2013

10. Jonathan O'Connell, Steven Rich and Peter Whoriskey. "Public Companies Received $1 Billion in Stimulus Funds Meant for Small Businesses." Washington Post. 1 May 2020
11. "New Research Brief Finds Banks Have Cashed in $19 Billion in Fees for Processing COVID Relief PPP Loans." University of Massachusetts Amherst. 8 Sept 2020
12. Stacy Cowley. "Despite Billions in Fees, Banks Predict Meager Profits on P.P.P. Loans." New York Times. 1 Oct 2020
13. Stacy Cowley and Ella Koeze. "1 Percent of P.P.P. Borrowers Got Over One-Quarter of the Loan Money." New York Times. 1 Feb 2021
14. Ryan Tracy. "Evidence of PPP Fraud Mounts, Officials Say." Wall Street Journal. 8 Nov 2020
15. "Trump Defends Tax Plan As 'Great Christmas Gifts' To Middle Class." Reuters. 16 Dec 2017
16. Carol Burris and Jeff Bryant. "Asleep At The Wheel." Network for Public Education. 2019

Tax Code

1. "The Moment of Truth." The National Commission on Fiscal Responsibility and Reform. December 2010
2. United States. Congress. "Two Years of Evidence Show 2017 Tax Cuts Failed to Deliver Promised Economic Boost." Joint Economic Committee. 28 Jan 2020
3. Allan Sloan and Cezary Podkul. "Donald Trump Built a National Debt So Big (Even Before the Pandemic) That It'll Weigh Down the Economy for Years." ProPublica. 14 Jan 2021
4. Jeff Stein and Yeganeh Torbati. "Trump's Former Treasury Secretary Expected to Launch Investment Fund, Seeking Backing of Persian Gulf State Funds." Washington Post. 23 Feb 2021
5. Jesse Drucker. "The Tax-Break Bonanza Inside the Economic Rescue Package." New York Times. 24 Apr 2020
6. William R. Emmons. "Housing and Consumer Spending Are Powering the Economy like Never Before." Federal Reserve Bank of St. Louis. September 2017

7. United States. Bureau of Economic Analysis. "Gross Domestic Product, 3rd Quarter 2018 (Advance Estimate)." 26 Oct 2018
8. United States. Department of Labor. Bureau of Labor Statistics. "The Employment Situation - December 2019." 10 Jan 2019
9. United States. Bureau of Economic Analysis. "Gross Domestic Product, Third Quarter 2019 (Advance Estimate)." 30 Oct 2019
10. Ben Leubsdorf and Richard Rubin. "U.S. Government Revenues Drop in Wake of Tax Cuts." Wall Street Journal. 12 July 2018
11. Howard Gleckman. "The Three Numbers to Know About the TCJA in 2018." Tax Policy Center. 18 Apr 2019
12. Tim Mahedy and Daniel J. Wilson. "Fiscal Policy in Good Times and Bad." Federal Reserve Bank of San Francisco. 9 July 2018
13. "Effects of the Tax Cuts and Jobs Act: A Preliminary Analysis." Tax Policy Center. 13 June 2018
14. "The Tax Cuts and Jobs Act, as Reported By Conference Committee: Static and Dynamic Effects on the Budget and the Economy." Penn Wharton Budget Model. 18 Dec 2017
15. Chye-Ching Huang and Brandon DeBot. "Corporate Tax Cuts Skew to Shareholders and CEOs, Not Workers as Administration Claims Eventual Spending Cuts or Tax Increases to Pay for Corporate Rate Cuts Could Leave Most Workers Worse Off." Center on Budget and Policy Priorities. 16 Aug 2017
16. Steve Wamhoff and Matthew Gardner. "Federal Tax Cuts In The Bush, Obama, And Trump Years." Institute on Taxation and Economic Policy. 11 July 2018
17. "Swamped." Public Citizen. 1 Dec 2017
18. Jesse Drucker and Jim Tankersley. "How Big Companies Won New Tax Breaks From the Trump Administration." New York Times. 30 Dec 2019
19. Jim Tankersley, Peter Eavis and Ben Casselman. "How FedEx Cut Its Tax Bill to $0." New York Times. 17 Nov 2019
20. Richard Rubin and Theo Francis. "Trump Promised a Rush of Repatriated Cash, But Company Responses Are Modest." Wall Street Journal. 16 Sept 2018
21. Sarah Chaney and Theo Francis. "Company Repatriations of Cash Surged, Then Moderated in 2018." Wall Street Journal. 27 Mar 2019

22. Austin Herrick. "Estimates of TCJA Repatriation of Foreign Earnings on Investment and GDP." Penn Wharton Budget Model (PWBM). 29 Aug 2018
23. United States. Congress. "Repatriating Offshore Funds: 2004 Tax Windfall for Select Multinationals." 112th Congress. 11 Oct 2011
24. United States. Board of Governors of the Federal Reserve System. "U.S. Corporations' Repatriation of Offshore Profits: Evidence from 2018." 6 Aug 2019
25. Chye-Ching Huang and Brandon DeBot. "Corporate Tax Cuts Skew to Shareholders and CEOs, Not Workers as Administration Claims Eventual Spending Cuts or Tax Increases to Pay for Corporate Rate Cuts Could Leave Most Workers Worse Off." Center on Budget and Policy Priorities. 16 Aug 2017
26. Toluse Olorunnipa. "Trump's Tax Promises Undercut by CEO Plans to Help Investors." Bloomberg. 29 Nov 2017
27. "What Are Businesses Saying About Tax Reform Now?" Federal Reserve Bank of Atlanta. 23 Mar 2018
28. "S&P 500 Q4 2018 Buybacks Set 4th Consecutive Quarterly Record at $223 Billion; 2018 Sets Record $806 Billion." S&P Global. 25 Mar 2019
29. Commissioner Robert J. Jackson Jr. "Stock Buybacks and Corporate Cashouts." U.S. Securities and Exchange Commission. 11 June 2018
30. Editorial Board. "How To Collect $1.4 Trillion In Unpaid Taxes." New York Times. 20 Mar 2021
31. Barry W. Johnson and Peter J. Rose. "Federal Tax Compliance Research: Tax Gap Estimates For Tax Years 2011-2013." Internal Revenue Service. September 2019
32. John W. Schoen. "Trump Defies Data With 6% GDP Growth Forecast." CNBC. 6 Dec 2017
33. "The Conference Board Economic Forecast for the U.S. Economy." 11 Dec 2019
34. "Corporate Tax Reform and Wages: Theory and Evidence." The Council of Economic Advisers. October 2017
35. "Table 1. Economic Projections of Federal Reserve Board Members and Federal Reserve Bank Presidents, Under Their Individual

Assumptions of Projected Appropriate Monetary Policy, December 2019." Board of Governors of the Federal Reserve System. 11 Dec 2019
36. United States. Congress. "Tax Cuts and Jobs Act of 2017." H.R.1. 115th Congress. 22 Dec 2018
37. United States. Internal Revenue Service. "Anti-Tax Law Evasion Schemes - Law and Arguments (Section II): The Meaning of Income: Taxable Income and Gross Income." 6 Nov 2018
38. William G. Gale, Hilary Gelfond, Aaron Krupkin, Mark J. Mazur, and Eric Toder. "Effects of the Tax Cuts and Jobs Act: A Preliminary Analysis." Tax Policy Center. 13 June 2018
39. "Distributional Analysis of the Conference Agreement for the Tax Cuts and Jobs Act." Tax Policy Center. 18 Dec 2017
40. Heather Long. "Trump's Stock Market Rally is Very Good, But Still Lags Obama and Clinton." Washington Post. 28 Dec 2019
41. Erik Sherman. "The S&P 500 Is at an All Time High – But Markets Still Performed Far Better Under Obama Than Trump." Fortune. 1 Nov 2019
42. Matthew Gardner and Steve Wamhoff. "55 Corporations Paid $0 In Federal Taxes On 2020 Profits." Institute on Taxation and Economic Policy. 2 Apr 2021
43. Christopher Ingraham. "Dozens Of America's Biggest Businesses Paid No Federal Income Tax – Again." Washington Post. 5 Apr 2021

In Defense of Rich People

1. "America's Top Charities 2019." Forbes. 14 Nov 2020
2. "Giving Statistics." Charity Navigator. 14 Nov 2020
3. Warren Buffett. "Stop Coddling the Super-Rich." New York Times. 14 Aug 2012
4. Karen Tumulty. "U-Va. is Investing $100 Million in Saving Democracy. Can It Make a Difference?" Washington Post. 3 June 2021
5. Jesse Eisinger, Jeff Ernsthausen and Paul Kiel. "The Secret IRS Files: Trove of Never-Before-Seen Records Reveal How the Wealthiest Avoid Income Tax." ProPublica. 8 June 2021

6. Stephen Engelberg and Richard Tofel. "Why We Are Publishing the Tax Secrets of the .001%." ProPublica. 8 June 2021

Finding Balance on a Tightrope

1. Neena Satija and Aaron Gregg. "Ten Years Ago, 241 Texas Power Plants Couldn't Take The Cold. Dozens Of Them Failed Again This Year." Washington Post. 6 Mar 2021
2. Hiroko Tabuchi. "Drillers Burned Off Gas At A Staggering Rate As Winter Storm Hits Texas." Washington Post. 26 Mar 2021
3. Abby Livingston. "Texas Lt. Gov. Dan Patrick Says A Failing Economy Is Worse Than Coronavirus." Texas Tribune. 23 Mar 2020
4. United States. Congressional Research Service. "Regulating Drinking Water Contaminants: EPA PFAS Actions." 26 Feb 2020
5. Nathaniel Rich. "The Lawyer Who Became DuPont's Worst Nightmare." New York Times. 6 Jan 2016
6. Cary Coglianese, Natasha Sarin, and Stuart Shapiro. "Deregulatory Deceptions: Reviewing the Trump Administration's Claims About Regulatory Reform." Penn Program on Regulation. 1 Nov 2020

Eight Bad Habits We Need to Break

Bad Habit One
The 2007-2009 Financial Crisis

1. Winston Churchill. "Air Parity Lost." House of Commons. 2 May 1935
2. United States. Congress. "Banking Act of 1933." H.R. 5661. 73rd Congress. 16 June 1933
3. United States. Congress. "Depository Institutions Deregulation and Monetary Control Act of 1980." H.R. 4986. 96th Congress. March 1980
4. United States. Congress. "Garn-St Germain Depository Institutions Act of 1982." H.R. 6267. 97th Congress. October 1982
5. Ronald Reagan. "Remarks on Signing the Garn-St Germain Depository Institutions Act of 1982." 15 Oct 1982

6. Timothy Curry and Lynn Shibut. “The Cost Of The Savings And Loan Crisis: Truth And Consequences.” FDIC Banking Review.
7. United States. Congress. “Financial Services Modernization Act of 1999, Commonly Called Gramm-Leach-Bliley.” S.900. 106th Congress. 12 Nov 1999
8. United States. Congress. “Commodity Futures Modernization Act of 2000.” 106th Congress. H.R. 5660 was incorporated by reference in the conference report to H.R. 4577. H.R. 4577, the Consolidated Appropriations Act 2001, became Public Law 106-554 on December 21, 2000.
9. Steve Schaefer. “Bernanke On Why Subprime Turned Out Worse Than the Dot-Com Bubble.” Forbes. 13 Apr 2012
10. “Kenneth Lay, Enron.” Time. 10 Aug 2010
11. Kathleen Day. “Study Finds ‘Extensive’ Fraud at Fannie Mae.” Washington Post. 24 May 2006
12. Kenneth Gilpin. “Freddie Mac to Pay $125 Million Fine.” New York Times. 10 Dec 2003
13. Terence O’Hara and Kathleen Day. “Riggs Bank Hid Assets of Pinochet, Report Says.” Washington Post. 15 July 2004
14. Elliot Blair Smith. “AIG Agrees to pay $1.64 Billion.” USA Today. 9 Feb 2006
15. Claudio Gatti and John Eligon. “Iranian Dealings Lead to a Fine for Credit Suisse.” New York Times. 15 Dec 2009
16. Lynnley Browning. “UBS to Pay $780 Million Fine Over Offshore Services.” New York Times. 18 Feb 2009
17. Tyler Atkinson, David Luttrell and Harvey Rosenblum. “How Bad Was It? The Costs and Consequences of the 2007 - 09 Financial Crisis.” July 2013
18. United States. Government Accountability Office. “Financial Regulatory Reform: Financial Crisis Losses and Potential Impacts of the Dodd-Frank Act.” January 2013
19. Roger Lowenstein. “Triple A Failure.” New York Times. 27 Apr 2008
20. Moody’s. Investor Relations. “Moody’s Reaches Settlement with U.S. Department of Justice, 21 U.S. States and District of Columbia.” 13 Jan 2017

21. Bob Ivry and Craig Torres. "Fed's Court-Ordered Disclosure Shows Americans' Right to Know.'" Bloomberg. 21 Mar 2011
22. "Federal Reserve, Banks Kept Huge Size of Bailout Secret, Records Show." Bloomberg. 28 Nov 2011
23. "Secret Fed Loans Gave Banks $13 Billion Undisclosed to Congress." Bloomberg. 27 Nov 2011
24. United States. Congress. "Emergency Economic Stabilization Act of 2008." H.R. 1424. 110th Congress. H.R.1424 is the vehicle for the economic rescue legislation. Division A is the Emergency Economic Stabilization Act of 2008; Division B is the Energy Improvement and Extension Act of 2008; and Division C is the Tax Extenders and Alternative Minimum Tax Relief Act of 2008.
25. United States. Congressional Budget Office. "Report on the Troubled Asset Relief Program." March 2018
26. "After Bailout, AIG Execs Head to California Resort." ABC News. 7 Oct 2008
27. "Merrill Lynch CEO Thain Spent $1.22 Million On Office." CNBC. 22 Jan 2009
28. Louis Story. "Judge Accepts S.E.C. Deal With Bank of America." New York Times. 22 Feb 2010
29. Martha Graybow and Rick Rothacker. "BofA Pays $2.4 Billion To Settle Claims Over Merrill." Reuters. 28 Sept 2012
30. Steven Davidoff. "A $50 Billion Claim of Havoc Looms for Bank of America." New York Times. 27 Sept 2011
31. Jessica Silver-Greenberg. "Justice Dept. Sues Bank of America Over Mortgage Securities." New York Times. 6 Aug 2013
32. Peter Eavis and Michael Corkery. "Bank Of America's $16 Billion Mortgage Settlement Less Painful Than It Looks." New York Times. 21 Aug 2014
33. Jessica Silver-Greenberg and Ben Protess. "JP Morgan Reveals It Faces Civil and Criminal Inquiries." New York Times. 7 Aug 2013
34. United States. Securities and Exchange Commission. "SEC Enforcement Actions: Addressing Misconduct That Led To Or Arose From The Financial Crisis." 26 May 2015
35. Steve Goldstein. "Here's the Staggering Amount Banks Have Been Fined Since the Financial Crisis." Market Watch. 24 Feb 2018

36. "President Trump Signs Biggest Rollback of Bank Rules Since Dodd-Frank Act." Bloomberg. 24 May 2018
37. "Finance, Insurance & Real Estate Sector: 2010-2018." Open Secrets. 14 May 2019
38. Ben Protess. "Wall Street Seeks to Tuck Dodd-Frank Changes in Budget Bill." New York Times. 9 Dec 2014
39. Haley Sweetland Edwards. "Why It Matters That Congress Just Swapped The Bank Swap Rule." Time. 12 Dec 2014
40. Federal Reserve Bank of Minneapolis. "The Minneapolis Plan to End Too Big to Fail." December 2017
41. "Global OTC Derivatives Market." Bank for International Settlements. 31 Oct 2018
42. "Lehman Ten Years On: More Has Changed Than Meets The Eye." Economist. 6 Sept 2018
43. Lisa Lee and Sarah Husband. "Biggest CLO Buyer Plots Return, Joining BofA and Pimco In Market." Bloomberg. 8 Apr 2021
44. Matthew Goldberg. "Top 15 Largest Banks In The U.S." Bankrate. 2 Mar 2021
45. "Dodd-Frank Progress Report." Davis Polk. 11 May 2021
46. Aline van Duyn. "Dilemmas Of Reforming the Rating Agencies." Financial Times. 11 June 2010
47. "Freddie Mac Toughens Policy on Risky Mortgages." New York Times. 27 Feb 2007

Bad Habit Two
Introduction

1. "Too Big Not To Fail." Economist. 18 Feb 2012
2. "The right Way To Redo Dodd-Frank." Economist. 11 Feb 2017
3. "Five Years Of Dodd-Frank." Davis Polk. 1 July 2015
4. Jayne O'Donnell and Fola Akinnibi. "How Many Pages Of Regulations Are In The Affordable Care Act?" USA Today. 23 Oct 2013
5. Glenn Kessler. "How Many Pages Of Regulations For 'Obamacare?'" Washington Post. 15 May 2013

6. Paul Bedard. "Obamacare Architect Rockefeller: It's 'Beyond Comprehension.'" Washington Examiner. 11 Apr 2013
7. Melanie Curtin. "33 Steve Jobs Quotes That Will Inspire You To Success." Inc.
8. "President Biden's American Families Plan: Budgetary And Macroeconomic Effects." Penn Wharton Budget Model. 5 May 2021

Infrastructure

1. United States. Department of Transportation. "Pocket Guide To Transportation." 1 Mar 2021
2. "2021 Report Card For American's Infrastructure." American Society of Civil Engineers

American Jobs Plan & American Families Plan

1. "President Biden's American Families Plan: Budgetary And Macroeconomic Effects." Penn Wharton Budget Model. 5 May 2021
2. Jeff Stein. "Treasury Targets Tax Cheats, Cryptocurrency in Proposal It Hopes Will Bring in $700 Billion." Washington Post. 20 May 2021
3. United States. Congressional Budget Office. "Trend In The Internal Revenue Service's Funding And Enforcement." 8 July 2020
4. United States. Government Accountability Office. "Payment Integrity: Federal Agencies' Estimates of FY 2019 Improper Payments." March 2020
5. Jeff Stein. "Biden Jobs Plan Seeks $400 Billion to Expand Caretaking Services As U.S. Faces Surge In Aging Population." Washington Post. 2 Apr 2021
6. Alan Rappeport. "Pandemic Inspector General Warns of Oversight Breakdown." New York Times. 1 May 2021
7. United States. Government Accountability Office. "Coronavirus Oversight: Overview." 24 May 2021
8. United States. Government Accountability Office. "Emergency Loans for Small Businesses." 24 May 2021
9. United States. Office of the Special Inspector General for Pandemic Recovery: January 1, 2021 – March 31, 2021."

10. United States. Congressional Budget Office. "DATA ACT: OIGs Reported That Quality of Agency Submitted Data Varied, and Most Recommended Improvements." July 2020
11. "Service Employees International Union." Open Secrets. 26 May 2021
12. Timothy F. Geithner, Jacob J. Lew, Henry M. Paulson Jr., Robert E. Rubin and Lawrence H. Summers. "We Ran the Treasury Department. This is How to Fix Tax Evasion." New York Times. 9 June 2021
13. Nick Noel, Duwain Pinder, Shelley Stewart and Jason Wright. "The Economic Impact of Closing the Racial Wealth Gap." McKinsey & Company. 13 Aug 2019

Bad Habit Three
Education

1. Matthew N. Atwell, Robert Balfanz, Eleanor Manspile, Vaughan Byrnes and John M. Bridgeland. "Building a Grad Nation: Progress and Challenge in Raising High School Graduation Rates Annual Update 2020." Civic and Everyone Graduates Center at the School of Education at Johns Hopkins University. 1 Oct 2020
2. United States. Department of Education. "2017 National Achievement-Level Results: Reading." National Center for Education Statistics. National Assessment of Educational Progress. 5 July 2019
3. United States. Department of Education. "2017 National Achievement-Level Results: Mathematics." National Center for Education Statistics. National Assessment of Educational Progress. 5 July 2019
4. "PISA 2018 Results." OECD, Programme for International Student Assessment (PISA). 2019
5. "Snapshot of Student Performance." OECD, Programme for International Student Assessment (PISA). 2019
6. "PISA 2018 Insights and Interpretations." OECD, Programme for International Student Assessment (PISA). 2019
7. "Back to School Statistics." Fast Facts, National Center for Education Statistics. 19 May 2021

8. “Academic Ranking of World Universities 2020.” Shanghai Ranking Consultancy. 29 Apr 2021
9. Michael T. Nietzel. “The 2019 Nobel Laureates: U.S. Universities Lead the Way Again.” Forbes. 14 Oct 2019
10. United States. Department of Health and Human Services. “About the Office of Head Start.” 29 Apr 2021
11. United States. Department of Health and Human Services. “Head Start Impact Study Final Report.” 15 Jan 2010
12. United States. Department of Health and Human Services. “Third Grade Follow-Up To The Head Start Impact Study.” October 2012
13. David Deming. “Early Childhood Intervention and Life-Cycle Skill Development: Evidence from Head Start.” American Economic Journal. 2009
14. Remy J. C. Pages, Dylan J. Lukes, Drew H. Bailey and Greg J. Duncan. “Elusive Longer-Run Impacts of Head Start: Replications Within and Across Cohorts.” Brown University. 2 Apr 2019
15. United States. Department of Health & Human Services. “FY2020 Head Start Funding Increase.” 11 Mar 2020
16. United States. Department of Health & Human Services. “FY2021 Head Start Funding Increase.” 19 Feb 2021
17. “Swiss Education System – Overview.” Switzerland. Ministry of Education. 21 May 2021
18. “Apprenticeship Positions.” Switzerland. Ministry of Education. 21 May 2021
19. “Vocational Education and Training (VET).” Switzerland. Ministry of Education. 21 May 2021
20. “Gold Standard: The Swiss Vocational Education and Training System.” Center on International Education Benchmarking. March 2015
21. Klaus Schwab. “The Global Competitiveness Report 2019.” World Economic Forum.
22. John F. Helliwell, Richard Layard, Jeffrey D. Sachs, and Jan-Emmanuel De Neve, Lara B. Aknin, Haifang Huang and Shun Wang. “World Happiness Report 2020.”
23. “World Top 20 Project.” New Jersey Minority Educational Development. 21 May 2021

Child Tax Credit

1. “The Family Security Act.” The Office of Senator Mitt Romney. 21 May 2021
2. Irwin Garfinkel, Laurel Sariscsany, Elizabeth Ananat, Sophie Collyer and Christopher Wimer. “The Costs and Benefits of a Child Allowance. Poverty & Social Policy Brief. 23 Feb 2021
3. Zachary Parolin, Sophie Collyer, Megan A. Curran and Christopher Wimer. “The Potential Poverty Reduction Effect of the American Rescue Plan.” Poverty & Social Policy Brief. 11 Mar 2021
4. “Poor Children in Rich Countries: Why We Need Policy Action.” Organization for Economic Cooperation and Development. October 2018
5. Chuck Marr, Kris Cox, Stephanie Hingtgen, Katie Windham and Arloc Sherman. “House COVID Relief Bill Includes Critical Expansions of Child Tax Credit and EITC.” Center on Budget and Policy Priorities. 2 Mar 2021
6.
7. Contributed by Greg J. Duncan; received August 25, 2021; accepted December 29, 2021; reviewed by Martha Farah and Joan Luby. “The Impact of a Poverty Reduction intervention on Infant Brain Activity.” PNAS. 24 Jan 2022

Welfare Reform

1. United States. 104th Congress. “Personal Responsibility and Work Opportunity Reconciliation Act of 1996.” Public Law 104-193. 22 Aug 1996
2. President William J. Clinton. “Statement on Signing the Personal Responsibility and Work Opportunity Reconciliation Act of 1996.” 22 Aug 1996
3. United States. Census Bureau. Jessica Semega, Melissa Kollar, John Creamer and Abinash Mohanty. “Income and Poverty in the United States: 2018.” September 2019
4. H. Luke Shaefer and Kathryn Edin. “Welfare Reform and the Families It Left Behind.” Pathways, Winter 2018.

5. Scott Winship. “Poverty After Welfare Reform.” Manhattan Institute. 22 Aug 2016
6. United States. “The War on Poverty: 50 Years Later.” House Budget Committee Report. 3 Mar 2014
7. Deja Thomas and Richard Fry. “Prior To COVID-19, Child Poverty Rates Had Reached Record Lows in U.S.” Pew Research Center. 30 No 2020
8. United States. Department of Health & Human Services. “TANF: Total Number of Recipients.” 17 July 2020
9. Melissa Healy. “Welfare Rolls Fall To Half Of ’96 Numbers.” Los Angeles Times. 23 Aug 2000

The Six Pillars

1. Jim Tankersley and Zolan Kanno-Youngs. “Biden Seeks to Use Infrastructure Plan to Address Racial Inequities.” New York Times. 1 Apr 2021
2. United States. Department of Labor, Bureau of Labor Statistics. “The Employment Situation – June 2021.” 8 July 2021
3. United States. Department of Labor, Bureau of Labor Statistics. “Table A-15. Alternative Measures of Labor Underutilization.” 8 July 2021
4. United States. Department of Labor, Bureau of Labor Statistics. “Civilian Labor Force Participation Rate.” 6 June 2021
5. W. E. Burghardt Du Bois. “A Litany of Atlanta.” The Book of American Negro Poetry. 1922
6. Allison Keyes. “The East St. Louis Race Riot Left Dozens Dead, Devastating a Community on the Rise.” 30 June 2017
7. Gregory Mixon. “Atlanta Race Riot of 1906.” New Georgia Encyclopedia. 27 Aug 2020

Bad Habit Four
Trade

1. United States. Executive Office of the President. “Canada.” United States Trade Representative. 12 May 2019

2. United States. Census Bureau. "U.S. Trade in Goods and Services - Balance of Payments (BOP) Basis." 27 Mar 2019
3. United States. Census Bureau. "Annual Trade Highlights 2018 Press Highlights." 12 May 2019
4. "Larry Kudlow on Fallout From Rising Trade Tensions with China." Fox News Sunday. 12 May 2019
5. Mary Amiti, Stephen J. Redding, and David E. Weinstein. "New China Tariffs Increase Costs to U.S. Households." Federal Reserve Bank of New York. 23 May 2019
6. Mary Amiti, Sebastian Heise, and Noah Kwicklis. "The Impact of Import Tariffs on U.S. Domestic Prices." Federal Reserve Bank of New York. 4 Jan 2019
7. Mary Amiti, Stephen J. Redding and David Weinstein. "The Impact of the 2018 Trade War on U.S. Prices and Welfare." International Trade and Regional Economics. 2 Mar 2019
8. Aaron Flaaen, Ali Hortacsu, Felix Tintelnot. "The Production Relocation and Price Effects of U.S. Trade Policy: The Case of Washing Machines." 18 Apr 2019
9. "Global Economic Prospects: The Turning of the Tide." World Bank Group. June 2018
10. "Global Economic Prospects: Darkening Skies." World Bank Group. January 2019
11. "World Economic Outlook." International Monetary Fund. 2019
12. Sam Meredith. "After China, the U.S. Will Ratchet Up Trade Tensions With the EU, OECD Chief Economist Warns." CNBC. 5 Apr 2019
13. Pablo D. Fajgelbaum, Pinelopi K. Goldberg, Patrick J. Kennedy, and Amit K. Khandelwal. "The Return to Protectionism." 10 Mar 2019
14. Joseph E. Gagnon. "Trump and Navarro's Mistaken Assumptions About Trade Deficits." Peterson Institute for International Economics (PIIE). 1 Nov 2018
15. Joseph E. Gagnon. "Do Governments Drive Global Trade Imbalances?" Peterson Institute for International Economics (PIIE). December 2017
16. Peter Eavis. "These Companies Wanted Tariffs. How Are The Faring Now?" New York Times. 10 July 2019

17. Davide Furceri, Swarnali A. Hannan, Jonathan D. Ostry and Andrew K. Rose. "Macroeconomic Consequences of Tariffs." October 2018
18. Carson Kessler. "Why Harley-Davidson Is Moving Production Overseas." Fortune. 26 June 2018
19. Joe Deaux. "America's Top Aluminum Maker Is Getting Hit by U.S. Tariffs." Bloomberg. 18 July 2018
20. Paul A. Eisenstein. "GM To Slash Over 14,000 Jobs From North American Workforce." NBC News. 26 Nov 2018
21. Joe Deaux, Jack Farchy and Masumi Suga. "Losers Outweigh Winners as Trump's Metal Tariffs Start Year Two." Bloomberg. 24 Mar 2019
22. Andrew Tangel and Josh Zumbrun. "Whirlpool Wanted Washer Tariffs. It Wasn't Ready for a Trade Showdown." Wall Street Journal. 16 July 2018
23. Karen Braun. "Trade Tiff Has Market Over-Thinking Slow U.S. Soy Sales to China." Reuters. 26 Apr 2018
24. P.J. Huffstutter and Adriana Barrera. "Exclusive: As Trump Trashes NAFTA, Mexico Turns to Brazilian Corn." Reuters. 22 Feb 2018
25. United States. Department of Agriculture. "Percentage of U.S. Agricultural Products Exported." 30 May 2018
26. Bryce Cooke and Hui Jiang. "Outlook for U.S. Agricultural Trade: FY 2019 Export Forecast Reduced by $3.0 Billion to $141.5 Billion; Imports Forecast at $127.0 Billion." 29 Nov 2018
27. Michael Hirtzer and Mario Parker. "Trump Trade Tweets Send Grain Markets Diving to 42-Year Low." Bloomberg. 6 May 2019
28. Justin Worland. "What President Trump's Tariff on Solar Panels Means for American Jobs." Time. 25 Jan 2018
29. Nichola Groom. "Billions in U.S. Solar Projects Shelved After Trump Panel Tariff." Reuters. 7 June 2018
30. "U.S. Authorizes $12 Billion in Farm Aid." Reuters. 24 July 2018
31. "Soybean Farmer Loses From Retaliatory Tariffs With No Bailout Funds In Sight." All Things Considered. NPR. 11 May 2019
32. Joseph Parilla and Mark Muro. "U.S. Metros Most Exposed to a Trump Trade Shock." Brookings Institution. 30 Jan 2017

33. Wendong Zhang and Alejandro Plastina. "ISU Survey: Iowa's Farmland Owners Continue to Age." Iowa State University. 29 June 2018
34. "Tariffs On Steel and Aluminum Are Creating Some Winners." Economist. 9 Aug 2018
35. Federal Reserve Bank of Philadelphia. "Manufacturing Business Outlook Survey." July 2018
36. Douglas A. Irwin. "Clashing Over Commerce: A History of U.S. Trade Policy (Markets and Governments in Economic History)." University of Chicago Press. 29 Nov 2017
37. "Global Wealth Report 2018." Credit Suisse Research Institute. October 2018
38. "China Has Designs on Europe. Here is How Europe Should Respond." Economist. 4 Oct 2018
39. "China Moves Into Latin America." Economist. 3 Feb 2018
40. "Global Economic Prospects: Darkening Skies." World Bank Group. January 2019
41. Ban Ki-moon. "Remarks to the 12th United Nations Conference on Trade and Development – 'We Can Do This'." Accra, Ghana. 20 April 2008
42. "BRICs And Beyond." Goldman Sachs Global Economics Group. November 2007
43. "World Economic Outlook: Cyclical Upswing, Structural Change." International Monetary Fund. April 2018
44. "S&P 500 2017: Global Sales." S&P Dow Jones Indices. August 2018
45. "Global Unease, From Commerce To Currencies, Rattles Raw Materials." Economist. 23 Aug 2018
46. Homi Kharas. "The Unprecedented Expansion of the Global Middle Class." Global Economy and Development at Brookings. February 2017
47. Homi Kharas and Kristofer Hamel. "A Global Tipping Point: Half the World is Now Middle Class or Wealthier." Brookings Institute. 27 Sept 2018

48. Daniel Mminele, Deputy Governor of the South African Reserve Bank. "The Role of BRICS in the Global Economy." North Rhine-Westphalia, Düsseldorf, Germany. 7 July 2016
49. "Global Economic Prospects: The Turning of the Tide." World Bank Group. June 2018
50. United States. Department of Labor. "Databases, Tables & Calculators by Subject: Labor Force Statistics from the Current Population Survey." 3 Nov 2018
51. United States. Census Bureau. "U.S. Trade in Goods and Services - Balance of Payments (BOP) Basis." 3 Nov 2018
52. "The Contradiction At The Heart of Trumponomics." Economist. 13 May 2017
53. "Definition of Triffin Dilemma." Financial Times. 31 Oct 2018
54. "Current Account Balance (BoP, Current US$)." World Bank. 12 May 2019
55. United States. Department of State. "Outcomes of Current U.S. Trade Agreements." 25 Aug 2018
56. United States. Office of the U.S. Trade Representative. "United States-Mexico-Canada Agreement Text." 27 Oct 2018
57. "Mexico Nominal Hourly Wages in Manufacturing." Trading Economics. 27 Oct 2018
58. "United States Average Hourly Wages in Manufacturing." Trading Economics. 27 Oct 2018
59. "Automotive Team: Industry Trade Data: U.S. Exports of New Passenger Vehicles and 60. Light Trucks, Value and Units." International Trade Administration. Office of Transportation and Machinery. 27 Oct 2018
60. "Dairy in Canada - Statistics & Facts." Statista. 27 Oct 2018
61. United States. Executive Office of the President. "Canada." United States Trade Representative. 22 Aug 2018
62. United States. Office of the U.S. Trade Representative. "TPP Full Text." 28 Oct 2018
63. United States. International Trade Commission. "Trans-Pacific Partnership Agreement: Likely Impact on the U.S. Economy and on Specific Industry Sectors." May 2016

64. Congressional Research Service. "The Trans-Pacific Partnership (TPP): Key Provisions and Issues for Congress." 14 June 2016
65. "Weighing Anchor." Economist. 10 Oct 2015
66. Peter A. Petri and Michael G. Plummer. "The Economic Effects of the Trans-Pacific Partnership: New Estimates." Peterson Institute for International Economics. January 2016
67. William Mauldin. "Donald Trump Withdraws U.S. From Trans-Pacific Partnership." Wall Street Journal. 23 Jan 2017
68. Eva Vergara and Luis Andres Henao. "11 Nations Sign Pacific Trade Pact as Trump Plans U.S. Tariffs." Associated Press. 8 Mar 2018
69. Adam Edelman. "Trump Says He Would Consider Trans-Pacific Partnership With 'Better Deal'." NBC News. 25 Jan 2018
70. Michael C. Bender. "Trump Asks Advisers to Study Rejoining Pacific Trade Pact Talks." Wall Street Journal. 13 Apr 2018
71. Takeshi Kumon. "U.S. Seeks Level Playing Field In Japan Trade Talks, Ambassador Says." Nikkei Asian Review. 18 Apr 2019
72. "The WTO." World Trade Organization. 28 Oct 2018
73. "Regional Trade Agreements." World Trade Organization. 31 Oct 2018
74. Judith L. Goldstein, Douglas Rivers, and Michael Tomz. "Institutions in International Relations: Understanding the Effects of the GATT and the WTO on World Trade." Cambridge University Press. January 2007
75. Ryan Brutger and Julia C. Morse. "Balancing Law and Politics: Judicial Incentives in WTO Dispute Settlement." The Review of International Organizations 10.2 (2015): , 10, 2, 179-205.
76. United States. "Economic Report of the President." Together with The Annual Report of the Council of Economic Advisers. February 2018
77. United States. Customs and Border Protection. "Section 232 Tariffs on Aluminum and Steel." 31 Oct 2018
78. World Trade Organization. "Article XXI Security Exceptions." 31 Oct 2018
79. "Tariff Rate, Applied, Weighted Mean, All Products (%)." The World Bank. 29 Oct 2018

80. Drew Desilver. "U.S. Tariffs Vary A Lot, But The Highest Duties Tend To Be On Imported Clothing." Pew Research Center. 28 Mar 2018
81. United States. International Trade Commission. "Economic Impact of Trade Agreements Implemented Under Trade Authorities Procedures, 2016 Report." June 2016
82. "The Doha Round." World Trade Organization. 29 Oct 2018
83. "Trade Facilitation." World Trade Organization. 29 Oct 2018
84. "Plurilaterals: Of Minority Interest." World Trade Organization. 29 Oct 2018
85. "Century Aluminum Company Reports Fourth Quarter And Full Year 2020 Results." Century Aluminum Company. 18 Feb 2021
86. Nathan Bomey. "Trump's Steel, Auto Tariffs Damage GM, Fiat Chrysler, Ford." USAToday. 25 July 2018

Bad Habit Five and Six
Health Care

1. "Universal Declaration of Human Rights." United Nations. 10 Dec 1948
2. "Sustainable Health Financing, Universal Coverage and Social Health Insurance." World Health Organization. World Health Assembly Resolution 58.33. 2005
3. "What is Health Financing for Universal Coverage?" World Health Organization. 10 Apr 2019
4. "Medicare For All is a Meaningless Slogan." Economist. 13 Oct 2018
5. Richard Alonso-Zaldivar. "'Medicare for All' Would Cost $32.6 Trillion Over 10 Years, Study Says." Associated Press. 29 July 2018
6. John Holahan, Lisa Clemans-Cope, Matthew Buettgens, Melissa Favreault, Linda J. Blumberg and Siyabonga Ndwandwe. "The Sanders Single-Payer Health Care Plan: The Effect on National Health Expenditures and Federal and Private Spending." May 2016
7. "Health Insurance Coverage of the Total Population." Kaiser Family Foundation (KFF). 2017

8. United States. Congress. "Budget Projections for FY2019." Congressional Budget Office. 29 Jan 2019
9. Bacchus Barua and Sazid Hasan. "The Private Cost of Public Queues for Medically Necessary Care, 2018." Fraser Institute. 23 May 2018
10. Micah Hartman, Anne B. Martin, Joseph Benson, Aaron Catlin, and the National Health Expenditure Accounts Team. "National Health Care Spending In 2018: Growth Driven By Accelerations in Medicare and Private Insurance Spending." Health Affairs. 5 Dec 2019
11. Andrea M. Sisko, Sean P. Keehan, John A. Poisal, Gigi A. Cuckler, Sheila D. Smith, Andrew J. Madison, Kathryn E. Rennie, and James C. Hardesty. "National Health Expenditure Projections, 2018–27: Economic And Demographic Trends Drive Spending And Enrollment Growth." Health Affairs. 20 Feb 2019
12. United States. Centers for Medicare and Medicaid Services. "NHE Fact Sheet." 20 Apr 2021
13. "Report for Selected Countries and Subjects." World Economic Outlook Database, April 2019. International Monetary Fund. 11 Apr 2019
14. Bob Herman. "Axios Analysis: Drugmakers Getting Richer." Axios. 13 May 2019
15. "Why Trump's Plan Will Not Cut Drug Prices." Economist. 19 May 2018
16. United States. Congress. "The Budget and Economic Outlook: 2019 to 2029." Congressional Budget Office. January 2019
17. Robert Sunshine. "CBO's Analyses and Projections of Federal Health Care Costs." Congressional Budget Office. 3 July 2018
18. Kaiser Family Foundation. "KFF Health Tracking Poll." February 2019

Bad Habit Seven
Immigration

1. United States. Department of Homeland Security. "Definition of Terms." 8 May 2021

2. Mark Hugo Lopez, Jeffrey S. Passel and D'Vera Cohn. "Key Facts About The Changing U.S. Unauthorized Immigrant Population." Pew Research Center. 13 Apr 2021
3. United States. "Southwest Border Sector Apprehensions FY1960-2019."
4. United States. Department of Homeland Security. "Table 39. Aliens Removed Or Returned: Fiscal Years 1892-2018." 8 May 2021
5. United States. Immigration and Customs Enforcement. "U.S. Immigration And Customs Enforcement Fiscal Year 2019 Enforcement And Removal Operations Report."
6. United States. Immigration and Customs Enforcement. "Fiscal Year 2018 ICE Enforcement And Removal Operations Report."
7. United States. Immigration and Customs Enforcement. "Fiscal Year 2017 ICE Enforcement And Removal Operations Report."
8. John Gramlich. "How Border Apprehensions, ICE Arrests And Deportations Have Changed Under Trump." Pew Research Center. 2 Mar 2020
9. United States. Department of Homeland Security. Mike Guo. "Immigration Enforcement Actions: 2019." September 2020
10. "Immigrants and Nobel Prizes: 1901-2020." National Foundation for American Policy. October 2020
11. "New American Fortune 500 in 2019: Top American Companies and Their Immigrant Roots." New American Economy. 22 July 2019
12. Ufuk Akcigit, John Grigsby and Tom Nicholas. "Immigration and the Rise of American Ingenuity." National Bureau of Economic Research. March 2017
13. Andrés Rodríguez-Pose and Viola von Berlepsch. "Does Population Diversity Matter for Economic Development in the Very Long-Term? Historic Migration, Diversity and County Wealth in the U.S." European Journal of Population. 23 Nov 2018
14. Francine D. Blau and Christopher Mackie, Editors. "The Economic and Fiscal Consequences of Immigration." The National Academies of Sciences Engineering and Medicine. 2017
15. "2020 Fast Facts." Open Doors. 9 May 2021
16. Robert Adelman, Lesley Williams Reid, Gail Markle, Saskia Weiss and Charles Jaret. "Urban Crime Rates and the Changing Face of

Immigration: Evidence Across Four Decades." Journal of Ethnicity in Criminal Justice. 29 Sept 2016
17. Anna Flagg. "The Myth of the Criminal Immigrant." The Marshall Project. 30 Mar 2018
18. Michael T. Light and Ty Miller. "Does Undocumented Immigration Increase Violent Crime?" Criminology. 25 Mar 2018
19. Alex Nowrasteh. "Criminal Immigrants in Texas Illegal Immigrant Conviction and Arrest Rates for Homicide, Sex Crimes, Larceny, and Other Crimes." Cato Institute. 26 Feb 2018
20. United States. Customs and Border Protection. "Criminal Noncitizen Statistics Fiscal Year 2021." 9 May 2021
21. United States. Customs and Border Protection. "CBP Border Security Report: Fiscal Year 2018." March 2019
22. United States. Federal Bureau of Investigation. "Gangs." 9 May 2021
23. David J. Bier and Alex Nowrasteh. "45,000 'Special Interest Aliens' Caught Since 2007, But No U.S. Terrorist Attacks from Illegal Border Crossers." Cato Institute. 17 Dec 2018.
24. United States. Department of State. "Country Reports on Terrorism 2019: Mexico." 9 May 2021
25. Amelie F. Constant. "Do Migrants Take the Jobs of Native Workers? Migrants Rarely Take Native Workers' Jobs, and They Boost Employment Effects in the Long Term." IZA World of Labor. George Washington University and Temple University, USA, and IZA, Germany. May 2014
26. Giovanni Peri. "Do Immigrant Workers Depress the Wages of Native Workers? Short-Term Wage Effects of Immigrants Are Close to Zero - And in the Long-Term immigrants Can Boost Productivity and Wages." IZA World of Labor. University of California, Davis, USA, and IZA, Germany. May 2014
27. Giovanni Peri, Kevin Shih and Chad Sparber. "Foreign STEM Workers and Native Wages and Employment in U.S. Cities." May 2014
28. Alex Nowrasteh and Robert Orr. "Immigration and the Welfare State: Immigrant and Native Use Rates and Benefit Levels for Means-Tested Welfare and Entitlement Programs." Cato Institute. 10 May 2018

29. Lisa Christensen Gee, Matthew Gardner and Meg Wiehe. "Undocumented Immigrants' State & Local Tax Contributions." The Institute on Taxation and Economic Policy. February 2016
30. United States. Central Intelligence Agency. "Mexico." The World Factbook. 9 May 2021
31. Peter J. Meyer and Clare Ribando Seelke. "Central America Regional Security Initiative: Background and Policy Issues for Congress." Congressional Research Service. 17 Dec 2015
32. United States. Government Accountability Office. "Secure Border Initiative: DHS Has Faced Challenges Deploying Technology and Fencing Along the Southwest Border." 4 May 2010
33. United States. Customs and Border Protection. "Border Wall System." 14 Sept 2020
34. Jeremy Schwartz and Perla Trevizo. "He Built a Privately Funded Border Wall. It's Already at Risk of Falling Down if Not Fixed." Texas Tribune. 2 July 2020
35. Chantal Da Silva. "Donald Trump's New Border Wall Contract Will Cost More Than $30 Million Per Mile." Newsweek. 20 May 20
36. United States. Government Accountability Office. "Southwest Border Security: CBP Is Evaluating Designs and Locations for Border Barriers but Is Proceeding Without Key Information." July 2018
37. Nick Miroff. "At America's Toughest Border Wall, A Hole Remains." Washington Post. 4 June 2018
38. Rodrigo Dominguez-Villegas and Victoria Rietig. "Migrants Deported from the United States and Mexico to the Northern Triangle: A Statistical and Socioeconomic Profile." Migration Policy Institute. September 2015
39. Tim Smyth. "Abuse of Migrants in Mexico Rises Even as Numbers Fall." Reuters. 16 Oct 2015
40. Adam Isacson, Maureen Meyer, and Hannah Smith. "Mexico's Southern Border: Security, Central American Migration, and U.S. Policy." The Washington Office on Latin America (WOLA). June 2017
41. Maureen Meyer and Adam Isacson. "The Wall Before the Wall: Mexico's Crackdown on Migration at its Southern Border." The Washington Office on Latin America (WOLA). December 2019

42. Laurence Iliff. "Bush Announces $1.4 Billion Drug Plan for Mexico." Dallas Morning News. 2 Nov 2007
43. "Just Don't Call it Plan Mexico." Economist. 25 Oct. 2007
44. "Colombia Aid Failed to Halve Drug Making, Report Finds." New York Times. 6 Nov. 2008
45. Simon Romero. "Colombia Inflates Rebel Toll With Slain Civilians." New York Times. 30 Oct 2008
46. "Army Chief Steps Down Amid Scandal." Dallas Morning News. 5 Nov 2008
47. Simon Romero. "Colombian Army Commander Resigns in Scandal Over Killing of Civilians." New York Times 5 Nov 2008
48. United States. Department of State. "Progress Report for the United States Strategy for Central America's Plan for Monitoring and Evaluation." May 2019
49. Britta Glennon. "How Do Restrictions On High-Skilled Immigration Affect Offshoring? Evidence From the H-1B Program." National Bureau of Economic Research. July 2020
50. Emmanuel Abuelafla, Giselle Del Carmen and Marta Ruiz-Arranz. "In the Footprints of Migrants." IDB and USAID. 2018

Bad Habit Eight
Government Reform

1. "Earmark." Merriam-Webster. 5 Nov 2020
2. "2020 Congressional Pig Book Summary." Citizens Against Government Waste.
3. Drew Griffin and Scott Bronstein. "Obama: No Earmarks for 2009." CNN.com. 15 Apr 2008
4. "Obama Signs 'Imperfect' Spending Bill Away from Cameras." ABCNews.com
5. Paul Kane and Scott Wilson. "Obama Signs Spending Bill, Vowing to Battle Earmarks." Washington Post. 12 Mar 2009
6. United States. White House. Office of Management and Budget. U.S. Department of Education.
7. United States. White House. Office of Management and Budget. U.S. Department of Energy.

8. United States. White House. Office of Management and Budget. U.S. Department of Justice.
9. Brendan McKenna. "Dallas-Area Projects Among Those Getting Millions from Federal Budget." Dallas Morning News. 7 Jan 2008
10. Robert Pear. "From Bush, Foe of Earmarks, Similar Items." New York Times. 10 Feb 2008
11. Trish Turner. "Lawmakers Defend Earmarks in Spending Bill." 4 Mar 2009
12. Wes Allison. "Florida Legislators Defend Earmarks as Obama Signs Bill Chock-Full of Them." TampaBay.com. 12 Mar 2009
13. Dana Milbank. "Senate's Bold Proposal for Iraq: Sugar Beets and Rural Schools -in the U.S." Washington Post. 29 Mar 2007
14. Charles Hurt. "Senate War Bill Features $20B in Pork." Examiner. 27 Mar 2007
15. Robert Pear. "New Billions in Earmarks Approach Enactment." New York Times. 25 Sept 2008
16. Jake Tapper. "Congress Sweetens Bill, Hopeful for Passage." ABC News. 2 Oct 2008
17. "Lobbying Data Summary." OpenSecrets.org. 17 Apr 2021
18. Michael Beckel. "Outsized Influence." Issue One. April 2021

Foreign Policy

1. "1 in 3 People Globally Do Not Have Access to Safe Drinking Water." World Health Organization. 18 June 2019
2. "Drinking Water." World Health Organization. 6 Sept 2020
3. United States. Department of State. "2020 Country Reports on Human Rights Practices: Saudi Arabia." 30 Mar 2021
4. "Saudi Arabia." Amnesty International. 6 Sept 2020
5. "World Report 2020: Saudi Arabia." Human Rights Watch.
6. "World Report 2021: Yemen." Human Right Watch. 7 June 2021
7. United States. Department of State. "2020 Country Reports on Human Rights Practices: China." 7 June 2021
8. "China." Amnesty International. 6 Sept 2020
9. "World Report 2020: China." Human Rights Watch.

10. Carlos Cisternas. “U.S. Dollars Replace Ecuador Currency.” Associated Press. 12 Sept. 2000
11. “Dollarization & Economic Reform in Ecuador.” Ministry of Tourism of Ecuador.
12. Richard Wike, Jacob Poushter, Laura Silver, Janell Fetterolf and Mara Mordecai. “America’s Image Abroad Rebounds With Transition From Trump to Biden.” Pew Research Center. 10 June 2021
13. “Global Unease With Major World Powers.” Pew Global Attitudes Project. 27 June 2007
14. “Positive Aspects of U.S. Image.” Pew Global Attitudes Project. 3 April 2009
15. United States. Congress. “Cuban Democracy Act of 1992.” H.R. 5323, 102nd Congress.
16. Paul Angelo and Rebecca Bill Chavez. “‘Gracias China!!!’” New York Times. 21 Apr 2020
17. Thomas Gibbons-Neff and Najim Rahim. “Elite Afghan Forces Suffer Horrific Casualties as Taliban Advance.” New York Times. 17 June 2021
18. Theodore Roosevelt. “Theodore Roosevelt: An Autobiography.” 1913

Afghanistan, Iraq, Syria and Turkey

1. “Afghanistan: Protection of Civilians In Armed Conflict.” The United Nations Assistance Mission in Afghanistan. First Quarter Update.
2. Thomas Gibbons-Neff. “American Special Forces Soldier Is Killed in Afghanistan.” New York Times. 22 Dec 2019
3. “Afghanistan: Protection of Civilians in Armed Conflict Annual Report 2018.” United Nations. February 2019
4. “Lessons from Afghanistan’s Reconstruction: 2001-2019.” Prepared Remarks of John F. Sopko Special Inspector General for Afghanistan Reconstruction. United States Naval Academy Annapolis, Maryland. 17 Jan 2019
5. The World Bank. “Afghanistan.” 26 July 2019

6. Craig Whitlock. "Afghan War Plagued by 'Mendacity' and Lies, Inspector General Tells Congress." Washington Post. 15 Jan 2020
7. United Nations. Security Council. "Protection of Civilians in Armed Conflict." 7 May 2019
8. Special Inspector General for Afghanistan Reconstruction. "Quarterly Report to the United States Congress." 30 Apr 2019
9. United Nations. Security Council. "Letter from the Chair of the Security Council Committee Pursuant to Resolutions 1267 (1999), 1989 (2011) and 2253 (2015) Concerning Islamic State in Iraq and the Levant (Da'esh), Al-Qaida and Associated Individuals, Groups, Undertakings and Entities Addressed to the President of the Security Council." 16 July 2018
10. Special Inspector General for Afghanistan Reconstruction. "U.S. Reconstruction Efforts in Afghanistan: Key High-Risk Areas to Persist into Future." Statement of John F. Sopko, Special Inspector General for Afghanistan Reconstruction. 9 Apr 2019
11. "Human Costs." Costs of War Project. Watson Institute, Brown University. September 2020
12. "Human Cost of the Post-9/11 Wars: Lethality and the Need for Transparency." Costs of War Project. Watson Institute, Brown University. November 2018
13. "Economic Costs." Costs of War Project. Watson Institute, Brown University. November 2018
14. United States. "Worldwide Threat Assessment of the U.S. Intelligence Community." Director of National Intelligence Daniel R. Coats. 29 Feb 2019
15. "Caliphate." Encyclopedia Britannica. 30 Mar 2018
16. Hugh Kennedy. "Caliphate: The History of An Idea." Basic Books. 2016
17. Anchal Vohra. "'Taste of Victory' for SDF, but ISIL Threat Remains." Al Jazeera. 23 Mar 2019
18. David Martin. "Nearly 1,000 U.S. Troops Still in Syria Months After Last ISIS-Held Territory Was Liberated." 22 July 2019
19. Ayla Jean Yackley. "U.S. Envoy Holds Talks in Ankara as Turkey Threatens to Invade Syria." Al-Monitor. 2 July 2019

20. Ben Hubbard and Hwaida Saad. "Having Won Syria's War, al-Assad Is Mired in Economic Woes." New York Times. Feb 26, 2021
21. "Twelve Million Syrians Now In The Grip of Hunger, Worn down By Conflict And Soaring Food Prices." United Nations World Food Program. 17 Feb 2021
22. United States. "Worldwide Threat Assessment of the U.S. Intelligence Community." Director of National Intelligence Daniel R. Coats. 29 Feb 2019
23. "Caliphate." Encyclopedia Britannica. 30 Mar 2018
24. Hugh Kennedy. "Caliphate: The History of An Idea." Basic Books. 2016
25. Anchal Vohra. "'Taste of Victory' for SDF, but ISIL Threat Remains." Al Jazeera. 23 Mar 2019
26. David Martin. "Nearly 1,000 U.S. Troops Still in Syria Months After Last ISIS-Held Territory Was Liberated." 22 July 2019
27. Ayla Jean Yackley. "U.S. Envoy Holds Talks in Ankara as Turkey Threatens to Invade Syria." Al-Monitor. 2 July 2019
28. Gordon Lubold and Yaroslav Trofimov. "Afghan Government Could Collapse Six Months After U.S. Withdrawal, New Intelligence Assessment Says." Wall Street Journal. 23 June 2021
29. Thomas Gibbons-Neff and Eric Schmitt. "Security in Afghanistan Is Decaying, U.S. General Says as Forces Leave." New York Times. 3 July 2021
30. Phil Stewart, Idrees Ali and Hamid Shalizi. "Special Report-Afghan Pilots Assassinated By Taliban As U.S. Withdraws." Reuters. 9 July 2021
31. JM Rieger. "The Biden Administration Has Given 9 Justifications For The Slow Evacuation of Afghan Allies." Washington Post. 18 Aug 2021
32. "The Military Balance." International Institute for Strategic Studies. 25 Feb 2021
33. Anthony H. Cordesman. "The Reasons for the Collapse of Afghan Forces." Center for Strategic and International Studies. 17 Aug 2021
34. David Zucchino. "Collapse and Conquest: The Taliban Strategy That Seized Afghanistan." New York Times. 18 Aug 2021

35. "Twelfth Report of the Analytical Support and Sanctions Monitoring Team Submitted Pursuant to Resolution 2557 (2020) Concerning the Taliban and Other Associated Individuals and Entities Constituting a Threat to the Peace Stability and Security of Afghanistan." United Nations Security Council. 1 June 2021
36. Missy Ryan and Souad Mekhennet. "After Taliban Triumph, Biden Faces Even Greater Test in Preventing Extremist Resurgence in Afghanistan." Washington Post. 16 Aug 2021
37. Mark Mazzetti, Julian E. Barnes and Adam Goldman. "Intelligence Warned of Afghan Military Collapse, Despite Biden's Assurances." New York Times. 17 Aug 2021
38. Adam Taylor. "The Taliban is Flaunting Captured U.S. Weapons That May Be Worth Billions. Can It Use Them?" Washington Post. 20 Aug 2021
39. Mark Landler. "Biden Rattles U.K. With His Afghanistan Policy." New York Times. 18 Aug 2021
40. John Hudson and Missy Ryan. "Withdrawal From Afghanistan Forces Allies and Adversaries to Reconsider America's Global Role." Washington Post. 17 Aug 2021
41. Linda Qiu. "Biden's Inaccurate Claims in Defending Afghanistan Withdrawal." The New York Times. 20 Aug 2021
42. United States. Embassy in Afghanistan. "Security Alert." 18 Aug 2021
43. Megan McCloskey, Tobin Asher, Lena Groeger, Sisi Wei, and Christine Lee. "We Blew $17 Billion in Afghanistan. How Would You Have Spent It?" ProPublica. 17 Dec 2015
44. Megan Rose. "What the U.S. Didn't Learn in Afghanistan, According to the Government's Own Inspector General." ProPublica. 19 Aug 2021
45. Lauren Leatherby and Larry Buchanan. "At Least 250,000 Afghans Who Worked With U.S. Haven't Been Evacuated, Estimates Say." New York Times. 25 Aug 2021
46. Sami Sadat. "I Commanded Afghan Troops This Year. We Were Betrayed." New York Times. 25 Aug 2021

47. Jonathan Swan, Hans Nichols, Glen Johnson. "A Living Hell": Leaked Email Describes Afghan Refugee Conditions." Axios. 24 Aug 2021zz
48. Farnaz Fassihi and Dan Bilefsky. "For Afghan Women, Taliban Stir Fears of Return to a Repressive Past." New York Times. 17 Aug 2021
49. Maggie Astor, Sharif Hassan and Norimitsu Onishi. "A Taliban Spokesman Urges Women To Stay Home Because Fighters Haven't Been Trained To Respect Them." New York Times. 24 Aug 2021
50. Charles Lane. "The U.S. Dare Not Betray the Students at the American University of Afghanistan." Washington Post. 24 Aug 2021
51. Helene Cooper, Eric Schmitt and David E. Sanger. "Debating Exit From Afghanistan, Biden Rejected Generals' Views." New York Times. 17 Apr 2021
52. Ken Thomas and Vivian Salama. "Biden Wanted to Leave Afghanistan. He Knew the Risks." Wall Street Journal. 17 Aug 2021
53. Nick Niedzwiadek. "'I Want To Talk About Happy Things, Man': Biden Chafes At Press Questions on Afghanistan." Politico. 2 July 2021
54. Vivian Salama. "Internal State Department Cable Warned of Kabul Collapse." Wall Street Journal. 19 Aug 2021
55. United States. Department of Defense. "U.S. Military Casualties - Operation Freedom's Sentinel (OFS) Casualty Summary by Month and Service." 27 Aug 2021
56. Matthieu Aikins and Najim Rahim. "Afghan Family Says Errant U.S. Missile Killed 10, Including 7 Children." New York Times. 30 Aug 2021
57. Susannah George. "10 Civilians Killed By U.S. Drone Strike in Kabul, Family Says." Washington Post. 30 Aug 2021
58. Sebastian Junger. "A Vast Criminal Racket": Sebastian Junger On How the U.S. Corrupted Afghanistan." Vanity Fair. 31 Aug 2021
59. Ivana Saric. "Thousands of Prisoners Freed By Taliban Could Pose Threat to U.S." Axios. 15 Aug 2021
60. "Global Terrorism Index 2020." Institute for Economics & Peace.
61. "Arabs Are Losing Faith In Religious Parties And Leaders." The Economist. 5 Dec 2019

62. "Muslim Publics Share Concerns About Extremist Groups." Pew Research Center. 10 Sept 2013
63. Farnaz Fassihi. "American University of Afghanistan Students and Relatives Trying to Flee Were Sent Home." New York Times. 29 Aug 2021

China

1. United States. Department of the Treasury. "Major Foreign Holders of Treasury Securities." 17 May 2021
2. "The World Bank in China." World Bank. 4 June 2021
3. "GDP, PPP." The World Bank. 13 June 2021
4. "This Is Where Xi's Belt and Road Initiative Stands After Six Years." Bloomberg. 24 Apr 2019
5. Sebastian Horn, Carmen Reinhart and Christoph Trebesch. "China's Overseas Lending." Kiel Institute. June 2019
6. United States. CIA. "China." The World Factbook. 15 Aug 2019
7. United States. CIA. "United States." The World Factbook. 15 Aug 2019
8. United States. Department of State. "2019 Country Reports on Human Rights Practices: China."
9. United States. Office of the Director of National Intelligence. "Annual Threat Assessment." 9 Apr 2021
10. Tom Fairless. "U.S. Set to Power Global Economic Recovery From Covid-19." Wall Street Journal. 7 Mar 2021
11. Steven Mufson and Brady Dennis. "Chinese Greenhouse Gas Emissions Now Larger Than Those of Developed Countries Combined." Washington Post. 6 May 2021
12. Kate Larsen, Hannah Pitt, Mikhail Grant and Trevor Houser. "China's Greenhouse Gas Emissions Exceeded the Developed World for the First Time in 2019." Rhodium Group. 6 May 2021
13. Jacob Poushter and Mara Mordecai. "Americans and Germans Differ in Their Views of Each Other and the World." Pew Research Center. 9 Mar 2020

14. Steven Erlanger and Michael D. Shear. "Shifting Focus, NATO Views China as a Global Security Challenge." New York Times. 14 June 2021
15. Kristine Lee. Politico. "It's Not Just the WHO: How China Is Moving On The Whole U.N." 15 Apr 2020
16. Sebastian Horn, Carmen Reinhart and Christoph Trebesch. "China's Overseas Lending." Kiel Institute. June 2019
17. Sophia Ankel. "The 15 Top Countries For Billionaires, Ranked By How Many Live There." Business Insider. 23 Feb 2020
Syria

###

Made in the USA
Middletown, DE
26 April 2022

64787872R00362